Worlds Apart?
Perspectives on Africa–EU Migration

The Institute for Pan-African Thought and Conversation (IPATC), at the University of Johannesburg in South Africa, sincerely appreciate the German Federal Foreign Office that provided the funding (2019–2020), through the Institut für Auslandsbeziehungen (IFA), to produce this invaluable edited book.

First published by Fanele, an imprint of Jacana Media (Pty) Ltd in 2022
10 Orange Street
Sunnyside
Auckland Park 2092
South Africa
+2711 628 3200

www.jacana.co.za

ISBN 978-1-77634-590-8

Cover design by Aimèe Armstrong
Editing by Glenda Younge
Proofreading by Lynn Taylor
Indexing by Janine Leodolff
Set in Crimson Text 10.5/14.5pt
Printed and bound by ABC Press, Cape Town
Job no. 003939

See a complete list of Jacana titles at www.jacana.co.za

Worlds Apart?
Perspectives on Africa–EU Migration

Edited by

Adeoye O. Akinola and Jesper Bjarnesen

Contents

Acronyms and abbreviations   9

About the contributors   15

PART I: INTRODUCTION

Chapter 1: Africa–EU migration: Worlds apart? – *Jesper Bjarnesen*   23

PART II: THE BIGGER PICTURE

Chapter 2: Africa's 'Boat People' encounter 'Fortress Europe':
      Conflict and Migration in Africa–EU relations
      – *Adekeye Adebajo*   47

Chapter 3: Governance challenges for migration in Africa:
      The missing link – *Khabele Matlosa*   73

Chapter 4: Beyond the Eurocentric gaze: Refugee and migration
      governance in Africa – *Franzisca Zanker*   95

Chapter 5: Remittances and development of Africa – *Adeoye O. Akinola*   115

PART III: REGIONAL PERSPECTIVES

Chapter 6: Migration: The Maghreb and the European Union
      – *Ibtihel Bouchoucha*   139

Chapter 7: Migration in the Horn of Africa and the European Union
      – *Linda Adhiambo Oucho*   167

Chapter 8: Legal pathways to migration: Labour migration arrangements
between West Africa and Europe – *Amanda Bisong* 193

Chapter 9: Migration: Southern Africa and the European Union (EU)
– *Pragna Rugunanan, Terri Maggott and Celine Meyers* 219

Chapter 10: Migration: The African Great Lakes and the European Union
– *Alfred Ombeni Musimwa and Sylvie Sarolea* 239

PART IV: CONTINENTAL PERSPECTIVES

Chapter 11: African Union–European Union relations in the light of
migration management – *Ahmed Bugre* 261

Chapter 12: Bridging the Mediterranean: Coherent European and
African long-term migration policy – *Jan Bade* 287

PART V: PERSPECTIVES ON ROOT CAUSES

Chapter 13: The root causes of African migration to Europe:
An African Perspective – *Jack Mangala* 315

Chapter 14: The root causes of African migration to Europe:
A European perspective – *Jesper Bjarnesen* 339

PART VI: CIVIL SOCIETY PERSPECTIVES

Chapter 15: The role of African civil society in implementing the
United Nations Global Compact on Migration
– *Willie Eselebor* 369

Chapter 16: The role of European civil society in implementing the
United Nations Global Compact on Migration – *Anna Knoll* 389

VII: UN PERSPECTIVES

Chapter 17: The role of the UN High Commissioner for Refugees
(UNHCR) in Africa–EU Migration – *Nompumelelo Ndawonde* 413

Chapter 18: Towards lasting solutions to the Africa–European Union
migration challenge – *Ahunna Eziakonwa*   441

Chapter 19: The role of the International Organization for Migration in
African–European Union migration – *Leonie Felicitas Jegen*   459

VIII: FUTURE OF AFRICA–EU MIGRATION GOVERNANCE

Chapter 20: Renegotiating Africa–EU migration governance
– *Adeoye O. Akinola*   485

Index   505

Acronyms and abbreviations

4A	Addis Ababa Action Agenda
4IR	Fourth Industrial Revolution
4MI	Mixed Migration Monitoring Mechanism Initiative
ACBC	African Capacity Building Centre on Migration Management (IOM)
ACHPR	African Commission on Human Rights and Peoples' Rights
ACIRC	African Capacity for Immediate Response to Crises
ACP	African, Caribbean and Pacific States
ACRWC	African Charter on the Rights and Welfare of the Child
ACSRM	African Centre for the Study and Research on Migration (in Mali)
AEP	Africa–EU Partnership
AfCFTA	African Continental Free Trade Area
AfDB	African Development Bank
AGL	African Great Lakes
AHA	Alternative Help Association
AIR	African Institute for Remittances
AMADPOC	African Migration and Development Policy Centre (Nairobi)
AMISOM	African Union Mission in Somalia
AMU	Arab Maghreb Union
AOM	African Observatory on Migration (in Morocco)

AU	African Union
AUC	African Union Commission
AU-COMMIT	African Union Commission Initiative Against Trafficking
AU-HOAI	AU-Horn of Africa Initiative
AU-MPFA	African Union Migration Policy Framework for Africa
BMM	Better Migration Management
BRI	Belt and Road Initiative (Chinese)
C2CMMD	Continent-to-Continent Migration and Mobility Dialogue
CAP	Common Agricultural Policy (EU)
CAR	Central African Republic
CEAS	Common European Asylum System
CIDO	Citizens and Diaspora Organisation (AU)
CIGEM	Centre for Migration Information and Management/ Centre d'Information et de Gestion des Migrations
CMSI	Central Mediterranean Sea Initiative (UNHCR)
CNN	Cable Network News
COC	Continental Operational Centre (in Sudan)
CONCORD	Confederation for Relief and Development
CRRF	Comprehensive Refugee Response Framework
CSO	Civil society organisations
DFID	Department for International Development (UK)
DRC	Democratic Republic of Congo
DTM	Displacement Tracking Matrix
EAC	East African Community
EAM	European Agenda on Migration
EASO	European Asylum Support Office
ECDPM	European Centre for Development Policy Management
ECGLC	Economic Community of the Great Lakes Countries
ECHO	European Civil Protection and Humanitarian Aid Operations
ECOWAS	Economic Community of West African States
ECHR	European Convention on Human Rights

ECtHR	European Court ruling on the ECHR
ECRE	European Council on Refugees and Exiles
EEAS	European External Action Service
EESC	European Economic and Social Committee
ELS	Employment and Labour Sector (SADC)
EMB	Election management body
EPA	Economic Partnership Agreement
ETM	Emergency Transit Mechanisms (UNHCR)
EU	European Union
EUTF/EUTFA	European Union Emergency Trust Fund/(for Africa)
FAO	Food and Agriculture Organization (UN)
FDI	Foreign direct investment
FES	Friedrich Ebert Stiftung
FLS	Frontline States
FMPs	Flow monitoring points (IOM)
FRA	EU Agency for Fundamental Rights
GCC	Gulf Cooperation Council
GCIM	Global Commission on International Migration
GCM	Global Compact for Migration
GCR	Global Compact on Refugees
GDF	Gathering and Departure Facility, Tripoli (UNHCR)
GDP	Gross domestic product
GFMD	Global Forum for Migration and Development
GoK	Government of Kenya
GSDRC	Governance and Social Development Resource Centre, University of Birmingham
HLPM	High-Level Panel on Migration for Africa
HoA	Horn of Africa
ICEM	Intergovernmental Committee for European Migration
ICM	Intergovernmental Committee for Migration
ICMPD	International Centre for Migration Policy Development
ICT	Information and Communication Technology

IDPs	Internally displaced persons
IGAD	Intergovernmental Authority on Development
IFFs	Illicit financial flows
ILO	International Labour Organization
IOB	Policy and Operations Evaluation Department, Ministry of Foreign Affairs, Netherlands
IOM	International Organization for Migration
IPATC	Institute for Pan-African Thought and Conversation
IPI	International Peace Institute
IPPSHAR	IGAD Promoting Peace and Stability in the Horn of Africa Region
IRC	International Rescue Committee
ISS	Institute for Security Studies
ISWAP	Islamic State West Africa Province
JAES	Joint Africa–EU Strategy
JEG	Joint Experts Groups
JLMP	Joint Labour Migration Programme
JVAP	Joint Valletta Action Plan
KISEDP	Kalobeyei Integrated Socio-Economic Development Plan
MADE	Migration and Development Civil Society Network
MATCH	Migration of African Talents through Capacity building and Hiring
MDG	Millennium Development Goals (UN)
MEDAM	Mercator Dialogue on Migration and Asylum
MEV	Multiple-entry visa
MIDAS	Migration Information and Data Analysis System
MIDSA	Migration Dialogue for Southern Africa
MMC	Mixed Migration Centre
MME	Migration, Mobility and Employment Framework
MMP	Missing Migrants Project (IOM)
MNC	Multinational company
MPF	Migration Partnership Framework
MPFA	Migration Policy Framework for Africa

MSME	Micro, small and medium enterprises
NAI	Nordic Africa Institute
NGO	Non-governmental organisations
NHRIs	National Human Rights Institutions
NISS	National Intelligence and Security Services (Ethiopia)
NPC	National Peace Committees
OACPS	Organisation of African, Caribbean and Pacific States
OAU	Organisation of African Unity
ODA	Official development assistance
ODI	Outward Direct Investment
OECD	Organisation for Economic Co-operation and Development
OLA	Oromo Liberation Army
PAFoM	Pan-African Forum on Migration
PANiDMR	Pan-African Network in Defense of Migrants' Rights
PCD	Policy coherence for development
PFMP	Free Movement of Persons, Right of Residence and Right of Establishment
PGA	People's Global Action
PICCME	Provisional Intergovernmental Committee for the Movement of Migrants from Europe
PICUM	Platform for International Cooperation on Undocumented Migrants
QIP	Quick impact project (UNHCR)
REC	Regional Economic Communities
RDPP	Regional Development and Protection Programme
R-MAP	Regional Migration Action Plan
RMPF	Regional Migration Policy Framework
RMRP	Regional Migrant Response Plan
RPP	Regional Protection Programme
ROCK	Regional Operational Centre in support of the Khartoum Process
RSA	Refugee Support Aegean

SADC	Southern African Development Community
SADCC	Southern African Development Coordination Conference
S&R	Search and rescue
SDG	Sustainable Development Goal
SIHA	Strategic Initiative for Women in the Horn of Africa
SINCE	Stemming Irregular Migration in Northern and Central Ethiopia
SME	Small and medium sized enterprises
SOHR	Syrian Observatory on Human Rights
SOAS	School of Oriental and African Studies
SPRS-UN	Support Programme to the Refugee Settlements and Host Communities in Northern Uganda
TDCA	Trade, Development, and Cooperation Agreement (EU/SA)
TOKTEN	Transfer of Knowledge Through Expatriate Nationals
TPLF	Tigray People's Liberation Front
UN	United Nations
UNAMA	United Nations Assistance Mission in Afghanistan
UNCTAD	United Nations Conference on Trade and Development
UN DESA	United Nations Department of Economic and Social Affairs
UNDP	United Nations Development Programme
UNECA	United Nations Economic Commission for Africa
UNECE	United Nations Economic Commission for Europe
UfM	Union for the Mediterranean
UNGMD	United Nations Global Migration Database
UNHCR	United Nations High Commissioner for Refugees
UNOCHA	United Nations Office for the Co-ordination of Humanitarian Affairs
UNODC	United Nations Office on Drugs and Crime
UNOHCHR	United Nations Office of the High Commissioner for Human Rights
WPS	Women, Peace and Security

About the contributors

Prof. Adekeye Adebajo is a Senior Research Fellow at the University of Pretoria's Centre for the Advancement of Scholarship, South Africa. He was the Director of the Institute for Pan-African Thought and Conversation (IPATC) at the University of Johannesburg from 2017 to 2021. Prior to this, he was Executive Director of the Centre for Conflict Resolution in Cape Town between 2003 and 2016. He served on the United Nations Missions in South Africa, Western Sahara, and Iraq, and was Director of the Africa Programme at the International Peace Institute in New York. He is the author of five books: *Building Peace in West Africa* (Lynne Rienner Publishers, 2002); *Liberia's Civil War* (Lynne Rienner Publishers, 2007); *The Curse of Berlin: Africa after the Cold War* (Oxford University Press, 2014); *UN Peacekeeping in Africa* (Lynne Rienner Publishers, 2011); and *Thabo Mbeki: Africa's philosopher-king* (Ohio University Press, 2017). He is co-editor or editor of eight books on managing global conflicts, the United Nations, the European Union, West African security, South Africa's and Nigeria's foreign policies in Africa, and Nobel Peace Prize laureates of African descent. He obtained his doctorate from Oxford University, where he studied as a Rhodes Scholar.

Dr Adeoye O. Akinola is Head of Research and Teaching at the Institute for Pan-African Thought and Conversation (IPATC) at the University of Johannesburg, South Africa. He obtained a PhD in Political Science from the University of KwaZulu-Natal (UKZN) in South Africa. Dr Akinola was a lecturer at Obafemi Awolowo University in Nigeria; a Post-doctoral Fellow at UKZN and the University of Zululand; and a visiting professor at the

United Nations University for Peace (UPEACE) Africa Programme in Addis Ababa. He is the author and editor of several books, including, *Globalization, Democracy and Oil Sector Reform in Nigeria* (Palgrave Macmillan, 2017); and *The Political Economy of Xenophobia in Africa* (Springer, 2018). He specialises in globalisation, African political economy, development studies, resource governance, and conflict and peace studies.

Mr Jan Bade started his career as an econometrician in 1987 at Free University in the Netherlands, where he researched international trade, commodities, land tenure, and enterprise development in Zimbabwe. In 1995, he joined the Agricultural Economics Research Institute in The Hague, where he worked on soil fertility and farm household modelling. In 1998 he became a policy adviser on trade and agriculture to the Ministry of Foreign Affairs and Development Cooperation. Within the Ministry he served as Head of Economic Development at the Netherlands Embassy in Rwanda, as an inter-ministerial budget coordinator, as an independent policy evaluator, and as a strategic adviser. Since 2019, he has served as the first secretary based in Addis Ababa.

Ms Amanda Bisong is a policy officer in the migration programme at the European Centre for Development Policy Management (ECDPM) in Maastricht, the Netherlands. She holds an MA in International Law and Economics from the World Trade Institute, Switzerland, and another MA in International Trade Policy and Trade Law from Lund University, Sweden. She is currently pursuing part-time doctoral studies on regional migration governance (with a focus on West Africa) at the Vrije Universiteit Amsterdam, the Netherlands. Her research focus is on migration agreements and labour migration, and exploring the links between trade and migration in Africa. She has published several research articles on migration governance.

Dr Jesper Bjarnesen has been a senior researcher at the Nordic Africa Institute (NAI) in Uppsala, Sweden, since September 2013, and an Associate Professor at the University of Uppsala. He holds a Master's degree in Anthropology and another in African Regional Studies from the University of Copenhagen, Denmark, and a PhD in Cultural Anthropology from the University of Uppsala. He has worked primarily on the grey zones between forced and voluntary migration in West Africa, in the context of the 2002–

11 civil war in Côte d'Ivoire. He has researched the generational variations of displacement, the dynamics of integration among urban youths, and the broader themes of urban resettlement and transnational families. His current research focuses on the effects of migration governance in terms of the in/visibilities produced by specific legal statuses, and on the 'soft infrastructures' of labour mobilities across and between secondary cities in West Africa. He is the cofounder of the African Migration, Mobility, and Displacement (AMMODI) research network.

DR IBITHEL BOUCHOUCHA is a statistician and demographer, with a PhD in demography from the University of Nanterre, France. Her dissertation examined migration decisions in Tunisia. She also holds a European research certificate in demography from the Max Planck Institute for Demographic Studies and the INED, and is a member of the International Research Centre (IDRC) Directory of Experts in CRVS systems. She works as a part-time professor at the University of Ottawa where she lectures in demography and advanced research methods in social sciences. Her research areas include immigration, gender, employment and development, demographic changes in the Maghreb, particularly in Tunisia, Big Data in e-learning, and student behaviours in online learning.

DR AHMED BUGRE is the Adviser to the Office of the Commissioner for Social Affairs in the African Union Commission in Addis Ababa, Ethiopia. He is a visiting lecturer at the IBS IT & Business School Oldenburg, Germany, where he gives courses on business ethics and corporate social responsibility. He is the founder and Executive Director of the Foundation for Shelter and Support to Migrants (FSM) in San Ġwann, Malta.

DR WILLIE ESELEBOR is a lecturer at the Institute for Peace and Strategic Studies at the University of Ibadan, Nigeria, where he obtained his PhD in Peace and Conflicts. He worked at the Nigerian Immigration Service (1980–2012), was the past President of the Society for Peace Studies and Practice (2011–16), and the Focal Person for the Border Regions in Transition Conference (BRIT 2018) held in Nigeria and the Benin Republic. He is on the Boards of the Association of Borderlands Studies (ABS), Building Blocks for Peace Foundation, and the Society for Peace Studies and Practice. He is a certified Negotiation and Mediation, and Monitoring and Evaluation practitioner. Dr Eselebor has published numerous journal articles and

18 chapters in books. He specialises in international borders, migration, conflict analysis, peacebuilding, and security studies.

Ms AHUNNA EZIAKONWA has a BA in Education from the University of Benin, Nigeria. She is a graduate of Columbia University's School of International and Public Affairs, and an alumnus of the Harvard Kennedy School Executive Programme. In 2018 she was appointed by the United Nations Secretary-General as the Assistant Administrator of the United Nations Development Programme (UNDP), and Director of the Regional Bureau for Africa, at the rank of Assistant Secretary-General. She oversees a billion-dollar development programme in 46 African countries. Her vision is 'Africa's Promise: The UNDP's renewed strategic offer in Africa'. She established the Africa Influencers for Development (AI4D); Africa's Money Works for Africa's Development; UNDP–Tony Elumelu Foundation Partnership; and the Africa Young Women Leaders Initiative. She chairs the UN Development Group in Africa, and spent 10 years as the UN Resident Coordinator in Ethiopia, Uganda, and Lesotho. As the head of UN OCHA in Africa, she oversaw responses to natural disasters, emergencies, and transitions to recovery.

Ms LEONIE FELICITAS JEGEN is a doctoral candidate at the Amsterdam Institute for Social Science Research (AISSR) at the University of Amsterdam in The Netherlands. Her research considers the externalisation of European border control in the context of the Senegalese migrant smuggling policy. Previously, she worked at the European Council on Refugees and Exiles and on research projects at the University of Freiburg and the Vrije Universiteit Brussels (VUB) that investigated European influence on West African migration governance.

Ms ANNA KNOLL is Head of the Migration Programme at the European Centre for Development Policy Management (EPCDM) in Maastricht in The Netherlands. She holds a BA in Philosophy and Economics (University of Bayreuth) and an MSc in International Political Economy (London School of Economics). Her interests and expertise lie in the field of migration and international cooperation between Africa and Europe. She is currently researching the interaction between migration, displacement, and development processes; the external and development dimension of the EU's migration and asylum policies; migration in European development policies, as well as African narratives, policies and processes on migration. She is currently also pursuing a PhD at the Maastricht School of Governance.

Ms Terri Maggott is a doctoral candidate in the Department of Sociology at the University of Johannesburg, and an administrator in the Centre for Sociological Research and Practice (CSRP) in the department. A former student leader in the Economic Freedom Fighters (EFF), her research interests are social and political movements in Africa, particularly student and education-specific movements. She is interested in how social movements are potential sites for the reproduction of class inequalities, and her PhD research focuses on the archive of the National Education Coordinating Committee (NECC), which was instrumental in driving the People's Education movement in South Africa in the 1980s.

Prof. Jack R. Mangala lectures in Political Science and Global Studies at Grand Valley State University in Michigan, United States, where he also serves as Chair of the Area and Global Studies Department. He was Director of the African and African American Studies Program, as well as Director of Area Studies at the university. He holds a PhD in International Law from the Catholic University of Louvain, Belgium, and completed post-doctoral work at the University of Michigan Law School. He is interested in the nexus between international law and human security with a particular focus on migration and governance questions. He has published extensively, most recently, *The Politics of Challenging Presidential Term Limits in Africa* (Palgrave Macmillan, 2020); *Africa and its Global Diaspora: The policy and politics of emigration* (Palgrave Macmillan, 2017); *Africa and the European Union: A strategic partnership* (Palgrave Macmillan, 2013); *New Security Threats and Crises in Africa* (Palgrave Macmillan, 2010); and *Africa and the New World Era: From humanitarianism to a strategic view* (Palgrave Macmillan, 2010).

Dr Khabele Matlosa, a political economist, obtained a PhD from the University of the Western Cape, and an MA from the University of Leeds, United Kingdom. After a stint as Governance Advisor at the United Nations Development Programme (UNDP), he was Director for Political Affairs at the African Union Commission in Addis Ababa, Ethiopia. He is also a visiting Associate Professor in African Diplomacy and Foreign Policy at the University of Johannesburg. Dr Matlosa co-developed the Principles for Election Management, Monitoring, and Observation in the Southern

African Development Community (SADC) region, and was also the lead author of the African Charter on Democracy, Elections, and Governance (ACDEG), which evolved between 2004 and 2006. He specialises in governance, migration, development, conflict transformation, and peace and security.

Ms CELINE MEYERS is a final year doctoral candidate at the University of Johannesburg and is coordinator at the South African National Resource Centre for the First-Year Experience and Students in Transition (SANRC). She holds BA Honours and an MA (both *cum laude*) in Sociology. She has received several prestigious scholarship awards from the Global Excellence and Stature 4.0 (GES), the National Research Foundation (NRF), and merit awards for academic excellence. She is currently focusing on the emerging field of 'digital migration studies', but her other research interests include transnationalism, gender, family, intersectionality, and higher education.

MR ALFRED OMBENI MUSIMWA is a doctoral candidate at the Université catholique de Louvain in Belgium. His research focuses on migration partnerships concluded at various levels between African countries and the European Union. He studies these in the light of the institutional, legal, and democratic openings offered by the Global Compact for Migration. He also holds a degree in Law (Bac+5) from the Official University of Bukavu in the Democratic Republic of Congo, and a complementary MA in Human Rights from the Université catholique de Louvain, the University of Namur, and the University Saint-Louis in Brussels, Belgium.

Ms NOMPUMELELO NDAWONDE, a researcher at the Institute for Pan-African Thought and Conversation (IPATC), is currently registered for a PhD at the University of Cape Town. She obtained an MA in Political Science, a BSc Hons in International Relations (*cum laude*), and a BA in International Studies (*cum laude*), all from the University of KwaZulu-Natal, South Africa. Ms Ndawonde was awarded academic exchange scholarships to study at the University of Calgary in Canada, and the University of Uppsala in Sweden. Her research interests include regional organisations, trade, and development.

DR LINDA ADHIAMBO OUCHO holds a PhD in Ethnic Relations from the University of Warwick, United Kingdom. She currently leads the African Migration and Development Policy Centre (AMADPOC), an independent think tank in Nairobi, Kenya. Dr Oucho returned to Kenya after 16 years abroad, studying in Ghana, Botswana, and the United Kingdom, where her experiences as a migrant fuelled her interest in African migration. As the Executive Director at AMADPOC, she specialised in African women's agency in their decisions to migrate. She has been a consultant at international agencies such as the IOM, the International Centre for Migration and Policy Development (ICMPD), the African Union Commission (AUC), the United Nations Development Programme (UNDP), and the Food and Agriculture Organization (FAO). She works in partnership with universities such as the University of Sussex (UK), the Open University (UK), Carleton University (Canada), the University of Ghana, and Eduardo Mondlane University in Mozambique. She represents AMADPOC as a co-chair for the United Nations Migration Network on Labour Migration in Kenya.

Prof. Pragna Rugunanan is an associate professor and current head of the Department of Sociology at the University of Johannesburg. She obtained a PhD in Sociology from the University of Johannesburg, and has been involved in NRF-funded research on migration and transnationalism, family, well-being and resilience, and social capital and citizenship. Prof. Rugunanan served on the executive of the South African Sociological Association (SASA) and is a group convener for the Industrial and Economic Group. Her current research focuses on the construction of African and South Asian migrant communities in South Africa and migration in the Global South. She specialises in the sociology of migration, labour studies, changing patterns of work, social networks, and community studies, and has published on migration, gender, xenophobia, education, and citizenship.

Prof. Sylvie Sarolea is a professor at the Université catholique de Louvain and teaches immigration law, private international law, and human rights law. She holds an MA in Law (1994) and a PhD (2004) both from the Université catholique de Louvain. Prof. Sarolea is also a lawyer, specialising in international law. Her main research interests are the relationship between national sovereignty and the rights of the migrant, and the harmonisation of EU asylum and migration law. She has been Director of the Equipe droits européens et migrations (EDEM) at UCLouvain since 2011. She is also an expert for the Council of Europe and a member of the Odysseus Network, an academic network for legal studies on migration and asylum in Europe.

Dr Franzisca Zanker holds a PhD in Political Science from the University of Tübingen, and is a senior researcher at the Arnold-Bergstraesser Institute (ABI) in Freiburg, Germany, where she heads the research cluster on 'Patterns of (Forced) Migration'. Before this, she worked at the German Institute of Global and Area Studies Institute in Hamburg. Her research interests include migration and refugee governance, peacebuilding, and civil society. Dr Zanker has been heading a research project on the political stakes of refugee governance in Africa, funded by the German Foundation for Peace Research (2019–21). Together with Jesper Bjarnesen, she co-founded the AEGIS Collaborative Research Group on African Migration, Mobility and Displacement (AMMODI).

Part I
Introduction

Africa–EU migration: Worlds apart?

Jesper Bjarnesen

Introduction

Samia Yusuf Omar became an international news story in 2008, when she represented Somalia in the women's 200 m sprint at the Summer Olympics in Beijing. Wearing a loose, light blue and white t-shirt and a pair of shoes she had been given by her Sudanese competitors, the 17-year-old Omar became a living symbol of the hardships facing Somalia after decades of political instability and the growing menace of the al-Shabaab Islamist militants. More importantly, her spirit was celebrated as a testament to the Olympic creed: 'The important thing in life is not the triumph, but the fight; the essential thing is not to have won, but to have fought well' (Olympics website, n.d.). Omar finished the race in last place by a considerable margin, but the crowd in the National Stadium gave her a standing ovation in recognition of her determination. In 2009, following death threats from al-Shabaab, she relocated with her family to a camp for internally displaced persons (IDPs) outside Mogadishu and eventually left Somalia to pursue her training in Addis Ababa, Ethiopia (Krug, 2012). In a 2010 interview, when asked about the hardships she had endured in Somalia, she responded, 'We Somalis don't look back at those things. We just keep going' (Krug, 2016). In April 2012, Samia decided to attempt to cross the Mediterranean Sea as an irregular migrant in search of better training facilities and a European coach, in the hope of competing at the 2012 Summer Olympics in London. Teresa Krug, a journalist who had followed Omar's career, reported:

> Pushing off with around 70 other people, they soon ran out of petrol, leaving the boat drifting in open water. When an Italian rescue ship finally found them, many of the migrants fought to grab hold of the ropes thrown down to them. In the chaos, many people were knocked into the water – including Omar. Witnesses said after treading water for a while, Omar eventually went under. She was never seen alive again. She was 21 years old (Krug, 2016).

Samia Omar's story is gripping because we had learned about her personal spirit and determination in the face of such difficult circumstances, and because she was an Olympian, in every sense of that word. It is a story that symbolises both the hardships and the hopes that drive so many to risk their lives on the journey in search of a better life in Europe. Her untimely death served as a reminder of the many tragedies and senseless loss of human life on the Mediterranean Sea, which has become so horrendously familiar over the past decade. On 3 October 2013, at least 365 migrants perished off the coast of the Italian island of Lampedusa after their boat caught fire. The African Union (AU) declared 3 November a day of mourning across the continent in commemoration of the victims, with United Nations (UN) Secretary-General Ban Ki-Moon issuing a call to 'the international community as a whole to take action to prevent such tragedies in the future, including measures that address their root causes and that places the vulnerability and human rights of migrants at the centre of the response' (UN, 2013). It is heartbreaking to contemplate the human suffering and loss of life that has continued on and around the Mediterranean Sea.

Samia's tragic fate – and those of so many other migrants – is often forgotten in the current debates around migration governance. It is an understatement to say that over the past decade, migration has become a central theme in relations between Africa and Europe. In fact, migration is a political and diplomatic issue that seems to have imposed itself on a range of policy agendas, from development cooperation to peacebuilding and counterterrorism, and from climate change mitigation to discussions around Africa's demographic transition. This volume offers a broad selection of reflections on how and why migration has gained such prominence in the relations between the two continents. Although the contributions differ in their approaches and conclusions, we begin our reflections from a shared observation that migration governance has become – and is likely to remain – a highly polarising issue on both continents, and in the political relations between them. Indeed, this volume sets out to explore the extent to which African and European understandings of, and approaches to, migration governance have grown worlds apart, and the chapters all offer reflections on how particular actors or agendas relating to migration governance may be mobilised to narrow this gap. In this endeavour, we do not dwell on the tragedy of Samia Omar or the thousands of other lives lost at sea, but we do carry with us an acute awareness of the human consequences of the political battleground around migration governance.

Founded on quantitative and qualitative methodology, the book critically engages Africa–EU migration dynamics. The contributors to this volume are from varied backgrounds with a broad range of experiences, from migration scholars, policy experts and academics with other core practitioners with direct experience of planning, negotiating, and implementing migration-related interventions in different African contexts. What we all share is a professional interest in migration-related issues, and an investment in various African contexts. The world remains an unequal place. International cooperation is still a one-way street; European governments rarely solicit the advice of their African counterparts, and interventions still tend to flow in one direction only – from the North to the South. To reflect this unfortunate reality, the focus of this volume, and the expertise of its authors, is centred on the forms of migration that are most relevant to this unequal relationship, namely African migration to Europe. This is the trajectory that has become so central, and debated, over the past decade, and this is the governance field that has come to define international cooperation across the two continents to a significant degree. In this optic, migration is also somewhat of a one-way street; European migration to Africa, or North–South migration more broadly, does not feature in many policy discussions or political debates, unless it concerns the return of African migrants from longer or shorter sojourns in Europe.

This is not to say that migration does not occur in the other direction. For example, as recent research has shown, between 100,000 and 150,000 Portuguese nationals moved to Angola between 2008 and 2014 in search of better opportunities as the global financial crisis wreaked havoc on the

Portuguese labour market (Åkesson and Orjuela, 2019). And as we should never forget, European colonialism imposed more than borders, languages, and labour regimes; it also imposed several generations of white settlers across the continent. At the dawn of decolonisation in the late 1950s, at least 5.5 million white settlers are estimated to have lived on the continent (World Book Encyclopedia, 1989). While these contemporary and historical forms of North–South migration deserve continued scrutiny and reflection, they are beyond the scope of this volume.

This introductory chapter offers a critical reading of the policy landscape and political debates around African migration to Europe, to set the overarching theme for the chapters that follow. The following section elaborates on the notion that African and European perspectives on migration governance have grown worlds apart, followed by a summary of the so-called European refugee crisis of 2015–16, which became a key catalyser for the current polarisation of migration debates in Europe and in Europe–Africa relations. It further proceeds by discussing governance in relation to the 2030 Agenda for Sustainable Development. In the next two sections, I discuss both European and African perspectives on migration governance, and then analyse the broader contours of the global political economy of migration governance as a context that is often forgotten in relation to migration governance. The final section concludes by outlining the structure of the volume as a whole.

Worlds apart: African migration as a polarising policy issue

African migration to Europe is still making headlines and filling the minutes of high-level summits. What is sometimes stated, and almost always assumed, is that the forms of migration implied are clandestine. In most public or political debates, the notion of 'African migration' has been reduced to the figure of the irregular migrant, travelling across the Sahara Desert and onwards across the Mediterranean Sea.[1] As we address throughout this volume, and further in this introduction, the face of African migration to Europe is a desolate one – and an unwanted one. This imagery, of course, not only fixates on the most superficial aspects of a particular moment of an irregular migrant's journey and life trajectory, it also betrays the realities of who African migrants are, statistically speaking, and how they usually arrive in Europe. The European Union (EU) receives approximately 400,000 Africa-born migrants per year through regular paths (Bjarnesen, 2020), most often via a late flight from an African capital and an early arrival in a European city the following morning, with a residence permit or a tourist visa in hand.

In comparison, approximately 125,000 migrants arrived irregularly in Europe during 2021 along the Mediterranean coast, with Tunisia (15,675 migrants), Egypt (8,654 migrants), and Bangladesh (7,848 migrants) being the top three sending countries, accounting for approximately 25 per cent of the total arrivals, according to the United Nations Humanitarian Commission for Refugees (UNHCR website). According to the International Organization for Migration (IOM), '[b]etween 2017 and 2020, 535,632 migrants arrived irregularly in Italy, Spain, Greece, Malta and Cyprus by sea and land … of which 151,869 individuals (27%) were nationals of countries in West and Central Africa' (IOM, 2021: 1), which translates into an average of around 38,000 per annum. According to the same estimates, approximately 12,000 migrants from West and Central Africa arrived irregularly in Europe in 2020, confirming that irregular arrivals have been declining considerably over the past five years. Even if these figures omit the significant numbers of migrants arriving in Europe from the Horn of Africa, these proportions illustrate that regular migration is by far the most common form of migration from Africa to Europe.

Nevertheless, the imagery of irregular migration from Africa to Europe underlies much of the political anxiety in European debates, which in turn informs the policies intended to stem these perceived flows. This has led the EU and its member states to scale up their efforts to control immigration by reinforcing border control (Cusumano, 2019; Lemberg Pedersen 2019), limiting legal entries (Bjarnesen, 2020), targeting human trafficking networks in sending regions (Sanchez, 2020), and boosting border patrols in third countries through externalisation strategies (Gammeltoft-Hansen, 2012; Spijkerboer, 2018; Liguori, 2019). In addition to these hard power measures, Europe has also engaged in softer strategies to prevent future migrants from reaching EU territory, including investments in information campaigns intended to discourage people from leaving their home regions (Brekke and Thorbjørnsrud, 2020; Vammen, Cold-Ravnkilde and Lucht, 2021) and the reframing of international development cooperation as addressing the so-called 'root causes' of (irregular) migration, most notably through the EU Emergency Trust Fund for Africa (EUTF) (see chapters 13 and 14 in this volume).

While the numbers of irregular entries have, indeed, decreased in recent years, many of these measures have been highly controversial, arguably contributing to the suffering and ill-treatment of migrants along Europe's outer borders and further afield. Most famously, EU support to the Libyan coastguard, to prevent migrants from using this North African country as a departure point across the Mediterranean, has been widely criticised. In a political context in which warring factions are staking their claims to state power, the Libyan coastguard has been widely accused of systematic abuse against migrants in inhumane detention centres and along migrant routes (Amnesty International, 2021a, 2021b). It is estimated that approximately 570,000 migrants are caught in limbo in Libya, unable to continue their onwards journeys, and unwilling or unable to return (IOM, 2022).

The much-criticised EU–Turkey deal, signed in March 2016 (Mandıracı, 2020), provided the EU with a way of denying Syrian refugees and other migrants an entry point to the EU, but the Turkish authorities are accused of neglecting the plight of the more than 3.6 million Syrians currently stranded in Turkey, and the lucrative deal has also enabled Turkey to invest in the construction of a Trumpian border wall along its border with Syria (Vammen and Lucht, 2017). As a final example of the effects of Europe's quest to seal its outer borders, the winter of 2021–22 saw horrendous reports from the Belarusian border with the EU, where the Lukasjenko regime seems to have deliberately organised the transportation of Afghani refugees and other migrants to its western borders, releasing them to cross into Poland and Lithuania on foot. This was perceived as a strategy to put pressure on the EU to lift its sanctions on his regime (Brady, 2021), but as Belarus' neighbours caught on to this ploy, they closed their borders, leaving migrants to starve and freeze in a desolate no-man's land (Tondo, 2022). This cynical tug-of-war is estimated to have led to at least 17 deaths in December 2021 alone (al-Najjar et al., 2021), and adds to the long and shameful list of the effects of Europe's uncompromising quest to restrict irregular entry.

In this context of growing political tensions around immigration issues in Europe, the AU has been slow to articulate its joint position on migration governance, but EU–AU negotiations on the issue have tended to pit two distinct positions against each other, with the European demands for increased border control and more permissive deportation agreements dominating the conversation (Mbiyozo, 2019). The AU member states have consistently questioned the justification for accepting the involuntary returns of their citizens, even when these agreements have been combined with promises of increased financial support. African actors have also insisted that migration, including African migration to Europe, is an important asset for the continent, as migrants send home remittances, pursue higher education, and establish transnational bonds through the vast and growing African diaspora (Gnimassoun and Anyanwu, 2019; Zeleza 2019). This proclivity is evident in the attention afforded by the AU to the diaspora, which it increasingly refers to as its 'sixth region', through initiatives such as the African Union Commission's Citizens and Diaspora Organisation (CIDO) and the African Union Diaspora Programme.

In other words, there are fundamental differences in the way the EU and the AU, as the central organising bodies in this field, perceive the role of migration. As discussed further below, EU immigration policy has consolidated its view of migration as a symptom of societal problems in the Global South, the 'root causes' of which must be treated through targeted policy measures. In contrast to this view, AU perspectives on South–North migration tend to be informed by the optimism that characterised the international agenda around migrant remittances a decade ago, when the combined funds that migrants sent back to their home communities surpassed the total budget for international development aid (Barne and Pirlea, 2019). African diasporas have increasingly claimed influence and visibility in national politics and development efforts in their home countries over the past two decades. While the role of remittances in poverty reduction may be less straightforward than previously assumed, this implies that transnational migration of African citizens to the Global North has, indeed, been an important and productive asset that the AU member states are obliged to protect in the current international policy climate.

Contrary to the European view of South–North migration as a problem to be solved, the AU reflects a view of the same movements as an asset to be valued and utilised. These broad strokes of the current migration policy landscape underlie many of the outcomes and challenges of Europe–Africa relations relating to migration in recent years. On this note, it is impossible to appreciate the stakes of global migration governance today without a thorough consideration of the so-called 'refugee crisis' of 2015–16 and its aftermath. This assertion does not presuppose that the European responses or political agendas emerging from this crisis should claim centre stage, as they have tended to do in much debate in academia and elsewhere. It simply means that the European refugee crisis has had a decisive and lasting impact on the ways in which global migration governance concerns are articulated and negotiated, and that this convergence around a singular reading of a delimited, and tragic, event must be critically analysed.

The 2015–16 European refugee crisis

In March 2011, the Bashar al-Assad regime in Syria clamped down on anti-government protests with deadly force, which initially sparked further protests and eventually marked the beginning of a devastating and complex civil war (see, for example, Loft et al., 2021), which is estimated to have claimed more than 500,000 lives over the past 10 years (SOHR, 2020). By the end of 2014, approximately 7.6 million Syrians were displaced within the country and more than 3 million Syrian nationals were registered as international refugees (according to UNHCR). In 2015 and 2016, approximately 2.2 million people applied for asylum in the EU, with Syrian nationals posting 650,000 or about 30 per cent of all applications (Connor, 2017). This number, however, only accounted about 5 per cent of all displaced Syrian nationals. It is in this sense that the so-called 'refugee crisis' in Europe in 2015–16 must be distinguished from the Syrian refugee crisis, which is still ongoing, and which had displaced more than half of the country's population by 2020, according to the UNHCR. As a starting point for understanding Europe's experience of receiving the largest numbers of refugees since World War II, it is important to emphasise that the events of 2015–16 did not involve the displacement of European citizens, but rather the irregular arrival of people from outside the EU.

What occasioned the unprecedented impact on European public debate and, eventually, policy thinking was, therefore, a bureaucratic crisis concerning the principles of asylum and the national and EU-level legal and administrative mechanisms for dealing with the large numbers of migrants arriving between the spring of 2015 and mid-2016. Characterising the European refugee crisis as a bureaucratic crisis does not suggest that the only problem or emergency worth considering at the time was administrative in nature. To the contrary, we wish to emphasise that while there were media reports on the scale and nature of the Syrian refugee crisis (of which the arrival of Syrian nationals on European territory was but a minor part), the images that created an impact on European audiences were primarily of

Syrian refugees and other migrants arriving on the shores of Italy, Greece and Spain, or walking the highways of central Europe, rather than the devastation and human suffering taking place in Syria and its neighbouring countries. Similarly, despite substantial grassroots mobilisations across Europe to 'welcome refugees' and counter the voices of anti-immigration rhetoric, the national agendas in most European countries were influenced markedly by the latter. The disproportionate attention and reactions to the comparatively minor challenge of accommodating people arriving in EU territory warrants us to treat the very notion of a 'refugee (or migrant) crisis' with considerable reservation. On that note, and for the purposes of this introduction, four key observations regarding the nature and scale of the so-called European refugee crisis warrant further elaboration.

As a first observation, the so-called 'refugee crisis' was *delimited in time*, spanning about a year from mid-2015 to mid-2016. By mid-2016, monthly arrivals were back to their pre-2015 levels, with the total number of registered arrivals dropping from more than 1 million in 2015 to approximately 374,000 in 2016 and around 185,000 in 2017. These numbers have continued to decline, with approximately 95,000 arrivals registered in 2020, according to the UNHCR.

Furthermore, as already implied, the European refugee crisis of 2015–16 was a direct effect of the intensification of *armed conflict in Syria*, with mass displacements accelerating from approximately 350,000 registered refugees in January 2013 to more than 2.3 million in January 2014 and 3.7 million in January 2015.[2] The vast majority of Syrians displaced across international borders continue to be located in the immediate subregion, with more than 3.7 million Syrians currently registered in Turkey alone.[3] In addition, up towards 7 million people are estimated to have been displaced *within* Syria, according to the UNHCR. It is particularly in light of these proportions that the notion of the 'refugee crisis' – so often evoked in discussions about the events of 2015–16 – seems so unapologetically Eurocentric. The reactions from European publics and decision-makers were not a response to the plight of Syrian nationals, among whom more than 10 million people – more than half of the total population – were displaced by 2016, but rather a response to the irregular entry of the relatively small proportion managing to make it to European shores.

Third, the number of migrants from sub-Saharan Africa remained *relatively stable* throughout the so-called refugee or migration crisis. From about 2005, irregular migration from Africa was given a new face, at first depicted by colourful fishing boats departing from Senegal and Mauritania towards the Canary Islands (Bjarnesen 2007), and later as overcrowded boats or inflatable rafts heading for Greece or Italy. Prior to this, irregular migration had been associated mainly with undocumented migrant workers, overstaying their visas to remain in Europe, having arrived by air. With the imposition of carrier sanctions on private airlines in the early 1990s,[4] security controls and visa requirements were ramped up at international airports, which led migrants without the right to regular entry to search for new options. Crossing the Mediterranean Sea to reach the Canary Islands was one such tactic. In 2005, 36,542 arrivals were registered across the Mediterranean, which was below the average of about 44,000 for the 10-year period between 2003 and 2013 (Fargues 2017: 26).[5]

A new chapter in European outlooks on irregular migration began in 2014, when the number of arrivals rose above 200,000, and news of migrants perishing at sea led to widespread outrage and a promise to 'never again' witness such calamities in the ports of Europe. On 2 October 2014, in her one-year commemoration of the Lampedusa tragedy, in which more than 365 migrants lost their lives, the EU Commissioner, Cecilia Malmström, emphatically described the tragedy as 'a terrible reminder of how we must strive to keep Europe open to those who seek protection'.[6] As we have seen, neither the numbers of arrivals and casualties nor the European reluctance to assist those in need of protection had seen its darkest days, as numbers surged in 2015, and political and policy responses across Europe turned increasingly restrictive. Nevertheless, throughout these dramatic and unprecedented times, the number of sub-Saharan African arrivals in Europe were proportionally negligent, and remained at similar levels in the years that followed. More recently, this consistency has seen a considerable decline, as the number of arrivals has dropped significantly. The effects of the EU externalisation policies in North Africa and the Sahel region led to a significant decrease in the number of arrivals, from 185,139 in 2017 to 95,031 in 2020, according to the UNHCR.

Finally, as already mentioned, throughout the previous decade, the proportion of Africa-born nationals entering the EU *legally* has far exceeded the number of irregular entries. The number of legal arrivals, expressed in the number of first residence permits issued, dropped significantly between 2008 and 2012 – from 442,000 to 270,000 – but has remained more or less stable since then, with 288,000 first residence permits issued in 2016 (European Commission, 2018:15). Figure 1.1 illustrates that, between 2008 and 2016, the most significant shift occurred for Moroccan nationals, who experienced a 52 per cent drop in the number of issued residence permits. Outside of the top-10 sending countries listed in Figure 1.1, the majority of African countries shared around one-third of all residence permits issued, but experienced less dramatic drops over the eight-year period surveyed.

Figure 1.1: First residence permits issued by the EU-28 to African citizens by citizenship, 2008–16, top-10 countries of origin listed (absolute numbers, in thousands)

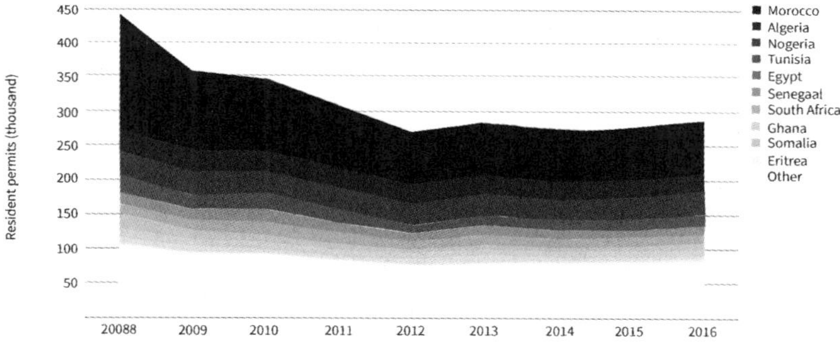

Source: European Commission (2018: 15)

The overall trend in African migration to Europe has been one of regular entries far exceeding irregular entries, and the number has been declining rather than increasing over the past decade. These trends become even more striking when one considers that the combined African population was growing by about 2.5 per cent per year, on average, over this period, which would warrant a gradual increase in the overall number of migrants.

What these observations amount to is that legal entries by Africa-born migrants to the EU fell dramatically between 2008 and 2012, primarily as a result of increasingly restrictive immigration policies, and that irregular entries have increased slightly over the past 15 years. Furthermore, the increases in irregular migration could be explained by the overall population growth rate rather than by changing mobility dynamics as such. The European refugee crisis, therefore, was first and foremost an EU-level *administrative crisis*, which exposed some of the underlying weaknesses of the Dublin and Schengen agreements and their practical implementation. Nevertheless, the impact of this bureaucratic crisis in Europe has had global repercussions. As South African migration scholar Loren Landau has commented, '[t]he focus on the Syrian refugee crisis, particularly its effects on Europe, will dominate discussions and frame any international compact for protecting refugee and migrant rights worldwide. What might work politically for Europe may well come down on the backs of migrants and refugees across Africa and elsewhere' (Landau, 2016).

The political economy of global migration governance

As several contributors to this volume point out, the disproportionate attention paid to how European member states were affected by the so-called refugee crisis – as well as the dominance of European agendas in migration governance between the two continents – cannot be fully understood without considering the broader structural, political, and economic relations between Africa and Europe. The Sixth EU–AU summit in Brussels in February 2022 was framed under the familiar banner of 'a partnership of equals', which has yet to translate into any genuine sense of mutuality (Aycart-Piquer, 2022; Maru, 2022). Regardless of the intentions of the Brussels summit, continental cooperation between the EU (with an estimated 2020 real GDP per capita of €29,890)[7] and the AU (with a GDP per capita of approximately €10,190)[8] is premised on one of the largest interregional socio-economic discrepancies in the world.

Furthermore, when Muammar Gaddafi famously threatened to unleash sub-Saharan African migrants on Europe were he not rewarded for keeping them out, his blunt and unapologetic style brought out sentiments that are often implied much more subtly in official statements. During a visit to Rome in August 2010, Gaddafi issued the threat in no uncertain terms:

> Tomorrow Europe might no longer be European, and even black, as there are millions who want to come in … We don't know what will happen, what will be the reaction of the white and Christian Europeans faced with this influx of starving and ignorant Africans … We don't know if Europe will remain an advanced and united continent or if it will be destroyed, as happened with the barbarian invasions (BBC News, 2010).

While Gaddafi's controversial rhetoric and politics are in no way representative of the way African decision-makers have approached the issue of African migration to Europe, Gaddafi's crude threat to unleash an 'influx of starving and ignorant Africans' may be read as a mirroring of Europe's most sinister politics around immigration – the fear of the racialised other – which continues to dominate political debates, although usually in more subtle ways. Since the fall of Libya's strongman, the country has remained central to European interests in stemming African migration, but the general tone from African stakeholders has become more unified around an alignment with European interests in reinforcing border controls and discouraging aspiring migrants from leaving their home regions. The xenophobic and racist undertones of European migration politics was spelled out with Gadaffiesque bluntness by Bulgarian Prime Minister Kiril Petkov in reaction to the arrival of Ukrainian refugees following the Russian invasion in February 2022:

> These are not the refugees we are used to … these people are Europeans … These people are intelligent, they are educated people … This is not the refugee wave we have been used to, people we were not sure about their identity, people with unclear pasts, who could have been even terrorists … In other words, there is not a single European country now which is afraid of the current wave of refugees (Brito 2022).

Although similar sentiments towards non-European refugees and other migrants are shared across the EU, they are obviously not representative of European public opinion overall, or of the motivations behind European migration policies. But it is necessary to address the fact that, in addition to and entangled with the socio-economic disparities between Africa and Europe, xenophobic and racist sentiments and politics constitute another underlying premise for the purported 'partnership of equals' between the two continents.

Migration and mobility dynamics are a central field of contestation in relation to these disparities. Rather than seeing the advances in transportation and communications technologies over the past decades as creating unproblematic 'free flows' of goods, people, capital, and ideas, increased openness resulting from globalisation has been more likely to lead to increased fragmentation and introversion, which are expressed through hyper-nationalism, xenophobia, and other forms of aggressive identity politics (Geschiere and Nyamnjoh, 2000). Although these tendencies occur throughout the globe, from Myanmar to South Africa and the United States to Australia, the wealthiest regions of the world still have the upper hand in shaping global access to mobility. In other words, through restrictive migration regimes, unfair terms of trade, transnational outsourcing of labour, and the perpetuation and expansion of shadow economies in the Global North, globalisation has tended to reinforce and aggravate socio-economic inequalities within and between nations, including a highly selective and restrictive distribution of transnational mobility.

This implies that the main obstacles to a less contested and costly regulation of migration globally are no longer primarily technological but, rather, are political and bureaucratic in nature. Notwithstanding the need to reduce carbon dioxide emissions and other environmentally detrimental effects, long-distance travel and communication have never been more efficient or affordable. What makes it difficult for aspiring migrants to travel, work, and settle in the ways they intend is primarily unfavourable labour market conditions – such as rigid and politically motivated demands on standardised diplomas; language skills; and increasingly even cultural assimilation – and restrictive immigration policies in the Global North. As the late Zygmunt Bauman (1998) argued, in the age of globalisation, access to international mobility has become a global currency, ensuring access and speed to the cosmopolitan elites and imposing restrictions and inertia on the vast majority of aspiring migrants.

The structural background to current debates and policy outlooks regarding sub-Saharan African migration, particularly to Europe, points to a series of historical and political factors that combine to create fundamental anxiety regarding immigration in the Global North and a counter-productive sense of continual emergency in migration governance regimes. In political and public discourse alike, these anxieties translate into an overly simplistic and criminalising understanding and representation of so-called economic migrants, and a growing tendency for European states to evade or limit their international responsibilities in burden sharing around asylum seekers and refugees.

Migration governance and the Sustainable Development Goals

Within the space of a few years, it has become the norm rather than the exception that immigration policies are high on national political agendas. Regardless of one's opinions in this regard, this inward-looking attitude to international migration is detrimental to policy thinking at all levels of migration governance, since it limits the scope of sustainable solutions to the current challenges, and sidesteps long-term investments in the development potential of transnational mobilities more broadly. Put differently, while particular notions of 'migration' are endlessly debated in domestic *political* terms, human mobility as a *policy* field has been caught in a virtual deadlock – particularly at the EU level – as illustrated by the lack of concerted action around the UN-led Global Compact for Safe, Orderly and Regular Migration (Kainz and Le Cos, 2022) and the current stalemate in the negotiations of the proposed EU Pact for Migration and Asylum (Hein, 2021). While this deadlock is, to a large extent, the outcome of European political sensibilities, migration scholars, policy analysts, and decision-makers are increasingly searching for ways to work around these broad political debates and ideals, to offer more delimited and practical solutions to break the impasse (Foresti, 2018).

In this spirit, the Institute for Pan-African Thought and Conversation (IPATC) convened a two-day policy dialogue, bringing together 30 senior officials, policy experts, and civil society actors to reflect on how to explore areas of convergence between Africa and the EU in the area of migration governance:

> Its three key goals were: first, to enhance dialogue and engagement between African and European policymakers and civil society on the challenges of conflict, governance, and migration; second, to offer concrete solutions to policymakers for the effective management of migration; and third, to engage and inform African and European publics about issues relating to migration and the implementation of the UN Global Compact (IPATC, 2019: 1).[9]

This volume is a direct outcome of these consultations, which also included an initial one-day policy dialogue in Brussels in October 2018, co-organised by the Friedrich Ebert Stiftung (FES) EU offices, the Organisation of African, Caribbean and Pacific States (ACP) Secretariat, and the IPATC (IPATC, 2018), and a total of four migration-themed webinars organised in collaboration with the Nordic Africa Institute (NAI) in 2020 and 2021 (IPATC and NAI, 2020, 2021).

The emphasis on the Global Compact for Safe, Orderly and Regular

Migration (GCM) signals the commitment of the IPATC and its collaborators, shared by the contributors to this book, to a less polarising and more holistic understanding of and approach to migration governance than the one that has prevailed in relation to African–EU relations in recent years. A key dimension of this holistic outlook may be expressed as a broader view of how development and migration interact. In this regard, it is important to remember that the GCM grew out of the 2030 Agenda for Sustainable Development and the Sustainable Development Goals (SDGs). While the preceding UN framework for global development, the Millennium Development Goals, were virtually silent on the matter, the SDGs are surprisingly nuanced in their treatment of the role of migration in relation to development. To a large extent, the complexity of what migration implies is reflected in the 2023 Agenda, and to some extent in the SDGs.

The most substantial statement of the overall view of migration is found in paragraph 29 of the introductory text of the Declaration of the 2030 Agenda for Sustainable Development. It states that the signatories 'recognize the positive contribution of migrants for inclusive growth and sustainable development', and 'also recognize that international migration is a multidimensional reality of major relevance for the development of countries of origin, transit, and destination, which requires coherent and comprehensive responses'. The signatories thereby pledge to 'ensure safe, orderly and regular migration involving full respect for human rights and the humane treatment of migrants regardless of migration status, of refugees and of displaced persons'. This overall statement provides a considerable counterbalance to the tendency of migrant-receiving states to criminalise irregular migrants to justify the harsh measures they take to avoid responsibility for their plight.

While the introductory statement of the 2030 Agenda invites a broadened and decriminalising view of migrants, involuntary and irregular forms of movement, not surprisingly, are a dominant theme in the SDGs. Of the 17 SDGs, only one (10.7) includes a migration-specific goal: 'Facilitate orderly, safe, regular, and responsible migration', and an additional six include migration-related subgoals or targets. In conjunction, these goals address the health (3.C); educational possibilities (4.B), labour rights (8.8); legal identity (16.9), as well as the measurability of migrants without limiting these ambitions to particular groups or statuses. But while these goals aim to improve the conditions for all migrants, an emphasis is placed on the regulation of migration, most specifically through goal 10.7 and the three subgoals addressing human trafficking (5.2, 8.7, and 16.2).

In this light, while far from ideal, the GCM provides an overarching framework that acknowledges in policy-applicable detail how the role of migration, in relation to global development, is more than just a concerning symptom of poverty, unemployment, armed conflict, and environmental disaster. People move across long distances and time to maintain, strengthen, or create bonds with their relatives or with other important counterparts. Many travel to seek out long-term or temporary opportunities in agriculture, trade, industry, or a range of other livelihoods. They travel to pursue further education. All these movements carry with them an immense development potential, which is evident in the AU's current efforts to stimulate continental free movement within the African Continental Free Trade Area (AfCFTA) agreement. This book, and the reflections initiated by IPATC on which it builds, may be read as a series of contributions to support and substantiate these initiatives intended to bring migration governance into a more holistic and less polarising conversation with global development. The overall challenge facing us in this regard is, simply put, to offer viable ways of governing both internal and international migration that would ensure the human rights of all migrants, and an active engagement with the development potential of migration. Rejecting the view that migration from and within the Global South is a problem to be solved, our fundamental orientation is that migration should be allowed to become even more central to the global development agenda, contributing to global poverty reduction and a range of other development targets. It is our hope that this book offers a small contribution in this regard.

Outline of the book

This comprehensive collection is structured into eight sections, each reflecting a central dimension for understanding and engaging with African and European perspectives on migration governance. In Part II, four chapters provide an overarching reflection on the structural dynamics affecting migration governance on the African continent, and on some of the systemic challenges that can be understood as drivers of off-continent migration. First, Adekeye Adebajo offers his analysis of Africa's security landscape and its effects on African migration within the continent and towards Europe. Next, Khabele Matlosa offers an Africa-centred discussion of the links between good governance and migration management, and Franzisca Zanker adds a a critical reflection on European priorities in international cooperation in relation to migration governance. Adeoye O. Akinola considers the roles of the diaspora, with a particular focus on providing a link between development and remittances.

In Part III, the chapters provide an in-depth analysis of migration dynamics across five geographical sending regions on the African continent. Ibtihel Bouchoucha's chapter focuses on the Maghreb; Linda Adhiambo Oucho's chapter looks at East Africa and the Horn of Africa; Amanda Bisong's chapter examines West Africa; Pragna Rugunanan, Terri Maggott and Celine Meyers discuss the dynamics in southern Africa; and Alfred Ombeni Musimwa and Sylvie Sarolea conclude the section with a chapter on the Great Lakes Region.

Part IV presents two chapters on the predominant governance agendas at the continental level, with Ahmed Bugre focusing on an African Union perspective and Jan Bade emphasising the European Union perspective. Part V then reflects on a central policy issue in current migration governance, namely the notion of 'addressing the root causes' of African migration to Europe. Jesper Bjarnesen first provides a Europe-centred perspective after which Jack Mangala offers an Africa-centred reflection on the same policy idea.

The following three sections shift attention to the key actors in African–EU migration governance. Part VI focuses on civil society, with Willie Eselebor offering an African perspective and Anna Knoll adding a European perspective. Part VII considers the role of the United Nations in relation to migration governance, with Nompumelelo Ndawonde's chapter highlighting the role of the UNHCR; Ahunna Eziakonwa focuses on the role of UNDP; and Leonie Felicitas Jegen reflects on the role of the IOM.

Part VIII presents the concluding chapter, where Adeoye O. Akinola draws together key insights from the contributors. The overall purpose of this volume is not to provide a unified reading of the realities of migration governance or policy, or of the potential or needs for policy reform. With this book, we intend to offer a series of reflections on key dimensions of African and European migration governance from writers engaged with these issues as policy analysts, decisions-makers, activists, or academics. It is our hope that these critical reflections will provide a nuanced insight into the complexities and challenges of Africa–Europe relations with regard to migration governance, and a toolbox of research-based reflections on how to understand the disparities within this policy field, and work towards more common ground and long-term policy solutions.

Notes

1 Although reliable data are difficult to come by, the European border agency, Frontex, suggests that the most common form of irregular entry into Europe (from any part of the world) remains by air, as migrants enter the EU on a temporary visa and then remain once the visa has expired, thereby becoming irregular migrants. For the purposes of this volume, however, the imagery of migrants crossing the Mediterranean Sea has become a shorthand for irregular African migration in the debates we wish to address.

2 See http://syrianrefugees.eu/

3 See https://data2.unhcr.org/en/situations/syria

4 Carrier sanctions place a primary responsibility for ensuring that travellers have the necessary permissions and documents on transportation companies. The 1990 Schengen Implementation Agreement integrated this principle into EU law, as a condition for EU member states to join the Schengen collaboration (see Baird 2017: 325).

5 During this decade, the number of sea arrivals to Europe fluctuated significantly, from as low as 9,851 in 2010 to as high as 70,471 the following year (Fargues, 2017: 26).

6 https://ec.europa.eu/commission/presscorner/detail/en/STATE-MENT_14_296.

7 Figures from Eurostat, https://ec.europa.eu/eurostat/databrowser/view/tec00001/default/table?lang=en.

8 Figures calculated from World Bank Data, https://data.worldbank.org/indicator/NY.GDP.PCAP.PP.CD.

9 The editors wish to reiterate their gratitude to Professor Adekeye Adebajo for initiating these consultations, and for his guidance and encouragement in preparing this volume.

References

Åkesson, L. and Orjuela, C. 2019. 'North–South migration and the corrupt other: Practices of bribery among Portuguese migrants in Angola', *Geopolitics*, 24(1): 230–50.

al-Najjar, M., Deeb, B., Van Dijken, K., Hebel, C., Kallsch, M. et al. 2021. 'A chronicle of refugee deaths along the border between Poland and Belarus', *Der Spiegel*, 22 December 2021.

Amnesty International. 2021a. Libya: 'No one will look for you': Forcibly returned from sea to abusive detention in Libya', Amnesty International, 15 July 2021, Index Number: MDE 19/4439/2021.

Amnesty International. 2021b. 'Libya: Unlawful lethal force and mass arrests in unprecedented migrant crackdown', Amnesty International, 11 October 2021.

Aycart-Piquer, L. 2022. 'AU–EU summit: One-sided partnership'. Overseas Development Institute (ODI), 24 February 2022.

Baird, T. 2017. 'Carrier sanctions in Europe: A comparison of trends in 10 countries', *European Journal of Migration and Law*, 19: 307–34.

Bauman, Z. 1998. *Globalisation. The human consequences.* Cambridge: Polity Press.

Barne, D. and Pirlea, F. 2019. 'Money sent home by workers now largest source of external financing in low- and middle-income countries (excluding China)', World Bank Data Blog, 2 July 2019.

BBC News. 2010. 'Gaddafi wants EU cash to stop African migrants', *BBC News*, 31 August 2010.

Bjarnesen, J. 2020. 'Shifting the narrative on African migration: The numbers, the root causes, the alternatives – get them right!', NAI Policy Notes 2020: 1. Uppsala: The Nordic Africa Research Unit.

Bjarnesen, J. 2007. 'On the move. Young men navigating paths towards adulthood in Gueule Tapée (Dakar)', Master's thesis No. 454, Department of Anthropology, University of Copenhagen.

Brady, H. 2021. 'Europe's sharper edges: EU migration policy after Lukashenko'. International Centre for Migration Policy Development (ICMPDP). ICMPD Research blog, 15 December 2021.

Brekke, J-P. and Thorbjørnsrud, K. 2020. 'Communicating borders: Governments deterring asylum seekers through social media campaigns', *Migration Studies*, 8(1): 43–65.

Brito, R. 2022. 'Europe welcomes Ukrainian refugees – others, not so much', AP News, 28 February 2022.

Connor, P. 2017. 'After record migration, 80% of Syrian asylum applicants approved to stay in Europe', 2 October 2017. Washington, DC: Pew Research Center.

Cusumano, E. 2019. 'Migrant rescue as organized hypocrisy: EU maritime missions offshore Libya between humanitarianism and border control', *Cooperation and Conflict* 54(1): 3–24.

European Commission. 2018. 'Many more to come? Migration from and within Africa'. Luxembourg: Joint Research Centre, Publications Office of the European Union. doi:10.2760/1702.

Fargues, P. 2017. *Four Decades of Cross-Mediterranean Undocumented Migration to Europe: A review of the evidence.* Geneva: International Organisation for Migration (IOM).

Foresti, M. 2018. 'More than outrage, we need to face hard lessons on migration', *The New Humanitarian*, 27 June 2018, Refugees Deeply.

Gammeltoft-Hansen, T. 2012. 'The externalisation of European migration control and the reach of International Refugee Law', in E. Guild and P. Minderhoud (eds). *The First Decade of EU Migration and Asylum Law.* Leiden: Brill, pp. 273–98.

Geschiere, P. and Nyamnjoh, F. 2000. 'Capitalism and autochthony: The seesaw of mobility and belonging', *Public Culture*, 12: 423–52.

Gnimassoun, B. and Anyanwu, J.C. 2019. 'The diaspora and economic development in Africa', *Review of World Economics*, 155: 785–817.

Hein, C. 2021. 'Looking for pact-makers: The debate on the deadlocked EU Migration and Asylum Pact'. Paris: Heinrich-Böll-Stiftung, 12 November 2021.

International Organization for Migration (IOM). 2022. 'Libya's Migration Report, January–February 2021. Round 35. Geneva: International Organisation for Migration (IOM).

International Organization for Migration (IOM). 2021. 'Irregular migration routes to Europe, West and Central Africa, January-December 2020'. Geneva: International Organisation for Migration (IOM).

IPATC. 2019. 'Implementing the United Nations (UN) Global Compact on Migration: Conflict, governance, and human mobility in Africa/European Union (EU) relations', *IPATC Policy Brief* 5, October 2019.

IPATC. 2018. 'Migration in the EU-ACP Partnership After 2020: Implementing the UN Global Compact', *IPATC Policy Brief No. 2*, November 2018.

IPATC and NAI. 2021. 'Centring the voices of African migrants in Africa/European Union (EU) migration debates', *IPATC Policy Brief 9*. Johannesburg: Institute for Pan-African Thought and Conversation and Uppsala, Sweden: the Nordic Africa Institute, June 2021.

IPATC and NAI. 2020. 'The impact of COVID-19 on Africa–European Union (EU) migration', *IPATC Policy Brief* 7. Institute for Pan-African Thought and Conversation (Johannesburg, South Africa) and the Nordic Africa Institute (Uppsala, Sweden), August 2020.

Kainz, L. and Le Coz, C. 2022. 'The winding road to Marrakech. Lessons from the European negotiations of the Global Compact for Migration'. Washington, DC: Migration Policy Institute, January 2022.

Krug, T. 2016. 'The story of Samia Omar, the Olympic runner who drowned in the Med', *The Guardian*, 3 August 2016.

Krug, T. 2012. 'Grieving for Somali Olympian Samia Omar', *Al-Jazeera*, 27 August 2012.

Landau, L. 2016. 'U.N. "Global Compact" may prove regressive for Africa's migrants', *The New Humanitarian*, 14 September 2016, Refugees Deeply.

Lemberg-Pedersen, M. 2019. 'Manufacturing displacement. Externalization and postcoloniality in European migration control', *Global Affairs*, 5(3): 247–71.

Liguori, Anna. 2019. *Migration Law and the Externalization of Border Controls. European state responsibility*. London: Routledge.

Loft, P., Harding, M. and Sturge, G. 2021. 'The Syrian civil war: Timeline and statistics', Research Briefing No. 9381, 29 November 2021. London: House of Commons Library.

Mandıracı, B. 2020. 'Sharing the burden: Revisiting the EU–Turkey migration deal'. International Crisis Group Commentary, 13 March 2020.

Maru, M.T. 2022. 'AU–EU Sixth Summit: Building the new post-pandemic partnership on migration and mobility', Migration Policy Centre (MPC) Blog, 23 February 2022.

Mbiyozo, A-N. 2019. *Returning Migrants. Europe's focus, but at what cost?* ISS Policy Brief No. 127. Johannesburg: Institute for Security Studies.

Olympics website. n.d. 'What is the Olympic creed?' Online at: https://olympics.com/ioc/faq/olympic-symbol-and-identity/what-is-the-olympic-creed (accessed 14 March 2022).

Sanchez, G. 2020. *Beyond Militias and Tribes: The facilitation of migration in Libya*. EUI Working Paper RSCAS 2020/09, European University Institute, Robert Schuman Centre for Advanced Studies, Migration Policy Centre.

Spijkerboer, T. 2018. 'The global mobility infrastructure: Reconceptualising the externalisation of migration control', *European Journal of Migration and Law*, 20(4): 452–69.

Syrian Observatory on Human Rights (SOHR). 2020. 'On International Human Rights Day: Millions of Syrians robbed of "rights" and 593 thousand killed in a decade', Syrian Observatory on Human Rights (SOHR), 9 December 2020.

Tondo, L. 2022. 'In limbo: The refugees left on the Belarusian-Polish border – a photo essay', *The Guardian*, 8 February 2022. Online at: https://www.theguardian.com/global-development/2022/feb/08/in-limbo-refugees-left-on-belarusian-polish-border-eu-frontier-photo-essay (accessed 14 April 2022).

United Nations (UN). 2013. Press Release: 'Saddened by reports of second capsized boat carrying migrants, Secretary-General calls on international community to prevent future tragedies'. United Nations, 12 October 2013. Online at: https://www.un.org/press/en/2013/sgsm15390.doc.htm (accessed 14 April 2022).

Vammen, I.M.S., Cold-Ravnkilde, S. and Lucht, H. 2021. 'Borderwork in the expanded EU–African borderlands', *New Geopolitics, Special Issue*, 15 December 2021. Copenhagen: Danish Institute for International Studies.

Vammen, I.M.S. and Lucht, H. 2017. *The EU–Turkey Deal on Migration: Refugees in Turkey struggle as border walls grow higher*, DIIS Policy Brief, December 2017. Copenhagen: Danish Institute for International Studies.

World Book Encyclopedia. 1989. 'Africa', in *World Book Encyclopedia*. Chicago, IL: World Book.

Zeleza, P.T. 2019. 'Leveraging Africa's global diasporas for the continent's development', *African Diaspora*, 11(1-2): 144–61.

Part II
The Bigger Picture

Africa's 'Boat People' encounter 'Fortress Europe': Conflict and migration in Africa–EU relations[1]

Adekeye Adebajo

Introduction

The phenomenon of Africa's 'Boat People' crossing the Mediterranean Sea to try to reach 'Fortress Europe' is one of the world's most underreported contemporary tragedies. About 30,000–40,000 African migrants attempt the crossing each year, resulting in at least 700 deaths annually.[2] Although much smaller in scale and more voluntary, these treacherous voyages on rickety boats still echo the aquatic graves of an estimated 12–15 million Africans over four centuries of the Transatlantic slave trade (Adebajo, 2021a). However, it is important to remember that most African migration occurs within the continent itself (see European Commission, 2018; IOM, 2021a), including 32 million Africans forcibly displaced by June 2021, 75 per cent of these within their own national borders. South Sudan had 4 million displaced persons at this time; Nigeria had 3.3 million; Ethiopia had 2.6 million; Sudan 2.5 million; and Burkina Faso, 1.2 million (Reliefweb, 2021).

This chapter assesses the root causes of African migration to Europe.

It focuses on issues such as conflict, the lack of opportunity, poor governance, and Africa's fragile security architecture, all of which have contributed to Africa's failure to achieve what the late Kenyan scholar, Ali Mazrui, described as a *Pax Africana* (Mazrui, 1967). This situation was exacerbated, from 2020, by the global COVID-19 pandemic, the impact of which is examined briefly. The often divergent African and European governmental (as opposed to civil society) perspectives on migration, including hostile European reactions to African migration are also assessed. The chapter then analyses the broader African Union (AU) geo-strategic relationship with the European Union (EU), which prioritises security, governance, and migration, before concluding with some brief reflections on future Africa–EU relations. It offers 10 policy recommendations for narrowing the divergence in African and European approaches to migration, based largely on the UN Global Compact for Safe, Orderly and Regular Migration (UN, 2018).

The root causes of Africa's insecurity lie in poor governance, political exclusion, and socio-economic inequalities (see, for example, Deng, 1993; Mwanasali, 2010). Africa's security architecture remains fragile, while the weakness of regional bodies like the AU, the Economic Community of West African States (ECOWAS), the Southern African Development Community (SADC), the Intergovernmental Authority on Development (IGAD), the Economic Community of Central African States (ECCAS), and the Arab Maghreb Union (AMU), and their failure to develop effective peacekeeping capabilities, have led to an overreliance on the UN in conflicts such as those in the Democratic Republic of the Congo (DRC), Mali, the Central African Republic (CAR), Darfur, and South Sudan (see, for example, Adebajo 2011, 2018). The collapse of the Muammar Gaddafi regime in Libya in 2011 created a safe haven for smugglers in an acephalous country with competing militias, and spread instability across the countries of the Sahel, such as Mali, Burkina Faso, and Niger (see Hoije, 2021; Taylor, 2021; Reuters, 2021).

The causes of African migration to Europe are partly a result of these conflicts, but also due to a lack of opportunities on a continent where 60 per cent of the population in 2021 was under the age of 25 years (IOM, 2020: 19). It is, however, important to remember – even in the data-scarce African environment – that Africa hosts more migrants than it sends to other regions of the world. In 2020, the continent hosted 25.2 million refugees, asylum seekers, internally displaced persons (IDPs), and stateless people

(UNSG, 2020). In 2019, according to the International Organization for Migration (IOM, 2020: 16), over half of all refugees in Africa were hosted by countries in East Africa (3.8 million), with significantly smaller numbers of refugees residing in Central and North Africa (1.4 million each), West Africa (383,000), and southern Africa (288,000). The key migrant-hosting countries were South Africa (4.2 million), Côte d'Ivoire (2.5 million), and Uganda (1.7 million).

To reinforce the point that most migrants stay within Africa, 2015 polling data showed that 40 per cent of those planning to migrate were intending to move to another African country, while a 2018 Afrobarometer survey saw only 20 per cent of African migrants planning to move to Europe (IOM, 2020: 19–20). An estimated 8 million Africans live as irregular migrants in Europe (UNDP, 2019). Many of the states from which these migrants come are countries in conflict, emerging from war, and/or suffering from poor governance. The correlation between conflict, poor governance and migration is, therefore, strong, although not always direct.

It is important to highlight the roles of African migrants themselves on their reasons for migrating. The 2019 United Nations Development Programme (UNDP) report, *Scaling Fences: Voices of irregular African migrants to Europe*, engaged the perspectives of over 1,000 African migrants from 39 African states residing in 13 EU countries. The report made it clear that Africa was at the stage of socio-economic development at which migration intensifies, as historically occurred in other parts of the world. Migration is thus a natural and unstoppable phenomenon that must be sensibly managed for mutual benefit. The UNDP report also confirmed that although socio-economic development is taking place in Africa, it is occurring at too slow a pace, with many countries remaining unstable, and the rewards of progress divided too unevenly to keep even educated young people at home (UNDP, 2019: 4–9). Contrary to popular myths of desperate, destitute illiterate youth, African migrants to Europe often have above average education. Most held steady jobs at home that were frequently better than the menial tasks they perform in Europe. However, 38 per cent of African migrants interviewed noted that their earnings were insufficient to get by and save. It was the lack of opportunities to fulfil their ambitions at home that most often drove these young migrants to embark on perilous voyages across the Mediterranean (See Fiedler, 2018).

AU leaders committed, at their February 2019 summit in the Ethiopian capital of Addis Ababa, to strengthen their national systems for preventing conflicts and the displacement of their citizens, and to create conditions that are conducive to the return, rehabilitation, and reintegration of refugees. To this end, the AU announced the establishment of a Continental Operation Centre (COC) in Sudan to help manage irregular migration, as well as an African Observatory on Migration (AOM) in Morocco to collect, analyse, and share data on continental initiatives.

The travails of AU–EU relations

It is important to understand the broader geo-strategic context of Africa–EU relations before one can contribute to resolving the migration challenges between both continents (Adebajo, 2021b). African security and governance challenges remain major priorities in this relationship. The AU declared a Continental Free Trade Area in January 2021 in a bid to unite a continent of 1.4 billion inhabitants in 55 territories, from the Cape to Casablanca. The 27-member EU has brought together 447 million people, from Sofia to Stockholm, to create the world's only truly supranational body. In reality, however, this is a club with two membership groups – the rich and the poor: while the EU had a GDP of US$15.2 trillion in 2020, Africa's GDP was about US$1.7 trillion; while 60 per cent of the EU's trade took place within its borders, only about 16 per cent of African commerce occurred within its own continent (Trade Law Centre, 2020; World Bank Data Portal, 2020).

A key source of tensions between both blocs has centred on migration. Several European governments and populations continue to view migration as a security threat, often scapegoating and criminalising African migrants. 'Fortress Europe' has thus resulted in EU governments sometimes violating refugee rights, and strengthening border security in contravention of their own free movement principles (Castillejo, 2017).

Contemporary Africa–EU relations can be dated to the first intercontinental summit in Cairo in April 2000 between the then Organisation of African Unity (OAU) and the EU (Adebajo and Whiteman, 2012; Carbone 2017). This process eventually culminated in the Joint Africa–EU Strategy (JAES) in December 2007, adopted at a second Africa–EU summit in Lisbon (it was not called an AU–EU summit because Morocco was not a member of the continental body at the time). The strategy intended to make the partnership more equal. Its 2008–10 Action

Plan identified eight priority areas: (1) peace and security; (2) democratic governance, and human rights; (3) migration, mobility, and employment; (4) regional economic integration, trade, and infrastructure; (5) the UN Millennium Development Goals (MDGs); (6) climate change; (7) energy; and (8) science, information society, and space. The third Africa–EU summit was held in Tripoli in November 2010, during which the 2011–13 Action Plan was adopted, reinforcing cooperation in the same eight priority areas as the first Lisbon Action Plan.

The Fourth Africa–EU Summit took place in Brussels in April 2014 under the central theme of 'Peace, Prosperity and People'. The meeting adopted the 2014–17 Roadmap, highlighting five priority areas for joint action: (1) peace and security; (2) democracy, 'good governance', and human rights; (3) human development; (4) sustainable and inclusive development and growth, and continental integration; and (5) global and emerging issues. The fifth summit was convened in the Ivorian city of Abidjan in November 2017 under the broad theme of 'Investing in Youth for a Sustainable Future', as European leaders worried increasingly about irregular African migration across the Mediterranean Sea. With 375 million African youths expected to reach working age by 2035 (Abebe and Maalim, 2020: 11), EU leaders were eager to find ways of keeping these young people at home.

Four strategic areas were identified in Abidjan: (1) mobility and migration; (2) economic opportunities for youth; (3) peace and security; and (4) cooperation on governance. But despite Brussels' constant assertion and rhetoric about 'equal partnership' and 'coherence', as well as its calls for a need to move away from a purely donor–recipient relationship, there were serious divergences between both sides: African governments emphasised aid and trade, while the EU championed security and migration (Carbone, 2017). These priority action plans have also been criticised for lacking concrete implementation plans and measurable mechanisms to monitor progress effectively. Furthermore, there have been calls to channel funding away from operational costs to capacity-building projects (Mabera, 2020).

The Sixth EU–AU Summit was held in Brussels in February 2022. The meeting prioritised migration, reiterating the usual pledges to prevent irregular migration; strengthen border management; improve return, readmission, and reintegration; halt human trafficking and smuggling; and create pathways for legal migration. Another major focus identified by African and European leaders was the need for increased cooperation in the area of peace and security. The Brussels summit agreed that these efforts would continue to focus on the 2018 AU–EU Memorandum of Understanding on Peace, Security, and Governance, which has sought to address the root causes of conflicts; combat instability and terrorism; strengthen African-led peace operations; and implement the Women, Peace, and Security (WPS) agenda (Sixth EU–AU Summit, 'A Joint Vision for 2030': 4–5).

The EU accounted for 36 per cent of Africa's external trade, and remained its largest investor at €261 billion in 2021 (Borrell, 2020: 4–5). Brussels also contributed €2.7 billion to the AU's African Peace Facility between 2004 and 2019 (European Commission, 2020). In February 2020, the German EU Commission President, Ursula von der Leyen, led a delegation of 22 of her commissioners to Addis Ababa for the tenth EU–AU Commission-to-Commission meeting. Two months later, the EU Commission unilaterally issued 'Towards a Comprehensive Strategy with Africa', outlining five priority areas: (1) migration and mobility; (2) peace and governance; (3) green transition and energy access; (4) digital transformation; and (5) sustainable growth and jobs (EU, 2020).

Contrary to the more recent and polarised relationship around migration governance, security cooperation between Africa and the EU has been consistent. In October 2020, the twelfth joint meeting of the AU Peace and Security Council and the EU Political and Security Committee discussed the security situations in the Sahel, Sudan and Somalia. The meeting condemned attacks on civilians by armed groups, and pledged support for the UN mission in Mali, as well as for the G5 Sahel Joint Force. Both the AU and the EU promised to continue supporting the efforts of the transitional government in Sudan, calling for donor pledges to be delivered. The two organisations also pushed for the acceleration of the restructuring of the Somali National Army (SNA) to take over responsibilities from the African Union Mission in Somalia (AMISOM), which was being heavily funded by the EU (AU PSC and EU PSC, 2020).

But the realities on the ground in Somalia were such that heads of state of the major troop-contributing countries (Uganda, Kenya, Ethiopia, and Burundi) often bypassed the AU Commission when making decisions on the mission, and there were constant complaints about the lack of AU capacity, even to administer AMISOM's budget.[3] The EU paid the salaries of AU peacekeepers, the UN reimbursed contingent-owned equipment, while the United States bilaterally provided military equipment to Kenya and Uganda. This support has thus not always been well coordinated for the greater good of the mission, and the AU was far from leading conflict management efforts in an operation run in its name. Even in the field of security cooperation, then, AU–EU relations have sometimes been characterised by a lack of transparency and coherent coordination.

Africa's security challenges as a driver of migration to Europe

It is important next to embark on a voyage around Africa's security architecture – from South Sudan to North Africa – in order to assess the critical connection between conflict and migration. Conflicts and governance challenges in Africa continue to push migrants to attempt the dangerous crossing of the Mediterranean Sea from Africa to Europe. When Portuguese UN Secretary-General António Guterres called for the observance of a global ceasefire in May 2020 because of the COVID-19 pandemic, warlords in Libya – the major transit point for African migrants to Europe, where about 43,000 migrants, in addition to 150,000 internally displaced persons were trapped – broke the ceasefire on the same day it was announced (Guterres, 2020; IOM, 2021a).

The sharp Horn

In East Africa in 2022, despite the presence of about 19,000 UN peacekeepers, South Sudan's five-year civil conflict had resulted in an estimated 400,000 deaths, and 1.6 million IDPs, and 2.2 million refugees spilling into neighbouring countries.[4] Somalia and Kenya have experienced tensions over mineral-rich border areas. About 2.6 million Ethiopians remain internally displaced by local conflicts, while the government struggles to manage discontent in its turbulent Oromia and Amhara regions.[5] Ethiopia's prime minister, Abiy Ahmed, went to war in November 2020 in a bid to pacify the Tigray region. The conflict also drew in the Eritrean army on the side of Addis Ababa. Massive human rights abuses were reported on all sides, including an estimated 10,000 people killed and 2 million displaced (Van Niekerk, 2021; Walsh and Dahir, 2021).

The Tigray People's Liberation Front (TPLF) retook the capital of Mekelle and surrounding areas from Ethiopian government forces in June 2021, and along with its Oromo Liberation Army (OLA) allies, was threatening to march to Addis Ababa to topple the Abiy administration in November 2021. This situation was halted by February 2022, but it resulted in 400,000 Tigrayans facing the threat of famine (*Africa Confidential*, 2021b; *The Economist*, 2021; *Africa Report*, 2022: 134–5). Maintaining social peace among the country's various feuding regions thus remains a major challenge, as groups like the Amhara and Oromo remain restive despite disputed elections in June 2021, which Abiy's ruling Prosperity Party won in a landslide. Ethiopia's filling of the next phase of the Grand Ethiopia Renaissance Dam has also resulted in further tensions with Egypt and Sudan over the waters of the Nile River. These disputes threaten a conflagration that could destabilise the entire Horn of Africa, and trigger more migrants to leave the region, including new attempts to breach 'Fortress Europe'.

Still in the Horn of Africa, Eritrea is one of the largest exporters of migrants to Europe as a result of internal repression and a lack of employment opportunities at home. Somalia has been without an effective central government for three decades. This acephalous country still required a 20,000-strong AU force to maintain stability in 2022, as it lacks an effective army of its own. The 10,000-strong Al-Shabaab militant group continues its attacks in Somalia, which have spilled over into Kenya, and killed an estimated 1,000 Somalis in 2021 (*Africa Report*, 2020: 140). Sudan's transitional government struggled to achieve stability and to revive economic growth, a situation compounded by unprecedented flooding in September 2020, which killed over 100 people and rendered 500,000 homeless (OCHA, 2020). Sudanese military strongman, General Abdel Fattah al-Burhan, effectively staged a coup d'état in October 2021, ending the fragile, two-year, power-sharing transition and removing the civilian technocratic prime minister, Abdalla Hamdok (Walsh, Dahir and Marks, 2021). The military junta continues to battle civil society groups, and at least 76 protesters were killed and 2,200 injured by security forces by January 2022 (Security Council Report, 'Monthly Forecast', February 2022: 6). Furthermore, there are continuing fears of famine ravaging parts of South Sudan and Somalia.

The volatile middle

In the Great Lakes region, the Democratic Republic of the Congo's two-decade long civil war has resulted in over 3 million deaths, while 6 million people have been displaced internally and across the region. The disputed presidential election of Félix Tshisekedi in January 2019 led to greater political squabbling and violence, and the eastern Congo continues to experience massacres and sexual violence. Burundi's instability also resulted in about 400,000 people being internally displaced, while the death of President Pierre Nkurunziza in June 2020, just before a transition of power to his successor, Évariste Ndayishimiye, increased political uncertainty. There are also continuing tensions between the governments of Burundi and Rwanda over harbouring and supporting each other's rebel groups.[6]

Even with the presence of 15,500 UN peacekeepers in September 2021, instability continued in the Central African Republic (CAR) between rival Christian and Muslim militias, who control an estimated 80 per cent of the country. These conflicts also involve farmers, herders, merchants, and reportedly Chadian and Sudanese mercenaries, and have resulted in over 1.5 million displaced persons,[7] while 63 per cent of the population (3.1 million people) was estimated to need humanitarian assistance in 2022 (Security Council Report, 'Monthly Forecast,' February 2022: 15). Further complicating the conflict, Russia's intervention in the historically French-dominated CAR since 2018 has involved about 200 mercenaries being sent to Bangui to protect politicians, and to guard gold and diamond mines (Ramani, 2021).

Chad suspended its constitution, and returned to full-fledged military rule following the death of its 21-year autocratic leader, Idriss Déby, in April 2021. In Cameroon, over 1 million people have been internally displaced by tensions between the central government and the Anglophone Northwest and Southwest regions under Paul Biya's 40-year autocracy, while 66,899 refugees have spilled into Nigeria. Cameroon hosted about 454,854 refugees in 2021, mostly from the CAR and Nigeria (UNCHR, 2021a). Across Central Africa, autocratic political dynasties were also desperately clinging on to power in Gabon, Congo-Brazzaville, and Equatorial Guinea in 2022.

The men on horseback

In West Africa, Nigeria continues to face the menace of Fulani herdsmen and widespread banditry, particularly in its Northern states. The terrorist scourge of Boko Haram and its breakaway Islamic State West Africa Province (ISWAP) had internally displaced 3.3 million Nigerians and killed about 350,000 people in the northeast by 2021 (Reliefweb, 2021;

and Al Jazeera, 2021). An estimated 1,436 schoolchildren were kidnapped in Nigeria's Northern states between December 2020 and October 2021 (Lawal and Umeh, 2021), while approximately 20 per cent of the population in the region had left their homes by July 2021 due to continuing instability. Thousands of Malian soldiers and about 250 UN peacekeepers have died in the conflict in its Northern Region since 2013, fuelled by militants reportedly with links to similar groups in Algeria and Mauritania. France has deployed 5,100 troops to the Sahel and backed the G5 Sahel Joint Force, whose members – Mali, Niger, Burkina Faso, Mauritania, and Chad – have suffered hundreds of fatalities, while thousands of civilians have been brutally killed, and over 2 million people were displaced (Hoije, 2021; Reuters, 2021; Taylor, 2021).

Intercommunal killings have also increased in Mali, which suffered its second coup d'état in nine months in May 2021, led by Colonel Assimi Goïta. Despite the presence of a 15,209-strong UN peacekeeping mission in November 2021, and the militarisation of the government in Bamako since August 2020, armed attacks continued unabated across the country in 2022. Mali's putschists accused France of meddling in its internal affairs and expelled its ambassador, Joël Meyer, from Bamako in February 2022. Soon after, Paris announced that it would withdraw all of its troops from the country and relocate them to Niger. The military junta in Mali withdrew from the G5 Sahel force in June 2022 over disagreements with French dominance of the initiative. Guinea similarly suffered a military putsch in September 2021, led by former French legionnaire, Colonel Mamady Doumbouya. About 1.5 million people have also been internally displaced in Burkina Faso as a result of attacks by local bandits, jihadists, and other terrorist groups, while the country hosted over 20,252 refugees in 2021, mainly from Mali (UNHCR, 2021b).

In January 2022, a coup led by Colonel Paul-Henri Sandaogo Damiba removed President Roch Kaboré from power in Burkina Faso. West Africa's 'men on horseback' – the military – in Mali, Guinea, and Burkina Faso seem increasingly prepared to defy ECOWAS by consolidating their grip on power. Niger, Guinea-Bissau, Côte d'Ivoire, Togo, and Benin are all vulnerable to similar putsches. Despite ECOWAS insisting on a rapid return to civilian rule, Burkina Faso's military rulers announced a three-year transition in March 2022; Mali's military brass hats proclaimed a two-year transition a month later; while Guinea's soldiers announced their own three-year transition a month after that. Overlaying these security challenges, Russia and France continue to battle for influence across the drought-stricken Sahel, while the United States military was active in an estimated 20 African countries by 2016, in addition to its 2,000-strong military base in Djibouti, and US$100 million drone base in Niger (Cooke and Downie, 2015; McDonald, 2015; Turse, 2015).

Cabo Delgado, crackdowns, and climate change

Despite the military assistance of about 3,000 Rwandan and SADC soldiers from South Africa, Botswana, Lesotho, Angola, and Zambia, Mozambique's insurgency in its northern mineral-rich Cabo Delgado Province, which started in October 2017, continued five years later. Fighting had displaced about 800,000 people by February 2022. Maputo has struggled to address the socio-economic challenges of the region's long-suffering inhabitants (Stark, 2022) Further afield in southern Africa, repression continued in military-dominated Zimbabwe and absolutist monarchy, Eswatini, in 2022, even as parties of change struggled to transform societies in Malawi and Zambia. Underlining the challenges of climate change, more cyclones are expected to hit southern Africa following the destructive 'Storm Ana' in January 2022, which killed 77 people in Madagascar, Mozambique, and Malawi, and destroyed tens of thousands of homes and scores of schools, hospitals, and bridges (Agence France-Presse, 2022). South Africa's KwaZulu-Natal province was similarly struck by heavy floods in April 2022 that resulted in 459 deaths and the destruction of over 4,000 homes (Mbatha, 2022).

Monarchical autocrats and street protesters

Finally, in North Africa, Egypt's pharaonic strongman, Abdel Fattah al-Sisi, has jailed civil society activists and muzzled the media, while his army continues to battle militants in the Sinai Peninsula. Cairo's switch of allegiance in neighbouring Libya, from warlord General Khalifa Haftar to the UN-recognised government in Tripoli, could, however, contribute positively to stability. Street protests by committed civil society activists also continued in Algeria and Tunisia in 2022. Amid rising food prices in Algeria, the military-backed regime of Abdelmadjid Tebboune continued to repress civil society and detain journalists. In Tunisia, Kais Saied – in a blatant power grab – sought to crown himself the new 'King of Carthage' by suspending parliament and seeking to convert a largely ceremonial presidency into a dictatorship. Civil society groups continued to resist this attempted civilian coup d'état (*Africa Report*, 2022: 184–91).

Fortress Europe and COVID-19

In 2020, attempts were made by 99,907 migrants to cross the Mediterranean Sea and other borders into the EU. Most came from Tunisia, Morocco, Algeria, Libya, Sudan, Somalia, Eritrea, Ethiopia, Côte d'Ivoire, Nigeria, Niger, Senegal, Guinea and Mali – countries in which governance and security challenges persist, as earlier highlighted. Other migrants came from Syria, Afghanistan, Iran and Bangladesh. Most of these migrants went to Spain, Italy and Malta. In 2020, 2,326 of these migrants died en route or were unaccounted for. In 2021, 151,417 migrants arrived in the EU, 72,425 of these from African countries, while 3,224 migrants perished or were declared missing.[8]

The COVID-19 pandemic, which erupted in 2020, has also greatly impacted Africa's security complex. Fragile health systems across Africa have increased the continent's vulnerability. Reflecting the global 'vaccine apartheid', by October 2021 only 4.4 per cent of Africans had been vaccinated, compared to 62 per cent of EU citizens (Mwai, 2021). According to a May 2020 policy brief on the impact of COVID-19 on Africa by UN Secretary-General, António Guterres, the continent's 25.2 million refugees, IDPs, asylum seekers, and stateless people are some of the most vulnerable to the pandemic (UNSG, 2020). In 2019, remittances to sub-Saharan Africa – a crucial source of revenue – reached US$48 billion, before falling 12.5 per cent in 2020 to US$42 billion (World Bank, 2021).

A dialogue of the deaf: African and European perspectives on conflict and migration

African and European governments have often engaged in a 'dialogue of the deaf' on migration issues. Both sides were the main players in negotiating the UN Global Compact in 2018, and agreed on several controversial issues despite their often divergent views on migration. Topics around the return of African migrants from Europe to their home countries were the most contentious, and nearly scuttled the negotiations. Most African delegates insisted that returns be voluntary – as stipulated in the 2016 New York

Declaration for Refugees and Migrants – while EU negotiators pushed for forced returns to be included in the compact. The compromise was to avoid use of the terms 'voluntary' or 'forced,' and to push instead for bilateral agreements to formalise returns between states.[9]

African and European governments, however, continue to maintain divergent approaches to managing this challenge. This issue must be viewed within the broader context of the politicisation of migration issues. Many of the EU's 27 governments view migration largely through a distorted security prism. Large sections of their citizenry have shown often irrational hostility to African migrants and asylum seekers, resulting in the electoral success of racist right-wing parties and the donning of xenophobic robes by extremist politicians in mainstream parties, not only in previously progressive Nordic countries such as Denmark and Sweden, but particularly in Hungary, Poland, Italy, Malta, the Czech Republic, Slovakia, Austria, and France (Miller, 2018; Pocock and Chan, 2018). The UN has consistently urged EU governments to live up to their legal obligations, while Amnesty International blamed the deaths of 721 migrants in June and July 2019 directly on Italy and Malta, for blocking rescue ships from their ports and allowing the Libyan coastguard to return migrants to the North African country (Tondo, 2021a, 2021b, 2021c). Some EU leaders have further proposed establishing 'hot spots' in Chad and Niger to process asylum seekers – an idea that many African governments have rejected.

'Fortress Europe' has resulted in several EU governments strengthening their border security. Spain, Greece, Hungary, and Slovenia went so far as to build and reinforce their border fences to keep out migrants. Several European states have also cynically struck deals with economically vulnerable African states, such as Mali and Niger, in a bid to keep migrants from reaching Europe. Denmark struck a controversial bilateral deal with Rwanda in 2021 for African asylum seekers to be forcibly transported to the central African country. Brussels has argued that 1 million migrants enter the EU annually, and that the 27-member bloc has sought to encourage legal circular migration in which migrants can return to their home countries after an agreed period. This proposal has operated mainly in the realm of theory, however, and not in the real world.

EU governments have further suggested draconian ideas such as forced returns of migrants and establishing 'disembarkation platforms' in autocratic

North African countries such as Egypt and Morocco. Rather than passing on lessons from Europe's border management system to enhance the free movement of Africans, Brussels often seems to be helping to restrict free movement across Africa. The EU took its harsh actions in Libya despite the ghastly, atavistic slave auction of black African migrants in the North Atlantic Treaty Organisation (NATO)-destroyed country, following its 2011 intervention that toppled the 42-year autocracy of Muammar Gaddafi. Structural issues – such as the EU's grotesque €55.7 billion annual Common Agricultural Policy (CAP), which provides wasteful subsidies to European farmers in a sector in which about 70 per cent of Africa's populations find employment also continue to create friction (European Commission, 2022).

The EU's 2016, €500 million Migration Policy Framework (MPF) – funds diverted from development financing – is a perfect example of the bloc's sometimes unilateral, transactional, and heavy-handed approach to dealing with African governments. The framework was devised in the wake of the 2015 'migrant crisis' when 1.3 million mostly Syrian, Afghan, Pakistani and Iraqi migrants descended on 'Fortress Europe'. Also among this number were migrants from conflict-affected Nigeria and Eritrea, where opportunities remain limited for their large number of unemployed youths. Through the MPF, Brussels sought to use EU muscle and resources to pressure African governments to take measures to curb migration from their countries. This approach has been controversial, even among EU members and institutions. While countries like Italy and several Central and Eastern European states such as Hungary and Poland hosting African migrants strongly back the MPF, others like Spain and Ireland are less keen (Castillejo, 2017: 6, 15). While the General Secretariat of the Council and the Directorate-General for Home Affairs support the heavy-handed framework, the European External Action Service (EEAS) and the EU Directorate-General for Development felt that the MPF would undermine other diplomatic and trade interests (Castillejo, 2017: 10). The framework identified Ethiopia, Mali, Niger, Nigeria and Senegal as its five priority countries. However, its negative incentives – with an obsession on negotiating the forced return of African migrants – often failed to achieve its desired objectives, while alienating governments, particularly in Addis Ababa and Abuja.

The EU's MPF is thus myopic and opportunistic, based unabashedly on its own parochial interests of securitising migration and forcibly sending migrants back to Africa, rather than protecting them and their rights. In a fit of alchemy, Brussels has unsuccessfully tried to use paltry short-term development funds to address the root causes of African migration, as well as to manage complex long-term challenges such as youth unemployment and rural livelihoods. European critics, such as British scholar Clare Castillejo, have noted that the draconian framework has undermined Brussels' human rights and development principles without drastically reducing migration. Curbing migration has thus become a major goal of EU development assistance programmes, and in the process, sometimes compromised a focus on poverty reduction. The plan of 'buying' cooperation for returns, by effectively bribing African governments, has not achieved much success, as African governments continue to view migration as a source of vital foreign currency income. The use of the EU Emergency Trust Fund (EUTF) in MPF countries was further devoid of local ownership. Implementation has also been slow, and selection processes have sometimes lacked transparency. The EU has struggled to convince governments in Ethiopia, Nigeria, Senegal, and Mali to cooperate with its policy of forced returns, and only in Niger did it have some limited success. These sensitivities came to the fore with angry African reactions during the Africa–EU summit in Abidjan in November 2017 (Castillejo, 2017: 1–3, 11).

In contrast to EU governments, their African counterparts have often argued that migration represents a developmental opportunity. They noted that 70 per cent of African migrants remain on their own continent; observed that only 20 per cent move to Europe; and highlighted that remittances from African diaspora communities were typically three times larger than development aid from rich countries. African governments also often observe that an estimated €20 billion annually is contributed to EU countries by African citizens living in Europe (African Union, 2020; Ratha, 2021).

The AU adopted a Migration Policy Framework for Africa and Plan of Action in May 2018, which updated a similar 2006 framework. Tied closely to the main areas of the 2018 UN Global Compact, nine key issues were prioritised: (1) migration governance; (2) labour migration and education; (3) diaspora engagement; (4) border governance; (5) irregular migration; (6) forced displacement; (7) internal migration; (8) migration and trade; and (9) cross-cutting issues. The framework advocated safe, orderly, and dignified migration; promoted the socio-economic wellbeing and legal rights of migrants; pushed for the free movement of African citizens across the continent; championed evidence-based policies and 'whole of government' approaches; supported the regional harmonisation of migration policies; advocated addressing the root causes of refugee movements; promoted the creation of comprehensive migration management systems and conflict management mechanisms to strengthen national and regional security; called for reversing Africa's 'brain drain'; and championed the crafting of effective policies to benefit from African diaspora communities (African Union, 2018).

The AU Migration Framework contains many sensible priorities but there remains a lack of institutional capacity for implementation; a failure of coordination with subregional bodies and African civil society; and a lack of consistent focus on migration issues at the highest decision-making institutions of this heads-of-state driven continental body. Several African governments, such as Eritrea, Nigeria, and Senegal, have also shown scant regard for the plight of their own citizens embarking on these perilous voyages across the Mediterranean in search of an elusive European El Dorado. Many have failed dismally to address the conditions of poor governance and massive youth unemployment that have provided the push factors for this contemporary African exodus, and have often done little to protect their citizens from, or speak out against, abuses in Europe.

Furthermore, some African governments have acted on the free movement of their fellow Africans across their own borders in as draconian a manner as the EU has done to African migrants. Only four AU states (Mali, Niger, Rwanda, and São Tomé and Principe) had ratified the AU Convention on the Free Movement of Persons by 2021. Despite about 75 per cent of African migration occurring on the continent, African governments have often securitised migration and restricted the free movement of continental migrants in clear violation of their own 2018 free movement protocol. Morocco has built a security fence with electronic sensors on its border with Algeria. Xenophobic acts against migrants from neighbouring countries have also occurred in South Africa, Angola, Libya and Nigeria (see, for example, Akinola, 2018; Moyo and Mpofu, 2020; Matambo, 2022).

More positively, ECOWAS and the East African Community (EAC) have established impressive and reciprocal open visa regimes that have led to some of the world's highest mobility rates, particularly in West Africa. However, two-thirds of African states still have illiberal visa regimes that make it difficult for continental citizens to travel between each other's regions. Concrete initiatives have not yet been taken to assess how African migrants can contribute substantively to African economies, in the same way that the contributions of African migrants in the EU are prioritised by many African governments (IOM, 2020: 148–9).

African governments have further been criticised by civil society groups for not prioritising migration, while EU negotiators tend to have a much firmer grasp of the key issues at joint migration summits than their African counterparts. African governments often leave the implementation of migration policies largely to UN agencies such as the IOM and the Office of the UN High Commissioner for Refugees (UNHCR).[10] The IOM has supported the AU and African subregional bodies to develop migration policies; has backed the Nairobi-based African Institute for Remittances (AIR); and has focused on protecting migrants, supporting policy debates, and promoting better understanding of migration issues. The UNHCR – which is leading the implementation of the 2018 UN Global Compact of Refugees – has sought to ease pressure on refugee-hosting countries; to extend access to refugees; to support country solutions; and to improve the conditions of refugees.[11] It would appear important for African and EU governments to engage both organisations more closely in order to bridge their differences.

Conclusion

Based on a critical reading of AU–EU relations in security cooperation, and on a security-informed reflection on current challenges relating to migration governance, this chapter has argued that there remains much mutual misunderstanding between African and European governments on the thorny issue of migration. The EU has been the most generous funder of peace and security efforts in Africa, financing about 90 per cent of the AU Peace Fund between 2004 and 2019 (European Commission, 2020: 8). But the AU–EU partnership has often been regarded by Africans as being shaped one-sidedly from Brussels according to its own interests. On the other hand, Eurocrats in Brussels have often complained about a lack of timely response to their proposals by their Afrocrat counterparts in the poorly capacitated AU Commission in Addis Ababa. The AU and African governments should, therefore, adopt more realistic and less illusory approaches to implementing their mandates on issues like migration, based on an accurate assessment of their financial and logistical deficiencies.

The AU's ambitious plans, first announced in 2003, to set up a 25,000-strong African Standby Force to manage conflicts on the continent by 2010 were postponed until 2015, even as talk of establishing an African Capacity for Immediate Response to Crises (ACIRC) continued. In December 2020, the AU simply declared the African Standby Force to be fully operational, despite the fantasy involved in such a statement. The date for 'Silencing the Guns by 2020' was postponed by a decade in the same month (Wondemagegnehu, 2021), further exposing the alchemy at the heart of a body whose huge ambitions frequently fail to match its achievements. *Pax Africana* will clearly not be achieved through empty declarations, but only through greater political commitment and increased resources from Africa's regional powers, led by Nigeria, South Africa, Algeria and Ethiopia, all of which, however, are suffering from their own internal challenges. More positively, by February 2022 the AU had raised US$315 million under its revised Peace Fund (Confidential communication, February 2022).

Although not legally binding, seven of the 23 key goals in the 2018 UN Global Compact on Migration provide some sensible ideas for moving this 'dialogue of the deaf' between Africa and Europe forward. Implementation at the domestic level will be particularly important. First, EU governments must ensure that evidence-based research and policies – rather than scare-mongering stereotypes and short-term populism – guide migration debates. Second, African governments should address the factors that push their citizens to leave their home countries at such great personal risk. Third, the movement of workers must be facilitated through free movement accords, visa-liberalisation regimes, and labour mobility cooperation – there must be a clear legal pathway to the regularisation of the status of migrants. Fourth, migrant deaths must be prevented as a matter of urgency and search and rescue operations should be decriminalised. Fifth, smuggling – which increasingly targets young children – must be thoroughly investigated and prosecuted. Sixth, any detention of migrants should be based on international human rights law, and migrants must have access to basic social services. Finally, African governments should incorporate migration into their development planning, while the more efficient use of remittances from African diaspora communities must be facilitated.

In addition, three more recommendations are critical to managing

Africa–EU migration more effectively. First, African actors should, in consultation with their EU counterparts, become directly involved in search and rescue missions in order to alleviate the current deficient system, which leaves African migrants vulnerable. Second, the EU should provide massive investment to labour-intensive economic sectors in Africa, such as agriculture, to promote socio-economic development and reduce incentives for migration. Finally, African and EU civil society must be granted a greater policy-making role on migration issues, which are still often dominated by governments on both continents.[12]

It is only through implementing some of these sensible ideas that Africa and the EU will be able to stem the continuing tragic deaths of thousands of African 'Boat People' as they cross the Mediterranean in a bid to breach 'Fortress Europe'.

Notes

1   The author would like to thank Nompumelelo Ndawonde, a researcher at the University of Johannesburg's Institute for Pan-African Thought and Conversation (IPATC), for her valuable assistance in completing the referencing.

2   See the reports by the International Organization for Migration (IOM), which produces annual data on African migration to Europe.

3   Confidential telephone interview with a senior diplomat, 2 May 2021.

4   These statistics are based on the UN Secretary-General reports to the Security Council on South Sudan; 'Africa in 2021,' The Africa Report, No 114, January–February 2021; and the monthly updates of the New York-based Security Council Report.

5   These statistics are based on 'Africa in 2021', The Africa Report, No. 114, January–February 2021; Reliefweb '32 million Africans forcibly displaced by conflict and repression', 17 June 2021 (reliefweb.int); and the monthly updates of the New York-based Security Council Report.

6   The statistics in this paragraph are based on UN Secretary-General reports to the UN Security Council on the DRC; 'Africa in 2021', The Africa Report, No. 114, January–February 2021; and the monthly updates of the New York-based Security Council Report.

7   These statistics are based on UN Secretary-General reports to the UN Security Council on the CAR; 'Africa in 2021,' The Africa Report, No. 114, January–February 2021; and the monthly updates of the New York-based

Security Council Report.

8   These figures are derived from reports of the IOM, notably 'Flow Monitoring.'

9   These insights draw from discussions at the Institute for Pan-African Thought and Conversation (IPATC)/Friedrich Ebert Stiftung (FES)/ African, Caribbean, and Pacific (ACP) Group policy dialogue, 'Migration in the EU/ACP Partnership After 2020: Implementing the UN Global Compact', held in Brussels in October 2018 (https://ipatc.joburg).

10 These insights draw from the IPATC policy dialogue, 'Implementing the United Nations Global Compact on Migration: Conflict, governance, and human mobility in Africa–EU relations', held in Johannesburg in October 2019 (https:ipatc.joburg).

11 These insights draw from the IPATC policy dialogue in 2019.

12 Some of these suggestions are drawn from the IPATC policy dialogue, 'Implementing the United Nations Global Compact on Migration'.

References

Abebe, T.T. and Maalim, H. 2020. *Relations Between Africa and Europe: Mapping Africa's priorities*, Africa Report 25, August 2020. Pretoria: Institute for Security Studies (ISS). Online at: https://issafrica.s3.amazonaws.com/site/ uploads/ar-25.pdf (accessed 10 May 2022).

Adebajo, A. 2021a. 'Pan-Africanism: From the twin plagues of European locusts to Africa's triple quest for emancipation', in A. Adebajo (ed.). *The Pan-African Pantheon: Prophets, poets, and philosophers*. Johannesburg: Jacana Media and Manchester: Manchester University Press, pp. 7–11.

Adebajo, A. 2021b. 'Strategic partnerships', in U. Engel (ed.). *Yearbook on the African Union*. Leiden: Brill, pp. 194–213.

Adebajo, A. 2018. '*Pax Nigeriana* versus *Pax Gallica*: ECOWAS and UN Peacekeeping in Mali', in T. Karbo and K. Virk (eds). *The Palgrave Handbook of Peacebuilding in Africa*. New York: Springer International Publishing, pp. 209–31.

Adebajo, A. 2011. *UN Peacekeeping in Africa: From the Suez Crisis to the Sudan conflicts*. Boulder, CO: Lynne Rienner and Johannesburg: Jacana Media.

Adebajo, A. and Whiteman, K. (eds). 2012. *The EU and Africa: From Eurafrique to Afro-Europa*. London: Hurst & Company and Johannesburg: Wits University Press.

Africa Confidential. 2021a. 'Abiy's war party digs', *Africa Confidential*, 62 (21), 22 October: 1–3. Online at: https://www.africa-confidential.com/article-preview/id/13623/Abiy%27s_war_party_digs_in (accessed 10 April 2022).

Africa Confidential. 2021b. 'Into the hell of war, again', *Africa Confidential*, 62 (21), 22 October: 3–4. Online at: https://www.africa-confidential.com/article/id/13624/Into_the_hell_of_war%2c_again (accessed 10 April 2022).

Africa Report, The. 2022. 'Africa in 2022', *Africa Report*, No. 118 January–February–March 2022 (accessed 10 April 2022).

Africa Report, The. 2021. 'Africa in 2021', *Africa Report*, No. 114, January–February 2021 (accessed 10 April 2022).

African Union. 2020. *Report on Labour Migration Statistics in Africa*, 2nd edition. Addis Ababa: African Union, Joint Labour Migration Programme. Online at: https://au.int/sites/default/files/documents/39323-doc-web254_184-10_english_2nd_edition_of_the_africa_labor_migration_statistics.pdf (accessed 10 April 2022).

African Union. 2018. *Migration Policy Framework for Africa and Plan of Action, 2018–30*. Addis Ababa: African Union Department for Social Affairs, May 2018. Online at: https://violenceagainstchildren.un.org/sites/violenceagainstchildren.un.org/files/documents/other_documents/35316-doc-au-mpfa_2018-eng.pdf (accessed 10 March 2022).

Agence France-Presse. 2022. 'Dozens killed in Tropical Storm Ana as southern Africa braces for more wild weather', *The Guardian* (London), 28 January 2022. Online at: https://www.theguardian.com/world/2022/jan/28/dozens-killed-in-tropical-storm-ana-as-southern-africa-braces-for-more-wild-weather (accessed 10 March 2022).

AU PSC and EU PSC. 2020. 'Joint Communiqué'. Issued after the 12th Annual Joint Consultative Meeting of the Peace and Security Council of the African Union and the Political and Security Committee of the European Union, Addis Ababa, 26 October.

Akinola, A.A. (ed.). 2018. *The Political Economy of Xenophobia in Africa*. New York: Springer International Publishing.

Al Jazeera. 2021. 'Northeast Nigeria conflict killed more than 300,000 children: UN', 24 June 2021.

Borrell, J. 2020. 'EU–African relations are a strategic issue: Here's why', Great Insights, 9(3): 3–4. Online at: https://ecdpm.org/great-insights/navigating-eu-au-post-covid/eu-african-relations-strategic-issue/ (accessed 16 May 2022).

Carbone, M. 2017. 'The European Union and International Development', in C. Hill, M. Smith and S. Vanhoonacker (eds). *International Relations and the European Union*, 3rd edition. Oxford: Oxford University Press, pp. 292–315.

Castillejo, C. 2017. 'The EU Migration Partnership Framework: Time for a rethink?' ECONSTOR Discussion Paper No. 28/2017. Bonn: Deutsches Institut für Entwicklungspolitik.

Cooke, J.G. and Downie, R. 2015. *Rethinking Engagement in Fragile States.* A Report of the CSIS Africa Program, July 2015. Washington DC: Centre for Strategic and International Studies (CSIS). Online at: https://csis-website-prod.s3.amazonaws.com/s3fs-public/legacy_files/files/publication/150722_Cooke_RethinkingEngagement_Web.pdf (accessed 20 April 2022).

Deng, F.M. 1993. *Protecting the Dispossessed: A challenge for the international community.* Washington, DC: Brookings Institution.

European Commission, 2022. 'The New Common Agricultural Policy: 2023–27'. Online at: https://ec.europa.eu/info/food-farming-fisheries/key-policies/common-agricultural-policy/new-cap-2023-27.

European Commission. 2020. 'African Peace Facility. Annual Report 2019'. Luxembourg: Publications Office of the European Union.

European Commission. 2018. 'Many More to Come? Migration from and within Africa.' European Commission Joint Research Centre. Publications Office of the European Union, Luxembourg.

European Union (EU). 2020. 'Joint Communication to the European Parliament and the Council: Towards a Comprehensive Strategy with Africa', April 2020.

European Union–African Union, 2022. Sixth European Union–African Union Summit: 'A Joint Vision for 2030'. Brussels, 17–18 February 2022.

Fiedler, A. 2018. *Migration from Sub-Saharan Africa to Europe: Reasons, sources of information and perception of German engagement.* Stuttgart: Institut für Auslandsbeziehungen.

Guterres, A. 2020. Speech by United Nations Secretary-General António Guterres, 23 March 2020.

Hoije, K. 2021.'France backs Chad military rulers, AU urges swift transition', *Bloomberg,* 23 April 2021. Online at: https://www.bloomberg.com/news/articles/2021-04-23/macron-signals-backing-for-chad-military-rulers-after-deby-death (accessed 1 April 2022).

International Organization for Migration (IOM). 2021a. IOM Libya Migrant Report, (May–June 2021), Round 37. Geneva: International Organization for Migration. Online at: https://dtm.iom.int/reports/libya-—-migrant-report-37-may-june-2021 (accessed 12 April 2022).

International Organization for Migration (IOM). 2021b. *Africa Migration*

Report: Challenging the narrative. Addis Ababa: International Organization for Migration. Online at: https://publications.iom.int/books/africa-migration-report-challenging-narrative (accessed 12 April 2022).

International Organization for Migration (IOM). 2020. *African Migration Report 2020*, chapter 2, 'African Migration: An overview of key trends'. Geneva: International Organization for Migration.

Lawal, I. and Umeh, K. 2021. 'Safe schools: "Over 12 million children traumatised, afraid to go to school," says Buhari', *The Guardian* (Nigeria), 27 October 2021, pp. 1–2. Online at: https://guardian.ng/news/safe-schools-over-12m-children-traumatised-afraid-to-go-to-school-says-buhari/ (accessed 10 May 2022).

Mabera, F. 2020. *A Revitalised EU-Africa Partnership in Peace and Security: Implications for EU financing for African peace and security architecture.* Friedrich Ebert Stiftung Report, October 2020. Online at: http://library.fes.de/pdf-files/bueros/fes-ua/16690.pdf (accessed 10 April 2022).

Matambo, E. (ed.). 2022. *Interrogating Xenophobia and Nativism in Twenty-first-century Africa.* Lanham, MD: Rowman & Littlefield.

Mazrui, A.A. 1967. *Towards a Pax Africana: A study of ideology and ambition.* Chicago, IL: University of Chicago Press.

Mbatha, A. 2022. 'Death toll from flooding in South Africa's KZN rises to 458,' Bloomberg. Online at: www.bloomberg.com (accessed 5 June 2022).

McDonald, S. 2015. 'Have US priorities in Africa changed? Do security concerns trump others?' *Harvard International Review*, 36(3): 18–22.

Miller, S.D. 2018. 'Xenophobia toward refugees and other forced migrants', World Refugee Council Research Paper No. 5. Online at: https://www.cigionline.org/publications/xenophobia-toward-refugees-and-other-forced-migrants/ (accessed 12 May 2022).

Moyo, D. and Mpofu, S. (eds). 2020. *Mediating Xenophobia in Africa: Unpacking discourses of migration, belonging and othering.* New York: Palgrave Macmillan.

Mwai, P. 2021. 'Covid-19 vaccinations: More than 50 nations have missed a target set by the WHO', *BBC Reality Check*, 1 October 2021. Online at: https://www.bbc.com/news/56100076 (accessed 15 May 2022).

Mwanasali, M. 2010. 'The African Union, the United Nations, and the responsibility to protect: Towards an African intervention doctrine', *Global Responsibility to Protect*, 2(4): 388–413.

Pocock, N. and Chan, C. 2018. 'Refugees, racism and xenophobia: What works to reduce discrimination?' Our World. Tokyo: United Nations University. Online at: https://ourworld.unu.edu/en/refugees-racism-and-xenophobia-what-works-to-reduce-discrimination (accessed 10 May 2022).

Ramani, S. 2021. 'Russia's strategy in the Central African Republic'. Royal United Services Institute (RUSI), London, 12 February 2021. Online at: https://rusi.org/explore-our-research/publications/commentary/russias-strategy-central-african-republic (accessed 10 April 2022).

Ratha, D. 2021. 'Keep remittances flowing to Africa', *Africa in Focus*, 15 March 2021. Online at: https://www.brookings.edu/blog/africa-in-focus/2021/03/15/keep-remittances-flowing-to-africa/ (accessed 10 April 2022).

Reliefweb. 2021. '32 million Africans forcibly displaced by conflict and repression,' 17 June 2021 (reliefweb.int).

Reuters. 2021. 'In tribute to friend Deby, Macron says France will not tolerate threats to Chad', 23 April 2021. Online at: https://www.reuters.com/world/africa/french-president-macron-says-he-will-not-let-anybody-threaten-chad-2021-04-23/ (accessed 10 March 2022).

Security Council Report. 2022 and 2021. 'Monthly Forecast'. Online at: https://www.securitycouncilreport.org/monthly-forecast/ (accessed 12 April 2022).

Stark, V. 2022. 'South Africa sending fresh troops to Mozambique to fight Islamist insurgents', Voice of America, 22 February 2022. Online at: https://www.voanews.com/a/south-africa-sending-fresh-troops-to-mozambique-to-fight-islamist-insurgents-/6454195.html (accessed 10 April 2022).

Stewart, H. and Mason, R. 2016. 'Nigel Farage's anti-migrant poster reported to police', *The Guardian* (London), 16 June 2016.

Taylor, P. 2021. 'In the Sahel, Macron faces his Afghanistan', *Politico*, 29 May 2021.

The Economist. 2021. 'Abiy against the World: Ethiopia is losing friends and influence', *The Economist*, 9 October 2021, pp. 45–6. Online at: https://www.economist.com/middle-east-and-africa/2021/10/09/ethiopia-is-losing-friends-and-influence (accessed 10 April 2022).

Tondo, L. 2021a '"It's a day off": Wiretaps show Mediterranean migrants were left to die,' *The Guardian* (London), 16 April 2021.

Tondo, L. 2021b 'More than 100 asylum seekers feared dead after shipwreck off Libya', *The Guardian* (London), 22 April 2021. Online at: https://www.theguardian.com/world/2021/apr/23/more-than-100-asylum-seekers-feared-dead-after-shipwreck-off-libya (accessed10 April 2022).

Tondo, L. 2021c. 'Libyan Coastguards "fired on and tried to ram migrant boat" – NGO', *The Guardian* (London), 2 July 2021.

Trade Law Centre (tralac). 2020. 'Intra-Africa trade update 2020'. Stellenbosch. Online at: https://www.tralac.org/documents/publications/trade-data-analysis/4365-intra-africa-trade-2020-update-infographic/file.html (accessed 10 April 2022).

Turse, N. 2015. *Tomorrow's Battlefield: US proxy wars and secret ops in Africa*. A Dispatch Books Project. Chicago, IL: Haymarket Books.

United Nations (UN). 2018. United Nations Global Compact for Safe, Orderly and Regular Migration. New York: United Nations, December 2018. Online at: https://refugeesmigrants.un.org/sites/default/files/180711_final_draft_0.pdf (accessed 10 April 2022).

United Nations Development Programme (UNDP). 2019. *Scaling Fences: Voices of irregular African migrants to Europe*. New York: United Nations Development Programme.

United Nations High Commissioner for Refugees (UNHCR). 2021a. 'Operational Data Portal on Cameroon'. Office of the United Nations High Commissioner for Refugees, 31 October 2021. Online at: https://data2.unhcr.org/en/country/cmr (accessed 20 March 2022).

United Nations High Commissioner for Refugees (UNHCR). 2021b. 'Burkina Faso Fact Sheet: Burkino Faso, 1 January–30 June 2021'. Office of the United Nations High Commissioner for Refugees. Online at: https://reporting.unhcr.org/sites/default/files/Burkina%20Faso%20Factsheet%201%20January%20to%2030%20June%202021.pdf (accessed 10 April 2022).

United Nations Office for the Coordination of Humanitarian Affairs (UN OCHA). 2020. Sudan Floods Situation Report No. 14, 14 September 2020.

United Nations Secretary-General (UNSG). 2020. 'Impact of COVID-19 in Africa, 2020'. Online at: https://unsdg.un.org/sites/default/files/2020-05/Policy-brief-Impact-of-COVID-19-in-Africa.pdf (accessed 20 March 2022).

Van Niekerk, P. 2021. 'Abiy's offensive against Tigray collapses: Dreams of a 'New Ethiopia' arise', *Daily Maverick*, 31 October 2021. Online at: https://www.dailymaverick.co.za/article/2021-10-31-abiys-offensive-against-tigray-collapses-dreams-of-a-new-ethiopia-arise/ (accessed 10 April 2022).

Walsh, D. and Dahir, A.L. 2021. 'Why is Ethiopia at war with itself?' *The New York Times*, 15 November 2021. Online at: https://www.nytimes.com/article/ethiopia-tigray-conflict-explained.html (accessed 10 April 2022).

Walsh, D., Dahir, A.L. and Marks, S. 2021. 'Sudan's military seizes power, casting domestic transition into chaos', *The New York Times*, 25 October 2021. Online at: https://www.nytimes.com/2021/10/25/world/africa/sudan-military-coup.html (accessed 10 March 2022).

Wondemagegnehu, D.Y. 2021. 'Peace and security', in U. Engel (ed.). *Yearbook on the African Union*. Leiden: Brill.

World Bank. 2021. 'Defying predictions, remittance flows remain strong during COVID-19 crisis', Press release, 12 May 2021. New York: World Bank.

World Bank Data Portal. 2020. 'Exports of Goods and Services (% of GDP) – European Union'. Online at: https://data.worldbank.org/indicator/NE.EXP.GNFS.ZS?locations=EU (accessed 10 April 2022).

Chapter 3

Governance challenges for migration in Africa: The missing link

Khabele Matlosa

Introduction[1]

This chapter argues that governance deficit is a critical push factor in Africa's increased displacement crisis and migration, most notably to Europe. Adopting a political economy approach, the chapter uses 'governance' to denote state–society power relations that are developmental, democratic, respectful of citizens' rights, and socially inclusive, providing citizens with decent living standards and full participation in national affairs (Mkandawire, 2007: 680). Governance deficit in this context, simply refers to a crisis in state–society relations, which forces some citizens to move from their countries, either to other African countries or to other continents, including Europe.

This chapter offers an in-depth analysis aimed at enhancing an understanding of the governance push factors associated with Africa's migration and forced displacement. African migration discourse needs to transcend the conventional lenses of development and peace deficits as the only push factors (see Castelli, 2018; European Union, 2018). This point is echoed by scholars such as Gimenez-Gomez et al. (2017), who aptly observe that the reasons for international out-migration from Africa to Europe cannot be confined to economic determinants. Beyond the economic motivations to move, these authors propose a human security[2] perspective for a holistic understanding of the factors responsible for people's movement.

Danziger (2017: 2) poignantly observes that migration is linked to the lack of a level playing field in the sending countries in Africa. He argues that,

> Without knowing the right people, being from the right community or having the money to buy their way into a job, [citizens] will never get ahead. This, in turn, is part of the broader problem of poor governance, which has resulted in everything from a sharp drop in the quality of education and other services, to investment in sectors that lead to impressive GDP growth indicators but result in little by way of job creation.

The principal thesis of this chapter is that loss of trust in governance systems and structures in African countries acts as a key factor for citizens to migrate. Corruption and illicit financial flows have contributed to out-migration, particularly of skilled professionals. Besides contributing to internal displacement, election-related violence has also triggered the outward movement of refugees and migrants. While triggers for intra-state conflicts in Africa are many and varied, key among these has been the mismanagement of diversity, especially by ethnic fault lines, leading Africans to flee from their own countries. Human rights violations have compelled Africans to run away from persecution and oppression. While all these are super-structural factors driving out-migration at the political level, a more structural factor propelling migration at the socio-economic level relates to deepening poverty and food insecurity. These compelling factors for out-migration notwithstanding, the current COVID-19 pandemic constitutes a major impediment to the movement of migrants, both within and outside the African continent.

The chapter comprises four sections. The first section sets the context and introduces global and continental normative frameworks governing forced displacement and migration, while the second delves into the governance challenges of international out-migration in Africa. The third section three identifies the COVID-19 pandemic as a major impediment to international migration from Africa and its implications for the future, and the fourth concludes.

Contextual and normative frameworks

Migration is a global phenomenon that has characterised human life from time immemorial. Today, the world has a total population of approximately 7.8 billion people (World Population Review, 2020). Of these, 272 million are migrants, constituting approximately 3.5 per cent of the global population (UNDESA, 2019). About 21 million migrants are Africans living within the continent (International Organization for Migration [IOM], 2020a). South Africa is the most preferred destination of African migrants, with 4 million migrants, followed by Côte d'Ivoire with 2.5 million (IOM, 2020a). In terms of out-bound migration, Europe is a top destination for African migrants. Despite the usual chants of 'African migrants flooding Europe', in 2019, only 12.9 per cent of the international migrants in Europe were originally from Africa (IOM, 2020a). This constitutes 10.6 million of the 82 million international migrants (IOM, 2020a). Africa hosts 25.2 million of the 70.8 million globally displaced people: 7.8 million refugees and 17.4 million internally displayed persons (IDPs) (UNHCR, 2019).

The world has seen the mushrooming of instruments aimed at improving the management of international migration, especially after European countries declared migration a 'crisis' in 2015. Most prominently, the New York Declaration for Refugees and Migrants, which was adopted on 19 September 2016, led to the development and adoption of the Global Compact on Refugees (GCR) on 26 June 2018, and the Global Compact for Safe, Orderly and Regular Migration (GCM) on 11 July 2018. African countries have participated actively in the development processes of both compacts. Between 2016 and 2018, prior to the adoption of the of the GCR, the Comprehensive Refugee Response Framework (CRRF) was developed using 15 pilot countries, eight of which are located in Africa, namely, Chad, Djibouti, Ethiopia, Kenya, Rwanda, Uganda, Zambia and Somalia.

Different frameworks have also been developed by the European Union, particularly for managing the flow of irregular African migrants destined for Europe. These include the EU's European Neighbourhood Policy, the Joint Valletta Action Plan (JVAP), the EU Partnership Framework on Migration, and the EU Emergency Trust Fund (EUTF).

The African continent also boasts a plethora of robust normative frameworks aimed at governing forced displacement and migration, including:

1. The 1969 Organisation of African Unity (OAU) Convention Governing the Specific Aspects of Refugee Problems in Africa;
2. The 1981 African Charter on Human and Peoples' Rights, which obligates state parties to protect and promote the rights of all persons, including refugees, asylum seekers, returnees, IDPs and stateless persons;
3. The 2018 African Union Migration Policy Framework for Africa (AU-MPFA) and the Plan of Action, 2018–2030, which updates the 2006 policy, and introduces a concrete plan of action aimed at facilitating safe, orderly, and dignified migration; and
4. The 2018 Protocol to the Treaty Establishing the African Economic Community Relating to Free Movement of Persons, Right of Residence and Right of Establishment.

The largest chunk of international African migration is not destined for Europe and North America as conventional wisdom would have us believe. Most African migration happens within the continent. Shimeles (2018: 2) reminds us that, '79 percent of sub-Saharan African migrants move within the same region. Less than 22 percent of migrants from Africa emigrate outside Africa, with less than 15 percent of African migrants emigrating to Europe and North America.' These facts are important to dispel the myth that outward migration from Africa, especially to Europe and North America, outweighs intra-Africa migration. This myth is 'influenced by media images of massive refugee flows and "boat migration", and alarmist rhetoric of politicians suggesting an impending immigrant invasion' (Flahaux and De Haas, 2016: 1). The apocalyptic myth of an African 'exodus' to Europe and the United States is simply a figment of the imagination of narrow nationalist, populist, and anti-immigrant politicians. It is merely an electioneering gimmick.

Key governance challenges

There is extensive literature on developmental and conflict determinants of international migration. What is missing is the critical analysis of international migration from the governance perspective. The state of governance in a particular country has a significant bearing on whether citizens stay or flee to seek refuge or greener pastures in other countries. I concur with Gimenez-Gomez et al. (2017: 4) that 'poverty, violent civil conflict, political persecution, human rights abuse and ethnic tensions have a substantial influence on migration'. Under such circumstances, citizens may lose faith in governance structures altogether, and opt to 'vote with their feet'. This section focuses on five main manifestations of poor governance, which may trigger migration, namely: (1) corruption and illicit financial flows; (2) electoral violence; (3) mismanagement of diversity; (4) human rights violations; and (5) poverty and food insecurity.

Corruption and illicit financial flows

Africa is home to some of the most corrupt countries in the world. That corruption is rife in countries characterised by poor governance, engulfed in protracted violent conflict or emerging from conflict is incontrovertible today. It is easy, therefore, to postulate the inextricable interface between poor governance, corruption and conflict in Africa. Countries with poor governance tend to be highly corrupt and conflict prone. The reverse is also true: countries with a demonstrable record of democratic governance are less corrupt and less conflict prone.

For instance, of the 180 countries surveyed globally by Transparency International, five of the 10 most corrupt countries are in Africa (Transparency International, 2020). These are Somalia (No. 180), South Sudan (No. 179), Equatorial Guinea (No. 173), Sudan (No. 173) and Libya (No. 168). All these countries are engulfed in violent conflict and/or face serious challenges in respect of democratic and participatory governance (see the Institute for Economics and Peace, 2020; Mo Ibrahim Foundation 2020 Ibrahim Index of African Governance). Countries with poor governance tend to exhibit high levels of corruption, are conflict-prone and, importantly, experience high levels of out-migration, particularly emigration of skilled labour – the so-called brain drain.

The flip side of this is also interesting, namely, that those African countries that enjoy durable peace and have institutionalised democratic governance perform remarkably well in combatting corruption. This means that peace and democracy are important antidotes for corruption. Globally, the five best performing African countries in terms of combatting corruption are Seychelles (No. 27), Botswana (No. 34), Cabo Verde (No. 41), Rwanda (No. 51) and Namibia (No. 56) (Transparency International, 2020). Interestingly, all these countries are relatively peaceful (see Institute for Economics and Peace, 2020) and perform well on continental rankings on democratic governance[3]. These countries tend to experience relatively low levels of out-migration, especially by skilled professionals.

Illicit financial flows (IFFs) are central to corruption in Africa. According to the 2012 United Nations Economic Commission for Africa (UNECA) High-Level Panel, led by the former President of South Africa, Thabo Mbeki, Africa lost an estimated US$1 trillion in IFFs over the last 50 years, equivalent to all the official development assistance (ODA) received by Africa in the same period (UNECA, 2012). UNECA (2012) estimates that Africa loses more than US$50 billion annually in IFFs. Commercial activities account for 65 per cent of IFFs, criminal activities for 30 per cent, and corruption for 5 per cent (UNECA, 2012). Trade mispricing, particularly in the extractive industries, are a major component of IFFs. Trade mispricing in the oil industry alone created over US$80 billion in IFFs between 2000 and 2010 (UNECA, 2012).

There is a similar trend between IFFs and migration corridors. While other players exist, including countries in the Middle East and South and East Asia, many of the IFFs from Africa are destined for Europe and the United States. African out-bound migration routes follow similar trends, with the majority leading to Europe. In 2019, for example, 10.6 million of the 39.4 million African migrants worldwide lived in Europe, followed by 4.6 million residents in Asia, and 3.2 million in North America (World Migration Report, 2020).

Africa's most corrupt countries are also among the leading sources of refugees and skilled migrants in Europe and globally. At the end of 2018, South Sudan and Somalia were among the top five countries of origin of migrants, totalling 2.3 million and 0.9 million, respectively (UNHCR, 2019). Sudanese migrants are also among the leading groups making the hazardous journey to Europe via the Mediterranean Sea. In 2016, 9,327 Sudanese reached Europe via the central Mediterranean route, although this declined to 1,600 in 2018, because Europe tightened its borders (Abebe, 2020).

While Europe and the United States are tightening their border controls against migrants, their borders are wide open when it comes to IFFs, which are hidden in safe havens through opaque systems that safe keep these proceeds of grand corruption in Africa. In short, Europe and the United States prefer the illegal proceeds of corruption over African migrants. It is possible that these poor migrants are simply following African resources siphoned off by Western countries.

One example of a massive siphoning of funds from Africa to Europe relates to Sani Abacha of Nigeria. Abacha, Nigeria's most ruthless and iron-fisted military strongman and dictator, ruled Nigeria during the country's darkest moments of authoritarian rule from 1993 till his death in 1998. During this five-year period, Abacha siphoned off public funds estimated by Transparency International at around US$5 billion (BBC, 2014), which were transferred illicitly to safe havens in Europe and United States. Currently, the government of Nigeria, under the leadership of Muhammadu Buhari, with the assistance of the World Bank, is making concerted efforts to recover these stolen assets 'to finance projects that will strengthen social security for the poorest sections of the Nigerian population' (BBC, 2017).

There is compelling evidence that corruption retards economic growth, damages a country's investment attractiveness, and denudes the integrity and public trust of national institutions (Spector, 2008). Similarly, IFFs reduce domestic expenditure and investment, both public and private, which curtails public service delivery, and undermines the viability of the financial sector. IFFs and corruption divert money from public spending to private use. This negatively affects the economy and sensitive sectors, such as security, health and education, are worse off. For example, Nigerian military officials stole about US$15 million, and the former national security adviser, Sambo Dasuli, allegedly diverted US$2 million that was meant to combat the Boko Haram's reign of terror in Nigeria (Centre for Democracy and Development, 2020: 4). Giraldo referred to this kind of fund diversion as 'petty corruption' (in Spector, 2008: 6). Thus, corruption contributes strongly to the existing push factors for migration from Africa, which include lack of educational and employment opportunities, poverty, food insecurity and conflict. Schneider corroborates this point and maintains that:

Corruption increases emigration among workers at all education[al] levels eroding living conditions. But different levels of corruption have different effects on workers of different skill levels. At low levels of corruption, medium- and low-skilled workers leave, but once corruption reaches a certain threshold, this emigration slows. Among highly-skilled and highly-educated workers, however, emigration rises with corruption. The emigration of highly-educated workers, in particular, reduces a country's growth prospects and can lead to a vicious cycle. Thus, reducing the level of corruption should be a major goal of governments (Schneider, 2015: 1).

AU Member States and other Regional Economic Communities (RECs) need to be proactive and make concerted efforts to combat corruption by implementing the principles enshrined in the 2003 African Union Convention on Preventing and Combatting Corruption. These five noble principles are:

1. respect for democratic principles and institutions, popular participation, the rule of law and good governance;
2. respect for human and peoples' rights;
3. transparency and accountability in the management of public affairs;
4. promotion of social justice to ensure balanced socio-economic development; and
5. condemnation and rejection of acts of corruption, related offences and impunity (AU, 2003).

AU Member States and RECs have an obligation to ensure effective implementation of all the recommendations of the report of the Mbeki High Level Panel on Illicit Financial Flows. The Mbeki report recommended, among others, that African countries should adopt a normative instrument in the form of a declaration to commit to combating IFFs (African Union and Economic Commission for Africa (AU/ECA), 2015). To this end, the AU adopted a declaration on IFFs in January 2015. Furthermore, the AU declared 2018 the anti-corruption year, under the stewardship of the Nigerian President, Muhammadu Buhari. It also developed the Common African Position on Assets Recovery, which was adopted during its Assembly of Heads of State and Government meeting in Addis Ababa, Ethiopia, in February 2020. This vital document constitutes Africa's unified voice against IFFs.

Furthermore, the global community should partner with Africa to curb IFFs. Western countries should demonstrate goodwill by supporting Africa and affected states to recover assets stolen from Africa and retrieve illicit funds held in safe havens abroad, particularly those in Europe and the United States. The United Nations should also partner Africa in this anti-corruption initiative by enacting a global legal instrument to curb IFFs, and enforce the rules on money laundering, and mandate the concerned Western states and institutions to return Africa's stolen assets and funds.

Electoral violence

Electoral violence can occur before, during or after an election. It involves a wide range of abuses, amounting to 'acts or threats of coercion, intimidation, or physical harm perpetrated to affect an electoral process or that arises in the context of electoral competition' (Sisk, 2008, in Birch and Muchlinski, 2020). The major objective of electoral violence is to secure election victory or call attention to electoral irregularities. Electoral violence is a common challenge facing the continent, leading to forced displacement, and increased out-bound migration. It is important to cite two cases of electoral violence, namely, Kenya (2007–8) and Zimbabwe (2008). Politics in Kenya has always mirrored the country's ethnic fault lines. During elections, politics in Kenya is ethnicised and ethnicity is politicised. This resulted in the devastating electoral violence of 2007–8, which resulted in the death of about 1,500 people, 600,000 being internally displaced and more than 300,000 rendered refugees (see Kagwanja and Southall, 2009; Matlosa and Shale, 2013).

Politics in general and elections in particular are militarised in Zimbabwe. The militarisation of politics is reinforced by politicisation of the military. The 2008 general election was the most violent in the country's history, claiming about 36 lives, leading to 3,000 internally displaced people and rendering scores more as refugees in neighbouring countries, including Botswana, Mozambique, and South Africa (Human Rights Watch, 2008). In both countries, part of the resolution of electoral violence led to power-sharing governments (Matlosa and Shale, 2013). Current trends indicate that young people are often both perpetrators and victims of electoral violence. Interestingly, young people constitute the bulk of forced displacement and migration because of electoral violence.

During the 13th Ordinary Session of the Assembly of Heads of State and Government, held in Sirte, Libya, in July 2009, the AU adopted the Panel of the Wise on Election-Related Disputes and Political Violence: Strengthening the Role of the African Union in Preventing, Managing and Resolving Conflict. This report provides a comprehensive set of strategies and approaches for the AU to tackle election-related disputes and political violence in Africa (IPI, 2010). The report mandated the Panel of Wise and other relevant institutions within the AU to address the root causes of electoral violence within the electoral cycle (election-related causes) as well as the structural factors (systemic causes). It further highlighted the need for the AU to commit more resources to preventive measures, and to early warning and early response mechanisms. A report by the International Peace Institute detailed the following far-reaching policy recommendations (IPI, 2010: 63–74):

1.   Risk mapping, preventive and early warning mechanisms;
2.   Electoral governance and administration;
3.   Coordination of electoral assistance;
4.   Post-election conflict transformation mechanisms;
5.   International cooperation and partnerships; and
6.   Strategic interventions by the Panel of the Wise.

Dealing with electoral violence requires investment in early warning systems, early response and preventive diplomacy. African countries need to move away from the current focus on conflict management, which amounts to a 'fire brigade approach'.[4] Despite the possibility that certain elections may trigger violent conflicts as a result of the tense atmosphere created by the political class and the divisive electoral system, too often African countries wait for the fire to break out and then retroactively unleash firefighters to contain the inferno. The design of the electoral system is also important in managing election-related conflicts. Evidence suggests that winner-take-all systems, applicable in many political transitions on the continent, are highly conflict prone.

Furthermore, the winner-take-all system has threatened power transitions in many African countries, where the incumbent office-holder tries to hold on to political power by all means, including using the state apparatus to suppress opposition parties. However, this often degenerates into large-scale violence. The most recent case was in Gambia, where the incumbent president, Yahya Jammeh, rejected the result of the general election, and deployed the military to quash the electoral violence that ensued. Dispute over the presidential election in Côte d'Ivoire, involving President Laurent Gbagbo, led to a devastating armed battle between the national security and defence forces loyal to Gbagbo and the Republican Forces of Côte d'Ivoire (FRCI), which supported his opposition, Alassane Dramane Ouattara. The violent conflict led to the death of at least 3,000 Ivorians, and about a million became refugees in neighbouring countries (Zounmenou and Lamin, 2011: 11).

In response, African countries should establish independent election management bodies (EMBs), where these do not exist, with adequate resources to ensure credible, transparent, and peaceful elections. Such institutions should also be answerable to the national legislature and not to the executive, thereby reinforcing the principle of checks and balances. The EMBs should work closely with national Infrastructures for Peace (I4Ps) to prevent electoral violence. I4P broadly refers to 'the building of institutional capacities for peace-building, prevention of violent conflict and recovery from post-war violence ... It is a dynamic network of interdependent structures, mechanisms, resources, values and skills which, through dialogue and consultation, contribute to conflict prevention and peace-building in a society' (Van Tongeren et al., 2012: 2). These institutions, platforms and networks conventionally take the form of National Peace Committees (NPCs) operating at local, district or provincial and national levels, involving all parties in conflict, governments, and civil society organisations (CSOs).

NPCs mediate in local conflicts and facilitate constructive dialogue among disputants, often using insider mediators and relying largely on customary and traditional alternative dispute resolution mechanisms. These mechanisms have worked well in most post-conflict situations. Odendaal (2012: 40) cautions that in designing NPCs, due regard should be given to four main elements, namely (1) the nature of their mandate; (2) clarity of their roles and functions; (3) the composition of their membership; and (4) their competence and technical expertise.

Mismanagement of diversity

African countries are socio-culturally diverse, and social groups often actively differentiate themselves from others to reinforce intra-group solidarity to promote and protect their interests. Key markers of diversity include ethnicity, religion, race, region, class, gender, age, among others. To quote Francis Deng (2008: 31), 'perhaps the most important challenge facing African countries today lies here: How does the African state transform its component identities – its ethnic diversities inherited from colonial boundaries – into nation-states.' Deng's observation clearly suggests that diversity, if properly managed, need not lead to adversity or become destructive. It need not be a political liability to nation-building, sustainable democratic governance and peacebuilding. Well understood and constructively managed, diversity can be a resource for national unity and for advancing the nation-state-building project in Africa. It can become an asset for democratisation, nation-building and peace in Africa.

The problem is not that African societies are diverse. Diversity should be an asset rather than a liability. The problem is that this diversity is mismanaged by the political elite for their self-serving political and economic gains. Because of its mismanagement, Africa's diversity often leads to adversity, which is accentuated during elections. Thus, ethnicity is politicised, and politics is ethnicised, especially around elections. Evidently, mismanagement of diversity has also triggered political instability and forced displacement of people within (as internally displaced persons) and outside their national borders (as refugees, asylum-seekers and forced migrants).

The United Nations Development Programme's (UNDP's) *Human Development Report 2004* presented a comprehensive exploration of possible policy reforms that could advance cultural liberty and present an opportunity for constructive management of socio-cultural diversity on regional and global levels. The UNDP (2004: 47–72) report proposes the following policy responses in five main domains:

1. Policies for ensuring political participation of diverse cultural groups through power sharing and consociationalism:
    a. Federalism
    b. Proportional representation electoral system
2. Policies on religion and religious practice:
    a. Freedom of belief
    b. Rights for religious minorities
3. Policies on customary law and legal pluralism:
    a. Access to justice for all
    b. Cultural recognition of justice
4. Policies on multiple languages:
    a. Language policy in schools
    b. Language policy in government institutions; and
5. Policies for redressing socio-economic exclusion:
    a. Addressing unequal social investments to achieve equality of opportunity
    b. Recognising legitimate claims to land and livelihoods
    c. Taking affirmative action in favour of disadvantaged groups.

Human rights violations

The discourse on the nexus between migration and human rights violations is two-pronged. First, the pervasive trend of human rights violations in Africa increases out-migration. Second, as migrants flee human rights violations in their countries of origin, they become susceptible to human rights abuses in both transit and destination countries. In fact, irregular or undocumented migrants are 'disproportionately vulnerable to discrimination, exploitation and marginalization, often living and working in the shadows, afraid to complain, and denied their human rights and fundamental freedoms' (UNOHCHR, 2019: 1). Abuses of the rights of migrants include denial of civil and political rights, such as the right to be free of torture; and denial of socio-economic and cultural rights, such as the right to health, education and housing. Denial of the rights and fundamental freedoms of migrants in countries of transit and destination may be propelled by sheer prejudice or xenophobia (UNOHCHR, 2019: 1).

There is documented evidence of horrendous human rights violations of migrants by Libyan state officials, armed militias, smugglers and traffickers since the collapse of the state system in 2011. These violations include unlawful killings, torture, arbitrary detention, gang rape, slavery, forced labour and extortion (UNOHCHR, 2018: 4). The violence that is often unleashed against African migrants in South Africa amounts to the denial of the rights of migrants, refugees and asylum seekers. While xenophobic attacks in 2008, 2015 and 2019 attracted international attention, cases of subtle discrimination of migrants have remained unnoticed. The problem continues partly because of the denial of state officials and the inefficiency of state security to maintain law and order. The hostility against migrants has led to a mass movement of African migrants from South Africa to other countries, including European countries. Apart from South Africa, other countries such as Ghana have recently displayed xenophobic attitudes towards migrants. Partly with a view to improve the protection and promotion of the rights of all, including those of migrants, the AU – under aspiration 3 of Agenda 2063, tagged 'The Africa We Want' – envisions an 'Africa of good governance, democracy, respect for human rights, justice and the rule of law' (AU, 2015).

While human rights violations are prevalent on the continent, they are more pronounced under conditions of authoritarian governance and violent conflict. It is largely under conditions inimical to democratic and participatory governance and peace that fundamental rights of citizens are abused and trampled underfoot. These violations include political persecution for holding views contrary to those who wield power and authority. This culture of impunity persists, despite the provisions of Article 4(h) of the Constitutive Act of the African Union, which gives the supranational body the power to intervene in cases of egregious human rights abuses, mass atrocities and genocide. Consequently, the initial perception of the early 2000s that the transition from the Organisation of African Unity (OAU) to the African Union (AU) presaged a paradigm shift from the old doctrine of non-interference in internal affairs of member states to the new doctrine of non-indifference to human rights abuses within member states, remains a distant mirage. This is largely because of the persistence of narrow national sovereignty and the principle of subsidiarity that governs relations between the AU and the RECs. These two factors constrain the AU's human rights agenda considerably.

Almost all AU Member States have ratified the 1981 African Charter on Human and Peoples' Rights and some have also ratified its various protocols on the rights of women enacted in 2003, the rights of older persons in 2016, and the rights of persons with disabilities in 2018. States have the responsibility to preserve, protect and promote human rights. Civil society actors have a duty to advocate for the protection and promotion of human rights. It is well-nigh impossible to promote and protect human rights at a national level without the establishment and adequate resourcing of independent National Human Rights Institutions (NHRIs) that are superintended by parliament and not the executive. It is through these NHRIs that a culture of human rights must be entrenched in Africa.

Poverty and food insecurity

Structural root causes of migration include underdevelopment, poverty, food insecurity, hunger, inequality and unemployment in conditions where socio-economic and cultural rights are in short supply. Poverty on the continent today illustrates what can be termed the African paradox. It is paradoxical that Africa is the richest continent in the world in terms of natural resource endowment, yet it is home to some of the poorest people and nations in the world. While accounting for only 2 per cent of the global gross domestic product (GDP), Africa is a repository of 15 per cent of the planet's crude oil reserves; 40 per cent of its gold; and 80 per cent of its platinum (Burgis, 2015). This situation lends credence to the conventional wisdom that Africa's natural resource endowment is more of a curse than a cure for the continent's development. This is vividly illustrated by the massive scale of illicit financial outflows, as the findings of the Mbeki report on IFFs demonstrate.

Poverty and food insecurity in Africa are, in part, a result of poor governance and violent conflicts. Yet, violent conflicts and instability are also caused by poverty and food insecurity. Somalia presents an interesting case study of how poverty, inequality and hunger combine with political instability as key drivers for out-migration. Key push factors for out-migration by Somalis, predominantly young males, include 'unemployment, lack of sufficient income, lack of jobs and livelihood opportunities, financial problems and debt and security reasons' (IOM, 2017: 2). One of the most preferred destinations for Somali migrants is Europe. But a considerable number of them have lost their lives on these perilous journeys due to 'hunger, heat and thirst or drowning as their boats sink or capsize in the Mediterranean Sea, the Gulf of Aden or the Black Sea' (Wasuge, 2018: 3).

Thus, there is a symbiotic and mutually reinforcing relationship between poverty and food insecurity, and among the four drivers of migration discussed earlier. The marginalised and vulnerable social groups, including women, children, people with disabilities, minorities and the elderly, tend to be the hardest hit by poverty, food insecurity and hunger. In fact, poverty, food insecurity, hunger, inequality and unemployment are some of the causal factors behind the popular protests, dubbed 'the Arab Spring,' in North Africa since 2010, spreading from Tunisia to Egypt, Libya and Algeria; and also in West Africa (Burkina Faso in 2016) and East Africa (Sudan in 2019).

Within the context of Agenda 2063 – 'The Africa We Want', and the global 2030 agenda on sustainable development, particularly Sustainable Development Goal (SDG) 1 on 'ending poverty' – an agriculture-led model for inclusive development should be the leading policy response to poverty, food insecurity and hunger (Mkandawire and Rukuni, 2015: 108). This is because all African countries are fundamentally agrarian societies. Ironically, poverty and hunger in Africa is more concentrated in rural areas due to the absence of effective agrarian reform. Mkandawire and Rukuni hit the nail on the head when they observe that 'given the significant reliance of African livelihoods on agriculture, either directly as smallholders or indirectly as farmworkers, the poor competitiveness of African agriculture compromises peoples' income earning capacity across the continent' (Mkandawire and Rukuni, 2015: 108). They conclude that, 'investing in farm productivity offers potentially the most effective strategy for lifting large numbers of Africans out of poverty' (Mkandawire and Rukuni, 2015: 113).

The impact of the COVID-19 pandemic on migration

Today, the world is reeling under the tight grip of a coronavirus disease (known as COVID-19), which was first detected in the city of Wuhan in Hubei province in China at the end of 2019. This deadly virus spread rapidly to other parts of Asia, Europe, and the Americas. It was declared a public health emergency of international concern on 30 January 2020, and subsequently a pandemic by the World Health Organisation (WHO) on 11 March 2020. In its third wave, the COVID-19 pandemic reached Africa, beginning with the first case reported in Egypt in February 2020. By June 2020, 54 AU Member States had recorded COVID-19 cases, including a monumental loss of human lives.

Essentially, COVID-19 is not only a health emergency, but also has severe implications for governance, peace, security and development. In its multi-dimensionality, COVID-19 adversely affects all aspects of social life, and the ferocious impact of this disease has spared no one. However, among the hardest hit are certainly refugees, asylum seekers, returnees, internally displaced persons and other migrants. Jason Gagnon reminds us that, 'while COVID-19 is not a migration issue, it is being viewed and managed as one' (Gagnon, 2020: 1).

Almost all countries have closed their borders, imposed states of emergency, states of disaster, curfews, and significantly restricted human movement under conditions of either partial or total lockdown. Given the tight restrictions on human movement and border closures, COVID-19 has triggered what the International Organization for Migration (IOM) has dubbed 'a near global international mobility deadlock' (IOM, 2020a: 1). Abebe (2020: 2) poignantly opines that migration from Africa to Europe is often perceived as a security threat (Abebe, 2020: 2). With COVID-19, migrants now face a double-jeopardy: they are perceived as a security threat as well as a health threat.

Consequently, migrants cannot move as they are trapped in their countries of origin, transit or destination. Some irregular migrants of African descent are being repatriated to their home countries. For instance, Ethiopian migrants have been repatriated from various countries in the Middle East (including Saudi Arabia, Yemen and Lebanon) and East Africa (including Djibouti) since the second quarter of 2020. These mass repatriations contravene international human rights and humanitarian laws, most notably the 1981 African Charter on Human and Peoples' Rights, as well as the 1948 Universal Declaration of Human Rights. The timing and conditions of these repatriations exposes 'migrants to the virus and pose ... challenges to countries of origin, which are already overstretched in responding to the pandemic' (Amani Africa, 2020: 3).

Even under normal circumstances, it is difficult for migrants to move from Africa to other continents. COVID-19 presents migrants with an additional dilemma. They are likely to face overt and covert incidences of intolerance, discrimination, dehumanisation, stigmatisation, and racism and xenophobia, as countries become more inward-looking and nationalistic in their policy responses to COVID-19. African migrants in the city of Gaunzhou in Gaundong province in China were subjected to acts of racism and xenophobia on mere suspicion that they had the virus; a development that triggered a political furore, which shook Sino-Africa relations (Human Rights Watch, 2020). The pandemic has generated fear-mongering, which provides 'the political space to push structural anti-migration policies through. This will be detrimental to the rights and health of migrants and the positive impact that migrants have on development' (Gagnon, 2020:1). COVID-19, therefore, compounds the governance challenges of Africa's out-migration – a trend that is likely to persist even after the pandemic.

Conclusion

This chapter interrogates the governance challenges of migration in Africa. It opposes the conventional wisdom that confines push factors for migration to development and peace deficits. It transcends the war-poverty discourse by bringing governance deficits to the centre of the analysis of the drivers of migration in Africa through a political economy lens. It identifies five indicators for poor governance in Africa and establishes their central role in driving out-migration, namely: corruption and illicit financial flows; electoral violence; mismanagement of diversity; human rights violations;

and poverty and food insecurity. It advances concrete policy proposals on how to deal with these governance deficits and resolve the migration issues.

Besides the specific thematic recommendations, three generic policy recommendations are in order. First, African countries should prioritise strengthening their democratic governance systems and structures to make them more accountable and responsive to stem out-migration. Second, because out-migration flows tend to constitute young people, in their governance reform measures, African countries should prioritise youth empowerment in social, cultural, economic and political spheres. Third, governance reforms in Africa should also privilege the economic empowerment of women, given that women are at the receiving end of the continent's socio-economic and political malaise.

The contemporary governance failures in Africa contribute immensely to political instability on the continent. The political crisis emanating from this instability propels disenchantment, frustration, even anger on the part of powerless citizens. Some of the disenchanted, frustrated and angry citizens opt to leave their countries and to seek solace elsewhere. They migrate under the assumption that the grass is greener on the other side. The COVID-19 pandemic has further compounded the governance challenges of international migration within and from Africa to other continents, including Europe.

The AU and the EU have vital roles to play in transforming migration within and across these two continents. For its part, the AU must prioritise two complementary continental integration agendas, namely the African Continental Free Trade Area (AfCFTA) and the free movement of persons, both of which are flagship projects of Agenda 2063 and key foundation stones of the 1991 Treaty Establishing the African Economic Community (AU, 2020). Considerable progress has been made on AfCFTA and the free trade formally commenced on 1 January 2021; however, negotiation for its full implementation remains ongoing. Little progress has been made on the free movement of persons, largely because of security fears, which have now been compounded by COVID-19. The dilemma is that AfCFTA will remain a distant mirage without the free movement of persons, given that free trade cannot succeed without the free movement of labour and business persons. In March 2020, the EU has published its policy document entitled, 'Towards a Comprehensive Strategy with Africa', with five pillars, one of which focuses on 'a partnership on migration and mobility' (EU, 2020).

While the COVID-19 pandemic has slowed the implementation of the strategy, it is imperative for the European Commission to focus attention on the governance drivers for migration, as elaborated in this chapter, so that the problem is tackled at its structural root. Only a strategy focusing on structural drivers of migration will address the problem more effectively. As the old English aphorism goes: prevention is better than cure.

Notes

1   The views expressed in this chapter are those of the author. They do not represent the official position of the African Union Commission (AUC). They are opinions of the author in his personal capacity as a scholar and researcher. I acknowledge comprehensive and useful comments from Tsion Abebe, Senior Researcher, Migration Programme, Institute for Security Studies (ISS), Addis Ababa, Ethiopia.

2   According to these authors, human security, taken at its most basic level includes, 'freedom from fear (threats to the safety of people), freedom from want (threats to basic needs), and freedom to live in dignity (threats to human rights and, by extension, access to services and opportunities' (Gimenez-Gomez et al., 2017: 3).

3   See the 2020 Ibrahim Index of African Governance: all the five countries are in the top 10 performers on democratic governance.

4   This is commonly used in Nigeria to describe government's act of responding to societal or governance issues at the last minute, and possibly when such intervention is too late.

References

Abebe, T. 2020. 'Fewer migrants to Europe, bigger problems for Africa', *ISS Today*, 7 April. Pretoria: Institute for Security Studies.

African Union (AU). 2020. 'The Status of Regional Integration in Africa', African Integration Report, Addis Ababa, Ethiopia, 30 June.

African Union (AU). 2015. Agenda 2063: 'The Africa We Want', Addis Ababa, Ethiopia.

African Union (AU). 2003. African Union Convention on Preventing and Combatting Corruption, Addis Ababa, Ethiopia.

African Union and Economic Commission for Africa (AU/ECA). 2015. 'Illicit Financial Flows. Report of the High Level Panel on Illicit Financial Flows from Africa'. Addis Ababa: African Union and Economic Commission for Africa.

Amani Africa. 2020. 'Insights on the Peace and Security Council: Briefing on the situation of IDPs, refugees and returnees in the COVID-19 crisis'. Addis Ababa: Amani Africa, Media and Research Services.

BBC. 2017. 'Abacha loot: Switzerland to return $320m to Nigeria', London.

BBC. 2014. 'Abacha loot: Nigeria to get $227m from Liechtenstein', London.

Birch, S. and D. Muchlinski. 2020. 'The dataset of countries at risk of electoral violence', *Terrorism and Political Violence*, 32(2), pp. 217–36.

Burgis, T. 2015. *The Looting Machine: Warlords, oligarchs, corporations, smugglers, and the theft of Africa's wealth*. New York: Public Affairs.

Castelli, F. 2018. 'Drivers of migration: Why do people move?', *Journal of Travel Medicine*, 25(1): 1–7.

Centre for Democracy and Development. 2020. *Buhari's Corruption Fight: A five-year assessment*. Abuja: Centre for Democracy and Development.

Danzinger, R. 2017. 'Voting with their feet? Why young Africans are choosing migration over the ballot box'. Geneva: World Economic Forum. Online at: https:/www.weforum.org.2017/07 (accessed 15 February 2021).

Deng, F. 2008. *Identity, Diversity and Constitutionalism in Africa*. Washington DC: United State Institute of Peace Press.

European Union (EU). 2020. 'Joint Communication to the European Parliament and the Council: Towards a comprehensive strategy with Africa'. Brussels: European Union, 9 March.

European Union (EU). 2018. *International Migration Drivers: A quantitative assessment of the structural factors shaping migration*. Luxembourg: Joint Research Centre Science for Policy Report.

Flahaux, M. and De Haas, H. 2016. 'African migration: Trends, patterns, drivers', *Comparative Migration Studies*, 4(1): 2–25.

Gagnon, J. 2020. 'COVID-19: Consequences for international migration and development', *Development Matters*, 2 April. Paris: OECD Development Centre. Online at: https://oecd-development-matters.org/2020/04/02/covid-19-consequences-for-international-migration-and-development/ (accessed 19 February 2021).

Gimenez-Gomez, J.G., Walle, Y. and Zergawu, Y. 2017. *Trends in African Migration to Europe: Drivers beyond economic motivations*. Centre for European Governance and Economic Development Research, Discussion Paper No. 330, pp. 1797–831.

Human Rights Watch. 2020. 'China: Covid-19 Discrimination Against Africans: Forced quarantines, evictions, refused services in Guangzhou'. New York, 5 May.

Human Rights Watch. 2008. '"Bullets for each of you": State-sponsored violence since Zimbabwe's March 29 elections'. Report, New York, 9 June.

Institute for Economics and Peace. 2020. *Global Peace Index 2020: Measuring peace in a complex world.* Sydney, Australia, June.

International Organization for Migration (IOM). 2020a. *World Migration Report.* Geneva: International Organization for Migration. Online at: https://publications.iom.int/system/files/pdf/wmr_2020.pdf (accessed 5 May 2020).

International Organization for Migration (IOM). 2020b. *COVID-19 Disease Response*, Situation Report No. 8. Geneva: International Organization for Migration.

International Organization for Migration (IOM). 2018. *World Migration Report.* Geneva: International Organization for Migration.

International Organization for Migration (IOM). 2017. Displacement Tracking Matrix (DMT)-Comprehensive Migration Flow Survey (CMFS). CMFS Brief: Somali Migrants (to Europe). Geneva: International Organization for Migration.

International Peace Institute (IPI). 2010. *Election-Related Disputes and Political Violence: Strengthening the role of the African Union in preventing, managing and resolving conflict*, African Union Series, pp. 63–74.

Kagwanja, P. and Southall, R. 2009. 'Preface', *Journal of Contemporary African Studies*, Special Issue on *Kenya's Uncertain Democracy: Election crisis of 2008*, 27(3).

Matlosa, K. and V. Shale. 2013. 'The pains of democratisation: The uneasy interface between elections and power-sharing arrangements in Africa', *Africa Review*, 5(1), January–June.

Mkandawire, T. 2007. 'Good governance: The itinerary of an idea', *Development in Practice*, 17(4/5): 679–81.

Mkandawire, R. and M. Rukuni. 2015. 'Eradicating Extreme Poverty and Hunger (MDG One),' in Mutasa, C. and M. Paterson. (eds). *Africa and the Millennium Development Goals: Progress, problems and prospects.* London: Rowman & Littlefield.

Mo Ibrahim Foundation. 2020. Ibrahim Index of African Governance, London, UK.

Odendaal, A. 2012. 'The political legitimacy of national peace committees', *Journal of Peacebuilding and Development*, 7(3): 40–53.

Organisation of African Unity (OAU). 1981. The African Charter on Human and Peoples' Rights, Addis Ababa: Organisation of African Unity.

Schneider, F. 2015. 'Does corruption promote emigration?' Online at: http://wol.iza.org/articles/does-corruption-promote-emigration-1.pdf. (accessed 5 May 2020).

Shimeles, A. 2018. 'Foresight Africa viewpoint – Understanding the patterns and causes of African migration: Some facts'. brookings, Africa in Focus, Thursday, 18 January.

Spector, I. 2008. *Fighting Corruption in Post-Conflict Countries: Practitioner guidance for negotiators and development assistance professionals*. Potomac, MD: Center for Negotiation Analysis.

Transparency International. 2020. Corruption Perceptions Index, 2020. Online at: https://www.transparency.org/en/cpi/2020/index/nzl (accessed 18 February 2021).

United Nations Department of Economic and Social Affairs (UNDESA). 2019. 'The number of international migrants reaches 272 million, continuing an upward trend in all world's regions', 17 September. New York: United Nations Department of Economic and Social Affairs.

United Nations Development Programme (UNDP). 2004. *Cultural Liberty in Today's Diverse World*. Oxford: Oxford University Press.

United Nations High Commissioner for Refugees. 2019. 'Desperate Journeys', January. Online at: https://bit.ly/2Vh7p2d (accessed 5 May 2020).

United Nations Office of the High Commissioner for Human Rights (UNOHCHR). 2018. *Desperate and Dangerous: Report on the human rights situation of migrants and refugees in Libya*. Geneva: United Nations Office of the High Commissioner for Human Rights.

United Nations Office of the High Commissioner for Human Rights (UNOHCHR). 2019. Migration and Human Rights, UNOHCHR Webpage (mimeo). Online at: https://www.ohchr.org/en/issues/migration/pages/migrationandhumanrightsindex.aspx (accessed 19 February 2021)

Van Tongeren, P., Ojielo, O., Brand-Jacobsen, K., McCandless, E. and Tschirgi, N. 2012. 'The evolving landscape of infrastructures for peace', *Journal of Peacebuilding and Development*, 7(3): 1–7.

Wasuge, M. 2018. 'Youth Migration in Somalia: Causes, consequences and possible remedies'. Research Report. Mogadishu, Somalia: Heritage Institute for Policy Studies.

World Population Review. 2020. 'World Population by Country'. Online at: https://worldpopulationreview.com/ (accessed 5 May 2020).

Zounmenou, D. and Lamin, A. 2011. 'Côte d'Ivoire's post-electoral crisis: Ouattara rules but can he govern?' *Journal of Elections*, 10(2): 6–21.

Chapter 4

Beyond the Eurocentric gaze: Refugee and migration governance in Africa

Franzisca Zanker

Introduction

In March 2020, the European Commission released its new strategy on European Union (EU)/African relations, calling on its 'principles of solidarity, partnership and shared responsibility' (European Commission, 2020). Although the strategy notes both challenges and opportunities, there is no significant change in perspective or approach regarding migration governance. Currently, European interests continue to dominate much of the strategy-making (Van Criekinge, 2016; Zanker, 2019). Yet, there is much more to tell when it comes to refugee and migration governance in Africa. Thus, this chapter seeks to highlight the roles of African states in dealing with refugee and migration governance.

Indeed, how states in the Global South approach migration governance has received scant attention in literature and public discourse. In most of the literature on the topic, African perspectives are seen as passive, working in the shadows of dominant European perspectives (see Berriane and De Haas, 2012; Adamson and Tsourapas, 2019b). Put differently, states are fundamental to protecting refugees and implementing migration governance, yet in the African setting, very little is known about what, how and why states choose to implement certain policies.[1] These blind spots persist even though migration has become a topic that can make or break elections or determine political alliances, with anti-migrant sentiment increasing across the world (Jaji, 2020). This chapter looks beyond a Eurocentric approach to migration politics and explores the response of African states to migration and refugee governance, acknowledging that references to European[2] political interests remain inevitable, given the dominant effect of the externalisation programmes in Africa.

First, most studies consider migration and displacement as two disparate concepts, but in reality, the two are interconnected for individuals on the move, as well as the political stakes involved (see also Bakewell and Bonfiglio, 2013). Frequently, the literature on migration focuses on economic immigration in/to countries in the Global North, and on refugees and forced displacement in/to countries in the Global South (Adamson and Tsourapas, 2019b). In addition to reiterating Eurocentric research biases, this discrepancy hides the political stakes that categorisations can hold. Categorising people on the move is highly politicised and often analytically blurry. The mobilities of refugees and other migrants often overlap; categorisations of mobility are ultimately legally or politically constructed; with a range of agency, choice and flexibility in individual journeys (for example, Crawley and Skleparis, 2018; see also Jaji, 2020). If we want to unpack the political constructions of refugees and migrants to understand how states are using these, we need to consider the different forms of movement in relation to each other.

Second, while migration governance remains largely a national matter (reiterating the importance of prioritising the place of African states), it is, nonetheless, tied to the transnational framing of both the actual mobility of people and the underlying governance frameworks (Castles, 2004). The different levels involved in migration governance were recognised by the 'African Agenda on Migration', presented to the African Union (AU) by King Mohammed VI in January 2018, which advocated for an 'approach based on national policies, sub-regional coordination, a continental vision and international partnership' (North Africa Post, 2018). Acknowledging this multidimensionality, this chapter will, however, for purposes of space, focus on state responses rather than on regional or continental initiatives.

Third, while migrants and refugees are often instrumentalised for political purposes, many positive contributions and advancements have been recognised and made in Africa, mostly at a continental level. Indeed, some of the most advanced refugee protection measures in the world exist in Africa. The 1969 Convention on Refugees, established by the Organisation of African Unity (OAU), advanced further than the International Geneva Convention, effectively granting African refugees the possibility of prima facie refugee status, side-lining the lengthy burden of proof that refugees face in asylum processes elsewhere (Abebe et al., 2019). The convention was promulgated at a time when Pan-African solidarity was particularly high, with decolonisation processes rapidly unfolding all over the continent.

Furthermore, in 2009 the AU proposed a convention to protect internally displaced people (IDPs), the first of its kind in the world. By now, 29 countries have ratified the Kampala Convention, which makes provision for addressing internal displacement caused by armed conflict and natural disasters, as well as large-scale development projects in Africa such as hotel developments, infrastructure projects like railways, dams or roads, or the exploitation for natural resources (African Union and Norwegian Refugee Council, 2013). Moreover, 10 years after the signing of the Kampala Convention, the AU declared 2019, The Year of Refugees, Returnees and Internally Displaced Persons.

In terms of migration governance, a Protocol to the Treaty Establishing the African Economic Community Relating to the Free Movement of Persons, Right of Residence and Right of Establishment ('The Free Movement Protocol') was adopted and signed in 2018 by 32 AU member states. In April 2019, the AU also launched the African Continental Free Trade Area agreement, with 28 ratifications. Despite these innovations and grand plans, dealing with migrants and refugees comes with both costs and potential benefits for African states, which will be discussed further as the chapter proceeds by outlining some of the challenges related to displacement and migration in Africa, and their role for domestic and external legitimacy.

Challenges of migration governance in Africa

The migration and refugee challenges confronting Africa are as varied and large as the continent itself. African governments often face a juxtaposition of two broad issues: one of the highest figures for refugee and internally displaced persons worldwide (see below), on the one hand, and a general understanding of mobility and migration as normality with important development repercussions, on the other hand (Adepoju, 2011; Okyerefo and Setrana, 2018; Jegen and Zanker, 2020).

A European agenda on migration in Africa, and especially on migration from Africa to Europe, favours a misreading of the complexities of the migration–development nexus, often resulting in localised development programmes, increasingly coopted by migration governance projects in order to *stop migration* to Europe (Bakewell, 2008; Kabbanji, 2013). While this chapter does not focus specifically on development challenges and opportunities, it will show how African governments considers this in their political calculations when they respond to displacements and movements across their borders.

Based on the most recent figures released by the United Nations High Commissioner for Refugees (UNHCR), around 31 per cent of the world's refugees (or 6.35 million people) are currently in sub-Saharan Africa (UNHCR, 2019a), and around 41 per cent of the 50.8 million IDPs live in Africa (Internal Displacement Monitoring Centre, 2020).[3] Of these, 19.2 million people were displaced due to conflict and nearly 2 million due to disasters. Causes of displacement related to conflict is pervasive in many contexts affected by longstanding instability and violence like the DRC, South Sudan, Nigeria, and Somalia. Other conflicts have seen more recent increases in displacement, including conflict in the Anglophone regions of Cameroon, and communal violence in Burkina Faso, Mali, and Niger. Natural disasters like flooding in Mozambique can also lead to displacement, as well as political instability or economic fragility, as is the case in Libya (Internal Displacement Monitoring Centre, 2020). These overwhelming numbers are coupled with massive problems of underfunding, and protracted situations where refugees and IDPs remain displaced for decades, leading whole generations to grow up in refugee camps.

In 2018, the situations of refugees from South Sudan in Kenya, Sudan and Uganda, as well as Nigerians in Cameroon and Niger, and refugees from the Democratic Republic of Congo (DRC) and Somalia in South Africa, became protracted cases (UNHCR, 2019a).[4] As the leading United Nations (UN) agency in charge of protecting refugees, the UNHCR is chronically underfunded. As of September 2018, the UNHCR only had 45 per cent of the funding required to ensure effective refugee protection. African states host four out of six of the most underfunded refugee situations globally. For example, in 2018 Burundi had only 28 per cent of the funds they needed

(UNHCR, 2018), while Rwanda, alarmingly, had only 2 per cent of their required funds at the beginning of 2019 (UNHCR, 2019b).

Considering the COVID-19 epidemic, the already challenging situation became increasingly complex in many ways. First, donor funding for refugees and displaced people is being slashed due to increased budget deficits. For example, the World Food Programme in Uganda has cut 30 per cent of its allocation in 2020 (Abebe and Abebe, 2020). Second, thousands of migrants and refugees have become stuck in dire circumstances, abandoned by smugglers or unable to return home, as borders are shut and travel undermined (Burke, 2020). Third, some states have used the pandemic to push through anti-migrant policies (Moyo and Zanker, 2020).

Having laid out some of the challenges related to displacement in Africa, the chapter presents two ways in which refugee and migration governance becomes politically instrumentalised: domestically and externally. Across the world, governments respond to displacement and migration in a politically calculated away. Governments have sought to counter domestic pressures by a variety of exclusionary rhetoric and practice, tied to a restrictive understanding of citizenship. These practices range from xenophobic discourse and tighter immigration controls to deportations. Such exclusionary posturing has been particularly relevant during election campaigns. External political gains can be made by using migration governance for humanitarian, donor and political leverage. Most importantly, this is not merely about gaining more revenue but also about resistance to external demands on migration control, as a new and growing research agenda shows (for example, Paoletti, 2010; Chou and Gibert, 2012; El Qadim, 2014). This will be discussed in more detail below.

Domestic legitimacy

Within Africa, many citizens face problems of high unemployment, economic inequality, and low access to public goods. In some countries, migrants or refugees are in direct competition for resources with the host society – especially in some refugee camps, where access to education, healthcare and other goods can create tensions between migrants and their host society, who face deprivation issues and social inequalities (Whitaker, 2002). Often the perception of refugees is negative even if the host community does actually benefit from the refugee neighbours, as in Uganda (see Kreibaum, 2016). Another study shows that the host community in Ghana believe that Liberian refugees have increased the costs of goods and services, brought pressure on facilities, increased social vices, and deteriorated environmental resources (Codjoe et al., 2013). Although the same study finds that refugees are also viewed as a source of income and trade partners, access to public resources is increasingly tied to citizenship, based on social hierarchies, and linked to people's ethnicities and indigeneity, which contributes to the marginalisation of displaced or migrant communities (Mosselson, 2010; Nyamnjoh, 2010; Daley, 2013). Some authors understand this resentment as a form of 'new nationalism', a term originally coined by Claude Ake, not in response to colonial powers but against non-citizens living in the country, shaped by socio-political exclusion (Kersting, 2009). Migrants, refugees, and IDPs often lack the power or voice to overcome these boundaries of exclusion and belonging (see Daley, 2013). Considering the structural inequalities that states are otherwise unable or unwilling to address, migrants and refugees are used by them as scapegoats to retain legitimacy.

In terms of discursive exclusionary practices, two of the most common scapegoat narratives are related to jobs and security.[5] This leads to an established narrative in which migrants supposedly steal jobs and symbolise a threat to the host societies (see also Okyerefo and Setrana, 2018; Jaji, 2020). The case of the former mayor of Johannesburg, South Africa, Herman Mashaba, comes to mind. During his two-year tenure, he made defamatory statements about migrants, often on the social media platform Twitter. In one incident, he conducted a citizen's arrest of a migrant selling cow's heads, and tweeted a statement insinuating that migrants were 'bringing Ebola' to the country. This case was taken up by the South Africa Human Rights Commission after which Mashaba had to undergo human rights sensitivity training (South Africa Human Rights Commission, 2019).

After resigning as mayor in late 2019, Mashaba launched a new political party, Action SA, in August 2020. Although his tone has become more balanced, a report from his new party notes that certain jobs should be kept for South Africans, who should also be prioritised for free access to public services, while the government should 'make foreigners pay for access' (People's Dialogue, 2020: 34). Such xenophobic discourse can become a source of mass mobilisation and motivation for violence against migrant and refugee communities, as has been the case in South Africa (Mosselson,

2010). While politicians mostly refrain from publicly endorsing violence, it is certainly fuelled by state (in)action, exclusive conceptions of citizenship, including the idea of South African exceptionalism, compared to the rest of the continent (Neocosmos, 2008; Mosselson, 2010).

In terms of direct exclusionary practices, many African states have used institutional mechanism to project anti-immigration sentiments. These range from immigration restrictions to outright deportations. In 2016, Swaziland announced policies banning 'Asian people' from entering the country and those already in the country were targeted for eviction. Local newspapers were supportive of this position (Ramdeen, 2017). A report in *The Economist* notes that 'Asians' (of unspecified origin) were accused of 'using cronyism to gain unfair economic advantages – thereby disrupting national development – and committing crimes'; and in the light of 'growing discord in Swaziland over an absence of political freedoms and a persistent economic slump, suggesting that illegal immigration, specifically targeting Asians, is becoming a scapegoat' (The Economist, 2016).

Exclusionary practices can also include deportations of migrants and refugees. Algeria has been expelling refugees and migrants back to Niger since 2014, 'citing concerns for Algeria's *security* and a desire to crackdown on drugs and weapons smuggling and human trafficking' (emphasis added; Beratto, 2018). Niger had signed an agreement with Algeria to allow for the reparation of Nigerien nationals, but Algeria commenced the deportation of *any* migrant and refugees to Niger, including Syrians, Yemenis and Palestinians, reaching 25,000 deportations to Niger in 2018 alone (Jegen, 2020).[6] These exclusionary practices – ranging from xenophobic rhetoric, and work and visa restrictions to threats of deportation and other measures against refugees – are made as political calculations to establish domestic control and improve legitimacy ratings. Thus, the threat to close the Dadaab refugee camp in Kenya (now overruled by the High Court) was almost cyclical with elections.

Some research has shown that the more that states follow an electoral democratic system, the more likely they are to try to profit from exclusionary practices towards migrants and refugees. In a comparison between Tanzania, Kenya and Guinea, Milner (2009) shows that Guinea, the least democratic of the three cases, is the most open to refugees, not having to account for domestic legitimacy to the same extent. Inversely, in Tanzania, domestic political calculations – including election results and inner-party divisions – explain a reluctance to fully implement generous naturalisation laws for refugees (Milner, 2013). Some analysts take this reasoning further, arguing that exclusionary political rhetoric is increased with higher electoral competition, since politicians will engage in identity politics in the absence of strong ideological differences among parties (see Whitaker, 2017; Whitaker and Clark, 2018). This is not only related to electoral competition but also applicable to the extension of political citizenship to migrant and refugee communities.

Consequently, when Tanzania had a more welcoming open-door policy through its naturalisation laws, it was under a one-party system where the political gain through votes of new citizens was always beneficial (Whitaker and Clark, 2018). Similarly, in the Gambia, the former long-standing dictator, Yahya Jammeh, who ruled the country for 22 years until 2017, allegedly favoured refugees from the Casamançe region in neighbouring Senegal. Generous refugee policies for this group, who have self-settled in villages close to the borders, have been linked to claims that Jammeh distributed naturalisation certificates and voter cards to increase his vote tally (Zanker, 2018).

In sum, exclusionary rhetoric and practice against migrant and refugee groups occur everywhere and can lead to (perceived) electoral gains. Certain types of policies can depend not only on electoral competition but also on the political citizenship possibilities of migrant and refugee communities. Beyond this domestic legitimacy question, the following section discusses the influence of external relations on refugee and migration governance.

External legitimacy

Migration and refugee governance plays several key roles for the construction of external state legitimacy. These roles can be divided roughly into humanitarian intervention, donor leverage, and political leverage, which are discussed in turn.[7]

First, some states have used migration and refugee governance policies to highlight their humanitarian credentials, which can improve both their domestic and external legitimacy. With the release of CNN footage of African migrants and refugees being auctioned off in slave markets in Libya in November 2017, major outrage unfolded across the continent (Cascais, 2017). Coinciding with the EU–Africa Summit in Abidjan, also in November

2017, the footage brought home the plight of African migrants to many governments. The revelations led Burkina Faso to recall its ambassador to Libya, and Niger to summon the Libyan ambassador for talks. In Senegal, the chargé d'affaires of the Libyan Embassy in Senegal was also summoned by the foreign minister, 'to notify him of the "profound indignation" of President Sall over the sale of Sub-Saharan African migrants on Libyan soil' (Bodian, 2018: 168). Furthermore, the International Organization for Migration (IOM) began to airlift migrants out of Libya, and countries like Nigeria also repatriated its citizens (Arhin-Sam, 2019; see also Mouthaan, 2019).

As a further reaction to the Libyan migration crisis, the UNHCR, AU and Rwandan authorities negotiated a deal in 2017 to evacuate hundreds of refugees from desolate Libyan detention camps to Rwanda, which was put into effect in 2019 (Jegen and Zanker, 2019b). In support of the deal, Rwandan President, Paul Kagame, stated his readiness to host up to 30,000 Africans trapped in Libya in response to the CNN footage. The recent evacuees were offered repatriation, resettlement or local integration in Rwanda, and the action was described as humanitarian, with the Minister in Charge of Emergency Management noting, 'Rwanda has not taken any money to honour the commitment to host African refugees from Libya. It was our proposal, and we are committed to it. We believe in African solutions to African problems. We don't have to wait for someone from outside to help us' (Kagire, 2019).

Another example comes from Niger, where a contested anti-smuggling law has attempted to prevent migrants from crossing the desert by further criminalising the popular transportation business since 2015. By many accounts, the law was introduced in response to European pressure and funding (Diallo, 2017; Molenaar, 2017; Frowd, 2019). But the very same law has also been shrouded in a humanitarian discourse by the Nigerien government, as a measure to protect migrants, referring to a tragedy in 2013, when a group of over 90 abandoned migrants died in the desert (Jegen and Zanker, 2019a).

Even beyond the continent, some African states, such as Mauritania and Sudan, went out of their ways to invite Syrian refugees to their countries. For example, Sudan has had a strong welcoming policy, with Syrian refugees welcomed as 'brothers and sisters', allowed to move around freely, and given access to educational opportunities. By the end of 2016, there were 200,000 Syrian refugees in Sudan (Bach and Deshayes, 2017). At the time, Syrians could easily access residency permits – the result of an agreement between the two countries that date back to the 1960s. According to one activist, 'the Syrian crisis is under the spotlight right now and, therefore, Sudan wants to look good on an international level as a supporter of the Syrian people, in hopes that the [Darfur] sanctions will be eased eventually' (Almajdoub, 2017; see also Malik, 2019).

Second, migration and refugee governance also play a big role in terms of donor leverage. As outlined earlier, the economic, political and socio-cultural pressures on receiving countries of large refugee populations are high, and the numbers are growing (UNHCR, 2019a). There is also a fundamentally asymmetric relationship between African states and donor states, especially given the neoliberal global agenda (Milner, 2009). With the market-reform-orientated structural adjustment plans, which many countries in Africa undertook throughout the 1980s, now putting them in highly indebted situations. Thus, those countries hosting the most refugees are also much less well off, making them dependent on global responsibility sharing to cover the basic needs of displaced populations. As shown previously, many refugee situations are severely underfunded. Consequently, states sometimes use refugees as leverage to gain donor funding, for example by threatening to close refugee camps (Whitaker, 2017). Such leverage, or 'the commodification of forced displacement' (Adamson and Tsourapas, 2019b), does not have to come at the cost of refugees or migrants.

In 2019, Ethiopia amended one of the most progressive pre-existing refugee laws worldwide, which granted refugees the rights to obtain work permits, open bank accounts and obtain drivers' licences. This progressive law is closely linked to the job compact; a US\$550 million agreement between the Ethiopian government and external donors (the United Kingdom, the European Union, and the World Bank) set to create 100,000 jobs (Department for International Development, 2019). The new industrial job park stemming from this would guarantee 30,000 jobs to refugees. It is potentially a win–win scenario, with the European Union creating incentives to stop the mobility of refugees and other migrants to Europe; and Ethiopia creating jobs for the local market.[8]

Moreover, the language of security can really pay off here, especially when migrants in particular can be linked – even remotely – to terrorism (Whitaker, 2017). Niger is an example of a country that has actively pursued

European policy interests in migration governance in recent years. In turn, the country has profited considerably through 12 national projects under the European Union Emergency Trust Fund (EUTF) in 2020, worth €253 million (European Commission, 2020b). But the link between migration and security was equally evoked by the Nigerien government, to gain much needed military support, state capacity building and development assistance (Jegen and Zanker, 2019a; see also Frowd, 2019; Jegen, 2020).

Third, states can use migration and refugee governance to gain more general political leverage. Adamson and Tsourpas (2019b: 16) note in their recent work that 'increasingly, states have an incentive to capitalize on cross-border mobility, treating both voluntary and forced migration as a commodity that can be utilized to enhance state revenue and power'. Like the case of Niger, migration-related projects can help to improve state revenues for capacity building, security sector and development projects the state might otherwise not be able to do (Jegen, 2020; see also Milner, 2009; Whitaker, 2017). However, beyond increasing state revenue, using migration governance to improve power or political leverage (externally rather than domestically) has so far been underresearched. Although international relations are multifaceted, the importance of migration and refugee governance cannot easily be downplayed. For example, Rwandan involvement in migration issues expands outside the borders of African states.

The country sealed several 'deals' with Israel, to accept 'voluntary' returns from Israel by African refugees, primarily of Eritrean and Sudanese origins (Gidron, 2020). Reports noted that the Israeli government had offered Rwanda (and Uganda) US$5,000 per person to accept African migrants currently in Israel. There were also allegations that part of these deals involved the supply of weapons, military training, and aid (Tumusiime, 2017). Both Rwanda and Uganda denied their participation in any such deals with Israel, and the whole transfer project later collapsed after widespread criticism, especially at the revelation that the terms for the return was involuntary and that refugees were threatened with detention if they failed to leave Israel (Gidron, 2020; see also Bouka, 2018).

Nonetheless, it bolstered what was already a good working relationship between Israel and Rwanda. As Gidron (2020: 154) notes, 'African leaders [like Kagame] ... were able to utilise Israel's geostrategic needs for their own ends'. In 2017, Israel announced its decision to open an embassy in Kigali and air routes between the two countries. At the opening of the embassy in April 2019, a statement from the Israeli foreign office stated, 'Rwanda is a true friend of Israel ... The opening of the embassy reflects the continued strengthening of relations between the two countries' (Israel Ministry of Foreign Affairs, 2019).

Milner argues that African states are externally constrained by the impositions of the neoliberal consensus and the imbalance in power relations in the international system, with the shots being called by the interests of donor states (Milner, 2009). The question is whether leverage has changed with the advent of the European migration agenda, and Europe's increasing interest to collaborate with African states, especially when it comes to return and readmission (see also Zanker, 2019). Thus, for some African states, capitalising on refugee and migration governance is no longer just about increasing donor leverage, but also about curtailing EU dominance and influence. Algeria, for example, despite its role in deporting migrants to Niger, has generally resisted the influence of the EU migration-related funding on the country's policy on migration (Beratto, 2018).

So far, this kind of political leverage has been raised, primarily by North African countries, with Libya, Algeria, and Morocco being prime examples (Paoletti, 2010; Adamson and Tsourapas, 2019a). El Qadim (2014) shows how brokering spaces in the transnational security field provides an avenue for Moroccan state actors to challenge the dominance of the North. Increasingly this may also occur in West Africa. As an example – and here we do return to the EU cooperation on migration – is the persistent efforts by the European Union to enforce return and readmission agreements with West African states. In addition to trying to reduce the number of migrants that can make it to Europe, European governments are desperate to try to return African citizens who did not succeed in claiming asylum. Such returns are highly contested, however, and come at huge potential domestic costs. This is because of the involuntary and sometimes violent nature of these returns, as well as the potential reduction in remittances (Mouthaan, 2019; Zanker et al., 2019). Despite the asymmetric relationship, European interests in return have largely failed so far, with formal agreements continuing to falter. Particularly symbolic was the self-imposed moratorium by the Gambian government in 2019, when the country refused to accept returnees from Europe in response to growing protests (Altrogge and Zanker, 2019). Although this moratorium was eventually overturned – and flights have resumed (only to be interrupted by the COVID-19 pandemic) – it was a strong stance for such a small country to take. In this light, future research can consider how actual practices of migration governance unfold to highlight such forms of adaptation and resistance (see El Qadim, 2014).

Conclusion

Although European interests do play a decisive role – and increasingly so – in African government policies on refugees, and migration in particular, it is important to take a more holistic approach to understanding the bigger picture. Governments in Africa – just as in Asia, Latin America, or Europe – use refugee and migration protection and regulations for their own purposes. This self-interest is oriented primarily towards domestic and external legitimacy. Domestically, there has been a growing trend towards exclusionary policies, which play into the idea of competition over scant resources and access to employment or public goods. Many politicians and political parties have capitalised on scapegoating rhetoric and other measures, including work and visa restrictions, and deportation measures.

Externally, refugee protection and migration can be used in several ways to cater for humanitarian assistance, donor support and political leverage. Although the necessity for more equal burden sharing is clearly there (see below), it would be far too simplistic to focus only on the relations in terms of donor funding. African states have also used their positions to gain political leverage, and the importance the European Union and its member states give to migration has become instrumental in this regard. As the COVID-19 pandemic has affected migrants and refugees across the continent, it remains to be seen how governments respond in its aftermath.

With governments all over the world scrambling to put together post-COVID rescue packages, it is sore time to revisit burden-sharing obligations and fulfill them. If contributions are made and not just promised, it would make donor funding for refugee camps less a political calculation for host states but rather something they could rely on. As for the AU and African states, they should use the innovation and strength of their refugee and displaced person frameworks to assure the humanitarian and legal protection of all those on move, including other migrants. This also means signing, ratifying, and effectively implementing, the AU Free Movement Protocol.

Notes

1 The reflections in this chapter are part of a research project on the political stakes of migration governance with a focus on Uganda and South Africa. The research is funded by the German Foundation for Peace Research and ran from 2019–2021. I thank Cita Wetterich and an additional anonymous reviewer for comments on earlier versions of this chapter; all errors remain my own.

2 European is used to describe the European Union and its 27 member states.

3 This is likely to be an underestimation. It is extremely difficult to count IDPs, especially those living in urban settings (see, for example, Jacobs and Kyamusugulwa, 2017)

4 Protracted displacement occurs when more than 25,000 refugees are displaced for over five years.

5 Refugee movements can sometimes be tied to security implications, whether from members of the refugee populations or other conflict actors (Fisk, 2014), nevertheless, such a security threat is often exaggerated or fabricated for political leverage.

6 For more on deportation practices in Africa, see Sylla and Schultz (2019).

7 Refugee movements can also play into regional conflict dynamics, as in the Great Lakes region (Rwanda, Burundi, and the DRC), but for reasons of space, this aspect will not be discussed here.

8 Which is not to say that the implementation and overall relationship between the European Union and Ethiopia always runs smoothly however (Abebe, 2018; see also Castillejo, 2017).

References

Abebe, T.T. 2018. 'Promises and challenges of Ethiopia's refugee policy reform'. Addis Ababa: Institute for Security Studies.

Abebe, T.T. and Abebe, A. 2020. 'How Africa can reduce COVID-19's impact on displaced persons'. Addis Ababa: Institute for Security Studies. Online at: https://issafrica.org/iss-today/how-africa-can-reduce-covid-19s-impact-on-displaced-persons (accessed 20 May 2020).

Abebe, T.T., Abebe, A. and Sharpe, M. 2019. 'After 50 years, Africa's refugee policy still leads'. Online at: https://issafrica.org/iss-today/after-50-years-africas-refugee-policy-still-leads (accessed 20 May 2020).

Adamson, F.B. and Tsourapas, G. 2019a. 'Migration diplomacy in world politics', *International Studies Perspectives*, 20(2): 113–28.

Adamson, F.B. and Tsourapas, G. 2019b. 'The migration state in the Global South: Nationalizing, developmental, and neoliberal models of migration management', *International Migration Review*, October. Online at: https://doi.org/10.1177/0197918319879057 (accessed 2 February 2021).

Adepoju, A. 2011. 'Reflections on international migration and development in sub-Saharan Africa', *African Population Studies*, 25(2): 298–318.

African Union and Norwegian Refugee Council. 2013. 'The Kampala Convention one year on: Progress and prospects'. Geneva: Internal Displacement Monitoring Centre. Online at: https://www.internal-displacement.org/publications/the-kampala-convention-one-year-on-progress-and-prospects (accessed 20 May 2020).

Almajdoub, S. 2017. 'Sudan welcomes its newest refugees', *Fair Observer*, 1 November 2017. Online at: https://www.fairobserver.com/region/africa/sudan-syrian-refugees-civil-war-middle-east-africa-news-11621/ (accessed 20 May 2020).

Altrogge, J. and Zanker, F. 2019. 'The political economy of migration governance in the Gambia'. Freiburg: Arnold Bergstraesser Institute. Online at: https://www.arnold-bergstraesser.de/sites/default/files/field/pub-download/medam_gambia_report_altrogge_zanker.pdf (accessed 20 May 2020).

Arhin-Sam, K. 2019. 'The political economy of migration governance in Nigeria'. Freiburg: Arnold Bergstraesser Institute.

Bach, J.-N. and Deshayes, C. 2017. 'Sudan', in A. Mehler, H. Melber, and K. van Walraven (eds). *Africa Yearbook Volume 13*. Leiden: Brill, pp. 368–78.

Bakewell, O. 2008. '"Keeping them in their place": The ambivalent relationship between development and migration in Africa', *Third World Quarterly*, 29(7): 1341–58.

Bakewell, O. and Bonfiglio, A. 2013. *Moving Beyond Conflict: Re-framing mobility in the African Great Lakes region*. IMI Working Paper Series, No. 71 (June). Online at: https://www.imi.ox.ac.uk/publications/wp-71-13 (accessed 20 May 2020).

Beratto, L. 2018. '"We can't stay here": Inside Algeria's mass expulsions of sub-Saharan migrants', 7 August 2018. Online at: https://www.worldpoliticsreview.com/articles/25435/we-can-t-stay-here-inside-algeria-s-mass-expulsions-of-sub-saharan-migrants (accessed 20 May 2020).

Berriane, M. and De Haas, H. 2012. 'Introduction: New questions for innovative migration research', in M. Berriane and H. de Haas (eds). *African Migrations Research*. Trenton, NJ: Africa World Press, pp. 1–31.

Bodian, M. 2018. 'Senegal 2017'. In A. Mehler, H. Melber, and K. van Walraven (eds). *Africa Yearbook Volume 14: Politics, economy and society south of the Sahara in 2017*. Leiden: Brill.

Bouka, Y. 2018. 'Rwanda', in A. Mehler, H. Melber, and K. van Walraven (eds). *Africa Yearbook Volume 14*. Leiden: Brill, pp. 342–52.

Burke, J. 2020. 'Coronavirus border closures strand tens of thousands of people across Africa', *The Guardian*, 5 May 2020, sec. World news. Online at: https://www.theguardian.com/world/2020/may/05/coronavirus-border-closures-strand-tens-of-thousands-of-people-across-africa (accessed 20 May 2020).

Cascais, A. 2017. 'Slave trade in Libya: Outrage across Africa', *Deutsche Welle*, 22 November 2017. Online at: https://www.dw.com/en/slave-trade-in-libya-outrage-across-africa/a-41486013 (accessed 20 May 2020).

Castillejo, C. 2017. 'The EU Migration Partnership Framework: Time for a rethink?' Discussion Paper No. 28/2017. Bonn: Deutsches Institut für Entwicklungspolitik. Online at: http://www.die-gdi.de/discussion-paper/article/the-eu-migration-partnership-framework-time-for-a-rethink/ (accessed 20 May 2020).

Castles, S. 2004. 'Why migration policies fail', *Ethnic and Racial Studies*, 27(2): 205–27.

Chou, M-H. and Gibert, M.V. 2012. 'The EU–Senegal mobility partnership: From launch to suspension and negotiation failure', *Journal of Contemporary European Research*, 8(4): 408–27.

Codjoe, S.N., Quartey, P., Tagoe, C.A. and Reed, H.E. 2013. 'Perceptions of the impact of refugees on host communities: The case of Liberian refugees in Ghana', *Journal of International Migration and Integration*, 14(3): 439–56.

Crawley, H. and Skleparis, D. 2018. 'Refugees, migrants, neither, both: Categorical fetishism and the politics of bounding in Europe's "migration crisis"', *Journal of Ethnic and Migration Studies*, 44(1): 48–64.

Daley, P. 2013. 'Refugees, IDPs and citizenship rights: The perils of humanitarianism in the African Great Lakes region', *Third World Quarterly*, 34(5): 893–912.

Department for International Development. 2019. 'Jobs Compact Ethiopia'. DevTracker Project. 2019. Online at: https://devtracker.dfid.gov.uk/projects/GB-GOV-1-300393 (accessed 17 February 2021).

Diallo, I.M. 2017. 'EU strategy stems migrant flow from Niger, but at what cost?', 2 February 2017. Online at: https://www.irinnews.org/special-report/2017/02/02/eu-strategy-stems-migrant-flow-niger-what-cost (accessed 10 February 2021).

El Qadim, N. 2014. 'Postcolonial challenges to migration control: French–Moroccan cooperation practices on forced returns', *Security Dialogue*, 45(3): 242–61.

European Commission. 2020. 'Towards a comprehensive strategy with Africa'. Factsheet, 9 March. Brussels: European Commission. Online at: https://eur-lex.europa.eu/legal-content/EN/TXT/PDF/?uri=CE-LEX:52020JC0004&from=FR (accessed 16 February 2021).

Fisk, K. 2014. 'Refugee geography and the diffusion of armed conflict in Africa', *Civil Wars*, 16(3): 255–75.

Frowd, P.M. 2019. 'Producing the "transit" migration state: International security intervention in Niger', *Third World Quarterly*, 41(2): 340–58.

Gidron, Y. 2020. *Israel in Africa*. London: Zed Books.

Internal Displacement Monitoring Centre (IDMC). 2020. 'Global Report on Internal Displacement 2020'. Geneva: IDMC.

Israel Ministry of Foreign Affairs. 2019. 'Israel Inaugurates Embassy in Rwanda, 1 April 2019'. Online at: https://mfa.gov.il/MFA/PressRoom/2019/Pages/Israel-inaugurates-embassy-in-Rwanda-1-April-2019.aspx (accessed 16 February 2021).

Jacobs, C. and Kyamusugulwa, P.M. 2017. 'Everyday justice for the internally displaced in a context of fragility: The case of the Democratic Republic of Congo (DRC)', *Journal of Refugee Studies*, 31(2): 179–96.

Jaji, R. 2020. *Deviant Destinations: Zimbabwe and North to South migration*. Lanham, MD: Lexington Books.

Jegen, L. 2020. 'The political economy of migration governance in Niger'. Freiburg: Arnold Bergstraesser Institute.

Jegen, L. and Zanker, F. 2020. 'The political economy of migration governance in West Africa'. In *2020 MEDAM Assessment Report*. Kiel: Kiel Institute for the World Economy (IfW).

Jegen, L. and Zanker, F. 2019a. *European Dominance of Migration Policy in Niger: 'On a fait les filles avant la mère'*. MEDAM Policy Brief No. 2019/3. Brussels: European Policy Centre.

Jegen, L. and Zanker, F. 2019b. 'Spirited away: The fading importance of resettlement in the emergency transit mechanism in Rwanda', *ECDPM* (blog). Online at: https://ecdpm.org/talking-points/spirited-away-fading-importance-resettlement-emergency-transit-mechanism-rwanda/ (accessed 17 February 2021).

Kabbanji, L. 2013. 'Towards a global agenda on migration and development? Evidence from Senegal', *Population, Space and Place*, 19(4): 415–29.

Kagire, E. 2019. 'Rwanda never received money to host refugees from Libya –

Kamayirese'. *KT PRESS* (blog), 10 September 2019. https://www.ktpress.rw/2019/09/rwanda-never-received-money-to-host-refugees-from-libya-kamayirese/ (accessed 17 February 2021).

Kersting, N. 2009. 'New nationalism and xenophobia in Africa: A new inclination?' *Africa Spectrum*, 44(1): 7–18.

Kreibaum, M. 2016. 'Their suffering, our burden? How Congolese refugees affect the Ugandan population', *World Development*, 78 (February): 262–87.

Malik, N. 2019. 'Sudan's reception of Syrian refugees proves popular will matters more than economic might', *The Correspondent*, 18 December 2019. Online at: https://thecorrespondent.com/182/sudans-reception-of-syrian-refugees-proves-popular-will-matters-more-than-economic-might/195050892036-871bd88a (accessed 17 February 2021).

Milner, J. 2013. *Two Steps Forward, One Step Back: Understanding the shifting politics of refugee policy in Tanzania*. New Issues in Refugee Research Series, Paper No. 255. Geneva: UNHCR.

Milner, J. 2009. *Refugees, the State and the Politics of Asylum in Africa*. London: Palgrave Macmillan.

Molenaar, F. 2017. *Irregular migration and human smuggling networks in Niger*. CRU Report. The Hague, Netherlands: Clingendael Institute.

Mosselson, A. 2010. '"There is no difference between citizens and non-citizens anymore": Violent xenophobia, citizenship and the politics of belonging in post-apartheid South Africa', *Journal of Southern African Studies*, 36(3): 641–55.

Mouthaan, M. 2019. 'Unpacking domestic preferences in the policy-receiving state: The EU's migration cooperation with Senegal and Ghana', *Comparative Migration Studies*, 7(1): 1–20.

Moyo, K. and Zanker, F. 2020. 'South Africa's xenophobic agenda is impeding its coronavirus response', *African Arguments* (blog). 9 April 2020. Online at: https://africanarguments.org/2020/04/09/south-africa-coronavirus-xenophobic-agenda-impeding-response/ (accessed 18 February 2021).

Neocosmos, M. 2008. 'The politics of fear and the fear of politics: Reflections on xenophobic violence in South Africa', *Journal of Asian and African Studies*, 43(6): 586–94.

North Africa Post. 2018. 'King Mohammed VI submits African Agenda on Migration to AU'. *The North Africa Post*, 29 January 2018. Online at: http://northafricapost.com/21977-king-mohammed-vi-submits-african-agenda-migration-au.html (accessed 17 February 2021).

Nyamnjoh, F.B. 2010. 'Racism, ethnicity and the media in Africa: Reflections inspired by studies of xenophobia in Cameroon and South Africa', *Africa Spectrum*, 45(1): 57–93.

Okyerefo, M.P.K. and Setrana, M.B. 2018. 'Internal and international migration dynamics in Africa', in Triandafyllidou, A. (ed.). *Handbook of Migration and Globalisation*. Cheltenham: Edward Elgar Publishing.

Paoletti, E. 2010. *The Migration of Power and North–South Inequalities: The case of Italy and Libya*. London: Palgrave Macmillan.

People's Dialogue. 2020. 'Participation and engagement report'. Online at: https://m.thepeoplesdialogue.org.za/ (accessed 20 February 2021).

Ramdeen, M. 2017. 'Swaziland', in A. Mehler, H. Melber and K. van Walraven (eds). *Africa Yearbook, Volume 13*. Leiden: Brill, pp. 508–13. Online at: http://dx.doi.org/10.1163/1872-9037_ayb_ayb2017_COM_0053> (accessed 17 February 2021).

South Africa Human Rights Commission. 2019. 'Mashaba, SAHRC reach settlement on Ebola Tweets', 5 December 2019. Online at: https://www.sahrc.org.za/index.php/sahrc-media/news/item/1722-mashaba-sahrc-reach-settlement-on-ebola-tweets (accessed 20 February 2021).

Sylla, A. and Schultz, S.U. 2019. 'Mali: Abschiebungen als postkoloniale Praxis', *PERIPHERIE-Politik, Ökonomie, Kultur*, 39(3): 389–411.

The Economist. 2016. 'Xenophobia against Swaziland's Asian minority intensifies', 2 November 2016. Online at: http://country.eiu.com/article.aspx?articleid=804777064&Country=Swaziland&topic=Politics&subtopic_6 (accessed 20 February 2021).

Tumusiime, J. 2017. 'Did Israel make a refugees-for-arms deal with Uganda?' *Hareetz*, 14 September 2017. Online at: https://www.haaretz.com/israel-news/did-israel-make-a-refugees-for-arms-deal-with-uganda-1.5450762 (accessed 17 February 2021).

United Nations High Commissioner for Refugees (UNHCR). 2019a. 'Global trends: Forced displacement in 2018'. Geneva: United Nations High Commissioner for Refugees.

United Nations High Commissioner for Refugees (UNHCR). 2019b. 'Rwanda as of February 2019'. Funding Update. Online at: https://reporting.unhcr.org/sites/default/files/Rwanda%20Funding%20Update%2006%20February%202019.pdf (accessed 16 February 2021).

United Nations High Commissioner for Refugees (UNHCR). 2018. 'Highlighted underfunded situations in 2018'. Geneva: UNHCR. Online at: http://reporting.unhcr.org/sites/default/files/UNHCR%20Brochure%20on%20Underfunded%20Situations%20-%20September%202018.pdf (accessed 15 February 2021).

Van Criekinge, T. 2016. 'The limits of the EU's external dimension of migration in Africa', in M. Carbone (ed.). *The European Union in Africa: Incoherent policies, asymmetrical partnership, declining relevance?* Manchester: Manchester University Press, pp. 258–82.

Whitaker, B.E. 2017. 'Migration within Africa and beyond', *African Studies Review*, 60(2): 209–20.

Whitaker, B.E. 2002. 'Refugees in Western Tanzania: The distribution of burdens and benefits among local hosts', *Journal of Refugee Studies*, 15(4): 339–58.

Whitaker, B.E. and Clark, J.F. 2018. *Africa's International Relations: Balancing domestic and global interests*. Boulder, CO: Lynne Rienner Publishers.

Zanker, F. 2019. 'Managing or restricting movement? Diverging approaches of African and European migration governance', *Comparative Migration Studies*, 7(1): 1–19.

Zanker, F. 2018. 'The Gambia: A haven for refugees?' *Forced Migration Review*, 57: 74–6.

Zanker, F., Altrogge, J., Arhin-Sam, K. and Jegen, L. 2019. *Challenges in EU–African Migration Cooperation: West African perspectives on forced return*. MEDAM Policy Brief, No. 2019/5. Brussels: European Policy Centre.

Remittances and development of Africa

Adeoye O. Akinola

Introduction

African–European relations date back to the precolonial era and include cooperation in many areas, such as migration. Therefore, migration governance has continued to occupy a decisive place in African–European Union (EU) relations. Migration is a significant characteristic of changes in population, and a 2019 report indicated that 3.5 per cent of the global population (272 million) were international migrants (IOM, 2019: 19). Currently, an estimated 280 million people are living outside their countries of origin. The past decades have witnessed the rise and intensity of mobility across borders, which has led to an increase in the volume of remittance flows to developing countries (ECLAC, 2021).

With the EU's foreign direct investment (FDI) in Africa reaching €222 billion in 2020, the EU is currently the largest investor on the continent, well ahead of the United States (€42 billion) and China (€38 billion) (EU, 2020: 6). Despite this partnership, the two continents have locked horns on migration governance and remittances as a result of their differing perspectives on migration. EU policy-makers have expressed reservations about the immigration of non-members of the Organisation for Economic Co-operation and Development (OECD), and have been ambivalent about the idea of migrants sending money back to their home countries, through formal channels such as remittances companies or banks, or through informal means such as family members.

Remittances play a vital role in enabling economic growth and prosperity. Remittances provide financial lifelines to innumerable families and communities in developing regions such as Africa. Across the world, and particularly in Africa, remittances have become one of the clearest and most measurable indicators of the real value that migration brings to the migrants' home countries (Natali and Isaacs, 2020: 117). One of the reasons for categorising migration governance as a top priority for African actors is because remittances from migrants constitute an important source of resilience for families on the continent, particularly since remittances have exceeded the income received in foreign aid (Naudé, 2012). Since the global financial crisis of 2008–9 and its rebounding in 2010, flows of remittances to low-income countries have steadily outgrown official development assistance (Dendir, 2017).

Remittances remain the most tangible and one of the least contentious connections between migration and development, both in sending and receiving countries (Mohapatra and Ratha, 2011: 3). This reinforces the importance of remittances to developing and poor countries in Africa, and beyond. Africa is generally known as one of the top receivers of remittances, with Nigeria and Egypt receiving over 50 per cent of the total remittance inflows to the region (World Bank/NOMAD, 2021: 119). For instance, in 2020, remittances to Egypt increased by about 11 per cent to an estimated record high of US$30 billion (World Bank/NOMAD, 2021: 28). While optimism among African stakeholders on the decisive contributions of migration and remittances to Africa's developmental scheme remain very high, several impediments orchestrated by European actors have become a stumbling block for increased remittances. For example, Africa has been the most expensive region to send money to and to make money transfer within, and South Africa has recorded the most expensive transactional cost on remittances.

Since the early 2000s, the EU has been engaged in 'the most extensive, sophisticated and far-reaching border enforcement programme in history, largely in an attempt to prevent "illegal" immigration – a category that generally refers to undocumented "economic migrants" and refugees from poor countries' (Carr, 2012). According to Carr, this includes the mobilisation of militarised border patrols on both land and the Mediterranean Sea, employing about 400,000 police and border personnel, including a new European border and coastguard agency (Frontex), as well as sophisticated surveillance technologies at the borders, and investments in computerised databases. Many European governments have been accused of mass deportations of asylum seekers, without considering their situations and claims, and migrants have lost their lives in the Mediterranean, where patrol guards have forced migrant boats out of European territorial waters (Carr, 2012).

This chapter engages the remittances debate and argues that through remittances, African migrants contribute to the development of their countries and the region. It is divided into nine sections: an introduction is followed by an overview of remittances, remittances as a pull factor, and case studies of remittance inflows to Africa. The chapter then discusses the prospects and challenges of remittances, the question of transfers costs, and perspectives on remittances and African–EU migration, before examining the impact of COVID-19 on remittances and concluding.

Understanding remittances

Remittances, which constitute the financial, monetary, or in-kind transfers made by migrants directly to individuals, associates, households and communities in their countries of origin (IOM 2019: 35), have become a major theme in discourses on Africa–EU migration, particularly during the 2020–21 COVID-19 pandemic. Generally, remittances are vital sources of income for developing countries, and migration is critical for African countries and the EU because remittances from migrants are recognised as an important source of resilience for households in African countries. The monetary value of remittances to Africa now exceeds that of aid.

While remittances are usually regarded as the transfer of money by migrants to their home countries, they also include the flow of non-cash assistance from sending to receiving countries (see Apatinga et al., 2021). This non-cash assistance, which includes food, clothing, mobile phones and computers, has contributed to the surviving strategies of many families in African countries such as Ghana. The concept is also used to account for the transfer of skills and cultural values (social or cultural remittances, as discussed by Levitt and Lamba-Nieves, 2011) and political values (political or democratic remittances, as explained by Piper and Rother, 2020). This chapter focuses on monetary remittances, although some observations are relevant to understanding other forms of transfer as well. Usually, remittances are conveyed through two channels: official or formal, and unofficial or informal. Formal channels rely on post-offices, banks and other financial providers, while informal channels include the transfer of remittances through relatives, friends and transport services (see Apatinga et al., 2021: 5). Remittances could be small-scale economic resources for individuals and families, or constitute larger-scale investment schemes, which in some communities are regarded as diaspora investments in support of developmental initiatives (Natali and Isaacs, 2020).

Generally, remittances to Africa seem to increase significantly after a natural disaster on the continent (Naudé, 2010). However, in the case of the COVID-19, a global pandemic, remittances initially declined in 2020 but have since increased as national governments have relaxed lockdown rules. The harsh economic realities of many Africans, exacerbated by the negative impact of COVID-19, have made many households dependent on remittances from migrants. The EU's increasingly restrictive immigration policies over the past decade have forced African migrants to risk their lives on informal routes through the dangerous Mediterranean Sea and Sahara Desert. That said, African–EU migration has been characterised by both regular and irregular migration, with around 280,000 African nationals per year settling legally in the EU (European Commission, 2018). Regular migration occurs through recognised, formal and authorised channels. Irregular migration, on the other hand, involves migrants who do not comply with the migration guidelines of origin, transit and destination countries, which usually means they have to rely on a collaborative effort with smugglers and human traffickers (Idemudia and Boehnke, 2020: 21).

The role and proportions of remittances

As with other migration corridors, there are several motivations, including political and socio-economic factors, behind African–EU migration. Naudé (2010) asserts that 'armed conflict and differences in the gross domestic product (GDP) growth have the greatest impact on international migration from Africa'. Poor governance and the protracted conflicts in the Sahel region, Mozambique, Libya and the Democratic Republic of Congo have forced Africans out of their countries into Europe. In the context of widespread unemployment and economic downturn, the prospects of seeking better employment and income opportunities and remitting money back home have become another driver of African–EU migration.

Of the US$528 billion remitted to developing countries in 2018, Africa received US$81 billion. In the same year, US$47 billion was derived from foreign direct investment (Kuhlcke and Bester, 2020). Over the years, remittance flows have become more stable than flows of private capital and now constitute the largest source of foreign inflows to Africa (Mohapatra and Ratha, 2011: 3). Indeed, remittances are perceived as more valuable and secure than foreign aid in Africa, as they do not have conditionalities and directly support the receivers.

In 2003, the inflow of remittances to developing countries was estimated at US$75 billion, while official development assistance (ODA) was recorded at US$52 billion (Adams, 2016: 1). In 2015, remittance flows to developing countries was recorded at US$440 billion, and hit a record high of US$548 billion in 2019, which was more than inflows of FDI (US$534 billion) and ODA (US$166 billion) (Dendir, 2017; World Bank, 2020a). At the global level, remittances increased from US$126 billion in 2000 to US$717 billion in 2019, and reduced to US$689 billion in 2020 (IOM, 2019: 11). Specifically, remittances in 2018 recorded a 9 per cent increase compared to 2017 when remittance was estimated at US$633 billion. Prior to 2017, there were recurrent declines in remittances; between 2014 and 2015, international (inward) flows of remittances decreased by about 1.2 per cent, from US$603 billion in 2014 to US$595 billion in 2015, and this further contracted by 1.1 per cent, to US$589 billion in 2016 (IOM, 2019).

Data from the World Bank indicate that global remittances declined from the US$719 billion recorded in 2019 to US$702 billion in 2020, which represented a 2.4 per cent reduction. Despite the COVID-19 pandemic and labour restrictions in the EU, remittances still surpassed FDI flows to low-income countries. In the same year, apart from China, remittance flows exceeded the entire sum of FDI and ODA. Therefore, remittances have 'become an important consumption smoothing mechanism for the recipient households and, as such, they form an increasingly important (private) element of global social protection systems' (World Bank/ NOMAD, 2021: vi). In 2019, remittances to sub-Saharan Africa increased by an estimated 0.5 per cent to US$48 billion (Ratha, 2021).

The World Bank initially projected a substantial decline of remittance flows to the region by 23.1 per cent to US$37 billion in 2020, while a recovery of 4 per cent was estimated for 2021. This projection did not materialise. The decline was attributed to two related factors: first, the COVID-19 pandemic has had a negative effect on the economies of destination countries in Europe and beyond. Second, Nigeria recorded a 27.7 per cent decrease in the inflow of remittances, which alone made up about 40 per cent of the remittance sent to sub-Saharan Africa. Indeed, remittances to other countries in Africa increased during this period. Thus, excluding Nigeria, the region recorded a rise of 2.3 per cent in remittance flows, demonstrating resilience during the COVID-19 pandemic (World Bank/NOMAD, 2021: 34). The World Bank Group President, David Malpass, reinforced the negative impact that the disease would have on remittances. He noted, 'remittances are a vital source of income for developing countries. The ongoing economic recession caused by COVID-19 is taking a severe toll on the ability to send money home and makes it all the more vital that we shorten the time to recovery for advanced economies' (World Bank, 2020b). However, against all expectations, US$42 billion was sent to Africa in 2020, which represented a 12.5 per cent decline in remittances, while US$43 billion was projected for 2021 (World Bank/NOMAD, 2021: 2).

To support households and development activities in Nigeria, migrants remitted US$25 billion to the country in 2019, and by 2020, money sent home by Nigerians in diaspora accounted for about 40 per cent of the remittances sent to sub-Saharan Africa (Adhikari et al., 2021: 62). The money remitted by both regular and irregular African migrants projects a picture of economic boom in Europe, which prompts new generations of migrants to move – sometimes at any cost. Ironically, this is a distorted picture of the reality of African migrants, who are resilient and committed to sending money to families and other beneficiaries amidst harsh labour conditions and to the detriment of their financial stability. In fact, migrants remit around 15 per cent of their earnings on average (Natali and Isaacs, 2020: 122).

The following section examines more closely the proportions of remittance flows to Africa.

Remittance inflows to Africa

Across the world, countries – both rich and poor – benefit from remittances. Many EU countries, such as Germany and France, which have imposed stringent conditions on the transfer of remittances and are hostile to migrants, continue to benefit from remittances. While Germany and France were among the top 10 receivers of remittances in 2020, the actual value of the inflows was less than 1 per cent of GDP in these two EU countries. In contrast, for example, Somalia, since 2020, is one of the most reliant on remittances in the world, with 35.3 per cent of its GDP made up of remittances. Surprisingly, and as shown in Table 5.1, only two African countries were among the top remittance-receiving countries in the world.

Table 5. 1: Top remittance receiving countries in 2020

	Countries	Total value of remittances (billion US$)	Percentage of change from 2019
1	India	83.1	–0.2
2	China	59.5	–13.0
3	Mexico	42.9	+9.9
4	Philippines	34.9	–0.7
5	Egypt	29.6	+10.5
6	Pakistan	26.1	+17.4
7	France	24.5	–8.8
8	Bangladesh	21.8	+18.4
9	Germany	17.1	–2.0
10	Nigeria	17.2	–27.7

Source: Cited in McCarthy (2021).

As Table 5.1 shows, receiving remittances is a global phenomenon, and is not limited to the Global South. However, many African countries tend to be dependent on remittances, which make up a more significant proportion of their GDP than in countries in other regions.

In Africa, remittance growth in comparison to the GDP in 2020 has been particularly evident in Zambia (37 per cent), Mozambique (16 per cent), Kenya (9 per cent), and Ghana (5 per cent).

Cape Verde – a small country with a population of about 550,000 population, which received remittance inflows of about US$144 million in 2010 (9 per cent of its GDP) – has the world's highest emigration rate at 38 per cent of the population (Mohapatra and Ratha, 2011: 43).

Table 5.2: Leading remittance-dependent African countries by share of GDP (average 2015–2018)

	Countries	Percentage of remittances in relation to GDP
1	Lesotho	20.9
2	Liberia	16.2
3	The Gambia	12.9
4	Comoros	12.8
5	Cape Verde	12.3
6	Senegal	10.1
7	South Sudan	9.5
8	Togo	8.6
9	Zimbabwe	8.2
10	Egypt	7.9

Source: Adapted by author from ECA (2020: 21).

Around 65 per cent of families in Cape Verde rely on remittances for their survival. In 2013, the country received US$175 million through remittances. While migration has been reduced due to the restrictive migration policies of destination countries in Europe and the United States, West African migrants continue to transit through the country to pursue irregular entry into Europe. In 2020, 33.5 per cent (186,312) of the population were migrants and of this, 63.6 per cent (118,607) moved onwards to the following EU countries: Portugal (60,543), France (24,545) and the Netherlands (12,601) (Diaspora for Development, 2020). In 2020, remittances constituted 12.1 per cent of GDP and remittance flows were estimated at US$247 million.

North and East Africa have had a greater share of the international migrant stock. At the global level, about 11.9 million migrants originate from North Africa, 48 per cent of whom reside in Europe and 33 per cent in Western Asia (Migration Data Portal, 2020a). As of 2020, migrants from North Africa represented 4.4 per cent of the global migrant population. At the time, about 1.7 million migrants from Algeria, 529,759 Tunisians, and

1.6 million Moroccans were hosted in Western Europe (Migration Data Portal, 2020a). Europe was the top destination for African migrants in 2018, as shown in Table 5.3.

Table 5.3: Population of African migrants per continent, 2018

s/n	Continent	Number of migrants
1	Europe	9,578,917
2	Asia	4,548,303
3	North America	2,652,606
4	Australia	505,100
5	South America	51,104
	Total	17,336,030

Source: CENFRI (2020: 8).

In 2010, remittances to Ethiopia and Kenya totalled US$3.2 billion (3 per cent of GDP) and US$1.9 billion (2 per cent of GDP), respectively (Dendir, 2017: 136). As noted by Dendir (2017: 125), the majority of recipients in Ethiopia (87 per cent) and Kenya (93 per cent) received their money through formal outlets such as banks or remittance companies.

In 2019, remittances became the highest source of foreign exchange in Kenya. A significant reduction in remittances would result in the decline of foreign reserves, which would negatively affect the country's exchange rate stability (Bisong et al., 2020: 11). In Nigeria, formal inflows of remittance (US$25.37 billion) accounted for 6.1 per cent of its GDP in 2019 – higher than its ODA – and 33 per cent of all remittance flows to sub-Saharan African countries. Adam's (2016) study on Ghana found that remittances reduced the level, depth and severity of poverty in the country. It shows that the poorest households under study received 22.7 per cent of their total income from international remittances. In 2018, Nigeria (US$22 billion) and Egypt (US$20 billion) were rated the fifth and sixth top destinations for remittances at the global level (Idemudia and Boehnke, 2020). In 2020, Egypt (US$29.6 billion) overtook Nigeria as the fifth largest remittance-receiving country in the world, Nigeria (US$17.2 billion) dropped to the 10th position, while India occupied the top position (McCarthy, 2021).

Prospects and challenges of remittances

In Africa, remittances have been vital resources for investment in education, land acquisition, the construction of houses, and payment for health services. Apart from engaging in money transfer, migrants have been involved in the development of their countries of origin through skills and knowledge transfer. Indeed, remittances to Africa have the potential to enhance the region's quest for innovation and technological development. As acknowledged by the IOM, migration is interrelated with innovation and technology, and 'international migration acts to support (and sometimes limit) the transfer of technology and knowledge, often working in tandem with investment and trade flows along historical, geographic, and geopolitical connections between countries and communities' (IOM 2019: 8). The development of globalisation and the moderate costs of accessing new technology have afforded migrants the opportunities to develop effective applications to support better integration in receiving African countries, and enhance social links and financial assistance to beneficiaries in origin countries. This is facilitated mostly through the use of 'mobile money' resources (IOM, 2019: 9).

Families use these remittances for empowerment initiatives and investment in human capital of children, and to reduce infant morbidity and mortality. Remittances are also insurance against hard times, and are used to make up for the shortfalls in relation to household consumption needs (Dendir, 2017). They are used to pay for health, education, daily expenditures, and other household needs. They help to augment agricultural incomes for many farmers, and constitute vital resources for starting businesses and investments, as well as for other socio-economic production. Recent studies found that about 75 per cent of the inflows of remittance are used for consumption and not investment (Natali and Isaacs, 2020: 122), but its contribution to improved livelihood and human development cannot be denied. Despite how important migration and remittances have become, actors from both continents have raised several concerns.

The emigration of skilled migrants is often described as the 'brain drain' – the flight of skilled human resources (Idemudia and Boehnke, 2020: 22) to Europe (UNDP, 2019) or other more affluent regions that offer higher wages and better employment opportunities. Zimbabwe has witnessed one of the worst brain drains on the continent due to political instability and a harsh economic reality, as migrants seek better opportunities in countries such as Britain and South Africa. The more successful the skilled migrants become in Europe, the higher the possibility of losing other young, skilled migrants – those who should be driving their communities and Africa's development agenda. In countries such as Nigeria, Ghana and Uganda, nurses and doctors have migrated in high numbers to European countries, thereby endangering the countries' health sectors and benefitting the destination countries (see Idemudia and Boehnke, 2020: 26). According to Collier (2021: n.p.), 'the British health service has been run by recruiting more than half its doctors from Africa and South Asia'. These kinds of exploitative relationships have prompted calls for the replacement of 'brain drain' with 'brain circulation' (Idemudia and Boehnke, 2020: 26).

While recipients of remittances on average spend more and save less, families with higher remittances are able to accumulate savings, which has reduced labour participation (Kim, 2007: 1; Dendir, 2017: 136). Remittances have the tendency to raise the reservation wages of many households without necessarily increasing national productivity, thereby impacting the labour supply in developing countries (Kim, 2007: 3). The lack of synergy between a rise in income and productivity has led to a shrinking labour force and the loss of export competitiveness in countries such as Jamaica (Kim, 2007: 6). The lack of reliable data is also a cause for worry. Despite the efforts of both state and non-state actors on gathering reliable data on remittances, the quantity of remittance flows to the African continent – including undocumented remittances through formal and informal channels – is conceived to be significantly larger than the official records (Mohapatra and Ratha, 2011: 3).

Remittances and the question of transfer costs

The World Bank and other international institutions, such as the UNDP, have persistently advocated for a reduction in the cost of money transfers. Migrants can pay as much as 6.5 per cent of the remittance in transfer costs from Europe to Africa, depending on the particular country and the service provider used (Bisong et al., 2020: 7). The Global Average, monitoring trends in the remittance costs worldwide, reported an average cost of 6.51 per cent in the fourth quarter (Q4) of 2020, and a decline to 6.38 per cent in the first quarter (Q1) of 2021 (World Bank, 2021), which were short of the financial body's expectations. The World Bank (2021) noted that if a remittance cost of 5 per cent were to be implemented globally, this would amount to a loss of about US$16 billion annually.

In 2015, the Addis Ababa Action Agenda (4A) was adopted in an attempt to support Africa's development agenda. Part of the outcomes was a deliberation on supporting African states to dismantle hindrances to international migration, as well as to integrate migration to Africa's development initiatives. Annex 40 of the agenda recognises the positive contribution of migrants to inclusive regional growth and sustainable development (UN, 2015: 13). The UN-led agenda acknowledges the place of remittances in Africa's economic growth, such as meeting the needs of recipient families, and highlights the difficulty of harnessing the benefits of remittances on the continent due to the higher costs involved in transferring money to Africa. Thus, the action plan set a target cost of an average of 3 per cent by 2030, with no corridor charging more than 5 per cent (Ratha et al., 2015; UN 2015: 13; Natali and Isaacs 2020: 120). The strategies for achieving this lofty objective remain unclear.

The high costs, which could militate against the willingness of some migrants to remit money back home, have led to a reduction in the remittance flows to Africa, thereby curtailing its potential to support regional development. The high cost of sending money home acts as a discouragement, while some of the funds that should be transferred end up as service charges. In the last quarter (Q4) of 2020, based on the World Bank Remittances Prices Worldwide, sub-Saharan Africa recorded an average transactional cost of 8.19 per cent, making it the most expensive region (World Bank/NOMAD, 2021: 35), with an estimated 8.02 per cent average transactional cost in the first quarter (Q1) of 2021 (World Bank, 2021).

The revised African Union Migration Policy Framework for Africa (AU-MPFA) and Plan for Action (2018–2030) aimed to promote safe, orderly and dignified migration, as well as achieve the AU's Agenda 2063 and the Sustainable Development Goals (SDGs), and promote international migration governance. The AU acknowledged that remittances to Africa was one of the conditions for attaining the SDGs on the continent (Idemudia and Boehnke, 2020: 4), and SDG 17.3 advocates for a 3 per cent limit on remittance transfer costs.

As remittances continue to rise, the cost of sending money to the developing countries also increases. In the third quarter (Q3) of 2020, transferring US$200 remittances to developing countries cost, on average,

8.5 per cent, representing a small decline from 9 per cent in 2019 (World Bank, 2020a). Table 5.4 shows the costs of sending US$200 from European countries to Africa.

Table 5.4: Average cost of sending US$200 from selected European countries

s/n	Countries	Transfer costs of sending US$200 (%)
1	France	5.93
2	Germany	7.23
3	Italy	4.76
4	Russia	1.00
5	Britain	6.44

Adapted from World Bank (2021: 12).

It is ironic that the region that seems to require more remittances has the most expensive transfer costs in the world.

While there are other channels for money transfer, banks remain the most expensive type of service provider, charging on average 10.66 per cent (World Bank, 2021). The high costs of sending remittances to Africa, and Nigeria in particular, is associated with the non-digitalisation of infrastructures for money transfer from Europe (Adhikari et al., 2021: 63). The UN (2015: 121) reports on the major causes of exorbitant remittance costs on the continent and identifies the following: '(a): liquid or "thin" currency markets; (b) limited competition; (c) bank-dominated markets; (d) high perceived risks of remittances; (e) cash-dominated markets; (f) low inflow volumes; and (g) a need to make profit'. However, remittance flows have led to the development of digital infrastructures, which in turn have increased the flows of remittances, despite the COVID-19 pandemic, with an estimated 65 per cent rise in remittances processed through mobile money, from US$7.7 billion in 2019 to US$12 billion in 2020 (World Bank/ NOMAD, 2021: 4). In Nigeria, the Naira4Dollar initiative,[1] which led to a reduction in the cost of remittances, has yielded significant benefits in the short run (Ardic et al., 2021). Kenya has developed its international money transfer facilities through mobile-to-mobile transfers, which are fast, convenient, wider in coverage, and cheaper (Natali and Isaacs, 2020: 117).

Perspectives on remittances and African–EU migration

Discourses on remittances within the broad conversation around African–EU migration is built on two major perspectives. First, African actors/stakeholders/decision-makers are optimistic about migration and see it as natural and an instrument for development. Second, their EU counterparts are generally pessimistic about migration and regard it as a problem to be solved, and a security concern to be addressed. The UNDP's *Scaling Fences* has thrown into question the EU's conversation around the prevention and reduction of migration through hostile policy response (UNDP 2019: 6). Migration policy experts in Africa believe that remittances could improve people's resilience to shocks and become an instrument to combat poverty through investments in health, education and other income-generating endeavours (African Union Commission, 2018: 5).

In Africa, migration and remittances have been seen as one of the practical ways to benefit from some of the wealth of the global powers, and former colonial masters. It also serves as a connection between diaspora communities and beneficiaries in their home countries. Through migration, Africans have acquired the skills and financial resources required for the development of their communities, thereby contributing to the national and regional development architecture.

Migration has also been interpreted as a threat to European culture and identity. As these sentiments are being reinforced and consolidated by right-wing voices within the EU, the attempts of African migrants to be gainfully employed and integrated into the EU labour chains are being jeopardised. Since the so-called 2015 'migration crisis' in Europe, African actors have tried to contend with alarmist reports about African migrants from a section of the European political class and the media. To militate against African–EU mobility, European governments have provided incentives (financial support, development aid and military support) for African leaders. However, these assistances have failed to stop migration, because migration is natural and African governments have been incapable of addressing the root causes of migration, among which are conflict, climate change, economic crises and unemployment, and infrastructural depletion (see Asiegbu, 2009).

As already implied, the AU recognises remittances as a tool for facilitating the economic and social development of Africa. The World Bank/NOMAD (2021: vi) is working towards the attainment of the SDGs, but this is dependent on increasing the volume of remittances as a percentage of GDP (SDG indicator 17.3.2) globally, and on reducing the cost of remittances (SDG indicator 10.c.1). The World Bank (2020) has tried to support member states in monitoring remittance flows through various channels, including ascertaining the costs and convenience of sending money, and protecting the financial integrity associated with such monetary flows. The aim of the World Bank, along with other partners such as UNDP and the G20 member states, is to reduce the costs of remittance and generally improve financial inclusion for poor individuals and households. Recognising the inadequacy of migration data, Article 4(a) of the African Institute for Remittances (AIR) relates to the need to capacitate member states to generate and compile remittance data (AU, 2012: 3).

The AU established the AIR with the aim of developing the capacity of Africa countries, migrants, recipients of remittances, and other partners to adopt effective tools and mechanisms to utilise remittances as development instruments for poverty alleviation. The AIR was established in January 2012 and became fully operational in 2015.

From the perspectives of migration and development, the AU Action Agenda failed to show more commitments to expanding regular channels of migration, which has been one of the central obstacles to sustainable African–EU migration governance. The more the regular channels are expanded, and the more remittance that flows into Africa, the fewer the incidences of irregular African–EU migration. Migration is beneficial for both continents. Europe has always required labour from African migrants. For instance, to fill the labour gaps in Southern Europe in the mid-2000s, Europe encouraged migration from African countries such as Morocco and Tunisia (Migration Data Portal, 2020a).

Globally, the population of those over the age of 60 years in 2017 was estimated to be 962 million and Europe made up the largest percentage (25 per cent) (IOM, 2019: 92). Africa's young population should be seen as an asset for European labour markets. The movement of this group to Europe has presented the EU member countries with the opportunity to use migrant labour in decisive sectors such as agriculture, industry, and hospitality. Despite this and the expectations of African decision-makers and migrants, European countries continue to implement hostile migration policies, resulting in the denial of visa issuance to migrants. As reflected in Table 5.5, nine African countries were among the top 10 countries with the highest rates of rejection of visas to enter Europe.

Table 5.5: Top 10 countries with highest visa rejection rates in 2018

	Country where consulate is located	Uniform visa applied for	Total uniform visa issued (including MEV)	Uniform visa not issued	Not issue rate for uniform visa	Share of MEVs
1	Nigeria	88.587	42.695	44.076	47.8%	38.2%
2	Iraq	64.726	32.909	30.908	47.8%	48.2%
3	Guinea	13.487	6.885	6.307	46.8%	26.3%
4	Democratic Republic of the Congo	9.122	5.203	4.197	46.0%	29.9%
5	Algeria	710.644	382.360	323.203	45.5%	29.7%
6	Ghana	43.664	24.988	18.137	41.5%	53.6%
7	Eritrea	2.155	1.275	874	40.6%	55.0%
8	Senegal	73.344	42.167	29.689	40.5%	31.4%
9	Comoros	1.709	1.035	633	37.0%	38.7%
10	Central African Republic	4.101	2.562	1.469	35.8%	21.4%

Source: Bisong (2020).

The list, which contains countries that usually experience visa denials in Europe, particularly multiple-entry visas (MEVs), featured Iraq as the only non-African country.

Impact of COVID-19 on remittances

Across the world, from Paris to Pretoria, the psychological, human, and socio-economic impacts of COVID-19 have been unprecedented. The global pandemic has transformed human relations with nature, and challenged the effective operations of important amenities and the life-support systems of societies the world over. The pandemic has been driving up poverty and expanding the inequality gap in Africa. The number of 'new poor' in 2020 is estimated to have increased by between 119 million and 124 million, in large part due to the pandemic, raising the number of individuals and households that require the support of migrants through remittances (World Bank/ NOMAD, 2021: 13).

The global COVID-19 pandemic has exposed the vulnerability of people, social relations and the financial systems that sustain the day-to-day existence of people. Indeed, remittance recipients in Africa and other regions have been affected by both the immediate and the longer-term socio-economic effects of COVID-19 (Kuhlcke and Bester, 2020). As reported, about 9.5 million formally documented Africans are living in Europe, many of whom send remittances back to the continent (Kuhlcke and Bester, 2020). As reported, 88 per cent of African migrants live in just five European countries (Italy, Germany, Belgium, France, and the Netherlands), which were under severe lockdowns during the initial outbreak of COVID-19 in January 2020. By June 2020, 25 per cent of land borders, 9 per cent of coastal entry points, and 6 per cent of airports were closed in the EU to prevent the spread of the disease (Migration Data Portal, 2020b). National economies have chosen to implement protectionist policies to cushion the effects of the pandemic on their citizens, amidst the pressures on infrastructures, labour, and economies.

A sharp decline in remittance inflows was projected in the first and second quarters (Q1 and Q2) of 2020, due to the spread of COVID-19, and the subsequent imposition of lockdowns by national governments to restrict movement and the spread of the disease. The lockdowns reduced migrants' prospects for employment in both the formal and informal sectors in many of the EU's foremost remittance-sending countries such as Germany and France (ECA, 2020: 21). Financial experts predicted that remittance flows between Europe and Africa would decline between 5 and 25 per cent in 2020, and global remittances would be reduced by about 20 per cent from the record US$554 billion in 2019 to US$445 billion in 2020 (World Bank, 2020a). The World Bank predicted the sharpest decline of remittances in recent history as a result of a fall in wages and the employment of migrant workers where they reside (including in the EU).

Despite the decline in remittances in the second quarter (Q2) of 2020, due to travel bans and the non-operation of money transfer offices in response to the COVID-19 crisis, the inflow recovered in the third and fourth quarters (Q3 and Q4). During the second quarter (Q2) of 2020, a particular remittance service provider experienced an 80 per cent decline in transactions in a week, which raised pessimism about the impact of COVID-19 on remittances (Kuhlcke and Bester, 2020). However, at the end of 2020, remittances to sub-Saharan Africa had increased by 12.5 per cent, and those to the Middle East and North Africa had risen by 2.3 per cent, while flows to Europe had fallen by 9.7 per cent (World Bank/NOMAD, 2021). Data gathered on the impact of COVID-19 on remittance flows to Africa reveals that,

> The resilience of remittance flows came as a result of migrants drawing on their savings to send money home, of shifting flows from unregulated channels, such as hand-carrying, to regulated remittance channels where accessible, and of migrants receiving cash transfers offered by host country governments where available (Ardic et al., 2021).

The desire to help families and associates in countries of origin, and implement cash transfer schemes and employment support initiatives in host countries also accounted for the increase in remittance flows to Africa (World Bank, 2021).

While remittance infrastructures showed great resilience during the 2008 financial recession and the 2014 Ebola epidemic, the negative impact of COVID-19 on national economies, through job losses and restrictions on human mobility and economic activities, continue to threaten remittances flows from Europe to Africa (Bisong et al., 2020). The World Bank had estimated a remarkable decline in global remittances of US$110 billion, while that of sub-Saharan Africa was projected to decline by about 23.1 per cent and North Africa by 19 per cent. Bisong et al. (2020: 5) note the initial estimate of money sent to sub-Saharan Africa, which was US$46 billion in 2019, and projected to rise to US$65 billion in 2020.

The persisting national lockdown measures across the world, including the EU, have created more uncertainties around migrants' employment opportunities. Migrants who have lost their jobs are unsure of when they may be employed again. While there has been job stability for migrant workers in the health, delivery, and agricultural sectors during the pandemic in Europe, migrants in the hospitality, tourism, construction and manufacturing sectors have struggled for job consolidation (Bisong et al., 2020: 1). In these situations, remittance senders that have been earning less income in the EU may choose to hold onto their savings or use them for personal survival amidst the economic and employment uncertainties (Bisong et al., 2020; Kuhlcke and Bester, 2020).

Despite general optimism regarding the resilience of remittances to Africa amidst the COVID-19 pandemic, African decision-makers know that remittances are important in the regional development projects and that these are conditional on labour security of migrants in the EU, and beyond. A consistent reduction in remittance flows to Africa would have devastating effects on household incomes, which would worsen the economic strains of the pandemic experienced by many African countries.

Conclusion: Towards a better management of remittances

This chapter has attempted to place the analysis of migration and remittances in relation to development discourse. Generally, African governments have been noted for their lack of institutional capacity to deal with natural disasters and economic strains, and instigate sustainable development, but the required evidence-based data needed to implement policies that would harness the use of remittances to enhance African development have been lacking. It is imperative to track the flow of remittances from sending countries to Africa. The EU and other sending regions, as well as non-state actors, should support African states to achieve this lofty objective.

The AU and its member states have realised the importance of maximising the developmental impact of remittances on the receiving African countries. Remittances have been categorised as an instrument of development by the AU and its member states. The large amounts of money transferred to the continent by migrants contribute to national and regional development. Natali and Isaacs (2020: 117) have suggested the following seven ways to harness the potentials of remittances:

(a) creating enabling regulatory framework for cross-bordering remittances; (b) improving domestic payments infrastructure with new technologies; (c) improving data collection; (d) increasing transparency; (e) improving access to remittance services for irregular migrants; (f) leveraging remittances as a tool for financial inclusion; and (g) moving informal transactions into the formal ones.

Furthermore, Africa and Europe should be focused on implementing effective and sustainable migration policies that assist African countries to benefit from migration and enhance their development projects, while also collaborating to reduce irregular migration to Europe. With genuine commitments from actors from both continents, a balance could be struck, which would benefit all parties, including the migrants who are usually neglected in migration policy discourse. The AU actors should push for policies that would create more opportunity for migrants to be gainfully employed and protect those who are already employed from the backlashes of the COVID-19 pandemic.

As noted by the AU, there is a need to enhance the efficiency of remittance transfer mechanisms, and drastically reduce remittance transfer costs, which limit its contribution to the developmental initiatives of receiving countries, and the continent (African Union Commission, 2018: 5). This declaration should be matched by commitment through effective dialogue with EU counterparts and other stakeholders on meeting the 3 per cent transfer cost limit, as provided for in the UN Global Compact. As a central aspect of this ambition, stakeholders from both continents must facilitate access to and adoption of digital financial services and mobile transfers to enhance the flows of remittance.

As observed, remittances to Africa tend to increase after a natural disaster, including the current global disruptive nature of the COVID-19 pandemic, when remittances to the continent have increased despite the earlier projection of a decline. Over time, remittances to receiving African countries have been much more stable than other financial assistance, and this emphasises the importance of Africa–EU migration as a source of stable financial inflows. Immigrants send money and resources back to their home countries through formal and informal channels such as remittances companies and relatives, respectively. It is vital to continue to develop remittance markets on the continent through government–private sector partnerships. This would facilitate the abolition of institutional impediments to the fast, cheap and convenient transfer of money from Europe to Africa.

Notes

1   This is the biggest e-currency exchange company in Nigeria. It operates online and provides the facility to transfer funds easily and cheaply at an international level.

References

Adams, R.H. 2016. *Remittances and Poverty in Ghana.* World Bank Policy Research Working Paper No. 3838. Washington, DC: World Bank.

African Union (AU). 2012. 'Statutes of the African Institute of Remittances (AIR)'. Online at: https://au.int/sites/default/files/treaties/36199-treaty-statute_african_institute_for_remittances_e.pdf (accessed 15 November 2021).

African Union Commission. 2018. *Migration Policy Framework for Africa and Plan of Action (2018–2030).* Addis Ababa: African Union, pp. 1–8.

Apatinga, G.A., Asiedu, A.B and Obeng, F.A. 2021. 'The contribution of non-cash remittances to the welfare of households in the Kassena-Nankana District, Ghana', *African Geographical Review*, 1–12. doi.org/10.1080/19376812.2020.1870511.

Ardic, O., Dashi, E., Baijal, H. and Natarajan, H. 2021. 'Ebb and flow: Remittances in a year of pandemic'. 15 June. Online at: https://blogs.worldbank.org/psd/ebb-and-flow-remittances-year-pandemic (accessed 15 November 2021).

Asiegbu, M. 2009. 'African migrants in spite of "Fortress" Europe: An essay in philosophy of popular culture', *OGIRISI: A New Journal of African Studies*, 6(1): 1–23.

Bisong, A. 2020. 'The new EU visa code and what it means for African countries'. Blog, 6 April. ECDPM. Online at: https://ecdpm.org/talking-points/new-eu-visa-code-what-it-means-for-african-countries/ (accessed 15 November 2021).

Bisong, A., Ahairwe P.E. and Njoroge, E. 2020. 'The impact of COVID-19 on remittances for development in Africa'. Discussion Papers No. 2, pp. 1–27. Online at: https://ecdpm.org/wp-content/uploads/Impact-COVID-19-remittances-development-Africa-ECDPM-discussion-paper-269-May-2020.pdf.

Carr, M. 2012. 'The trouble with Fortress Europe'. Open Democracy, 21 November. Online at: https://www.opendemocracy.net/en/trouble-with-fortress-europe/ (accessed 15 November 2021).

Centre for Financial Regulation and Inclusion (CENFRI). 2020. 'Exploring the impact of COVID-19 on livelihoods in Africa'. Cenfri, 20 March. Online at: https://cenfri.org/wp-content/uploads/Exploring-the-impact-of-COVID-19-on-livelihoods-in-Africa_Effect-on-remittances.pdf (accessed 15 November 2021).

Collier, P. 2021. 'Beyond the bottom billion'. *In Pursuit of Development* podcast. Online at: https://in-pursuit-of-development.simplecast.com/episodes/

paul-collier/transcript (accessed 15 November 2021).

Dendir, S. 2017. 'Saving out of remittances: Evidence from Ethiopia and Kenya', *International Migration*, 55(4): 118–140.

Diaspora for Development. 2020. 'Diaspora Engagement Mapping: Cabo Verde'. Online at: https://diasporafordevelopment.eu/wp-content/uploads/2020/07/CF_Cabo-Verde-v.3.pdf (accessed 15 November 2021).

Economic Commission for Latin America and the Caribbean (ECLAC). 2021. *The Coronavirus Disease (COVID-19) Pandemic: An opportunity for a systemic approach to disaster risk for the Caribbean.* UNDRR and ECLAC Report. Geneva: UN Office for Disaster Risk Reduction. Online at: https://repositorio.cepal.org/bitstream/handle/11362/46732/1/S2000944_en.pdf (accessed 15 November 2021).

Economic Commission of Africa (ECA). 2020. *COVID 19 in Africa: Protecting lives and economies.* Addis Ababa: ECA Printing and Publishing Unit.

European Commission. 2018. 'Many more to come? Migration from and within Africa'. European Commission, Joint Research Centre. Luxembourg: Publications Office of the European Union. doi 10.2760/1702, JRC 110703.

European Union (EU). 2020. 'Joint Communication to the European Parliament and the Council: Towards a comprehensive strategy with Africa'. Brussels: European Commission. Online at: https://ec.europa.eu/international-partnerships/system/files/communication-eu-africa-strategy-join-2020-4-final_en.pdf (accessed 15 November 2021).

Idemudia, E. and Boehnke, K. 2020. 'Psychosocial experiences of African migrants in six European countries', *Social Indicators Research Series*, 81: 15–31.

International Organization for Migration (IOM). 2019. *World Migration Report 2020*. Geneva: IOM.

Kim, N. 2007. *The Impact of Remittances on Labor Supply: The case of Jamaica.* World Bank Policy Research Working Paper No. 4120, pp. 1–18. Online at: https://openknowledge.worldbank.org/bitstream/handle/10986/7152/wps4120.pdf?sequence=1&isAllowed=y (accessed 15 November 2021).

Kuhlcke, K. and Bester, H. 2020. 'COVID-19 and remittances to Africa: What can we do?' 27 March. Online at: https://cenfri.org/articles/covid-19-and-remittances-to-africa-what-can-we-do/ (accessed 15 November 2021).

Levitt, P. and Lamba-Nieves, D. 2011. 'Social remittances revisited', *Journal of Ethnic and Migration Studies*, 37(1): 1–22.

McCarthy, N. 2021. 'These countries are the world's top remittance recipients'. Geneva: World Economic Forum, 19 May. Online at: https://www.

weforum.org/agenda/2021/05/infographic-what-are-the-world-s-top-remittance-recipients/ (accessed 15 November 2021).

Migration Data Portal. 2020a. 'Migration data in Northern Africa'. Online at: https://migrationdataportal.org/regional-data-overview/northern-africa#recent-trends

Migration Data Portal. 2020b. 'Migration data in Europe'. Online at https://www.migrationdataportal.org/regional-data-overview/europe (accessed 15 November 2021).

Mohapatra, S. and Ratha, D. 2011. 'Migrant Remittances in Africa: An overview', in *Remittance Markets in Africa*. Washington, DC: World Bank, pp. 3–70.

Natali, C. and Isaacs, L. 2020. 'Remittances to and from Africa', in A. Adepoju, C. Fumagalli and N. Nyabola, *African Migration Report: Challenging the narratives*. Addis Ababa: International Organization for Migration, pp. 117–31.

Naudé, W. 2012. 'Migration, remittances and resilience in Africa', 19 September. Tokyo: United Nations University. Online at: https://unu.edu/publications/articles/migration-remittances-and-resilience-in-africa.html#info (accessed 15 November 2021).

Naudé, W. 2010. 'The determinants of migration from sub-Saharan African countries', *Journal of African Economies*, 19(3): 330–56.

Piper, N. and Rother, S. 2020. 'Political remittances and the diffusion of a rights-based approach to migration governance: The case of the Migrant Forum in Asia (MFA)', *Journal of Ethnic and Migration Studies*, 46(6): 1057–71.

Ratha, D. 2021. 'Keep remittances flowing to Africa', *Foresight Africa 2021*. Brookings, 15 March. Online at: https://www.brookings.edu/blog/africa-in-focus/2021/03/15/keep-remittances-flowing-to-africa/ (accessed 15 November 2021).

Ratha, D., Macdermott, J. and Plaza, S. 2015. 'Addis Ababa Action Agenda (4A): On harnessing migration for financing development, we are almost there!' World Bank blog, *People Move*. 17 July. Online at: https://blogs.worldbank.org/peoplemove/addis-ababa-action-agenda-4a-harnessing-migration-financing-development-we-are-almost-there (accessed 15 November 2021).

United Nations. 2015. *Outcome document of the Third International Conference on Financing for Development: Addis Ababa Action Agenda*. A/CONF.227/L.1. Online at: https://www.un.org/ga/search/view_doc.asp?symbol=A/CONF.227/L.1 (accessed 15 November 2021).

United Nations Development Programme (UNDP). 2019. 'Scaling Fences: Voices of Irregular African Migrants to Europe'. Online at: https://www.

undp.org/publications/scaling-fences#modal-publication-download (accessed 15 November 2021).

World Bank. 2021. 'An analysis of trends in cost of remittance', *Remittance Prices Worldwide Quarterly*, Issue 37, March. Online at: https://remittanceprices. worldbank.org/sites/default/files/rpw_main_report_and_annex_q121_ final.pdf (accessed 15 November 2021).

World Bank. 2020a. 'World Bank predicts sharpest decline of remittances in recent history', 22 April. Washington, DC: World Bank. Online at: https:// www.worldbank.org/en/news/press-release/2020/04/22/world-bank- predicts-sharpest-decline-of-remittances-in-recent-history (accessed 15 November 2021).

World Bank. 2020b. COVID-19: 'Remittance flows to shrink 14% by 2021', 29 October. Press Release No: 2021/054/SPJ. Online at: https://www. worldbank.org/en/news/press-release/2020/10/29/covid-19-remittance- flows-to-shrink-14-by-2021 (accessed 15 November 2021).

World Bank/NOMAD. 2021. 'Resilience: COVID-19 crisis through a migration lens', *Migration and Development Brief*, No. 34, pp. 1–40. Online at: https:// reliefweb.int/sites/reliefweb.int/files/resources/Migration%20and%20 Development%20Brief%2034.pdf (accessed 15 November 2021).

Part III
Regional Perspectives

Chapter 6

Migration: The Maghreb and the EU

Ibtihel Bouchoucha

Introduction

The Maghreb countries represent Africa's gateway to Europe. Their wealth in human and natural resources, as well as their strategic location on the Mediterranean Basin, have been of great interest to European countries, who historically have tried to exploit these assets through colonisation or, in the case of Tunisia, through protection agreements. This colonisation is in reality 'a long history of inequitable power relations' (Rahali, 2017), linked to dependency and the underdevelopment of African countries (Rodney, 1973). This unequal historical relationship accounts for the initial movements of North African labour to Europe and largely explains the continuity and intensity of the current flows (Charef, 2009). However, it is also important to recognise the effects of bad governance and the lack of crisis management by successive governments in Tunisia and Libya over the last decades.

Clearly, emigration has exposed the unemployment problems and deterioration of living standards in the Maghreb countries. Indeed, since their independence, the Maghreb economies have remained highly dependent on the agricultural sector, which was virtually destroyed by strong competition from industrial economies. With the failure of agrarian reforms, this sector no longer has the capacity to absorb agricultural labour, causing massive rural exodus (Charef, 2009). Rural–urban migration created a strong imbalance in the labour market in many regions, which over time became relays to international migration. Indeed, their geographical location and their proximity to Europe have positioned these countries as favourite destinations of 'sub-Saharan migrants who circulate in this region to reach Europe', making the Maghreb 'a transnational space of departure, circulation, return, transit and installation' (Alioua, 2007: 40).[1]

Apart from unemployment, Maghreb countries have experienced labour market imbalances, internal regional inequalities and the underdevelopment of rural areas. This problematic and complex context has resulted in the evolution of several forms of internal and international migration, with an increase in irregular migration, especially after the European Union (EU) adopted restrictive migration policies.

To rectify these economic difficulties and the imbalance in the labour market, the Maghreb countries have developed policies in favour of economic migration. They have facilitated the integration of their emigrants to the development of their origin country. Overall, the Maghreb states consider economic emigration as an essential element for labour market stability and enhancement of their economic and social development. In fact, migration is considered to be a solution, providing new economic dynamics that can create new jobs.

Therefore, the Maghreb states tend to encourage emigration and adjust to the demands of international labour markets, particularly those of European countries. This positive political orientation towards emigration has inspired reforms in education, favourable policies towards emigrants in the diaspora upon return, as well as bilateral agreements with destination countries. However, the EU countries, in response to the increase in irregular migration, have developed policies to reduce immigration. But these policies and measures have not achieved their desired goals; instead, they have contributed to the proliferation of irregular migration from politically unstable countries such as Libya and Tunisia.

This chapter engages the debate on Africa–EU migration and reflects on migration policies in the Maghreb. It examines the socio-economic and political context in the Maghreb countries and explores its influence on international migration and migration policies in these countries. It aims, finally, to offer practical recommendations on effective migration policies on both continents. The chapter comprises three sections. The first analyses the main factors that determine the number and characteristics of migrants, while the second presents the historical perspective of migration in the Maghreb countries. The last section assesses the migration policies of Maghreb countries.

Socio-economic development in the Maghreb: The backdrop of international migration

Migration is often linked, directly or indirectly, to labour market imbalances, and specifically to the problem of unemployment – or underemployment – and low wages. Indeed,

> large income disparities between the origin and destination countries, and the high levels of unemployment in North Africa, remain significant drivers of migration. As of 2019, almost 12 million North Africans were living outside their countries of birth, with roughly half in Europe and 3.3 million living in Gulf States (IOM, 2019: 66).

Thus, migration in North Africa is no longer an unskilled migration that involves mainly unemployed men; the profiles of migrants have changed. Migration today affects both women and men, unskilled and highly skilled people, as well as workers and the unemployed. The push factors are mainly economic reasons (finding a job, raising the level of wages) to improve their living conditions (Bouchoucha, 2013; UNDP, 2019).

This section presents an overview of the demographic changes and socio-economic development in the Maghreb countries. It analyses the evolution of some indicators on young and adult men, and women's schooling and poverty. The underlying premise of this analysis is that it is difficult to ignore the link between poverty and migration. As several research studies have shown, internal or international migration (Massey et al., 1993; Diarra, 2003; Zohry, 2006; Haffad, 2007) sometimes represents, for poor populations, the only way to improve their income.

Fully aware of the importance of demographic balance to their development after independence, the Maghreb countries have adopted a demographic policy of fertility regulation. In fact, the governments have tried, through political, legal, health and other measures, to influence the demographic behaviours of their populations. The results have been remarkable. Indeed, the region's total fertility rate (TFR) has fallen significantly since the 1960s. It went from approximately seven births per woman in 1960 to almost half of that in the early 1990s. The TFR has now almost reached the replacement rate of around 2.3, except in Mauritania where the fertility level remains high (on average four children per woman) (data from the World Bank: World Development Indicators). Such evolution had an important effect on the level of population growth and on its structure.

Figure 6.1: Fertility rate, total births per woman

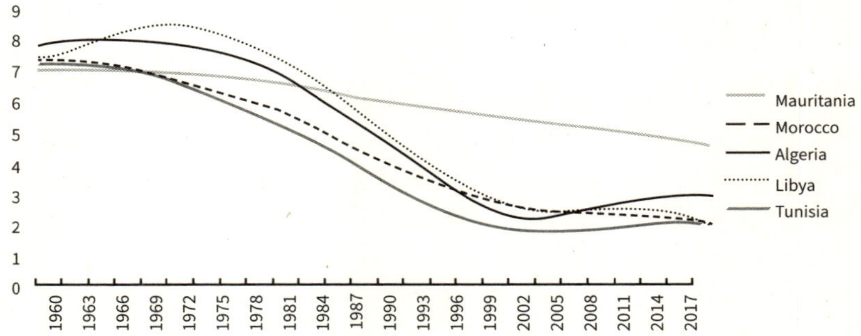

Source: Data from the World Bank: World Development Indicators

Overall, the population in the Maghreb countries expanded rapidly in the 1950s, followed by a dramatic decline in fertility from the 1960s, especially in Tunisia, until the population growth stabilised in the early 2000s. These demographic changes influenced the population structure and raised the proportion of young people of working age. These developments had a positive influence on the dependency ratio. This has been improved over time and it reached an average of two people in the working-age population per dependent person (young or old). However, the growth in the active population has created a strong demand for jobs, but the capacity of the labour market is very limited, which has raised the number of potential migrants.

Figure 6.2: Age dependency rate (% of the working-age population)

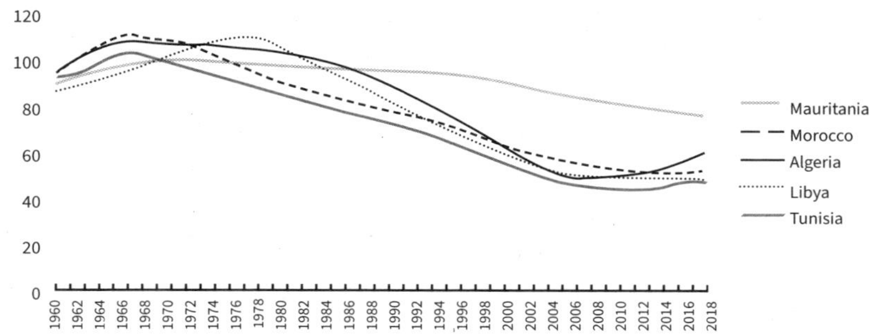

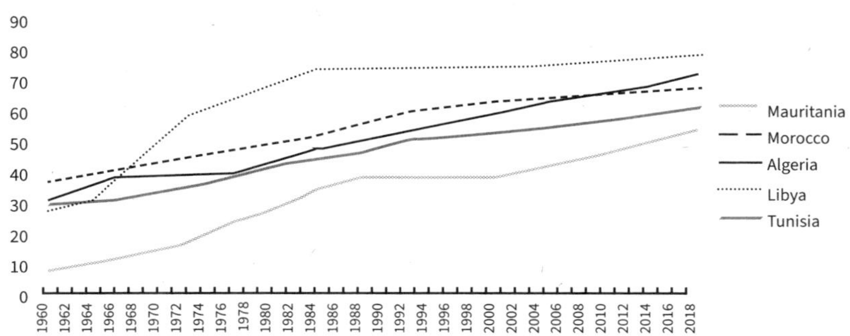

Source: Data from the World Bank: World Development Indicators

These dynamics have also led to a strong and rapid level of urbanisation. Today, in all Maghreb countries, more than half of the population lives in urban areas. In Libya, Algeria and Tunisia, more than two-thirds of the population live in urban areas. This proportion is explained primarily by the importance of internal migration and the rural exodus. International migration is not accessible to all, and many people rely on internal migration for job opportunities and improvement in their living standard. For some, internal migration becomes a step towards international migration.

Figure 6.3: Urban population (% of total population)

Source: Data from the World Bank: World Development Indicators

The evolution of the health status of the population is not only an indicator of the standard of living, but also a sign of the overall development of the region. This development also reflects access to public services and the efficacy of the health infrastructure, which is one of the main elements necessary for a better quality of life. The evolution of the health status of the population, then, indicates an entire context that may or not be favourable to migration flows.

Figure 6.4: Life expectancy at birth, total (years)

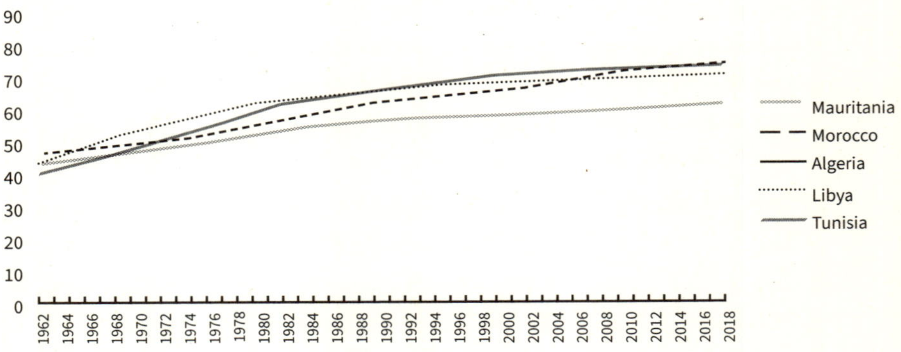

Figure 6.5: Mortality rates, under 5 years (per 1,000 live births)

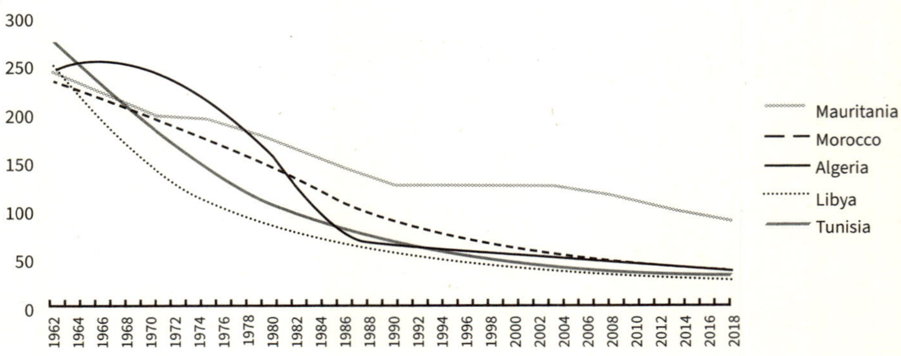

Source: Data from the World Bank: World Development Indicators

Health policies in the Maghreb countries have resulted in an improved access to care and a decent quality of health services. As shown in Figure 6.5, from 1962 onwards, the under-five mortality rate declined rapidly.

Between 1962 and 2018, it fell by at least 163 points, from around 250 per cent (Mauritania, 239.8 per cent; Morocco, 227.4 per cent; Algeria, 243.4 per cent; Libya, 244.2 per cent; Tunisia, 272.9 per cent) to less than 76 per cent (Mauritania, 75.6 per cent; Morocco, 22.4 per cent; Algeria, 23.5 per cent; Libya12 per cent; Tunisia, 17 per cent). The decline in under-five mortality obviously reflects general progress in health, and improvement in living standards resulting from socio-economic progress. Moreover, a decrease in illiteracy, an increase in the age at marriage, a decrease in fertility, medical densification, and urbanisation are decisive factors in the decline in infant mortality. Notably, during the same period, following a similar trend as mortality, life expectancy grew rapidly between1970 and 1980. From 1962 to 2018, it rose between 19 and 33 points, from a value between 43 and 49 years (Mauritania, 45.8 years; Morocco, 49.3 years; Algeria, 47.1 years; Libya 45.8 years; Tunisia 43.4 years) to between 64.7 and 76.5 years (Mauritania, 64.7 years; Morocco, 76.4 years; Algeria, 76.7 years; Libya 72.7 years; Tunisia 76.5 years) (World Bank: World Development Indicators). The promotion of education has been another decisive factor in the Maghreb countries' sustainable development process. The considerable improvement in access to education, for both girls and boys, has been remarkable for all Maghreb countries. With the exception of Mauritania, almost all young people aged between 15 and 24 years were enrolled in school (Tunisia 96.2 per cent in 2014; Algeria 97.4 per cent in 2018; Morocco 97.7 per cent in 2018; and Libya 99.6 per cent in 2014).

Like many other African countries, unemployment is a serious challenge in the Maghreb region. The unemployment rate differs greatly from one country to another, as seen in Tables 6.6a to 6.6e. In Tunisia, the recorded unemployment rate was 15 per cent in 2019, Libya's stood at 19 per cent in 2012, while Morocco registered only 9.3 per cent unemployment in 2016. In Mauritania and Algeria, the unemployment rate reported in 2017 was 10.3 per cent and 13.6 per cent, respectively. Overall, however, unemployment is high among young women aged 15–24 years, although there are significant differences between the different countries. The unemployment rate of young women in Algeria was a staggering 82 per cent in 2017, compared to 24.9 per cent in Mauritania. In Tunisia, the rate observed in 2015 was 37.4 per cent compared to 22.7 per cent in Morocco. The most recent statistics available for Libya are for 2012, which reveal an unemployment rate of 67.8 per cent for young women. Given the deteriorating security situation in

Libya from 2012, this number is likely to be even higher today. In Tunisia, the unemployment rate for women (22.18 per cent) in 2019 was almost double that of men (12.27 per cent).

Clearly, from these statistics, unemployment affects young people in particular, especially those with university degrees; for example, in Tunisia in 2015, the unemployment rate of women with advanced education was 37.37 per cent compared to 17.78 per cent for men. The inability of the labour market to absorb the growing number of university graduates, have put pressures on available employment opportunities. However, unemployment affects women much more than men, especially highly educated young women. Unemployment, high levels of poverty and the deterioration of the standard of living have pushed many, especially young women, to take precarious, underpaid or even unpaid jobs. The increasing number of sub-Saharan immigrants in the Maghreb countries, and their integration into the economy, constitutes a challenge for the government of member states that are keen to reduce unemployment. Indeed, migrants from sub-Saharan Africa occupy different professions and many of them, especially the irregular ones, accept precarious jobs with low wages and deplorable working conditions (Monia, 2009).[2]

Figure 6.6a: Unemployment rate, Libya, 2012

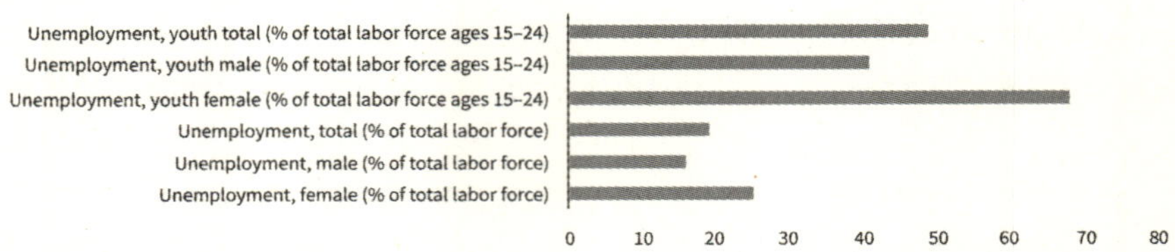

Figure 6.6b: Unemployment rate, Morocco, 1997/2016

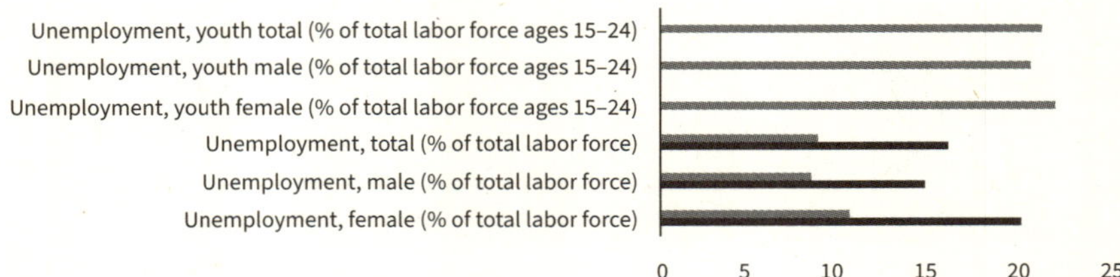

Figure 6.6c: Unemployment rate, Tunisia, 1997/2019

Figure 6.6d: Unemployment rate, Algeria, 1997/2017

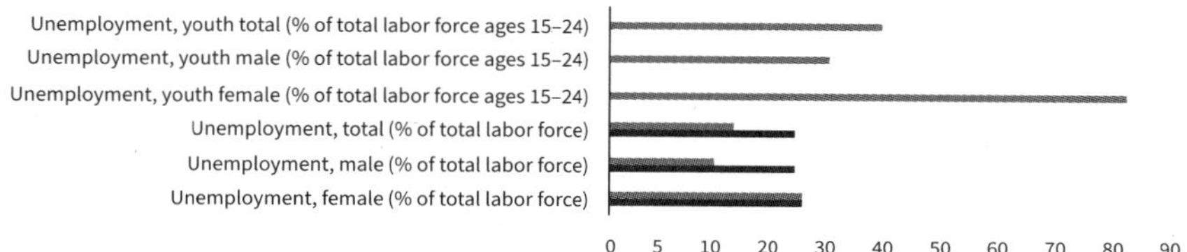

Figure 6.6e: Unemployment rate, Mauritania, 2012/2017

Source: Data from the World Bank: World Development Indicators

The relationship between migration and employment is evident in several studies, confirming that job search is one of the root causes of migration (Mzali, 1997; Boubakri, 2010). Thus, it is undeniable that in the Maghreb countries, unemployment and working conditions are the two main causes of internal and international migration, particularly for men. Women's involvement in international migration (regular or not) has increased but it remains low compared to men. The gender effect that still weighs heavily on female migration has been a major factor (Bouchoucha, 2013, 2018). Indeed, fertility rates have decreased and stabilised around the replacement rate, and population growth has stabilised at a very low level, which has influenced the structure of the population. A population structure that extends the working age between 18 and 59 years should favour the Maghreb countries, but given the socio-economic and political crises in the region today, these countries are unable to harness this dividend. Therefore, desperate young people in the lowly paid job market and unskilled workforce are always motivated to cross borders to live the 'European dream'.

In many cases, the imbalance between local and international labour markets determines the decision to migrate. Figure 6.7 shows the unemployment rate and gross domestic product (GDP) per capita in the Maghreb countries and the three main destination countries (France, Italy, and Spain). As shown on the graph, the GDP per capita clearly reflects the differences between the Maghreb countries and the main destination countries. While, youth unemployment remains a major problem for all Maghreb countries such as in Tunisia, which recorded 29 per cent, it is very low in France compared to other countries. However, unemployment rates of highly qualified people are low in EU countries like France (5.1 per cent), Italy (5.7 per cent) and Spain (8.61 per cent).

Figure 6.7: GDP per capita and youth unemployment by country in 2019

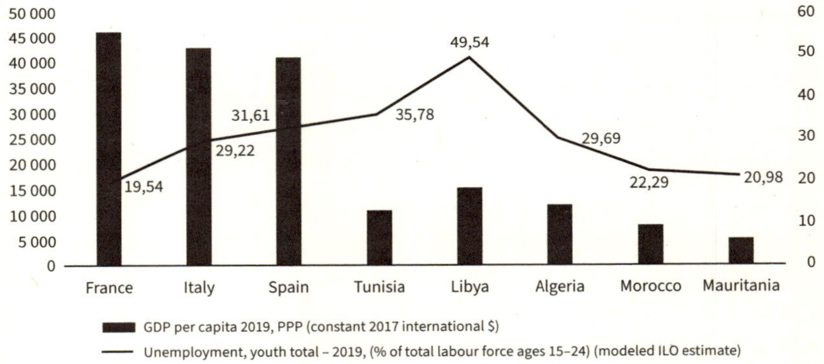

Source: Data from the World Bank: World Development Indicators

Finally, Figure 6.8 shows that the poverty level decreased significantly in the Maghreb region in 2019, but inequality remains high (World Bank, 2016).[3]

Other statistics also reveal a clear improvement in housing conditions in the region. For example, the proportion of housing connected to the electricity grid has continued to expand, reaching almost 100 per cent in Algeria, Tunisia and Morocco in 2018. In Mauritania, the number of homes connected to the electricity grid doubled between 2000 and 2018, from 22 per cent to 44 per cent. In Libya, this indicator has fallen as a result of the protracted armed conflict since 2012.

Figure 6.8: Access to electricity (% of the population)

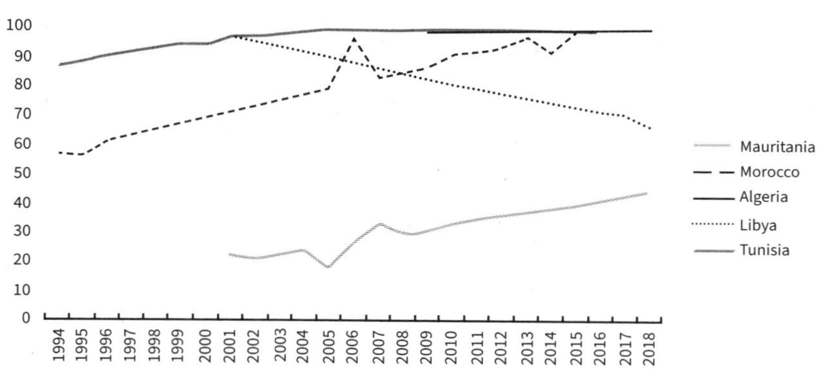

Source: Data from the World Bank: World Development Indicators

These statistics reveal the social context of international migration in the Maghreb. In addition, it is vital to recognise the importance of geographical and historical factors that favour mobility, especially towards Europe. Indeed, the demographic trends in all Maghreb countries are characterised by an increasing control of fertility. Today, all the Maghreb countries, with the exception of Mauritania, are experiencing changes in their population structure; they are increasingly registering an expansion of the younger population and, consequently, the working-age group. Thus, with the development of education, on the one hand, and the stagnation of the labour markets, on the other, the unemployment rates, especially among highly qualified people, have increased. After the revolution in Tunisia and the crisis in Libya, the GDP per capita remained stagnant while inflation increased, which led to the deterioration of the purchasing power and the standard of living of the populations in these countries. The damaging effects of the COVID-19 pandemic across the world since early 2020 have aggravated the economic crises and led to further job losses. Ultimately this has increased mobility flows to Europe from countries such as Tunisia, which still suffers from great political and economic instability.

However, the levels of development in the Maghreb countries are not uniform. Tunisia, for instance, has been affected by economic crises and political and social instability since the revolution in 2011, and especially because of its close economic relations with Libya, which was also a favourite destination of many Tunisian migrants. Likewise, the economic effects of COVID-19 will not be felt uniformly in the Maghreb, and countries like

Morocco and Tunisia will undoubtedly be more severely affected since tourism and the services sectors are key to their economic growth. This evolution and other changes that have occurred since the 1950s have had important effects on the quantitative and qualitative evolution of international migration in the Maghreb countries, which has changed from assisted migration to voluntary and clandestine migration (Charef, 2009).

Migration in the Maghreb in historical perspective

According to the United Nations (UN) report, in 2019 there were more than 6 million international migrants from Maghreb countries, which represents 2 per cent of the total number of international migrants recorded worldwide. Maghreb migration is concentrated in Europe, representing 6 per cent of the migration stock in Europe. France is the preferred destination: it receives almost half of these migrants, which represent 37 per cent of its total migrant stock. Migration from the Maghreb represents 13 per cent and 10 per cent, respectively, of the number of international migrants in Spain and Italy.

Table 6.1: International migrant stock from Maghreb countries, 2019

Country or area of destination	Country or area of origin							
	Total	Algeria	Libya	Mauritania	Morocco	Tunisia	Maghreb countries	
WORLD	271,642,105	1,944,784	180,586	128,506	3,136,069	813,213	6,203,158	2%
EUROPE	82,304,539	1,759,610	85,974	32,531	2,781,506	638,385	5,298,006	6%
Italy	6,273,722	22,877	35,852	834	450 557	109,387	619,507	10%
Spain	6,104,203	57,140	1,000	8,781	711 792	2,832	781,545	13%
France	8,334,875	1,575,528	2,588	19,563	1,020,162	427,897	3,045,738	37%

Source: United Nations (2019)

Maghreb/EU migration, particularly to France, is the result of a long history of migration that began after the First World War in 1919 with the recruitment of soldiers from the Maghreb and later to help France restore its economy (Charef, 2009). Since then, the migration movement has accelerated and has taken several forms depending on changes in the political, economic and social climate. In the 1960s, migration was desired and assisted to meet the labour demand in Europe, and particularly in France, which was the colonial centre. This migration was temporary and limited to unskilled labour, mainly young males from poor populations in rural areas, where emigration was the only solution to ameliorate their poor living conditions (Charef, 2009). The 1960s was a time of restructuring after a long period of colonisation, so although governments in the Maghreb were not keen on emigration, the lack of opportunity in the local markets and poor living conditions, especially in rural areas, compelled them to accept it, as it seemed like the only viable solution to the region's crisis.

After the 1970s, because of the economic upheaval of the first 'oil crisis', the unemployment rate increased, and European countries closed their borders, established visa application processes, and encouraged family unification. Consequently, migration ceased to be assisted and temporary, and became voluntary and permanent due to the unemployment crisis, which created a steady supply of skilled labour from the region. Despite changing global conditions, this dynamic has been consolidated to the extent that the 'Maghreb is increasingly becoming a skill migration hub' (Musette et al., 2006: 21) and has become a labour exporter to other regions, with a majority still moving to France. In fact, labour emigration is no longer a short-term response to fluctuations in the needs of foreign and domestic labour markets, but has become a deliberate strategy in many Maghrebi states. For example, Tunisia has developed a massive schooling programme to meet the requirements of the international as well as the domestic labour markets. Maghreb countries now export a specialised labour force (in higher education, in information technology, and computer engineering) and, increasingly, women have become involved in migration.

Over the years, emigration from the Maghreb has shifted from being purely economic migration of unskilled or low-skilled labour to a migration of skilled labour for different reasons, such as economic, family, or educational factors. Thus, over time, many diasporas who are well established in host countries, particular in France, facilitate the movement of others. While earlier generations of women migrated through marriage or accompanying other family members, women's migration is no longer limited to the family setting. Women now migrate independently and for a variety of reasons, such as studies and employment. Migration from the Maghreb to Europe has evolved, and its causes and composition have changed over time in response to structural shifts at global, regional, national and sub-national levels. Indeed, although many European countries have faced economic and political difficulties, including employment, they still receive significant migration flows from the Maghreb – even if their unemployment rates are sometimes higher than in the countries of origin. Apart from economic factors, colonial history has played an important role in Maghreb–Europe migration.

Table 6.2 summarises the overall trends of this mobility. Since the early 1960s, three Maghreb countries (Algeria, Morocco and Tunisia) have recorded significant international mobility, with European countries as their main destinations. Between 1962 and 1977, estimated net migration from Morocco was 3,833,330 and from Mauritania 5,057; while Algeria and Tunisia recorded 220,632 and 102,038, respectively. From 1977 to 2017, Morocco and Algeria continued to have large emigration. In fact, because migrants from the Maghreb have similar destinations, it seems that economic and political crises in any one of the destination countries influences the migration flows from the entire region. For example, in 1967, there was a significant decrease in net migration from Tunisia and Algeria, which could be explained by the return of migrants or by a decrease in the flow of migration after the independence of these countries. However, Morocco recorded a significant increase in net migration in this period. It seems that European countries facilitated the migration of Moroccans to make up for the shortfall from Tunisia and Algeria. Likewise in 2017, data show a large increase in migration flows from Libya and Tunisia, while there was a significant decrease in net migration from Morocco and Algeria. This shows that the Europeans countries restricted migration from these two countries to manage migration from the region. Table 6.2 also shows that, until the early 1990s, Libya was primarily a host country rather than a sending country, and it was the favourite destination for many Tunisians. By the end of the 1990s, Libya began to record a negative net migration, especially from the beginning of the revolution which ended with the fall of Muammar Gaddafi in 2011. In 2012, Libya had the highest number of departures in its recent history, registering a negative net migration of −300,002 migrants.

Table 6.2: Net migration

	1962	1967	1972	1977	1982	1987	1992	1997	2002	2007	2012	2017
Mauritania	–1,820	–2,760	–5,950	–9,700	–16100	–39,998	–466,627	–44,003	–10,004	10,001	25,002	25,002
Morocco	–239,800	–121,335	–508,947	–309,839	–320,659	–430,184		–53,2581	–654,821	–565,140	–367,108	–257,096
Algeria	–282,941		–25,3436	–224,833	–81,020	–,93,302	–128,679	–164,413	–205,228	–357,340	–143,268	–50,002
Libya	45,891	48,002	58665	57,534	113,380	5,490	3,965	–57,368	–20,569	–118,555	–300,002	–9,997
Tunisia	–142,495	–96,523	–97,065	–72,068	85,582	48,999	140,341	–39,804	–143,045	–40,641	–150,000	–20,000

Source: Data from the World Bank: World Development Indicators

Increasingly over the past 50 years, the governments of the Maghreb countries have seen emigration as a solution to revive their economies and mitigate unemployment, and to improve the living conditions of the population. However, currently only Tunisia and Morocco are benefitting from the remittance flows linked to international migration. In fact, the level of money transfers from Europe to Algeria, Libya and Mauritania remain relatively low: remittances for Algeria contribute 1.22 per cent of total GDP; Libya 0.03 per cent and Mauritania 0.42 per cent of total GDP. On the other hand, in Tunisia and especially in Morocco, the level of remittances is relatively high: 4.17 per cent of GDP in Tunisia and 6.21 per cent in Morocco.

Figure 6.9: Personal remittances received (% of GDP)

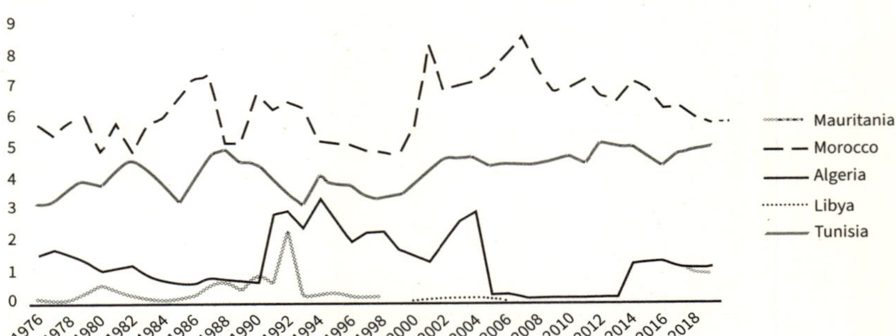

Source: Data from the World Bank: World Development Indicators

Indeed, the remittance levels have fluctuated over time, reflecting not only the effect of national and international economic and political conditions, but also the shifts in the nature and forms of migration. For example, remittance levels in Algeria follow the trend in the number of asylum seekers. Thus, we should mention that France was the main destination of these asylum seekers, especially during the 1990s, but currently these migrants are moving to the Netherlands, Germany, Canada and other countries (Collyer, 2005). As these migrants enter the host country, they try to help their families left behind. Those who obtain a legal residence status generally start the procedures to reunite their family, which explains the decrease in the level of remittances.

Figure 6.10: Inflows of asylum seekers

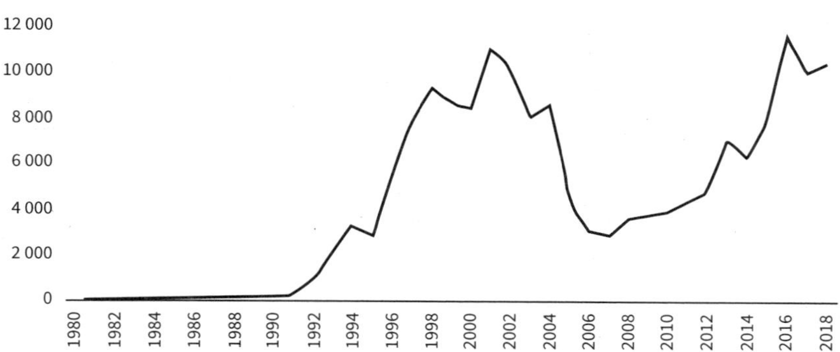

Source: Data from the World Bank: World Development Indicators

Thus, with the improvement of the status of women and their integration into the labour market, and especially because of their higher education status and their diverse specialisations, the number of job seekers has increased, while the skilled job market has remained stagnant. In turn, a lack of employment opportunities at home has led to a significant increase in the number of potential migrants, as indicated by the high number of young people expressing the desire to emigrate (Hammouda, 2008; Bouchoucha et al., 2010) and, consequently, an increase in emigration flows. The high cost of migration and the restrictive policies and regulations adopted by the European countries, including the daunting complexity of visa regulations, are some of the principal factors that limited migration flows. Thus, for many, especially young men, emigration has become an unattainable dream. This lack of access to legal options pushes those who intend to leave into irregular migration. As research on Tunisia has demonstrated (Bouchoucha, 2013), most migrants originate from the most developed regions or affluent families, or from areas with easy access to their migration networks.

Bouchoucha (2013) also notes that internal migration is very prevalent in Tunisia, mainly because of the lack of job opportunities, especially for high-skilled young people, and the difficult economic conditions in western Tunisia, which pushes people to migrate to the east, especially to Tunis, the capital. For some, this internal migration could be a step towards international migration. It is important to emphasise that individual characteristics are not sufficient to explain the decision-making processes in terms of international migration (Bouchoucha, 2013). Indeed, studies in both developed and developing countries have shown that the economic status of the region plays an important role in explaining both internal and international migration. A lack of employment opportunities, due to weak economic structures and a large working population, is one of the main causes of migration (Massey 1994; Arango, 2000; Zoltnik, 2003). Inadequate health conditions, education difficulties and low living standards also push people to leave for a more favourable environment for family life. Hence, it is important to study the socio-economic context in which international migration has developed to understand the link between development and migration, which is important for designing effective migration policies in both the Maghreb and Europe.

Migration policies in the Maghreb

The governments of the Maghreb countries are fully aware of the positive effect of emigration on the development of their respective countries and especially on mitigating the unemployment challenges discussed earlier. Despite this positive view on emigration, Maghrebi states have generally failed to develop adequate measures to strengthen the link between migrants and their countries of origin. In addition, they have failed to mobilise the intellectual and financial capacities of the diaspora to contribute to the economic and socio-cultural development of their countries. There are several factors that hamper migrants, reintegration into their countries of origin. Besides the problems of unemployment and low wages in destination countries, factors that impede migrants' investment in their country of origin include high competition from the local population and the red tape (Bouchoucha et al., 2010; 2012).

A study of the Tunisian diaspora and migrant participation in the development of their country of origin noted that the Tunisian state provides support for migrants to strength their link with Tunisia. It had also introduced a welcome home programme and measures to facilitate migrant reintegration on their return (Bouchoucha et al., 2012). Despite these efforts, Tunisians abroad are still reluctant to invest in their country of origin because there are no clear economic and financial incentives for them to do so. On the contrary, they encounter many difficulties (such as a lack of information, a poor legal framework, an absence of strong ties with the home country, and bureaucratic bottlenecks), which accounts for their low involvement in the state's development initiative. In short, although migration is perceived as an important solution to the economic and social problems of the country, there are no clear and efficient policies to harness the contribution of the diaspora.

Thus, with the oil crisis at the beginning of the 1970s, the demand for foreign labour decreased in European countries and new restrictive migration policies were developed; they closed their borders and started to encourage family reunification. They adopted various measures to reduce the number of immigrants: they introduced visa restrictions, developed major border security measures, and signed readmission agreements for illegal and clandestine migrants with neighbourhood countries of origin or transit. European countries thus imposed sanctions based on their relationships with particular Maghreb countries.

European countries defined their immigration policies without considering the consequences of these on the economies of the sending countries. As a result of the increase in the number of irregular migrants from Africa to Europe, European governments threatened to impose sanctions on 'erring' Maghreb countries. Since the end of the 2000s, they have tried to improve the level of cooperation with the partner countries in the 'readmission of rejected asylum seekers or irregular migrants by offering the prospect of visa facilitation', and have used various negative sanctions, such as the 'reduction of development cooperation', 'visa restrictions', and 'sanctions in other policy areas' (Kipp et al., 2020). In fact, the EU 'wants to use all policy areas for its migration policy objectives' (Kipp et al., 2020: 2–3). However, the system of readmission has not been warmly welcomed by the North African countries, particularly Morocco and Tunisia. Thus, today, many European actors believe that the Maghreb countries have failed to protect their borders. Recently, Italy threatened to cancel all its development assistance to Tunisia (Buzzi, 2020),[4] thus forcing the Tunisian government to cooperate in carrying out the expulsion of more than 4,000 migrants from Italy to Tunisia; they had landed in Italy in July and had been quarantined because of COVID-19.[5]

It should be noted that irregular and clandestine migrations were and continue to be subjects of discussion and negotiation between European and Maghreb countries, in particular, Morocco and Libya. In fact, the EU had tried to exert increasing pressure on Maghreb countries to sign readmission agreements, which became 'the prerequisite for negotiations' with the EU to obtain 'development money'. The readmission agreements also become 'an effective negotiating tool with donors to obtain funds to manage the "migration risks"' (Wa Kabwe-Segatti, 2009: 147). The case of Morocco and especially Libya are perfect examples of the capacity of African countries to negotiate and illustrate the pressure they can exert on European countries. Following President Gaddafi's agreement to no longer condone irregular migration, Libya was able to obtain significant funding to manage its borders, build detention centres for irregular immigrants, and train its staff (Kalush, 2020). Indeed, it seems that the EU is much more concerned with border management than development, democratic governance and human rights. Its agreement with the Gaddafi regime is a good illustration of this political orientation (Wa Kabwe-Segatti, 2009). However, it seems that EU migration policies are out of step with their demographic and economic realities, which clearly show a growing need for foreign labour. Thus, regularisation operations, as well as policies to encourage high-skill migration, clearly show this dichotomy between economic reality and migration policies (Charef, 2006).

Overall, European countries have continued to invest in similar measures and policies, despite their failure and the negative effects on the socio-economic stability of origin countries. Indeed, through these measures, the EU countries aim to keep migrants at home, reduce the number of immigrants, and develop selective migration. But, as El-Sayed Hassan has argued, 'these new regulations stimulated the illegal migration. We can look to the illegal migration as a reaction of closing doors in front of North African immigrants' (Hassan, 2009: 4), and adding another complex problem to manage.

European policies have been designed without alternative options for legal migration, or measures to strengthen the sustainable development of these countries, including measures to reduce the pressure on domestic employment markets, which have been a central driver of migration, and irregular migration in particular. Thus, during the 2015/16 'refugee crisis' in Europe, the EU broadened its political approach to border management by trying to involve the entire African region by strengthening its links with the African Union (AU). However, this orientation was not appreciated by North African countries (De Groof and Bossuyt, 2019). Although they have expressed interest in border management, the 'North African countries are resistant to managing migration on behalf of the EU and criticise the EU's lack of policy coherence' (De Groof et al., 2019: 20), and they think that the EU should note that the region comprises not only countries of origin, but also countries of transit, and flagged the high number of migrants crossing their borders to reach Europe.

Thus, by trying to externalise border management, the EU countries tied development aid to migration management, without making any concerted efforts to help alleviate the problem of unemployment and the economic and social difficulties experienced by these countries of origin. Indeed, the new EU's migration politics and measures (focusing on the security aspects and on border protection, imposing sanctions, and reducing development aid to African countries) have, undoubtedly, had a negative effect on the evolution of the crises in these countries. These restrictive policies have also had a negative effect on the standard of living in African countries, since many families depend on remittances.

Figure 6.11 presents the net official development assistance received by the Maghreb countries. Note the fluctuating tendency and the significant differences between countries, which reflect its non-stability and the negotiation level and the collaboration of each country. In fact, Morocco's geographical location and the importance of its migrant population (Morocco has more than 3 million emigrants in Europe, which represents nearly half of the Maghreb population abroad) has translated into increased negotiating power, which has allowed the Moroccans to defend their interests effectively and benefit from their collaboration with the EU on the issue of migration, border management and aid disbursement. Also, the level of development assistance to all the Maghreb countries, except Morocco, was higher between 1960 and 1970 than in recent decades, although the region's economic difficulties have increased considerably. The trend for Tunisia shows a slight increase after the 2012 revolution, but this increase is not very significant, especially considering the challenges facing the country during this difficult transitional phase.

The Maghreb countries are also among those that benefitted from the European Union Emergency Trust Fund for Africa (EUTF). They obtained a total of €712,317,427, which represents 15.3 per cent of the total funding given to African countries. Apart from Morocco, Libya benefitted much more than the other countries. Indeed, Algeria did not obtain any funding under this programme, while Tunisia received funding of only €12,800,000 for one project. Morocco, on the other hand, was able to benefit from funding of €182,943,500 for seven projects, while Libya was able to obtain about €309,923,927 for 13 projects. Almost all of this funding was intended 'to improve migration management', except for Mauritania, which received funding of €30,000,000 for two projects, €25,000,000 of which was intended for 'greater economic and employment opportunities'. Morocco also got €8,000,000 for improving governance and conflict prevention. This confirms the absence of policies on development and job creation in the EU's political perspectives towards the Maghreb countries.

Figure 6.11: Net official development assistance received (constant 2015 US$)

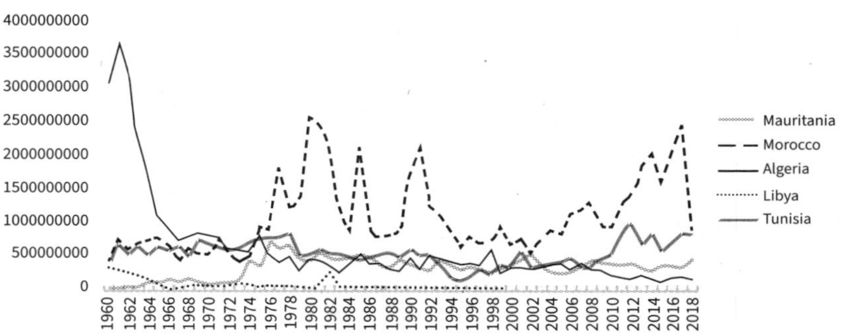

Source: Data from the World Bank: World Development Indicators

Conclusion

Sustained economic development across the Maghreb region has not eliminated the problem of unemployment, which has remained high since the 1960s. This has been one of the failures of the region's economic policies. Consequently, high unemployment, especially among university graduates, accounts for a deterioration in the standard of living. This chapter has argued that unemployment among skilled workers has been one of the main causes of the migration flows, particularly towards Europe, since the independence era. This has led to the establishment of irregular migration routes – through the Mediterranean Sea – as European immigration policies have become increasingly restrictive. Considering these realities, the Maghreb countries have generally failed to develop clear migration policies that would have allowed them to fully exploit the socio-economic and financial benefits of Maghreb/EU migration.

Since the beginning of the 1980s, the EU member states have developed many policies and procedures aimed at border closure to reduce the number of new immigrants, integrating old immigrants, and regularising the status of irregular immigrants. To a significant extent, these measures have been counterproductive insofar as the closure of borders, without providing alternative livelihood options, has led to the expansion of irregular migration from the Maghreb region. This chapter highlights the procedures and policies adopted by the EU in the aftermath of the '2015/16 refugee crisis', which were developed without substantial measures to encourage people from the Maghreb to stay in their home countries. Furthermore, Europe failed to develop alternative migration options, which is particularly problematic in a context where migration is perceived by origin countries as a viable solution to mitigate unemployment and poverty.

The ineffectiveness of the EU attempts to halt irregular migration is mainly a result of policies being formulated without taking account of the context in which these migration flows have developed. In light of the specific economic and social problems in the Maghreb context, border closures may not be the solution to reducing irregular migration flows. There is a need to find more sustainable and effective alternatives. The overall migration governance approach has to be beneficial for both the EU and the Maghreb countries. Europe also needs to be very supportive of the efforts of the Maghreb countries of origin to overcome their current crises, which include the armed conflict in Libya, the pressure on domestic labour markets, and other socio-economic challenges facing most of the countries in the region. It is also important to think about measures that promote the sustainable development of domestic economies, including concerted investments to promote job creation, and circular migration, which could be a better alternative for both European and Maghreb states. In fact, this would make it possible to respond to specific demands in the European labour market while reducing the pressures on the Maghreb labour markets. Overall, measures must be developed to encourage emigrants to participate in the development of their home countries, especially by enhancing the standard of living of poor households, and promoting investment and job creation through their remittances.

Notes

1   Author's translation from: 'migrants subsahariens qui circulent dans cette région en vue de rejoindre l'Europe, le Maghreb développe aussi ses propres

migrations, intérieures (migration nationale interne à chaque pays et migration entre pays du Maghreb) et internationales (dont l'essentiel des flux se focalisent sur l'Union Européenne), devenant en même temps un espace transnational de départ, circulation, retour, transit et installation' (Alioua, 2007: 40).

2 For more information, see Monia (2009).

3 For more information, see World Bank (2016).

4 https://www.corriere.it/politica/20_luglio_31/di-maio-dobbiamo-distruggere-barconi-un-emergenza-nazionale-b4d22296-d297-11ea-9ae0-73704986785b.shtml

5 https://www.seneweb.com/news/International/en-italie-des-migrants-tunisiens-menaces_n_326530.html

References

Alioua, M. 2007. 'Nouveaux et anciens espaces de circulation internationale au Maroc', *Revue des mondes musulmans et de la Méditerranée*, pp. 119–20. DOI: https://doi.org/10.4000/remmm.4113 (accessed 23 June 2021).

Arango, J. 2000. 'Explaining migration: A critical view', *International Social Journal*, 52(165): 283–96.

Kabwe-Segatti, Wa, A. 2009. 'Dimension extérieure de la politique d'immigration de l'Union européenne', *Hommes et migrations*, 1279: 140–53. Online at: http://journals.openedition.org/hommesmigrations/342 (accessed 23 June 2021).

Boubakri, H. 2010. 'Migration, marché du travail et développement en Tunisie'. In S. Tobin (ed.) *Migration, Labour Market and Development in North and West Africa Project*. Geneva: International Institute for Labour Studies/ ILO. Online at: http://www.ilo.org/public/french/bureau/inst/download/tunisie.pdf (accessed 23 June 2021).

Bouchoucha I. 2018. 'The migration of women in Tunisia: Between tradition and modernity', in K. Hiralal and Z. Jinnah (eds). *Gender and Mobility in Africa*. London: Palgrave Macmillan.

Bouchoucha, I. 2013. 'Genre, emploi et migrations en Tunisie. Sous la direction de Maria Eugenia Casio-Zavala'. Thèse de doctorat en démographie, Université de Paris-Ouest, Nanterre La Défense, p. 402.

Bouchoucha, I., Fourati, H. and Zekri, L. 2012. *Quels liens les Tunisiens résidant en Europe gardent-ils avec le pays d'origine?* OIM-Tunis (publié en trois langues: arabe, français et anglais). Online at: http://tunisia.iom.int/sites/default/files/resources/files/Etude%20OIM%20TUDO%20-%20participation%20 des%20Tunisiens%202012.pdf (accessed 23 June 2021).

Bouchoucha, I., Pieroni, L. and Lanari, D. 2010. *Second Migration in the Maghreb.* Paris: Lundi de l'INED.

Buzzi, E. 2020. 'Di Maio: "We have to destroy the boats, it's a national emergency"'. Online at: https://www.corriere.it/politica/20_luglio_31/di-maio-dobbiamo-distruggere-barconi-un-emergenza-nazionale-b4d22296-d297-11ea-9ae0-73704986785b.shtml (accessed 23 July 2021).

Charef, M. 2009. *Le Maghreb central face à ses migrations: le cas du Maroc. Regards sur les migrations tunisiennes.* Agadir (Maroc): Editions Sudcontact, pp. 307–38.

Charef, M. 2006. Jeux et enjeux des Migrations internationales dans le Développement au. Maroc. ORMES/MIGRINTER Université Ibn Zohr Agadir Maroc.

Collyer, M. 2005. 'When do social networks fail to explain migration? Accounting for the movement of Algerian asylum-seekers to the UK', *Journal of Ethnic and Migration Studies*, 31(4): 699–718.

De Groof, E. and Bossuyt, J. 2019. 'Mixed messages from Europe and Africa stand in the way of an intercontinental deal. North Africa's double pursuit – Part 1'. ECDPM paper, 28 February.

De Groof, E., Bossuyt, J., Abderrahim, T. and Djinnit, D. 2019. 'Looking North and moving South: Little enthusiasm for a continent-to-continent approach. North Africa's double pursuit – Part 1'. 28 January 2019.

Diarra, S. 2003. Migrations et Pauvreté au Mali. Communication présentée au séminaire, 'Questions de population au Mali: des enjeux internationaux aux perspectives locales', Bamako, 6–7 janvier.

Haffad, T. 2007. 'Migration et développement au Maghreb'. Communication présentée au 3ème colloque international: La nouvelle politique européenne de voisinage. Université de Tunis El Manar, FSEG, Hammamet, 1–2 juin. Online at: http://www.ps2d.net/media/tahar_haffad.pdf (accessed 25 July 2021).

Hammouda, N. 2008. *Le Désir de migration chez les jeunes Algériens: analyse micro-économétrique.* Report number: CARIM-AS 2008/42, Affiliation: CARIM RSCAS UEI.

Hassan, K.E. 2009. 'Levels and trends of international migration in North Africa'. A paper submitted to the XXVI International Population Conference. Online at: https://www.academia.edu/8279848/Levels_and_Trends_of_International_Migration_in_North_Africa (accessed 21 July 2021).

International Organization for Migration (IOM). 2019. The *World Migration Report 2020*, McAuliffe, M. and B. Khadria (eds). Geneva. IOM. Online at:

DOI: https://doi.org/10.1787/eco_surveys-usa-2018-en (accessed 23 June 2021).

Kalush, R. 2020. 'Migration beyond the crisis: Libyan policy and practice', in: A. Abusedra, S. Toperich and N. Kirkesh (eds). *Unheard Voices of the Next Generation: Emergent leaders in Libya.* Washington, DC: Brookings Institution Press.

Kipp, David, Nadine Knapp, and Amrei Meier (2020) "Negative Sanctions and the EU's External Migration Policy", SWP Comment; pp. 1-4. https://www.swp-berlin.org/publications/products/comments/2020C34_NegativeSanctions.pdf.

Lee, E. 1966. 'A theory of migration', *Demography*, 3(1): 47–57. Online at: http://www.jstor.org/stable/2060063 (accessed 22 July 2021).

Manchon. P-Y. 2016. 'L'union Européenne et la crise des réfugiés (2015–2016)'. Online at: https://www.academia.edu/30246548/LUnion_Europ%C3%A9enne_et_la_crise_des_r%C3%A9fugi%C3%A9s_2015_2016_ (accessed 23 June 2021).

Massey, D. 1994. 'The social and economic origins of immigration'. This article is reprinted with permission from the Bulletin of the Inter-American Parliamentary Group on Population and Development, 920 Broadway, NY 10010. Online at: http://www.thesocialcontract.com/pdf/four-three/massey.pdf (accessed 23 June 2021).

Monia, B. 2009. 'La répression des migrations clandestines en Tunisie', in Dans: A. Bensaâd (ed.). *Le Maghreb à l'épreuve des migrations subsahariennes: Immigration sur émigration.* Paris: Karthala, pp. 267–78. Available at: https://doi.org/10.3917/kart.bensa.2009.01.0267 (accessed 23 June 2021).

Musette, M.S., Alouane, Y., Khachani, M. and Labdelaoui, H. 2006. 'Summary report on migration and development in Central Maghreb'. Online at: https://www.ilo.org/wcmsp5/groups/public/---ed_protect/---protrav/---migrant/documents/publication/wcms_201461.pdf (accessed 23 June 2021).

Mzali, H. 1997. 'Marché du travail, migrations internes et internationales en Tunisie', *Revue Région et Développement*, N° 6-1997. Online at: http://region-developpement.univ-tln.fr/en/pdf/R6/Mzali.pdf (accessed 23 June 2021).

Rahali M. 2017. 'État et société au Maghreb, le poids de l'Histoire et la nécessité des réformes politiques, une dialectique inachevée', *État et société au Maghreb, le poids de l'Histoire*, 12(13): 46–59.

Rodney, W. 1973. *How Europe Underdeveloped Africa.* London: Bogle-L'Ouverture Publications, and Dar-Es-Salaam: Tanzanian Publishing House. Transcript from 6th edition, 1983.

The World Bank. 2016. 'Poverty has fallen in the Maghreb, but inequality persists', 16 October. Online at: https://www.worldbank.org/en/news/feature/2016/10/17/poverty-has-fallen-in-the-maghreb-but-inequality-persists (accessed 23 June 2021).

United Nations. 2019. 'International Migrant Stock 2019: Documentation'. Online at: https://www.un.org/en/development/desa/population/migration/data/estimates2/docs/MigrationStockDocumentation_2019.pdf (accessed 23 June 2021).

United Nations Development Programme (UNDP). 2019. *UNDP Scaling Fences: Voices of irregular African migrants to Europe*. Online at: https://www.ng.undp.org/content/nigeria/en/home/library/mdg/undp-scaling-fences---voices-of-irregular-african-migrants-to-eu.html (accessed 23 June 2021).

Zlotnik, H. (2003). 'Théories sur les migrations internationales', in G. Cazalli and J. Vallin (eds). *Démographie: analyses et synthèse IV: les déterminants de la migration*. Paris: Ed Ined, pp. 55–78.

Zohry, A. 2006. *Egyptian Youth and the European Eldorado: Journeys of hope and despair*. DIIS Working Paper No. 18. Copenhagen: Danish Institute for International Studies (DIIS).

Chapter 7

Migration in the Horn of Africa and the European Union

Linda Adhiambo Oucho

Introduction

The Horn of Africa (HoA) is a diverse region with a long history of mixed migration patterns. The countries in the region are interconnected by several migration corridors: to the east, heading to the Gulf States via Yemen; to the north, heading to Europe via North Africa, and to the south, with migrants bound for southern Africa. While there are a multitude of reasons why people migrate to these different destinations – most of them economically motivated – the region has been best known for the scale of internal and international displacement. Regional Economic Communities (RECs), and especially the Intergovernmental Authority on Development (IGAD), have been instrumental in coordinating migration responses adapted to the realities within and between the member states. The IGAD, headquartered in Djibouti, comprises eight countries from the Horn of Africa, the African Great Lakes, and the Nile Valley. These efforts have led to the development of frameworks, protocols and conventions to address the migration flows to, from and within their respective countries.

The European Union (EU) and other international organisations have collaborated with IGAD and its member states by providing the support needed to strengthen migration governance in the region. This includes allocating resources and building capacities of the personnel handling asylum seekers and refugees, at the same time buttressing facilities operational at the border. Countries in the HoA region have, therefore, established working relationships with these international organisations to address the negative impacts of migration, while harnessing the positive impacts that contribute to the development of their citizens. The chapter elucidates the migration realities in the region: how member states, especially Kenya, Uganda, Ethiopia, Somalia and Eritrea, have been responding to the mixed migration flows; it also expounds on the role and impact that EU support has had on strengthening migration governance and management in the region. Uganda and Kenya are included in this chapter as they are integral to understanding mobility in the Horn of Africa as transit and destination countries to neighbouring states. Furthermore, they are members of the IGAD, which has designed migration-related frameworks and guidelines, which include them. Thus, it examines HoA/EU migration and proffers sustainable policy options for its management.

This chapter starts with a general overview, followed by a discussion of the different HoA migration corridors: northern, eastern and southern corridors. It then engages the realities of mixed migration in the region, followed by the policy responses to this. Thereafter it presents the responses of the IGAD to migration, followed by the EU's engagement with the Horn of Africa on migration issues, before concluding.

The Horn of Africa migration corridors

The Horn of Africa is the focal point of several migration corridors, which migrants use to access destination countries. Some may be former trade routes through which migrant smuggling and human trafficking took place, while others are formalised routes where the necessary legal documents give people access and safe passage to and/or through a country. Within the Horn of Africa, there are three primary migration corridors:

1.   The *northern* corridor to Europe via North Africa;

2.   The *eastern* corridor to the Middle East via Djibouti and Somalia; and

3.   The *southern* corridor to South Africa via Kenya, Malawi, Zimbabwe, Mozambique and Zambia.

Map 7.1. presents the routes in and out of the Horn of Africa.

Map 7.1: Migration corridors from the Horn of Africa

Source: African Center for Strategic Studies (2019)

The northern and eastern corridors were historically trade routes, which have subsequently evolved into irregular pathways towards migration destinations in Africa and beyond. Determining the difference between a victim of human trafficking and a voluntary migrant is often a challenge as there is evidence that some people end up being trafficked in the process of soliciting services from a smuggler, who often wears several hats (United Nations Office on Drugs and Crime, 2018a: 31). According to the International Organization for Migration (2018), the majority of movements take place within the HoA region, with 52.41 per cent moving to neighbouring countries, while the eastern corridor has reported the highest movement (with 37.76 per cent) of those moving to the Gulf Cooperation Council (GCC) states,[1] as outlined in Table 7.1.

Table 7.1: Movements by migration corridors

Route	Movements	Percentage
Horn of Africa (intra-regional)	437,432	52.41%
Eastern route	315,172	37.76%
Southern route	47,545	5.70%
Northern route	32,824	3.93%
Other routes	1,692	0.20%

Source: International Organization for Migration (2018)

Both regular and irregular migration patterns occur within these routes. In terms of irregular migration, the primary countries that are sources of migrant smuggling are Somalia, Djibouti, Ethiopia and Eritrea with varied destinations in the north, east and south, as illustrated in Table 7.2.

Table 7.2: Source, transit and destination countries for migrant smuggling

Source country	Transit countries/ territories	Destination countries
Somalia	Djibouti, Kenya, Malawi, Mozambique and United Republic of Tanzania	Europe, Kenya, South Africa and Yemen
Djibouti		Yemen
Ethiopia	Djibouti, Kenya, Libya, Malawi, Mozambique, Puntland, Somalia, Somaliland. Sudan, United Republic of Tanzania, Yemen, Zambia and Zimbabwe	Europe, Lebanon, Saudi Arabia, South Africa and United Arab Emirates
Eritrea	Libya, Kenya and Sudan	Europe, Egypt, Israel and Kenya

Source: Regional Mixed Migration Secretariat (2013)

The flows of HoA migrants to the different regions has led to a diversification of livelihoods, especially for fishermen. They often lease their boats or operate as part of the value chain in smuggling activities (Majidi and Oucho,

2016: 62). Addressing the challenges brought about by the clandestine and dynamic nature of migrant smuggling and human trafficking is a key agenda among governments in the Horn of Africa and is of interest to the EU, which will be discussed later.

Those adopting more regular pathways to migration are more likely to engage the services of a recruitment agency, or other migration brokers that facilitate the processes for them, especially for those countries with a memorandum of understanding to provide employment. This is the case with governments in the Gulf States, which offer employment to nationals from countries such as Ethiopia, Somalia, Kenya and Uganda.

Eastern migration corridor

The unstable political conditions in the Horn of Africa, and especially in Somalia, have driven many migrants to seek asylum in neighbouring countries such as Ethiopia, Kenya and Uganda, with some using refugee camps as transit stations en route to Europe via North Africa. The eastern corridor is the window to the Middle East as migrants, mostly Ethiopian (80 per cent), travel through Somalia, Somaliland and Djibouti to transit through Yemen via the Red Sea. This is a dangerous route given the current instability in Yemen. Migrants tend to be mostly male, single and with little education (United Nations Office on Drugs and Crime, 2018: 76). The solicitation of the services of smugglers is usually initiated through contacts from the country of origin, and usually through a recommendation from a migrant or family member that may have used a similar path (Tinti, 2017).

The strategies of smugglers have changed in recent years, for example, in the increased use of social media platforms to advertise their services, giving the potential migrant more agency in the decision to migrate, based on the assessment of the information provided. Migrants from Ethiopia travel on foot through Wajale border post in Somaliland and proceed to Bosaso in Puntland – an arid region in north-east Somalia. From Bosaso, they usually travel by boat to Yemen. Whereas migrants smuggled through Djibouti from Ethiopia travel through the transit hubs – Obock and Tadjourah – and then move onto Yemen. Loyada border post in Djibouti has remained a key entry point for Somali migrants smuggled through Djibouti on to one of its towns, Tadjourah. However, over the years, Loyada has become dormant as Somali migrants cross directly to Yemen from Somalia. The flow through the eastern route declined around 2017 because of the growing insecurity in Yemen and the Saudi Arabian response to irregular migrants.

Northern migration corridor

Typically, migrants from the Horn of Africa, who dominate migration patterns to North Africa and to Middle East via Yemen, are of Somali and Eritrean origin. As mentioned earlier, there are a number of drivers of migration associated with political and economic security in the countries of origin. HoA nationals often take pathways already known to them or their family members. However, these routes have become more dangerous, which has led to violation of human rights of migrants along the northern migration corridor, such as sexual and physical abuses of men and women, and in some cases fatalities (Davy, 2017). The northern corridor has received global attention because of the concerns raised in the destination countries in Europe. According to a report by the Sahan Foundation and the IGAD Security Sector Program (2016), Ethiopians, Eritreans, and Somalis have used Ethiopia as a primary crossroads for migration out of the region. Those taking the northern route travel via Sudan and Libya, and use the refugee camps as transit points, where they connect with smugglers destined for North Africa.

Eritrean migrants, however, face the risk of being trafficked and ransomed to their family members in Eritrea or in the destination countries. Those migrants who opt to reach Europe via irregular routes are often diverted, owing to the complexity of locating the correct routes. Given that many do not know the terrain, they base their trust on the smuggler. According to a joint study by the School of Oriental and African Studies (SOAS), the Strategic Initiative for Women in the Horn of Africa (SIHA) Network, and the International Refugee Rights Initiative, Italy's push-back against irregular migrants, which returned irregular migrants to Libya, led to the utilisation of the Sinai trafficking routes where, it is estimated, 25,000–35,000 migrants, who were kidnapped in Sudan between 2009 and 2013, have been victims of trafficking in Sinai (SOAS, SIHA Network and IRRI, 2017). It is estimated that over US$600 million was paid for ransom cases between 2009 and 2013 (Belloni, 2019).

Migrants face a particular risk of being trafficked and/or ransomed between Sudan and Libya, because the payments for the journey are made in phases as there are different actors involved along the migration corridor, which include the recruiters at the country of origin, the smuggler who organises the trip, and the transporters, all at varied prices (UN Office on Drugs and Crime, 2010). Furthermore, migrants have no guarantee of reaching the final or chosen destinations without facing other risks (physical or otherwise). This route offers no guarantees of safe passage, and is plagued by corrupt practices and human rights abuses. In light of these dangers, the few Sudanese migrants destined for Europe often opt to travel via Egypt to access transport via Alexandria (Sahan Foundation and IGAD Security Sector Program, 2016: 10).

The conditions for irregular migrants in Libya have been documented by international media, such as Cable Network News (CNN) and Al Jazeera, and deemed to be modern slavery. The destabilisation of Libya has affected mobility to and through the country, which has seen a rise in criminal activities since 2012, raising the insecurity experienced by migrants in the country, whether they are regular or irregular. Some migrants have been detained indefinitely in deplorable and crowded condition in Libya. Stemming the flow of migrants from this region required the joint efforts of African countries with support from international organisations, including the EU. This partnership is discussed further in the subsequent section.

Southern migration corridor

The southern corridor has received less attention than those leading eastwards and northwards. However, media reports and ongoing studies have provided insights into the migration southwards. Migrants are often destined for South Africa, where the perceived economic opportunities drive them to adopt different means to access the country. Most migrants from the Horn of Africa using the southern corridor are Somalis and Ethiopians, and the mode of transport and route determines the cost of their travel (Majidi and Oucho, 2016). This is outlined in Table 7.3. These fees are not fixed as they are determined by the risks and the immigration conditions put in place in transit and the destination countries.

Table 7.3: Smuggling fees by destination/route

Destination/Route	Mode of transport	Nationality	Fees (US$)
Kakuma/Dadaab Camp Kenya → South Africa	Road	Somalis	3,000
Ethiopia → Zambia → South Africa	Road	Ethiopians Somalis	4,000–5,000
Ethiopia/Somalia → Malawi → South Africa	Road	Ethiopians Somalis	4,218
Ethiopia → Kenya/Tanzania → Malawi	Road	Ethiopians	850

Source: Majidi and Oucho (2016)

Not all migrants bound for countries in southern Africa travel by land. Migrants use sea routes via Somalia – from Kismayo and Mogadishu – to unregulated ports in Mombasa, Kilifi and Lamu in Kenya, where other boats may carry passengers to Mozambique, from where they may proceed to South Africa by land (Majidi and Oucho, 2016: 60). A small proportion of migrants use the southern route to access pathways to Latin America (Sahan Foundation and IGAD Security Sector Program, 2016). The lack of attention paid to migrant smuggling to southern Africa has allowed certain activities to go unchecked at border points, and security systems require strengthening to curb the migration to the southern region.

Furthermore, the region lacks a formal governmental response strategy to address irregular movement. As the region's primary destination country, South Africa has enacted stringent laws and regulations on migration and border management, as well as measures relating to asylum seekers and refugees, including the recent changes made to the Refugee Amendment Act at the end of 2019. This limits the rights of refugees and asylum seekers. However, this has not reduced the flow of migrants to the region as some of the transit countries have weak migration management and governance systems, which allow for continued irregular migration and settlement. Although countries such as Tanzania and Malawi have arrested irregular migrants travelling by road using large containers, they have yet to come up with a coherent strategy to address irregular migration to and through their respective countries (IOM, 2015). It is, therefore, important for countries in the region, through the Southern African Development Community

(SADC), to develop a regional response to migration management, especially when addressing the challenges associated with irregular migration.

Realities of mixed migration in the Horn of Africa

According to the Mixed Migration Centre (MMC), mixed migration refers to the 'cross border movements of people, including refugees fleeing persecution and conflict, victims of trafficking and people seeking better lives and opportunities' (MMC, 2020). The literature on migration patterns within the Horn of Africa depicts it as an area rife with conflict, with large groups of people displaced internally and within the region. As noted, there is evidence of both regular and irregular forms of migration within the HoA region. Regular forms of migration are often associated with labour migrants moving within a country or to a neighbouring country, using legal and safe pathways. Irregular migration patterns, on the other hand, are associated with individuals in search of economic opportunities in destinations where they have families. However, they lack the documentation and the resources to adopt safe and legal pathways to migrate and stay in the identified destinations. The International Organization for Migration's (IOM's) Flow Monitoring Report in 2018 suggests that 66.4 per cent of HoA migrants are more likely to move within the region compared to 28.8 per cent moving out of the region, and only 4.9 per cent migrating internally (IOM, 2018).

Internal displacement is a key concern for many HoA countries as the persistent conflict in South Sudan and the protracted insecurity in Somalia since 1991 has led to the internal displacement of about 1,352,000 in South Sudan, and over 2,648,000 in Somalia because of conflict and natural disasters by the end of 2019. Recent data by the IOM, monitoring displacement in the Horn of Africa, showed that the drivers of migration range from access to services (for example, health and social services), economic factors (such as employment), and family reunification, to war/conflict and natural disaster, and persecution. Data collected in December 2018 from Ethiopia, Somalia, and Djibouti highlighted the push and pull factors of migration from these countries (see Figure 7.1). Natural disasters and family reunion were identified as the overall drivers across the three major migration corridors. Surprisingly, economic factors were not part of the top three drivers, which may be reflective of the conditions in the countries in the region. Countries such as South Sudan, Ethiopia and Somalia have recorded high numbers of displaced people. Furthermore, natural disasters, ranging from droughts to floods, have pushed people to migrate internally in the respective three countries. Indeed, those forced to migrate due to war/conflict are more likely to move to neighbouring countries in search of refuge.

Figure 7.1: Drivers of migration in the Horn of Africa

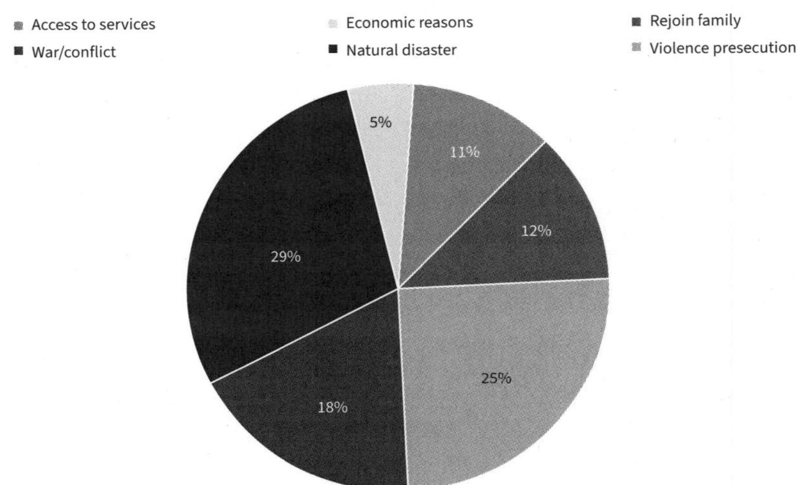

Source: International Organization for Migration (2018)[2]

However, a closer look at the specific drivers by migration corridor shows that economic reasons are the primary driver of migration, as illustrated in Figure 7.2. As shown, economic factors in each corridor are the main drivers of migration in the region. Of all the drivers of migration in the Horn of Africa, economic reasons remain the most important at 29 per cent, followed by family reunion, which scored 28 per cent.

Those displaced within the region often seek asylum in neighbouring countries, such as South Sudanese in Uganda, and Somalis in Kenya. These countries, which have experienced relative economic and political stability, have become safe havens for many of the displaced populations from the Horn of Africa. They also serve as migration corridors to other parts of Africa, especially for Ethiopian and Somali migrants bound for South Africa. According to the United Nations Humanitarian Commission for Refugees (UNHCR) data of 30 April 2020, Uganda hosts the largest asylum seeker and refugee population at 1,423,742, mostly from South Sudan (880,367), while Ethiopia hosts 761,819 displaced people. Kenya's refugee and asylum-seeker numbers dropped from 593,881 in 2016 to 494,649 in April 2020 (IOM, 2018).

Figure 7.2: Drivers of migration in the Horn of Africa, calculated by migration corridor

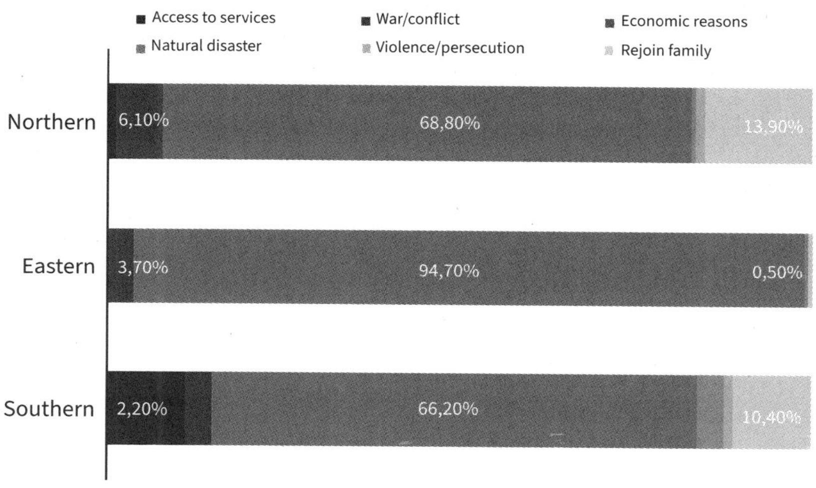

Source: International Organization for Migration (2018)

The Horn of Africa is also known for being a source of some of the irregular migration to Europe, including migrant smuggling and human trafficking. Irregular migration is a key concern for member states in the Horn of Africa. Most of the migrants that take up irregular pathways are from Somalia, Eritrea and Ethiopia, travelling through countries such as Djibouti, Sudan, Kenya and Somalia. These latter countries are primary transit countries for migrants destined for Europe via North Africa; the Middle East via Djibouti and Somalia; and southern Africa via Kenya. The MMC[3] has documented irregular migration in the Horn of Africa, providing insights into the changing nature of this type of migration, which is continuing at significant rates, despite the creation of laws and policies to monitor and curb this migration.

Migration from Eritrea is generally linked to the political, economic, and social conditions that exist in the country. It has experienced emigration flows since the 1960s due to poverty, war and human rights violations, which has resulted in a 30-year-long liberation struggle in the country. Most migrants fled within the region, using irregular pathways to countries such as Sudan, while others continued to the Middle East, the United States and Europe. Even though independence was achieved in 1991, large numbers of Eritreans have continued to flee the country, especially as a result of the conflict with Ethiopia in 1998, which led to the mass displacement of Eritreans expelled from Ethiopia to Sudan (GSDRC, 2016). In 2019, the ongoing border conflict with Ethiopia came to an end with the signing of an agreement between Prime Minister Abiy Ahmed of Ethiopia and President Isaias Afwereki of Eritrea.

Despite this positive step towards peace, Eritreans continue to flee the country, especially men under the age of 40 because of the government requirement for all to serve in the national service indefinitely (SOAS, SIHA Network and IRRI, 2017). This has led to the suppression of the social, political and economic rights of Eritrean nationals. Put differently, young Eritreans continue to migrate because their individual aspirations do not align with the national interests, which has increased tensions between the government and the youth (Mac-Ikemenjima and Gebregiorgis, 2019: 1321). The government's approach can be traced back to the national recovery plan in the 1990s, which – in order to boost the national economy after a 30-year war – included a heavy investment in human capital. The focus on self-reliance meant developing a national service programme, where wartime values were preserved, and the integrity of the country safeguarded. The primary critique of this national service was the indefinite period of conscription, which prompted many young men and women to flee. Furthermore, young people seeking employment once they completed their higher education, had limited opportunities available to them. According to Muller (2004), these limitations are the result of the lack of resources allocated by the government for the development of a more inclusive higher education system.

Research on voluntary labour migration has focused mostly on international migration, more recently, to the Gulf States. There have been few studies on internal migration patterns, which account for a much larger proportion of HoA migrants. Most countries do not collect data on internal migration patterns, although Kenya and Uganda have attempted to capture this through the Housing and Population Census. However, data on international labour migration, which was collected for migrants in the GCC in January 2019, estimated that there were 500,000 Ethiopians resident in the Kingdom of Saudi Arabia, most of whom were irregular migrants (IOM, 2019).

Economic factors continue to dominate and influence the migration decisions of individuals seeking better opportunities beyond their place of origin. Some have sought out those opportunities in neighbouring countries that are seen to offer economic, social and political safety, whereas others have opted to seek opportunities in international locations in the Gulf States, Europe and southern Africa. The choice of destination and the means by which they get there varies depending on the resources available to them and, in some instances, their nationality determines the cost of migration.

Policy responses to migration in the Horn of Africa

The regional response to migration has been steered by the continental approach led by the African Union, which has been instrumental in providing guiding documents and frameworks that have been agreed on by its member states. The establishment of the Regional Economic Communities (RECs) within Africa, through the 1980 Lagos Plan of Africa for the Development of Africa, and the Abuja Treaty, has created an environment in which greater African integration is pursued by strengthening regional integration. In this light, migration policy responses require a regional and coordinated strategy between and among the HoA states, from potential origin, transit and destination countries. As such, REC member states are guided by principles and strategies discussed and passed in the African Union, which include:

1. OAU Convention Governing the Specific Aspects of Refugee Problems in Africa, 1969;
2. African Charter on Human and Peoples' Rights, 1981;
3. African Charter on the Rights and Welfare of the Child (ACRWC), 1990;
4. African Common Position on Migration and Development, 2006;
5. Declaration on the African Union Border Programme, 2007;
6. AU Commission Initiative against Trafficking (AU-COMMIT) Campaign, 2009;
7. AU Convention for the Protection and Assistance of Internally Displaced Persons in Africa (Kampala Convention), 2009;
8. Joint Labour Migration Programme (JLMP), 2015;

9. Khartoum Declaration on AU–Horn of Africa Initiative on Human Trafficking and Smuggling of Migrants, 2015;
10. Declaration on Migration, 2015;
11. Migration Policy Framework for Africa, 2018;
12. Treaty Establishing the African Economic Community relating to Free Movement of Persons, Right of Residence and Right of Establishment and Draft Implementation Roadmap, 2019;
13. African Free Continental Free Trade Area (AfCFTA), 2019.

The IGAD is the primary area of interest in this chapter. Its member states include Somalia, Eritrea, Djibouti, Ethiopia, Sudan and South Sudan, Kenya, and Uganda. Most countries in Africa have overlapping memberships across different RECs, which is also true within the Horn of Africa.

The IGAD response to migration

The IGAD has played an instrumental role in providing guiding principles in response to migration within the region. Discussions and dialogue at regional level, based on the conventions, frameworks and guiding principles outlined at AU level, led to the development of the Regional Migration Policy Framework (RMPF) in 2012. The AU adopted a Regional Migration Action Plan (R-MAP) aimed at assisting member states to address some of the weaknesses related to migration management and governance between their member states. At the same time, there was a need for member states to develop their own national migration policies, guided by the RMPF and the African Union's Migration Policy Framework for Africa (AU-MPFA). Alongside the RMPF were additional policies to guide their migration strategy in the region, including but not limited to:

1. Durable Solutions for Somali Refugees and Reintegration of Returnees in Somalia;
2. Nairobi Declaration Action Plan for Somali Refugees and the Comprehensive Refugee Response Framework;
3. Khartoum Declaration on AU–Horn of Africa Initiative on Human Trafficking and Smuggling of Migrants, 2015; and
4. Towards Free Movement and Transhumance in the IGAD Region, 2020.

In collaboration with some international and/or non-governmental organisations such as the IOM, the United Nations Humanitarian Commission for Refugees (UNHCR) and the EU, IGAD has been able to develop projects aimed at implementing some of these regional instruments at a national and/or regional level. The IOM, for instance, outlines an annual Regional Migrant Response Plan (RMRP) for the Horn of Africa with a 'migrant focused humanitarian strategy for vulnerable migrants from the Horn of Africa, specifically those from Somalia, Djibouti and Ethiopia, moving bi-directionally to and from Yemen' (IOM, 2018: 4). UN agencies have been working with governments in the Horn of Africa and the Gulf States to respond to the migration issues affecting key countries. This has resulted in the development of the Sana'a Declaration, focused on eight key areas of interest (IOM, 2018: 11):

1.   Understanding the *drivers of migration*;
2.   *Strengthening law enforcement and mechanisms* to stem trafficking and smuggling;
3.   Providing increased *support for return programmes*;
4.   *Enhancing cooperation in employment opportunities* in destination countries through regularised labour agreements;
5.   *Awareness-raising campaigns* focused on highlighting the dangers of irregular migration;
6.   Promoting *regional and international cooperation*;
7.   Undertaking *data collection and analysis* to produce a better understanding on mixed migration in the region; and
8.   Developing a *follow-up mechanism.*

Hence, the IGAD has many frameworks and guiding documents to assist member states to address the migration challenges they are facing at a regional level. The main challenge has been on the resources and abilities to implement some of these initiatives and mainstreaming these regional guidelines into national policies.

However, there have been some challenges in the implementation of the projects where there has been the need for economic support. In addition, changing global perceptions of refugees have affected and limited resources to support certain initiatives targeted at refugees, including resettlement programmes. Reduced levels of burden sharing have also strained the resources of the host countries that are exploring alternative cost-effective strategies to achieve some of the durable solutions. The

Government of Kenya, for instance, embarked on a mission in May 2016 to reduce the asylum-seeking and refugee numbers to less than 150,000, primarily by shutting the largest and oldest refugee camp in the country, Dadaab,[4] located in Garissa County. The government was concerned about the growing insecurity in the region and the move was taken to protect its citizens from terrorist activities associated with Al Shabaab. In partnership with the UNHCR, the Government of Kenya began a Comprehensive Refugee Programme, which aimed to repatriate Somali refugees to safe zones identified in Somalia for those willing to voluntarily return.

This programme attracted considerable criticism, as there were many Somali refugees who had been born in Kenya and, therefore, had no connection with Somalia. There were also cases of intermarriages with Kenyans, so addressing the needs of these households was a delicate issue. In addition, some Kenyan nationals were registered as refugees to access the services available at the camp. Nevertheless, 75,659 Somali refugees returned to Somalia from Dadaab, between 2014 and 2018, and an additional 96,369 expressed willingness to return (UNHCR Weekly Update: Voluntary Repatriation of Somali Refugees from Kenya, 2018). As such, the Government of Kenya is making strides in achieving this durable solution. They are also exploring local integration through the establishment of the Kalobeyei Integrated Settlement in Turkana County, next to Kakuma Refugee Camp. Funded by the World Bank, the Kalobeyei Integrated Socio-Economic Development Plan (KISEDP) was designed in such a way that the host and refugee population benefit jointly in services and opportunities available in the settlement area (Betts et al., 2020). This settlement allows refugees to contribute to the local economy, and eventually become self-sufficient with the support of the Government of Kenya and its international and local partners (UNHCR, 2018). The role of international organisations and agencies has been critical in dealing with some of the limitations of the IGAD member states, especially in terms of financial and human resources, as well as meeting some of the capacity-building needs in specific countries.

European Union's engagement with the Horn of Africa

The EU has a long history of collaboration and engagement with African countries either bilaterally or through the AU on some initiatives and frameworks related to migration, which has had a trickle-down effect on the RECs and their member states. Since migration became a key Sustainable

Development Goal (SDG), the EU's approach to migration has shifted from a multilateral to a bilateral engagement with a strong focus on curbing irregular migration destined for European countries via North Africa (Castillejo, 2019). The development of the EUTF was meant to provide support to African countries to mainstream the Joint Valletta Action Plan (JVAP), specifically on legal migration and mobility under domain 2 (Castillejo, 2019). In this regard, the Valletta Action Plan allowed the EU to support regional and sub-regional frameworks that created legal pathways to migration. Within the Horn of Africa, some frameworks and guiding principles have been established as a result of long-term engagement with international guidelines on migration. Abebe (2017) documents the following engagements in her studies:

1. EU–African Dialogue on Migration and Development (Rabat Process), 2006;

2. Joint Africa–EU Declaration on Migration and Development (Tripoli Process), 2006;

3. Joint Africa–EU Partnership on Migration, Mobility and Employment, 2007;

4. EU–Horn of Africa Migration Route Initiative (Khartoum Process), 2014; and

5. Valletta Summit on Migration Action Plan, 2015.

Migration programmes have been developed and implemented across all or some member states in the Horn of Africa. These programmes are targeted at:

1. *strengthening the capacities of migrants[5] and the host population,* targeting the youth and women through technical and vocational education and training (TVET), to increase their employability;

2. developing a multi-sectoral approach to support countries to *strengthen the resilience of communities* at risk of being displaced as a result of climate change, which may lead to food insecurity and diversification of livelihoods;

3. supporting national governments in the region to strengthen their migration management *to promote safe, orderly and regular migration in line with the Global Compact of Migration (GCM).* This includes providing resources to monitor irregular migration, as well as raise awareness of the risks of irregular migration to stem this kind of migration; and

4. supporting the *improvement of governance and conflict prevention* by strengthening capacities to enable the differentiation between a victim of trafficking and cases of migrant smuggling (European Union Trust Fund, 2019).

Therefore, the EU's role is to reduce the factors that push people to migrate regularly, as well as irregularly. The projects initiated at the national level focus on creating a conducive environment – where youth and women, in particular, have access to opportunities, including employment – and reducing the risk of displacement by strengthening the resilience of populations at risk. At the same time, the project empowers government officials, through capacity building, to manage the irregular migration flows from, to and through their respective countries. Each programme has a specific focus, such as improving migration governance or reducing drivers of migration in source locations.

Within the Horn of Africa, Somalia, Ethiopia, and Sudan have benefited financially from the EUTF funding. Somalia has received €307.5 million since December 2019, which is the largest EUTF funding in the region. The funding primarily targeted resilience building, economic development, and security governance (Oxfam, 2020: 16). Sudan's funding, on the other hand, targeted development-focused projects more unequivocally, prioritising economic development and resilience building (totalling €39.9 million in the same period). Funding in Ethiopia, amounting to €270.2 million, which started in December 2017, has targeted mainly return and readmission programmes for Ethiopian returnees.

The Better Migration Management (BMM) programme, for instance, was aimed at strengthening migration governance and building the capacities of government officials in the IGAD member states between 2016 and 2019 (Phase I) and 2020 and 2023 (Phase II) to curb irregular migration in the region. It focused on improving the rights and security of migrants. Like many of the programmes, the BMM has implementing partners such as the IOM, the UN Office on Drugs and Crime, among others, that support different aspects of their programming. A key target met by the BMM programme was the design and implementation of a postgraduate course on migration studies in 2018, which trained government officials from East Africa and the Horn of Africa on migration. A list of the projects by country, focused specifically on migration in selected locations in the Horn of Africa, is outlined in Table 7.4.

The EU's projects on migration in Eritrea have focused on creating an enabling environment to improve the economic conditions of the youth in the country and reduce their need to migrate. They have concentrated on strengthening education and its links to employment opportunities, which was identified as one of the many drivers of migration, especially for the youth. However, for as long as the Government of Eritrea requires its citizens to serve indefinitely in national service, migration is unlikely to reduce because the driver is associated with citizens' social, political and human rights (GSDRC, 2016; and SOAS, SIHA Network and IRRI, 2017).

Table 7.4: EU–IGAD Migration Projects

PROJECTS	DJIBOUTI	SOMALIA	SUDAN	S. SUDAN	ETHIOPIA	ERITREA	UGANDA	KENYA
Strengthening the ability of IGAD to promote resilience in the Horn of Africa	X	X	X	X	X		X	X
Sustainable solutions for the most vulnerable host populations, refugees and migrants in Djibouti	X							
Refugee empowerment through education, access to social protection services and economic opportunities	X							
IGAD Promoting Peace and Stability in the Horn of Africa Region (IPPSHAR)	X	X	X	X	X	X	X	X
Stemming Irregular Migration in Northern and Central Ethiopia (SINCE)					X			
Stimulating economic opportunities and job creation for refugees and host communities in Ethiopia in support of the Comprehensive Refugee Response Framework (CRRF)					X			

PROJECTS	DJIBOUTI	SOMALIA	SUDAN	S. SUDAN	ETHIOPIA	ERITREA	UGANDA	KENYA
Promoting stability and strengthening basic services delivery for host communities, refugees and other displaced populations in the Gambella Regional State of Ethiopia					X			
Towards free movement and transhumance in the IGAD Region	X	X	X	X	X		X	X
Enhancing self-reliance for refugees and host communities in Kenya								X
Piloting private sector solutions for refugees and host communities in North West Kenya								X
RE-INTEG: Enhancing Somalia's responsiveness to the management and reintegration of mixed migration flows		X						
Better Migration Management programme	X	X	X	X	X	X	X	X
Response to increased environmental degradation and promotion of alternative energy sources in refugee-hosting districts							X	
Regional Operational Centre in support of the Khartoum Process and the AU-Horn of Africa Initiative (ROCK)	X	X	X	X	X	X		X
Protection of Persons of Concern (PoC) and vulnerable migrants along migratory routes in Sudan (PROTECT)			X					
Delivering durable solutions to forced displacement in the IGAD region through the implementation of the Global Compact on Refugees (GCR)	X	X	X	X	X	X	X	X

PROJECTS	DJIBOUTI	SOMALIA	SUDAN	S.SUDAN	ETHIOPIA	ERITREA	UGANDA	KENYA
Strengthening resilience of IDPs, returnees and host communities in West Darfur			X					
Integrating refugee children into the Sudanese education system			X					
Regional Development and Protection Programme (RDPP): Support Programme to the Refugee Settlements and Host Communities in Northern Uganda (SPRS-UN)							X	
Collaboration in cross border areas of the Horn of Africa Region		X	X		X			X
Facility on Sustainable and Dignified Return and Reintegration in Support of the Khartoum Process	X	X	X	X	X	X	X	X

Source: Compiled by author from European Union Trust Fund for Africa (2019) (Online at: https://ec.europa.eu/trustfundforafrica/region/horn-africa/regional/better-migration-management-programme_en)

The EU and African countries, however, have experienced challenges in balancing the implementation process as the EU focus has been primarily on finding ways of curbing or reducing irregular migration, without considering the benefits and positive impact of migration in source, transit and destination countries. This has meant that the EU's agenda takes precedence over the needs and expectations of African member states, including in the IGAD region (Castillejo, 2019). Migrants have also questioned the intentions behind the regional body's programmes, which some felt were geared to stopping migration from the region, specifically to Europe. Some of the funded programmes in North Africa have been criticised for contributing to an insecure environment for transit migrants, who face human rights abuses in countries such as Libya. In January 2020, Raphael Shilhav, the EU migration policy adviser, noted that:

European governments seem determined to prevent migration at any cost. They are putting short term wins over strategies that work in the long run, at the expense of those most in need. The EU needs to stop undermining its own values and make sure that all of its engagements in Africa promote stability, democracy and resilience – not the opposite (in Oxfam, 2020).

In Ethiopia, the return and readmission programme for Ethiopian returnees was criticised by civil society and human rights organisations because of data protection issues around sharing the personal details of returnees with the Ethiopian National Intelligence and Security Services (NISS) of the previous government, known for its human rights violations against Ethiopian protestors, which posed a risk to those returning (Oxfam, 2020: 14).

As a way forward, Oxfam has recommended the removal of the conditional requirements on some of the EU's collaborations with AU/IGAD member states, and the development of flexible financial instruments, in line with humanitarian and development objectives and principles. There is also a call to refocus their migration-related activities to 'reduce vulnerabilities, address needs and promote resilient development' (Oxfam, 2020: 5). The Oxfam report further suggests that, 'the amount of spending should be decided according to evidence based projections, not on political positioning', as stated by Mr Shilhav. This line of criticism evokes the idea of having an inclusive process driven by the IGAD member states, with national and community-based stakeholders being part of the process. In response to such criticism, many revisions are expected to take place at regional and national levels as some programmes enter their second phase. In this process, there is a need to review the financial and human resources required for the implementation process and the capacity needs of each member state. The recent COVID-19 pandemic has further hampered efforts in the region as funds have been diverted towards responses to the pandemic, which further increases the risks, and the protection needs of refugees. Funds have been reallocated to strengthen Water, Sanitation and Hygiene (WASH) standards, especially in the refugee settlement areas and camps to flatten the COVID-19 curve. Hence, going forward, the EU and IGAD member states will have to factor health concerns into their programming activities.

Conclusion

Addressing migration management in the Horn of Africa is a complex task due to the dynamism of mixed migration flows to, through and from the region. Data is key to understanding how trajectories and proportions are changing and whether the policies and regulations in place are having an impact on governing migration flows and creating an enabling environment. Clearly, IGAD member states have demonstrated their political will by putting in place regulations, protocols and agreements to address the challenges of migration, while trying to balance restrictive measures with the positive impact migration brings to a country. The states do not lack the required frameworks and guiding principles to undertake projects and initiatives on or related to migration but are limited by capacity and resources to implement some of the migration policies that have been highlighted.

The collaborative work with international actors, including the EU, has been able to address some of the resource gaps that the region or some member states face, but challenges remained. Thus, it is important to ensure that the agenda of the IGAD member states and not that of the EU is guiding the process. The discussions regarding funding, programming, monitoring and evaluation of migration projects funded by the EU are currently underway during the global public health crisis caused by the COVID-19 pandemic. Key to this process is ensuring that programmes are sustainable beyond the EU funding period, which requires member states to own the process. IGAD member states should also take strategic measures to budget effectively for migration needs, including the capacity and resources needed to meet the regional and national targets.

Notes

1   The Gulf Cooperation Council (GCC) is a political and economic union of Arab states bordering the Gulf. It was established in 1981 and its six members are the United Arab Emirates, Saudi Arabia, Qatar, Oman, Kuwait and Bahrain. See Netherlands Worldwide, 'GCC countries. Online at: https://www.netherlandsworldwide.nl/doing-business-in-the-gulf-region/other-sectors-in-the-gulf-region/gcc-countries (accessed 1 February 2021).

2   The data from the IOM Flow Monitoring Report are based on data captured at flow monitoring points (FMPs) and are conducted on a regular basis. The

data represented in this and other graphs in this chapter were based on a sample of 15,000 respondents in 2018.

3   In their monitoring of migration patterns in the region, the MMC has developed an innovative mechanism called the Mixed Migration Monitoring Mechanism Initiative (4Mi) to map the migration corridors digitally, and identify hotspots where corruptive practices are taking place, including human rights violations.

4   The camp was established in 1991, initially to host refugees from Somalia displaced by conflict and natural disasters. By 2015, it was hosting over 600,000 refugees.

5   Including IDPs and refugees.

References

Abebe, T.T. 2017. *Migration Policy Frameworks in Africa.* Addis Ababa: Institute for Security Studies.

Belloni, M. (2019) *The Big Gamble: Migration of Eritreans to Europe*, California: University of California Press.

Betts, A., Omata N., and Sterck, O. (2020) 'The Kalobeyei Settlement: A Self-reliance Model for Refugees?' *Journal of Refugee Studies* Vol. 33, No. 1; pp. 189-223.

Castillejo, C. 2019. *The Influence of EU Migration Policy and Regional Free Movement in the IGAD and ECOWAS Regions.* Discussion Paper. Bonn: Federal Ministry for Economic Cooperation and Development.

Davy, D. (2017). Unpacking the Myths: Human smuggling from and within the Horn of Africa, *RMMS Briefing Paper* 6, 1–26.

European Union Trust Fund. 2019. *EUTF for Africa: Tackling the root causes of instability, forced displacement and irregular migration in the Horn of Africa.* Online at: https://ec.europa.eu/trustfundforafrica/sites/euetfa/files/eutf_hoa_factsheet_.pdf (accessed 30 May 2020).

Governance and Social Development Resource Centre (GSDRC). 2016. *Rapid Fragility and Migration Assessment for Eritrea*, Rapid Literature Review. Birmingham: University of Birmingham.

International Organization for Migration (IOM). 2020. *Regional Migrant Response Plan for the Horn of Africa and Yemen, 2018–2020.* Geneva: IOM.

International Organization for Migration (IOM). 2018. *Migration Flows in the Horn of Africa and Yemen: Overview 2018.* Geneva: IOM. Online at: https://migration.iom.int/sites/all/themes/fmp/pages/data_story_hoa_and_yemen/index.html (accessed 26 May 2020).

Mac-Ikemenjima, D. and Gebregiorgis, H. 2019. 'Eritrea's youth migration challenge: The role of aspirations and opportunity', *African Human Mobility Review*, 4(2): 1310–1330.

Majidi, N. and Adhiambo Oucho, L.A. 2016. 'East Africa', in M. McAuliffe and F. Laczko (eds). *Migrant Smuggling Data and Research: A global review of the emerging evidence base.* Geneva: International Organization for Migration, pp. 55–84.

Mixed Migration Centre (MMC). 2020. *The Mixed Migration Centre.* Online at: http://www.mixedmigration.org/about/ (accessed 30 May 2020).

Muller, T. 2004. '"Now I am free": Education and human resource development in Eritrea: Contradictions in the lives of Eritrean Women in Higher Education', *A Journal of Comparative and International Education*, 34(2): 215–29.

Ngunyi, M. and Oucho, J.O. 2013. *Migration and Human Security in the East and Southern African Region: The state of play on mechanisms and gaps,* Volume 1. Djibouti: Inter-Governmental Authority for Development.

Oxfam. 2020. *The EU Trust Fund for Africa: Trapped between aid policy and migration politics.* Briefing Paper. London: Oxfam.

Regional Mixed Migration Secretariat. 2013. *Migrant Smuggling in the Horn of Africa and Yemen: The political economy and protection risks.* Nairobi: Mixed Migration Research Series No. 7.

Sahan Foundation and IGAD Security Sector Program. 2016. *Human Trafficking and Smuggling on the Horn of Africa–Central Mediterranean Route.* Project Report. Djibouti: Sahan Foundation and IGAD Security Sector Program.

SOAS, SIHA Network, and IRRI. 2017. *Tackling the Root Causes of Human Trafficking and Smuggling from Eritrea: The need for an empirically grounded EU policy on mixed migration in the Horn of Africa.* Project Report. London: SOAS, SIHA and IRRI.

United Nations Humanitarian Commission for Refugees (UNHCR). 2020. *UNHCR Operational Portal – Refugee Situations: Uganda.* 04 30. Online at: https://data2.unhcr.org/en/country/uga (accessed 31 May 2020).

United Nations Humanitarian Commission for Refugees (UNHCR). 2018a. *Kalobeyei Integrated Socio-Economic Development Plan in Turkana West: Phase One: 2018–2022 Comprehensive Refugee and Host Community Plan in Turkana West, Kenya.* Strategy Report. Nairobi: UNHCR.

United Nations Humanitarian Commission for Refugees (UNHCR). 2018b. *Weekly Update: Voluntary Repatriation of Somali Refugees from Kenya.* Online at: https://www.unhcr.org/ke/wp-content/uploads/sites/2/2018/05/Voluntary-Repatriation-Analysis-06042018.pdf (accessed 31 May 2020).

Chapter 8

Legal pathways to migration: Labour migration arrangements between West Africa and Europe

Amanda Bisong

Introduction

This chapter analyses how labour migration arrangements between European and West African countries create legal pathways to migration between the two continents. European and African policymakers, in a bid to stem the migration flows through irregular channels to Europe, are creating legal pathways to migration, in addition to their investments in other aspects of migration governance. For West African actors, the objective of these pathways is to provide increased opportunities for their nationals seeking to migrate to Europe. At the state level, these pathways facilitate migration cooperation between European and West African countries and form the basis for further cooperation on returns and readmissions. This chapter examines the validity of these assertions in the West African context, drawing on textual analyses of the policy documents relating to these labour migration arrangements. It concludes that while these arrangements may generate incentives to promote cooperation between states, they create limited opportunities to improve accessibility for individuals seeking to migrate to Europe through legal pathways.

Labour migration is a feature of contemporary labour markets and the future of work (ILO, 2017). Current global labour market trends reveal that an increasing number of migrant workers make up the labour force in important countries of destination in Western Europe, North America, the Middle East, and the Gulf cooperation countries (UN, 2020). Although labour migration slowed down because of the COVID-19 pandemic, the trend in increased labour mobility has continued as governments and individuals adjust to the new normal (Papademetriou and Hopper, 2020). Migrants represent 3.5 per cent of the world's population but contribute an equivalent of nearly 10 per cent of the gross domestic product (Okai, 2020). In 2019 it was estimated that there were about 281 million international migrants globally. According to the International Labour Organization (ILO), there are 169 million international migrant workers around the world (McAuliffe and Triandafyllidou 2021). African migrant workers are mostly in the Middle East, North America, and Western Europe (UNDESA, 2019).

Migration policies play a decisive role in facilitating, restricting, and mediating access to labour market opportunities in countries of destination. Therefore, migration policies of countries should reflect the labour market realities and create opportunities to attract migrant workers to fill the domestic labour shortages, which result from skills gaps or demographic changes (Martin, 2015). Migration policies have been determined by factors including foreign relations among countries. This has fostered cooperation and enhanced soft power relations among states and regional hegemons.

In recent times, European migration policies have been politicised by governments and influenced by the domestic interests of nationalist parties in countries such as Italy, Malta and Greece. This has led to a lessened focus on labour market needs and the economic effects of migration for the labour market, thus making it difficult to adopt a pragmatic approach (Geddes et al., 2020). Migration flows between Europe and Africa have been portrayed as mainly irregular, with photographs of boat people used to portray migration from West Africa to Europe (Baldwin-Edwards et al., 2019). These untenable and largely unsubstantiated perceptions of African migration to Europe contribute to the negative public opinion in Europe, which hinders a more constructive and pragmatic approach to labour migration between both continents (Bjarnesen, 2020).

Many European and African countries have jointly committed to enhance legal pathways to labour mobility and migration through bilateral and multilateral agreements. Examples of these arrangements are the 2008 mobility partnerships with Cape Verde; the 2007 bilateral agreement between Spain and Senegal the 2015 European Agenda on Migration and the cooperation with partnership countries, and more recently, the 2020 European Pact on Migration and Asylum (especially through the Talent Partnerships). These measures are intended to create options for the nationals of partner countries, such as Nigeria, Senegal, and Morocco, to migrate to the European Union (EU) using legal channels. They also aim to promote cooperation between states to advance the readmission and return of migrants in an irregular situation to their countries of origin (European Commission, 2017).

The 2015 European Agenda on Migration (EAM) is the basis for the cooperation between EU and African counties on migration. This policy framework stipulates the areas of cooperation of EU member states and third countries. The four main pillars of the policy are: (1) improving border management at the EU's external borders and supporting the development of border management in third countries; (2) reducing incentives for irregular migration by addressing the root causes of migration; (3) reforming the Common European Asylum System (CEAS); and (4) developing a new policy on legal migration (European Commission, 2015).

Linked to this agenda, the 2015 Valletta Summit on Migration between European and selected African countries – mainly from North, West, Central and the Horn of Africa, such as Morocco, Algeria, Libya, Ghana, Nigeria, Gabon amongst others – established the European Union Emergency Trust Fund for Africa (EUTF).[1] The main objectives of the EUTF were to support stability, save and protect migrants, and create economic opportunities in countries or regions of origin, and legal pathways for migration within and outside Africa (European Court of Auditors, 2018). The second priority area of the EUTF was to enhance cooperation on legal migration and mobility between African and European countries, and among African countries (Valletta Summit Action Plan, 2015).

The thematic areas, which focus on improving border management measures, addressing the root causes of migration through economic empowerment, reintegrating the returned migrants, and promoting migration dialogues, have received increased funding and support from the EUTF.[2] However, enhancing legal pathways to migration through labour migration and mobility has received limited funding and support (Kervyn and Shilhav, 2017). From the perspective of the European Commission, the objective of facilitating legal pathways to labour migration is to promote the admission of certain categories of workers from African countries to Europe, to promote cooperation in combatting irregular migration, and better organisation of circular mobility between partner states on both continents (European Commission, 2014; 2017).

These legal pathway programmes have been fraught with implementation challenges for the EU. The EU has set up the cooperation framework through the EAM and provided the financial and technical assistance for these measures, but until the introduction of the Talent Partnerships, it lacked the tools to design and implement them. Member states have the competence through national regulations to determine if, whether and to what extent these programmes would be used, and with which third countries to partner based on their domestic priorities and interests.[3] Therefore, cooperation with the EU on legal pathways is limited to the demand from member states.

Currently, there are examples of cooperation on legal pathways with African countries through pilot projects on labour migration in specific sectors. Most of these projects partner with North African countries like Morocco, Tunisia and Egypt (Stefanescu, 2021). In West Africa, there are pilot programmes with Senegal and Nigeria, while other programmes are still in various stages of design. West African countries have the second highest number of irregular migrants to Europe after North African countries (IOM, 2019). In 2018 and until early 2020, there has been a significant reduction in the number of arrivals from West African countries (Abebe, 2020). Without considering Spain, current data from national governments hold that, Tunisia and Côte d'Ivoire are 'the most frequently reported country of origin among all registered arrivals to Europe (14 and 13 per cent respectively)' between January and March 2021 (IOM, 2021). The region has more formalised cooperation with the EU, both at member state and regional levels (Bisong, 2019). Furthermore, the Sahel window of the EUTF, to which most West African countries belong, has the largest disbursement of funds under the EUTF (European Commission, 2019b). Senegal and Nigeria, which are partner countries for the pilot projects, are priority countries under the EU's 'new partnership framework' for migration cooperation with third countries (European Commission, 2016).

Cooperation between the EU and third countries on enhancing legal pathways to migration are based on non-legally binding joint declarations or memoranda of understanding between states. Thus, I refer to them in this chapter as 'arrangements'. The chapter analyses the cooperation on enhancing labour migration through legal pathways between European and West African states at two levels – the individual level and the state level – identifying the narratives and the politics driving state cooperation, and assessing how these translate into national policy frameworks that are implemented through practices at the individual level. It examines the extent to which these arrangements create opportunities for individuals seeking to migrate and to what extent they promote cooperation between states.

The next section examines the evolution of the discourse on legal pathways between European and West African countries, which is followed by an examination of the characteristics of the new categories of labour mobility arrangements between West African and European countries. Thereafter the chapter analyses the assertions that labour migration agreements create increased accessibility for migrants and further cooperation between states. The final section concludes that while these arrangements may create incentives for further state cooperation, limited opportunities are created for a subset of migrants at the individual level.

The evolution of legal mobility pathways between European and West African countries

Cooperation on labour migration through circular and other mobility schemes between West African and European countries began in the early 2000s. Seasonal migration schemes were organised between Spain and France, on the one hand, and Senegal, Mali and Mauritania, on the other hand. A centre for promoting legal migration – the Centre for Migration Information and Management (Centre d'Information et de Gestion des Migrations [CIGEM]) – was established in 2008 in Bamako, Mali. In 2008, a mobility partnership was also signed between Cape Verde and the EU, one of the objectives being the promotion of labour migration. Some additional measures to promote legal migration resulted from bilateral cooperation.

European states have used these circular and labour migration programmes to fill domestic labour shortages in specific sectors, including agriculture and construction. The design of European migration policies has been influenced by neoliberal ideas such as market-oriented liberalisation of mobility and the flexibilisation of labour (Maisenbacher, 2015). Market forces and economic reasons have driven the design and conceptualisation of migration policy instruments at the national and regional levels. From a long-term macro-economic perspective, liberal labour migration policies are in the interest of the domestic labour force as they promote the competitiveness of labour, raise the wages of domestic workers and promote the protection of labour (workers), in cases where these measures are combined with welfare policies (Cottier and Sieber-Gasser, 2015).

European states, aware of the limitations of the domestic workforce in filling the labour market needs, create migration instruments to attract, retain and expel these labour migrants with the objective of promoting domestic economic growth. These measures may be accessible to all nationalities or have strict preferences for nationals from other countries within the region, for example, in free movement schemes. With the increasing need for leverage on migration cooperation, these agreements have become bilateral in nature and are used in negotiation cooperation within realist contexts, based on power dynamics between states (Bisong, 2020a). This focus on foreign relations and power dynamics, in short, has contributed to side lining the needs of the labour market and filling domestic gaps. States view control of their borders as inherent to their sovereignty and have designed their migration policies to determine which categories of migrants should gain access to their territory.

The EU has a history of migration worker programmes with migrants from other geographical areas outside of Africa, including Latin America, South East Asia, and the West Balkans. These programmes target different sectors, including seasonal jobs in agriculture and longer-term opportunities in nursing (Hooper, 2019). In previous European labour mobility programmes, such as temporary foreign worker programmes, migrants were expected to work for one or more years abroad and then return to their countries of origin (Martin, 2015). Labour mobility programmes changed over the years, with governments increasing requirements for employers to prove that they need migrant workers.

More restrictive migration policies have also contributed to the difficulties of implementing labour migration programmes, which have grown larger and lasted longer than anticipated, creating dependency in migrant workers and employers, and leading, in some cases, to the resettlement of these workers in their destination countries (for example, Germany and Turkey). In most current agreements, states, either unilaterally or in negotiations with partner countries, stipulate the conditions for labour migration programmes. These measures target a particular industry, occupation, or geographic area, such as North African (like Morocco) or West Balkan countries (like Kosovo). They stipulate the unique admission criteria of migrants, the length of stay, and employer requirements. Sometimes employers are made to undergo certifications, and are required to sign bonds for each migrant; in other cases, each recruitment is subject to an economics needs test.

These circular mobility programmes have had seemingly low success rates. Migrants often choose to settle in the host countries and not to return to their countries of origin. It is estimated that about 25 per cent of migrant workers in Europe did not return to their countries of origin following the post-World War II guest worker programmes in the 1950s and 1960s (Martin, 2015). Employers equally benefit from these increased sets of skilled workers when migrants choose to stay in the host countries. Subsequently, guest worker programmes in the 1990s were based on foreign policy considerations. Spain and Italy had migration cooperation agreements with the governments of countries of origin, and admitted legal migrants from these countries in order to promote the return of unauthorised migrants, and with a view to curb irregular migration. An example of this model is the cooperation between Spain and Morocco. These worker programmes had little to do with employment needs in the host countries and were crafted mainly for foreign policy and political reasons (Martin, 2015).

Furthermore, circular migration has limited welfare provisions because social standards for labour migrants are scarcely included in these agreements (Triandafyllidou, 2013; Martin, 2015). There are also limited benefits in terms of training and education as employers rarely want to spend money on training temporary employees. Another disadvantage is that migrants may not earn enough money during the short residency abroad to reinvest in sustainable economic activities on their return to their countries of origin (Triandafyllidou, 2013).

Circular migration projects re-emerged in the 2000s with the renewed emphasis on migration and development, through the establishment of the Global Forum for Migration and Development (GFMD) and other similar dialogues. A closer examination of the European Commission policy documents, and their development from 2007 to 2019, reveals an orientation towards labour market needs and a proactive liberalisation of legal migration. This priority was intended to ensure the competitiveness of sectors and enterprises in the EU, such as the agricultural sector and specific services sectors. Therefore, legal channels for migration were described as a way 'to facilitate circular migration, which will help EU Member States address their labour needs' (European Commission, 2007a: 2). These mobility agreements were to be based on the identified labour needs of countries of origin and destination. This led to cooperation between European and West African states, like Spain and Senegal, through bilateral cooperation measures. However, the agreements were also aimed at stemming irregular flows of migrants through cooperation and creating legal pathways for migrant workers in the fishing and agricultural sectors in Spain, where there was a shortage of domestic labour (Kabbanji, 2013).

In Senegal, legal agreements with France in 2008 and Spain in 2007 were aimed at facilitating labour migration while reducing irregular flows and supporting returns of irregular migrants (Toma, 2014). These agreements involved the use of quotas, visas, and circular and student mobility schemes to promote bilateral cooperation between states, and the supply of labour to match the needs of specific sectors like agriculture, retail and fishing, in the partner countries (Toma, 2014). They also included pre-departure training and education in countries of origin. The diaspora community in host countries were equally involved in the design and implementation of these measures (Panizzon, 2011). National institutional frameworks were set up to jointly implement these agreements with international organisations. The Comité de suivi du Crédit d'impôt pour la compétitivité et l'emploi brought together different state agencies and ministries with the aim of implementing and monitoring these agreements. However, with the 2008 financial crisis, consequent unemployment and reduced funding in European countries, these programmes were unilaterally suspended (Toma, 2014).

New generation of labour mobility and migration arrangements

The renewed cooperation on legal pathways began during the 2015 Valletta Summit and the creation of the EUTF – linked to the European Agenda on Migration adopted earlier that year. In the lead up to the Valletta Summit, the African Union (AU) developed a 'Common Perspectives Paper', which included labour migration as one of the important themes for discussion (Knoll and De Weijer, 2016). During the negotiations, of the four evident themes that were observed, two were about creating legal migration pathways (Knoll and De Weijer, 2016). African countries viewed legal migration (within and outside of the continent) as an opportunity for livelihoods and long-term development. Their focus (during the summit and afterwards) is on facilitating and managing migration flows more effectively, and creating opportunities for the legal migration of workers, researchers and students to Europe. From the European perspective, migration is perceived by some countries as a threat to their national security and socio-economic welfare (Knoll and De Weijer, 2016), therefore it was necessary to expand cooperation with third countries with a view to increasing returns and readmissions (Kipp, 2018).

For the European countries, migration cooperation emphasised the containment of unregulated and irregular migration, and reducing the number of irregular arrivals in Europe. Their discussions also envisaged that labour migration would be a reward for cooperation on returns and readmission. On the other hand, African countries sought to increase the possibility for legal migration through orderly and freer flow of movements, and to minimise the negative aspects of migration through policies targeted at better integration of migrants in their host communities.

Consequently, African policymakers demanded these legal pathways as part of a holistic approach to migration cooperation (Hauck et al., 2015). This insistence resulted in an increase in the number of scholarships for African students and researchers, and a commitment to promote the legal pathways principle, which was eventually made the second pillar of the EUTF, as reinforced in the statement by Donald Tusk at the Valletta Summit (EU Council, 2015)

> What we have agreed is a crucial step in reinforcing our cooperation. We have adopted a Political Declaration and a Valletta Action Plan. We now need to get moving on implementing it, in partnership and solidarity. The elements of the Action Plan are designed to: One, address the root causes of migration; Two, enhance cooperation on legal migration and mobility…

However, in the context of the 2015 migration crisis and the ensuing Valletta Summit, the discussions on legal pathways were framed around facilitating migration cooperation between states to improve further cooperation on returns and readmissions. As noted by some authors, 'the EU was prepared to make concessions to partner countries that help it achieve its goal of containing migrants outside Europe' (Knoll and De Weijer, 2016). Limited emphasis was placed on the role of the safe and orderly migration through legal pathways in contributing to the development of countries of origin and destination, and migrants contributing to filling evident labour market shortages in destination countries.

While these narratives may be oversimplified representations of the realities in the negotiating positions, they played a key role in determining the outcome of the Valletta Summit and subsequent cooperation. Both European and African countries may have comprehensive migration frameworks on paper, but there are divergent positions in practice, depending on the countries and their perception of migration. In both Europe and African countries, there are concerns about perceived or real threats of migrants crowding the labour markets and promoting economic competition, which may result in hostilities, instability and xenophobia between the migrants and host communities.

The United Nations (UN) Global Compact on Safe, Orderly and Regular Migration (GCM) also promoted the use of legal pathways. Objective 18 of the GCM encourages states to:

> Engage in bilateral partnerships and programmes in cooperation with relevant stakeholders that promote skills development, mobility and circulation, such as student exchange programmes, scholarships, professional exchange programmes and trainee or apprenticeships that include options for beneficiaries, after successful completion of these programmes, to seek employment and engage in entrepreneurship (UN, 2018).

As stipulated in the GCM, Objective 18 also encourages countries to build global skills partnerships that strengthen the training capacity of both countries of origin and destination, and involving multiple relevant stakeholders, including the private sector and trade unions. This is in line with the UN Sustainable Development Goal (SDG) target 10.7, to 'facilitate orderly, safe and responsible migration and mobility of people'.

In September 2017, the European Commission announced that it would launch pilot projects on legal migration with African countries. These pilots are aimed at curbing irregular migration flows by enhancing the opportunities for legal migration and reducing the incentives for migrants to use irregular channels (European Commission, 2017). However, these pilot projects have delivered mixed results in various partner countries. Factors such as high operational costs and difficult administrative procedures in both countries of origin and destination make it difficult to scale up these projects into more permanent pathways and fit them into a broader EU strategy on legal migration (Hooper, 2019).

This new approach to labour migration involves dialogue on migration issues and projects proposed and implemented by EU member states, in cooperation with international organisations and intergovernmental organisations, such as the International Organization for Migration (IOM), and implemented by member state development agencies. The pilot projects have different requirements regarding skill levels, sectors and duration of stay. These requirements also differ between the various European and African countries, based on their priorities. This approach also emphasises the benefits for individual migrants, and sending and destination countries. The benefits for sending countries include receiving remittances and training of skilled workers, whose experience has the potential for knowledge transfers, which can promote and spur innovation in the countries of origin.

In West Africa, pilot projects have been implemented in Nigeria and Senegal, and involve experts from the information and communication technology (ICT) sector.[4] The 'Digital Explorer' project between Nigeria and Lithuania is designed around three main themes: labour migration, development of the digital economy, and migration and development (Afriko, 2019). The programme brings together ICT specialist firms in Nigeria and Lithuania, and builds networks across these private-sector actors, providing an environment for mutual learning, exchange and development (Afriko, 2019). This internship project is implemented by Enterprise Lithuania and the International Centre for Migration Policy Development (ICMPD), in collaboration with about 15 private companies located in Nigeria and Lithuania. It provides an option for temporary legal migration of up to 50 ICT experts from Nigeria to Lithuania to enhance their digital skills and fill the labour gaps in Lithuania. The project offers a paid traineeship for ICT experts from Nigeria in ICT firms in Lithuania for a period of 6–12 months (*Baltic Times*, 2019). On completion of the internship, these experts will be supported in 'reintegrating' into Nigerian society to promote the productive use of the skills and networks gained during the sojourn abroad. Thus, return to the country of origin is an integral part of the project.

The Migration of African Talents through Capacity building and Hiring (MATCH) project, implemented by the IOM in collaboration with the Netherlands, Senegal and the Africa Business Council (NABC) in Nigeria, is aimed at promoting temporary work placements of up to 210 ICT experts from the two West African countries in the Netherlands (IOM, 2020a). The selected experts are given the opportunity to upgrade their skills to increase their employability in Europe and in their home countries. Recruited experts can work either remotely in the country of origin or they have the option to migrate temporarily to the country of destination for a fixed work period. The project focuses on ICT, technology, and the digitalisation sectors, and brings together different public, non-profit and private actors in partner countries to collaborate in its implementation. It feeds into future labour mobility schemes by emphasising the benefits of both countries of origin and destination. The MATCH project is part of a larger programme implemented in Belgium, Luxembourg, the Netherlands and Italy.

These projects offer training or work experience based on a temporary stay in countries of destination in Europe through work placements in these countries or exchange programmes. Some of these projects make provisions for extending the stay in the country of destination for a limited time; however, this depends on the possession of an employment opportunity. Some projects offer an additional training component, which includes technical training and training on soft skills such as work ethics, presentation, and time management. The travel and training costs are covered by the government of the destination country, non-governmental organisations (NGOs) or employers. Most projects involve recruiting people who are already qualified to work in a profession and then offering an additional layer of training on soft skills, or vocational training to equip the migrants to work abroad (IOM, 2020a).

Table 8.1: Labour migration arrangements involving European and West African countries

Countries with agreements	Scope (fulltime/ temporary employment	Duration	Training component	Sector	Re-integration support	Possibility for extended stay in country of destination	Implementation partner / period
Nigeria – Lithuania	Traineeship in destination country	6–12 months	No training in country of origin (soft skills)	ICT	Yes	No. Brain circulation is a key component of the project	ICMPD (1.01.2019 –30.09.2020)[5]
Nigeria – Netherlands	Employment in country of origin (remote work) or destination country	12–24 months	Skills development; knowledge transfer; peer-to-peer capacity building	ICT	Unclear	Unclear	IOM/NABC (01.01.2020 – 01.01.2023)
Senegal – Netherlands	Employment in country of origin (remote work) or destination country	12–24 months	Skills development; knowledge transfer; peer-to-peer capacity building	ICT	Unclear	Unclear	IOM/NABC (01.01.2020 – 01.01.2023)

Source: compiled by the author

Having realised, through failed attempts, the importance of involving key stakeholders to achieve the objectives, the projects also collaborate with a broad range of stakeholders to design, implement and promote the schemes. These stakeholders include: labour and trade unions; workers' groups; the private sector in the relevant industries; training institutions; and different government ministries and agencies, including labour, foreign affairs or ministries responsible for labour migration and domestic labour needs, migration policy, integration and entrepreneurship. Other stakeholders include the city councils and police. The projects also focus on the links between employment and the educational sector in these countries of origin, especially in projects where a training component is carried out in the countries of origin. The projects envisage benefits for both destination and origin countries, as migrants on return to their countries of origin can contribute to domestic development through their acquired skills. Migrants who choose to stay in the host countries, where the conditions allow, can also contribute through remittances sent back to their families.

Legal pathways: Implications for individuals and states

Enhancing legal pathways for migration between the EU and third countries is based on two broad narratives, as seen from the earlier sections. The first is that enhanced legal pathways will facilitate accessibility of migrants to European countries. However, migration cooperation between the EU and other regions such as the West Balkan states, and Moldova or Georgia in particular, reveals that the visa facilitation agreements or circular mobility schemes between the EU and partner countries do not improve the mobility of services and people, but rather that restrictions to individual mobility to EU countries remain (Brouillette, 2018). The national policies or programmes established and the practices in implementing these programmes differ from the narratives, and in practice limited opportunities are available for individuals to migrate through legal channels. On the other hand, through the existence of these schemes, the European Commission increases its leverage in readmission negotiations with partner countries. Thus, in the second broad narrative, cooperation on the legal benefits of migration is linked with reducing illegal migration and implementing an effective return policy in collaboration with third countries (Brouillette, 2018 ; Barslund et al., 2019). And evidently, the narrative on creating legal pathways to reduce irregular migration through return and cooperation on readmissions is the one that primarily facilitates the cooperation between European and non-European states at present.

These narratives, in turn, influence the politics of states that drive migration cooperation. Although the transmission mechanisms are not clearly defined, these narratives and politics equally contribute to the design of national policy frameworks on labour migration and how these frameworks are implemented in practice (Geddes et al., 2020). Thus, while the narratives and their ensuing politics may contribute to facilitating cooperation at state level, policy frameworks and practice define accessibility at the individual level. This concept, as summarised in Figure 8.1, is used to analyse legal migration arrangements between European and West African countries. It highlights the narratives and politics of cooperation between states and illustrates how these broad principles translate into increased accessibility for migrants at the individual level.

Figure 8.1: Concept analysing legal migration arrangements between European and West African countries

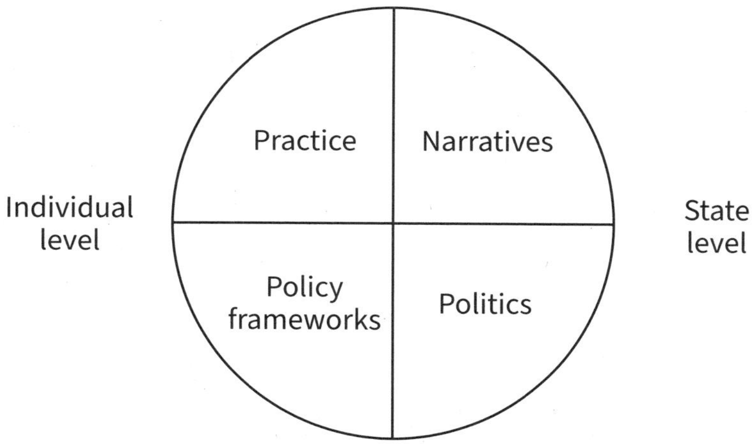

Source: compiled by the author

Legal pathways and migration cooperation between the EU and third countries

Legal pathways are a key component of the EU strategy to strengthen cooperation with third countries (European Commission, 2017). The EU has designed its migration cooperation with third countries to include the use of incentives and leverages to achieve its objectives, as stated in the EAM. The partnership framework was designed by the EU as part of this holistic and coordinated approach. There are five priority countries in the partnership framework, three of which are in West Africa – Nigeria, Mali and Senegal. Simply put, the EU has leveraged on its partnership with third countries through the implementation of some 'carrot and stick' measures, primarily to improve cooperation on returns and readmissions.

There are currently 23 readmission agreements and practical arrangements between West African countries and EU member states (European Commission, 2019b). These practical arrangements enable EU member states to facilitate the returns of nationals to their countries of origin. It also improves the cooperation between officials of European states and third countries in the identification of nationals, and the issuance of emergency travel documents to facilitate the return of these identified persons. Although the EU has been successful in signing these arrangements and securing the cooperation of West African states, the actual number of returns conducted still remains low for other structural reasons.

Furthermore, there has also been improved dialogue on migration between the EU and West African countries. While the EU has many dialogue platforms and processes on migration with West African countries at national, regional and continental levels, most of these processes are stuck. This is a result of the migration crisis; the negative treatment of African migrants in Europe; and the practices of European states which lead to the deaths of African migrants in the Mediterranean Sea. Moreover, African policymakers believed that their views were ignored by their European counterparts, especially on creating legal pathways for migration. However, the commencement of the pilot projects, mentioned earlier, has improved cooperation between countries on both sides. These pilot projects appear to be an extension of the goodwill of European states to improve on their cooperation with African states. They are also an indication that European states are listening to the demands of their African counterparts and are willing to compromise.

As already indicated, European states have mainly leveraged these labour migration arrangements to promote increased cooperation on border management and joint surveillance. As a result, liaison officers from European states are posted to West African countries to assist in the implementation of border management solutions. These officials also assist in joint surveillance patrols to detect and identify migration through irregular channels, such as migrant smuggling networks. These joint operations, carried out by the national agencies with the assistance of European states, has led to high profile arrests of smugglers and large rescue missions of irregular migrants. In addition, the collaboration on legal migration arrangements provides an avenue to build the capacity of West African state agencies, ministries and other stakeholders on various aspects of migration, including irregular and labour migration.

Thus, the European Commission and its member states, through legal migration arrangements, have improved their cooperation with non-European states on migration with the aim of reducing irregular migration and implementing returns.

Creating increased accessibility for migrants

There are no official figures on irregular migrants from West African countries to Europe. However, it was estimated that half of the irregular migrants from West Africa to the EU are a result of overstays of short-stay entry visas (European Commission, 2008). Contrary to common beliefs, migration from West Africa to Europe between 2011 to 2017 was mostly regular (IOM, 2019); but during the same period, both regular and irregular entries to the EU reduced overall. Generally, about 53 per cent of African migrants remain in Africa and move within their regions (Flahaux and De Haas, 2016). Migrants from West Africa to Europe are motivated by economic factors, low governance indices, exclusion from the society, and aspirations for an improved wellbeing (Kirwin and Andersson, 2018; UNDP, 2019).

There is limited information about the socio-economic profile of irregular migrants from West African counties. Countries with the highest number of irregular migrants in the EU are Nigeria, Ghana, Senegal and Guinea. A recent study conducted by the IOM shows that among these migrants, about one-third had completed a lower secondary education (IOM, 2019). Another study conducted by the UN Development Programmes (UNDP, 2019) revealed that most respondents were typically educated above the average levels in their home countries. Migrants who arrived in Europe using irregular channels were highly educated, employed or enrolled in higher education at the time of their departure to Europe (UNDP, 2019). From the sample of 3,096 respondents, 43 per cent had completed secondary school, 6 per cent had completed some type of vocational training, and 8 per cent had studied to tertiary-level education. Thus, these studies reveal the varying levels of education among irregular migrants from West Africa, so the stereotype of irregular migrants as lacking education and skills is contentious.

Regular migrants within Europe have been measured using the proxy of first residence permits issued (IOM, 2019). While the total number of first residence permits issued for African migrants increased between 2011 and 2018, the number of permits issued to West African nationals decreased from 19,397 in 2011 to 17,752 in 2018, representing an 8 per cent drop.[6] Only 33 per cent of permits were issued to nationals from West African countries, with Nigerians, Senegalese and Ghanaians getting the highest number of permits (IOM, 2019). In addition, the number of residence permits granted for work purposes fell sharply over the same period. These permits were issued mostly for family reunification purposes (59 per cent), educational purposes (25 per cent), and for work (16 per cent) (IOM, 2019).

Furthermore, between 2016 and 2018, there was a significant reduction in the number of short-stay visas, including visas for study issued to nationals of West African countries. Nigeria is the most significant country in this regard, with an estimated 50 per cent decline in the number of successful applications (Bisong, 2020b). This reduction in the number of successful visa applications makes it difficult for third country nationals from West African states to gain access to the EU through legal channels. Interviews with irregular migrants confirm that they initially attempted to gain access to Europe for work or to study using legal channels but were denied entry visas (UNDP, 2019).

There is a diversity of migrants from West Africa seeking to gain access to Europe for a variety of reasons. However, the limited scope of the legal mobility arrangements target only experts within specific sectors of the economy. The narratives by the European states on creating channels for legal access to Europe do not translate into practical options for most migrants from West Africa. While these narratives are ongoing at the political level, there is a disconnect between these narratives and the practices of state institutions. For example, although commitments were made at the Valletta Summit by European and African states to increase the opportunities for scholarships and research under various educational programmes, including Erasmus and Marie Curie fellowships, the number of first residence permits issued to West African nationals for educational purposes has reduced (IOM, 2019). Therefore, in practice, labour migration arrangements do not create significantly more opportunities, outside existing avenues, for migrants to gain access to Europe.

Conclusion

A comprehensive approach to migration has been portrayed by the European Commission as being essential to replace irregular and unsafe pathways with legal, orderly and safe channels for those in need of protection, and attractive and efficient channels for those needed in European labour markets. These measures are proving difficult to implement, however, especially in terms of aligning the employment needs of migrant-producing countries with the foreign policy interests of EU member states. Thus, in adopting a comprehensive approach to migration cooperation, West African and European states need to create legal pathways and options that are feasible to aspiring labour migrants.

The current arrangements do not fit these needs and cannot be scaled up sustainably. For these measures to be effective in creating opportunities at the individual level, it is important to create programmes that match the skills profiles of potential users of irregular migrant routes. Also, cooperation needs to go beyond pilot projects and involve the private sector more comprehensively, and not only selected companies, to achieve a more sustainable result and impact. Migrants should have increased opportunities to upgrade and acquire skills, which can be used on return and in the host communities. The European Commission, its member states and West African countries should have a coordinated approach to monitoring these pilot projects and identifying the aspects that can be scaled up to promote legal migration.

More concretely, while acknowledging that the EU has a limited mandate to implement labour migration programmes, it can mobilise and support its member states to create such programmes, beyond pilot projects. The European Commission can contribute to the knowledge sharing and experiences of countries implementing these programmes. It can highlight the positive or negative experiences of countries implementing these pilots. This can be done through expert exchanges or dialogues involving the key partners in both migrant sending and receiving states. These dialogues should highlight the successful points of the cooperation and the areas for improvement. These experiences can contribute to reforming and shaping the EU's policy guidelines on such labour migration programmes. Beyond providing guiding policies, it is difficult for the EU to push states to create these pathways as it is beyond the mandate of the commission. Also, the EU can further its activities on blue card measures with a view to harmonising the regulations relating to the entry and stay of migrant workers within the EU.

This research has shown that – following the Valletta Summit and the commitment by policy makers to improve opportunities for migrants – no immediate measures were taken at the national level to promote legal pathways. For example, the first pilot project with Nigeria began four years after the Valletta Summit. Furthermore, there was even a decline in the number of first resident permits issued and the number of successful visa applications for nationals from West African countries. Therefore, the EU needs to show a genuine commitment to providing legal pathways. This can be done by increasing the scale of such legal programmes and through better coordination between actors. The declining numbers of admissions of regular migrants should be communicated to the European public. This could help to gain public support for legal measures for admitting migrants, with a limited backlash from the EU public and politicians, especially given the role of migrant workers in Europe – both formal and informal sectors – during the pandemic and the renewed sense of appreciation for these workers.

Notes

1 There were 36 African countries present at the Valletta Summit. The African Union was also present, along with other African regional economic communities. Online at: https://www.consilium.europa.eu/media/23727/v-summit-2015-trombinoscope.pdf (accessed 2 February 2021). Twenty African countries and six Regional Economic Communities were not invited to participate at the Valletta Summit (Knoll and De Weijer, 2016).

2 Funding on EUTF projects along four thematic areas: migration management – €1,392,048,627; strengthening resilience – €1,193,153,505; governance and conflict prevention – €1,011,102,960; and greater economic employment opportunities – €858,864,827 (EUTF website).

3 Although the 1999 Treaty of Amsterdam provides the EU with a formal mandate for labour migration from outside the European Economic Area, states are unwilling to cede their sovereignty to the EU and hesitant to harmonise their labour migration policies (Geddes et al., 2020).

4 Table 8.1 provides an overview of the projects.

5 An extension to the project and possible scaling up is currently being discussed with the project partners.

6 According to Eurostat data, there were 472,597 first residence permits issued to migrants from West African countries between 2011 and 2017, which amounts to 33 per cent of the total issued to nationals from northern and western African countries during this period.

References

Abebe, T. 2020. 'Fewer migrants to Europe, bigger problems for Africa'. Addis Ababa: Institute for Strategic Studies (ISS). Online at: https://issafrica.org/iss-today/fewer-migrants-to-europe-bigger-problems-for-africa (accessed 7 April 2020).

Afriko. 2020. ICT4D project/Digital Explorers. Online at: https://www.afriko.lt/ict4dprojectdigitalexplorers/ (accessed 7 April 2020).

Baldwin-Edwards, M., Blitz, B. and Crawley, H. 2019. 'The politics of evidence-based policy in Europe's "migration crisis"', *Journal of Ethnic and Migration Studies*, 45(12): 2139–55.

Baltic Times. 2019. '"Digital explorers" at the forefront of EU–Africa Digital Partnership'. Online at: https://www.baltictimes.com/_digital_explorers__at_the_forefront_of_eu_-_africa_digital_partnership/ (accessed 20 February 2021).

Barslund, M., Di Salvo, M., Laurentsyeva, N., Lixi, L. and Ludolph, L. 2019. 'An EU–Africa partnership scheme for human capital formation and skill mobility'. CEPS Project Report. June 2019.

Bisong, A. 2020a. 'The new EU visa code and what it means for African countries'. ECDPM Talking points. Maastricht: European Centre for Development Policy Management. 06 April 2020.

Bisong, A. 2020b. 'Migration Partnership Framework and the externalization of European Union's (EU) migration policy in West Africa: The case of Mali and Niger', in G. Rayp, I. Ruyssen and K. Marchand (eds). *Regional Integration and Migration Governance in the Global South.* Heidelberg and London: Springer, pp. 217–37.

Bisong, A. 2019. 'Trans-regional institutional cooperation as multilevel governance: ECOWAS migration policy and the EU', *Journal of Ethnic and Migration Studies*, 45(8): 1294–309.

Bjarnesen, J. 2020. *Shifting the Narrative on African Migration: The numbers, the root causes, the alternatives – get them right!* Nordic Africa Institute. NAI Policy Notes 2020: 1. Online at: https://reliefweb.int/report/world/shifting-narrative-african-migration-numbers-root-causes-alternatives-get-them-right (accessed 28 February 2021).

Brouillette, M. 2018. 'From discourse to practice: The circulation of norms, ideas and practices of migration management through the implementation of the mobility partnerships in Moldova and Georgia', *Comparative Migration Studies*, 6(1): 1–21.

Cottier, T. and Sieber-Gasser, C. 2015. 'Labour migration, trade and investment: From fragmentation to coherence', in M. Panizzon, G. Zurcher, E. Fornalé and G. Zürcher (eds). *The Palgrave Handbook of International Labour Migration*. London: Palgrave Macmillan, pp. 41–60.

European Commission. 2019a. Progress report on the implementation of the European Agenda on Migration. Communication from the commission to the European Parliament, the European council and the Council. COM (2019) 126 final, 6 March 2019. Online at: https://ec.europa.eu/home-affairs/sites/homeaffairs/files/what-we-do/policies/european-agenda-migration/20190306_com-2019-126-report_en.pdf (accessed 20 February 2021).

European Commission. 2019b. Progress report on the Implementation of the European Agenda on Migration. Communication from the commission to the European Parliament, the European council and the Council. 16 October 2019. Online at: https://ec.europa.eu/home-affairs/sites/homeaffairs/files/what-we-do/policies/european-agenda-migration/20191016_com-2019-481-report_en.pdf (accessed 20 February 2021).

European Commission. 2018a. Enhancing legal pathways to Europe: an indispensable part of a balanced and comprehensive migration policy. Communication from the commission to the European Parliament, the European council and the Council. 12 September 2018. Online at: https://ec.europa.eu/commission/sites/beta-political/files/soteu2018-legal-pathways-europe-communication-635_en.pdf (accessed 20 February 2021).

European Commission. 2018b. Managing Migration in all Its Aspects: Progress Under the European Agenda On Migration. Communication from the commission to the European Parliament, the European council and the Council. 4 December 2018. Brussels: European Commission.

Online at: https://ec.europa.eu/commission/sites/beta-political/files/eu-communication-migration-euco-04122018_en_1.pdf (accessed 20 February 2021).

European Commission. 2017. Delivery of the European Agenda on Migration. Communication from the commission to the European Parliament, the Council, the European Economic and Social Committee and the Committee of the Regions. 27 September 2017. Online at: https://ec.europa.eu/home-affairs/sites/homeaffairs/files/what-we-do/policies/european-agenda-migration/20170927_communication_on_the_delivery_of_the_eam_en.pdf (accessed 20 February 2021).

European Commission. 2016. Communication from the Commission to the European Parliament, the Council, and the European Investment Bank on establishing a new partnership framework with third countries under the European Agenda on Migration. COM (2016) 0385 final, 7 June 2016. Online at: https://eur-lex.europa.eu/resource.html?uri=cellar:763f0d11-2d86-11e6-b497-01aa75ed71a1.0001.02/DOC_1&format=PDF (accessed 20 February 2021).

European Commission. 2015. *A European Agenda on Migration*. Communication from the Commission to the European Parliament, the Council, the European Economic and Social Committee and the Committee of the Regions. COM (2015) 240 final, 13 May 2015. Online at: https://ec.europa.eu/anti-trafficking/sites/antitrafficking/files/communication_on_the_european_agenda_on_migration_en.pdf (accessed 20 February 2021).

European Commission. 2014. Communication from the Commission to the European Parliament and the Council on the implementation of Directive 2009/50/EC on the conditions of entry and residence of third-country nationals for the purpose of high qualified employment (EU Blue Card). COM (2014) 287 final, 22 May 2014. Online at: https://www.europarl.europa.eu/meetdocs/2014_2019/documents/com/com_com(2014)0287_/com_com(2014)0287_en.pdf (accessed 20 February 2021).

European Commission. 2008. Accompanying document to the communication from the Commission to the European Parliament, the Council, The European Economic and Social Committee and the Committee of the regions preparing the next steps in border management in the European Union impact assessment. 13 February 2008. Online at: https://eur-lex.europa.eu/LexUriServ/LexUriServ.do?uri=COM:2008:0069:FIN:EN:PDF (accessed).

European Commission. 2007. Communication from the Commission to the

European Parliament, the Council, The European Economic and Social Committee and the Committee of the regions on circular migration and mobility partnerships between the European Union and third countries. 16 May 2007. Online at: https://eur-lex.europa.eu/LexUriServ/LexUriServ.do?uri=COM:2007:0248:FIN:EN:PDF (accessed 20 February 2021)

European Union Council. 2015. Remarks by President Donald Tusk at the press conference of the Valletta Summit on Migration, 12 November 2015. Online at: http://statewatch.org/news/2015/nov/eu-africa-Valletta-Summit-tusk-final-remarks.pdf (accessed 20 February 2021).

European Court of Auditors. 2018. 'European Union Emergency Trust Fund for Africa: Flexible but lacking focus'. Special Report No. 32. Online at: https://www.eca.europa.eu/Lists/ECADocuments/SR18_32/SR_EUTF_AFRICA_EN.pdf (accessed 20 February 2021).

Flahaux, M.L. and De Haas, H. 2016. 'African migration: Trends, patterns, drivers', *Comparative Migration Studies*, 4(1): 1.

Geddes, A., Hadj-Abdou, L. and Brumat, L. 2020. *Migration and Mobility in the European Union*, 2nd edition. The European Union Series. London: Red Globe Press.

Hauck, V., Knoll, A. and Cangas, A.H. 2015. 'EU Trust Funds: Shaping more comprehensive external action'. European Centre for Development Policy Management Briefing Note, No. 81.

Hooper, K. 2019. *Exploring New Legal Migration Pathways: Lessons from pilot projects*. Washington, DC: Migration Policy Institute.

International Labour Organization (ILO). 2017. 'Addressing governance challenges in a changing labour migration landscape'. Report IV, International Labour Conference, 106th Session, 2017. Geneva.

International Organization for Migration (IOM). 2021. 'DTM Europe: Displacement Tracking Matrix (DTM) (January – March 2021) - Quarterly Regional Report, Q1 2021'. Online at: https://reliefweb.int/report/world/dtm-europe-displacement-tracking-matrix-dtm-january-march-2021-quarterly-regional (accessed 4 May).

International Organization for Migration (IOM). 2020a. 'Migrant Integration – MATCH'. Online at: https://iom-nederland.nl/en/migrant-integration/match (accessed 20 February 2021).

International Organization for Migration (IOM). 2020b. 'Migration of African talent through capacity building and hiring'. Project information sheet. Online at: https://belgium.iom.int/sites/default/files/Gallery/MATCH-Info-Sheet-EN-online.pdf (accessed 20 February 2021).

International Organization for Migration (IOM). 2019. 'African Migration to the EU: Irregular Migration in Context'. GMDAC Briefing Series: Towards safer migration on the Central Mediterranean Route. Global Migration Data Analysis Centre, Berlin. Online at: https://gmdac.iom.int/sites/default/files/03_-_residence_permits-bbb.pdf (accessed 20 February 2021).

Kabbanji, L. 2013. 'Towards a global agenda on migration and development? Evidence from Senegal', *Population, Space and Place*, 19(4): 415–29.

Kervyn, E. and Shilhav, R. 2017. 'An emergency for whom? The EU Emergency Trust Fund for Africa – migratory routes and development aid in Africa'. 15 November 2017. Nairobi: Oxfam.

Kipp, D. 2018 *From Exception to Rule: The EU Trust Fund for Africa*. SWP Research Paper 2018/RP13, December 2018. Online at: https://www.swp-berlin.org/en/publication/eu-trust-fund-for-africa/ (accessed 20 February 2021).

Kirwin, M. and J. Anderson. 2018. 'Identifying the factors driving West African migration', *West African Papers*, N°17. Paris: OECD Publishing.

Knoll, A. and De Weijer F. 2016. *Understanding African and European Perspectives on Migration: Towards a better partnership for regional migration governance?* ECDPM Discussion Paper No. 203. November 2016. Online at: https://ecdpm.org/wp-content/uploads/DP203-Understanding-African-European-Perspectives-Migration-November-2016.pdf (accessed 20 February 2021).

McAuliffe, M. and A. Triandafyllidou (eds.), 2021. World Migration Report 2022. International Organization for Migration (IOM), Geneva.

Maisenbacher, J. 2015. 'The political economy of mobility partnerships: Structural power in the EU's external migration policy', *New Political Economy*, 20(6): 871–93.

Martin, P. 2015. 'Low-skilled labour migration and free trade agreements', in M. Panizzon, G. Zurcher, E. Fornalé and G. Zürcher (eds). *The Palgrave Handbook of International Labour Migration*. London: Palgrave Macmillan, pp. 205–30.

Okai, A. 2020. 'Five ways to keep remittances flowing in COVID-19'. UNDP. 16 June 2020. Online at: https://www.undp.org/content/undp/en/home/blog/2020/five-ways-to-keep-remittances-flowing-in-covid-19.html.

Panizzon, M. 2011. 'Franco-African pacts on migration', in R. Kunz, S. Lavenex and M. Panizzon (eds). *Multilayered Migration Governance: The promise of partnership*. London: Routledge, pp. 207–48.

Papademetriou, D. and Hooper, K. 2020. Commentary: How is COVID 19 reshaping labour migration? International Migration. doi: 10.1111/imig.12748 Online at: https://onlinelibrary.wiley.com/doi/epdf/10.1111/

imig.12748 (accessed 20 February 2021).

Stefanescu, D. 2021 Partnerships for Mobility at the Crossroads: Lessons learnt from 18 months of implementation of EU pilot projects on legal migration. ICMPD, MPF. Brussels.

Toma, S. 2014. 'Policy and institutional frameworks: Senegal country report'. Technical Report, INTERACT Research Report, Country Reports, 2014/16. Florence, Italy: Migration Policy Centre.

Triandafyllidou, A. (ed.). 2013. *Circular Migration between Europe and its Neighbourhood: Choice or necessity?* Oxford: Oxford University Press.

United Nations Development Programme (UNDP). 2019. *Scaling Fences: Voices of irregular African migrants to Europe.* Geneva: UNDP.

United Nations, Department of Economic and Social Affairs, Population Division (2019). International Migration 2019: Report (ST/ESA/SER. A/438).

United Nations. 2018. Global Compact on Safe, Orderly and Regular Migration. Online at: https://refugeesmigrants.un.org/sites/default/files/180711_final_draft_0.pdf (accessed 6 February 2021).

United Nations. 2020. 'Policy Brief: COVID-19 and people on the move'. June 2020. Online at: https://www.un.org/sites/un2.un.org/files/sg_policy_brief_on_people_on_the_move.pdf (accessed 6 February 2021).

United Nations. 2018. Global Compact on Safe, Orderly and Regular Migration. Online at: https://refugeesmigrants.un.org/sites/default/files/180711_final_draft_0.pdf (accessed 6 February 2021).

Valletta Summit Action Plan. 2015. Online at: https://www.consilium.europa.eu/media/21839/action_plan_en.pdf (accessed 20 February 2021).

Chapter 9

Migration: Southern Africa and the European Union (EU)

Pragna Rugunanan, Terri Maggott and Celine Meyers

Introduction

The movement of people, labour and goods is not a new phenomenon in the southern African context. It stretches back from the arrival of Europeans in Africa in the 1400s through to the 1820s and the Mfecane Wars, and to the 1860s during the mineral revolutions in what is now Johannesburg and Kimberley. Present-day migration in southern Africa can be described as mixed. It is made up of several migration flows, including documented and undocumented migrants. Labour migration, mainly from Botswana and Zimbabwe, is embedded in a long history that centres on South Africa's many gold, platinum and diamond mines. Although much of the migration flows occur intra-regionally (African Union Commission, 2018), since the end of colonial rule, from about the 1980s, there has been an increase in emigration from southern Africa to Europe due to perceptions that economic and social opportunities are greater there.

To locate the study within the social and political reality in which migration trends occur, it is important to note at the outset, a few important characteristics of the region. Southern Africa is home to approximately 67 million people and South Africa is the African country with the largest white population. Within the region, a sending–receiving dichotomy exists between the more industrialised economic centres of South Africa, Botswana and oil-rich Angola, and the sending countries such as the Democratic Republic of Congo (DRC), Mozambique and Zimbabwe (United Nations, 2020). In addition, southern African countries such as Mozambique, South Africa, and Zimbabwe gained their independence from colonial rule comparatively late compared, for example, to their West African counterparts. This has, in some instances, resulted in what has been described as a pattern of circular migration, in which people who were regionally displaced by anticolonial violence in the 1980s have since returned to their home countries. A diverse region, both economically and culturally, southern Africa records migration related to the pursuit of economic opportunities, political instability, as with, for example, the DRC and Zimbabwe, and, more recently, changing environmental factors (UN, 2020).

This chapter unpacks migration flows and trajectories, and analyses how these migration streams are shaped by both policy frameworks implemented by European and southern African states, and by political instability and the pursuit of a better life by southern African migrants. First, it discusses the nature of southern Africa–European Union (EU) migration governance, providing the context in which, increasingly, bilateral agreements between member states are agreed and implemented (or not). Second, it presents migration trends between southern Africa and the EU, the vice versa, and from within Africa to southern Africa. Finally, it examines policy debates surrounding migration governance in the region, drawing explicit lessons from the analysis of these trends to southern African–EU migration policy issues.

Migration governance in southern Africa

While most of the migration within Africa occurs intra-continentally, and most migration in southern Africa occurs intra-regionally, increased focus and resources have been directed at addressing the challenges of Africa–EU migration (AU Commission, 2018: 21). For example, in 2015 the European Trust Fund for Africa (EUTF) was established to deliver an integrated and coordinated response to the root causes of irregular migration and forced displacement, such as political instability, the lack of economic opportunities, and environmental crises. Its geographic scope covered three regions, namely, the Sahel and Lake Chad, the Horn of Africa, and North Africa. EUTF funds have contributed significantly to the gross domestic product (GDP) of recipient countries, such as Niger and South Sudan.

However, focusing only on African migration to Europe ignores the realities of southern African migration, which occurs mostly intra-regionally. Policies and Africa–EU partnerships around migration and mobility in southern Africa, emerge largely as a result of bilateral agreements between EU Member States and southern African governments, such as between the Netherlands and South Africa, and the DRC and Belgium. Bilateral agreements are commonplace within the continent generally (Nakayama, 2018: 29), and this is also the case in the southern region.

There is no single guiding document or policy framework that regulates migration between the EU and southern Africa, but rather sets of bilateral agreements between states that dictate migration governance within the region. Migration governance and policy in the region is guided by the AU's Migration Policy Framework for Africa (MPFA), which is invested in the value of free movement and ensures a series of protections and rights for migrants, refugees, asylum seekers and migrant workers (Nakayama, 2018). Indeed, bilateral agreements inform the nature and scope of international movement within the countries in agreement, and as such operate over or parallel to policy frameworks that require international cooperation, because the latter require multistate ratification, which has been difficult to achieve. As a result, an array of visa options overlap in different countries. For example, EU citizens arriving in Botswana, Namibia and South Africa are automatically granted a visa exemption, which allows them to stay for up to ninety days, which is no different from the exemptions afforded to regional passport holders (Stiftung Entwicklung und Frieden [SEF], 2016). However, SADC countries such as Botswana and Namibia also offer visa-free entry to other countries such as the United States of America and Canada, which suggests that this visa-free trend is part of a larger plan by these (developing) countries to attract foreign direct investment (FDI) and tourism (Urso and Hakami, 2018).

Policy debates highlight that often when South–North migration occurs, a humanitarian or political crisis needs to be managed, whereas when North–South migration occurs, at least in the post-colonial period, the narrative is one of tourism and travel, and not migration or labour migration. The EU and the SADC signed an Economic Partnership Agreement (EPA) in 2016 with a view to improving opportunities for trade and exports. However, issues of migration are not included in this pact. The narrative around the migration trajectory from the EU to southern Africa is one of travel and tourism. This ignores the trend of Europeans working and living within the SADC, in countries such as South Africa and Namibia.

Trajectories from Europe to southern Africa

The history of European migration to southern Africa is not a new phenomenon, dating back to the colonial conquests of the Portuguese in the late 1400s, the Dutch East India Company in the 1600–1800s, and the British in the 1820s. In his classic book, *Heart of Darkness*, Joseph Conrad depicts the treacherous travels of male European explorers to the vast Congo Basin in modern-day DRC, where decades of instability can be traced back to European conquest (Conrad, 1902). The mineral revolutions in Botswana, Namibia, Zimbabwe and South Africa were another milestone in the trajectories of European–southern African migration, bringing British, German and Dutch mine managers and technicians from the 1870s to the present day (Armbruster, 2010). This North–South trajectory was underpinned by racism, evangelism, and rape of Africans and the abundance of resources on the continent. This exploitation was disrupted by decades of anti-colonial movements organised by the emerging, European-educated African elite (Lonsdale, 1990: 398), from as early as 1912, when the African National Congress (ANC), the oldest anti-colonial movement in Africa, was formed. During one such period of unrest in Mozambique in 1975, almost 250,000 European descendants fled to Portugal or were expelled from the country (Åkesson and Orjuela, 2017). Similar trends were observed in Angola and South Africa, during and after the transitions to democratic rule (Segatti, 2011; Åkesson and Orjuela, 2017). Since apartheid ended in 1994, and the South African borders were demilitarised, the southern African region has been liberalised in terms of movement and global economic, political and cultural integration (Nshimbi and Fioramonti, 2014).

Within the SADC, the focus on Europeans migrating to the region is rather limited compared to the focus on the migration of Africans to southern Africa (Flahaux and Schoumaker, 2016). It is important to note that the region is home to both South Africa, the African country with the largest population of migrants within its borders, and the DRC, one of the most populous African countries. A 2011 study by Statistics South Africa (Stats SA) showed that 'immigrants from the Europe region had the second highest percentage of international migrants in South Africa, after those from the SADC region, a percentage higher than migrants from other African countries outside the SADC' (Stats SA, 2011: 145). Åkesson and Orjuela (2017) highlight the trend of Portuguese citizens migrating to Angola, a former Portuguese colony, to seek better economic and job opportunities. Although this case seems 'exceptional' (Åkesson and Orjuela, 2017), it suggests that the trajectory of southern Africa–EU migration is not unidirectional, from southern Africa to Europe, but is actually nuanced and multidirectional: people move from the EU to southern Africa; from southern Africa to the EU; and, most predominantly, within the region. In addition, South Africa attracts highly skilled labour, particularly in the financial sector and the motor industry (Migration Data Portal, 2020).

The trend of Europeans migrating to countries within the southern African region differs from country to country. For example, Namibia has recently launched a retiree residency programme for EU citizens hoping to retire in a quiet and picturesque setting. In 2014, about 220,000 Portuguese nationals were residing in Angola (Åkesson and Orjuela, 2017). In contrast, in the DRC, the migration of Europeans to the region after independence in 1960 has remained low, largely due to the political instability in the region since the 1990s (Flahaux and Schoumaker, 2016). South Africa remains the African country with the most European migrants within its borders (MDP, 2020), which can be attributed to its economic dominance within the region and the continent more broadly, because of its historical economic hegemony through settler colonialism.

Trend from southern Africa to Europe

Although southern Africans were colonial subjects from the 18th century to as recently as the 1990s, their mobility to Europe was restricted and reserved primarily for the educated elite. Recent research suggests that migration within the region is more desirable and accessible to southern Africans (EC, 2018: 14) than it is to Europe. During regime changes, there has been a pattern of African citizens of European descent migrating back to Europe. For example, when the DRC was granted independence from Belgium in 1960, the state administration suffered immensely as civil servants, mostly Europeans, fled the country for fear of a backlash from the black majority (Flahaux and Schoumaker, 2016). Similarly, in South Africa in 1990, during the dismantling of apartheid 333,000 – mostly white – South Africans emigrated; this number stood at 900,000 in 2017 (UN Department of Economic and Social Affairs, 2019). Another more recent dimension of migration from the region to the EU is that of refugees and asylum seekers from countries where prolonged political crises, such as the DRC and Zimbabwe, have driven people to seek a better life in countries such as France and Belgium, and the United Kingdom, respectively. The EU New Pact on Migration and Asylum has been designed and implemented to manage this movement.

Europe has been the second most popular destination for African migrants, after countries within Africa itself (Nakayama, 2018: 28). Three countries show a different pattern from this overall trend: South Africa, Madagascar and Mauritius. Both Madagascar and Mauritius have large diasporas in the EU, namely in France and the United Kingdom, respectively (Natale et al., 2018: 12). South Africa, the African country with one of the world's most diverse emigration patterns, has remained a sending country to Europe, mostly to Britain and Germany (Natale et al., 2018: 12). For example, 6,000 South Africans emigrated to Germany in 2020 and more are expected as Germany encourages skilled workers to move there (Destasis, 2020). In the case of migration between Mauritius and the EU, the 2009 Visa Waiver Agreement granted Mauritians free access to travel and conduct business in the Schengen. This is the exception rather than the rule, given that for most southern African countries, such as the DRC and Zimbabwe, mobility and migration to the EU have been marked by crises and restrictions (Flahaux and Schoumaker, 2016).

The major instrument for migration governance between the two continents is the Euro-African Dialogue on Migration and Development, or the Rabat Process of 2006, to which no southern African country is currently a signatory. The Migration Dialogue for Southern Africa (MIDSA) also regulates international migration flows. As expected, policy debates have focused largely on regional migration, given that 68 per cent of the movement of people occurred within the region in 2011 (Stats SA, 2011: 145). By 2020, about 80 per cent of African migrants travel within Africa (African Centre for Strategic Studies, 2020). However, a large percentage of the southern Africans on the move are highly skilled and young professionals migrating to other continents, including the EU. For example, in 1979, the German Democratic Republic and socialist Mozambique entered into a labour agreement under which thousands of black Mozambicans emigrated to East Germany on work contracts. Forty years later, many of their descendants have remained in Germany. Documented migrants in the EU in 2008 were mostly 'South Africans (126,065), Zimbabweans (86,075), Congolese (73,905), and Angolans (49,645)' (Ellis and Segatti, 2011: 72). This type of movement is conceptualised largely as emigration or as the 'brain drain', which occludes the nuanced nature of southern Africa–EU migration and the diverse reasons for why southern Africans choose to move.

Issues of poverty, discrimination, economic growth and freedom, prompt skilled graduates from predominantly health, engineering and technology sectors in southern Africa to migrate to developed countries (Docquire, 2014; Crush, 2019). In sub-Saharan Africa, the health sector is one of the primary divisions linked to the 'brain drain' debate. For instance, the number of physicians from southern African in the United States increased by 38 per cent between 2002 and 2011. Liberia was the most affected – it lost 77 per cent of its physicians (Tankwanchi et al., 2013). Although the 'brain drain' phenomenon has detrimental effects for southern Africa, it is also considered to be beneficial for growth and development, human capital, remittances and a return of highly skilled migrants (Docquire, 2014).

Southern African intracontinental migration

Much like migration between Europe and Africa, migration within the African continent is an age-old phenomenon, predating the arrival of Europeans on the continent in the late 1400s. Within the southern African region, the movement of people from one community and region to another dates back millions of years to when *Homo erectus* spread throughout East Africa and into southern Africa. The century-long movement of Bantu people from West Africa to southern Africa has contributed to the formation of large ethnic groups, such as the Zulu nation. The Mfecane Wars between the second and third decades of the 19th century triggered large migration flows within the region and displaced one to two million people, the figure generally agreed on by scholars. More recently, the white minority apartheid regime in South Africa, until 1994, influenced the region in terms of both political and trade relations, and the movement of people by destabilising the Frontline States (FLS) as part of its Total Strategy.

The Southern African Development Coordination Conference (SADCC) was a loose organisation of southern African states, initiated in the 1980s. It opposed the lingering colonialism and apartheid, the abolishment of which led to the establishment of the Southern African Development Community (SADC) in 1992, in line with the AU's vision of regional economic integration through Regional Economic Communities (RECs).

Since 2020, the SADC has had 16 member states: Angola, Botswana, Comoros, DRC, Lesotho, Madagascar, Malawi, Mauritius, Mozambique, Namibia, Seychelles, South Africa, Swaziland, Tanzania, Zambia, and Zimbabwe. There is an increasing need to harmonise migration policy within the SADC (Dodson and Crush, 2015: 1), given the weak influence it exerts over its member states and the continued dominance of South Africa and its securitisation of migration governance. The need for regional integration is vital, especially given the high levels of intraregional migration within southern Africa. Oucho (2007) shows that South Africa, Botswana and Namibia are the preferred destinations for regional migrants, and in 2019, the UN Department of Economic and Social Affairs reported that four of the top five countries of origin for SADC migrants, were SADC countries – Mozambique, Zimbabwe, Angola, and Lesotho (MDP, 2020).[1] This shows that intraregional migration is the mainstream of migration in southern Africa, which research has found is essential for regional integration and redistribution, given the importance of remittances in countries such as Lesotho. Economic hardship, environmental disasters and political instability are additional driving factors of intraregional migration in southern African.

As already implied, intraregional migration in the SADC occurs within a context of 'unharmonized and contradictory legal frameworks' (Dodson and Crush, 2015: 6). In a recent report, the AU evaluated the effectiveness of Africa's RECs and found that the SADC was one of the weaker regional bodies, given its inability to influence policy formulation and the migration governance strategies of its member states (Urso and Hakami, 2018: 41; see also EC, 2018). Dick and Schraven (2018: 6) argue that this is due to the multi-membership of SADC countries to various regional bodies, which have clashing bureaucracies and overlapping interests. The regional policy instrument framing migration governance is the SADC Protocol of the Facilitation of Movement of Persons (SACD, 1992), which 'focuses on the progressive elimination of obstacles to the freedom of movement' (Abebe, 2017: 4). Migrants from the region enjoy a visa-free entry for up to 90 days within the SADC zone. This is a progressive move in a historically restricted context, however, member states have been reluctant to ratify the SADC Protocol into their respective national legislative frameworks. By 2016, only six countries – Botswana, Lesotho, Mozambique, South Africa, Swaziland and Zambia – had ratified it. A series of bilateral agreements and memoranda of understanding (MOUs) exist between states, with South Africa at the centre of a vast web of bilateral agreements. The tendency to manage migration bilaterally and not regionally has meant that a parallel system of migration governance exists between states, especially with regard to labour migration (MiWorc, 2013: 80), echoing the SADC's initial ideals of 'free movement' outlined in its Protocol. The trend towards bilateralism is, therefore, only affirmed and not addressed by the Protocol (MiWorc, 2013: 56), since the Protocol has to be ratified by a minimum of two-thirds of the member countries.

A 2016 SEF study on regionalism in Africa suggests that Botswana, Namibia and South Africa have approached migration governance from a security lens, choosing to follow national migration policy that is framed in terms of perceived threats to national security rather than, for example, from a developmental perspective (SEF, 2016: 28). In the case of South Africa, this is perhaps evidence of a continuation in the migration regimes that the ANC inherited from the apartheid state and consolidated after 1994 (Ellis and Segatti, 2011). For example, South Africa has one of the most expansive deportation programmes globally; it deported 2.5 million people between 1988 and 2005, most of whom were Zimbabweans and Mozambicans (Nshimbi and Fioramonti, 2014: 58). According to Nshimbi and Fioramonti (2013), and contrary to its stated ideals, the SADC Protocol focuses on controlling the movement of people, from a security lens – thus, not on fostering development through migration. Furthermore, there is no regional mechanism to ensure that states comply with the Protocol or compel states to change their legislative frameworks to mirror those of the Protocol.

In addition to a trend towards securitisation, there is a tendency to view the movement of people as a secondary process to the migration of labour. In 2014, the SADC Heads of State developed the SADC Labour Migration Policy Framework and the SADC Protocol on Employment and Labour, which aimed to 'promote policies for regional labour mobility and migrant workers' rights, including social protection' (Urso and Hakami, 2018: 32). This category of migration is highly regulated and institutionalised because of the long history of migrants seeking work in South African mines (Nakayama, 2018: 67). Within the region, mining, agriculture, domestic work, and, increasingly, informal trading, are the main occupations for migrants; the latter is probably due to the precarity of securing these types of work. In terms of migrant rights, Dodson and Crush (2015: 10) show that the SADC Protocol on Employment and Labour provides migrant workers with access to non-citizen rights and labour protections, which transcend 'narrowly defined workers' rights'. The SADC Regional Labour Migration Action Plan (2013–2015) is 'the first proper regional initiative on labour migration' and its 'members have committed to harmonising labour data collection systems' (SEF, 2016: 25). Yet, the security regime of regional powers and receiving countries, especially South Africa, dominate policy formulation. The informal and irregular nature of labour migration has meant that reliable data are not readily available to inform policy design and implementation.

Migration governance trends and challenges

In recent years, following instability in Libya and Mali, and the 2015 'EU migration crisis', migration from Africa to Europe has been viewed pejoratively and as a security threat to states within the EU. It is not only the EU that has instituted policies to keep migrants out – some African countries (such as South Africa, Botswana, Egypt, Algeria and Morocco) have also restricted the entry of migrants from low-income countries by implementing strict visa rules (Abebe, 2020).

Research findings from the Institute for Security Studies (ISS) show that the securitised approach has a negative impact on countries. From a breakdown in livelihoods to increased regional political instability, the continued smuggling of marginalised and displaced persons has led to a growing violation of migrants' human rights and a breakdown in national and government relations (Abebe, 2020). For example, prior to the COVID-19 outbreak in 2020, increased securitisation was linked to tightening migration for unskilled migrants, and attracting more skilled people. The onset of the pandemic provided heightened political opportunism to intensify securitisation and xenophobia in South Africa.

This window of opportunity led to the deportation of non-nationals in South Africa (Maple et al., 2021; Moyo et al., 2021) and an intensification of nationalism; and the securitised approach promulgated the 'erecting [of] new border fences, the expulsion of migrants from urban areas and the exclusion of migrants and refugees from key services and provisions' (Maple et al., 2021). The construction of a 40-kilometre fence on the border between South Africa and Zimbabwe to exclude refugees and migrants because of 'perceived' health risks (Zanker and Moyo, 2020) is a clear indication of the exclusionary practices of the South African state and its policy of securitisation.

There is a need to see migration in a broader context – one that transcends framing migration as a security issue. The smuggling 'industry' simply adapts its strategy in response to increased securitisation. For example, Sudanese smugglers replaced Nigerian smugglers, while finding new routes to Libya, via Chad and Sudan (Abebe, 2020). The securitised approach increases the vulnerability of migrants, opens them to increased human rights abuses, and exposes them to racial and xenophobic violence. Notable events of xenophobic attacks in South Africa date back to 2008, when small shops owned by non-nationals such Ethiopians, Somalis, Bangladeshis and Pakistanis were attacked (Rugunanan, 2020; Zanker and Moyo, 2020). The 2019 riots in Johannesburg also resulted in the death of a number of non-nationals in South Africa.

While the notion of state security is paramount, those forced to migrate do so at the expense of their personal safety. Indeed, they are often forced to move because of a lack of security. Migration is a risky business and the threat to their personal safety is always prevalent, both in the home countries and on their journey, where they are exposed to hazardous conditions. Unaccompanied women and children are more vulnerable to gender-based violence throughout the migration process. The possibility of encountering border control obstacles, difficult terrains, sharp fences, isolated forests, robbers, sexual violence, and hygiene and food issues is heightened when migrants undertake irregular pathways as undocumented persons (Meyers, 2022). Cheap labour and sexual services are root causes of human trafficking, and conditions such as relative poverty and underdevelopment exacerbate the vulnerabilities of many aspirant migrants (Martens and Christiansen, 2012: 10). Life in the country of destination is also not without risk, as migrants often live and work under irregular and poor conditions. Many experienced exploitative labour practices, a lack of access to healthcare services, xenophobia and racism, and they are always at the risk of deportation (Rugunanan, 2016).

Alongside the view of migration as a security risk, is the idea of migration governance reform, which has gained momentum in Africa over the last decade as intraregional migration has increased. Spurred on by the EU migration-related investments and the creation of the EUTF, and the recognition that migration promotes development, African governments have begun to insert migration into their national development strategies and policy domains of health and education (Le Coz and Pietropolli, 2020). Non-nationals in southern Africa face considerable challenges in accessing healthcare (Vearey, 2014), and the number of migrant students from selected parts of sub-Saharan Africa is increasing steadily as they search for quality education (Tati, 2014). Le Coz and Pietropolli (2020) show that 71 per cent of migrants born in sub-Saharan Africa continue to reside there, yet scholarly and policy debates have continued to pay greater attention to international migration and the enduring challenges in Africa, such as the civil wars plaguing the continent, famine, drought and overpopulation. Little attention has been given to the intraregional flows of migration between African countries and the interplay of 'economic development, social dynamics and security' (Le Coz and Pietropolli, 2020).

The SADC Employment and Labour Sector (ELS) Committee endorsed the Labour Migration Policy Framework and adopted a Protocol on Employment and Labour in 2014 (SADC, 2014). The policy framework was used to stimulate SADC members to implement national labour migration policies by 2020. The International Labour Organization (ILO) and International Organization for Migration (IOM) provided the technical assistance to facilitate this process. In South Africa, after a long process of consultation and social dialogue with the relevant stakeholders and social actors, the government published the *White Paper on International Immigration for South Africa* (2017). This was intended to regularise semi-skilled and unskilled economic migrants, including domestic workers, and provided an outline for integrating international migrants in South Africa and augmenting social cohesion. Despite these progressive steps, the rhetoric by some South African politicians has served to inflame xenophobia, and resulted in pervasive outbursts of xenophobic attacks against foreign nationals between 2008 and 2020. The intensity and violent nature of these attacks on foreign nationals contradict the gains of inclusivity and social cohesion (ILO, n.d.).

Abebe (2020) points out that any attempt to curtail African migration to the Global North would spell doom for many African countries that are dependent on remittances from migrants to sustain their families and communities, and improve their economies. In 2018, remittances amounting to US$46 billion were received in Africa (Abebe, 2020). Remittances continue to be the biggest benefits of migration to African countries; however, African countries have also experienced a devastating loss of skilled professionals – the brain drain is not matched by a brain gain. In contrast to severe problems triggered by the brain drain, remittances have to some extent filled the gap as an important survival mechanism for Africans and their communities (Adepoju, 2010). At the community level, remittances supplement much-needed resources to fulfil housing, education, and healthcare needs. Recent figures from the World Bank suggest that US$7 billion in remittances were received in selected countries in southern Africa (World Bank, 2020). These remittances are an important source of capital in most southern African countries, but the costs continue to be among the highest globally (World Bank, 2020). For example, in 2019, the highest number of remittances in the sub-region were received by the Democratic Republic of the Congo and Lesotho (World Bank, 2020). Further estimations show that remittances to sub-Saharan Africa will decline by 14.6 per cent as a result of the COVID-19 pandemic (World Bank, 2020).

The deteriorating financial situation the world over has resulted in a brain gain for countries in sub-Saharan Africa, with many highly skilled migrants returning to countries such as South Africa after 1994, and to Botswana. South Africa attracts the largest inflow of Chinese and Indian migrants on the continent (Huynh et al., 2013). It has become the preferred choice for skilled male migrants from India (Rugunanan, 2017), particularly in the information and communication technology (ICT) and engineering sectors. India has a liberal migration policy that supports the temporary migration of highly skilled workers. The IOM (2020) also points to the 'brain circulation' within sub-Saharan Africa, which has seen skilled professionals from poor African countries move to the rising economies of Gabon, Botswana, Namibia and South Africa over the years. Botswana and South Africa, for example, have attracted a significant number of

Zimbabwean doctors, who relocated following the state's economic collapse (IOM, 2020). Migration trends have changed and there is a need to reflect more on South–South migration and what it means for the African continent (Rugunanan and Xulu-Gama, 2022). One of the most serious stumbling blocks for effective migration management and policy is the lack of accurate and consistent data on who is migrating, their destinations, and their reasons for migration. The lack of formal documentation of migrants undermines the migration policy process and further undermines migrant rights (Rugunanan and Xulu-Gama, 2022).

It is anticipated that by 2050 there will be 1.3 billion people of working age in Africa (Abebe, 2017) and in sub-Saharan Africa, the population is growing at 2.7 per cent a year, which is more than twice as fast as South Asia (1.2 per cent) and Latin America (0.9 per cent) (*The Economist*, 2020). Despite the looming increase in population, no African country is developing a commensurate, effective economic growth and development plan to ensure sufficient livelihood opportunities. As projected, migration will continue to increase in the coming years, as the digital age provides greater access to opportunities in other countries, including South–South migration, as access to resources and a wider range of networks increase the mobility of younger generations. At the same time, the COVID-19 pandemic may alter the course and trajectories for many countries and change the course of migration forever. The 'threat of COVID-19 "migrating" across remains high, as borders in southern Africa are notoriously porous. Border closures do not necessarily prevent traversing borders, but rather escalate the hidden networks that perpetuate illegal border crossings' (Rugunanan, 2020: 1).

In the same breath, the Fourth Industrial Revolution (4IR) and digital age will change migration processes, the ways of migration streams, and managing migration through policy and policing. It will also impact the securitisation of migration. The technologies of the 4IR will certainly create new opportunities for migrants: from the creation of new business ventures – migrants are known for their entrepreneurship, especially if they receive training on skills such as robotic applications (Eldridge et al., 2017) – to the migration of ideas, skills development via remote technologies, virtual healthcare and virtual education; the opportunities are endless and expansive. The COVID-19 pandemic has illustrated how technology can be an enabler in the development of society and how dependent we are on it.

Conclusion

In summary, the growing number of African and European frameworks encompass actions for better management of migration; establishing the free movement of people; advocating a humanitarian approach to address refugee issues; eradicating human trafficking and human smuggling; prioritising migration and development on government's agendas, and finally, focusing on migration governance, peace, and security (Abebe, 2017: 19). While great strides have been made in the development of these policies to manage migration, the implementation across the continent has not been as effective. The securitisation of migration policies and practices in the southern African subregion requires attention, as it needs to be less exclusionary and more inclusionary. There should also be a focus on the implementation of gender-sensitive labour migration policies and practices. The place of women and children in the migration process tends to be overlooked, yet these are the more vulnerable groups of people. The intraregional migration of skilled personnel should be facilitated to benefit and enhance the sustainable development of the region, and ensure peace and security.

This chapter has explored the historical and contemporary trajectories of migration from southern Africa to the EU, from the EU to southern Africa, and within Africa and the southern African subregion. It has shown that the SADC, as the main regional body, has been relatively weak in implementing migration governance reform, as only a third of its 16 member states have ratified its migration policies to date (SEF, 2016: 24). As discussed, most of the migration and mobility of southern Africans occurs within the region. Although southern African–EU migration does occur on a smaller scale, it is seen largely as emigration or as the 'brain drain'. When Europeans migrate to southern Africa, they are attracted mostly to Botswana, Namibia and South Africa. Other SADC countries, such as the DRC and Zimbabwe, have established long-standing trajectories to South Africa and, to a much lesser extent, to Europe as refugees and asylum seekers. Countries such as South Africa, Mauritius and Madagascar show a trend towards both regular and irregular migration to the EU. This chapter draws explicit lessons from the analysis of migration trends to policy issues. In this respect, we draw attention to the blind spots between migration trends and policy priorities, and the power balances at play in the implementation of policy.

It examines the migration flows between the EU and southern Africa, but also looks at intra-African migration, an often overlooked area of migration studies on the continent. What is clear is that migration to the Global North is set to continue, but newer migration streams to the Global South and newer destinations must be given scholarly attention. Indeed, greater attention also needs to be paid to women and children, who are migrating in ever-increasing numbers.

This chapter also reviewed some of the policy initiatives from the EU to Africa, and argues that effective migration governance would benefit both continents. The securitisation of migration has had more negative consequences than positive effects on migration from Africa.

Notes

1 The fifth and final country was Burundi.

References

Abebe, T.T. 2017. 'Migration Policy Frameworks in Africa', Africa Report 2, December. Johannesburg: Institute for Security Studies. Online at: https://issafrica.org/research/africa-report/migration-policy-frameworks-in-africa (accessed 21 February 2021).

Abebe, T.T. 2020. 'Fewer migrants to Europe, bigger problems for Africa', *ISS Today.* Johannesburg: Institute for Security Studies. Online at: https://issafrica.org/iss-today/fewer-migrants-to-europe-bigger-problems-for-africa (accessed 21 February 2021).

Adepoju, A. 2010. 'Introduction: Rethinking the dynamics of migration within, from and to Africa', in A. Adepoju (ed.). *International Migration Within, To and From Africa in a Globalised World.* Accra: Sub-Saharan Publishers, pp. 9–45.

African Centre for Strategic Studies. 2020. 'African Migration Trends to Watch in 2021'. Online: https://reliefweb.int/report/world/african-migration-trends-watch-2021 (accessed 27 April 2022).

African Union Commission. 2018. 'Migration Policy Framework for Africa and Plan of Action'. Addis Ababa: African Union.

Åkesson, L. and Orjuela, C. 2017. 'North–South migration and the corrupt other: Practices of bribery among Portuguese migrants in Angola', *Geopolitics*, 24(1): 230–50.

Anderson, D.M. 2010. 'Sexual threat and settler society: "Black Perils" in Kenya, c. 1907–1930', *The Journal of Imperial and Commonwealth History*, 38(1): 47–74.

Armbruster, H. 2010. 'Realising the self and developing the African', *Journal of*

Ethnic and Migration Studies, 36(8): 1229–46.

Conrad, J. 1902. *Heart of Darkness and the Secret Sharer.* New York: Bantam Classics.

Crush, J. 2019. *Rethinking the Medical Brain Drain Narrative.* SAMP Migration Policy Series No. 81. Online at: https://media.africaportal.org/documents/SAMP81.pdf (accessed 21 February 2021).

Dick, E. and Schraven, B. 2018. *Regional Migration Governance in Africa and Beyond: A framework of analysis.* German Development Institute, Discussion Paper 9/2018. Bonn: German Development Institute.

Docquire, F. 2014. 'The brain drain from developing countries'. Online at: https://wol.iza.org/uploads/articles/31/pdfs/brain-drain-from-developing-countries.pdf?v=1 (accessed 21 February 2021).

Dodson, B. and Crush, J. 2015. 'Migration governance and migration rights in the Southern African Development Community (SADC): Attempts at harmonization in a disharmonious region'. Accessed 28 October 2021, https://scholars.wlu.ca/samp/9/.

Eldridge, R., Koser, K., Levin, M. and Rai, S. 2017. 'What does the Fourth Industrial Revolution mean for migration?' *Global Agenda.* Geneva: World Economic Forum. Online at: https://www.weforum.org/agenda/2017/06/what-does-the-fourth-industrial-revolution-mean-for-migration/ (accessed 21 February 2021).

Ellis, S. and Segatti, A. 2011. 'The role of skilled labour', in: A. Segatti and L. Landau (eds). *Contemporary Migration to South Africa: A regional development issue.* Washington DC: The International Bank for Reconstruction and Development/The World Bank, pp. 67–78.

European Commission, Joint Research Centre. 2018. "Many more to come? Migration from and within Africa." Publications Office of the European Union, Luxembourg. DOI: 10.2760/1702

Fin Global. 2020. 'Immigrating to Germany from South Africa.' *Fin Global.* Accessed 27 October 2022, https://www.finglobal.com/2020/04/06/immigrating-to-germany-from-south-africa/.

Flahaux, M.L. and Schoumaker, B. 2016. 'Democratic Republic of the Congo: A migration history marked by crises and restrictions', *Migration Information Source*, 20 April. Online at: https://www.migrationpolicy.org/article/democratic-republic-congo-migration-history-marked-crises-and-restrictions (accessed 6 September 2020).

Frigeri, D. 2016. 'Migrants, Women and Young People in the 5+5 Countries. Managing Migration Policies beyond the Security Approach', R. Albinyana and D. Ruiz-Giménez Coderch (eds), *The 5+5 Dialogue as a Mechanism of Integration and Regional Cooperation*, Barcelona: European Institute of the

Mediterranean and the Med Think 5+5 Network.

Huynh, T., Rugunanan, P. and Park, Y.J. 2012. 'Chinese and Indian women migrants in South Africa: A preliminary and comparative examination of women's role in globalisation and new geo-political, economic engagements'. Unpublished research report. FAHAMU, South Africa.

International Labour Organization (ILO). n. d. 'Strengthening labour migration governance through tripartism and social dialogue in the formulation and implementation of evidence-based and gender-sensitive labour migration policies, legislation and practices'. Online at: https://www.ilo.org/africa/areas-of-work/labour-migration/thematic-areas/WCMS_673562/lang--en/index.htm (accessed 21 February 2021).

International Organization for Migration (IOM). 2020. *Migration Report: Challenging the narrative.* Online at: https://publications.iom.int/system/files/pdf/africa-migration-report.pdf (accessed 21 February 2021).

Le Coz, C. and Pietropolli, A. 2020. 'Africa deepens its approach to migration governance, but are policies translating to action?' *Migration Information Source.* Migration Policy Institute. Online at: https://www.migrationpolicy.org/article/africa-deepens-approach-migration-governance (accessed 21 February 2021).

Lonsdale, J. 1990. 'Mau Maus of the mind: Making Mau Mau and remaking Kenya', *The Journal of African History*, 31(3): 393–421.

Maple, N., Walker, R. and Vearey, J. 2021. 'COVID-19 and people on the move in Africa: The impact of state responses to the pandemic on migrants, refugees, asylum-seekers and internally displaced people', ACCORD, Conflict and Resilience Monitor, 30 June. Online at: https://www.accord.org.za/analysis/covid-19-and-people-on-the-move-in-africa-the-impact-of-state-responses-to-the-pandemic-on-migrants-refugees-asylum-seekers-and-internally-displaced-people/ (accessed 21 February 2021).

Martens, J. and Christiansen, J. 2012. *Counter Trafficking and Assistance to Vulnerable Migrants. Annual Report of Activities 2011.* International Organization for Migration. Online at: https://reliefweb.int/sites/reliefweb.int/files/resources/Annual_Report_2011_Counter_Trafficking.pdf (accessed 21 February 2021).

Meyers, C. 2022. 'Digital-mediated migration and transformative agency: African women negotiating risk in Johannesburg, South Africa'. Unpublished PhD thesis: University of Johannesburg.

Migration Data Portal. 2020. 'Migration Data in the Southern African Development Community'. Online at: https://migrationdataportal.org/regional-data-overview/southern-africa (accessed 11 October 2020).

Moyo, K., Sebba, K.R. and Zanker, F. 2021. 'Who is watching? Refugee protection during a pandemic – responses from Uganda and South Africa', *Comparative Migration Studies*, 9(37), 10 August. doi.org/10.1186/s40878-021-00243-3.

Nakayama, Y. 2018. 'Migration Governance: Migration within and from Africa'. Development, Migration, and Resources Series, African Studies Centre, Tokyo University of Foreign Studies Working Papers.

Natale, F., Migali, S. and Münz, R. 2018. *Many More to Come? Migration from and within Africa*. European Commission Joint Research Centre Technical Reports, EUR 29106 EN. Luxembourg: Publications Office of the European Union. Luxembourg, doi:10.2760/1702, JRC110703.

Nshimbi, C. and Fioramonti, L. 2014. 'The will to integrate: South Africa's response to regional migration from the SADC Region', *African Development Review*, 26(1), 52–63.

Oucho, O. 2007. *Migration Management in Southern Africa: Migration management initiatives for SADC member states,* Institute for Security Studies Papers, No. 157.

Republic of South Africa. 2017. *White Paper on International Migration for South Africa*. Department of Home Affairs. Online at: http://www.dha.gov.za/WhitePaperonInternationalMigration-20170602.pdf (accessed 21 June 2021).

Rugunanan, P. 2020. '"South Africa belongs to all who live in it": COVID-19 showed it does not', *Mixed Migration Review 2020*. Online at: https://www.opendemocracy.net/en/pandemic-border/south-africa-belongs-to-all-who-live-in-it-covid-19-showed-it-does-not/ (accessed 21 February 2021).

Rugunanan, P. 2020. 'Africa must be ... one place, one country': Xenophobia and the unmediated representation of African migrants in South Africa. In: Moyo, D. Mpofu, S. (eds) *Mediating Xenophobia in Africa*. Palgrave Macmillan, Cham. https://doi.org/10.1007/978-3-030-61236-8_12.

Rugunanan, P. 2017. '"Fitting in": Social cohesion among migrant Indian women and host diasporic communities in South Africa', *Alternation*, 24(1):170–96.

Rugunanan, P. 2016. 'Forged communities: A sociological exploration of identity and community amongst immigrant and migrant communities in Fordsburg.' PhD thesis. Department of Sociology, University of Johannesburg.

Rugunanan, P. and Xulu-Zama, N. 2022. *Migration in Southern Africa*. Heidelberg: Springer Press.

Southern African Development Community (SADC). 2014. *Protocol on Employment and Labour*. Online at: https://www.sadc.int/files/5714/6193/6406/Protocol_on_Employment_and_Labour_-_English_-_2014.pdf (accessed 21 February 2021).

Segatti. A. 2011. 'Migration to South Africa: Regional challenges versus national instruments and interests', in: A. Segatti and L. Landau (eds). *Contemporary Migration to South Africa: A regional development issue.* Washington DC: The International Bank for Reconstruction and Development/The World Bank, pp. 9–29.

Statistics South Africa. 2011. *Census 2011: Migration Dynamics in South Africa.* Pretoria: Statistics South Africa.

Stiftung Entwicklung und Frieden (SEF). 2016. *Regional Migration Governance in the African Continent: Current state of affairs and the way forward.* Bonn: Stiftung Entwicklung und Frieden (Development and Peace Foundation).

Tankwanchi A.B.S., Özden, Ç. and Vermund, S.H. 2013. 'Physician Emigration from Sub-Saharan Africa to the United States: Analysis of the 2011 AMA Physician Masterfile', *PLOS Medicine*, 10(12): 10. doi.org/10.1371/annotation/64ffd514-00bb-4a5e-9e2e-584763637d14.

Tati, G. 2014. Differentials in educational motives and return among African students at the Western Cape University. Research workshop on Researching Migration, Integration and Transnationalism. Online at: https://journals.openedition.org/cres/2602 (accessed 21 June 2021).

The Economist. 2020. 'Africa's population will double by 2050', The Economist Special Report, 28 March. Online at: https://www.economist.com/special-report/2020/03/26/africas-population-will-double-by-2050 (accessed 21 June 2021).

United Nations Department of Economic and Social Affairs, Population Division. 2020. *International Migrant Stock Database 2020.* Online at: https://migrationdataportal.org/regional-data-overview/southern-africa (accessed 21 June 2021).

Urso, G. and Hakami, A. 2018. *Regional Migration Governance in Africa: The African Union and Regional Economic Communities.* European Commission Joint Research Centre Technical Reports. Luxembourg: European Commission.

Vearey J. 2014. 'Healthy migration: A public health and development imperative for South(ern) Africa', *South African Medical Journal/Suid-Afrikaanse Tydskrif vir Geneeskunde*, 104(10): 663–4. doi.org/10.7196/samj.8569.

World Bank. 2020. *World Development Report 2020: Trading for development in the age of global value chains.* Washington, DC: World Bank. Online at: https://openknowledge.worldbank.org/handle/10986/32437 (accessed 21 June 2021).

Zanker, F. L. and Moyo, K. 2020. 'The coronavirus and migration governance in South Africa: Business as usual?' *Africa Spectrum*, 55(1): 100–12. doi: 10.1177/0002039720925826.

Migration: The African Great Lakes and the European Union

Alfred Ombeni Musimwa and Sylvie Sarolea[1]

Introduction

Migration is part of human history. While it is relatively stable in proportion (Docquier, 2018: 3), there are wide geographical variations. About 3 per cent of the global population are migrants. They are not evenly distributed, and their direction of movement and their regions and countries of origin, transit, and destination constantly change. Migration issues have now, more than ever, become a matter of concern on both the political-cooperative and legislative levels. International migration raises new legal questions every day (Sarolea, 2018: 7). It is also the subject of lively debates at all levels – international, regional, subregional and national – including academia. These debates focus largely on two aspects of (irregular) migration from Africa to the European Union (EU): the organisation and management of African migration, which is upstream and the least explored; and the European management of African migration, and to some extent its cooperation with African states of origin and/or transit. Unlike the first aspect, it is downstream and attracts more attention, especially from the media.

This chapter examines migration to and from the African Great Lakes (AGL) region. The geographical and historical delineation of this region is unclear and the overlap of cooperation bodies under the name 'Great Lakes' leads to confusion. In general, confusion could arise from the establishment in 2000 of the International Conference on the 'Great Lakes Region' (ICGLR), pursuant to United Nations Security Council (UN) Resolutions 1291 and 1304; or by reference to the Framework Agreement on Peace, Security and Cooperation in the 'Great Lakes Region', signed in Addis Ababa, Ethiopia, on 24 February 2013 by 11 African countries, which were joined by two others on 31 January 2014; or by consideration of the Economic Community of the 'Great Lakes' Countries (ECGLC) comprising Burundi, the Democratic Republic of Congo (DRC) and Rwanda; or finally, by reference to the East African Community (EAC), which includes Burundi, Kenya, Rwanda, South Sudan and Tanzania.

These institutional initiatives do not correspond to the AGL's geohistorical delineation. Ultimately, these point to the instability of the AGL region, which influences migration flows. Indeed, there is no single and easily identifiable economic community that brings together all the states sharing the Great Lakes highlands. These states are Burundi, the DRC, Uganda, Rwanda and Tanzania (Muhinduka Di-Kuruba, 2010: 128), all of whom also have a common migratory history dating back to the colonial period. As a geohistorical delineation, these states comprise the AGL region in this chapter.

A further delimitation of this chapter concerns the concept of migration. Although the idea of a clear distinction between economic migrants and migrants eligible for international protection (refugees/asylum seekers) is useful, not only for policy prescriptions but also for the status of refugees – which is well established in international law – it is impossible to separate these completely. This ambiguity applies especially in the context of the AGL region, where the condition of migrants eligible for international protection and economic migrants is structural and long-term (Frigeri, 2016: 107). Moreover, the national and/or migration cooperation policies developed by states affect the condition of both economic migrants and those eligible for international protection.

The AGL has been particularly affected by war and remains unsafe, especially in the eastern part of the DRC. For a quarter of a century, this situation has led to significant human rights violations, deterioration of governance and the socio-economic fabric, and significant mixed migratory movements, both within the subregion and to the EU. To overcome these difficulties, the AGL states are making multiple cooperative efforts, including the creation of subregional economic communities, such as the ECGLC and the EAC, to ensure integration by establishing a free movement of persons. This chapter seeks to contribute to a better understanding of the AGL's migration context, the state of cooperation and migration law in the subregion, before exploring its cooperation with the EU on migration, and discussing the prospects for cooperation offered by the Global Compact for Safe, Orderly and Regular Migration (GCM).

Historical overview of the AGL's migration context

Historically, the AGL region has seen considerable migration, which has been both voluntary and forced, depending on the political situation in each state. While the forced movement of people across borders has been on an unprecedented scale since 1994, it remains important to note that the free movement of people across AGL borders has been organised and effective since the colonial period. Uganda and Tanzania were first German and then British colonies after the German defeat of 1918, and the other three AGL countries were Belgian colonies.

The international conventions that established the borders between these territories organised migration through the colonies.[2] For a period of six months, inhabitants of the border regions between Ruanda-Urundi and Buganda could settle freely with their portable goods on the other side of the border (Jentgen, 1957: 32). In addition, the Belgian Congo granted migration facilities to residents of Buganda and Tanganyika (present-day Tanzania). They could enter the Congo without a visa by showing their identity card or passport (Office of Information and Public Relations for Belgian Congo and Ruanda-Urundi, 1958: 149). In addition, several migration programmes from Ruanda-Urundi to the Belgian Congo were implemented after 1938, either to relieve congestion in Ruanda-Urundi, or to meet labour needs in the Congo (Nicolaï, 2009: 304). Moreover, in 1948, the significant migratory flows between these colonies led the Belgian and British colonial authorities to set up annual conferences to discuss migration issues and migrant workers' rights (Trusteeship Council, 1952: 27).

The political turmoil and inter-ethnic wars, which marked the first years of independence of the AGL states, did not allow them to focus on migration cooperation. At the same time, these political crises led to major migratory movements in the subregion, including the very first political refugees from sub-Saharan Africa (Chrétien, 1996: 112–14). In August 1966, these widespread crises, and their subregional migration repercussions, led to the establishment of security cooperation between Burundi, Rwanda and the present-day DRC. The ECGLC was borne out of this security cooperation.

The law and framework for migration cooperation within the AGL region

This section focuses on the regulation of migration within the ECGLC. This chapter includes Uganda and Tanzania, particularly in view of the strong migratory interactions between these states and their geographical membership of the AGL region. We shall discuss immigration law in the EAC for the following two reasons. First, the EAC currently includes four of the five AGL states: Uganda and Tanzania since 1967, and Burundi and Rwanda since 2007. In addition, the DRC is considering joining. Second, unlike the ECGLC, the EAC is becoming the more predominant in the area of free movement, and the right of establishment and residence, while the ECGLC is stagnating.

Regulation of migration within the ECGLC framework

The ECGLC was created by the Convention of 20 September 1976 between Burundi, Rwanda and the DRC. These three states were all once administered by Belgium. Moreover, Burundi and Rwanda were already administratively united in 1925 with the present-day DRC (De Clerck, 2006: 187), forming an economic union (Muhinduka Di-Kuruba, 2010: 128). Strongly inspired by the EU and the Benelux Union (Galand and Van de Casteele, 2006: 5), the ECGLC pursues – among other objectives – the promotion and intensification of the movement of people (ECGLC, 1978: 51). At its inception, the ECGLC was one of the most dynamic and ambitious organisations in terms of the free movement of people in Africa. In December 1979, visas were abolished in favour of national identity cards as the only required travel document within the Congo–Rwanda border zones (Kabamba Kazadi, 2000: 54). In December 1980, an Arrangement on the Free Movement of Civil Servants introduced the ECGLC special card and the ECGLC identity card, allowing civil servants and ECGLC citizens to move freely within the Economic Community without a visa (Kabamba Kazadi, 2000: 54). The same right to free movement is granted to any holder of an ECGLC special movement authorisation. In addition, students from Rwanda and Burundi benefit from ECGLC scholarships to continue their studies in Congolese universities (Musila, 2005: 10).

The ECGLC's most striking achievement was the signing of the Convention on the Free Movement of Persons, Capital, and the Right of Establishment within the Community on 1 December 1985. The novelty of this convention is twofold. First, it covers almost all migrant persons: workers, students, family members, refugees, including more specific categories such as lawyers and doctors. Second, while setting a timetable, this convention opened the way to a right of establishment and citizenship rights for all ECGLC nationals, including refugees. However, this ambitious convention did not enter into force due to lack of ratification by Burundi and Zaire (now the DRC). In 1986, the treaty was ratified by Rwanda's President Juvénal Habyarimana, who saw it as a solution to the demographic problem raised by the return of Rwandan refugees from Burundi and Zaire (Kabamba Kazadi, 2000: 54).

Since the 1990s, ECGLC member states have been numbed by political and ethnic conflicts. On 6 April 1994, the plane carrying the President Juvénal Habyarimana, and the President of Burundi, Cyprien Ntaryamira, crashed in Rwanda, which brought the ECGLC activities to a halt. The ensuing Rwandan genocide, the two wars in the DRC (1996–97 and 1998–2002), and the persistence of armed groups and rebel movements in Kivu (the Congolese province bordering Burundi and Rwanda), which had subregional ramifications, impeded any cooperation. In 2004, Belgium initiated the revitalisation of the ECGLC[3] but this did not restore the momentum of the 1970s and 1990s. Moreover, the ambitious 1985 project was never discussed again. Tense diplomatic relations brought an end to a new attempt to revitalise the convention in 2010 (Kabamba Kazadi, 2000: 71). Free movement within the ECGLC has been reduced to a minimum. Nationals of each member state, including foreign legal residents, in possession of a passport or a special ECGLC travel permit (Berwouts, 2009: 2), receive a free entry visa valid for 90 days upon arrival in the other member states. In addition, two types of cross-border documents have been introduced: the market and visit tokens. These are issued at the border and are valid for one day. They allow the free cross-border movement of people between neighbouring towns in the ECGLC states. However, without ambitious cooperation, irregular migration remains a huge challenge.[4]

Regulation of migration in the EAC framework

The EAC was founded on 1 December 1967 between Kenya, Uganda and Tanzania. It collapsed in 1977 but was relaunched and entered into force on 7 July 2000. Burundi and Rwanda joined in 2007 and South Sudan in 2016. In addition to the Summit of Heads of State, the Council, and the Secretariat, the EAC has established a Community Legislative Assembly and a Community Court of Justice. This court is competent to interpret and apply the Treaty for the Establishment of the East African Community (EAC), and particularly in matters of fundamental rights by any person residing in a member state. It also ensures the interpretation and application of the protocols to this treaty, including the protocol on the free movement of persons adopted under Article 104 of this treaty.

In addition to the Economic Community of West African States (ECOWAS), the EAC is one of the most promising organisations of the African Regional Economic Communities in terms of the free movement of persons. Article 104 of the treaty, which established the regional institution, makes free movement one of the objectives of the EAC. On 20 November 2009, the regional body created a Protocol for the Establishment of the EAC Common Market, which entered into force in July 2010, after ratification by all five EAC member states (EAC, 2009). It establishes a right for any citizen of a member state in possession of a travel document or a national identity card, to move freely, and reside and settle in any other member state. This protocol is of particular interest to migrant workers, because Article 10 prohibits any discrimination against migrant workers or members of their families to seek employment or self-employment. The only permissible limitation applies to employment in public services.

This protocol recognises the right of every EAC migrant worker to be accompanied by their spouse, children and dependants (EAC, 2009: 12). They all enjoy the right of residence and have the right to be employed or to carry out any other economic activity. To give effect to Article 10, the member states agree to mutually recognise diplomas and professional qualifications acquired in any other member state, and to harmonise their systems of study, and their labour policies and legislation. Ultimately, this protocol institutes a right of establishment, which allows immigrants to set up and manage a business and have access to social security. This right, like the right to free movement, is not absolute and may be limited by the state for reasons of public order, public security, or public health.

It should be noted, however, that this protocol provides only a partial response to the need for an ambitious migration cooperation solution in the specific context of the AGL region. In this region, and particularly in Burundi and Rwanda, the question of refugees and access to land are among the most challenging issues confronting migration cooperation. It is important to provide consensual and sustainable solutions to the challenge of refugees and access to land. These issues are intimately linked and reinforce each other, and they could cause a new crisis in the region in the future. As far back as 1951, a United Nations' mission underscored the fact that the overpopulation of Rwanda and Burundi, the difficulties of access to land in these two states, and the demographic imbalance in the subregion, constituted a permanent threat to the stability and prosperity of the subregion (Trusteeship Council, 1952: 26). In addition, it was recognised as early as 31 December 1949 that allocating the available land would leave 180,000 families without land. So even if Burundi and Rwanda did manage to improve their food production, they would still be in a permanently precarious situation (Trusteeship Council, 1952: 12). The outbreak of inter-ethnic conflicts in the years of independence confirmed these fears.

Today, three of the five AGL countries (Rwanda, Burundi and Uganda) are the most densely populated in Africa, and access to land is a permanent source of conflict. Rwanda ranks first with about 499 inhabitants per square kilometre. It is followed by Burundi with about 435 inhabitants per square kilometre, and Uganda is in fourth place (behind Nigeria) with about 213 inhabitants per square kilometre (Food and Agriculture Organization and World Bank, 2018). The other two AGL countries, the DRC and Tanzania, are among the least populated on the continent, and are among the few countries where land remains available. For example, the DRC has only about 37 inhabitants per square kilometre, and Tanzania about 64 inhabitants per square kilometre (Food and Agriculture Organization and World Bank, 2018). As a result, emigration is one of the major solutions to the overcrowding and conflicts in the AGL region. However, within the EAC, Articles 7.8 (about refugees) and 15 (on access and use of land) of the protocol under review limit the application of this solution. Article 7.8

is less ambitious in that it does not offer a more contextual treatment of community refugee issues, while Article 15 paves the way for discrimination against non-nationals, differential treatment between states, and potential conflicts.

Moreover, all member states would benefit from ambitious migration cooperation. Migration allows for the circulation of knowledge, the availability and accessibility of labour, the repatriation of funds, and living together. In short, it is a tool for development. The context of the AGL states make the emergence of such cooperation more relevant, because they are the largest senders and receivers of migrant and refugee flows in the subregion, as illustrated in Table 10.1:

Table 10.1: Migrant and refugee flows within the AGL region

Country ↓	Immigrant, refugee and asylum-seeking populations by nationality				
	Burundian	Congolese	Rwandan	Ugandan	Tanzanian
Burundi		173,417	66,530	921	28,951
		77,764	1,387	18	21
DRC	41,654		298,652	6,637	*
	103,690		215,122	17	*
Rwanda	64,729	231,438		92,521	42,927
	72,007	76,853		5	*
Uganda	64,092	298,749	108,638		35,789
	48,275	415,118	17,526		9
Tanzania	208,949	105,174	692	5,788	
	207,074	76,571	104	26	

■ : Immigrants; ■ : Refugees and asylum seekers; ■ : Not applicable * : No data

Source: IOM and UNHCR[5] (our calculation)

Table 10.1, which includes statistics mainly from the end of 2019 and 30 June 2020, shows considerable flows of migrants and refugees across the five AGL states' borders. Overall, these states constitute the top five countries of origin and destination/transit of migrants and refugees from the subregion. However, the persistence of conflicts (particularly in Kivu and Ituri) and the deterioration of trust between states are factors that hinder the return to genuine cooperation in the subregion. Moreover, the overlapping of regional communities, the absence of the ECGLC, and the weakness of the EAC to implement ambitious immigration policies and protect the rights of migrants (Carlier and Sarolea, 2016: 594), are all ingredients for irregular migration within the subregion, and to the EU. This relative governance vacuum informs migration cooperation between the AGL region and the EU.

Migration cooperation between the AGL and the EU

Despite its relative remoteness from the EU, migration from the AGL region to the EU remains considerable. However, the EU has shown little interest in terms of cooperation, as reflected in this section.

Overview of AGL migration to the EU

The AGL region is one of the main origins of African migrants to the EU. This is justified in particular by its German–British–Belgian colonial past, the persistence of socio-political crises, the size of its population, and the deterioration of its economy and its labour market. Most of the migrants from the AGL region to the EU remain regular. As an illustration, according to Schengen statistics, Belgium, who represents 20 European states in Kigali, Rwanda, for the processing of short-stay visas, issued 8,251 visas for entry into the Schengen area in 2019 out of 10,639 visa applications submitted. In Kinshasa, DRC, where Belgium manages the European Visa Centre representing 20 European States, 17,344 visas were issued out of 24,910 visa applications submitted in 2019. In the same year, Germany issued 3,708 visas out of 4,565 applications submitted in Kampala, Uganda. In Bujumbura, Burundi, France issued 47 visas out of 48 applications submitted in 2019; and Belgium, representing 17 European states, issued 2,212 visas out of 3,720 applications received. During 2019, out of the 1,828 Schengen visa applications processed by France in Dar es Salaam, Tanzania, 1,361 visas were issued. Over the same period and in the same country, Germany issued 2,568 visas out of 2,891 applications received. In addition, each EU state, or the member state representing it in each AGL state, issues long-stay visas, in particular for study, work, or family reunification.

Overall, migration from the AGL region to the EU has remained relatively stable in relation to global population growth. Figure 10.1, based on data from the Organization for Economic Co-operation and Development (OECD), illustrates the evolution of this migration.

Figure 10.1: Evolution of migration from AGL region to the EU from 2000 to 2017

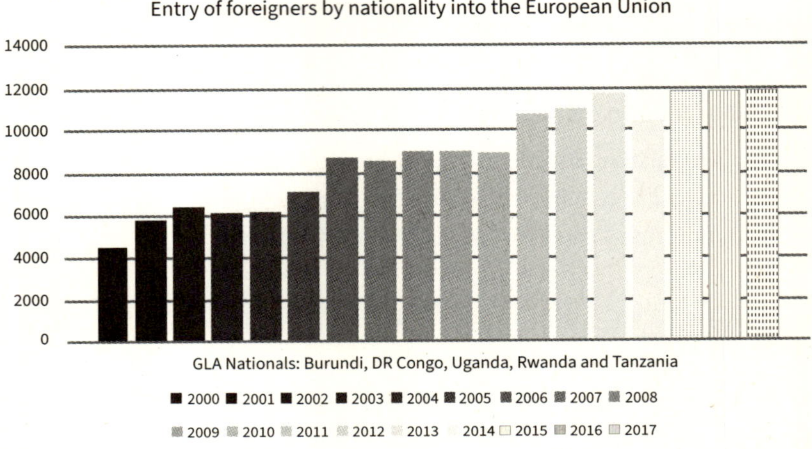

Source: Based on OECD data (our calculation)

According to the OECD, these figures are based on population registers or residence permit files. They may, therefore include temporary migrants (for example, Italy and Portugal) and international students who usually return home at the end of their stay. In addition, these statistics might contain asylum seekers (for example, Ireland). Based on residence permits, these data could also include EU residents who changed or renewed their status. Moreover, obtaining a visa from Africa to the EU remains a struggle. The EU and its member states have been restricting entry (Pascouau and Labayle, 2011: 22; Carlier and Crépeau, 2017: 464) and residence conditions over the years. This contributes to an increase in the number of irregular migrants. Every year, European states refuse hundreds of AGL nationals at the European borders, as illustrated in Table 10.2.

The number of AGL nationals attempting to cross EU borders irregularly has been growing steadily since 2015. Nationals from the DRC account for more than half of the nationals of the subregion who are denied access to the EU. This is because the DRC, and particularly its eastern part (Kivu and Ituri), is the only AGL country that has been at war for nearly 25 years. According to the UN High Commissioner for Refugees (UNHCR), the DRC has nearly five million internally displaced persons, nearly one million Congolese refugees live in another country in Africa (UNHCR, 2019: 1), and some 12,830 Congolese nationals have been granted refugee status in the EU in the last 10 years.

Table 10.2: AGL nationals denied at EU external borders (EU28)

Country of origin ↓	2015	2016	2017	2018	2019
Burundi	30	25	40	20	20
DRC	435	485	485	395	485
Uganda	60	55	55	55	90
Rwanda	35	50	70	90	45
Tanzania	40	60	75	50	50
Total	600	675	725	610	690

Source: Based on Eurostat statistics (our calculation)

As a result, migration flows from the AGL region to the EU are often mixed, combining economic migrants and migrants eligible for international protection. This reality is often ignored, and this accounts for the recurrent expulsions of AGL migrants by EU member states. On several occasions, the European Court of Human Rights has condemned European states who have carried out collective expulsions in the absence of a prior administrative or judicial decision and of an examination of the individual situation of the migrants.[6]

Existing migration cooperation frameworks between the AGL region and the EU

Unlike the regions closer to the Mediterranean Sea, such as the Arab Maghreb Union (AMU) or ECOWAS, the EU is not intensifying its migration cooperation with AGL states. Nevertheless, some or all AGL states do participate in migration cooperation frameworks with the EU, as we elaborate below. Overall, while the EU has been implementing an AGL refugee support programme in Tanzania for more than 12 years, migration cooperation with other AGL states remains limited.

Scope and limits of AGL–EU migration cooperation

The nature and limits of AGL–EU cooperation on migration can be analysed at three levels: the continental level within the overall framework of the Cotonou Agreement; the regional level within the framework of regional processes; and the subregional level within the framework of European strategies targeted at African subregions.

At the continental level, the Cotonou Agreement was signed on 23 June 2000 between the African, Caribbean and Pacific (ACP) states and the EU and its member states. Article 13 of this agreement governs migration cooperation between the ACP states and the EU. In essence, Article 13 covers:

1. Respect for the human rights of migrants;
2. Non-discrimination;
3. Improvement of living conditions in countries of origin;
4. Cooperation to facilitate access to education for students from ACP states, including through the use of new technologies;
5. Most importantly, the return of irregular migrants to their countries of origin, at the sole request of the State Party on whose territory they find themselves, and without further formalities; and
6. The conclusion – at the request of a Party – of bilateral agreements governing specific obligations for the readmission and return of nationals, including those of third countries and stateless persons.

However, Article 13 has been difficult to implement fully, particularly because of unequal power relations between the EU and the AGL region, which favour the EU priority on the unconditional return and readmission of irregular migrants, without offering prospects for relaxing (or abolishing) the formalities for regular migration. As a result, Article 13 has not actually served the cause of African migrants, especially those from the AGL region. A major point of contention is the inability of the parties to agree on its revision. The Cotonou Agreement expired on 1 March 2020 (Article 95), and a new deadline was set for 31 December 2020. Expectedly, the new agreement under negotiation will be more ambitious and more balanced on this important wand sensitive issue.

The most decisive criterion for the non-existence of a migration cooperation mechanism between the EU and the AGL member states is the physical distance between them. There are two flagship mechanisms for regional migration cooperation between the EU and African states: the Khartoum Process and the Rabat Process. Interestingly, no AGL state is part of the 'EU–Horn of Africa Migration Route Initiative' (the Khartoum Process), and only the DRC is a member of the 'Euro–African Dialogue on Migration and Development' (the Rabat Process), as part of Central Africa. These processes aim to provide a framework for consultation and coordination among stakeholders, who are mainly countries of origin, transit, and destination, to jointly address the challenges posed by migration and explore its benefits. Thus, the AGL states see their fate discussed in forums where they have little to no presence. The absence of the AGL states – which are an important source of economic migrants and refugees who are Europe-bound – remains one of the major weaknesses of the two processes.

In addition to the continental and regional frameworks that address migration governance explicitly, the EU has promoted cooperation with other groups of African states where migration is addressed indirectly. For example, Uganda is the only participant in the EU's Khartoum Process, which includes the states of the Intergovernmental Authority on Development (IGAD) and Eritrea. It was only in 2015 that the EU adopted a Regional Action Plan to support the Khartoum Process and push for legislative changes. The implementation of this initiative is sufficiently recent to allow for an assessment of its real impact on the ground.

In 2014, the EU instituted a 'Strategy for the Gulf of Guinea' and a year later, an 'Action Plan on Maritime Security', involving Burundi and the DRC. These two initiatives aim (secondarily) to combat migrant smuggling networks by strengthening maritime security in the Gulf of Guinea. Partnership between these states and the EU in the implementation of the initiatives constitute the European counterpart to its support for the implementation of the Code of Conduct concerning the prevention and repression of acts of piracy and illicit maritime activities in West and Central Africa, which was adopted by 19 African states in Yaoundé, Cameroon, in June 2013. The impact of these European unilateral initiatives on irregular migration has still to be studied.

Despite the relative lack of migration-specific collaboration, the EU understands that the AGL region is a major focus for migration. It has established a pilot programme (the Regional Protection Programme, RPP) with Tanzania for the regional protection of refugees from the subregion.

However, the distribution of the EU Trust Fund for Africa (a financial programme aimed at combatting the root causes of irregular migration), reveals little European interest in the AGL region.

As noted earlier, Tanzania's political stability has made it a preferred destination for many refugees, mainly from Burundi and the DRC. To protect itself against the influx of these refugees, the EU identified Tanzania as a priority country with which to experiment its new approach to international protection. The European philosophy of RPPs is to improve the capacity to protect refugees of areas close to the regions of origin by creating the necessary conditions for the implementation of one of the following three durable solutions: repatriation, local integration and resettlement. Of these solutions, the first two are prioritised and the third is rarely considered, particularly if it involves resettlement in the EU.

Several RPP projects have been implemented in Tanzania since 2007, notably by the UNHCR. They consist mainly of capacity-building training for public officials, magistrates, lawyers, and human rights defenders, to enable them to inform refugees on the registration process, repatriation, local integration, and resettlement possibilities. Although the results are generally positive, this cooperation is far from sufficient and provides only a partial solution to the issue of refugee flows within the AGL region and to the EU.

As noted earlier, the European RPP for the AGL region prioritises repatriation or the local integration of refugees and neglects the third option of resettlement in another country, especially if it is European. For example, from 2004 to 2008, of the 12,471 mainly Burundian, Congolese, and Rwandan refugees in Tanzania, most were resettled in the United States, Canada, and Australia, while the RPP resettled only 434 of these refugees in the EU.[7] Moreover, several reports indicate increasing pressure on Burundian refugees and asylum seekers to return to Burundi.[8] By prioritising repatriation and local integration, and by going to great lengths to prevent third country resettlement in Europe, the EU is compromising its international responsibility towards legally recognised refugees. Finally, to provide more sustainable conditions for repatriated refugees, local integration should be accompanied by strong measures, involving the host communities, to prevent or manage possible conflicts.

In recent years, the EU's highest priority in terms of migration management has been the fight against irregular migration to the EU. The main European instrument to combat irregular migration from Africa is the EU Trust Fund for Africa (EUTF). The EUTF was established in November 2015, following the Euro-African Summit on Migration held in Valletta, Malta. In 2018, the EUTF amounted to more than €4 billion. According to the European Commission, the fund 'contributes to better migration management, and helps tackling the root causes of destabilization, forced displacement and irregular migration by promoting economic and equal opportunities, security and development' (European Commission, 2019: 7). The African countries covered by this fund are shown in Figure 10.2.

Figure 10.2: Countries covered by the EUTF

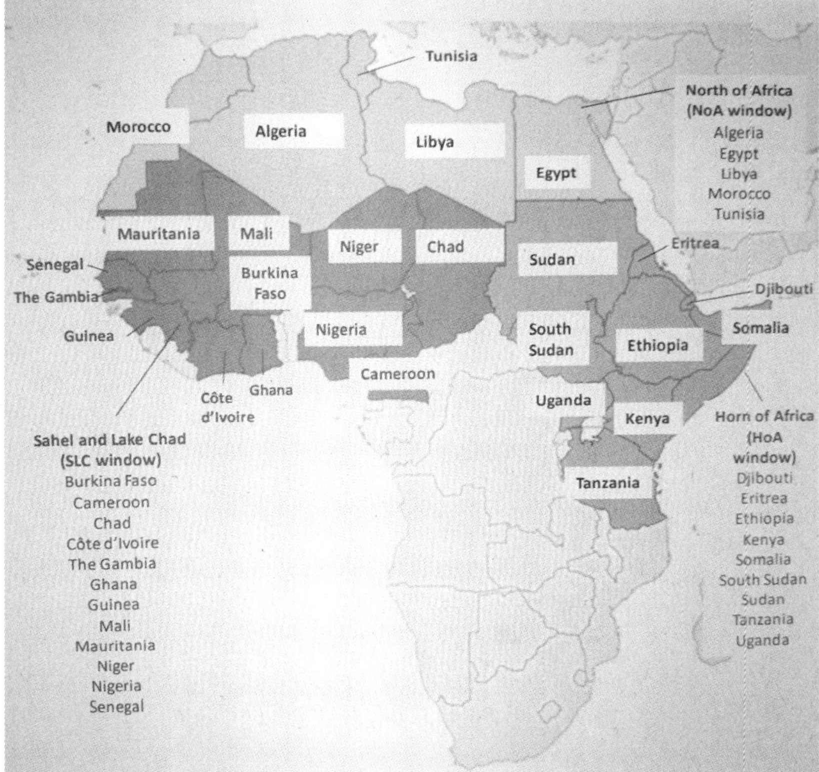

Source: European Commission (2018: 9)

While Uganda and Tanzania are covered by the EUTF, Burundi, Rwanda and the DRC are not. The case of the DRC is striking in view of the number of its nationals who cross from Central to North Africa in the hope of migrating (irregularly) to Europe. In Morocco, for example, Congolese nationals account for 12.8 per cent of irregular migrants, just behind nationals from Nigeria, Mali and Senegal (Rais, 2018: 66–7). Moreover, each year, an average of 8,758 Congolese, Burundian and Rwandan nationals, who are denied entry at the European external borders, are in an irregular situation or are required to leave European territory. Table 10.3 presents these figures by year and by reason for refusal or repatriation.

Table 10.3: Irregular migration and residence of Burundian, Congolese and Rwandan nationals in the EU (EU28)

Country of origin →	Burundi, the DRC and Rwanda					
Migration indicator ↓	2014	2015	2016	2017	2018	2019
Refusal at external borders	400	500	560	595	505	550
Identified in an irregular situation	1,655	1,870	1,400	2,265	2,510	4,150
Subject to an obligation to leave the territory	6,050	6,180	5,565	5,595	5,245	6,955
Total	8,105	8,550	7,525	8,455	8,260	11,655

Source: Based on Eurostat statistics (our calculation)

These figures from the Statistical Office of the EU reflect the weight of irregular migration from Burundi, the DRC, and Rwanda: three of the five AGL countries not covered by the EUTF. Admittedly, these figures reflect only official statistics, and consider the situation only around the EU borders. The reality would, therefore, be much more significant. Moreover, outside the overall framework of Article 13 of the Cotonou Agreement, the EU has not signed any readmission agreements with any AGL state.[9] This lack of partnership with some states of origin shows how partially the EU is addressing the challenges of irregular migration.

As an overarching framework for ensuring a more holistic EU–Africa collaboration on migration governance, the UN-led GCM for *safe, orderly and regular migration* should be employed more consequentially. This instrument provides a common understanding of the opportunities and challenges of migration and the need for more substantial/extensive/ decisive cooperation between countries of origin, transit and destination.

In particular, the GCM emphasises the fact that no single state has the capacity to address the challenges and opportunities of migration on its own (GCM, para. 11). It thus encourages states to build balanced and mutually beneficial partnerships at all levels, while respecting the human rights of migrants (GCM, Objective 23). These partnerships should, inter alia, address irregular migration, including the return of irregular migrants (GCM, Objective 21), the flexibility and accessibility of regular migration channels (GCM, Objective 5), as well as the participation of migrants in the development of both host and home countries (GCM, Objectives 19 and 20).

Not only does the GCM make no distinction of migratory status regarding the respect of fundamental rights, but it also defends the principle of non-regression and relaunches the concept of the shared responsibility of states. This concept should mitigate the claims of sovereignty of states at the border (Guild, 2018: 663). Non-binding but ambitious (Newland, 2018: 660), the success of the GCM depends entirely on cooperation between the states of origin, transit and destination of migrants (Tardis, 2019: 21). This imperative for cooperation also applies to the migration of AGL citizens via North Africa to Europe.

Conclusion

There are still challenges ahead for the AGL states to establish a substantial/extensive/coherent migration management cooperation, among themselves and with the EU, which can provide joint responses to the shared challenges raised by migration. Internally within the AGL region, a migratory interdependence characterises all these states. Rwanda, Burundi, and Uganda are among the top four overpopulated African countries where problems of access to land and resources are already causing conflict. The other two AGL states, the DRC and Tanzania, are among the least populated countries on the continent where land and resources remain fairly available and underexploited. An ambitious migration cooperation agreement would not only solve the difficulties in overpopulated countries, but would also create wealth in the underpopulated countries. In short, it would boost development in the subregion.

In terms of the EU, this chapter demonstrates that the relative geographical distance between the two blocs has little impact on AGL migration to the EU. The main reasons for this include the region's colonial past, socio-political conflicts, population growth, and the deterioration of the economic and labour market fabric of the AGL countries. For example, the curve of AGL migrants entering the EU has been rising since 2000, as have migrants from the subregion who attempt to cross the EU borders irregularly or who remain there irregularly. However, compared to the potential of regular migration, irregular migration is not beneficial to the states of origin, transit or destination, nor is it conducive to human rights. This calls for the development of ambitious migration cooperation between Africa and the EU. To take full advantage of this migration and make it more regular, the European bloc must relax the requirements for regular migration, and the African bloc must fight against the root causes of irregular migration and facilitate the return and readmission of its nationals who are irregularly in the EU.

More than ever, opportunities for partnership are emerging in view of the gradual stabilisation and normalisation of cooperation in the subregion, including the African and global dynamics around migration. In January 2018, Africa embarked on a path of free movement of people within its borders, based on these regional economic communities, including those of the AGL states. In December of the same year, almost all UN member states adopted the GCM. The African and European consensus that presided over the adoption of the GCM should thus enable concerted actions for its implementation.

Ultimately, although cooperation with the EU remains necessary, it is time for the LGA region – and African governments in general – to guarantee their citizens well-defined migration policies and processes. Indeed, the experimentation with African solutions or alternatives are a new line of thought.

Notes

1   Sylvie Sarolea and Alfred Ombeni are members of the Research Team on European Laws and Migration (EDEM) at UCLouvain. (Online at:https:// uclouvain.be/en/research-institutes/juri/cedie/edem.html).   They   thank Trésor Maheshe, another member of this team, for his proof reading.

2   These include the convention of 8 November 1884 between Germany and the International Association of the Congo; the Brussels Convention of 11

August 1910 between Germany and Belgium delimiting the border between the Belgian Congo (now the DRC) and Ruanda-Urundi (now Rwanda and Burundi), and between Ruanda-Urundi and Buganda (now Uganda); the German–British arrangements signed in Berlin on 1 July 1890 and 19 May 1909. For more details on these different conventions, see Jentgen (1957: 12–49).

3   That year, the foreign ministers of Burundi, Rwanda and DRC came to the Palais d'Egmont in Brussels on 11 July at the invitation of the Belgian Foreign Minister, Louis Michel, to discuss the modalities for reviving the ECGLC.

4   See among many others, *La libre Afrique*, 'La RDC expulse plusieurs centaines de burundais "en séjour illegal"', 18 March 2020. Online at: https://afrique.lalibre.be/47881/la-rdc-expulse-plusieurs-centaines-de-burundais-en-sejour-illegal/; International Organization for Migration (IOM), 'Undocumented migrants expelled from Tanzania to receive humanitarian aid', 30 August 2013. Online at: www.iom.int/news/undocumented-migrants-expelled-tanzania-receive-humanitarian-aid; BBC, 'Des burundais expulsés du Rwanda', 12 June 2016. Online at: www.bbc.com/afrique/region/2016/06/160612_burundi-rwanda; Sahel-intelligence, 'RDC: expulsion de rwandais', 26 November 2018. Online at: http://sahel-intelligence.com/12468-rdc-expulsion-de-rwandais.html (all accessed 18 December 2020).

5   Table 10.1 combines statistics from the IOM (2017), www.iom.int/fr/la-migration-dans-le-monde, and the Office of the United Nations High Commissioner for Refugees (UNHCR) (current as of 30 June 2020), https://data2.unhcr.org/fr/countries/, supplemented by other UNHCR data (2019), www.unhcr.org/refugee-statistics/download/?url=R1xq.

6   ECtHR, 5 February 2002, Conka v. Belgium, No. 51564/99, 61–63, 85; ECtHR, 23 February 2012, Hirsi Jamaa and Others v. Italy, No. 27765/09, 185–186; ECtHR, 21 October 2014, Sharifi and Others v. Italy and Greece, No. 16643/09, 221–225; ECtHR, 25 June 2020, Moustahi v. France, No. 9347/14, 134–137, 161–164.

7   European Resettlement Network, Regional Protection Programmes. Online at: www.resettlement.eu/page/regional-protection-programmes (accessed 2 March 2021).

8   See among others UNHCR, 'Refugee returns to Burundi must be voluntary and not under pressure', 28 October 2019. Online at: www.unhcr.org/news/press/2019/10/5db6ffed4/refugee-returns-burundi-must-voluntary-

under-pressure.html; Amnesty International, 'Tanzania: Confidential document shows forced repatriation of Burundi refugees imminent', 6 September 2019. Online at: www.amnesty.org/en/latest/news/2019/09/tanzania-confidential-document-shows-forced-repatriation-of-burundi-refugees-imminent/ (accessed 2 March 2021).

9   In legal terms, the readmission by a state of its nationals (irregular migrants) is a customary obligation arising from the principle of the territorial sovereignty of any state, according to which it sets the requirements for entry into and stay on its territory, even in a way that discriminates against nationals of certain states. Moreover, in the context of EU–ACP cooperation (including the GLA), this obligation is written into Article 13 of the Cotonou Agreement. However, there are several difficulties with the unilateral implementation of this obligation, including the procedure for identifying irregular migrants and the issuance of travel documents. Indeed, a state is obliged to readmit only its own nationals. Readmission agreements, among other things, make it possible to resolve these practical difficulties.

References

Berwouts, K. 2009. 'Grands Lacs: La libre circulation des personnes et des biens au sein de la CEPGL', *European Network for Central Africa*: 56.

Carlier, J.-Y. and Crépeau, F. 2017. 'De la "crise" migratoire européenne au pacte mondial sur les migrations: exemple d'un mouvement sans droit?' *Annuaire Français de Droit International*, 2017(1): 461–99. Paris: CNRS Editions.

Carlier, J.-Y. and Sarolea, S. 2016. *Droit des étrangers*, 1st edition. Brussels: Larcier.

Chrétien, J.-P. 1996. 'Ethnicité et politique: les crises du Rwanda et du Burundi depuis l'indépendance', *Guerres mondiales et conflits contemporains*, 181.

De Clerck, B. 2006. *History of Rwanda: From the beginning to the end of the twentieth century*. Revised and trans. from French. Online at: https://medialibrary.uantwerpen.be/oldcontent/container49546/files/Burundi/ethnic/NURC16.pdf (accessed 3 March 2021).

Docquier, F. 2018. 'Long-term trends in international migration: Lessons from a macroeconomic model', *Economics and Business Review*, 4(18/1): 3–15.

East Africa Community (EAC). 2009. The East African Community Common Market Protocol for Movement of Labour. https://www.eac.int/documents/category/protocols (accessed 4 June 2021).

ECGLC. 1978. 'Convention Establishing the Economic Community of the Great

Lakes Countries: Concluded at Gisenyi on 20 September 1976.' No. 16748. https://wits.worldbank.org/GPTAD/PDF/archive/CEPGL.pdf (accessed 4 June 2021).

European Commission. 2019. *EU Emergency Trust Fund for Africa. 2018 Annual Report,* Brussels. European Commission. 2018. *The European Union Emergency Trust Fund for Africa: A flexible but focused instrument,* Special Report. Online at: https://op.europa.eu/en/publication-detail/-/publication/2c11f4a9-1a0a-11e9-8d04-01aa75ed71a1/language-en/format-PDF (accessed 28 February 2021).

Food and Agriculture Organization and World Bank. 2018. *Population density.* Online at: HYPERLINK «https://data.worldbank.org/indicator/EN.POP.DNST?most_recent_value_desc=true»https://data.worldbank.org/indicator/EN.POP.DNST. (accessed 2 March 2021).

Frigeri, D. 2016. 'Migrants, Women and Young People in the 5+5 Countries. Managing Migration Policies beyond the Security Approach', R. Albinyana and D. Ruiz-Giménez Coderch (eds), *The 5+5 Dialogue as a Mechanism of Integration and Regional Cooperation,* Barcelona: European Institute of the Mediterranean and the Med Think 5+5 Network.

Galand, P. and Van de Casteele, A. 2006. *La Communauté Économique des Pays des Grands Lacs,* Report to the Belgian Senate, 2005–2006, No. 3-1578/1.

Guild, E. 2018. 'The UN Global Compact for Safe, Orderly and Regular Migration: What place for human rights?' *International Journal of Refugee Law,* 30(4): 239–252.

Jentgen, P. 1957. *Les frontières du Ruanda-Urundi et le régime international de tutelle,* Royal Academy of Colonial Sciences, Memoirs in-8°, New Series, Vol. XIII, fasc. 2.

Kabamba Kazadi, B. 2000. 'Interrégionalité des pays des Grands Lacs africains: élaboration d'un modèle d'intégration régionale en Afrique et son application à la région des Grands Lacs (Burundi, République démocratique du Congo, Kenya, Ouganda, Rwanda et Tanzanie)'. PhD thesis, Vol. 1, University of Liège.

Muhinduka Di-Kuruba, D. 2010. 'Gestion additive, biens publics et fourniture de l'électricité dans la région de Bukavu, RD Congo'. PhD thesis in Political and Social Sciences, University of Louvain.

Musila, C. 2015. 'Entre Grands Lacs et Afrique australe: quel positionnement régional pour la RDC?' *Notes de l'Ifri*: 1–21. Online at: www.ifri.org/sites/default/files/atoms/files/note_rdc_afriqueaustrale.pdf (accessed 1 March 2021).

Newland, K. 2018. 'The Global Compact for Safe, Orderly and Regular Migration: An unlikely achievement', *International Journal of Refugee Law,*

30(4): 657–60.

Nicolaï, H. 2009. '*Progrès de la connaissance du Congo, du Rwanda et du Burundi de 1993 à 2008*', *Belgeo*: 3–4. https://journals.openedition.org/belgeo/7306.

Office of Information and Public Relations for Belgian Congo and Ruanda-Urundi. 1958. *Congo belge et au Ruanda-Urundi: Guide du voyageur*, 4th edition. Brussels.

Pascouau, Y. and Labayle, H. 2011. *Les conditions d'accès au regroupement familial en question: une étude comparative dans neuf Etats membres de l'UE*. Brussels: European Policy Centre and King Baudouin Foundation.

Rais, M. 2018. *Les accords communautaires de réadmission des migrants en situation irrégulière: Aspects juridiques et dilemmes politiques*. Rabat, Maroc: Konrad-Adenauer-Stiftung.

Sarolea, S. 2018. *Immigration et droits: Questions d'actualité*, 1st edition. Brussels: Larcier.

Tardis, M. 2019. '*Le pacte de Marrakech: vers une gouvernance mondiale des migrations?*' *Notes de l'Ifri*: 1–30. Rabat, Maroc: Policy Centre for the New South and Centre Migrations et Citoyennetés. Online at: www.ifri.org/sites/default/files/atoms/files/tardis_pacte_marrakech_2019.pdf (accessed 1 March 2021).

Trusteeship Council, 1952. *Report on the Visiting Mission to Trust Territories in East Africa (1951)*, New York.

UNHCR. 2019. *RD Congo*. Online at: https://data2.unhcr.org/en/documents/download/73406 (accessed 23 February 2021).

UNTAD. 2021. Economic Development in Africa: Migration for Structural Transformation, https://unctad.org/en/Pages/ALDC/Africa/EDAR2018-Key-Statistics.aspx

Cases

European Court of Human Rights. 25 June 2020. *Moustahi v. France*, No. 9347/14.

European Court of Human Rights. 21 October 2014. *Sharifi and Others v. Italy and Greece,* No. 16643/09.

European Court of Human Rights. 23 February 2012. *Hirsi Jamaa and Others v. Italy*, No. 27765/09.

European Court of Human Rights. 5 February 2002. *Conka v. Belgium*, No. 515

Part IV
Continental Perspectives

African Union–European Union relations in the light of migration management

Ahmed Bugre

Introduction

Migration is a human phenomenon that has existed for as long as human civilisation. Migration dynamics are interlinked, *inter alia*, with history, global politics, socio-economic realities, demographics, environmental changes, and cultural practices, as well as pandemics – as recently witnessed with COVID-19. These factors reflect the complexities of what it means to be human, namely, our dreams and our fears, and our search for freedom, opportunities, and a better life (Dakash, 2018).

The history of Africa is characterised by migration and human mobility. These movements, whether voluntary or forced, have contributed to the contemporary demographic landscape of the continent. Human mobility in Africa is often not limited by post-colonial political boundaries. Communities in many parts of Africa extend across two or three nation-states. Cross-border migration is an important livelihood and coping strategy during times of disaster, conflict, violent extremisms and economic downturns. Moreover, the lack of employment and decent work is key to understanding and forecasting the onset of migratory movements and humanitarian responses (AU, 2018). Based on United Nations (UN) estimates, the current population of Africa, which stands at 1.3 billion – equivalent to 16.7 per cent of the total world population – is projected to rise to 2.5 billion by 2050 (UN, 2018). By then, the continent will have the largest population growth of any geographical region. It is estimated that in 2050, a quarter of the world's working-age population will live in Africa (UN, 2018).

While Africa is often seen as a continent of mass emigration, recent research has contradicted these perceptions, which are based on stereotypes rather than empirical research. According to the UN Conference on Trade and Development (UNCTAD), international migration in Africa occurs primarily within the continent. For instance, in 2017, 80 per cent of international migrants residing in East, Central and West Africa were from the same African region (UN, 2018). It is worth noting that while 90 per cent of North African migrants moved outside the continent, nearly 70 per cent of sub-Saharan Africans migrated to neighbouring countries or within their sub-region. Western and eastern Africa are the most dynamic regions in terms of sending and receiving countries, with about 97 per cent and 67 per cent intra-regional migrants, respectively. These movements highlight the role of the Regional Economic Communities (RECs) in these regions in facilitating the free movement of persons, although the right to reside and work remains controlled. Furthermore, the evidence from a range of countries suggests that internal migration (rural–urban migration) is rising and could become the dominant migration pattern across sub-Saharan Africa (Mercandalli and Losch, 2017).

Moreover, according to the United Nations High Commissioner for Refugees (UNHCR), Africa was home to over a third of the 71 million forcibly displaced persons globally in 2018, including 6.6 million refugees and asylum seekers, and 17.8 million internally displaced persons (IDPs) (UNHCR, 2021).

The contribution of migration to African development

Historically, migration in Africa has been perceived in a positive light, and plays a constructive role as a catalyst of economic growth. Although the predominant narrative from developed countries tends to report migration in a negative way, migration and human mobility is a significant contributor to development. Migrant workers across all skill ranges fill labour market gaps, promote trade and investment, and bring innovation, skills and knowledge to both host and origin countries. According to UNCTAD, intra-African migration can positively impact structural transformation in destination countries. It forecasts that migration in Africa could lead to an increase in GDP per capita of US$3,249 by 2030, growing at a compound annual growth rate of 3.5 per cent from 2016 (UNCTAD, 2021). For instance, the inflow of remittances to developing countries was estimated at US$548 billion in 2019, which was more than foreign direct investment (FDI) (US$534 billion) and also exceeded official development assistance (ODA) (US$166 billion) (World Bank, 2020). Currently, remittance inflows to Africa account for half of all private capital flows into the continent and have risen from US$38.4 billion on average in 2005–2007, to US$64.9 billion in 2014–2016 (UN, 2018). The African diaspora is not only a potent force for the development of origin countries through remittances, but also, importantly, through the promotion of trade, investments, research, innovation, knowledge, and technology transfers.

Remittances benefit local households in countries of origin by sustaining daily living, providing investment funds for education, health services, housing, and businesses. At the national level, remittances contribute to the balance of payments by providing much needed foreign exchange. At the same time, migrants are agents of development in terms of human social capital, such that the return of migrants can maximise the impact of migration through skills transfer (or 'brain circulation').

The African Union's position on migration

The African Common Position on Migration and Development[1] and the Migration Policy Framework for Africa and Plan of Action 2018–2030 (MPFA)[2] are the two most important AU policy frameworks on migration adopted to date.

The MPFA provides comprehensive policy guidelines to AU Member States and Regional Economic Communities as well as guidelines in nine thematic areas: (1) Migration governance; (2) Labour migration and education; (3) Diaspora engagement; (4) Border governance; (5) Irregular migration; (6) Forced displacement; (7) Internal migration; (8) Migration and trade; and (9) Other cross-cutting issues (AU, 2018). It offers a strategic framework to guide member states and RECs in the management of migration. Annexed to the MFPA is a Plan of Action that documents activities to be undertaken by the AU Commission to facilitate the coherent management of migration in Africa for the period 2018 to 2030. The plan of action further takes into consideration work that is already underway on the continent, seeking to forge synergies with institutions that are working on the identified activities. Taken together, the MPFA (2018 – 2030) and its Plan of Action, the Protocol to the Treaty Establishing the African Economic Community (Abuja Treaty 1991) Relating to the Free Movement of Persons, Right of Residence and Right of Establishment, and the Protocol to the 1991 Abuja Treaty establishing the African Continental Free Trade Area (AfCFTA), signal a commitment to fully utilise and leverage socio-economic opportunities in Africa, through mobility management, to harness Africa's development potentials (AU, 2006a).

The ACP presents the AU position on 11 priority policies related to migration and recommendations for actions on the national, continental and global level. The policy priority areas outlined are: migration and development; human resources and the brain drain; labour migration; remittances; the African diaspora; migration and peace, security and stability; migration and human rights; migration and gender; children and youth; the elderly; and regional initiatives (AU 2006a: 4–7). Of particular importance for the analysis of multi-level governance of migration, the ACP underlines the fact that regional migration management policies within the RECs should consider national and regional specificities, and that the promotion of capacity-building would foster and facilitate ownership of migration processes by African countries (Urso and Hakami, 2018). To ensure that the challenges migration posed to African and developed countries are addressed effectively, it became necessary to establish a common strategy for the management of migration, which associates countries of origin, transit and destination, in order to find solutions that consider the interests of the countries concerned (AU, 2006a). In addition, the importance of cooperating, to develop a 'concerted effort' to assist transit and destination countries to manage migration, is highlighted. Finally, cooperation on labour migration should ensure the 'systematised and regular movements of labourers; responding to the supply and demand needs of domestic and foreign labour markets; promoting labour standards; and reducing recourse to illegal and irregular movements' (AU, 2006a: 12).

The position of the AU with regard to migration governance is summarised in the following recommendation for action in the ACP:

> It would be indeed illusory to try to treat the problems of migration by recourse only to security measures; hence the need for a comprehensive, integrated, concerted and balanced solution, whose objectives, policies and measures will be long-lasting. This approach should involve the treatment of problems of the movement of persons (legal, illegal and irregular migration), the protection of the rights of communities that are legally established, as well as the linkage between migration and development (AU, 2006a).

Since the adoption of the Abuja Treaty in 1991 by the AU, migration and human mobility has been identified as a tool for regional integration. The free movement of persons, goods and services are key components of regional integration, which is expected to lead to increased economic prosperity and poverty reduction. On the one hand, voluntary migration can enhance economic development by stimulating intraregional trade and promote political integration and closer social interaction between countries. The AU has always acknowledged the migration–development nexus, the benefits of migration to households and communities, and its contribution to national development. As the ACP states,

> Migration can be an effective tool for development by enhancing income distribution, promoting productive work for growth in Africa, enhancing women's empowerment and gender equality, combatting HIV/AIDS, Malaria and Tuberculosis amongst migrant populations and improving partnership amongst the developed and African countries and other stakeholders (AU, 2006).

On the other hand, forced migration, including irregular migration, has the tendency to work against regional integration of the continent (Klavert, 2011). In this regard, poverty is one of the main root causes of migration. The AU acknowledges that creating development opportunities in countries of origin would mitigate the main reasons for young people to engage in migration, thereby also dealing with the problem of the brain drain (AU, 2006a).

Africa–EU Partnership on Migration

The Africa–EU Partnership (AEP) is the formal political channel through which the EU and AU work together, engage in political and policy dialogues, and define their cooperative relationship. Established in 2000 at the first Africa–EU Summit in Cairo, the AEP strives to bring Africa and the EU closer together through strengthening economic cooperation and promoting sustainable development (AU/EU, 2017). Against this backdrop, both continents are determined to work together on a strategic, long-term footing to develop a shared vision for Africa–EU relations in a globalised world. Their common interests include issues such as climate change, global security, and the UN Sustainable Development Goals (SDGs). Although, the relations between Africa and the EU are complex and multi-levelled, the AEP focuses primarily on cooperation at a continental level and specifically on the relationship between the two regional institutions, the EU and the AU. As such, it complements the EU's existing frameworks of cooperation with sub-Saharan Africa and with the EU neighbourhood at bilateral and regional levels (AU/EU, 2017).

On the subject of migration, the joint declaration by African and EU leaders at the Cairo Summit 'acknowledge that a comprehensive and integrated approach is needed to tackle the issue of migration and the separate but related issue of asylum, and will co-operate in this field' (OAU/EU, 2000). The summit also underlined the need for further cooperation to address the root causes of migration, both in countries of origin and transit, as well as in recipient countries, and pledged support for the principle of the Free Movement of Persons in the spirit of the Abuja Treaty. The treaty encourages African states to adopt employment policies that allow the free movement of persons within the African Economic Community through the establishment and strengthening of labour exchanges that ensure optimal redistribution of skilled labour (OAU/EU, 2000). Furthermore, the signatories of the joint declaration, recognise the need for measures to secure the respect, the dignity and protection of migrants' rights, to which they are entitled under agreed international conventions, and,

> Reaffirm our will to continue to provide substantial assistance to those refugees and internally displaced persons, and to support their repatriation and reintegration, in conformity with international humanitarian law and, more specifically, using relevant OAU

Conventions as an important guide in addressing the specific aspects of refugee problems in Africa (OAU/EU, 2000: 8).

Lastly, the signatories 'emphasise the role of the UNHCR and human rights organisations, and the right of asylum seekers to protection' (OAU/EU, 2000: 8).

Apart from the AEP, the African, Caribbean, and Pacific (ACP)–EU Partnership Agreement (also known as the Cotonou Agreement), which involves African countries and the Pacific and Caribbean Group of States, provides an additional framework informing Africa–EU relations. In this regard, the AEP, with its continental approach, has offered an instrumental platform for political dialogue and cooperation, overarching and complementing existing development collaborative frameworks between the EU and African countries.

The Joint Africa–EU Strategy

The Africa–EU Partnership is implemented through the Joint Africa–EU Strategy (JAES), adopted at the 2007 Lisbon Summit. The JAES is an overarching long-term framework for Africa–EU relations, which is implemented through successive short-term action plans and enhanced political dialogue at the continental and regional levels, resulting in concrete and measurable outcomes in all areas of the partnership. It is also a non-legally binding consultative policy framework for Africa–EU relations, which aims to enhance the strategic and political partnership between the two continents.

According to the political declaration of the Lisbon Summit, the purpose of 'this Joint Strategy is to take the Africa–EU relationship to a new, strategic level with a strengthened political partnership and enhanced cooperation at all levels' (AU/EU, 2007). Furthermore, the partnership was to be constructed on a Euro-African consensus on values, common interests and common strategic objectives, and would strive 'to bridge the development divide between Africa and Europe through the strengthening of economic cooperation and the promotion of sustainable development in both continents, living side by side in peace, security, prosperity, solidarity and human dignity' (AU/EU, 2007).

The JAES is the first EU framework to 'treat Africa as one' (Helly et al., 2014), as opposed to other frameworks that still regulate EU relations with

African countries in terms of whether they are north or south of the Sahara. These frameworks comprise the Cotonou Partnership Agreement with the ACP group of states; the Barcelona Process, which involves partnership among southern European countries, North Africa and the Middle East; the Euro-Mediterranean Partnership (now the European Neighbourhood Policy) with North African countries; and the Union for the Mediterranean (UfM). The EU also has a special relation with the Republic of South Africa based on the Trade, Development and Cooperation Agreement (TDCA).

The JAES is implemented through a consultative structure, which is carried out through a biannual Joint Task Force, bringing together representatives of the African Union Commission (AUC) and the EU, member states and experts, including civil society. Notably, civil society involvement has been limited to some extent. The activities are carried out, on a voluntary basis, by thematic Joint Experts Groups (JEGs), one for each of the eight thematic partnerships, which are co-chaired by a European and an African partner. Despite the optimism surrounding the JAES partnership, dialogue has been complex, there was confusion about the level of implementation at national, regional, and continental levels, and there was no effective link with the vital decision-making bodies (Helly et al., 2014). However, the partnership provided space for the exploration of innovative solutions to some gridlocks in Africa–EU relations.

The Migration, Mobility, and Employment (MME) Framework

Both continents also partnered on migration, mobility and employment through the Joint Strategy and Action Plan (2008–2010), embedded in eight separate Africa–EU thematic partnerships. The Action Plan outlines the Priority Actions for the MME partners in three key areas: (1) Implement the declaration of the Tripoli Ministerial Conference on Migration and Development; (2) Implement the Africa–EU Plan of Action on people trafficking (AU, 2006b); and (3) Implement and follow-up the 2004 Ouagadougou Declaration of Action on Employment, Poverty Eradication and Inclusive Development in Africa (AU, 2014; AU, 2006a; AU/EU, 2007). The Africa–EU Declaration on Migration and Development, which adopted the AU Action Plan to Combat Trafficking in Human Beings, Especially Women and Children, led to the establishment of the EU–Africa Partnership on Migration, Mobility and Employment (MME). The MME is a key part of the EU–Africa strategic partnership within the framework of the Joint Africa–EU Declaration on Migration and Development adopted at a ministerial conference in Tripoli on the 22–23 November 2006 (AU/EU, 2006). It is important to note that this meeting follows the adoption of the Africa Common Position on Migration and Development by the AU General Assembly in Banjul in July 2006 (AU, 2006c). The MME, among other things, focuses on the issues of irregular migration, concern for the human rights and wellbeing of migrants, migration management challenges, opportunities for regular migration, human resources and the brain drain, migration and development, peace and security, the protection of refugees, and sharing best practices.

Since the adoption of the JAES framework, migration has received more political attention from the EU. The political cooperation is framed in a number of so-called 'migration dialogues'. Migration dialogues are basically tools to foster governmental discussions and enhance interstate dialogue on migration policy issues. They also contribute to the reinforcement of international migration cooperation, which, according to the EU, facilitates the development of regional and global concepts and systems for more manageable migration. In the recent past, cooperation on migration and asylum policy between the EU and the AU has been framed within four dialogue-led processes, namely, the Rabat Process; the Khartoum Process; the Support to the Africa–EU Migration and Mobility Dialogue; and the Joint Valletta Action Plan.

The Rabat Process: Euro-African Dialogue on Migration and Development

The Euro-African Dialogue on Migration and Development (the Rabat Process) was established at the first Euro-African Ministerial Conference on Migration and Development organised in Rabat in 2006. This conference brought together the countries of origin, transit and destination – along the West African migration route to Europe through the central Mediterranean – to discuss the issues of migration and development. At the time, major migration routes crossed the Strait of Gibraltar or led to the Canary Islands. The conviction that it was not exclusively the responsibility of Spain and Morocco to manage these migration routes gave the impetus to France, Morocco, Senegal and Spain to create the Rabat Process (Rabat Process, 2020).

The objective of the Rabat Process is to enhance dialogue and cooperation on migration more broadly, including legal migration and mobility; the prevention of irregular migration and measures to counteract it; migration and development; international protection, as well as to identify common priorities to develop operational and practical cooperation (European Commission, 2015). It is primarily a dialogue between national administrations and international organisations, both at political and technical levels. The dialogue involves 29 African and 28 Europeans countries (which included the UK until Brexit), the European Commission (EC), the Economic Community of West African States (ECOWAS), the United Nations High Commission for Refugees (UNHCR), the International Organization for Migration (IOM), and civil society organisations (CSOs). International organisations, as well as several CSOs, are increasingly involved in the dialogue due to their ability to contribute relevant expertise (Rabat Process, n.d.-b). According to information on the official website of the Secretariat, the Rabat Process allows a shared understanding of migratory matters, with a consensual approach to new challenges. The location for each meeting and training session alternates between Africa and Europe, and the approach on migration also ensures a balance of African and European issues on the agenda (International Centre for Migration Policy Development, 2017).

In terms of governance, the Rabat Process is based on a network of active National Focal Points who animate the dialogue, guarantee the continuity of the actions, and support the commitment of each state. There is also a steering committee, which is the strategic governing body of the dialogue. The committee is made up of Belgium, Burkina Faso, Equatorial Guinea, France, Italy, Mali, Morocco, Portugal, Senegal, Spain, the EC and ECOWAS. Its function is to stimulate cooperation between the partnering countries and prepare the political orientations of the Rabat Process. The Rabat Process is facilitated by a Secretariat and implemented by the International Centre for Migration Policy Development (ICMPD).

The Rabat Process is funded by the European Union as part of the Euro-African Dialogue on Migration and Mobility (MMD) Support Project. The total budgetary contribution to the MMD facility is €18.5 million, of which the EC is to contribute €17.5 million and the Swiss Development Corporation €1 million. The specific objective of the MMD facility is to improve the governance of migration and mobility within Africa and between Africa and the EU, and to enhance the protection of migrant rights. The fund will be implemented through three interrelated components: (1) The Euro-African Dialogue on Migration and Development; (2) Continental management of migration and mobility; and (3) Support to African Diaspora as development actors (EC, 2020).

Following the fourth Euro-African Ministerial Conference on Migration and Development in November 2014 in Rome, the Rome Declaration and Programme (2014–2017) was adopted, which identified two main priorities: (1) strengthening the link between migration and development, and (2) the prevention and fight against irregular migration and related crimes, namely trafficking in human beings and smuggling of persons (International Centre for Migration Policy Development, 2017). Furthermore, the Rome Declaration introduced four thematic pillars, namely:

1. Organising mobility and legal migration;
2. Improving border management and combatting irregular migration;
3. Strengthening the synergies between migration and development; and
4. Promoting international protection.

At the fifth Euro-African Ministerial Conference on Migration and Development in May 2018 in Marrakesh, the Marrakesh Declaration and Action Plan (2018–2020) defined 10 objectives and 23 actions, and paid particular attention to fostering coherence and complementarity with the outcomes of the Valletta Summit on Migration of 2015. The objectives of the Rabat Process's Marrakesh Action Plan are aligned to the five domains defined by the Joint Valletta Action Plan (JVAP):

1. Development benefits of migration and addressing root causes of irregular migration and forced displacement;
2. Legal migration and mobility;
3. Protection and asylum;
4. Prevention of and fight against irregular migration, migrant smuggling and trafficking in human beings; and
5. Return, readmission and reintegration.

Furthermore, the Marrakesh Action Plan introduced a unique commitment mechanism through which each partner country, on a voluntary basis, could pledge to make particular efforts to implement one or more of the actions defined in the plan (Rabat Process, n.d.-a).

The Khartoum Process: EU–Horn of Africa Migration Route Initiative

The EU–Horn of Africa Migration Route Initiative (known as the Khartoum Process) was launched on 28 November 2014 following the Ministerial Conference of the EU–Horn of Africa Migration Route Initiative in Rome (IOM, 2014). As a platform for political cooperation among the countries along the migration route between the Horn of Africa and Europe, the Khartoum Process is an intercontinental consultation framework, which aims at:

1. establishing a continuous dialogue for enhanced cooperation on migration and mobility;
2. identifying and implementing concrete projects to address trafficking in human beings and the smuggling of migrants; and
3. giving a new impetus to the regional collaboration between countries of origin, transit, and destination regarding the migration route between the Horn of Africa and Europe (EU/ICMPD, n.d.).

The thematic focus of the Khartoum Process is 'to prevent and tackle the challenges of human trafficking and smuggling of migrants between the Horn of Africa and Europe, in a spirit of partnership, shared responsibility and cooperation' (IOM, 2014).

The process leading to the Khartoum Process is based on the AU initiatives to counteract the smuggling of migrants and the trafficking in human beings, as guided by the AU Migration Policy Framework for Africa, the Ouagadougou Action Plan and the AU Commission Initiative against Trafficking, which culminated in the AU General Assembly Declaration. There was also the first regional ministerial conference, the AU Horn of Africa Initiative (AU–HOAI) on human trafficking and smuggling, which was established in October 2014. Furthermore, since 2002, the EU has adopted directives aimed at combatting smuggling of migrants as part of its Global Approach to Migration and Mobility (EC, 2011b).

The Khartoum Process, funded by the EU, brings together over 40 countries, consisting of EU Member States, Norway and Switzerland, countries in the Horn of Africa, North African countries, the European External Action Service, the European Commission, the African Union Commission (AUC), and seven regional organisations. The dialogue is led by a Steering Committee made up of five EU countries, five African countries, the EC, the European External Action Service (EEAS), and the AUC. Its €40 million budget represents the largest deployment of funds secured through the Valletta Process for the EU Emergency Trust Fund for Africa. The Valletta Process offers the opportunities to integrate origin countries to demonstrate to both European and African audiences that concerted action on Africa–EU migration has received due attention.

The Joint Valletta Action Plan

The Joint Valletta Action Plan was adopted by European and African Heads of State and Government at the EU–Africa Migration Summit held in Valletta, Malta, in November 2015. The summit was convened in response to the tragic loss of lives of migrants in the Mediterranean Sea and Europe's so-called refugee or migration crisis, in an effort to strengthen Africa–EU cooperation, and address the challenges and the opportunities of international migration. A Political Declaration and an Action Plan were agreed at the end of the Valletta Summit with the aim of tackling five priority areas, as incorporated in the Rome Declaration (Council of the European Union, 2015).

The Political Declaration highlighted the 'sharp increase in flows of refugees, asylum seekers and irregular migrants', and emphasised the need to 'save lives and do everything necessary to rescue and protect the migrants whose lives are at risk' (Council of the European Union, 2015). Furthermore, the declaration focused on the management of migration flows in all its aspects, and the determination to strengthen the fight against irregular migration, as well as the implementation of bilateral arrangements on return and readmission, giving preference to voluntary return, and reaffirming that all returns must be carried out in full respect of human rights and human dignity. The EU, in particular, stressed the need for the 'return and sustainable reintegration, which can only enhance migration and mobility policy and make it more effective and comprehensive' (Council of the European Union, 2015). The Valletta Summit stakeholders called for the implementation of 16 priority initiatives by the end of 2016, in response to the challenges of migration and mobility, at the appropriate level and with a gender perspective, allowing for the necessary degree of differentiation through region- and country-specific approaches. The EU also launched the Emergency Trust Fund for Africa (known as the EUTF) to foster stability and address the root causes of irregular migration and displaced persons in Africa (EC, 2021a).

According to data on the official website, the EUTF for Africa is worth over €5 billion, with over 88 per cent of the contributions coming from the EU, and 12 per cent from EU Member States and other donors (EU, 2021a). The EUTF will complement prevailing EU aid assistance to Africa, which totalled over €10 billion until 2020 (EC, 2021a). Since June 2020, over 220 initiatives and actions have been approved or implemented across the three regions of Africa, involving 26 African countries and costing approximately €4.4 billion, as follows: (1) Horn of Africa: €1.6 billion; (2) North Africa: €807 million; and the Sahel and Lake Chad Region: €2.0 billion. Over 31 per cent of the projects implemented relate to migration management. In July 2021, the EUTF donated about €107 million to eight countries in the Horn of Africa to strengthen ongoing programmes for sustainable peace, security, and development (EC, 2021a).

The EUTF for Africa is governed by the Strategic Board and the Operational Committee, which are both chaired by the EC and comprise representatives of the European External Action Service (EEAS), EU and non-EU donors (as full members), and representatives of the concerned African partner countries and regional organisations (as observers). In 2018, the Board of the EUTF prioritised six areas[3]:

1. Return and reintegration;
2. Refugee management;
3. Completing progress on the securitisation of documents and civil registry;
4. Anti-trafficking measures;
5. Essential stabilisation efforts in the Horn of Africa and in the Sahel/Lake Chad region;
6. Supporting migration dialogues.

Although, the Valletta Action Plan called for joint action between Africa and the EU, actions under the mandate have been driven by EU Member States development agencies, international NGOs, international organisations or UN agencies, notably through the EU–IOM Initiative focusing of 'assisted voluntary returns' (EC, 2021a).

Defining a new partnership of 'equals': From Abidjan to Kigali

Since 2015 and the so-called refugee crisis, the dialogue between the EU and African countries on migration issues has assumed a new intensity. A key influence of the EU in relation to the AU positioning on migration and asylum lies in the way the EU has elevated migration as a key issue within the EU–AU partnership. Spurred on by the impetus of an increased number of people arriving from Libya and the Sahel region, migration has become an issue of unprecedented importance in EU–Africa relations (Tardis, 2018).

The Fifth African Union–European Union Summit held on 29–30 November 2017 in Abidjan, Côte d'Ivoire – 10 years after the adoption of the Joint Africa–EU Strategy under the central theme 'Investing in youth for a sustainable future' – Heads of State and Government from both continents adopted the Abidjan Declaration, which outlined the new priorities in AU–EU relations. In the area of migration and mobility, the leaders agreed,

> To promote a positive, and constructive and multidimensional approach to migration that takes place in a safe, orderly and regular manner. Taking into account and complementing existing dialogues and frameworks, we commit to deepen our cooperation and dialogue on migration and mobility in a strengthened and regular manner between Africa and Europe. We express our strong political commitment to address the root causes of irregular migration and forced displacement. We stress the importance of effectively managing irregular migration in a spirit of genuine partnership and shared responsibility, in full respect of national law, international law and human rights obligations to maximise the development potential for both Africa and Europe (AU, 2017: 3).

The Abidjan Declaration also included a strong commitment to mobilise financial and technical resources to support joint priority projects. On the one hand, the EU noted the efforts by EU Member States to collectively achieve the target of 0.7 per cent of gross national income (GNI) for official development assistance (ODA) (AU, 2017: 5). On the other hand, the AU was to encourage efforts by its Member States to follow up on the AU Summit Decision to introduce a levy of 0.2 per cent on eligible imports to finance the AU (AU, 2017: 5). Furthermore, the two Unions reiterated their 'determination to give a new impetus to our Partnership through the establishment of effective and inclusive joint mechanisms and structures, which include annual Joint Ministerial meetings' (AU, 2017: 5).

Since the Abidjan Summit, the EU has steered significant financial support towards migration-related projects and policies in its partnership with Africa. According to figures published by the EU, as of 2017, nearly €10 billion had been allocated to migration-related projects in sub-Saharan Africa (Barbe, 2017). By the end of 2020, 254 initiatives and projects had been funded by the EUTF in three regions of Africa, mainly North Africa, the Sahel and Lake Chad Basin, and the Horn of Africa, at a cost of approximately €4.9 billion. This was divided as follows: Horn of Africa: €1808 million; North of Africa: €900 million; Sahel/Lake Chad: €2145 million (EC, 2021b). Of these, 31 per cent (€1.52 billion) were related to migration management. Between 2017 and 2020, the EUTF for Africa, through the EU–IOM Initiative, supported the voluntary return of about 90,000 vulnerable migrants, mostly from Libya and Niger and the creation of 132,000 jobs (EC, 2021b). These migrants were also supported after their return. Embedded in these projects and initiatives has been a focus on cooperation that is geared towards an increase in the return and readmissions of irregular migrants to countries of origin and transit, while also requiring these countries to enhance their efforts on border security and management.

In other words, the EU has used the migration dialogues under the Khartoum Process, the Rabat Process, and the Joint Valletta Action Plan to influence its externalisation of migration policies in Africa. Essentially, the EU has used financial diplomacy to influence migration governance in African states, and in the AU as a continental body. This approach has contributed to the trend of securitising European development assistance; ODA has been used increasingly to support border security and management in Africa. Under the EUTF, for example, countries such as Mali, Niger, and Libya have received support geared to enhancing the capacity of their law enforcement agencies and border control, while development-oriented projects have been contained (Grant et al., 2017). This securitised approach has resulted in the erosion of migrant protection along dangerous routes (Scazzieri, 2018). In short, there has been a misalignment between the short-term or immediate imperatives of the EU and the long-term goals of the AU. While much has been achieved since the Abidjan Summit, there is growing disappointment among AU Member States that little progress has been made under the second pillar of the JVAP in terms of opening legal pathways for migration, in comparison to border security and the return of migrants to countries of origin.

Despite these inherent tensions on priorities, the EU financial support under the Joint Africa–EU Strategy has contributed to positive developments in normative advancements for migration at the AU level. Under the MMD, which required the 'development, monitoring and implementation of pan-African migration and mobility frameworks', the AU achieved the milestone of developing the Migration Policy Framework for Africa and Plan of Action (2018–2030) (Miyandazi et al., 2018). The AU also adopted the Protocol to the Treaty Establishing the African Economic Community relating to the Free Movement of Persons, Right of Residence and Right of Establishment (PFMP). The PFMP obliges the AU to monitor and coordinate the implementation of the protocol, and thus places the AU at the epicentre of collaboration with RECs and Member States in the formulation of free movement policy regimes and procedures. While 33 Member States have signed the PFMP, it is yet to come into force because only four out of the required 15 Member States have ratified the protocol. The AU has also leveraged the resources under the partnership agreement to enhance its institutional capacity and to play a role in the convening and facilitating of key national, intra and inter-regional platforms for migration and asylum dialogue. One such initiative is the Pan-African Forum on Migration (PAFoM).

Established in 2015, the PAFoM invites African regional institutions and partners to disseminate contemporary information on migration trends, patterns and dynamics, with a view to finding durable solutions to migration challenges in Africa. The PAFoM focus areas include, migration governance, regional integration, the facilitated free movement of persons, facilitated trade, integrated border management, visa regimes, and combatting irregular migration (IOM, 2015). Furthermore, in 2019, the AU facilitated 'The Year of Refugees, Returnees and IDPs: Towards durable solutions to forced displacement in Africa', which was the theme of the Eighth High-Level Dialogue of the African Governance Architecture (AGA) held in December 2019. Finally, with the EU funding, the AU established three specialised migration agencies and centres: the African Observatory on Migration in Morocco (AOM), the African Centre for the Study and Research on Migration in Mali (ACSRM), and the Continental

Operational Centre in Sudan (COC).

The second AU–EU Summit, scheduled to take place in November 2020 in Kigali, Rwanda, was postponed until October 2021 due to the COVID-19 pandemic. The Kigali Summit would build on the achievements of the targets set in the 2018 Abidjan Summit. The summit was aimed at renewing the commitment of the two regional institutions to deepen their cooperation and dialogue on migration and mobility, and to further commit themselves to a balanced, coherent and comprehensive approach, guided by the principles of solidarity, partnership and shared responsibility, in full respect of international law, including international human rights law. Another joint initiative under discussion between the EU and AU is the development of a Joint Framework for Continent-to-Continent Migration and Mobility Dialogue (C2CMMD), with the aim of further 'structuring cooperation' on migration and mobility by 'adding value to, and complementing, the other dialogues' (ICMPD, 2021).

There are still key challenges that exist between the AU and EU, particularly on migration and mobility. First, the perspectives of the AU and EU diverge. While migration remains a development issue for Africa, the EU has prioritised the control of Africa–EU migration as a security issue. Second, the impact of COVID-19 on African migrants is a major concern. Migrants were the first to face job losses or the shutdown of their businesses, especially those in the informal sector. The pandemic will have long-term impacts on migration management and integration policies, as it has resulted in a surge of unemployment and underemployment in both Africa and Europe. The mass expulsion or push for the return and readmission of migrants affected by the COVID-19 crisis will be high on the agenda for the foreseeable future.

Third, while the EU has prioritised return, readmission and reintegration of irregular migrants to countries of origin, in the foreseeable future, the AU is likely to call for the integration of migrants working within the EU into their European countries of residence. Fourth, the issue of the readmission of African migrants working in the EU is another area where the EU and the AU do not see eye to eye. The AU is vehemently opposed to obliging African countries to readmit their nationals in the absence of the EU making any progress on the expansion of legal pathways for migrants from Africa. The AU prefers voluntary assisted return as opposed to the forced return and detention of asylum seekers. Thus, the AU always underlines the importance of both unions working together on all aspects of irregular migration, in accordance with international law, the AU Constitutive Act, its regulations and instruments, including return, readmission and reintegration of African nationals, the principle of non-refoulement, and other applicable international legal processes.

Recommendations for future AU–EU relations on migration and mobility

As noted earlier, significant progress has been achieved by the AU and EU in relation to migration and mobility since the Fifth AU–EU Summit in Abidjan in 2018. The next phase of the EU–Africa Strategy should consolidate the gains made since Abidjan, but in a manner consistent to all the priority areas set out in the Joint Valletta Action Plan. The EU has focused most of its funding on border management and return, readmission and reintegration, areas that are asymmetrical to the long-term objectives of the AU. The Common African Position (CAP) on Migration and Development and the Migration Policy Framework for Africa (MPFA) serve as a policy framework and roadmap of a more Afro-centric understanding of migration dynamics, as well as the interventions required to ensure the continent derives the developmental benefits of migration.

Therefore, as the AU and the EU attempt to forge an equal partnership in relation to migration, I would like to propose the following areas of cooperation:

1. The AU and the EU should renew the commitments made at the Fifth AU–EU Summit in Abidjan, in particular, to deepen cooperation and dialogue on migration and mobility, and to take a balanced, coherent and comprehensive approach, guided by the principles of solidarity, partnership and shared responsibility, in full respect of international laws, including international human rights law.

2. Harmonise the AU–EU migration dialogue frameworks, including the EU-led dialogues (Rabat and Khartoum Processes, the Joint Valletta Action Plan) and AU-led dialogues (the Pan African Forum on Migration and the AU-EU-UN Task Force for Libya).

3. Immediately establish the Joint Framework for Continent-to-Continent Migration and Mobility Dialogue (C2CMMD). This process should be co-chaired and funded by the AU and the EU, with the aim of

institutionalising the AU–EU Partnership on migration and mobility. This framework would provide the platform to address the specificities in managing irregular migration, combatting the trafficking in persons and the smuggling of migrants, and developing joint actions on return and reintegration of stranded migrants.

4.   Expand the legal pathways for African migrants to enter Europe legally through the development of forward-looking labour migration and mobility strategies, in full respect of national competencies, and exchange programmes for students, researchers, academics and entrepreneurs; including the recognition of qualifications and vocational training programmes aligned with the needs of the labour markets in Africa and Europe.

5.   The AU and the EU should continue to collaborate to fully operationalise the relevant AU frameworks and instruments on migration, forced displacements,and humanitarian interventions in Africa, through capacity-building and strategic financial instruments targeting the AU and its organs.

6.   All AU Member States should ratify the AU Free Movement of Persons, Right of Residence, and Right of Establishment Protocol (PFMP) to enhance safe, orderly and regular migration within Africa; and operationalise the African Continental Free Trade Area (AfCFTA). The free movement of goods and capital cannot be realised fully without the free movement of people in Africa. In these procedures, the EU could support a robust campaign for the ratification and operationalisation of the PFMP, shifting its priorities from border control to more long-term strategies for migration governance.

Notes

1   Adopted by Executive Council Decision – EX.CL/Dec.305(IX) in Banjul, July 2006; see AU (2006a).

2   Adopted in Banjul, July 2006, as the AU Migration Policy Framework and revised in May 2018; see AU (2018).

3   For full information, check the website of the EU.

References

African Commission. 2006. 'Ouagadougou Action Plan to Combat Trafficking in Human Beings, Especially Women and Children, As adopted by the Ministerial Conference on Migration and Development'. African Commission. Online at: https://au.int/sites/default/files/pages/32899-file 3._ouagadougou_action_plan_to_combat_trafficking_en_1.pdf (accessed 6 October 2021).

African Union (AU). 2006a. 'African Common Position on Migration and Development'. Addis Ababa: African Union. Online at: https://www.unhcr.org/protection/migration/4d5257e09/african-common-position-migration-development.html (accessed 6 October 2021).

African Union (AU). 2006b. 'Ouagadougou Action Plan to Combat Trafficking in Human Beings, Especially Women and Children'. Online at: https://www.africa-eu-partnership.org/sites/default/files/documents/doc_au_commit_ouagadougou_ap_en_0.pdf (accessed 6 October 2021).

African Union (AU). 2006c. 'The Migration Policy Framework for Africa'. Addis Ababa: African Union.

African Union (AU). 2014. 'Declaration on Employment and Poverty Alleviation in Africa'. Addis Ababa: African Union. Online at: https://au.int/sites/default/files/newsevents/workingdocuments/27983-wd-draft_declaration_-english.pdf (accessed 6 October 2021).

African Union (AU). 2017. 'Investing in Youth for Accelerated Inclusive Growth and Sustainable Development'. African Union–European Union Summit 2017. Online at: https://au.int/sites/default/files/documents/37754-doc-5th_au-eu_abidjan_declaration.pdf (accessed 6 October 2021).

African Union (AU). 2018. *The Revised Policy Framework for Africa and Plan of Action (2018–2027)*. Addis Ababa: AU Department for Social Affairs. Online at: https://au.int/sites/default/files/newsevents/workingdocuments/32718-wd-english_revised_au_migration_policy_framework_for_africa.pdf (accessed 6 October 2021).

African Union Commission. 2006. 'African Union Commission Initiative against Trafficking'. Online at: http://www.ohchr.org/Documents/Issues/Trafficking/Dakar_Protection_Kapp-Marais.pdf (accessed 6 October 2021).

African Union Commission. 2018. 'Migration Policy Framework for Africa and Plan of Action'. African Union. Online at: https://au.int/sites/default/files/documents/35956-doc-au-mpfa-executive-summary-eng.pdf (accessed 6 October 2021).

African Union/European Union (AU/EU). 2006. 'Joint Africa–EU Declaration

on Migration and Development.' 22–23 November. Online at: https://
au.int/sites/default/files/pages/32899-file-4._the_joint_africa_eu_
declaration_on-migration_and_development_2006.pdf (accessed 6 October
2021).

African Union/European Union (AU/EU). 2007. 'The Africa–EU Strategic
Partnership: A Joint Africa–EU Strategy'. Online at: https://africa-eu-
partnership.org/sites/default/files/documents/eas2007_joint_strategy_
en.pdf (accessed 6 October 2021).

African Union/European Union (AU/EU). 2017. 'The Partnership and Joint
Africa–EU Strategy'. European Union. Online at: https://www.africa-eu-
partnership.org/en/partnership-and-joint-africa-eu-strategy (accessed 6
October 2021).

Barbe, J. 2017. 'European Union Trust Fund Financials: State of play and
financial resources'. Brussels: European Commission. Online at: https://
ec.europa.eu/trustfundforafrica/content/trust-fund-financials_en
(accessed 6 October 2021).

Council of the European Union. 2015. 'Valletta Summit, 11–12 November 2015'.
Valletta Summit on Migration, Malta. Online at: https://www.consilium.
europa.eu/media/21841/political_decl_en.pdf (accessed 6 October 2021).

Dakash, S. 2018. 'The future of human mobility'. The UNDP, Europe and
Central Asia'. United Nations Development Programme. Online at: http://
www.eurasia.undp.org/content/rbec/en/home/blog/2018/the-future-of-
human-mobility-4-things-to-keep-in-mind-when-debat.html (accessed 6
October 2021).

EU/ICMPD. n.d. 'The Khartoum Process. EU–Horn of Africa Migration
Route Initiative'. Online at: https://www.khartoumprocess.net/about/the-
khartoum-process (accessed 6 October 2021).

European Commission (EC). 2005. 'EU plan on best practices, standards and
procedures for combatting and preventing trafficking in human beings',
Official Journal of the European Commission, 311(1). Online at: https://
ec.europa.eu/anti-trafficking/sites/default/files/eu_action_plan_on_
combating_human_trafficking_en_1.pdf (accessed 6 October 2021).

European Commission (EC). 2011a. 'Directive 2011/36/EU', *Official Journal
of the European Union*. Online at: http://eurlex.europa.eu/LexUriServ/
LexUriServ.do?uri=OJ:L:2011:101:0001:0011:EN:PDF (accessed 6 October
2021).

European Commission (EC). 2011b. 'Global Approach to Migration and
Mobility (GAMM)'. European Union. Online at: https://eur-lex.europa.eu/

legal-content/EN/ALL/?uri=CELEX:52011DC0743 (accessed 6 October 2021).

European Commission (EC). 2015. 'The European Union's cooperation with Africa on migration'. European Union. Online at: https://ec.europa.eu/commission/presscorner/detail/en/MEMO_15_4832 (accessed 6 October 2021).

European Commission (EC). 2020. 'Commission Implementing Decision on the financing of the 2020 annual action programme for the Thematic Programme on "Global Public Goods and Challenges in the area of Migration and Asylum" to be financed from the general budget of the Union'. Online at: https://ec.europa.eu/international-partnerships/system/files/aap-gpc-migration-asylum-c2020-5741-f1_en.pdf (accessed 6 October 2021).

European Commission (EC). 2021a. 'EU Emergency Trust Fund for Africa'. Brussels: European Union. Online at: https://ec.europa.eu/trustfundforafrica/index_en (accessed 6 October 2021).

European Commission (EC). 2021b. 'EUTF for Africa'. Online at: https://ec.europa.eu/trustfundforafrica/sites/default/files/factsheet_eutf-for-africa_january_2021_0.pdf (accessed 6 October 2021).

European Union (EU). 2013. 'The EU Strategy Towards the Eradication of Trafficking in Human Beings 2012–2016'. European Commission. Online at: https://ec.europa.eu/anti-trafficking/sites/antitrafficking/files/eu_strategy_towards_the_eradication_of_trafficking_in_human_beings_2012-2016_1.pdf (accessed 6 October 2021).

Grant, A., Rossi, A., Sagna, S., Stetter, E., Tocci, N. and Venturi, B. 2017. 'The Security–Migration–Development Nexus Revised: A perspective from the Sahel'. Online at: https://www.iai.it/sites/default/files/9788868129729.pdf (accessed 6 October 2021).

Helly, D., Bekele, E.A., Fassi, S. and Galeazzi, G. 2014. 'The Implementation of the Joint Africa–Europe Strategy: Rebuilding confidence and commitments'. European Parliament. Online at: https://ecdpm.org//wp-content/uploads/2014-European-Parliament-Study-Implementation-Joint-Africa-Europe-Strategy.pdf (accessed 6 October 2021).

International Centre for Migration Policy Development (ICMPD). n.d. 'Migration Dialogues'. Online at: https://www.icmpd.org/our-work/migration-dialogues/ (accessed 6 October 2021).

International Centre for Migration Policy Development (ICMPD). 2021. 'Migration and Mobility Dialogue Support Programme'. Online at: https://www.icmpd.org/our-work/projects/migration-and-mobility-dialogue-support-programme (accessed 6 October 2021).

International Centre for Migration Policy Development (ICMPD). 2017. 'Rabat Process Factsheet'. Online at: https://www.icmpd.org/fileadmin/2017/ Rabat_Process/EN_RP_Factsheet_Rabat.pdf (accessed 6 October 2021).

International Organization for Migration (IOM). 2015. 'Pan-African Forum on Migration'. International Organization for Migration. Online at: https:// www.iom.int/pan-african-forum-migration (accessed 6 October 2021).

International Organization for Migration (IOM). 2014. 'Declaration of the Ministerial Conference of the Khartoum Process: EU–Horn of Africa Initiative'. European Council on Refugees and Exiles. Online at: https:// ecre.org/wp-content/uploads/2014/12/italia2014.eu_media_3785_ declaration-of-the-ministerial-conference-of-the-khartoum-process.pdf (accessed 6 October 2021).

Klavert, H. 2011. 'African Union frameworks for migration: Current issues and questions for the future'. European Centre for Development Policy Management. Online at: https://ecdpm.org/wp-content/uploads/2013/11/ DP-108-African-Union-Frameworks-Migration-Issues-Questions-Future-2011.pdf (accessed 6 October 2021).

Mercandalli, S. and Losch, B. (eds). 2017. *Rural Africa in motion. Dynamics and drivers of migration South of the Sahara.* Rome: Food and Agriculture Organization of the United Nations. Online at: http://www.fao.org/3/ I7951EN/i7951en.pdf (accessed 6 October 2021).

Miyandazi, L., Apiko, P., Abderrahim, T. and Aggad-Clerx, F. 2018. 'AU–EU relations: Challenges in forging and implementing a joint agenda', *South African Journal of International Affairs*, 25(4), 461–80. Online at: https://doi. org/10.1080/10220461.2018.1548974 (accessed 6 October 2021).

Organisation of African Unity/European Union (OAU/EU). 2000. 'Africa–EU Summit: Cairo Declaration'. *Conseil/00/901.* 3–4 April. Online at: https:// africa-eu-partnership.org/sites/default/files/pres-00-901_en_0.pdf (accessed 6 October 2021).

Rabat Process. n.d.-a. 'Multi-annual Cooperation Programmes. Rabat Process'. Euro-African Dialogue on Migration and Development'. Online at: https://www.rabat-process.org/en/about/rabat-process/335-strategic-framework-ministerial-declarations (accessed 6 October 2021).

Rabat Process. n.d.-b. 'Rabat Process: Partners'. Euro-African Dialogue on Migration and Development. Online at: https://www.rabat-process.org/ en/about/our-partners/336-our-partners (accessed 6 October 2021).

Rabat Process. 2020. 'Equatorial Guinea: Current Rabat Process Chair'. Euro-African Dialogue on Migration and Development. Online at: https://www.

rabat-process.org/en/about/rabat-process/current-chairmanship (accessed 6 October 2021).

Scazzieri, L. 2018. 'To manage migration, the EU needs to rethink its neighbourhood policy'. Brussels: Centre for European Reform. Online at: https://www.cer.eu/sites/default/files/insight_LS_17.5.18.pdf (accessed 6 October 2021).

Stern, M. 2015. 'The Khartoum Process: Critical assessment and policy recommendations', *IAI Working Papers*, 15(49): 1–19.

Tardis, M. 2018. 'European Union Partnerships with African Countries on Migration: A common issue with conflicting interests'. Paris: French Institute of International Relations. Online at: https://www.ifri.org/en/publications/notes-de-lifri/european-union-partnerships-african-countries-migration-common-issue (accessed 6 October 2021).

United Nations (UN). 2018. *Economic Development in Africa Report 2018: Migration for Structural Transformation*. Brussels: United Nations Conference on Trade and Development. Online at: https://www.icafrica.org/fileadmin/documents/Publications/Economic_Development_in_Africa_Report_2018.pdf (accessed 6 October 2021).

United Nations High Commissioner for Refugees (UNHCR). 2021. 'Global trends forced displacement in 2019'. Online at: https://www.unhcr.org/statistics/unhcrstats/5ee200e37/unhcr-global-trends-2019.html (accessed 6 October 2021).

Urso, G. and Hakami, A. 2018. *Regional Migration Governance in Africa: AU and RECs*. Luxembourg: Publications Office of the European Union. Online at: https://publications.jrc.ec.europa.eu/repository/bitstream/JRC112055/african_migration_governance_pubsy.pdf (accessed 6 October 2021).

World Bank. 2020. 'COVID-19: Remittance flows to shrink 14% by 2021'. Press Release No: 2021/054/SPJ, 29 October. Online at: https://www.worldbank.org/en/news/press-release/2020/10/29/covid-19-remittance-flows-to-shrink-14-by-2021 (accessed 11 October 2021).

Chapter 12

Bridging the Mediterranean: Coherent European and African long-term migration policy[1]

Jan Bade

Introduction

European and African countries have different views on migration, primarily because of differences in levels of prosperity and demography. This chapter discusses the drivers of migration on both continents and indicates how both could benefit in the longer term from coherent migration policies that take into account both the positive and negative effects of migration for each continent. By mitigating the negative effects and stimulating the positive effects, safe, orderly, and regular migration could become a tool to bridge the divide between the European Union (EU) and African Union (AU), paving the way for more cooperation and mutual benefits in a geopolitically changing world.

The EU position on migration is also the result of historical developments within Europe. Member countries cannot agree on migration and asylum policies, in part due to the colonial history of some European countries, the large number of Europeans that migrated to the Americas, the freedom to move within the Schengen Area, and the differences in their wages and dependence on foreign labour. Yet a common position is required for the stability of EU's external relations. African actors stress the importance of international solidarity with respect to the costs of protection and shelter of refugees. They also highlight the benefits of better access to work, remittances, networks, trade and investment, education, and a more affluent diaspora.

This chapter investigates how cooperation can bridge the divide between Africa and Europe on migration issues by developing a common view on the factors that determine migration and asylum, and on ways to influence these jointly. The chapter starts with the current state of Africa–EU migration, including perspectives on migration, and demographics in Europe and in Africa, and then gives an overview of the literature on determinants of migration. After discussing European and African policies, conclusions are drawn on how both continents can cooperate on migration and asylum, and on the potential benefits of migration.

European perspectives on contemporary migration

For a long time, less than 3 per cent of the world's population lived in a country that was not their country of origin or birth. Since the year 2000, there has been an upward trend in migration, culminating in 3.5 per cent in 2019 (IOM, 2019: 21). This increase cannot be explained by an increase in international prosperity gaps. In fact, inequality between countries has decreased since 2000 (UNDESA, 2020). The rise in the number of refugees caused about one-third of this worldwide increase in migrants. Regional integration such as intra-European migration and globalisation, including the reduction in transport and other migration costs, and the expansion of international networks also contributed to the rise. The rest of the increase is probably the result of political, social, demographic and climate-related factors.

In 2000, the number of Europeans that had settled on another continent was still comparable to the number of immigrants that had settled in Europe. However, in recent years, Europe has become a net immigration region with about 78 million migrants in 2017, which is roughly 10 per cent of the European population and thus a lot more than the global average. The majority (41 million) were from Europe itself. Most of the other 37 million immigrants are from Asia, Central and South America, and North Africa. These include more than 3 million refugees and asylum seekers, especially from Syria (1 million), Afghanistan (400,000), Iraq (300,000), Eritrea

(200,000), Somalia (125,000) and Iran (120,000) (UNDESA, 2018).

Another characteristic of recent immigration in Europe is the growth of so-called 'irregular' forms – entering a country without permission. Estimates vary from 10 per cent of the total migration to over a third. This irregular migration has increased because of the rise in the number of refugees, as well as more restrictive admission policies. Between 2009 and 2013, about 100,000 people entered Europe annually in an irregular way (Frontex, 2017). This number rose in 2014, and in 2015 there were over 1 million 'illegal border crossings',[2] mostly by refugees originating from Syria, Afghanistan and Iraq. By 2019, the number of irregular immigrants was back to around 100,000 (IOM, 2020), with fewer refugees and more irregular labour migrants, in particular from West Africa. Most irregular migrants entering the EU apply for asylum. Over the years, the EU member countries allowed on average half of the asylum seekers to stay (Eurostat, 2020). Of these around 50 per cent got refugee status.[3] The others were allowed to stay because they came from a country that was regarded as unsafe for people to return (subsidiary protection) or for humanitarian reasons. Whereas refugees are entitled to cross a border irregularly, three-quarters of the irregular migrants into the EU are not. Nevertheless, only a quarter of them return to their country of origin.

Free movement within the Schengen Area is an important aspect of EU migration policy. The free movement of persons is a fundamental right guaranteed by the EU to its citizens. It enables every EU citizen to travel, work and live in any EU country without special formalities. It is a recent phenomenon that has caused substantial intra-European migration and has influenced the discussions on migration within Europe. As Figure 12.1 shows, net migration is strongly correlated with GDP, and people generally move from East to West.

There are also significant differences between Eastern and Western European countries in their acceptance of immigrants. The Gallup Migrant Acceptance Index (2020)[4] shows these large differences. The index score for EU countries in Western Europe is 6.73 compared to 2.77 for EU countries in Central and Eastern Europe. This divide in public attitudes toward immigrants illustrates why the EU has had such difficulty creating a common and cohesive policy on migration and asylum. Acceptance is positively correlated with the level of education and income, and negatively with age.

Figure 12.1: Net migration rates in Europe (2017)

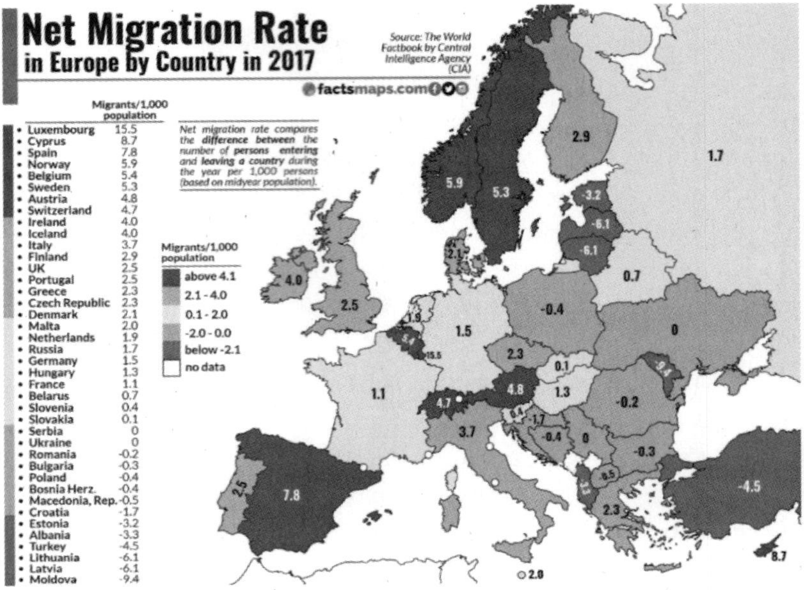

Source: The World Fact Book, CIA

Figure 12.2 (De Wulf, 2020) shows that Europe is ageing with a relative decline of the working population. The Joint Research Centre (JRC) published a scenario study on ageing and potential labour supply in the EU-28 (so including the UK), making scenarios until 2060, based on immigration and fertility rates. In the base scenario, the size of the working-age population will drop from 306 million in 2015 to 256 million in 2060 (Lutz et al., 2019: 21). Without any immigration, the working-age population would be only 222 million in 2060. This means that in the base scenario there are 34 million more workers in 2060 than in the scenario without immigration. This requires at least 750,000 immigrants per year. Immigration is, therefore, compensating for reduced fertility. In the high migration scenario needed to keep the working-age population stable (given base scenario fertility rates), rather than the total population, immigration would have to be three times the current levels, resulting in a 20 per cent increase in total population in 2060.

Figure 12.2: Population pyramid of Europe (2019)

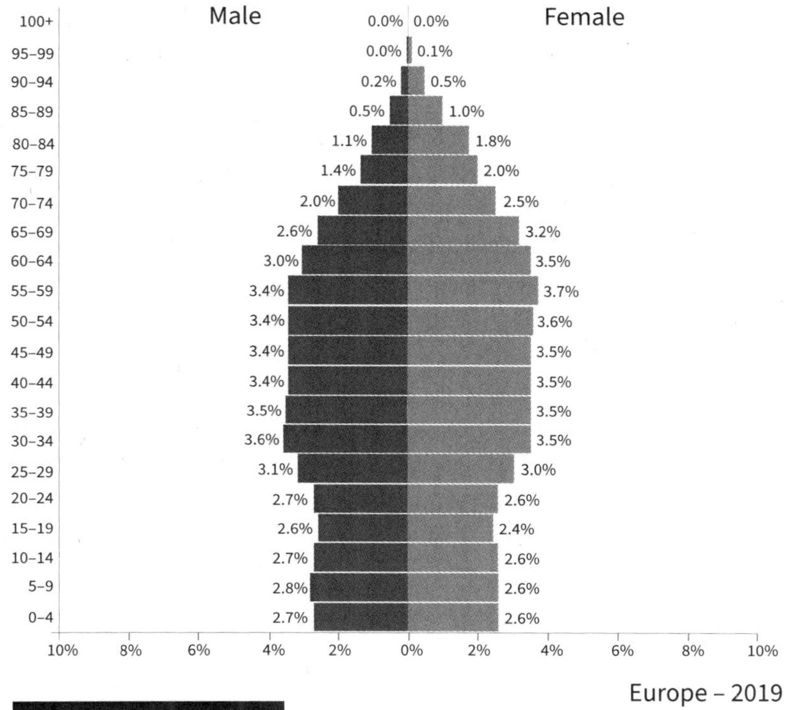

Source: De Wulf (2020)

Unlike a change in fertility, immigration would make little improvement in the long-term on reducing the proportion of people of non-working age relative to those of working age. This is because immigrants also grow older. Increasing immigration will not stop the population from ageing. The JRC scenario study concludes that if the EU needs more labour, which is uncertain and will depend on technical progress and globalisation, a combination of higher labour market participation, higher fertility rates and more immigration seem advisable, depending on social acceptance of these three factors and the integration of immigrants.

African demographics and migration dynamics

Unlike Europe, Africa currently has a very young population, mostly under 20 years of age (50.7 per cent), as Figure 12.3 shows (De Wulf, 2020). As a result, the labour force will increase in the coming decades, both as a percentage of population and in absolute terms. Every year, 15–20 million young people will enter the African labour market. There is high population growth, but labour productivity and the number of jobs lag far behind (IOB, 2018b). Many young people have unproductive and badly paid work in the informal sector.

Figure 12.3: Population pyramid of Africa (2019)

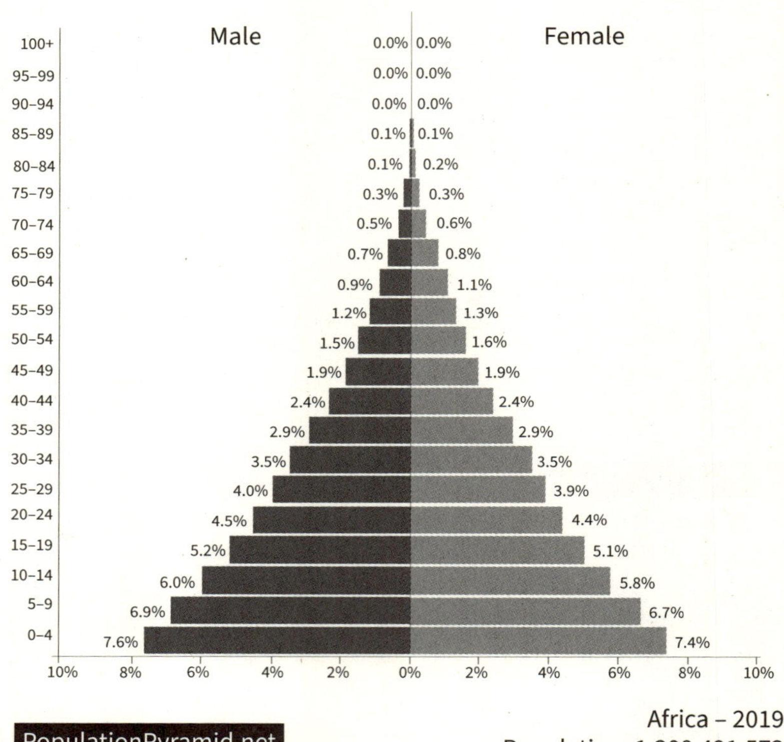

Between 1990 and 2017, the population of Africa doubled, as Figure 12.4 shows. This growth continues. According to the 2019 revision of the World Population Prospects of the United Nations (UN), the population of the continent will reach the 2 billion mark in the 2040s. In fact, as Figure 12.4 shows, population growth is the main reason for the increase in the number of migrants from Africa to other continents such as Europe. Furthermore, contrary to growth of intercontinental migration, growth of intra-African migration is lagging behind population growth.

Figure 12.4: Development of population and migration in Africa (1990–2017)

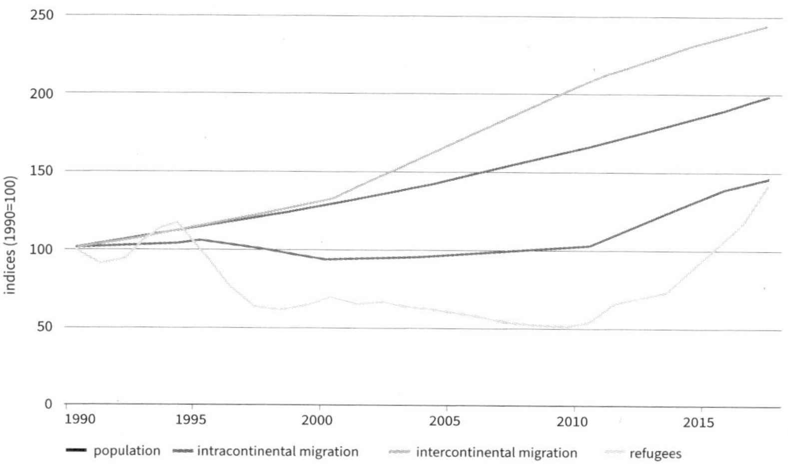

Source: IOB (2018a), based on UNDESA, UNHCR and WDI data

Within Africa, migration takes on many forms. Except for Liberia, South Africa, Egypt and Ethiopia, all African countries became independent in the last 70 years. In those countries, there are still people who were born under colonial rule when borders and nations states were less important and the difference between a native and a migrant[5] less articulated. Language and ethnic backgrounds still seem to matter more than borders. Nomadic pastoralists have always looked for greener pastures across borders. In West Africa, young people have for centuries worked in coastal areas where the climate is more suitable for cash crops and the larger cities provide better chances than the countryside. South Africa's mining industry has attracted labourers from all over the continent. On the one hand, discussions on migration and border control have regained momentum recently, with the EU pushing for border control in the Sahel. On the other hand, African regional blocs are allowing free movement and the African Union (AU) is trying to push a continent-wide freedom to move.

The largest portion of African migrants, including refugees, live on their own continent. In 2000, about 70 per cent of migrants born in Africa also lived in Africa (Beauchemin, 2018), and this estimate has barely changed. The main destination countries include South Africa, Côte d'Ivoire, Nigeria, Kenya and Ethiopia (Awumbila, 2017). Sometimes, like in the case of Ethiopia, Kenya, Sudan and Uganda, conflicts in neighbouring countries cause immigration. West Africa has a long migration tradition for economic reasons, also influenced by the large number of small countries (Flahaux and De Haas, 2016), since emigration figures in smaller countries are often relatively high (Lucas, 2015).

Most migrants from poorer African countries (such as Mali, Niger and Burkina Faso) reside in neighbouring countries (such as Côte d'Ivoire), whereas Africans from more developed countries such as South Africa, Nigeria and North African countries are more likely to emigrate to Europe (Lucas, 2015; Flahaux and De Haas, 2016; Beauchemin, 2018). This may be due to capital constraints in poor countries or higher aspirations in more developed African countries (see determinants of migration, below).

Figure 12.5: African migration. Where do migrants come from (Stock data, 2017)

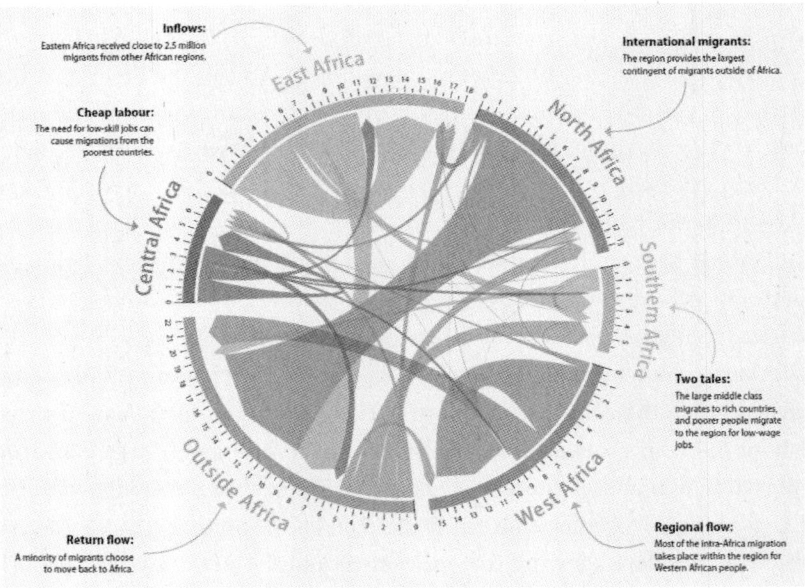

Source: African Development Bank. *Annual Development Effectiveness Reviews* (2018)

Figure 12.5 presents migration of Africans in one graph. It presents stock data for 2017. The ring indicates the number of migrants. It shows, for instance, that in 2017 around 1.5 million migrants in Southern Africa originated from East Africa. It also illustrates that migrants in Africa stay predominantly in their own regions. Interestingly, there has been very little migration between East Africa and West Africa. This confirms that language, trade relations, and a common colonial past have influenced migration patterns in Africa (Lucas, 2015).

As in Europe, the Gallup World Poll also calculated the Gallup Migrant Acceptance Index (2020) for African countries. In 2016, sub-Saharan Africa turned out to be very migrant friendly. Seven sub-Saharan countries made it to the top 15 worldwide, with three (Rwanda, Mali and Sierra Leone) in the top five behind Iceland and New Zealand. With an average score of 6.47, sub-Saharan Africa scores almost as high as Western Europe. North Africa on the contrary scores 4.49, which seems low but is still higher than the Middle East (3.50) and the EU countries in Central and Eastern Europe (2.77).

The percentage of Africans living outside their continent has gradually increased from 0.9 per cent in 1990 to 1.2 per cent in 2017 (UNDESA, 2018). More than half of this migration involves migration from North Africa (with an emigration rate of 4.6 per cent), especially to the Middle East (Saudi Arabia and the United Arab Emirates) and Europe (France, Spain and Italy). The percentage of people born in sub-Saharan Africa but living outside Africa rose from 0.3 per cent in 1990 to 0.7 per cent in 2017, or from roughly 3 million to 7 million people. About half of these live in Europe, while others have found a destination in the Middle East or in the United States. The increase to those latter two destinations was relatively higher than the increase in migration of Africans to Europe.[6]

Determinants of migration

People migrate for various reasons. Migration can be voluntary, for example, in search of adventure, for marriage or to get a (better) job, or it can be forced, as in the case of fleeing from war or through human trafficking. Most migration is for various reasons, in between forced and voluntary, and is often called 'mixed'. An overview of the determinants of migration will assist in assessing which policies are likely to be successful.

Violence is an obvious reason to flee from one's home, but often not a reason to leave the country. Typically, the size of the country, the spread of the conflict, and the distance to the border plays a role. Conflict and political insecurity have an impact on living conditions as well as on economic opportunities (De Haas, 2011; Cummings et al., 2015). People stay until the physical threat begins to outweigh the cost of fleeing, including what one is forced to leave behind (Adhikari, 2013). Changes to personal circumstances, such as the loss of income or possessions or a threat to one's safety, frequently tip the balance (Cummings et al., 2015). De Haas et al. (2019) conclude that authoritarian regimes do not necessarily have higher emigration figures than more democratic ones. An authoritarian state can increase aspiration levels, but also effectively limit the possibility of migrating (as in the case of North Korea). De Haas et al. (2019) conclude that a combination of violent conflict and the absence or collapse of an effectively functioning central state (as in Somalia) is more likely to lead to emigration. Knowing that most European countries will grant asylum is also an important factor.

Traditional neoclassical migration theories explain migration primarily by wage and prosperity differentials. The decision to migrate is based on a consideration of expected costs and benefits, on preference in time (the willingness to invest), on the length of time that the benefits are expected to last, and on the perception of and the willingness to take risks. This theory reinforces the basis for policies to strengthen border control and fight migrant smuggling. Research shows that international income disparities and international wage differentials do in fact provide an important explanation for migration (World Bank, 2018). An increase of 10 per cent in income disparity between two countries will increase migration by 3 per cent, according to a study by the OECD (2016). The neoclassical theory provides an explanation (prohibitive costs and capital constraints) for the relatively low level of emigration from the poorest countries. The theory cannot, however, explain why total migration from some poor countries initially increases when there is growth in prosperity (De Haas, 2010a; Clemens, 2014a; OECD, 2016; Dao et al., 2018). Between 1995 and 2015, the relative income disparities between several emerging countries and high-income countries decreased by 45 per cent on average, but migration from the first to the latter increased by 86 per cent (OECD, 2016).

Apart from wage differentials and income disparities, other factors also play a role. This recognition has led to push and pull approaches (Van Hear et al., 2018). The charm of the notion is in its relative simplicity: there are push factors that cause people to want to leave their current community or country, and pull factors that cause them to want to go to certain new destinations. Push factors include conflict, unemployment, a lack of economic prospects, low wages, natural disasters, food insecurity, poor healthcare, and persecution. Pull factors are usually complementary, for example, the prospect of economic prosperity, employment opportunities, high wages, good educational systems, technology, safety and security.

The approach is appealing from the point of view of policy: if emigration or immigration is deemed undesirable, then in principle it should be possible to tackle the root causes by reducing the push factors. The main weakness is that it explains migration by a more or less unlimited and random list of factors that cause people to migrate. The framework is static and does not analyse how migration, in turn, influences the factors that contribute to migration (De Haas, 2010a). A third criticism is that the approach is based on external factors and not people's intrinsic motivation (De Haas, 2011; 2014). The assumption is that people respond in the same way. This begs the question: why are more people not migrating?

Migration transition theories view migration as a process that is an inherent part of development, economic and demographic transition, and globalisation (De Haas, 2014; De Haas et al., 2019).[7] The transition approach predicts an initial increase rather than a decrease of emigration with growing prosperity. De Haas (2011; 2014) analyses migration as a function of people's ambitions and opportunities to migrate. The pivotal idea is that as a country develops, more people have the opportunity to migrate. In addition to opportunities, aspirations play a key role. These aspirations change over time, influenced by socio-economic and cultural developments. Usually, people first migrate from rural areas to the city and only at a later stage to another country (De Haas, 2014; IOB, 2018a). Opportunities for migrating will continue to grow with development, but the aspiration to migrate will fall when a certain level of development is reached. According to De Haas and the American economist Michael Clemens, empirical evidence confirms the existence of a 'migration hump', whereby emigration generally peaks at a per capita income of around US$7,000-13,000 or a human development index of 0.75 (De Haas; 2010a; 2010b; 2011; 2017; and Clemens, 2014a).[8]

Despite data problems, it is clear that the number of people entering Europe irregularly has gone up in recent years, if only because of the Syrian refugees. Allowing asylum seekers in while restricting labour migrants, who intend to enter regularly, leads to substitution (De Haas, 2018). Labour migrants continue to come, but irregularly, and they apply for asylum to prolong their stay, thereby congesting and overloading the system at the expense of genuine refugees, who are forced to take the same dangerous routes, pay the same high prices to smugglers, and have to wait longer to get asylum.

Regular and irregular migration are influenced largely by the same drivers, but the chance of succeeding differs greatly, as success is determined by the odds of reaching Europe, of being deported, and of making a living. For irregular labour migrants, the latter depends on the availability of informal work, as they do not generally have work permits or identity cards.

Figure 12.7: Size of the shadow economy in European countries, 2016 (percentage GDP)

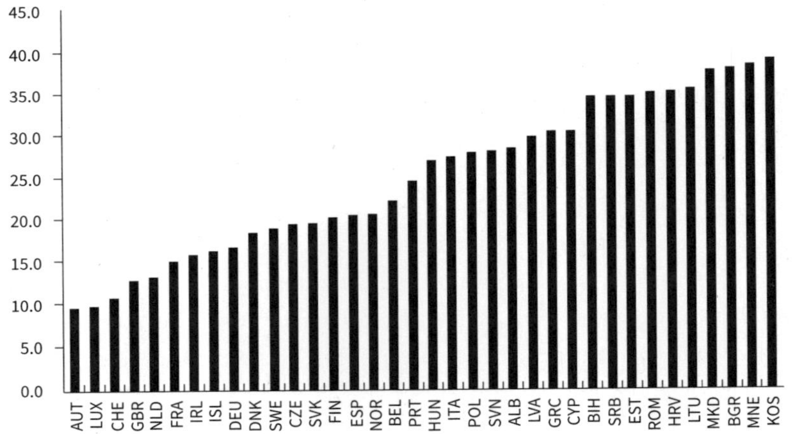

Source: IMF staff calculations

Figure 12.7 from an IMF Working Paper by Kelmanson et al. (2019) shows the extent of the informal sector in Europe. The paper presents estimates that show that the relative share of the shadow economy is constant over time at around 23 per cent of GDP on average for the EU, and at about 20 per cent for the more advanced countries where many irregular migrants stay. The shadow economy consists mainly of jobs in agriculture, cleaning, domestic labour, care, catering, construction, garment manufacturing, prostitution, and drugs. A very rough estimate indicates that the shadow economy of the EU could include the equivalent of 40 million full-time jobs.

The drivers of regular and irregular migration do not differ much, but irregular migrants often risk their lives and need to be prepared to work for precarious wages in the informal sector. The main difference is that informal labour is a far more important driver for irregular migration than for regular migration.

European migration and asylum policy

Two out of every three refugees have fled a country in Africa or the Middle East. Although more than 80 per cent are given shelter in their own region, the concern of policy actors in Europe is the possibility of these refugees reaching Europe in large numbers. Another concern is that many irregular labour migrants will come in their wake and request asylum or stay illegally in Europe. As indicated earlier, in 2019 only 26 per cent of the asylum seekers were granted a refugee status, but 82 per cent of all asylum seekers stayed in Europe (Eurostat, 2020).

In 2015, the EU presented a new European Agenda on Migration, emphasising full implementation of the Common European Asylum System (CEAS), fighting irregular immigration, securing the external borders, and reviewing the policy on legal immigration. This policy is based on the view that it is possible to curb irregular migration through international cooperation and partnerships. Asylum seekers are only a small part (around 15 per cent) of total immigrants into the EU. Other categories are legal labour migrants, students, and migrants for family reunion. Contrary to common perceptions, legal entry and family reunion have become less restricted over the last decades, particularly for highly skilled and unskilled workers, and students. However, border controls, return policies and measures against irregular migration have become more restrictive (De Haas, 2017; Migali et al., 2018) and the key subject of EU–AU cooperation. The EU offers African countries support to manage their borders, stimulates voluntary return of rejected asylum seekers, and emphasises the agreements on forced return and readmission. The EU also supports the fight by African countries against trafficking and human smugglers.

In the aftermath of the European refugee crisis, EU member states have been unable to agree on ways to reform the current asylum system. Disagreement within the EU focuses particularly on the admission and resettlement of refugees. Some member states do not wish to accept any resettlement of asylum seekers, or even of recognised refugees. Apart from very limited numbers of resettled refugees, and asylum seekers that were able to get tourist visas, the system does not allow for the regular arrival of asylum seekers, so their entry into EU territory is often irregular and concentrated in a few countries, such as Greece, Italy and Spain (IOM, 2020). Disagreement concerning the admission and resettlement of refugees may have a negative impact on the EU's foreign policy in general, and on the credibility of its value system. Thus, the EU has a key interest in this area that is much broader than asylum policy. Therefore, the EU currently explores the opportunities for combining the international community's shared responsibility for people who legitimately invoke the Refugee Convention, with the principle of subsidiarity.[9] Given that the Czech Republic, Hungary and Poland voted against the 2018 United Nations (UN) Global Compact for Safe, Orderly and Regular Migration (GCM), while Austria, Bulgaria, Latvia, Italy, Romania, Slovakia and Switzerland abstained or did not vote, this creates a situation in which a majority of EU countries imposes obligations on a minority. This is neither in the interests of the EU nor in those of migrants and refugees. It is, therefore, a top priority for the EU to agree on a future-proof migration policy.

A logical first step towards a better European refugee policy is to reduce the number of refugees worldwide, particularly those headed for Europe. This, in fact, is part of the EU-supported Comprehensive Refugee Response Framework (CRRF) and the Global Compact on Refugees (GRF), adopted in December 2018 by the UN General Assembly. It aims at easing the (mainly financial) pressures on host countries, enhancing refugee self-reliance, expanding access to third-country solutions, and supporting return in safety and dignity.

Addressing the root causes of irregular migration by targeted international cooperation is one of the concrete policy measures taken by the EU and its member states. The idea is that trade and investment can be substitutes for migration, offering jobs in countries of origin and importing goods and services rather than people. Development assistance is another instrument for addressing the root causes. The EU Emergency Trust Fund for stability and addressing the root causes of irregular migration and displaced persons in Africa (the EUTF for Africa) is the flagship of this policy. It attempts to integrate migration politics, foreign policy and partnerships for development.[10]

African migration and asylum policy

In 2001, the AU decided on the outline of a migration policy framework based on three objectives: (1) ensuring the integration of migration into the agenda for security, stability, development, and cooperation agenda; (2) working towards the free movement of people; and (3) facilitating the participation of migrants, particularly those in the diaspora, in the development of their own countries of origin (AU, 2018). In 2006, the AU Migration Policy Framework for Africa (MPFA) was adopted. In 2016 the AU member states and the Regional Economic Communities (RECs) acknowledged changes in migration trends and patterns on the continent. As a result, in 2018 the AU adopted the revised 'MPFA and Plan of Action (2018–2030)' (AU, 2018). This comprehensive policy on migration and asylum focuses on potential advantages of emigration for countries of origin, while mitigating the negative effects, elegantly summarised as follows by the OECD (2016):

1. Relieve pressure on the labour market, while avoiding shortages. Emigration helps to decrease unemployment and increase wages.
2. Maximize financial remittances by migrants.
3. Stimulate 'social remittances', such as the transfer of knowledge and skills and values and standards both via networks and via returning migrants, while minimizing the cost of separation of family members.
4. Promote 'brain gain' and 'brain circulation' effects, and counter brain drain.
5. Facilitate trade with and investments in the countries of origin, e.g. via the diaspora.

In addition, the MPFA calls for improved border governance and addressing irregular migration, as well as the prevention of cross-border forced displacement and the protection of refugees and asylum seekers, including durable solutions, and addressing the root causes of refugee movements (AU, 2018).

The adoption of the MPFA has already yielded some promising developments. In July 2016, the AU passport was unveiled in Kigali, Rwanda, with the adoption of the AU Decision on the Free Movement of Persons. In 2019, the AU launched the operational phase of the African Continental Free Trade Area (AfCFTA) at a summit in Niamey, Niger. The work of the High-Level Panel on Migration for Africa (HLPM), headed by the former President of Liberia, Ellen Johnson Sirleaf, is also important in this context.

Building bridges

Contemporary European views on migration are influenced by recent intra-European migration, by the influx of refugees from Syria, by differences in migrant acceptance, and by the negative effects of irregular migration. African policies, on the other hand, generally stress the importance of international solidarity with respect to the costs of the provision of protection and shelter of refugees, and highlight the benefits of better access to work, remittances, networks, promoting trade and investment, education, and a more affluent diaspora. To develop common policies, Europe and Africa need a common view on migration and asylum and on ways to influence and regulate these movements. Despite the polarisation around these issues in recent years, AU–EU relations need not be hijacked by different views and expectations on migration. To bridge the divide, the two continents should put migration in a broader perspective – one that looks first at geopolitics, international economic cooperation, including policy coherence for development and demographics, and only then at migration and asylum policy as a means to a common end.

Geopolitics

In his book, *World Order: Reflections on the character of nations and the course of history*, Henry Kissinger (2014) examines how the world is changing under the influence of technology and globalisation. He divides the world based on political power and value systems.[11] He describes four systems of historic world order: the Westphalian Peace in Europe; the central imperium philosophy of China; the religious supremacism of political Islam; and the democratic idealism of the United States. Kissinger notes that these factors have led to the current emergence of various power blocs, such as the ones led by the United States, the EU, China, Russia, Saudi Arabia and Iran. There is increased international cooperation and liberalised cross-border trade within these blocs, but less so between them. The first signs of this change are already evident. Multilateral agreements on climate change, international trade, chemical weapons and non-proliferation are under threat. The annexation of Crimea, the transformation of reefs in the South

China Sea into military bases, the Chinese Belt and Road Initiative (BRI), the conflict between Saudi Arabia and Iran, and the trade war between the United States and China already shape the contours of a new global order. Kissinger regards the EU as a separate bloc and believes that the United States and the EU are slowly drifting apart. In this view, the geopolitical framework in which migration policy is pursued will be determined by the role to which Europe aspires or ends up playing, and by Africa's choice of bloc. The EU has an open economy with external trade, as a percentage of GDP, three times larger than that of the United States and more than twice that of China;[12] it has 8,000 kilometres of land borders with its eastern neighbours and 80,000 kilometres of sea borders in the south, almost half of which are in the Mediterranean. In a multipolar world, the EU needs to remain a powerful bloc to protect its interests.

To become a global power, independent of the United States, the EU would have to harmonise and centralise its foreign policy and add Africa to its political sphere of influence. This requires reinventing the relationship with Africa, away from post-colonialism, which it can achieve by entering into more 'partnerships of equals', providing a counterweight to superpowers such as the Unites States, China, Russia, and to a lesser extent, India. In the future, Europe will have to offer Africa more, rather than less, in exchange for influence, market access and migration management. Externally, the EU should function as a unit and act in unison. Internally, this requires a robust EU migration and asylum policy that is acceptable to member states in Eastern and Southern Europe. An ability to influence Africa and the countries bordering the Black Sea[13] is crucial to Europe's power and security position. Since migration policy is part of foreign policy, if the EU does not live up to the global rules on migration (the Global Compact on Migration), there could be repercussions for forms of global governance that are of vital importance to the EU, such as trade. Migration policy should contribute to the EU's geopolitical interests. Improved cooperation with Africa on migration and labour market policy in the EU, and subsidiarity for the member states in Eastern Europe, are elements of a migration policy that would do just that.

International cooperation

It is important to improve the overall relationship between Africa and the EU. Thus, the EU should strive to have a mature economic relationship with Africa; one that is not related to financial aid. The EU needs to rethink what it takes to limit the influence of China, the Arab world and even the United States, and to retain access to Africa's natural resources and expanding consumer markets. Together the EU and AU can form a strong economic bloc. Notwithstanding human mobility, Africa and Europe are already close to being a free trade area.

There are at least four ways in which migration policy and economic cooperation can reinforce one another. First, the network effects of migration can strengthen economic cooperation between the continents rather than weaken it. Second, trade needs to be stimulated to create demand for labour-intensive goods. Crucially, the production of such goods in Africa can reduce migration by creating jobs. Third, foreign investment in Africa should be encouraged to focus much more on increasing productivity, transferring technological expertise, and supplying options for local businesses. Fourth, the EU can share with Africa the experience and knowledge it has acquired in creating and implementing the four freedoms – the free movement of goods, capital, services and labour. Both the AfCFTA and the implementation of the AU Free Movement Protocol could benefit from such an exchange.

Fundamentally, European migration policy needs to meet the criteria set for policy coherence for development (PCD). Exploring how the EU and AU can combine migration and asylum policy with development cooperation is thus imperative. The agenda for aid, trade, and investment would need to focus on stimulating labour-intensive economic growth. A joint effort focusing on the agricultural sector, the stimulation of labour-intensive industry (including the processing of agricultural products) and a modern services sector, and private entrepreneurship in micro-enterprises is more effective than a direct labour market policy in the form of business training, wage subsidies and employment services. Research on promising transformation processes indicates that the effort should consist of a framework policy around land rights, infrastructure, financing, innovation, competition, legal protection and quality assurance (IOB, 2018a; 2018b). Rural development can slow down urbanisation and, by extension, reduce irregular emigration, which usually takes place from cities. Improving education in rural areas can also affect urbanisation and contribute to less irregular migration. Increasing the enrolment of girls in secondary schools and providing easy access to contraceptives are effective instruments to slow down population growth and, therefore, migration. Given demographic and labour market developments in Europe, and considering the positive effects of migration on development, development funds could be used to organise circular migration and skills-based partnerships. Under certain conditions, this extension of legal pathways could curb irregular migration.

Reframing migration and asylum policy

To promote the provision of regional protection and shelter in Africa, the EU, above all, will have to contribute substantially to the associated costs, since the countries neighbouring conflict states are almost without exception developing countries, without the means to bear the burden. Europe and Africa need to agree on the implementation of the Global Compact on Refugees, including the Comprehensive Refugee Response Framework. Besides durable solutions for refugees, the EU and countries neighbouring conflict states have to ensure that the host communities – local people living near the refugees – also benefit. Durable solutions have to aim at enabling refugees and host communities to support themselves. Given the high costs associated, this would mean a major change in development cooperation policy and would require a substantial increase in European official development assistance (ODA).

If refugees enter the EU through resettlement, like in Canada, rather than by visa overstay and irregular border crossing, the EU could allow for differences in the willingness and ability of the member states to absorb refugees. It would also make it possible to allow the immigration of additional numbers of selected refugees, depending on European labour market demand, for instance, recruiting highly skilled refugees, awarding scholarships to refugees, and even selecting refugees for circular migration.

The EU cannot assume that African countries will agree to restrict labour migration to Europe, since migration is highly lucrative for Africa in terms of remittances, skills and networks, and because African governments lack the resources and institutions to curb migration. Enhanced one-sided border controls by the EU can act as a restraint and slow down irregular migration because it increases the price of smugglers, but these controls are insufficient on their own, as the case of the US–Mexico border demonstrates. To manage irregular migration effectively, cooperation with countries of origin and transit is needed. Partnerships based on more legal migration, in exchange for collaboration in preventing irregular labour migration, can guarantee that the benefits are mutual and can end the tragedies and extortions that come with human smuggling. Allowing larger numbers of regular migrants will not automatically reduce irregular migration. Circular labour migration, however, can act as a substitute for irregular migration, but only if the incentives for irregular migration are reduced simultaneously.

Structures can be put in place to ensure that legal circular and non-circular forms of labour migration benefit migrants, as well as the countries of origin and destination. The advantages to migrants and their families should be so apparent that they are willing to wait a few years to move to the EU legally rather than trying to reach Europe irregularly by taking the perilous maritime route. Various institutional efforts are required to achieve this. In Africa, setting up systems for selection, security screening, preparation, skills training and language teaching can provide the right incentives, improve recruitment and limit the probability of failure of migrants. In the EU, the creation of attractive migration arrangements is needed, including incentives to promote the return of circular migrants. An interesting form of legal migration is the result of 'skills partnerships' whereby employers in the EU pay for migrants' educational and travel costs, while simultaneously investing in training infrastructure in their countries of origin (Clemens, 2014b). This approach can be combined with circular migration tailored to the EU labour market.

The EU needs to discourage irregular labour migration by combatting employment in the informal sector, which acts as a magnet in this regard, and by implementing an effective return policy. Africa could benefit from a gradual substitution of the informal labour of emigrants living in Europe by more formal labour, as improved wages will push up remittances. In return, African countries will need to assist in preventing human smuggling and implement the international agreements on readmission of irregular migrants and an effective returns policy.

There are already many agreements and dialogues between the EU and Africa that deal with migration, such as Mobility Partnerships, the Rabat and Khartoum Processes, the Organisation of African, Caribbean and Pacific States (ACP)–EU Dialogue on Migration, the (to be renewed) ACP treaty, The EU–Africa Partnership on Migration, Mobility and Employment, the Valletta Action Plan, and many readmission agreements. However, there is no comprehensive agreement between the EU and the AU that addresses all issues and puts them in a broader geopolitical perspective.[14]

Conclusions

Europe and Africa have different views on migration. Africa emphasises the advantages of migration intra-Africa and to other continents for development, whereas Europe fears mass irregular immigration and struggles with internal differences in net migration and the acceptance of immigrants. Bridging this divide would benefit both continents. Strategically, Europe needs to maintain good relationships with Africa for geopolitical and security reasons, and to guarantee access to its raw materials and the growing African consumer markets. Africa needs trade, investment and development assistance, and can benefit from good relations with Europe in a multipolar new world order. Migration policy should add to improving relationships rather than being a divisive fungus.

With respect to migration and asylum, Europe wants Africa to shelter and protect refugees and help them to become self-reliant through return, resettlement, or integration. This engagement should contribute to Europe's overarching objective of minimising irregular immigration. African countries need external funding to relieve the financial burden of hosting refugees. Africa benefits from remittances, investment and brain gain from the diaspora, and should be willing to improve migration management to help prevent irregular migration in return for 'enhanced availability and flexibility of legal pathways for regular migration'; objective 5 of the Global Compact on Migration. Migration management includes the acceptance of the return and readmission of irregular migrants from Europe.

Addressing the root causes of irregular migration also provides scope for cooperation. Stimulating trade and investment in labour-intensive sectors such as agriculture, agricultural processing and productive services (the public sector, construction and tourism) would be effective, especially in middle-income countries. In poorer countries, targeted development assistance can contribute to development and reduce the aspirations for (irregular) migration. Employment creation, education and skills development for employment is effective, and so is rural development in general, because it slows down urbanisation and consecutive migration. Rural education also decreases urbanisation. One cannot expect large effects, however, if budgets are not in line with the size of the challenges.

The most important pull factor for migration is work, and the most important pull factor for irregular migration is informal work. An estimated 40 million jobs in Europe are informal, mainly in agriculture, domestic work, construction, cleaning, catering, the garment industry, crime, and prostitution. Europe needs to address this root cause. By doing so, demand for regular immigration will gradually substitute the demand for irregular immigration.

Europe's population is ageing and without net immigration, it will decrease by a million people per year. The African population, on the other hand, is growing and on average very young. Migration cannot solve the problematic population growth in Africa. However, improving enrolment in (secondary) education for girls and access to sexual and reproductive health and rights can decrease population growth substantially. Immigration can solve labour market shortages in Europe, but only if those migrating have the right skills, which requires proper management of legal migration through predictable migration procedures, emigration services, selection, skills development and mobility partnerships. Circular migration may be a way to let more people benefit and increase European acceptance of migrants.

Migration cooperation can lead to mutual benefits and better understanding. Europe will get fewer irregular migrants and fewer migrants will be exploited or drown. The EU will get the kind of labour it needs and Africa will get more international cooperation, more knowledge (from the diaspora and from returnees) and better networks, and it will probably get more remittances. In a multipolar new world order, this mutuality around migration governance would pave the way for both continents to become an integrated geopolitical bloc.

Notes

1   This chapter benefits from earlier work. It includes revised parts of IOB (2018a) and an unpublished MFA internal working paper. Permission was granted by the co-authors, Antony de Kemp (IOB, 2018a) and Huub von Frijtag Drabbe (unpublished MFA working paper). Responsibility for this article remains with the author.

2   In 2015, Frontex registered 1.8 million illegal crossings by migrants at Europe's external borders, but this includes many instances of double counting on the Western Balkan route.

3   Eurostat (2020) data show that in 2019 in the EU-27 (i.e. excluding the UK), 26 per cent of asylum cases resulted in a refugee status.

4   The Gallup Migrant Acceptance Index is based on approximately 1,000

interviews per country. It asks people if they think immigrants living in their country, becoming their neighbours, and marrying into their families, are good or bad things. The higher the score, the more accepting the population is of migrants. The maximum possible score on the index is a 9.

5   The term migrant refers to a person attempting and/or succeeding to settle in a country other than his or her country of birth.

6   According to OECD data (OECD, 2020), in 2000 about 100,000 migrants from sub-Saharan Africa entered the EU. Ten years later that number was 150,000, a small portion of which (10,000 migrants) entered through irregular channels. A change subsequently occurred in 2015, when the number of migrants increased by 100,000 to 250,000, mostly attributable to irregular migration. This mainly involved refugees from Eritrea and Somalia, as well as migrants from several countries in West Africa. Recently irregular migration from Africa to Europe has gone down again.

7   This approach originates from the work of American geographer Wilbur Zelinsky (1971).

8   The 'migration hump' theory has been challenged in several studies. The IOB (2018a) concludes that there is a migration hump, but its intensity is stronger for small countries than for large countries, and it is more pronounced in the West and Latin America than in Africa or Asia. Benček and Schneiderheinze (2019) conclude that, although cross-section analysis shows an inverse U-shaped curve, more rigorous, fixed effects panel estimations show a negative relation between income and emigration, independent of the initial level of a country's income. They therefore doubt the causal interpretation of the migration hump.

9   An idea often suggested is to finance the CEAS from the EU budget, funded by all member states, but only allocated to those that take in refugees. In this way, the EU can combine a common interest with subsidiarity.

10 For critical remarks on the mixed objectives of the EUTF, see Kipp (2018) and Oxfam International (2020).

11 According to Kissinger, the characteristics of world order are power and legitimacy.

12 Total trade (imports and exports of goods and services) in value terms as a percentage of GDP in 2018 according to the World Bank Data was 28, 38 and 88 for the United States, China, and the Euro zone, respectively.

13 Specifically, Moldova, Ukraine, Georgia, Armenia, Azerbaijan and Turkey. The total combined population of these countries is almost 150 million.

14 Geddes and Maru (2020) provide a checklist and suggested future direction for African and European migration diplomacy.

References

Adhikari, P. 2013. 'Conflict-induced displacement, Understanding the causes of flight', *American Journal of Political Science*, 57(1): 82–9.

African Development Bank. 2018. *Annual Development Effectiveness Reviews 2018*. Abidjan, Ivory Coast: AfDB.

African Union (AU). 2018. *Migration Policy Framework for Africa and Plan of Action (2018–2030)*. AUC, Addis Ababa.

Awumbila, M. (2017). 'Drivers of Migration and Urbanization in Africa: Key Trends and Issues'. *International Migration*, 7, 8, pp. 1-8.

Beauchemin, C. (ed.). 2018. *Migration Between Africa and Europe*. New York: Springer Publishing.

Benček, D. and Schneiderheinze, C. 2019. *More Development, Less Emigration to OECD Countries: Identifying inconsistencies between cross-sectional and time-series estimates of the migration hump*. Kiel Working Paper No. 2145. Kiel: Kiel Institute for the World Economy, Christian Albrechts Universität.

Clemens, M. 2014a. 'Does development reduce migration?', in R.E.B Lucas (ed.) *International Handbook on Migration and Economic Development*. Cheltenham: Edward Elgar Publishing, pp. 152–85.

Clemens, M. 2014b. *Global Skill Partnerships: A proposal for technical training in a mobile world*. CGD Policy Paper No. 40. Washington, DC: Center for Global Development.

Cummings, C., Pacitto, J., Lauro, D. and Foresti, M. 2015. *Why People Move: Understanding the drivers and trends of migration to Europe*. ODI Working Paper No. 430. London: Overseas Development Institute.

Dao, T.H., Docquier, F., Parsons, C. and Peri, G. 2018. 'Migration and development: Dissecting the anatomy of the mobility transition', *Journal of Development Economics*, 132: 88–101.

De Haas, H. 2018. *European Migrations: Dynamics, drivers, and the role of policies*. Luxembourg: Publications Office of the European Union.

De Haas, H. 2017. *African Migration: Drivers of migration in Africa*. Addis Ababa: UN Economic Commission for Africa.

De Haas, H. 2014. *Migration Theory: Quo vadis?* DEMIG Project, Working Paper No. 100. Oxford: International Migration Institute, University of Oxford.

De Haas, H. 2011. *The Determinants of International Migration: Conceptualising policy, origin and destination effects*. Working Paper No. 32. Oxford: International Migration Institute, University of Oxford.

De Haas, H. 2010a. 'Migration and development: A theoretical perspective', *International Migration Review*, 44(1): 227–64.

De Haas, H. 2010b. *Migration Transitions: A theoretical and empirical inquiry into the developmental drivers of international migration.* Working Paper No. 24. Oxford: International Migration Institute, University of Oxford.

De Haas, H. 2008. 'The myth of invasion: The inconvenient realities of African migration to Europe', *Third World Quarterly*, 29(7): 1305–322.

De Haas, H. Czaika, M., Flahaux, M., Mahendra, E., Natter, K., Vezzoli, S. and Villares-Varela, M. 2019. 'International migration: Trends, determinants and policy effects', *Population and Development Review*, 45(4): 885–922.

De Wulf, M. 2020. PopulationPyramid.net based on open access UN data. Online at: www.populationpyramid.net/europe/2019/ and www. populationpyramid.net/africa/2019/ (accessed 8 June 2020).

Eurostat. 2020. Asylum Statistics. Online at: https://ec.europa.eu/eurostat/ statistics-explained/index.php/Asylum_statistics (accessed 8 June 2020).

Flahaux, M.L. and De Haas, H. 2016. 'African migration: trends, patterns, drivers', *Comparative Migration Studies*, 4(1): 1.

Frontex. 2017. *Africa-Frontex Intelligence Community Joint Report 2016.* Warsaw: Frontex.

Gallup Migrant Acceptance Index. 2020. Online at: www.gallup.com (accessed 8 June 2020).

Geddes, A. and Maru, M.T. 2020. *African and European Migration Diplomacy: A checklist and suggested future direction.* Online at: https://blogs.eui.eu/ migrationpolicycentre/african-and-european-migration-diplomacy-a-checklist-and-suggested-future-direction/ (accessed 25 September 2020).

IOB 2018a. *Development and Migration.* The Hague: Ministry of Foreign Affairs, Report No. 427.

IOB 2018b. *Transition and Inclusive Development in Sub-Saharan Africa: An analysis of poverty and inequality in the context of transition.* The Hague: Ministry of Foreign Affairs, Report No. 422.

International Organization for Migration (IOM). 2020. Flow monitoring Europe. Online at: https://migration.iom.int/europe?type=arrivals (accessed 8 June 2020).

International Organization for Migration (IOM). 2019. *World Migration Report 2020*, International Organization for Migration, Geneva, 2019.

Kelmanson, B., Kirabaeva, K., Medina, L., Mircheva, B. and Weiss, J. 2019. *Explaining the Shadow Economy in Europe: Size, causes and policy options.* IMF Working Paper No. 19/278. Washington DC: IMF.

Kipp, D. 2018. *From Exception to Rule – the EU Trust Fund for Africa.* SWP Research Paper 13.

Kissinger, H. 2014. *World Order: Reflections on the character of nations and the course of history*. London: Penguin Books.

Kuschminder, K., De Bresser, J. and Siegel, M. 2015. *Irregular Migration Routes to Europe and the Factors Influencing Migrants' Destination Choices*. Maastricht: Maastricht Graduate School of Governance.

Lucas, R.E. 2015. 'African migration', in R. Chiswick and P.W. Miller (eds). *Handbook of the Economics of International Migration*, Volume 1. Amsterdam: Elsevier, pp. 1445–596.

Lutz, W. (ed.). Amran, G., Bélanger, A., Conte, A., Gailey, N., Ghio D., Grapsa, E., Jensen, K., Loichinger, E., Marois. G., Muttarak, R., Potančoková, M., Sabourin, P. and Stonawski, M. 2019. *Demographic Scenarios for the EU – Migration, Population and Education*. EUR 29739 EN. Luxembourg: Publications Office of the European Union. doi:10.2760/590301, JRC116398.

McAuliffe, M. and Koser, K. (eds). 2017. *A Long Way to Go: Irregular migration patterns, processes, drivers and decision-making*. Acton: Australian National University (ANU) Press.

Mercator Dialogue on Asylum and Migration (MEDAM). 2019. *2019 MEDAM Assessment Report on Asylum and Migration Policies in Europe*. Kiel: Kiel Institute for the World Economy.

Migali, S., Natale, F., Tintori, G., Kalantaryan, S., Grubanov-Boskovic, S., Scipioni, M., Farinosi, F., Cattaneo, C., Benandi, B., Follador, M., Bidoglio, G., McMahon, S. and Barbas, T. 2018. *International Migration Drivers. A quantitative assessment of the structural factors shaping migration*. Joint Research Centre, Science for Policy Report, JRC 112622, EUR 29333 EN.

Organization for Economic Co-operation and Development (OECD). 2020. International Migration Database. Online at: https://stats.oecd.org/Index.aspx?DataSetCode=MIG (accessed 8 June 2020).

Organization for Economic Co-operation and Development (OECD). 2018. *International Migration Outlook 2018*. OECD Publishing, Paris.

Organization for Economic Co-operation and Development (OECD). 2016. *Perspectives on Global Development 2017: International Migration in a Shifting World*. Paris: OECD Publishing.

Oxfam International. 2020. *The EU Trust Fund for Africa: Trapped between aid policy and migration politics*. Oxford: Oxfam.

United Nations Department of Economic and Social Affairs (UNDESA). 2018. Trends in International Migrant Stock: Migrants by Destination and Origin. Online at: https://www.un.org/development/desa/pd/themes/international-migration (accessed 20 June 2018).

United Nations Department of Economic and Social Affairs (UNDESA). 2019. *Population Facts.* No. 2019/6. New York: UNDESA.

United Nations Department of Economic and Social Affairs (UNDESA). 2020. *World Social Report 2020: Inequality in a rapidly changing world.* New York: UNDESA.

Van Hear, N., Bakewell, O. and Long, K. 2018. 'Push-pull plus: Reconsidering the drivers of migration', *Journal of Ethnic and Migration Studies*, 44(6): 927–44.

World Bank. 2018. *Moving for Prosperity: Global migration and labor markets.* Policy Research Report. Washington, DC: World Bank.

Zelinsky, W. 1971. 'The hypothesis of the mobility transition', *Geographical Review*, 61(2): 219–49.

Part V
Perspectives on Root Causes

The root causes of African migration to Europe: An African perspective

Jack R. Mangala

Introduction

Against the backdrop of the so-called 'refugee and asylum crisis' in Europe, addressing the root causes of African migration to Europe has become a core policy tenet of European Union (EU)–Africa relations. This was illustrated by the establishment, in 2015, of the EU Emergency Trust Fund for Africa (EUTFA), as elaborated in Chapter 11. The trust was designed explicitly as a financial mechanism to 'address the root causes of destabilization, forced displacement and irregular migration' (EUTFA website) in countries and regions that constitute the African migration routes to Europe. Even though the reality of African migration to Europe is far from the crisis narrative that seems to dominate much of the discourse in Europe, addressing the root causes of African migration has been elevated to a policy mantra, repeated at every major gathering of African and EU leaders and echoed in countless policy documents and strategy papers adopted over the past decade.

According to the most recent estimates, African-born immigrants in Europe total approximately 9 million, which amounts to 1.3 per cent of Europe's and 0.7 per cent of Africa's total population (see, for example,

European Commission, 2018: 10). To put the African migration landscape into perspective, the narrative of overwhelming numbers of Africans on the move is overblown: only 3.5 per cent of Africans migrate, and 53 per cent of these remain on the continent; 36 per cent travel to the Organisation for Economic Co-operation and Development (OECD) countries; and 11 per cent to other countries (European Commission, 2018). While it is true that over the past decade there has been an increase in the average number of African migrants to European countries to around 400,000 per annum, this figure is still far from the dominant narrative of an African 'invasion' of Europe. As previously stated, African international migration is primarily of an intraregional character. Moreover, the increase in the average annual number of arrivals in Europe must be assessed against the backdrop of two important trends: first, the expanding population in Africa as a result of the continent's demographic transition; second, the sharp decline in African legal immigration to Europe, which stood at 288,000 in 2016, down from 442,000 a decade earlier (Bjarnesen, 2020: 4–5). Considering the aforementioned migration figures and demographic trends, an objective assessment of African migration to Europe points to a great deal of stability, and not the 'crisis' narrative that has been used to justify a host of preventive measures and policies, among which is the root causes approach that increasingly forms the backbone of 'Fortress Europe' (Gebrewold, 2007). As it has been observed, 'the unspoken assumption of most protagonists in such debates is that migration of the poor should be prevented or deterred' (Castles and Van Hear, 2011: 288).

While seemingly intuitive and well-intended, the idea of addressing the root causes of migration hinges on deep-seated issues of framing, history and agency between Africa and Europe, which are rarely addressed in the policy debate (McKeon, 2018). At its core, addressing the root causes of migration is about geopolitics: 'ultimately … [root causes] lie in the imbalances of power and resources in the global political economy, and addressing them would require a major transformation in the distribution of power and resources worldwide' (Castles and Van Hear, 2011: 287). In current policy thinking, however, a much more narrow and one-sided understanding of the root causes of migration is deployed, with the EU dominating the conversation and African stakeholders caught in a Faustian deal of accepting this premise in order to further international collaboration and goodwill.

The main objective of this chapter is to offer an African perspective on the root causes of African migration to Europe. The following section briefly summarises the history of the concept of root causes in relation to migration policy, emphasising its Eurocentric origins and early applications. The second section analyses the African Union (AU) approach to understanding the root causes of African migration, arguing, on the one hand, that the fundamental chasm between European and African approaches to migration governance is clearly expressed in the approach to the notion of root causes and, on the other hand, that the past decade has seen the AU engage in a partial alignment with regard to migration governance. The final section engages with recent migration scholarship in order to reflect critically on the framing and premise of the root causes argument.

The rise of the root causes approach in migration policy

In migration policy circles, the notion of root causes encompasses a wide range of 'measures designed to reduce migration by dealing with the supposed driving factors in origin countries, especially violence, human rights violations, disparities in living standards, and poverty' (Castles and Van Hear, 2011: 287). As discussed in Chapter 11, the root causes approach emerged as a policy tool in the 1970s in the context of debates about forced displacement. Faced with a surge of asylum seekers, as a result of decolonisation and other post-colonial conflict situations in the Global South, European governments responded with a two-pronged approach, which included stricter border control, on the one hand, and addressing the so-called 'root causes' of displacement, on the other. By actively engaging in humanitarian action aimed at preventing violence, limiting human rights abuses, and facilitating peacebuilding and reconstruction in origin countries, the policy assumption was that the flows of asylum seekers from conflict-affected countries could be contained through socio-political stabilisation.

Parallel to forced migration, the root causes approach was also applied to more voluntary forms of migration in light of the increase in the number of migrants whose motivation for reaching Europe was believed to be essentially economic. The policy response to this second category of migrants took the form of development measures intended to reduce poverty and create jobs in countries of origin. Countries such as France, Italy and Spain came to champion 'co-development policies' with a dual objective: to stem the flow of economic migrants and to incentivise origin countries to accept returnees in exchange for development investments.

In the early 1990s, the social, political and economic turmoil following the fall of the Iron Curtain in the former Soviet Union created new migratory movements towards central and northern Europe. The complex interplay between economic drivers and political insecurity blurred the lines between forced and economic migration, challenging European policy-makers to think outside the confines of the traditional understanding of forced and voluntary migration as being categorically different. Although such complexity can be assumed to characterise most migration experiences, the end of the Cold War prompted the growing realisation that people moving 'were fleeing violence and persecution (and were thus "asylum seekers"), but they were seeking to build new lives and to send remittances to dependants back home (so they were also "economic migrants")' (Castles and Van Hear, 2011: 292). New scholarly developments highlighting a continuum between forced and voluntary migration inspired governments and international agencies in the Global North to establish new policy frameworks. Concepts such as 'mixed migration' and 'the migration–asylum nexus' emerged in the early 2000s to capture the new policy approach that blurred the lines between the two types of migration. This carried new legal implications for the migrants in terms of their prospects for being seen as eligible to protection, and it also increased political pressure on countries of origin to contain their citizens.

Within the specific context of African–EU migration, this paradigm shift has been accompanied by two significant policy trends. First, there is a renewed tension and growing rift between the proponents of strict border control and those who advocate an emphasis on addressing the root causes of migration as the best approach to managing mixed migration. Second, there is a resurgence of the development discourse in migration policy – informed by the idea of the so-called 'migration–development nexus'. This second trend warrants further comment.

Over the past decade, the migration–development nexus has become a core tenet of development thinking and strategies, an idea brought to the fore by a host of studies, policy analyses and global consultation processes (see, for example, Plaza and Ratha, 2011; Ratha et al., 2011; Mangala, 2017). Simply put, the migration–development nexus has two dimensions. The first calls on countries to harness the development potentials of emigration by strategically engaging with their diaspora. The second reiterates the old idea that development of migrants' home countries is the key to reducing migration, and is thus a revival of the root causes approach to economic migration as first formulated in the 1970s. Even though the assertion that increased development will reduce migration has long been debunked by migration research (see, for example, De Haas, 2007, 2020), it has not subsided in the EU national policy circles, where the dominant idea seems to be that 'migration and refugee movements are driven by poverty, underdevelopment, and unemployment, and that tackling these "root causes" can help keep people at home' (Castles and Van Hear, 2011: 297). As it has unfolded over the past decade, the new migration–development nexus discourse has expanded, conceptually, the root causes conversation to include the role of diasporas. Members of diaspora communities, as a result of their development activities and impacts, are increasingly acknowledged by receiving countries and international agencies as key partners in addressing the root causes of migration in their countries of origin.

While the initial root causes approaches – which developed separately in relation to forced and economic migration in the 1970 – sought to address the socio-political and development conditions in origin countries through a 'neutral humanitarianism', which emphasised peacebuilding, post-conflict reconstruction and the provision of aid, there has been a significant shift towards a more interventionist approach, that is, a 'new humanitarianism'. As controversial as the 'new humanitarianism' might be in the 21st century, it pursues 'a much more active policy of political, economic, and (sometimes) military intervention designed to transform whole societies' (Castles and Van Hear, 2011: 298). While always present in the idea of addressing the root causes of migration in countries of origin, the transformational agenda is more overt in the new policy approach, which seeks, among other things, to partner with diasporas in this transformative project. As Castles and Van Hear note,

> The notion of enlisting conflict-induced diaspora ... to transform conflict societies into stable, sustainable communities has now become a project of relief and development agencies, and the last twist on the root causes approach – for if diasporas can be enjoined to help address the root causes of displacement, they may supplement intervention by humanitarian and development agencies, or even supplant the need for them (Castles and Van Hear, 2011: 301).

Even though the migration research literature has long questioned the static and restrictive logic underlying the root causes approach, the latter continues to occupy the forefront of policy deliberations at national and regional levels. It became the centrepiece of the EU response in the wake of the so-called migration 'crisis' in Europe, which led to the 2015 Valletta Summit and the establishment of the EUTFA. It figured prominently on the agendas of several global consultations that culminated in the adoption of the UN Global Compact for Safe, Orderly and Regular Migration in 2018, objective 2 of which seeks to 'minimize the adverse drivers and structural factors that compel people to leave their country of origin' (Global Compact for Migration, 2018: 5). The Global Compact does not explicitly use the 'root causes' language, and frames the issue in different and less simplistic terminology than the Valletta Declaration.[1] So far, however, the Global Compact has not had a significant impact on European policy priorities, which are centred on preventing unwanted flows of migrants from the Global South to the North where they are seen increasingly as a problem.

This restrictive view on international migration stands in stark contrast to the overall approach of African policy priorities at national, regional and AU levels. As already implied, the root causes approach has been driven primarily by European actors. African actors, on the other hand, emphasise the benefits of international migration and the need to expand legal pathways for African migrants to Europe, while engaging with the root causes rationale as an entry point to negotiate development cooperation arrangements. It is against the backdrop of the evolution of the root causes approach to policy that we now consider an African perspective on the notion of root causes in more detail.

The AU approach to the root causes of African migration

Until the early 2000s, the issue of migration was not given much priority in the AU policy agenda. The new discourse on migration and development promoted by international organisations and the series of global consultations on migration, which followed the establishment of the UN Global Commission on International Migration (GCIM) by Secretary-General Kofi Annan in 2003, provided the impetus for the AU to engage in policy discussions on the migration–development question with the goal, among other things, of formulating a unified African position. Since this initiative, the AU has produced a number of policy documents that reference, to various degrees, the causes of migration in and out of the continent (see, for example, Abebe, 2017). To illustrate AU priorities and rationales around addressing the root causes of African migration, this section analyses the 'African Common Position on Migration and Development', which was endorsed by the AU Executive Council at its summit in Banjul in July 2006, and the *Migration Policy Framework for Africa and Plan of Action (2018–2030)*.[2] The Common Position was intended 'to enable Africa to ensure that its concerns are properly reflected at the Africa/Europe dialogue and other international fora' (AU Executive Council, 2006). In its introductory statement, the Common Position notes,

> The root causes of migration are numerous and complex. The push–pull framework gives insight into the different forces at work to explain migration. In Africa, poor socio-economic conditions, such as low wages, high levels of unemployment, rural underdevelopment, poverty and lack of opportunity fuel out-migration. These factors are usually brought about by a mismatch between the rapid population growth and available resources, low level of requisite technology to exploit the available natural resources and capacity to create employment and jobs in the countries of origin.
>
> In addition, various political and social factors induce migration. Among these are poor governance, nepotism and corruption, human rights violations, political instability, environmental factors, conflict and civil strife, the real and perceived opportunity for a better life, high income, greater security, better quality education and health care at the destinations influence decision to migrate. Lower costs of migration, improved communication, greater information availability and the need to join relatives, families and friends are among the factors, which amplify push–pull factors (AU Executive Council, 2006).

The language and structure of this introductory statement is significant in many ways. First, the fact that socio-economic conditions (which reflect broader development issues) are addressed first, and the remaining factors are introduced by the phrase 'in addition', seems to indicate an implicit hierarchy that sees migration as primarily driven by underdevelopment. Second, the notion of root causes is only mentioned in the opening sentence, while the remainder of the statement goes on to consider the 'forces at work', 'factors [that] induce migration', and 'factors which amplify push–

pull factors'. The listing of these various forces and factors shows that the AU considers the root causes to include the broader structural drivers and determinants of migration. Root causes are often referred to by the general term 'drivers' of migration, which encompasses all the 'factors which get migration going and keep it going once it has begun' (Van Hear et al., 2018: 930). Even though these various factors often overlap, it is important to distinguish root causes from drivers (mechanisms that eventually produce migration outcomes, such as social networks and access to information) and determinants of migration (which refer to quantitative modelling and the search for data that might explain and predict migration patterns, for example, the size of the diaspora in a destination country). Conceptually, then, while root causes are among the factors inducing migration, not all inducing factors are categorised as root causes. Third, the AU approach is theoretically situated within the push–pull framework, which 'identifies economic, environmental and demographic factors which are assumed to push people out of places of origin and pull them into destination places' (De Haas et al., 2020: 45). As migration scholars have argued for some time, this theoretical framework offers only a limited perspective on the drivers of migration. As recently observed (Van Hear *et al.*, 2018: 929), the push–pull model has been critiqued in part for presenting a descriptive account of migration-inducing factors, rather than offering an analytical framework to explain their underlying dynamics (cf. Skeldon, 1990), and in part for being unable to account for the fluctuating and contextual nature of these factors (cf. De Haas, 2011). Finally, by plainly stressing that poor governance, nepotism, corruption and human rights violations are among the factors inducing migration, the opening statement stands in contrast to the usual diplomatic parlance and represents a damning indictment of African governments.

In the preamble, the AU member states convey a more holistic understanding of root causes. While being 'aware that conflicts, poverty, poor governance, underdevelopment, lack of opportunities, and environmental factors are some of the underlying causes of migration and to effectively manage migration, the root causes of migration should be addressed', they remain 'concerned that the emphasis on addressing illegal and irregular migration has been only on security considerations rather than on broader development frameworks and on mainstreaming migration in development strategies' (AU Executive Council 2006, paragraphs 3 and 5).

The remainder of the document reflects a development-centred approach to the root causes of migration.

Overall, the links between migration and development constitute the most central policy issues addressed in the Common Position. It is noted that, 'poverty is one of the main causes of migration. Creating development opportunities in countries of origin would mitigate the main reasons for young people to engage in migration, thereby also dealing with the problem of brain drain' (AU Executive Council, 2006, section 3.1). The role of the African diaspora in contributing – through remittances and other transfers – to development in origin countries and thus helping to address poverty as a central root cause of migration is also emphasised (AU Executive Council, 2006, section 3.4 and 5). On the links between migration and peace, security and stability, it is observed that 'conflict is a root cause of forced displacement … Conflict prevention and resolution as well as good governance contribute to addressing the root causes of migration' (AU Executive Council, 2006, section 3.6). In terms of the critical question of human rights, it is disappointing that, instead of expanding on the preamble by further stressing human rights violations in origin countries as a root cause of migration, the Common Position focuses exclusively on deprivation of the basic human rights of migrants and other racist and discriminatory practices in transit and destination countries (in section 3.7).

The cross-cutting issues of the AU Common Position deal with health, the environment, trade and access to social services. The issues of health and access to social services are addressed in relation to the rights of migrant populations and their vulnerabilities in destination countries. A causal reference to migration appears only in regard to the environment and trade. As it relates to the former, the Common Position notes that 'environmental factors play a role in causing population movements' (section 4.2). With regard to trade, the document singles out the specific questions of subsidies by, and market access to, developed countries. Thus, 'measures to address the related issues of trade distorting agricultural subsidies of certain developed countries as well as the issue of market access for the products of developing countries, should form part of strategies to deal with the push factors of migration' (section 4.3).

In its conclusion, the Common Position outlines a series of recommendations aimed at ensuring a better management of migration by associating countries of origin, transit and destination 'in order to find balanced solutions that take into account the interests of the countries concerned' (section 5). It is further emphasised that '[i]t would be illusory to treat the problems of migration by recourse only to security measures' (section 5). The balanced approach advocated by the AU calls for specific actions at the national and continental levels, while seeking greater cooperation at the international level, in addressing 'the fundamental causes of this phenomenon, which are disparities in development, conflicts and political instability' (section 5).

In its revised *Migration Policy Framework for Africa and Plan of Action (2018–2030)* (MPFA), the overall tone and approach is essentially an extension of the 2006 Common Position, with its emphasis on intra-African migration, and a potentially productive link between migration and development (see also Bacon and Robin, 2018). This tone is reaffirmed with explicit reference to the shifts in the European migration governance agenda in the decade following the inauguration of the Common Position: 'Despite the international focus on migration flows to Europe, more than 80 per cent of African migration takes place in Africa' (AU, 2018: 20). Although the proportions of intra-African migration in relation to off-continent migration remains a debated issue (see Rodrigues and Bjarnesen, 2020), it is clear that the MPFA is articulated more actively in relation to, and in partial opposition to, its European equivalents (see Chapter 11). The core contrast between the AU approach and its EU equivalents is, in many ways, much clearer in the MPFA than in the Common Position, and is most clearly expressed in its migrant-centred understanding of the overarching objective of migration governance as such:

> Better migration governance as the overarching objective of the MPFA aims at facilitating safe, orderly and dignified migration. It advocates for the socio-economic well-being of migrants and society through compliance with international standards and laws. The security of migrants' rights and addressing the migration aspects of crises are key elements (AU, 2018: 10).

While similar notions may be found in EU frameworks on migration, we would argue that the European approach tends to prioritise a more state-centred understanding of migration governance, reflected in the restrictive understanding of the notion of root causes, as discussed earlier. The AU approach to migration governance, in this sense, may be seen as more in alignment with the approach of the UN Global Compact for Safe, Orderly and Regular Migration considered earlier, with its emphasis on the human rights of all migrants.

Although the MPFA retains the overarching approach of the AU to migration governance, the concept of 'root causes' is used more frequently in the 2018 revision, primarily with reference to refugee and IDP displacement, but also in the generic phrase 'root causes of mass migration and forced displacement', repeated in different sections of the framework. The conflation of forced migration and a broader notion of 'mass migration' seems to align with the European notion of African migration as being associated mainly with irregular migration towards Europe. Most tellingly, section 9.5 of the MPFA is entitled 'Migration, poverty and conflict' and explicitly encourages a strategy to,

> Include migration in the formulation of continental, regional and national development frameworks with the purpose of supporting the economic and social development of the regions (rural and urban) from which migrants originate in order to address the root causes of migration and to reduce poverty (AU, 2018: 74).

Bearing in mind the earlier discussion of the migration–development nexus, this shift towards the inclusion of migration in African development frameworks may be read as a partial alignment with the European agenda on addressing the root causes of African migration. This alignment is also evident in the considerable attention devoted to 'migrant smuggling' (section 5) in the MPFA, with one of the section's recommendations simply suggesting the need to 'Tackle the root causes leading people to leave their countries' (AU, 2018: 50). Although listed in a section explicitly addressing irregular migration, such formulations do seem to contradict the overall emphasis on migration as a viable livelihood strategy.

In addition to expanding and refining its approach to migration governance, and the partial alignment with EU terminology and priorities, the AU Commission has also recently established the African Migration Observatory in Rabat, Morocco, and the African Centre for the Study and Research on Migration (CARIM) in Bamako, Mali, as a means of 'building the capacity of Member States and RECs in the area of migration governance, an issue that is fundamental to the coherent management of migration on the continent' (AU, 2021). It remains to be seen what the priorities of these two centres will be, and whether these new centres will be invested with the necessary resources to have an impact on migration policy thinking at AU and member state levels. Nevertheless, this investment in research infrastructure relating to migration governance does confirm the overall impression that migration policy has become more important to the AU. The geographical location of the two institutions might also be a confirmation of the shift towards an emphasis on irregular migration off the continent, and away from the earlier emphasis on free movement and the importance of migration and mobility as livelihood strategies in many African contexts.

To gain a more research-informed understanding of the AU approach to the root causes of African migration, the following section summarises some of the key themes raised by migration scholarship in this regard.

Drivers of migration: Research insights on the notion of root causes of African migration

While the notion of addressing the root causes of migration has become central to policy thinking in Europe and elsewhere, migration scholarship rarely uses this concept to explain how or why migration occurs. In this regard, the broader concept of 'drivers' of migration is more commonly evoked, as mentioned earlier. Adapting the outline of the UNECA report titled 'Drivers of migration in Africa' (2017), this section focuses on the relationship between migration and six core issues that help to explain African migration dynamics: (1) labour demand, (2) development and inequality, (3) urbanisation, (4) education, (5) environmental factors, and (6) armed conflict. These themes provide empirical entry points and conceptual nuance to the notion of root causes discussed earlier.

In discussions about the drivers of African migration, *labour demand* is often overlooked or underplayed in favour of factors such as conflict, poverty and environmental degradation. Empirical evidence suggests that the changing structure and dynamics of labour demand in African and overseas markets represent a central driver of African migration, both within and outside the continent:

The segmentation of European and Middle Eastern labour markets into a highly skilled, formal sector and a lower skilled, often informal sector, together with rising living standards and levels of education, as well as ageing, has led to a persistent demand for migrant labour in the informal labour markets of comparatively wealthy destination societies, in which case migrant workers typically do the manual jobs that local workers are unwilling to do (UNECA, 2017: 3).

The same labour market dynamics are also at play when considering rural to urban, and other forms of intra-African migration (Amira, 2003; Awumbila et al., 2017; Rodrigues and Bjarnesen, 2020). Despite the dangers, humiliation and violations of basic human rights experienced by migrants in overseas labour markets, the long-term economic and educational benefits for the migrants and their families seem to outweigh the personal and psychological costs incurred in the short and medium terms (see UNDP, 2019). The demand for labour in segmented European labour markets, in other words, is a key factor driving African migration to Europe and it deserves proper policy consideration.

Second, and contrary to what push–pull models of migration would predict, another important factor driving African migration has to do with *improved development indicators* in sending contexts, for example, in the form of rising incomes, increasing education and improved infrastructure connectivity. These processes 'shape the conditions that initially tend to increase people's aspirations and capabilities to migrate' (UNECA, 2017: 4). Improvement of these conditions in many African countries continue to result in more, not less, emigration from the continent as more people – especially the young and more educated – are afforded the opportunity to fulfil migration aspirations that have been frustrated due to a lack of income, education and the general stagnation of other development markers in origin countries. This phenomenon helps to explain why African countries with relatively higher levels of economic and human development, such as Morocco, Algeria, Tunisia, South Africa, Ghana and Senegal, tend to have comparatively higher extra-continental emigration rates than the poorest countries such as Chad, Niger or South Sudan, as illustrated in Table 13.1 (see also Flahaux and De Haas, 2016). As Adepoju has pointed out, the continent's primary migrant-*sending* states are also among its main migrant-*receiving* destinations, which implies that 'countries are no longer neatly classifiable as either the origin or destination of migrants but a mixture of these, and transit countries' (Adepoju, 2003: 38).

Table 13. 1. Emigration numbers and rates to Europe and the United States for selected African countries[3]

Country	Migrant stock 2020[4]	Migrants per 100,000	Population 2020 in million[5]
1. Morocco	3,061,648	82,949	36.91
2. Algeria	1,926,033	43,923	43.85
3. Nigeria	921,160	4 469	206.14
4. Tunisia	857,691	72,562	11.82
5. Egypt	603,552	5,898	102.33
6. Somalia	540,924	34,042	15.89
7. South Africa	525,336	8,857	59.31
8. Ghana	509,861	16,410	31.07
9. Ethiopia	436,283	3,795	114.96
10. Senegal	403,132	24,082	16.74
46. Niger	13,923	575	24.21
47. Chad	13,733	836	16.43
48. Djibouti	12,805	12,934	0.99
50. South Sudan	6,350	567	11.19
51. Namibia	5,809	2,287	2.54
52. Botswana	5,436	2,313	2.35

Source: UN Global Migration Database (2020)

In other words, while it seems intuitive to see poverty as a key driver of African migration, migration research points to a more complex and nuanced relationship between poverty and migration than the simplistic and stereotypical view of desperate, poor Africans on the move, which is often portrayed in policy analyses and approaches, as well as in media reports on irregular crossings of the Mediterranean Sea. A growing body of scholarly work locates the decision to migrate at the level of the household rather than the individual, and questions the linear assumption about the relationship between poverty and migration. It notes that, 'in situations of poverty and constraints migration is generally part of deliberate, carefully planned, and largely rational strategies by families in order to improve their long-term social and economic wellbeing' (UNECA, 2017: 5). There is now an established scholarly consensus that the poorest tend to migrate less than the relatively well off, who are in a position to harness the requisite resources and capabilities to migrate, especially internationally. Looking at the socio-economic profile of African migrants to Europe from countries such as Ghana, Senegal and Morocco, many empirical studies have confirmed this core finding, which stresses a positive link between access to resources and the ability to migrate over long distances (see, for example, De Haas, 2003; Bleibaum 2009; UNDP, 2019). To put this observation in more conceptual terms, the bulk of African migration seems to be driven by 'relative poverty resulting from rising aspirations combined with better opportunities and more attractive lifestyles elsewhere ... rather than by absolute poverty' (UNECA, 2017: 4). *Inequality*, rather than poverty, is a main driver of migration in general, including African migration to Europe (Bjarnesen, 2020).

Third, *urbanisation* remains a key arena for thinking about African migration (see also Teye and Awumbila, 2018; Rodrigues and Bjarnesen, 2020). Although Africa is the least urbanised continent in the world, its rates of urbanisation are among the highest. The percentage of Africans living in urban areas has risen from an estimated 14 per cent in 1950 to 40 per cent in 2015, and is projected to reach 56 per cent in 2050 (Cilliers et al., 2011). Historically, urbanisation has been seen as an engine of growth because of its links to many of the processes that contribute to economic development and technological changes. Despite the challenges accompanying high urbanisation rates, such as poor and inadequate housing, water and sanitation, or transportation and healthcare services, the same processes of social and economic transformation, which have historically accompanied urbanisation elsewhere in the world, are under way in Africa. Within the broader context of rural–urban transformation, rising incomes and improved infrastructures, generally associated with urbanisation, function as 'a key driver of many forms of migration within and across borders' (UNECA, 2017: 5). These processes are driving subregional as well as off-continent migration. Some of these trajectories are step-wise and may lead migrants from rural homes through regional urban centres onwards across international borders, and sometimes towards destinations in Europe, the United States, or the Middle East (see Schapendonk and Steel, 2014). Urban centres thereby function as mobility nodes, providing migrants with opportunities to accumulate the capital needed for onwards travel, and serving as infrastructural nodes where both air and overland transportation are centred (Kleist and Bjarnesen, 2019).

Fourth, *education* is becoming a central driver of African migration. The migration literature has identified three overlapping dynamics related to the migration-stimulating role of education. First, due to profound inequities in the supply of and access to primary and secondary education between rural and urban areas in many countries on the continent, the desire to acquire an education is an important driver of rural-to-urban mobility in Africa. Second, the attainment of a certain level of education in rural areas tends to contribute to urban migration 'essentially because it tends to increase the desire to migrate in order to fulfil newly set material and immaterial life goals' (UNECA, 2017: 10; see also Williams, 2009). Third, the completion of a secondary education tends to generate more international migration through the unequal supply and demand relating to higher education (see, for example, Hallberg Adu, 2019). In fact, a survey of African student mobility found that Africa has the highest share of outbound student mobility in the world, with 58 per cent of enrolled tertiary students going outside their homelands for tertiary study (Kritz, 2015).

Against the backdrop of Africa's demographic transition, this trend is likely to continue, and possibly increase in the future:

> [A]n increasing number of young Africans completing secondary school will inevitably sustain the demand for higher tertiary education, which is likely to sustain international student migration, either to other African countries, such as South Africa and Morocco, or to destinations such as Europe, North America, Russia or China. It may also encourage people to migrate abroad for work, particularly if domestic economic growth and job creation levels are relatively low (UNECA, 2017: 11).

Although student mobility, especially at the graduate and postgraduate levels, has a long history in Afro–European relations, education is becoming increasingly important as a driver of African migration to Europe, as well as to other destination regions within and outside the continent. In the colonial and early postcolonial eras, such mobility was less regulated than today but, nevertheless, restricted to a very limited elite. In addition to the quest for high-quality education, these journeys were also driven by the tendency at many African universities for academic programmes to be interrupted by the lack of teaching resources, or by armed conflict or other forms of political destabilisation, delaying graduation and leading students and their families to search for other options. Today, scholarship programmes and a growing middle class have enabled more African students to invest in overseas mobility as part of their educational trajectories. At the same time, European immigration regimes have made it increasingly difficult to access such opportunities in an EU member state, once again pushing aspiring migrants to consider irregular migration in the hope that their status can be regularised once on European ground (see, for example, Alpes, 2017; UNDP, 2019).

Fifth, with the rise of climate change to the top of the international agenda, the link between *environmental factors* and migration has become a key topic of public interest, policy discourse and scholarly investigation. Climate change (and its impact) is often cited among the key drivers of contemporary migration from the Global South to the North. According to Zickgraf (2019), the 2014 assessment of the Intergovernmental Panel on Climate Change (IPCC) suggested that,

> African regions are expected to be the most affected by climate change and climate vulnerability, including hotter and drier conditions, rainfall variability, and extreme events such as floods, as well as more gradual environmental changes including sea-level rise, land degradation, and desertification. Sub-regionally, weather pattern projections vary of the twenty-first century including an increase in drought and heavy rainfall in southern and East Africa, more intense precipitation in West Africa, and more frequent heat waves in the north (350).

Given Africa's particular vulnerabilities to climate change, public discourse has centred on the apocalyptic predictions that see millions of environmental migrants wandering across the continent with considerable outpour on European shores. Over the past few years, the tragic situation of thousands of migrants from sub-Saharan Africa, particularly from the Sahel countries, trying to reach Europe at great peril via the Mediterranean Sea, has sometimes been attributed to 'a combination of climate change, environmental degradation and population growth' (UNECA, 2017: 11) and presented as a premonition of what is to come.

If such predictions and imageries make for good headlines, they are misleading because they suggest a deterministic link between environmental factors and migration, even though a growing body of literature has established that 'the role of environmental factors in migration processes is much more complex, subtle and indirect than popular discourses suggests … in short, there is little to no evidence that climate change directly effects migration patterns' (UNECA, 2017: 11; see also Bukari, Sow and Scheffran, 2019). Instead of thinking about the climate change-migration nexus in causal terms, the migration literature considers how environmental stresses affect the livelihoods of vulnerable people, including their aspirations and capabilities to migrate in order to cope with such stress (Foresight, 2011). This line of inquiry stresses the methodological challenges of singling out environmental factors as 'root causes' of migration (see Jonsson, 2010; Foresight, 2011; Beine and Parsons, 2015). In other words, while it is true that environmental factors play an important part in people's livelihoods and migration decisions, it is misleading to seek to establish its causal relationship with migration. Thus, environmental factors 'should be seen in relation to other political, economic, social, and cultural factors that eventually determine standards of living and inequality of access to resources' (UNECA. 2017: 12; see also Zickgraf, 2019).

In short, the relationship between environmental factors and migration is more complex and nuanced than the deterministic and sensationalist view of climate change creating hordes of African environmental migrants en route to Europe. The same complex relationship also applies to the links between forced migration and political oppression and violence.

Finally, since the post-independence era, *armed conflict* and other forms of political destabilisation have been considered to be important drivers of forced migration and displacement within and from Africa. While the role of conflicts and authoritarianism in generating mass displacement and fuelling the 'asylum crisis' in Europe dominates the news and features prominently in policy documents, migration research underscores a rather complex relationship between violence/oppression and forced migration. Most crucially, the assumption that armed conflict or political oppression necessarily leads to increased displacement overlooks that,

> while violence and oppression can obviously motivate people to get on
> the move, the same factors that motivate their flight can also prevent

them from fleeing ... [P]eople living under authoritarian regime[s] may more often wish to migrate, but authoritarian states may also have a higher willingness and capacity to control and restrict emigration (UNECA 2017: 14; see also Lubkemann, 2008; De Haas and Vezzoli, 2011).

Much like the poorest segments of a population, those living under authoritarian regimes are more likely to be suffering involuntary immobility (see Carling, 2002); and much like migrants moving to mitigate environmental degradation, those able to move are more likely to remain in their immediate subregions. This set of observations is corroborated by a study of global migration data that finds no clear correlation between the level of political freedoms and levels of emigration (De Haas, 2010). While these scholarly findings underscore the role of violence and political oppression in generating forced migration in Africa, they show that the reality of violence/oppression-induced migration is far removed from the deterministic view that dominates the popular imagery of asylum seekers and refugees, the vast majority of whom stay close to the countries of origin, without making concerted efforts to reach Europe.

Conclusion

Over the last decade, addressing the root causes of forced and irregular migration in Africa has become a central part of African–EU relations. While African migration to the EU is not a new phenomenon, recently this issue has received a renewed institutional interest and focus, which is reflected in the EU's response to the so-called migration 'crisis' in Europe. This response led to the establishment of the EUTFA in 2015, as a funding mechanism for the implementation of the EU's core policy objective on African–EU migration, in which the notion of addressing the root causes of African migration was a key pillar. The series of global consultations, which culminated in the adoption of the UN Global Compact in 2018, also contributed to the policy debate on the root causes of migration. The Global Compact is aimed at addressing global migration governance, and transforming migration to a matter of choice and not of necessity.

An inquiry into the notion of the root causes of migration, informed by the AU's position and the findings of academic migration scholarship, has shown its conceptual limitations, methodological weaknesses and policy shortcomings. Positing migration as a problem has resulted in migration policy focusing on addressing its root causes, which is a restrictive and static approach that conveys the false impression that migration can be prevented through development investments. Despite the conceptual flaws associated with the root causes conversation and policy intervention, the new iteration of the policy on migration carries a transformational agenda that aims to radically reshape the status of origin countries in order to 'overcome the economic underdevelopment and political instability that are seen as the main determinant of migration and refugee flows' (Castles and Van Hear, 2011: 298).

A discussion of the AU's assessment of the root causes of migration in and from Africa has revealed the impact of the following broad range of issues: poverty, rural underdevelopment, population growth, conflicts, environmental degradation, human rights violations, and political instability. However, a review of the migration research has stressed a more complex and nuanced relationship between migration and the aforementioned drivers of migration. Indeed, a genuine conversation on the root causes would note that the deterministic and simplistic view of migration, which is often portrayed in media and popular imagery, and sometimes echoed in policy documents, does not capture the complex reality of a multicausal phenomenon that does not lend itself to policy mantras.

Notes

1   See Chapters 11 and 12.

2   For a more comprehensive analysis of the African Union position on migration, see Chapter 11 in this volume.

3   The table is based on data from the UN Global Migration Database, which offers emigration data ordered by country and world region. The UNGMD lists a total of 57 African territories, including Saint Helena, Eswatini, Western Sahara, and Réunion. The countries in the table are selected as illustrative of the general trend discussed here, with the numbers in the first column indicating the country's rank among the 57 territories listed by the UNGMD in terms of total migrant stock in Europe and the United States at mid-year in 2020. It should be noted that when migrant stock is calculated in relation to the population size of the sending country (as in column three), the ranking changes slightly, although with the same overall trend of emigration rates to Europe and the United States being dominated

by North African states and other relatively developed states.

4 Cf. UN Global Migration Database (UNGMD).

5 Cf. Statista. Online at: https://www.statista.com/statistics/1121246/population-in-africa-by-country/ (accessed 12 May 2022).

References

Abebe, TT. 2017. *Migration Policy Frameworks in Africa*. ISS Africa Report No. 2, December 2017. Pretoria: Institute for Security Studies. Online at: https://issafrica.org/research/africa-report/migration-policy-frameworks-in-africa (accessed 20 May 2022).

Adepoju, A. 2003. 'Migration in West Africa', *Development*, 46(3): 37–41.

Alpes, M.J. 2017. *Brokering High-Risk Migration and Illegality in West Africa: Abroad at any cost.* London and New York: Routledge.

Amira, A. 2003. 'Gender, forced migration and paid domestic work: case studies on refugee women domestic workers in Cairo'. MA thesis, The American University in Cairo.

African Union (AU). 2021. 'Official inauguration of the African Centre for the Study and Research on Migration'. Online at: https://au.int/en/pressreleases/20210313/official-inauguration-african-centre-study-and-research-migration (accessed 13 March 2021).

African Union (AU). 2018. *The Revised Policy Framework for Africa and Plan of Action (2018–2030)*. Addis Adaba: AU Department of Social Affairs. Online at: https://au.int/sites/default/files/newsevents/workingdocuments/32718-wd-english_revised_au_migration_policy_framework_for_africa.pdf (accessed 13 March 2021).

African Union Executive Council. 2006. 'African Common Position on Migration and Development', Banjul 2006, EX.CL/DEC.305 (IX), Preamble. Online at: https://www.iom.int/sites/g/files/tmzbdl486/files/jahia/webdav/shared/shared/mainsite/microsites/rcps/igad/african_common_position_md.pdf (accessed 13 March 2021).

Awumbila M., Deshhingkar, P., Kandilige, L., Teye, J.K. and Setrana, M. 2017. *Brokerage in Migrant Domestic Work in Ghana: Complex social relations and mixed outcomes.* Working Paper No. 47, Migration out of Poverty Research Programme, University of Sussex. Online at: http://www.migratingoutofpoverty.org/files/file.php?name=wp47-awumbila-et-al-2017-brokerage-in-migrant-domestic-work-in-ghana.pdf&site=354 (accessed 20 May 2022).

Bacon, L. and Robin, N. 2018. 'State of the Art – The root causes of irregular migration in the region of the Rabat Process'. Study commissioned by the Steering Committee of the Rabat Process in preparation of the October 2018 Paris thematic meeting on the root causes of irregular migration. Online at: https://www.rabat-process.org/images/TM-root-causes/EN_Study_State-of-the-art.pdf (accessed 10 May 2022).

Beine, M. and Parsons, C. 2015. 'Climatic factors as determinants of international migration', *The Scandinavian Journal of Economics*, 117(2): 723–67.

Bjarnesen, J. 2020. 'Shifting the narrative on African migration: The numbers, the root causes, the alternatives – get them right!' *NAI Policy Notes* 2020:1.

Bleibaum, F. 2009. 'Senegal case study report', EACH-FOR Environmental Change and Forced Migration Scenarios.

Bukari K.N., Sow P. and Scheffran J. 2019. 'Real or hyped? Linkages between environmental/climate change and conflicts: The case of farmers and Fulani pastoralists in Ghana', in M. Behnassi, H. Gupta and O. Pollmann (eds). *Human and Environmental Security in the Era of Global Risks*. New York: Springer International Publishers.

Carling, J. 2002. 'Migration in the age of involuntary immobility: Theoretical reflections and Cape Verdean experiences', *Journal of Ethnic and Migration Studies*, 28(1): 5–42.

Castles, S. and Van Hear, N. 2011. 'Root causes', in A. Betts (ed.). *Global Migration Governance*. Oxford: Oxford University Press.

Cilliers, J., Hughes, B. and Moyer, J. 2011. *African Futures 2050: The next forty years*. ISS Monograph No. 175, 27 January 2011 Pretoria: Institute for Security Studies. Online at SSRN: https://ssrn.com/abstract=2690239 or http://dx.doi.org/10.2139/ssrn.2690239 (accessed 12May 2022).

De Haas, H. 2020. 'Paradoxes of Migration and Development', in T. Bastia and R. Skeldon (eds). *Routledge Handbook of Migration and Development*. London: Routledge, pp. 17–31.

De Haas, H. 2011. *The Determinants of International Migration: Conceptualizing policy, origin and destination effects*. IMI Working Paper No. 32. Oxford: International Migration Institute.

De Haas, H. 2010. *Migration Transitions: A theoretical and empirical inquiry into the development drivers of international migration*. IMI Working Paper No. 24. Oxford: International Migration Institute.

De Haas, H. 2007. 'Turning the tide? Why development will not stop migration', *Development and Change*, 38(5): 819–41.

De Haas, H. 2003. 'Migration and development in southern Morocco: The disparate socio-economic impact of out-migration on the Todgha Oasis

Valley'. Nijmegen: Radboud University.

De Haas, H., Castles, S. and Miller, M. 2020. *The Age of Migration*. London: The Guilford Press.

De Haas, H. and Vezzoli, S. 2011. *Leaving Matters: The nature, evolution and effects of emigration policies*. IMI Working Paper 34. Oxford: International Migration Institute.

European Commission. 2018. 'Many more to come? Migration from and within Africa'. European Commission Joint Research Centre. Luxembourg: Publications Office of the European Union.

EUTFA website, https://ec.europa.eu/trustfundforafrica/index_en.

Flahaux, M-L. and De Haas, H. 2016. 'African migration: Trends, patterns, drivers', *Comparative Migration Studies*, 4(1). https://doi.org/10.1186/s40878-015-0015-6.

Foresight. 2011. 'Migration and global environmental change'. London: Government Office for Science.

Gebrewold, B. (ed.). 2007. *Africa and Fortress Europe: Threats and opportunities*. Aldershot: Ashgate.

Global Compact for Migration. 2018. Global Compact for Safe, Orderly and Regular Migration (A/RES/73/195). Intergovernmentally negotiated and agreed outcome, 13 July 2018. Online at: https://refugeesmigrants. un.org/sites/default/files/180713_agreed_outcome_global_compact_for_ migration.pdf (accessed12 May 2022).

Hallberg Adu, K. 2019. 'Student migration aspirations and mobility in the global knowledge society: The case of Ghana', *Journal of international Mobility*, 7(1): 23–43.

Jonsson, G. 2010. *The Environmental Factor of Migration Dynamics: A review of African cases*. IMI Working Papers No. 21. Oxford: International Migration Institute.

Kleist, N. and Bjarnesen, J. 2019. *Migration Infrastructures in West Africa and Beyond*. MIASA Working Paper 2019(3). Accra: University of Ghana.

Kritz, M. 2015. 'International student mobility and tertiary education capacity in Africa', *International Migration*, 53(1): 29–49.

Lubkemann, Stephen. 2008. *Culture in Chaos. An anthropology of the social condition in war*. Chicago, IL: University of Chicago Press.

McKeon, N. 2018. 'Getting to the root causes of migration in West Africa: Whose history, framing and agency counts?' *Globalizations*, 15(6): 870–85.

Mangala, Jack. 2017. 'Engaging diasporas in development: contours and outcomes of international policymaking', in J. Mangala (ed.). *Africa and its Global Diaspora: The policy and politics of emigration.* New York: Palgrave Macmillan, pp. 3–37.

Plaza, S. and Ratha, D. (eds). 2011. *Diaspora for Development in Africa.* Washington, DC: The World Bank.

Ratha, D., Mohapatra, S., Özden, C., Plaza, S., Shaw, W. and Abebe, S. 2011. *Leveraging Migration for Africa: Remittances, skills, and investments.* Washington, DC: World Bank. https://openknowledge.worldbank.org/ handle/10986/2300 License: CC BY 3.0 IGO.

Rodrigues, C.U. and Bjarnesen, J. 2020. 'Intra-African Migration'. Study for the European Commission DEVE Committee. Policy Department for External Relations, Directorate General for External Policies of the Union. PE 603.514 – October 2020. Online at: https://www.europarl.europa.eu/ thinktank/en/document/EXPO_STU(2020)603514 (accessed 10 May 2022).

Schapendonk, J and Steel, G. 2014. 'Following migrant trajectories: The im/ mobility of sub-Saharan Africans en route to the European Union', *Annals of the Association of American Geographers,* 104: 262–70.

Skeldon, R. 1990. *Population Mobility in Developing Countries: A reinterpretation.* London: Belhaven.

Teye, J. and Awumbila, M. 2018. 'Factors of migration and urbanization in Africa'. Presentation at the Rabat Process thematic meeting on Root Causes of Irregular Migration, Paris, 23–24 October 2018.

Van Hear, N., Bakewell, O. and Long, K. 2018. 'Push-pull plus: reconsidering the drivers of migration', *Journal of Ethnic and Migration Studies,* 44(6): 927–44.

UNDP. 2019. *Scaling Fences. Voices of irregular African migrants to Europe.* United Nations Development Programme. Online at: https://www. undp.org/publications/scaling-fences#:~:text=October%2021%2C%20 2019,originating%20from%2039%20African%20countries (accessed 10 May 2022).

UNECA. 2017. 'African Migration: Drivers of migration in Africa', Draft Report commissioned by the UN Economic Commission for Africa African Migration, October 2017.

Williams, N. 2009. 'Education, gender, and migration in the context of social change', *Social Science Research,* 38(4): 833–96.

Zickgraf, C. 2019. 'Climate change and migration crisis in Africa', in C. Menjívar, M. Ruiz and I. Ness (eds). *The Oxford Handbook of Migration Crises.* Oxford: Oxford University Press, pp. 347–65.

Chapter 14

The root causes of African migration to Europe: A European perspective

Jesper Bjarnesen

Introduction

In recent years, the notion of 'addressing the root causes of irregular migration' has become a central reference point among decision- and opinion-makers in the Global North, and especially within the European Union (EU). In this context, the approach is intended to counteract irregular migration to the EU through investments in socio-economic development, as well as conflict prevention and mitigation. These measures, furthermore, increasingly focus on irregular migration from sub-Saharan Africa. Briefly stated, the underlying assumption of the 'root causes' approach is that these measures will create more favourable conditions at home, thereby disincentivising potential migrants from leaving. Most articulations of the 'root causes' approach specify that the target of these interventions is *irregular* migration, with some proponents emphasising the imperative of securing Europe's international borders, and others stressing the humanitarian imperative of sparing future migrants the hardships and risks of such journeys. In other renditions, the emphasis on irregularity is either implied or omitted, leaving the impression that Europe is working to discourage African migrants writ large. But what is the reasoning behind the notion of 'addressing the root causes of (irregular) migration'? What are the implications of the policies designed and implemented in its name? And what does the 'root causes' approach tell us about contemporary European migration management?

As a contribution to this volume's overall ambition to explore the gaps between African and European migration governance, this chapter examines the notion of root causes from a European, or analytically Eurocentric, perspective. It explores the role of the root causes approach in the European policy landscape before and after the 2015–16 so-called 'refugee crisis', and argues that political rhetoric and, to a lesser extent, public opinion has been instrumental in limiting the scope for policy-makers to think and work through long-term sustainable policies around migration. The transnational migration of citizens from sub-Saharan Africa to the Global North is currently seen in a very limited and politicised perspective, and this chapter suggests that the root causes approach provides a key to understanding some of these limitations.

It traces the origins of the concept, reflects on its implications, and suggests how and why it has gained such traction in European policy thinking and public discourse. The analysis, although focused on European public and policy discourses, advocates a migrant-centred approach by reflecting on the perspectives of people on the move – those whose lives are most directly, and often severely, affected by the understandings and opinions of actors far removed from these realities. In addition to this migrant-centred agenda, the chapter reflects on the broader question of integrating migration governance into the global sustainable development agenda. The following two sections provide some conceptual and historical context, respectively, for understanding the notion of 'addressing the root causes of (irregular) migration'. It then analyses the root causes approach in relation to scholarship on the links between migration and development, before the conclusion outlines three brief recommendations for addressing the shortcomings of this policy agenda in relation to migration governance.

The migration–development nexus

As an initial conceptual delimitation, it is worthwhile considering the root causes approach as a subset of ideas within the broader field of thinking about the connections between migration and development – or what is increasingly referred to as the 'migration–development nexus' (Nyberg-Sørensen et al., 2002; Bastia and Skeldon, 2020). To begin with, it may be useful to ask what *migration* actually implies in this juxtaposition. Obviously, not all movements may be categorised as migration, and some forms of migration are more desirable to a host country or region than others. In public discourse, highly skilled migrants – and especially those moving from relatively well-off sending countries, and even more particularly those that identify as racially white – may not be thought of as migrants at all. Their motives or capabilities are rarely questioned, and even if they do not have their papers in order, they are rarely seen as a problem to the host country. An American investment banker bending the immigration rules in Germany to set up a business is more likely to be seen as a resourceful entrepreneur than an 'irregular migrant'. A Zimbabwean minister of finance, on the contrary, may have a hard time getting through security at a European airport. Some of these selective readings of what migration is and is not sometimes seep into migration policy thinking, reinforcing a host of colonial and deeply oppressive power dynamics. As Kenyan author and activist Nanjala Nyabola emphatically states, 'we are once again in the situation where racism and fear of the other is being used to shape how we control human mobility, instead of beginning from a point of inclusion and providing safety' (Nyabola, 2021: 5).

If we look beyond these politicised notions of what migration is, we may say that from the perspectives of (all) migrants, migration is a means to an end. We do not usually strive to become migrants – we migrate to achieve something. In other words, we become migrants to become something else: workers, providers, students, life partners, etc. In this light, it is important to acknowledge that most migrants, and those aspiring to become migrants, generally set out with the intention to *work* (Carling, 2017; Bjarnesen, 2020; Aslany et al., 2021), even when the journey takes place in illegal, undocumented, or irregular ways.

The ability to realise one's migrant aspirations may be thought to be primarily a matter of one's financial means. In the broadest sense, we may say that pace and distance is a privilege of the most affluent (see Baumann, 1992). But that picture is deceiving. While it is true that the global visa regime favours the wealthiest nations and individuals, it is much cheaper to travel from Bamako to Paris by air with a visa than it is to undergo the same journey as an irregular migrant.[1] The cost of migration, then, is not equally distributed, and financial capital is not enough to ensure easy access to migration. As most African academics travelling to a conference in Europe will tell you, the global visa regime imposes restrictions and hardships on travellers depending on their citizenship or passport (Melber et al., 2020). European immigration authorities generally use a similar standard to assess applications for work or residence permits. In the global hierarchy of nation-states, access to international migration is closely tied into geopolitical hierarchies, as they are reflected in international visa regimes and other measures that restrict the movement of some, and facilitate the movement of others. At the same time migration scholarship has consistently pointed out that people's abilities to move do depend to a considerable degree on their financial resources to do so (De Haas, 2007; Angelucci, 2015; Bazzi, 2017; Clemens and Postel, 2018a). Whether in relation to relatively voluntary migration, such as long- and short-distance labour migration, or in relation to forced migration in response to armed conflict or natural disasters, migration is costly. Those able to cross national, regional and continental borders tend to be better off than those who aspire to leave but remain in place (Carling and Schewel, 2018).

What is more unequivocal still is the fact that migration, whether irregular or regular, tends to contribute to migrant household income. Due to the vast differences in salary levels and labour market demand, South–North migration in particular is, more often than not, worth the trouble. And the benefits of migration do tend to benefit sending communities through financial and social remittances (Clemens and McKenzie, 2018) to an extent that is difficult to replace through society-wide development efforts. 'Migration *is* development', as migration scholar Ronald Skeldon has famously stated (Skeldon, 1997 in de Haas, 2020: 25). Although fairly intuitive, this understanding does seem to run counter to the current policies of using targeted development interventions in countries with relatively high out-migration in order to disincentivise future aspiring migrants from leaving. To offer an understanding of why the root causes approach has gained such centrality in European migration governance, despite these apparent contradictions, the following section traces the emergence and variations of the root causes approach to migration management.

A brief history of 'root causes' in migration policy thinking

Although roots generally tend to be associated with plants, the notion of 'root causes' has a distinctly medical ring to it. We refer to the idea of treating the cause, rather than the symptom of an illness, with the term 'root' underlining the botanical imagery of an underlying and vital source of such causes. This imagery has found its way into everyday parlance, and the *Oxford English Dictionary* lists more than a hundred uses of the word 'root' in conjunction with other words to that effect, such as 'root problem', 'root question', 'root reason', and 'root system'. In relation to human mobility, the term was first used strictly in relation to conflict-related forced migration in the early 1980s, with a focus on humanitarian interventions to end violence and human rights abuses, and to contribute to peacebuilding (Carling, 2017: 2; Castles and Van Hear, 2011: 288).

As research and policy thinking increasingly became aware of the grey zones between voluntary and forced migration (see Bjarnesen, 2016), this 'preventative logic' (Carling, 2017: 2) was also applied to more voluntary forms of migration, informed by the expectation that investments in broader societal development, such as poverty reduction, education and employment, would decrease the incentive to migrate. Such policies gained in appeal among decision-makers and publics in Western Europe in the aftermath of the 1973 oil crisis, as its post-war reliance on foreign, mainly low-skilled, labour to staff its industrial production gave way to more inward-looking policies (Castles and Van Hear, 2011: 289). This shift also influenced development economists to rethink the benefits of labour migration for sending countries. In the post-war period, most mainstream economists had argued that labour emigration would benefit sending countries by relieving pressure on local labour markets and boosting economies through remittances. By the mid-1970s, analysts inspired by dependency theory and world systems theory were finding more resonance for their arguments that immigration to former colonial centres was reproducing colonial geopolitical power dynamics and hindering 'modernisation' in the former colonies:

By the 1980s, the dominant view was that Europe would no longer need migrant workers, and that globalized capital investment would bring about accelerated development in poor regions of the world, leading to a trend towards equilibrium in productivity and incomes between North and South (Castles and Van Hear, 2011: 290).

The end of the Cold War shifted European migration policy priorities from this more long-term, structural and developmentalist approach to a more short-term and humanitarian response to rising numbers of forced migrants from Eastern Europe. This influx initially consisted of people fleeing persecution in the aftermath of the dissolution of the Soviet bloc following the failed coup on 18 August 1991, and subsequently from the effects of the onset of the war in the Balkans in late 1992. The turmoil in Eastern Europe alerted decision-makers in Western Europe to two emerging trends in international mobility. First, forced migration from Eastern Europe highlighted the risk of immigration overwhelming European asylum and integration structures, including the potential of future influxes from Europe's former colonies, as the total number of asylum applications in the EU increased almost tenfold from a decade low of around 70,000 in 1983 to a peak of almost 700,000 in 1992 (see Figure 14.1). Second, these conflict-related displacements emphasised that the 'majority of refugees were now fleeing not from conflicts *between* countries, nor from individual acts of persecution, but from conflicts *within* a State' (Spencer, 1996: 251–2, emphasis added). These developments raised concerns over policies that were too narrowly focused on the reception of forced migrants, leading the European Commission to call for 'a response which must go beyond management of immigration in the host country to deal with the causes of emigration in the source country' (European Commission, 1991: 9, in Spencer, 1996: 152).

Figure 14.1: New asylum applications in the OECD and EU since 1980

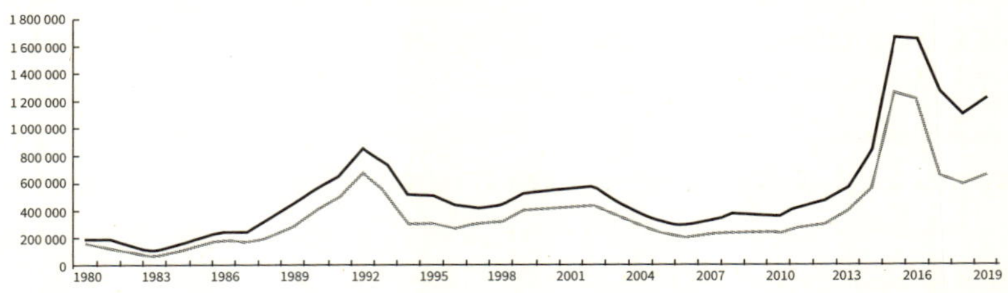

Source: OECD (2020: 35)

The combination of European disenchantment with the idea of labour migration as a driver of development and the rise in the number of international asylum seekers brought on by the Balkan war, influenced migration policy thinking to seek to reduce what was referred to as an increasing 'migration pressure' (see, for example, European Commission, 1994, cited in Spencer, 1996: 254). A key pillar of this approach was to intervene in the sending countries through diplomatic and developmental collaboration to reduce economic and conflict-related migration to Europe, rather than simply relying on stricter immigration control in host countries. This incentive was strengthened further by growing suspicions among European opinion-makers that aspiring immigrants were abusing the asylum system. While these policy priorities foreshadowed the current emphasis on 'root causes', relatively little was actually done to implement these ideas at the time (Carling, 2017: 2). This is clear from Spencer's report to the European Commission in 1996, which concludes: 'It is fair to say that the EU has not, to date, developed a root causes strategy which is integrated in practice into the relevant arms of its external policies' (Spencer, 1996: 260).

It is also important to specify that perceptions of what the underlying or root causes of migration are have changed considerably over the past 30 years. In 2002, a report from the European Committee on Migration stated:

> Dialogue should place migration into a broader foreign and trade policy context, linking it with discussions about trade and capital flows. Origin countries are unlikely to co-operate in taking steps to reduce emigration flows unless the *root causes* of those flows, expressed in sharp differences in standards of living, are tackled. Trade policies that restrict the ability of origin countries to market their products may well be counter-productive where there is also an aim to reduce immigration pressures (European Committee on Migration, 2002: 28, emphasis added).

At the turn of the new millennium, then, European foreign and trade policies – as components of a global political economy – were considered to be part of the root causes of migration. The same report also addressed the idea of using development aid to reduce emigration (a principle that has become central to the current policy thinking around 'root causes', explored later) but argued that such an approach seemed unlikely to work in practice:

> First, it is not clear how aid can be targeted to reduce emigration. Secondly, any resulting economic growth in origin countries has the

effect in the short and medium terms of increasing emigration from them. Third, using economic growth in origin countries as a vehicle for reducing emigration pressures raises other issues, such as trade agreements and remittance flows, which may lead to new foreign and trade policy difficulties. Finally, donors may seem to be operating from selfish motives, leading to a tension between origin and destination states not easily resolved. For these reasons, neither development assistance nor the creation of free trade zones, though an important part of the policy equation, may be regarded as substitutes for comprehensive migration policies (European Committee on Migration, 2002: 14).

It is worth remembering that around the year 2000, the EU was still focused primarily on migration and mobility from Eastern Europe to Western Europe, rather than arrivals from non-OECD countries. In fact, the African continent was mentioned only once in the European Commission on Migration strategic outline, and only in passing as a prediction of potential future challenges relating to demographic disparities, rather than a relevant geopolitical region in relation to migration management (see Spencer, 1996: 251). This preoccupation was driven by significant changes in global mobility dynamics. While the 1980s had seen a more diverse geographical spread of asylum seekers to Europe – with Turkey (243,000 applicants), Poland (214,000), the Islamic Republic of Iran (152,000) and Sri Lanka (106,000) making up the top four countries of origin for the decade – the 1990s saw a significant surge in arrivals from within Europe (See figure 14.2). The break-up of the former Republic of Yugoslavia, in particular, lead to a rise in asylum applications from a total of 68,000 in the 1980s to 877,000 in the 1990s. Romanian asylum seekers were the second-largest group (402,000 applications), followed by Turkish (337,000) and Iraqi (229,000) nationals (UNHCR, 2001: viii–ix).[2]

As a 2001 UNHCR report summarised, 'the share of European asylum applicants in the total number of asylum seekers in Europe increased from 27 per cent in the 1980s to 42 per cent in the 1990s, making Europe the largest source region of asylum seekers' (UNHCR, 2001: viii). Many things changed on 11 September 2001. Following the attacks on the World Trade Centre and the Pentagon, which claimed almost 3,000 lives, the Bush administration ushered in the American 'war on terror'. The revamped US-led alliance against Islamic terrorism eventually led to the invasions of Afghanistan in late 2001 and Iraq in early 2003.[3] These renewed conflicts kept Iraq and Afghanistan atop the lists of displaced people throughout the early 2000s, including the lists of asylum applications to the EU (see, for example, UNHCR, 2001; Wagner, 2011). The fact that the root causes of these new displacements were so obvious to European policy-makers may explain why the policy agenda on asylum and migration shifted more towards humanitarian responses to armed conflict, and to the shared responsibility of the European member states to receive approved asylum seekers through the so-called quota refugee programme. Somewhat paradoxically, it was not until the escalation of violence in Syria in 2014, and the ensuing exodus from Syria in 2015–16, that the root causes approach gained a new and unprecedented prominence in European migration governance.

Figure 14.2: Asylum applications lodged in Europe by origin, 1980s and 1990s

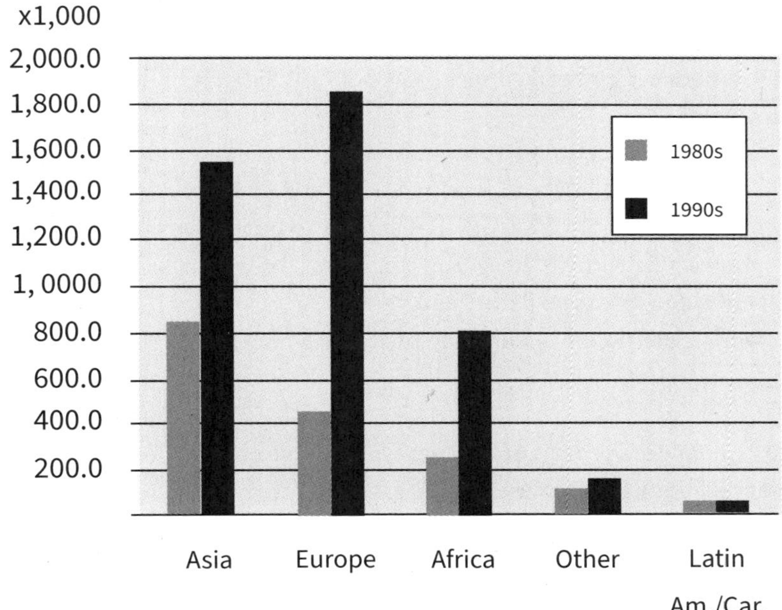

Source: UNHCR (2001: viii, https://www.unhcr.org/3c3eb40f4.pdf).

EU Trust Fund for Africa

Much has already been said in this book, and elsewhere, about the events and effects of what is commonly referred to as the 2015–16 European refugee, or migration, crisis. For the purposes of this chapter, and for understanding the paradox of how a humanitarian emergency in the Middle East came to fundamentally reshape the EU's outlook on African migration, it is worth noting that – as the introductory chapter summarised – this so-called crisis was delimited in time; that is was a direct effect of the intensification of armed conflict in Syria; that the number of migrants from sub-Saharan Africa remained relatively stable throughout this period; and that the proportions of Africa-born nationals entering the EU legally have far exceeded the number of irregular entries. Nevertheless, in addition to the humanitarian responses to the needs of migrants on the Mediterranean Sea or arriving on European shores, the EU quickly engaged with African states to address the broader political problem of sub-Saharan African nationals arriving irregularly in Europe. Already in November 2015, the Valletta Summit on Migration brought together European and African Heads of State in an effort to 'strengthen cooperation and address the current challenges but also the opportunities of migration' (Valletta Summit political statement, 2015). The meeting resulted in a joint political declaration and an action plan vowing to:

1. address the root causes of irregular migration and forced displacement
2. enhance cooperation on legal migration and mobility
3. reinforce the protection of migrants and asylum seekers
4. prevent and fight irregular migration, migrant smuggling and trafficking in human beings and
5. work more closely to improve cooperation on return, readmission and reintegration.

In this new agenda on Euro–African migration governance, the notion of addressing the root causes of migration centred 'on reducing poverty, promoting peace, good governance, rule of law and respect for human rights, supporting inclusive economic growth through investment opportunities and the creation of decent jobs, improving the delivery of basic services such as education, health and security' (Valletta Summit political statement, 2015). The statement continued to assert that '[r]ekindling hope, notably for the African youth, must be our paramount objective'. Remembering the European Commission's earlier approach to the notion of root causes, it is notable that this rekindling of the hope of Africa's potential future migrants was located exclusively in African states themselves. While the global political economy had previously been considered a root cause of (irregular) migration, the Valletta Summit cemented the idea that African states were to look inwards, not outwards, to explain and redress the emigration of their citizens. On this foundation, the Valletta Summit revived the notion of addressing the root causes of irregular migration with an emphasis on the internal development and stabilisation of sending states. The scale and impact of this policy lifted the 'root causes' idea from the drawing boards of European policy-makers to the centre of political debates across the EU; and one framework in particular, the Emergency Trust Fund for Africa, established at the Valletta Summit, has become key for this ascension (Carling, 2017: 2).

One of the enduring policy responses to the so-called refugee crisis has been the EU Trust Fund for Africa (EUTFA). Tellingly, the EUTFA was initially called the EU Emergency Trust Fund for Africa, but the 'emergency' has been gradually written out of the framework, as it were, indicating that the acute and exceptional circumstances of its creation has contributed to a more lasting shift in EU–African relations around migration governance. The notion of root causes has been placed at the centre of European migration policy through this framework, with one of the stated goals of the fund being 'to address the root causes of instability, forced displacement and irregular migration and to contribute to better migration management' (EUTFA website).

The Constitutive Agreement to officially establish the EUTFA was signed during the Valletta Summit on Migration by the European Commission, 25 EU member states, as well as Norway and Switzerland on 12 November 2015. The overall aim of the agreement was summarised as providing 'a new impetus for EU cooperation on migration by creating a platform to reinforce political engagement and dialogue with partner countries in Africa, pooling together EU and other donors' resources, and enlarging the EU evidence base to better understand the drivers and dynamics of migration', as well as 'to build a comprehensive approach to support all aspects of stability, security and resilience, aiming at addressing the conditions that could be conducive to violence and destabilisation' (EUTFA website). The rationale behind the framework quickly became engrained in political discourses across Europe (Clemens and Postel, 2018a: 1). For example, speaking at the high-level Leaders' Summit on Refugees held in New York on 20 September 2016, then British International Development Secretary Priti Patel stated:

I am clear that the only viable long-term response to the migration
crisis is to address its root causes – conflict, disease, poverty and a lack
of opportunities. If we do not tackle these issues which are forcing
people from their homes then we will not reduce mass migration
(Gov.UK 2016).

While the summit was organised specifically to address responses to refugee
situations, the statement illustrates a slippage that would become common
in political discourse, namely, the convergence of refugee displacements
with both regular and irregular migration from the Global South into one
joint notion of 'mass migration', uniformly framed as a problem facing
the countries of the Global North. This slippage was less explicit, but no
less present, in the founding statutes of the EUTFA, exposing a highly
Eurocentric agenda in the new framework for managing African migration
to the EU. In other words, although the Valletta Summit brought European
and African actors together, with 17 African heads of state in attendance,
in addition to representatives from the African Union (AU), the Economic
Community of West African States (ECOWAS), and all major international
organisations involved in migration governance, the EUTFA's Constitutive
Agreement was a European affair, intended to foster coordination among
European states. As the name implies, this coordination is envisioned as
anchored in EU-level development policy, with most funding channelled
through existing EU mechanisms. According to the EUTFA website,
'Resources currently allocated to the EU Trust Fund for Africa amount to
EUR 5.0 billion including EUR 4.4 billion from the European Development
Fund (EDF) and EU financial instruments including DCI, ENI, HOME and
ECHO funding. EU Member States and other donors (Switzerland and
Norway) have contributed and fully paid around EUR 620 million' (EUTFA
website).[4]

The fund, in other words, remains primarily funded by the European
Development Fund (see Figure 14.3), which has redirected, or more
precisely, reframed a significant portion of its resources to migration-focused
interventions. These investments target the African states understood to
be likely to generate the largest numbers of irregular migrants to Europe,
with the Sahel and Lake Chad countries of West Africa receiving the largest
share of these funds (see Figure 14.4).

Figure 14.3: Resources allocated to the EUTFA

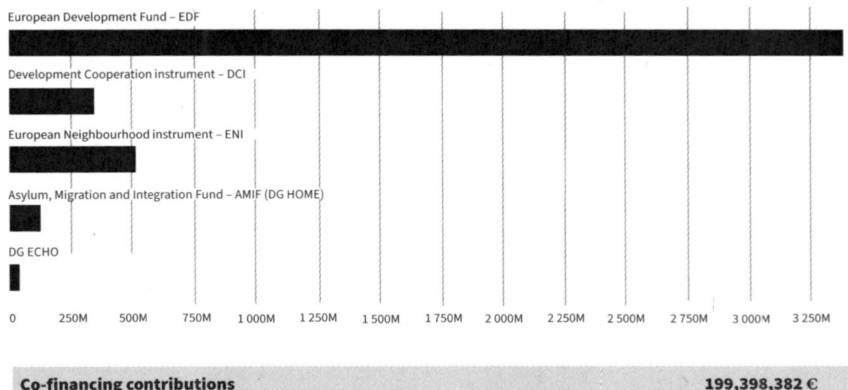

Source: https://ec.europa.eu/trustfundforafrica/content/trust-fund-financials_en

The EUTFA framework, furthermore, is unequivocally centred on the stated assumption of a direct connection between (in)security and irregular migration, which is explored in more detail below. Finally, as the previous citation illustrates, the spirit of the EUTFA is to be both exploratory, in the sense of prioritising a shared evidence base, and holistic, in the sense of linking migration governance to broader issues of security and resilience. More specifically, the EUTFA revolves around four 'lines of action':

1. Greater economic and employment opportunities;
2. Strengthening the resilience of communities and particularly the most vulnerable, including refugees and other displaced people;
3. Improved migration management in countries of origin, transit and destination;
4. Improved governance and conflict prevention and the reduction of forced displacement and irregular migration.

While broad in scope, the thrust of the EUTFA is not geared towards migration governance reform in the short term, but rather towards providing 'alternative opportunities for communities to foster growth and development in the long term' (EUTFA website).

Figure 14.4: EU Emergency Trust Fund for Africa funding

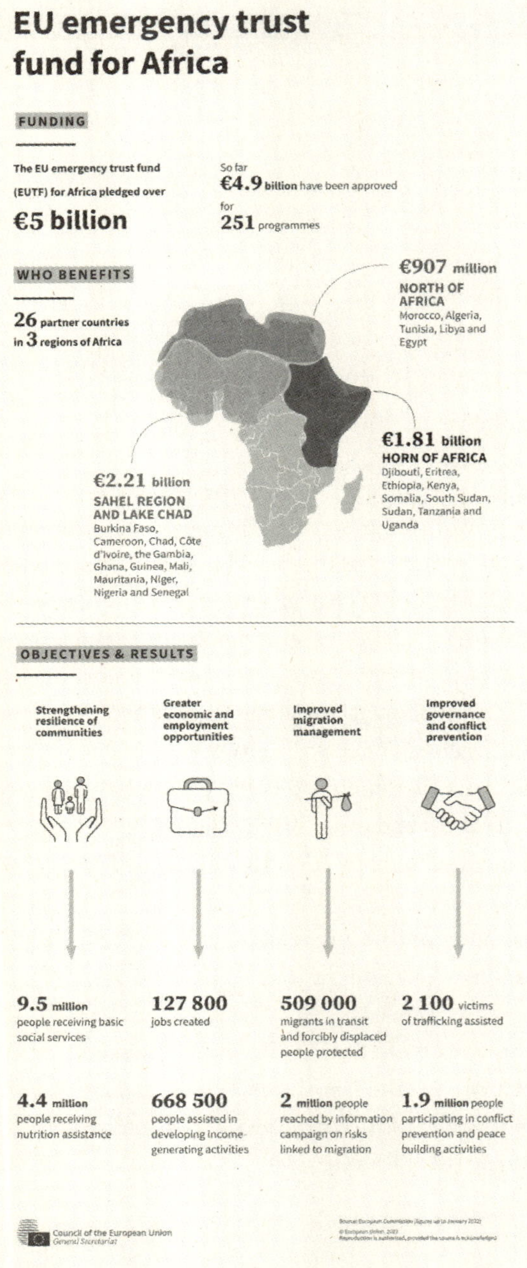

Source: https://www.consilium.europa.eu/en/infographics/africa-trust-fund/

A recent review of EUTFA spending noted, however, a tendency to increase funding for migration governance projects and a corresponding decline in projects focusing on development cooperation (Oxfam, 2020: 12). This shift, which seems to undermine the spirit and mandate of the EUTFA, suggests at the very least that the long-term and holistic approach to migration governance is easier said than done. In the remainder of this chapter, I offer some analytical reflections on the idea of 'addressing the root causes of (irregular) migration' on the basis of this brief history of the notion in European policy thinking, and its most elaborate articulation in the EUTFA framework.

Root causes and the migration–development nexus

Building on the four lines of action of the EUTFA, it seems appropriate to ask the most fundamental question at the outset of this analytical reflection: why would holistic interventions targeting long-term improvements of overall development and security problems be at the heart of a framework designed as a response to the much more specific field of migration governance? The 'root causes' approach may be understood as the bridge between conventional development policies and the post-2015 European migration governance agenda. In order to avoid the costly and indefinite struggle to intersect vessels at sea, coordinate rescue operations, combat networks of human smugglers, and mobilise humanitarian assistance to new arrivals – in addition to handling the asylum applications of tens of thousands of migrants with all the accompanying administrative and political complications at EU and national levels – the reasoning goes, interventions are needed to put an end to (irregular) migration from Africa once and for all. In other words, all these measures to deal with migrants already on the move may be understood as intended to treat the symptoms of an underlying illness or problem: the fact that new generations of migrants are likely to be equally inclined to leave their countries of origin in the future.

In their review of pre-2015 'root causes' approaches in migration governance, Castles and Van Hear summarise their rationale in a strikingly similar way:

> 'Root causes' approaches developed as a reaction to two trends: first, the growth in international movements of asylum seekers and lower skilled workers; and second, the gradual comprehension that border control

measures on their own were ineffective in the face of the powerful forces causing mobility, especially from poor to rich countries, in the epoch of neo-liberal globalization. To put it more generally, the 'root causes' notion involves a recognition that migration cannot be dealt with in isolation from other global issues, and that migration policies cannot be separated from other issues of global governance (Castles and Van Hear, 2011: 302).

Spanning the broad expanses of conventional development policy, conflict prevention and migration governance, and doing so in a holistic and long-term perspective, is an almost unsurmountable task for any bridge, which has led to confusion around what the concept of 'root causes' actually implies. As Clemens and Postel summarise,

> It is not always clear what 'root causes' of migration targeted by aid are. The EU Trust Fund for Africa, for example, identifies four key policy areas: employment creation, basic local service provision, migration management, and governance – including conflict prevention and border management. Yet few details are published on key project mandates under these broad umbrellas; specific targeting of so-called migration drivers is even less clear (Clemens and Postel, 2018b: 1–2)

Such confusion seems to put both decision-makers and implementing agencies in a politically vulnerable position vis-à-vis their constituencies and funders. Investing in long-standing development sectors such as poverty reduction, youth employment and education should not need to be rationalised as anti-immigration efforts. Not only are those intentions unlikely to be fulfilled, at least not in the foreseeable future, but they also risk undermining the viability of the development interventions in and of themselves. For example, the underlying migration-related agenda may promote a tendency to rush interventions to produce immediate results, or place policy-makers and practitioners in a position where they are expected to plan, administer and report on an overwhelming set of impact variables. This policy overreach may explain the gap between intentions and implementation. Clemens and Postel's review of development interventions targeting migration from Africa to Europe concluded that, despite the increased reliance on the 'root causes' logic and narrative,

An index of migration-relevant aid, including commonly identified 'root causes' interventions, yields no clear evidence that aid systematically targets 'root causes' of migration. That is, migration-relevant sectors do not seem to receive more funding in major migrant-origin countries than the average aid recipient. A worldwide wave of new 'root causes' aid is unlikely (Clemens and Postel, 2018b: 2).

In addition to the broad scope, which leads to confusion around the actual priorities and rationales of interventions under this banner, the root causes approach relies on a particular understanding of how and why people choose to leave their countries of origin and become international migrants. As we have seen, addressing the root causes of (irregular) migration implies looking beyond the short-term challenges of border control and anti-trafficking measures involving people currently on the move, to measures that could prevent future migrants from even aspiring to leave their countries of origin. The notion that migrant aspirations can be discouraged through development measures, however, is based on several flawed assumptions about the causal mechanisms of migration.

To be more specific, current policies under the 'root causes' banner, tend to lack a clear understanding of the way migration chains work. For example, there is a glaring conceptual gap between migrant aspirations and the specific routes and means that migrants end up using to realise those aspirations (Carling and Talleraas, 2016). Most aspiring migrants would probably prefer the cheapest and safest route to their desired destination. In the case of most African migrants travelling to Europe, the cheapest and safest route would arguably be by air with a valid visa. As already mentioned, travelling by land to the North African coast and onwards across the Mediterranean Sea is not only exceedingly more dangerous, but the accumulated costs of that journey – including the costs of paying various brokers and officials along the way – generally surpass the costs of regular migration several times over. Furthermore, migration scholars have increasingly argued that even if development interventions were to reach their targets in terms of increasing the standard of living in a sending country, emigration is more likely to increase rather than decrease (see, for example, De Haas, 2007; Carling, 2017). It is rarely the poorest segments of a population that migrate outside their region, let alone continent, of origin. What is important to acknowledge here is that people do not generally aspire to become irregular migrants. They aspire to a different set of circumstances, which they believe are achievable through migration. Migration is not the goal, but the means to achieve that goal. In this sense, the specific routes and conditions of a journey to Europe are separate from the root causes of why people wish to migrate in the first place.

Furthermore, income inequality between the world's richer and poorer countries continues to attract migrants to the former – and to make the journey worthwhile. Given the historically marginal impact of development interventions on these macroeconomic inequalities, migration-targeted development aid stands a poor chance of changing the underlying reasons why people may want to become migrants in the first place (Clemens and Postel, 2018b). The question that remains in this regard then becomes whether development may have a deterring effect on *irregular* migration specifically, which seems equally questionable. These fundamental weaknesses in the root causes approach have led to widespread criticism, and accusations that the motives behind the redirection of aid are primarily political – intended to appease an immigration-hostile segment of European voters – rather than genuinely about development effectiveness:

> There is an increasing concern that the EUTF[A] is being used as a political tool focusing on quick-fix projects with the aim to stem migratory flows to Europe, which is not the purpose of ODA according to the EU's own Lisbon Treaty. There is also a concern that some funding from the EUTF[A] contributes unintentionally to inhumane treatment of migrants and refugees, as in the case of Libya. In addition, the EU strategy of 'quick-fixes' is very likely to fail since addressing the drivers of forced migration requires a long term, coherent and sustainable approach, respecting the basic principles of development aid (CONCORD, 2018: 6)

The Global Compact for Safe, Orderly and Regular Migration represents a global framework that connects migration governance explicitly to the Sustainable Development Goals in such a spirit, but since its signing in 2018, European policies have continued to prioritise deterrence strategies. Revitalising this global framework in European policy thinking not only ensures a more holistic anchoring of the migration–development nexus but may also offer a way out of the political deadlock that hinders progress at the European level, since the framework is founded on truly global consultations rather than a narrow, Eurocentric understanding of migration management. Even if the root causes approach were to be openly justified as a politically motivated investment in stemming irregular entries to Europe, I would add, it still seems unlikely to succeed given the macroeconomic factors discussed earlier (see also Castles and Van Hear, 2011: 287).

Furthermore, the most instrumental efforts to reduce irregular migration and combat human trafficking have been argued to be counterproductive. For example, an analysis of the impact of EU migration policies on central Saharan migration routes (Tubiana *et al.*, 2018) concludes that EU-funded anti-trafficking measures have tended to actually increase rather than reduce migration by diversifying, rather than preventing, human trafficking; for instance, by pitting traffickers against one another, which adds to migrant insecurity; and by empowering local militia and other irregular security actors as allies, which further destabilises the already overburdened Sahel region.

In light of the politically charged atmosphere around European migration governance, the inconsistent implementation of policies, and of several more conceptual contradictions implicit in the approach, the prospects for root causes approaches to succeed in stemming (irregular) migration from Africa to Europe seem to have the odds stacked against them. This conceptual and practical failure is nothing new. In their 2011 reflection on root causes approaches to migration governance, Castles and Van Hear conclude that these measures remained limited in at least three respects:

> [F]irst, they did not seek to address fundamental North–South inequalities; second, they remained based on the implicit assumption that the migration of poorer people was a bad thing that should be curtailed; and third, 'root causes' approaches remained poor cousins of the migration control measures, in the sense that governments were willing to spend far more on the latter. Thus, 'root causes' approaches have on the whole failed to bring about substantial changes in migration dynamics, and especially in the unequal power relationships between migrant origin and destination states (Castles and Van Hear, 2011: 302).

The three limitations outlined by Castles and Van Hear may be said to speak to the structural, strategic and practical shortcomings of the root causes approach, respectively. First, at a structural level, while it may seem utopian to expect migration governance measures to effect a significant change in fundamental North–South inequalities, these conclusions do hold important lessons for post-2015 root causes approaches. Whether or not one agrees that such global inequalities can (or should) be fundamentally changed, their role in shaping current and future global migration and mobility dynamics cannot be underestimated. This observation leads to the second, strategic shortcoming. By allowing for a conceptual slippage between refugee displacements, irregular migration and South–North migration writ large, the 'root causes' approach not only causes unnecessary and politically polarising confusion, it also deprioritises the mutually beneficial effects of South–North migration. Even irregular migrants send remittances back to their families, and European shadow economies rely on undocumented migrants for cheap and exploitable labour (see, for example, Holston and Appadurai, 1996; Kelmanson et al., 2019). Stating these circumstances does not imply condoning the exploitation of migrant labour, but adds necessary nuance to the understanding of the drivers of African migration to Europe.

Third, the lack of genuine European commitment to development interventions and the prioritisation of migration control measures remains true of the post-2015 era. This priority signals that the commitment to 'addressing the root causes of irregular migration' is, if not outright disingenuous, then at least secondary to more suppressive measures to stem irregular entries to Europe. More importantly, it makes the success of the long-term development interventions highly unlikely. As Clemens and Postel (2018b: 2) argue, even if current investments in macro-economic growth and youth unemployment were tripled overnight, the rates of growth needed to reduce income inequality enough to discourage future migration would take more than a generation. In the concluding section, I summarise the main findings of the analysis and provide a brief outline of three broad policy recommendations to address some of these shortcomings.

Conclusion

This chapter has traced the emergence and transformation of the notion of 'addressing the root causes of (irregular) migration' in European policy thinking, emphasising its centrality in political rhetoric and migration governance in the aftermath of the so-called European refugee crisis. The notion was present, although relatively dormant, in European policy thinking in the 1980s and 1990s, but gained prominence under somewhat counterintuitive circumstances, namely in reaction to a humanitarian crisis in and around Syria in 2014–15. Even more unexpectedly, the root causes approach soon came to centre on the prevention of irregular migration from sub-Saharan Africa across the Mediterranean Sea, leading policy responses in the direction of long-term investments in poverty reduction, livelihood creation, and education, rather than the more immediate sectors of conflict mitigation and prevention in and around Syria. The approach, in other words, came to bridge short-term humanitarian responses with long-term development interventions, shifting the attention from conflict-related displacement and the breakdown of the EU asylum system to so-called 'economic migration'. This chapter also illustrated that the meaning of the term 'root causes' has changed over time, from emphasising unequal terms of trade and income levels at a global scale in the 1990s to an understanding that centres on national development in the Global South, and particularly in sub-Saharan Africa.

Reviewing the origins and development of the 'root causes' narrative over time, it is easy to understand why the idea of 'addressing the root causes of (irregular) migration' seems intuitive and compelling. First, it makes sense to treat the (root) cause, rather than the symptom of any problem. In migration governance, the unfolding tragedy on the Mediterranean Sea clearly calls for determined and sustainable solutions to prevent the unnecessary loss of human lives, and rescue operations and humanitarian assistance clearly do not address the underlying reasons why people end up in such circumstances. Second, given the delimited nature of the Syrian refugee crisis, it is reasonable to include irregular migration from sub-Saharan Africa in forward-looking policy thinking, since the number of arrivals from that region to Europe has been consistent for more than a decade.

However, as most migration scholars agree, current approaches under the 'root causes' banner tend to neglect a series of factors that would be necessary to consider as fundamental for shaping global migration and mobility dynamics. First, the humanitarian imperative to rescue migrants at sea and assist them on their arrival to European shores should not be undermined by utilitarian motives of reducing South–North migration.

Not only is it unethical and in violation of international refugee law to disregard the rights and needs of people seeking international protection, it is also bad policy. Most acutely, shifting priorities to deterrence strategies in sending regions undermines the legal principles of asylum, which in turn may challenge the very foundation of the principles of national sovereignty and regional collaboration.[5] Second, even if investments in long-term development were successful, it is far from evident that increased development would decrease migration. On the contrary, most migration scholars insist that in the short- and medium-term, more people are likely to leave if they acquire the means to do so.

Third, as the 'root causes' approach has come to rely primarily on development cooperation in sending countries, the broader challenges of addressing inequality within the global political economy have been silenced (Glick Schiller, 2020: 35). Viewing sending states or subregions in isolation from these structural problems, in many ways amounts to the exact opposite of treating the root causes of (irregular) migration; it treats the symptoms of systematic underdevelopment as if these symptoms were not intimately linked to a global political economy. Even if we accept that dependency theorists may sometimes stretch their argument into conspiratorial territory, a simple comparison of income levels between sending and receiving regions is enough to remind us that even if many African countries have seen significant progress over recent decades, global income inequality will continue to make labour migration an attractive and reasonable strategy for several generations to come.

Fourth, the 'root causes' approach – and the European debates around (irregular) migration from the Global South more broadly – wilfully ignores that EU legislation and patrolling are also root causes of unsafe migration in their own right. By criminalising northbound mobility from Agadez in Niger, for example, EU-driven legislation to restrict irregular migration to Europe has contributed to boosting demands for human trafficking, which exploits migrants and leads to ever-more dangerous routes through the Sahara Desert, with grave human consequences. The European support to the Libyan coast guard and other armed actors in a state in the throes of civil war has also been argued to put migrants at further risk of exploitation and abuse in Libyan detention centres, once intercepted in international waters. By investing heavily in deterrence measures alongside the 'root causes' approach, in other words, the EU is complicit in creating the circumstances that foster irregular and unsafe migration. This is also true of the increasingly restrictive policies around legal entry to Europe. Without a realistic chance to migrate regularly, migrants are effectively pushed to irregular migration by such policies.

To redress some of these failures and fundamental flaws in current European migration management approaches, epitomised by the notion of 'addressing the root causes of irregular migration', I would suggest that more concerted efforts are devoted to (1) addressing and rethinking the intertwinement of European asylum and migration concerns; (2) resuscitating the virtually defunct Global Compact for Safe, Orderly and Regular Migration as an overarching framework for global migration management; and (3) reconceptualising the notion of 'root causes' to include factors that are not restricted to the national and regional context of sending countries. To conclude, I briefly elaborate on these three broad recommendations.

First, much of the political polarisation that is fuelling European policy thinking around migration management concerns the virtual collapse of the EU asylum system during the so-called refugee crisis.[6] To open up more space for policy thinking to move beyond the political pressure to reduce irregular entries to Europe at all costs, the European asylum system must be reformed in a way that is palatable to the most immigration-hostile member states, without compromising on the legal and moral obligation to assist and protect international refugees. The new EU Pact for Migration and Asylum is facing considerable resistance in this regard, but migration governance reform is unlikely without such a framework.

Second, as already implied, the notion of addressing the root causes rather than the symptoms of an illness or a problem seem misplaced as a guiding metaphor for migration management, especially when the delimitation around irregular migration is more or less wilfully forgotten. From the perspectives of migrants, migration is a means to an end, and this end is often to improve the lives of oneself and one's family.

Finally, the notion of 'addressing the root causes of (irregular) migration' could provide a useful metaphor for migration management reform, but in its current framing, it is – ironically – too often restricted to a narrow focus on national and subregional contexts. As Castles and Van Hear argued in the pre-2015 era, '[i]n the long run, migration governance needs to go beyond both border control and root causes approaches, to take account of the interdependence of migration with other key areas of global relations, including trade, investment, development cooperation, security, and international politics' (Castles and Van Hear, 2011: 302–3). One step in this direction would be to reemphasise global inequality as a fundamental driver (or root cause) of African migration to Europe, as well as to highlight the counterproductive effects of deterrence policies in criminalising migrants and enabling irregular alternatives.

To conclude, by investing heavily in addressing the 'root causes' of irregular migration, on the one hand, and patrolling the North African coast, on the other, current policy solutions are missing out on the potentials that are currently hidden in the conceptual gap between migrant aspirations and the routes used to reach Europe. In this gap, considerations of how to proactively reshape migration flows remain subdued by the predominant narratives on how to 'fix' the problem of South–North migration. Any possibility for tapping the immense development potential of international migration remains out of sight. And by treating the symptoms rather than the structural causes, of the administrative deficiencies of European immigration regimes and asylum procedures at both national and EU levels, temporary reductions in the numbers of migrants crossing the Mediterranean Sea are likely to change into renewed 'migration crises' in the future.

Notes

1   For example, while the total revenue from the Central Mediterranean route is estimated to have decreased more than ten-fold between 2017 and 2019, the average cost for the individual migrant is estimated to have tripled during the same period – from €500–€1000 to around €3,000 (Frontex 2020). Considering the amount of money irregular migrants spend just reaching a departure point on the North African coast, it should be clear that the irregular journey is as disproportionately expensive as it is disproportionally dangerous.

2   These numbers accounted for applications to the EU member states, as well as Norway and Switzerland.

3   The former conflict is estimated to have caused at least 32,000 direct civilian deaths over its first ten years (UNAMA, 2019), while the latter is estimated to have caused at least 120,000 direct civilian deaths over a similar time span (IBC 2013).

4   The acronyms in the quote are spelled out in Figure 13.3, except for ECHO, which is the European Civil Protection and Humanitarian Aid Operations.

5   This trade-off is abundantly clear from the current debates surrounding the proposed EU Pact for Asylum and Migration, which has further polarised EU member states over the principle of a shared responsibility to accommodate international refugees.

6   This intertwinement of asylum and migration concerns is nothing new. In 2003, the UNHCR addressed the UN General Assembly, contending that, 'Although different in scope and nature, efforts to develop better systems for migration and for asylum go hand in hand. Asylum systems cannot function effectively without well-managed migration; and migration management will not work without coherent systems and procedures for the international protection of refugees' (UNGA, 2003: 11, quoted in Castles and Van Hear, 2011: 295).

References

Angelucci, M. 2015. 'Migration and financial constraints: Evidence from Mexico'. *Review of Economics and Statistics* 97 (1): 224–228.

Aslany, M., Carling, J., Bålsrud Mjelva, M. and Sommerfelt, T. (2021). 'Systematic review of determinants of migration aspirations', *QuantMig deliverable* 2, 2. Southampton: University of Southampton.

Baird, T. 2017. 'Carrier sanctions in Europe: A comparison of trends in 10 countries', *European Journal of Migration and Law*, 19: 307–34.

Bakewell, O. 2008. 'Keeping them in their place: The ambivalent relationship between development and migration in Africa', *Third World Quarterly*, 29(7): 1341–58.

Bastia, T. and Skeldon, R. 2020. 'Introduction', in T. Bastia and R. Skeldon (eds). *Routledge Handbook of Migration and Development*. London and New York: Routledge, pp. 1–13.

Bazzi, S. 2017. 'Wealth heterogeneity and the income elasticity of migration'. *American Economic Journal: Applied Economics* 9(2): 219–55.

Bjarnesen, J. 2020. *Shifting the Narrative on African Migration: The numbers, the root causes, the alternatives – get them right!* NAI Policy Notes, 2020: 1. Uppsala: The Nordic Africa Institute. Online at: https://nai.uu.se/download/18.a830d416fee1c2549339e3/1581412859413/NAI%20Policy%20Notes%202019%201_Migration_Jesper%20Bjarnesen_Final%20version.pdf (accessed 12 May 2022).

Bjarnesen, J. 2016. 'Between labor migration and forced displacement: Wartime mobilities in the Burkina Faso-Côte d'Ivoire transnational space', *Conflict and Society*, 2: 52–67.

Carling, J. 2017. 'How does migration arise?', in M. McAuliffe and M. Klein Solomon (eds). *Ideas to Inform International Cooperation on Safe, Orderly and Regular Migration*. Geneva: IOM.

Carling, J. and Talleraas, C. 2016. *Root Causes and Drivers of Migration*. PRIO Paper. Oslo: Peace Research Institute Oslo.

Carling, J. and Schewel, K. 2018. 'Revisiting aspiration and ability in international migration', *Journal of Ethnic and Migration Studies*, 44(6): 945–63.

Castles, S. and Van Hear, N. 2011. 'Root causes', in A. Betts (ed.). *Global Migration Governance*. Oxford: Oxford University Press.

Commission of the European Communities (CEC). 2002. Communication from the Commission to the Council and European Parliament on Integrating Migration Issues in the European Union's Relations with Third Countries. COM 2002 703 Final, Brussels: Commission of the European Communities.

Clemens, M. 2014. *Does Development Reduce Migration?* Working Paper No. 359. Washington, DC: Center for Global Development.

Clemens, M. and McKenzie D. 2018. 'Why don't remittances appear to affect growth?' *The Economic Journal*, 128(612): F179–F209.

Clemens, M.A. and Postel, H.M. 2018a. *Deterring Emigration with Foreign Aid: An overview of evidence from low-income countries.* CGD Policy Paper. Washington, DC: Center for Global Development. Online at: https://www.cgdev.org/publication/deterring-emigration-foreign-aid-overviewevidence-low-income-countries (accessed 15 march 2022).

Clemens, M.A. and Postel, H.M. 2018b. 'Can development assistance deter emigration?' CGI Brief. Washington, DC: Center for Global Development.

Crush, J. 2015. 'The EU–ACP migration and development relationship', *Migration and Development*, 4(1): 39–54.

CONCORD Europe. 2018. Partnership or Conditionality? Monitoring the Migration Compacts and EU Trust Fund for Africa. European NGO Confederation for Relief and Development. Brussels: CONCORD Europe.

De Haas, H. 2020. 'Paradoxes of Migration and Development', in T. Bastia and R. Skeldon (eds.) *Routledge Handbook of Migration and Development.* London and New York: Routledge, pp. 17–31.

De Haas, H. 2007. 'Turning the tide? Why development will not stop migration', *Development and Change*, 38(5): 819–41.

European Commission. 2018. Many more to come? Migration from and within Africa. Joint Research Centre, Publications Office of the European Union, Luxembourg.

European Commission. 1995. The European Union and the external dimension of human rights policy: from Rome to Maastricht and beyond. Communication from the Commission to the Council and European Parliament (COM(95) 567 final, paragraphs 72/74).

European Commission. 1994. Communication from the Commission to the Council and the European Parliament on immigration and asylum policies (COM(94) 23 final), Brussels, Foreword, 23 February 1994.

European Commission. 1991. Commission communication to the Council and the European Parliament on immigration (SEC(91) 1855 final), Brussels, S9, 23 October 1991.

European Committee on Migration. 2002. 'Towards a Migration Management Strategy', November 2002, Strasbourg. Online at: https://www.coe.int/t/dg3/migration/archives/Documentation/Migration%20management/Towards_Migration_Management_Strategy_en.pdf (accessed 12 May 2022).

EUTFA. 2019. The EU Emergency Trust Fund for Stability and Addressing Root Causes of Irregular Migration and Displaced Persons in Africa. Brussels: European Union External Action. Online at: https://ec.europa.eu/trustfundforafrica/index_en (accessed 12 May 2022).

Fargues, P. 2017. *Four Decades of Cross-Mediterranean Undocumented Migration to Europe: A review of the evidence.* Geneva: International Organisation for Migration (IOM). Online at: https://publications.iom.int/system/files/pdf/four_decades_of_cross_mediterranean.pdf (accessed 12 May 2022).

Flahaux, M-L. and De Haas, H. 2016. 'African migration: Trends, patterns, drivers', *Comparative Migration Studies,* (4)1. DOI: https://doi.org/10.1186/s40878-015-0015-6.

Frontex. 2020. 'After the money: Prices for people smuggling on Central and Western Mediterranean routes', (europa.eu). News release, 23 June 2020. Online at: https://frontex.europa.eu/media-centre/news/news-release/after-the-money-prices-for-people-smuggling-on-central-and-western-mediterranean-routes-EHDfJg (accessed 15 April 2022).

Glick Schiller, N. 2020. 'Migration and development. Theorising changing conditions and ongoing silences', in T. Bastiaand and R. Skeldon (eds). *Routledge Handbook of Migration and Development.* London and New York: Routledge, pp. 32–42.

Gov.UK 2016. Prime Minister pledges new UK support to help tackle migration crisis. Online at: https://www.gov.uk/government/news/prime-minister-pledges-new-uk-support-to-help-tackle-migration-crisis (accessed 18 March 2022).

Holston, J. and Appadurai, A. 1996. 'Cities and Citizenship'. *Public Culture* 8: 187-204.

Iraq Body Count (IBC). 2013. 'The war in Iraq: 10 years and counting. Analysis of deaths in a decade of violence'. Iraq Body Count, press release, 19 March 2013. Online at: https://www.iraqbodycount.org/analysis/numbers/ten-years/ (accessed 12 May 2022).

Kelmanson, B., Kirabaeva, K., Medina, L., Mircheva, B. and Weiss, J. 2019. *Explaining the Shadow Economy in Europe: Size, causes and policy options.* IMF Working Paper No. 19/278. Washington DC: International Monetary Fund.

Martin, P.L. and Taylor, J.E. 2001. 'Managing migration: The role of economic policies', in A.R. Zolberg and P.M. Benda (eds). *Global Migrants, Global Refugees: Problems and solutions.* New York and Oxford: Berghahn.

Melber, H., Bjarnesen, J., Hallberg Adu, K., Lanzano, C. and Mususa, P. 2020. *The Politics of Citizenship. Social contract and inclusivity in Africa.* NAI Policy Notes 2020: 8. Uppsala: The Nordic Africa Institute. Online at: http://www.diva-portal.org/smash/get/diva2:1508597/FULLTEXT01.pdf (accessed 15 March 2022).

Nyabola, N. 2021, 'First AMMODI Keynote Lecture', June 2021. Online at: http://www.ammodi.com/events (accessed 15 March 2022).

Nyberg-Sørensen, N., Van Hear, N. and Engberg Pedersen, P. 2002. 'The migration–development nexus: Evidence and policy options', *International Migration*, 40: 49–73.

OECD. 2020. *International Migration Outlook 2020.* Paris: OECD Publishing. Online at: https://doi.org/10.1787/ec98f531-en (accessed 15 March 2022).

Oxfam. 2020. 'The EU Trust Fund for Africa: Trapped between aid policy and migration politics'. Oxfam Briefing Paper, January 2020. Nairobi: Oxfam. Online at: https://reliefweb.int/report/world/eu-trust-fund-africa-trapped-between-aid-policy-and-migration-politics (accessed 15 March 2022).

ReliefWeb. 2016. 'Prime Minister pledges new UK support to help tackle migration crisis', World/ReliefWeb. Online at: https://reliefweb.int/report/world/prime-minister-pledges-new-uk-support-help-tackle-migration-crisis (accessed 15 March 2022).

Skeldon, R. 1997. *Migration and Development: A Global Perspective.* London: Longman.

Sirkeci, I. 2005. 'War in Iraq: Environment of insecurity and international migration', *International Migration*, 43(4): 197–214.

Spencer, S. 1996. 'Tackling the root causes of forced migration: The role of the European Union', in European Commission DG 10 (ed.). *The European Union in a Changing World*. Brussels: European Commission.

Tapinos, G.P. 1990. Development Assistance Strategies and Emigration Pressure in Europe and Africa. Washington DC: Commission for the Study of International Migration and Co-operative Economic Development.

Tubiana, J., Warin C. and Saeneen, G.M. 2018. *Multilateral Damage: The impact of EU migration policies on central Saharan routes*. CRU Report, September 2018. Clingendael: Netherlands Institute of International Relations.

UNAMA. 2019. 'Civilian deaths from Afghan conflict in 2018 at highest recorded level – UN Report. United Nations Assistance Mission in Afghanistan, Press release, 24 February 2019. Online at: https://unama.unmissions.org/civilian-deaths-afghan-conflict-2018-highest-recorded-level-%E2%80%93-un-report (12 May 2022).

United Nations General Assembly (UNGA). 2016. New York Declaration for Refugees and Migrants (Resolution 71/1). New York: United Nations.

United Nations General Assembly (UNGA). 2015. Transforming Our world: The 2030 Agenda for Sustainable Development Resolution, 70/1. New York: United Nations.

United Nations General Assembly (UNGA). 2003. 'Strengthening the Capacity of the Office of the UN High Commissioner for Refugees to Carry its Mandate'. Note by the Secretary-General A/58/410 (3 October 2003).

United Nations High Commissioner for Refugees (UNHCR). 2001. Asylum Applications in Industrialized Countries: 1980–1999. Trends in asylum applications lodged in 37, mostly industrialized countries. Geneva: Population Data Unit, Population and Geographic Data Section, November 2001.

Wagner, M. 2011. 'Quantitative overview of asylum seekers from Afghanistan in European countries', in *Conference Reader: Conference on asylum related questions regarding Afghanistan*, Vienna, 31 March–1 April 2011. ICMPD and the County of Origin Information Unit of the Austrian Federal Asylum Office.

Part VI
Civil Society Perspectives

The role of African civil society in implementing the United Nations Global Compact on Migration

Willie A. Eselebor

Introduction

This chapter examines the role of African civil society organisations (CSOs) in the implementation of the Global Compact for Safe, Orderly and Regular Migration (GCM). Up until the so-called 'refugee crisis' of 2015–16, migration was a low priority on the global policy agenda. In the face of widely mediatised images of migrants dying in the Mediterranean Sea en route to Europe, the United Nations (UN) General Assembly issued a declaration calling for greater international cooperation on migration in 2016. This prompted intergovernmental fora to engage with other stakeholders in setting up the GCM for migration governance in 2018, with African CSOs mobilising to influence the global agenda. The assumption underlying the framing of the GCM is that migration does have positive attributes, which should be managed. This engaged the attention of the proponents of the global policy agenda themed *safe, orderly and regular migration*, which aligns with target 10.7 of the Sustainable Development Goals (SDGs) (Agenda

2030). The GCM is the first international instrument that addresses problems of irregular migration through a coordinated global action.

Although it is difficult to strictly separate the interests of the Global North from those of the Global South, most African CSOs were coordinated by the Migration and Development Civil Society Network (MADE) in the process of developing the migration compact. From 28–29 August 2017, the CSOs' consultation in Africa was piloted by the Pan-African Network in Defense of Migrants' Rights (PANiDMR) and MADE-Afrique in Mali. Prior to this, these networks traditionally focused more on the smuggling of migrants, trafficking in human beings or migrants' human rights, rarely paying much attention to policy implementation, which this chapter aims to address. More recently, CSOs have become increasingly involved in the policy-making arena, raising new questions about interests, capacities and strategies. However, sustainable policy outcomes depend on accurate understandings of existing problems and stakeholders, and CSOs are renewing their claims to relevance in this regard.

It further examines the role of African civil society in the implementation of the GCM, with a point of departure in two central policy instruments: the 2018 UN GCM and the African Union (AU) Revised Migration Policy Framework for Africa (MPFA) of 2018. The chapter argues that these two policy documents are similar in many regards, and that their overall approaches and recommendations are closely connected to other regional and Regional Economic Communities' (RECs) instruments. It is also argued that these share a fundamental flaw in their failure to assign specific roles to these African CSOs in the implementation process at all levels. This explains the absence of any standard operating procedure in either framework to empower African CSOs to function optimally.

The GCM is a set of 23 actionable objectives – which are consistent with the 17 Goals of Agenda 2030 (target 10.7: facilitate orderly, safe and responsible migration and mobility of people) – that address migration management. The AU revised Migration Policy Framework for Africa (AU-MPFA) and Plan of Action (2018–30) is about migration governance, which aims to facilitating safe, orderly and dignified migration. It consists of eight pillars and aligns with the AU Agenda 2063, with 20 Goals (target 8: a united Africa on migration). The GCM is global in nature, whereas the MPFA is regional and specific to Africa. However, both documents uphold the sovereignty of states, and are not legally binding, while fostering a collaborative effort in the context of migration management (GCM) or governance (MPFA). The chapter reflects on the limitations of CSOs in setting the agenda around global migration governance and examines the opportunities for strengthening their impact on migration policy action plans in the future.

The analysis is based on a selective review of academic and grey literature on migration governance, migration policy and the workings of CSOs. The GCM and the AU-MPFA documents were purposively selected for analysis to determine the role of African CSOs in the implementation process. Grey literature from the International Organization for Migration (IOM), the UN High Commission for Refugees (UNHCR), the International Labour Organization (ILO), the UN Department of Economic and Social Affairs (UNDESA), and the World Bank were submitted to content analysis. Treaties, protocols and policy briefs from governments and research institutions were also considered.

Understanding migration governance

Migration governance is not a new concept, but as a policy domain it has become increasingly visible and contested, especially in defining the relationship between the Global North and the Global South. For more than a decade, a cornerstone in measuring the performance of a democracy has been the principle of good governance. Several critical factors are implied in this principle, such as transparency, accountability, inclusiveness, and unhindered associational life, beyond state influence. Governance is thus presumed to be good, although it is difficult to achieve if it is not based on the rule of law, efficient, and responsive to the needs of the citizens. This understanding of good governance is not just important for politicians and lawmakers but is also seen as a central tenet of development cooperation and poverty reduction.

According to Anan (2002: 51): 'Good governance is perhaps the single most important factor in eradicating poverty and promoting development.' Increasingly, since the 1980s, donors have been demanding good governance as a condition for granting aid packages to developing nations, including African countries, because of previous abuses, corruption, and the politics of exclusion. The new demands were also based on global responses to curtailing dictatorships and human rights abuses, and to promote a Western model of democracy. Global migration governance follows this trajectory, and as a field of policy-making, it is particularly apt in illustrating the underlying power asymmetries of global North–South relations.

While formal government bureaus may be understood to be the lead agents in policy-making and implementation, in practice, governance may be conducted by a combination of corporate, international, national and local transactional agencies. Most African governments play a key role in border and migration governance and tend to be relatively unhindered when it comes to exercising their power as to whom to include or exclude in their decision-making processes. From this vantage point, governments may be inclined to work primarily with formal or informal groups, whose scope and activities do not pose a significant threat to the government's policy agenda. The principles of good governance, such as participation, consensus, accountability, transparency, responsiveness, efficiency, inclusiveness and the rule of law are thus recognised and adhered to, but often only to the extent that the government finds appropriate.

The general principles and workings of (good) governance are also reflected in global migration governance. Migration governance, according to the IOM (2015: 3) can be understood as 'the traditions and institutions by which authority on migration, mobility and nationality in a country is exercised, including the capacity of the government to effectively formulate and implement sound policies in these areas'. This understanding aligns with the concept of good governance, but in the context of the GCM and other regional instruments, adherence to international best practices may not necessarily translate into meeting the socio-economic wellbeing of the affected migrants. As a highly politicised policy field, migration governance has tended to be directed more towards the priorities of the Global North than to the realities and needs of the sending countries in the Global South. As the IOM (2015: 5) has noted, this tendency to prioritise policies that steer clear of political controversy may be justified as an effort not to stir anti-immigrant sentiments and other fears stoked by European populist politics.

However, the assumption that global governance instruments will alleviate the unfulfilled aspirations of the African youth cohorts, who want to escape the harsh realities of life and migrate to Europe, can be illusory. Good governance has not solved the problems of corruption in Africa either. The inhumane detention centres in Libya and elsewhere, in part funded by the European Union, will not change the irregular surge. It is in response to these fundamental shortcomings in migration governance that CSOs have attempted to create a wider space for advocacy and direct policy dialogue, appealing to the general principles of inclusive governance considered earlier.

Understanding the role of civil society organisations

As previously discussed, policy-making is carried out through a process of consultation with relevant stakeholders, and this has become a guiding principle of most states and multilateral bodies. Migration is a multifaceted social phenomenon, which makes it imperative to involve a broad range of institutions at different times and stages of the policy-making and implementation process. While policy-making used to be an exclusive domain of the state, the devolution of power from states to international and supra-national authorities (the UN, the AU and RECs) has enhanced the opportunity to include non-state actors such as the private sector, the media, and civil societies in public decision-making processes.

There is no consensus on which agencies or actors should be classified as CSOs, non-governmental organisations (NGOs) or community-based organisations. Generally, the World Economic Forum (2013: 8) and the African Development Bank (AfDB, 2012:10) understand NGOs as CSOs. Examples of CSOs involved in policy-making and aid delivery include faith-based organisations, community-based organisations, cultural groups, and professional associations, among others. CSOs reflect the circumstances and challenges of their respective domains of operation. The AfDB posits that civil society is 'the voluntary expression of the interests and aspirations of citizens organised and united by common interests, goals, values or traditions and mobilised into collective action' (AfDB, 2012: 10). This definition serves well to capture the broad areas of civic involvement in migration governance, ranging from employment policies to family dynamics, and from money transfers to the central issue of diaspora relations.

The evolution of CSOs has revealed that they target their roles in policy implementation in terms of transparency and accountability. However, there is a need to question *which* role they should play on migration governance, whose interests they serve, and whether they have the capacity and competencies to deliver on those responsibilities. In compiling this study focusing on the mandate, the civic space and the specialisation of African CSOs working on migration, it became apparent how little information exists about these actors. For example, an online search for African CSOs on migration governance delivered no substantial results. By contrast, searches on international NGOs like Missing Migrants or ActionAid, and multilateral agencies like the International Organization for Migration (IOM), the International Labour Organization (ILO), and the United Nations High Commission for Refugees (UNCHR) provide easy access to details of their respective mandates, what they do and how they operate. The web absence reflects much less visibility of African CSOs working on migration governance.

In terms of their mandates and operational modalities, African CSOs seem to be following the inclination summarised by Florini (2000: 213), who observed that, '[s]ome civil society groups are moving beyond the role of advocate and monitor, providing services directly, implementing governmental policies'. Indeed, inadequate funding has made existing CSOs rely on small projects to generate income as survival strategies. The following section elaborates on the role of CSOs in migration governance, with particular emphasis on African organisations and stakeholders.

Understanding civil society involvement in migration governance

The growing relevance of migration governance globally brings the need to include civil society content to the fore to create spaces and invigorate trust-building for an engagement with state actors and advocacy in the field of migration. This is not unconnected to the roles that CSOs, in collaboration with other alliances, played in pushing for development as a precursor to the UN Millennium Development Goals (MDGs 2015), now replaced by UN Agenda 2030, which accords priority to migration and development (target 10.7).

Migrant and migration advocacy groups, including diasporas, became more formally organised and held wider consultations in Mali in 2017 to deliberate on a common agenda as part of the pre-GCM negotiation. This is not to suggest that African CSOs working in the field of migration governance did not exist before, but that they fundamentally changed the recognition accorded to migration at the UN level, as well as the expectations of their roles going forward in this unfolding scenario. This process created an expanded space for CSOs dealing with transnational organised crime, migrants' action, labour matters, diasporas and remittances. Another factor that boosted the entry of several non-state actors into the field of migration, was an increase in the UN funding of migration-related issues.

There are some CSOs pushing for a broad, human rights-based approach to migration and development. For instance, the People's Global Action on Migration, Development and Human Rights (PGA) is of particular interest because it combines the UN 2030 Agenda for Sustainable Development with migration issues. However, there is insufficient research on CSOs by African scholars; this is supported by Betts (2010a) who identified the near absence of critical academic studies into what roles CSOs should play in migration in terms of visioning or formulating migration policies that enhance human development.

Migration and its governance policies have become central themes in global discourses, yet it has not been resolved. It is important to recognise that research on the involvement of CSOs in global governance have been introduced by scholars from the Global North like Kalm and Uhlin (2015), Piper and Grugel (2015), and Rother (2018), who provided understandings on policy practices through evidence-based processes. These contributions are pivotal, but literature at the African regional level is sadly lacking. It is recognised that scientific research could enrich the engagement of CSOs, which would impact positively on more balanced global narratives on governance.

Scholte (2011) has argued for the critical need to engage CSOs to improve migration governance processes. Linking migration to the Sustainable Development Goals may also provide the opportunity to leverage on the experience of similar CSOs attuned to development interventions. Migration-related CSOs are important to Africa, because sending, transit, and receiving countries benefit from assistances rendered, which governments alone cannot cover adequately. In addition, Africa generates but also accommodates refugees and asylum seekers. Areas in which African CSOs should be active include conducting surveys and situation analyses of migration flows, which would be useful for planning as well as migration management, especially where data is identified as lacking. This is the domain of academic research and migration training institutes. This aligns with the GCM priority focus of promoting data-driven migration discourse, policy and planning.

Linking data sourcing to migration management would confirm or confute the contested narratives on the smuggling of migrants, and the return and reintegration of irregular migrants. The roles of CSOs in Africa are generally hindered by a lack of access to institutions that collect official data, which are mostly border security agencies. Data collected by CSOs from diasporas, and community and faith-based organisations are sometimes unreliable, and the official statistics from national bureaus are often outdated. Building synergy in the areas of data management requires the collaborative effort of all migration stakeholders. This would greatly assist in determining migration numbers, trends of inflow and outflow, and analyses of irregular migration to assist in planning responses at the continental level.

The protection of asylum seekers and refugees, and the search for durable solutions remains underresourced. The UN Convention 51 stipulates the principle of non-refoulement and the protection of persons affected by war or life-threatening circumstances, who are forced to relocate and migrate across borders for safety reasons. This also includes return and readmission formalities. The involuntary return and outright expulsion of migrants can be dehumanising – this is another sphere where CSOs engaged in human rights and humanitarian actions are most needed. Currently there are other unfolding dimensions of statelessness in Africa, which are presenting difficulties. For instance, the Kingdom of Morocco and the Polisario Front are unable to reach agreement on claims to separation in the Western Sahara, which has dislocated large numbers of Sahrawi people, who are living in camps in Algeria as stateless persons.

The pre-GCM negotiations in 2017 and 2018 to refine principles around labour, migrant workers' rights and obligations attracted the attention of the policy drafters. The final document on labour migration was captured in UN (2018a) Objective 5, which calls on states to consider options of 'temporary, seasonal, circular, and fast-track programmes in areas of labour shortages' to '[e]nhance availability and flexibility of pathways for regular migration'. This speaks to the comprehensive nature of the compact and the technical inputs from several UN organs. ILO conventions stipulate equal treatment for migrant workers, yet these are the most vulnerable and abused in destination countries.

Significant inputs were made in the GCM regarding the role migrants play in development and how to engage the diaspora for national development and harnessing remittances. Suggestions were made to ensure the involvement of the diaspora in the development of host communities and sending nations. The GCM, like the MPFA, created an enabling environment for diaspora activities to thrive, through recognition of dual citizenship, skills, and ease of remittance of earned income and benefits. This will foster development and change the negative perception of Africans migrating to the Global North as economic migrants.

CSOs and the UN Global Compact for Safe, Orderly and Regular Migration

CSOs are represented in the MPFA to assist and complement governments on issues related to the protection, return and readmission of migrants, as well as research, and advocacy for migrants' rights. The CSOs support vulnerable migrants, and asylum and refuge seekers in terms of service delivery, not limited to humanitarian interventions. They advocate for best practices in migration governance, especially when it comes to migrants' rights and safety, including decisions to regularise stays and work permits. This also includes facilitating regular migration and addressing irregular migration. The CSOs are clearly active in advocacy for the protection of minors, unaccompanied children, trafficking in persons and smuggling of humans in all ramifications.

The Global Compact for Safe, Orderly and Regular Migration, which is often referred to simply as the GCM, was conceived to address the shortcomings of global migration governance, especially as these shortcomings were made visible during the 2015 European refugee crisis. The CSOs participated in all the processes leading to the final document signed in 2018, but the roles they are expected to play in the implementation process need to be scrutinised. Since the aim, objectives and guiding principles of the GCM are outlined in the policy document, it is important to interrogate the challenges facing African CSOs in the implementation process.

The GCM adopted by the United Nations General Assembly in 2018 is an outcome of the New York Declaration of 19 September 2016, a resolution of the UN General Assembly, which enjoined stakeholders, including national governments to improve coordination and governance of migration globally. Thus, 152 member nations, except for Algeria and

Libya in Africa, endorsed the GCM. The GCM (2018: 2) sits on three pillars of *common understanding, shared responsibilities* and *unity of purpose regarding migration*; and the envisaged success rests on trust, determination and the solidarity of stakeholders to accomplish the objectives and commitments set forth for implementation. For Africa, the GCM's focus is on cross-cutting issues that are germane at the national and subregional levels. The strategy followed a comprehensive approach calling for the inclusion of migration in the key sectors of education, health, the economy and development planning.

The guiding principles include the following: it is people centred, with a strong human dimension; it is based on international cooperation; it affirms the rights and sovereignty of nations to determine their migration policy; and it upholds the rule of law and due process in migration governance. Other key principles are sustainable development, human rights, child sensitivity and gender responsiveness. Finally, it involves both government and society in migration governance. The GCM framework consist of 23 objectives; strategies for implementation and evaluation. The objectives are all intended to support dialogue and deepen collaboration on migration issues.

This initiative represents a model in evidence-based policy, in which five thematic areas of demographic imbalances, economic inequalities, conflict, disaster, and the impacts of climate change, will be examined, taking into consideration the input from relevant CSOs.

What has become obvious is that the AU cannot bear the migration burden alone, thus the need to build synergy with stakeholders to overcome the challenges, which have become threatening. The AU held a meeting with CSOs in this regard, after the adoption of the GCM in Marrakech in December 2018, to determine actionable strategies that would benefit migrants in Africa.

In the area of demographic imbalance, the CSOs have committed to promote fact-based and data-driven migration discourse, policy and planning, which were elaborated in Objectives 1 and 3 of the GCM. To address issues related to economic inequality and poverty, the CSOs committed to engage with the diaspora, who are contributors to development, both in host and sending countries. This aligns with Objectives 18, 19 and 20 of the GCM. There are several areas outlined in the objectives of the GCM (23) that enables CSOs to practise in the field of migration. These include supporting migrants' associations, innovations in monetary transfers, youth and women empowerment, and skills acquisition for vulnerable groups.

In response to the growing political and policy concerns about migration governance, international migration research is expanding in the fields of politics, economics, security and social and development studies, but there is surprisingly little academic research by scholars of African descent. This explains why awareness of the GCM is generally low on the continent, thus challenging South–South academic exchanges.

CSOs are becoming important in managing borders in a well-secured and coordinated manner, which reduces incidences of abuse, corruption, conflicts, and disaster-induced migration. Climate action is also recognised as a field of advocacy, where CSOs have proven their mantle of leadership in Africa. This is contained in Objective 2 of the GCM, which deals with natural disasters, the adverse effects of climate change, and environmental degradation. Currently there is a focus on transhumance and the mobility of herders from the Western Sahel southward, which continues to engender conflicts.

CSOs and the AU Revised Migration Policy Framework for Africa

In 2018 the AU revised its Migration Policy Framework for Africa (MPFA) and Plan of Action (2018–30) to cover new areas, including the diaspora, migrant labour, migrants' rights, internal migration, migration data management, and development. The MPFA and Plan of Action is a parallel policy at the regional level. It is non-binding and contains guidelines to assist RECs and national authorities in migration governance. The revised MPFA and Plan of Action is the result of a performance evaluation of the initial 2006 MPFA draft document. In context, it facilitated other policy reforms that cumulated in the African Continental Free Trade Area, 2018, the AU Protocol to the Treaty Establishing the African Economic Community Relating to the Free Movement of Persons, Right of Residence and Right of Establishment adopted in 2018 and Agenda 2063.

The Economic Community of West African States (ECOWAS), in a retreat held with the UNHCR, agreed to jointly address issues of protection and mixed flows. Mixed flow refers to the movement of asylum seekers, refugees and economic migrants. Finding durable solutions to this form of irregular migration is engaging the attention of ECOWAS, the Southern African Development Community (SADC) and UNCHR under a collaborative framework, in which they will focus on voluntary returns and local integration efforts. ECOWAS has committed to the principles of the Global Compact on Refugees (GCR) adopted by the UN General Assembly on 17 December 2018, which aims to build a Comprehensive Refugee Response Framework (CRRF) and measures to implement sustainable solutions to issues on refugees. The CRRF is an action plan on burden- and responsibility-sharing, under collaborative arrangement between the UNCHR, and regional and national mechanisms. It involves procedures for funding, partnerships, and data gathering and sharing in the domain of needs and support for refugees.

In similar collaboration in 2019, involving Regional Economic Communities (RECs) in Africa, the UNHCR also signed a memorandum of understanding with the SADC on the protection of refugees and stateless persons in the region, in alignment with the provisions of the CRRF and in furtherance of the spirit of the GCR. The GCR lays out the guidelines for a comprehensive response to the crisis of refugees. It calls for greater support for refugees and the countries that host them.

Challenges facing African CSOs in migration governance

In addition to the specific shortcomings and restraints of the two policy frameworks considered above, African CSOs face a range of additional challenges to making an impact on migration governance. First, migration governance is often handled in conjunction with the security sector, and border controls cannot be divorced from state sovereignty. The autonomy of the state still subsists, despite the prevalence of supranational authority, which imposes some limits on nation-states. The principles of non-intervention in the governance of migration still dominate. This is why Nigeria partially closed its borders due to escalating security concerns, despite ECOWAS's policy on open borders. The misuse of what constitute national security in West Africa has also enabled some EU member states to contract third countries to control borders to reduce migrant flows from the Global South to the North. In context, therefore, while the benefits of migration in some instances far outweigh the negative impacts, the phenomenon remains a challenge for both sending and receiving states.

In these ways, the migration–security nexus severely complicates and limits the scope of CSOs' involvement and impact. The inability to control the entry of not only migrants, but also harmful substances into a country can lead to instability and insecurity. This explains why the United States withdrew from the GCM in December 2017. Border security is about promoting safe, orderly, and regular migration, or reducing irregular migration. Therefore, competent control filters the good from the bad. Whereas the GCM is a subtle pathway to non-threatening migration governance, the non-binding approach makes it suspect when it comes to independent monitoring and enforcement of procedures. African CSOs have never been welcomed as monitors and watchdogs on governmental institutions exercising sovereign controls over national borders. They have been perceived more as spies and sometimes as activists or enemies of the government. The disdain for these groups has not changed fundamentally despite democracy and the enthronement of the rule of law. This, in part, explains the reluctance to mainstream CSOs into policy debates and decision-making. This is especially true because most of the recognition accorded to migration policy is fairly recent and driven by external actors, rather than the African states themselves.

Another major challenge is the issue of funding and limited investment in charity in most African states. The reluctance to embrace corporate social responsibility may be due to suspicion about the transparency and accountability of CSOs, as well as a lack of incentive to invest in measures to improve the wellbeing of the less privileged. Mechanisms for monitoring and reporting are often lacking and attempts to monitor the earnings of civil societies are also resisted. Of course, this reluctance is not limited to African CSOs.

Furthermore, African CSOs are still a relatively new phenomenon, and they generally have weak organisational foundations. These institutions need to mature over time. This immaturity also extends to a limited access to in-field experience, which limits the possibility for consolidating and expanding staff competence. Because most CSOs in Africa are poorly funded, they have limited access to training to update their knowledge, skills and attitudes. Humanitarian work is technical in nature, dealing with supply-chain management, fund raising, and the distribution of relief materials, especially when working with refugee and asylum camps.

Contrary to the major international NGOs, CSOs and smaller NGOs struggle to recruit and retain qualified staff, which further inhibits their capacity to operate effectively.

Strengthening African CSOs in migration governance

The UN and AU frameworks for migration governance also hold potential for more decisive CSO involvement in migration governance. Indeed, both the GCM and MPFA innovatively depoliticised migration problems by bringing together different stakeholders and, most importantly, by adopting a holistic approach involving both government and society in solving the problems of irregular migration. This created a space for CSOs to engage with the trajectories of irregular migration. The GCM facilitated a dialogue between sending and receiving countries on joint problem-solving. The co-option of different UN multilateral agencies, like the IOM, the UNCHR and the ILO, to produce a compact document is evidence of synergy at the global level, which should be replicated at the regional level. It represents a significant milestone regarding labour migration, the rights of migrants, the protection of refugees and asylum seekers, and the rescue of irregular migrants in distress in the Mediterranean Sea.

Further analysis of the GCM and MPFA established the links between migration and development, which explains why the UN Agenda 2030 and the AU Agenda 2063 are important for addressing poverty, which is often touted as a factor responsible for irregular migration. Others include an absence of peace, security, and climate change. Conflicts, wars and instabilities are triggers for asylum and refugee flows in Africa. Both documents created opportunities for migrants and diasporas to be recognised as contributing to sustainable development. This includes issues relating to remittances and improved legislations in Africa to cater for migrant workers.

The GCM also allowed for technical mobility agreements to be negotiated between European partners and the AU on migration challenges. This has engendered several cooperative interventions by the EU in capacity-building on good border management, the funding of returns, and reintegration activities in focal sending countries like Nigeria. Overall, African CSOs need to take ownership of the policy cycle in relation to migration governance and claim a leading role in formulating and owning policies designed to achieve economic, social, environmental, and other development goals.

In this light, there are several opportunities for African CSOs working in the field of migration governance. CSOs need to research migration-related problems and dynamics to represent the realities on the ground from a more actor-oriented perspective. This work requires funding, which raises the question of the capacity and competencies of CSOs in Africa. Situational and stakeholder analysis are important tools for migration governance. While situational analysis can be predictive, serving the purpose of early warning, stakeholder analysis enables one to identify the primary, secondary and tertiary actors, or potential spoilers, who may obstruct policy implementation. In addition, influencers with close links to policymakers should be consulted. This is evident in the role of state-centric (immigration, police, anti-trafficking agencies) institutions in Africa that are desirous of adapting new ideas from the external world.

In addition to providing up-to-date analyses of the realities, CSOs in Africa have the opportunity to be not only implementers, but also mobilisers for action with larger international organisations as well as local communities and stakeholders. Gaining active support from actors that see the policy as desirable or beneficial requires lobbying of interest groups, the legislature, faith-based organisations, and other agencies or persons who are directly or indirectly affected by and involved in such interventions.

In terms of their organisational structures and practices, African CSOs need to articulate and delimit their contributions in relation to other actors in the field, and work to strengthen their operations. It is unlikely that they will be able to match the resources and influence of the major international NGOs in the field of migration governance, but based on the accepted principles of civic inclusion in policy-making processes, they do have a particular niche which they should use. African CSOs must learn to build coalitions and alliances to strengthen their position and capacity to intervene and to influence decision-making. Alliances with the media, public health providers, criminal justice systems, and faith-based organisations are crucial in this line of work.

Seeking common cause should also extend to other CSOs. Collaborative governance is about partnering, cooperation and joint problem-solving, but some CSOs engage in mutual competition rather than building synergy. CSOs need to pool their resources and improve the quality of local partnerships and technical support. In short, CSOs in Africa need to rethink their roles in relation to migration governance and adjust their policies and practices accordingly. CSOs can also strengthen their bid by improving their dialogue with strategic change agents. The key to influencing policy is access to policy- and decision-makers, and to be ready to offer well-articulated and context-specific policy solutions. Such engagement requires organisations to be able to adapt continuously and adjust their messaging, and also to remain humble to the fact that agencies and organisations are complex institutions that do not change easily.

In addition, there are advantages in clearly stating organisational values, ethics and standards. Value statements help to profile an organisation in an increasingly crowded policy field and provide guidance and consistency in interventions. A clear value statement is seen as one aspect of the overall strategy to build trust around what a CSO commits to do, how it intends to achieve this, and how it could be of benefit to others. African CSOs need to be skilled in monitoring and evaluating their programmes, and comply with international standards for reporting and accountability, to earn the trust of their international partners.

Conclusion

The GCM has facilitated new vistas for Africa to influence how migration should be governed at the national, regional and continental levels. The traction gained by the GCM also connects with other policy frameworks, including the UN's Agenda 2030 and Agenda 2063, the AU's MPFA, and other REC mechanisms. These are strategic policy spheres around which the role of African civil society has been interrogated in this chapter. The discussion has focused on how the CSOs are involved in implementation rather than policy design or political advocacy, since the current agenda on migration governance has been characterised by a growing emphasis on the challenges of multilateral implementation practices. Migration has also expanded into the sphere of international development cooperation, especially the Sustainable Development Goals (target 10.7) and Agenda 2063 (target 8), requiring holistic multisectoral approaches. In short, there are clearly roles for CSOs in the implementation of policies concerning migration governance, and a need for informed reflection on how these roles may be defined and achieved. African scholars should be able to play a much more central role in this reflection than has been the case thus far.

This chapter's examination of the role of African civil society in the implementation of the GCM has provided several reflections on the potential space created by the GCM and strategies on which African CSOs may rely. In addition to the above, the following strategies are suggested:

First, the GCM is a new and non-binding agreement, which makes it fluid and non-mandatory for nations to implement. This means that for African CSOs, the unfolding scenario of a 'whole-of-government' approach is innovative and a departure from previous regimes of migration governance. However, in the context of a 'whole-of-society' approach, the non-state actors are not as organised as formal government structures. In essence it calls for the involvement of multi-stakeholders in two aspects: horizontal links across governmental ministries and vertical connectedness traversing administrative levels, including non-state actors like civil society and research institutions. This also entails strengthening cooperation and coordination mechanisms at all levels.

Second, African CSOs generally have not developed into coalitions, because some of the prop-up cells are formless and have not evolved as institutions with enduring structures. Coalition and partnership are required to manage migration, since it is multisectoral in nature. No one agency can boast of a complete pool of expertise, so collaboration with similar agencies become imperative. One can learn from how all the UN specialised agencies collaborated in drafting the GCM, with buy-in from the majority of nations and interested stakeholders. CSOs operating at the community and grassroots levels are still lacking competencies on migration issues. This hurdle needs to be overcome through training, capacity-building and learning on the job, to make them effective.

Third, the expansion and inclusion of multisectoral coalitions require building the capacity of the new actors on diverse migration-related issues. For example, the inclusion of a ministry of education in migration issues requires building-capacity on curriculum development; and involving a department of health requires a set of new skills to deal with transnational health-related issues, such as the COVID-19 pandemic. Dealing with data collection for analyses of situations, demographics and patterns of flow, means developing new skills to address gaps in capacities. Practically, the geography and routes of irregular migration are shifting continuously, requiring expert knowledge in geographic information systems. These are new technologies that should be mainstreamed into migration governance.

Fourth, this study also uncovered a variety of multilevel policy instruments, which accounts for the lack of coordination among multisectoral actors. Steps to improve migration governance should include consolidating the roles of non-state actors and civil society, including aligning them with local, national and regional policies. REC mechanisms are more firmly rooted in dealing with identified problems, but they may have changing priorities and conflicts of interest on how to align national and regional migration plans into a compact agenda. Funding migration remains a huge challenge in Africa because of limited resources.

In conclusion, a comprehensive mapping of African CSOs and specific areas in which they have expertise should be identified. This could be disaggregated into various streams such as protection, returns, migrant health, gender issues, legal requirements and migrant labour. In addition, specialities like asylum, refugees, statelessness, programme monitoring and evaluation should be included. Currently, there are very few institutions that train to building competencies in this field in Africa. Research institutions must consider migration as a contemporary problem that requires further research to achieve more efficient service delivery in the future.

References

Anan, K. 2002. 'Democratic governance for human development'. Excerpt from *Human Development Report 2002: Deepening democracy in a fragmented world*. New York: UNDP.

African Union Commission (AUC). 2018. *Migration Policy Framework for Africa and Plan of Action (2018–2030)*. Online at: https://au.int/sites/default/files/documents/35956-doc-2018_mpfa (accessed 20 April 2020).

African Union Commission (AUC). 2015. Agenda 2063: 'The Africa We Want', pp. 1–24. Online at: https://au.int/en/au-nutshell (accessed 28 April 2020).

African Development Bank (AfDB). 2012. *Framework for Enhanced Engagement with Civil Society Organisations*. Abidjan: African Development Bank.

Betts, A. 2010a. 'Global Migration Governance: The emergence of a new debate'. Global Economic Governance Programme, University of Oxford, Oxford. Online at: https://www.migrationinstitute.org/files/news/global-migration-governance_paper_2010.pdf (accessed 28 April 2020).

Betts, A. 2010b. 'The refugee regime complex', *Refugee Survey Quarterly*, 29(1), 12–37.

Brinkerhoff, D. and Crosby, B. 2002. *Managing Policy Reform: Concepts and tools for decision-makers in developing and transitioning countries*. Bloomfield, CT: Kumarian Press.

Florini, A.M. (ed.). 2000. *The Third Force: The rise of transnational civil society*. Tokyo: Japan Center for International Exchange and Washington, DC: Carnegie Endowment for International Peace.

Grindle, M.S. and J.W. Thomas. 1991. 'Implementing reform: Arenas, stakes and resources', in M.S. Grindle and J.W. Thomas (eds). *Public Choices and Policy Reform: The political economy of reform in developing countries*. Baltimore, MD: Johns Hopkins University Press, pp. 121–50.

International Organization for Migration (IOM). (2015). Migration Governance Framework. Council Decision C/106/40 Online at: https://governingbodies.iom.int/system/files/en/council/106/C-106-40-Migration-Governance-Framework.pdf (accessed 28 April 2020).

Kalm, S. and Uhlin, A. 2015. *Civil Society and the Governance of Development. Opposing global institutions*. Basingstoke: Palgrave Macmillan.

Piper, N. and Grugel, J. 2015. 'Global migration governance, social movements and the difficulties of promoting migrant rights', in C.-U. Schierup, R. Munck, B. Likic-Brboric and A. Neergaard (eds). *Migration, Precarity and Global Governance. Challenges for labour*. Oxford: Oxford University Press, pp. 261–79.

Rother, S. 2018. 'The Global Forum on Migration and Development (GFMD) as a venue of state socialization: A stepping stone for multi-level migration governance?' *Journal of Ethnic and Migration Studies*, 45(111): 1–17.

Scholte, J.A. (ed.). 2011. *Building Global Democracy? Civil society and accountable global governance*. Cambridge: Cambridge University Press.

World Bank. 1997. *World Development Report 1997: The state in a changing world*. Oxford: Oxford University Press.

World Bank. 1991. *World Development Report 1991*. Oxford: Oxford University Press.

World Economic Forum. 2013. *The Future Role of Civil Society*. World Economic Forum in collaboration with KPMG International.

United Nations. 2019. The Global Compact for Safe, Orderly and Regular Migration, in General Assembly Resolution 73/195, adopted on 19 December 2018, UN Doc. A/RES/73/195 (19 January 2019).

United Nations. 2017. *International Migration Report 2017*. Department of Economic and Social Affairs, Population Division. Online at: https://www.un.org/en/development/desa/population/migration/publications/

migrationreport/docs/migrationreport2017.pdf (accessed 10 May 2020).

United Nation. 2016. Resolution 71/1 – New York Declaration for Refugees and Migrants. Online at: https://www.un.org/en/development/desa/population/migration/generalassembly/docs/globalcompact/A_RES_71_1.pdf (accessed 10 May 2020).

The role of European civil society in implementing the United Nations Global Compact on Migration

Anna Knoll

Introduction

Over the years, migration has become a complex phenomenon. One state or actor in isolation cannot manage the challenges and opportunities of transnational migration. Successful migration governance requires not only cooperation across government actors but also involves a whole-of-society engagement, which includes non-state actors such as civil society, businesses, universities and the media. These actors increasingly build informal and formal relationships with governments, while also critically observing, challenging and contributing to migration governance.

The United Nations (UN) Global Compact for Safe, Orderly and Regular Migration (GCM), adopted by 164 nations in 2018, is the first of its kind and lays out the key principles for international migration governance. It includes 23 objectives covering a comprehensive migration governance agenda. By setting out actionable commitments, ranging from the collection and utilisation of data for evidence-based policies, and pathways for regular migration, to combatting trafficking and strengthening the transnational response to migrant smuggling, the GCM aims to comprehensively guide international cooperation on migrants and human mobility. The GCM recognises the role of civil society and includes commitments to a 'whole-of-society' approach. With the GCM, nations have pledged to 'implement the Global Compact in cooperation and partnership with migrants, civil society, migrant and diaspora organisations, faith-based organisations, local authorities and communities, the private sector, trade unions, parliamentarians …' (UN General Assembly, 2019: §44).

Most of the European Union (EU) member states adopted the GCM, with a smaller number opting out of the framework. While the GCM is a state-led process, European civil society groups played an important role in the lead up to the GCM, by organising consultative sessions, inputting into the process, and advising on key priorities in the European migration context. They did so at the national levels as well as through global processes such as the Civil Society Days of the Global Forum on Migration and Development (GFMD). During the 2017 Berlin meeting of the GFMD, civil society organisations had the idea to develop a 'Global Compact from below', which led to over 230 civil society actors issuing 'Ten Acts for the Global Compact – A civil society vision for a transformative agenda for human mobility, migration and development' (MADE, n.d.).[1]

This chapter explores the roles of European civil society actors in the implementation of the GCM and European migration governance more broadly. It briefly reviews the state of play of GCM implementation in the EU and highlights some trends and challenges that European civil society organisations face in the migration sector, specifically looking at Search and Rescue, provision of services to migrants, and their role as critical observers of European border governance.

Roles of civil society actors in GCM implementation

European civil society plays a variety of roles in the implementation of the GCM and in European migration governance more broadly. While there is no universally accepted definition of 'civil society', the EU understands it as forms of 'social action carried out by individuals or groups who are neither connected to, nor managed by, the state.'[2] The United Nations describe it as the 'third sector', next to government and private business.[3]

Civil society actors active in migration include non-governmental and non-profit organisations, foundations, diaspora organisations, social or political movements related to migration, faith-based or religious institutions, trade unions, and advocacy groups, among others. Several umbrella organisations or networks[4] also exist, pursuing the specific joint perspectives and interests of their members. In the European context, these include networks dedicated solely to migrant or refugee issues, such as the European Council on Refugees and Exiles (ECRE), the Migration and Development Civil Society Network (MADE),[5] and the Platform for International Cooperation on Undocumented Migrants (PICUM). They also include broader civil society umbrella organisations dealing with migration together with other topics, such as the European non-governmental organisation (NGO) Confederation for Relief and Development (CONCORD). As laid out in the treaty of the EU, the European Economic and Social Committee (EESC) represents civil society at an EU level, advising the other EU bodies such as the European Parliament, Council, and the Commission.[6] Since 2015, the EESC has organised five editions of the 'European Migration Forum' – a platform for dialogue between civil society and the European institutions.

This diverse set of civil society actors forms an integral and critical part of migration infrastructures (Xiang and Lindquist, 2014) and pursues a variety of roles and objectives, ranging from organisations providing services to migrants and refugees, to carrying out research and sharing knowledge. They thus fulfil several important functions for the implementation of the various elements of the UN GCM. European governments and institutions often rely on NGOs to play a part in certain migration governance processes. While filling the space between the state and irregular service providers, they may act on behalf of the government, as well as challenge, defy and act in conflict with the state. Collaboration between governments and civil society actors can, therefore, be harmonious but also fragile 'carry[ing] economic and political costs for both parties' (Spencer and Delvino, 2018: 4). Some of the key functions and roles, which may overlap, are summarised below.

The first role relates to advocacy for policy change and input to policy and normative frameworks or strategies. This includes contributions to public and policy debates, inputs to policy processes, lobbying and representing migrant interests. This can take several forms, ranging from close cooperation with policy-makers, and indirect influence at the more technical level to influence at the operational level, like providing services on behalf of governments (Spencer, 2017). In doing so, they often focus on rights-based principles and inclusive and transparent processes. This is more important as migrants often lack representation in European migration policy debates.

The second role relates to monitoring, holding accountable, producing and communicating knowledge, and fostering learning. Civil society actors often monitor the effectiveness of policies and programmes. They are well placed to do so, not only because they are independent of governments, but also because they have 'accurate grassroots intelligence regarding the conditions under which migrants transit, work and live (to which governments often have limited access)' (Banulescu-Bogdan , 2011: 2), as well as an understanding of what migrants need and want. This provides them with better knowledge on how policies 'land on the ground'. Given the non-legally binding status of the GCM, holding governments to account is an important part of its implementation. Civil society actors can effectively engage with the EU Commission and EU member states when they devise and implement strategies that are counter to the provisions of the compact (ECRE and PICUM, 2019). Some European states that have endorsed the GCM, have adopted restrictive asylum and reception policies, clashing with the GCM provisions. For instance, civil society organisations (CSOs) have expressed strong concern about the EU's recast of the Returns Directive, noting that the provisions included fall below the standards agreed as part of the GCM (ECRE and PICUM, 2019).

Third, through implementing programmes and interventions, civil society actors provide services to migrants, such as access to food, healthcare, or legal advice, and help vulnerable migrants access their rights. Civil society actors do so either with the financial resources and support from state authorities (such as when implementing activities and programmes on behalf of governments or the EU) or independently (for instance, to counterbalance effects that government policies or non-action may have on migrants) (EESC, 2016). For example, under the EU Trust Fund for Africa, about 14 per cent of all activities focused on migration management, and assistance to displaced and migrant affected communities, are implemented by CSOs such as Action Against Hunger and the International Rescue Committee (IRC).[7]

The implementation of the GCM in the EU

The EU is not itself a signatory to the GCM, although it has stated its support throughout the process. The EU delegation to the UN actively participated in the negotiation process and the EU Commission noted that the provisions of the GCM are in line with EU priorities. The EU does not have an exclusive competence around migration, yet it has become increasingly involved in internal and external policies and practices governing migration (see Vosyliūtė, 2020). EU frameworks thus have implications also for EU member states, even though cooperation and agreement has become increasingly difficult in a politicised climate during the past years.

CSOs had the vision that the GCM would become a key framework guiding EU policies, strategies and funding decisions. This is far from what is being observed. Since the adoption of the GCM, the EU Commission or EU Council presidencies have rarely mentioned it as a reference point or framed it in strategies and communications to EU member states. Neither have EU member states used the framework as a starting point in discussions or non-papers on specific thematic areas of migration at the EU level. A key example is the recently proposed EU Pact on Migration and Asylum, which does not include a single mention of the GCM, even though it covers most of its elements (European Commission, 2020a). The EU institutions and some EU member states do, however, communicate or 'repackage' initiatives and activities on migration as contributions to the GCM's implementation.[8]

This may not be surprising, given the controversies around the GCM in Europe, with some EU member states, including Hungary, Poland and Austria, opting out of the framework. But it falls short of the expectations of civil society actors, some of whom have pointed out that the EU's external dimension of migration should follow stronger coherence with the GCM (European Commission, 2020b: 28). For instance, in relation to the new EU Pact for Migration and Asylum, (PICUM) has stressed that the EU Commission proposal opposes some of the GCM's objectives, such as the provision of accurate and timely information (Objective 3 of the GCM) or the use of migrant detention (Objective 13 of the GCM) (PICUM, 2020).

While the European External Action Service and the EU Commission still stand behind the GCM (see EEAS and European Commission, 2020), the real implementation activity takes place at the national levels of EU member states that are signatory to the CGM. Some EU member states played an active role in the first formal regional review process for Europe, held in November 2020. Belgium, Croatia, Denmark, Finland, Germany, Greece, Malta and Portugal have published their input for the regional review.[9] This is, thus, also where civil society actors focus their attention and target their lobbying efforts in relation to the GCM specifically. At the European level, much of the advocacy on migration follows European frameworks and strategies rather than the GCM. Yet, some challenges have been encountered at national levels. Even in countries committed to the GCM, such as Germany, formal coordination processes to implement the GCM objectives have been missing.[10]

EU/civil society relations on migration governance

At EU and its member state levels, state–civil society relations in areas covered by the GCM have followed the parallel development of trust, cooperation and involvement, on the one hand, and increasing tension on the other. Civil society actors are consistently involved in initiatives of the EU Commission and member state governments, be it through consultations, participation in working and expert groups, or as implementing partners. For many new initiatives, such as the recently announced 'Skills and Talent Packages' in legal migration, the EU relies on CSOs, among other actors, to suggest ways to improve EU frameworks.[11] At the national level, CSOs are part of expert commissions, providing strategic advice to European governments. In Germany, for example, the federal government convened a Commission on the Root Causes of Displacement in July 2019. The president of the German Red Cross chairs this commission, which will present its report in early 2021.

Portugal goes a step further and includes NGOs as key actors in the implementation of the national Strategic Plan for Migration, which spells out detailed provisions on the anticipated role of civil society actors in migration governance (Spencer and Delvino, 2018). Engagement and access differ, however, depending on the thematic area, the EU member state involved, and the different ministries and departments of EU member state governments.[12] Because NGOs play a significant role in providing services to migrants and refugees (such as providing access to basic needs, offering legal, medical and psychological support, or supplying and distributing food items),[13] since the 2015 refugee crisis, the EU and its member states have had to rely more on their cooperation. This has given NGOs more credibility and a louder voice in operational matters. However, such engagement does not automatically translate into a stronger influence for civil society actors on EU or EU member states' migration policies. During past years and in the context of growing irregular migrant movements towards the EU, migration policy-making has become more politicised and decisions are often taken at the highest level, which leaves little room for manoeuvre. Despite NGOs' important role in implementation of activities for migrants, 'it has not, by and large, brought them a role around the table when policy proposals are discussed' (Spencer, 2017: 31).

Moreover, relations have become increasingly strained due to the growing securitisation of European migration governance. In the field of migrant smuggling and search and rescue, both noted in the GCM, visible clashes have emerged between EU governments and their state agencies and NGOs. The GCM commits governments to 'develop procedures and agreements on search and rescue of migrants, with the primary objective of protecting migrants' right to life, that uphold the prohibition of collective expulsion, guarantee due process and individual assessments [...] and ensure that the provision of assistance of an exclusively humanitarian nature for migrants is not considered unlawful' (UN General Assembly, 2019: §24).[14] Many CSOs, such as SOS Méditerranée or Médecins Sans Frontières, have engaged in humanitarian search and rescue (S&R) activities aimed at protecting lives at sea and promoting human rights. For their operations in the Mediterranean and at land borders, they have faced strong criticism and increasing criminalisation by the EU and its member states (Gordon and Lerson, 2020). In 2017, the director of the EU's border and coastguard (Frontex) told a German newspaper that 'NGOs who rescue people [...] are encouraging traffickers who profit from dangerous Mediterranean crossings' (Wintour, 2017), accusing them of ineffective cooperation with security actors. Italian authorities have viewed S&R NGOs as competitors rather than partners and have vilified and restricted their activities.

In addition, during 2017, courts in the Italian cities of Trapani and Palermo opened preliminary investigations into NGOs involved in S&R operations. The public prosecutor of Catania, Carmelo Zuccaro, accused NGOs of colluding with and receiving funding from migrant smugglers, as well as having political aims to destabilise the Italian economy (Cuttita, 2018). Most controversial has been the code of conduct, which the Italian authorities introduced and asked NGOs to sign. The code sets limits to the activities of NGO rescue ships off the coast of Libya. Observers have argued that its provisions are 'redundant or counterproductive' while 'violat[ing] humanitarian principles without increasing existing rescuing capabilities' (Cusumano, 2019:107).[15] EU member states have actively prosecuted NGOs engaging in rescue activities and have impounded their vessels. The EU Agency for Fundamental Rights (FRA) notes that, since 2018, EU member states have initiated about 40 administrative and criminal proceedings against crew members or vessels of NGO S&R operators for alleged crimes such as human smuggling, the facilitation of irregular migration, and money laundering, among others (EU Agency for Fundamental Rights, 2020).

Since 2018, both Italy and Malta have also prevented vessels operated by civil society S&R actors from disembarking in their ports. The COVID-19 pandemic,[16] which started in late 2019 and later spread across the world, has exacerbated this situation as Italy, Malta and Greece, under the pretence of COVID-19 protocols, have placed restrictions on landing possibilities for CSO ships, effectively leading many of them to cease their operations.[17] The EU Commission has not taken active steps against such practices and the Italian code of conduct seems to have been endorsing it. As a response, and in relation to the recent EU Commission proposal for a new EU Pact on Migration and Asylum, a joint statement by over 70 CSOs noted that the EU should 'strengthen the exemptions of humanitarian action and other independent civil society activities from criminalisation and remove obstacles to civil society actors providing life-saving and other humanitarian assistance on land and at sea' (Statewatch, 2020b).

But S&R is not the only role being curtailed. Civil society actors have pointed out that their role in independently scrutinising EU anti-smuggling and border security activities, and their impacts on migrants, is being diminished. The approach of Frontex towards civil society actors illustrates the tension between viewing CSOs as partners, which need to be consulted and cooperated with, on the one hand, and organisations whose activities should be diminished if they impede border governance and smuggling activities, on the other. In 2011, Frontex set up a Consultative Forum on fundamental rights, including NGOs, which are able to lobby Frontex and request information on fundamental rights and operations. This forum is meant to assist Frontex with independent advice on human rights issues. While such NGOs should be able to access information first-hand, in practice there are limitations, especially concerning access to operational reference and guiding documents (Gianetto, 2020). Another example is the process of establishing an Operational Platform for the Eastern Mediterranean Route, which is set out in the Vienna Declaration[18] and aims to bring together EU and Western Balkan governments, the EU Commission, Frontex, the European Asylum Support Office (EASO), Europol, the International Centre for Migration Policy Development (ICMPD) and other relevant international partners in a structured way to jointly coordinate operational measures. Civil society or even parliamentary scrutiny, however, is absent in these processes (Statewatch, 2020a).

Overall, while there is strong collaboration, the EU and EU member states have engaged in several practices that have hindered and curtailed the ability of active NGOs to carry out their work in support of GCM provisions when this has clashed with their own priorities. In a context in which the GCM has not become the most dominant strategic reference framework for migration governance, this does not bode well for the implementation of the whole-of-society commitments of the GCM.

Challenges for civil society in implementing the GCM

In the context of migration governance, several other challenges impede European civil society's ability to play a constructive role in implementing the GCM. These relate to the shrinking of space for progressive civil society activities, the changing nature of the CSO sector, upholding norms and values, and the setting of red lines.

Shrinking space for progressive CSOs active in asylum and migration

The earlier discussion on civil society actors active in S&R serves as an example of a wider trend towards a more hostile environment for progressive civil society in general. While Europe, and especially the EU, remains a region with strong open civic space and is seen to uphold democratic and political rights, as the research of Civicus shows, 'the conditions for civil society continue to deteriorate' (Civicus, 2019). Democratic regression across Europe has led to governments restricting the work of civil society actors, resulting in a narrowed civic space (Negri, 2020). In 2019, both Malta and Serbia[19] regressed, while instances of restrictions were also visible in other EU member states (Civicus, 2019). As migration has become an increasingly politically sensitive topic, the space for NGOs that provide services to migrants or help in the defence of their rights has been narrowed. In many EU member states, the 'political discourse against non-governmental organisations in the field of asylum and migration has intensified and fuelled unprecedented hostility by local groups against civil society' (RSA, 2020: 1).

Greece is one of the countries in which this trend impacts CSOs active on migration and asylum. Public attitudes and perceptions towards NGOs have shifted over time. The Greek government introduced new legislation in April 2020 requiring NGOs operating in the areas of asylum and social integration to be part of a registry, which is linked to tighter requirements for continuing operations. Human rights organisations have voiced concerns that the new law compromises the freedom and independence of NGOs and imposes onerous and burdensome requirements, which obstruct their work. For some NGOs, these demands have been impossible to comply with (Amnesty International, 2020a).

Such government actions have simultaneously fuelled an already tense public perception of NGOs, which ultimately resulted in a 'series of attacks against refugees, journalists, NGO workers, activists and members of organisations on Chios, Lesvos and Kos' (Amnesty International, 2020a: 2). In Poland, liberal civil society actors working on migration have fewer chances of receiving government funding and are targeted by defamation campaigns by members of the governing party, PiS (Novakova, 2020). Amnesty International has also recorded cases of restrictions and the criminalisation of CSOs assisting migrants in Croatia, France, Italy, Malta, Spain and the United Kingdom (Amnesty International, 2020b). COVID-19 is likely to increase this pressure on civil society actors: not only have they been strongly hit by COVID restrictions and other challenges related to the pandemic, but their funding base is also likely to suffer in the future, and they are being left out of the EU's recovery measures (Pornschlegel, 2020).

As Negri (2020) points out, civil society actors counter such developments actively by deploying several strategies, including increased coalition building, stronger coordination at European level across EU member states, and more forceful grassroots mobilisation. Yet not all have been resilient enough to continue their activities on migration.

Changing nature of CSOs on migration and asylum

Some of the restrictions and the backlash against progressive NGOs working on migration and asylum is due to the changing nature of the CSO sector more generally. The civil society landscape has evolved over the years, with more conservative and partially 'right-wing' radical civil society actors[20] emerging. These CSOs organise their own activities in the form of 'smear campaigns' or countering the efforts of NGOs focusing on migrant rights (see Youngs, 2018). These new actors have pursued an anti-immigration agenda and were instrumental in introducing 'fake news' with the aim of diminishing public support for the GCM ahead of its adoption, and in pressuring governments to withhold their support for the pact, as was the case in Belgium. In Germany, over the past few years, the number of registered clubs with a right-wing leadership has tripled, according to Nattke (see Nattke interview by Körmeling, 2020).

Some right-wing NGOs have engaged actively in activities similar to those of liberal NGOs in the field of migration, but with opposite aims. An example is the group 'Die Identitären' (Identitarian Movement), active in Germany and Austria (DW, 2019; Ebner, 2019). This movement has been behind a number of activities, including 'Defend Europe', in which they hired a ship and engaged in search activities in the Mediterranean with the aim of preventing people from reaching Europe. A nationalist NGO, 'Alternative Help Association (AHA)', has claimed to be active in Syria and Lebanon to prevent the (onward) movement of people to Europe. To do this, the AHA, posing as a humanitarian help organisation, provides funding for families and individuals. At the same time, these grassroots projects are committed to influencing political attitudes in Germany and Austria towards more anti-immigration and anti-Islam stances (Vohra, 2018).[21]

In Poland, the government has engaged in systematically strengthening conservative civil society actors, while reducing support to liberal CSOs focusing on migrant rights. This has also affected the distribution of the EU Fund for Asylum, Migration and Integration by the Polish Ministry of the Interior. Since 2015, the calls to which CSOs could apply for funding have become irregular and unpredictable, and no CSO has received any funding despite being prior beneficiaries. In the context of a reduction in international funding, CSOs working on migrant protection have had to either cease operations or reduce their staff count. When the government has cooperated with civil society, it has favoured conservative CSOs as partners and recipients of funding (Novakova, 2020).

The diversification of civil society actors and their different stances to the GCM and its implementation has made it more challenging for a strong implementation agenda to take hold in EU member states. Liberal NGOs that support the implementation of the pact face an increasing number of adversaries, which makes the context for GCM implementation more difficult.

Setting boundaries: Red lines of NGO–EU cooperation and EU funding

Given the politicisation and growing externalisation of the migration agenda in Europe, civil society actors have also had to define more clearly the 'red lines' of cooperation with the EU – especially when implementing specific EU-funded projects. This has become increasingly important for NGOs in the humanitarian and development sectors, with the reframing of parts of the EU's development cooperation under a migration agenda. There have been shifts in the framing, objectives and instruments of EU member states under the EU Trust Fund for Africa (Knoll and Sherriff, 2017). In most cases, the politically motivated objectives of these funds did not resonate well with NGOs. NGO implementers have responded with mixed levels of confidence in the Trust Fund's objectives and approach to interventions (Oxfam, 2020).

NGOs have adopted a variety of approaches to react to this new reality. Some have gone along with the political reframing of development assistance while ensuring that the objectives and implementation of their projects still follow their desired development-led priorities. In the Netherlands and at the EU level, 'civil society organisations were initially doubtful whether to apply for [migration-related] funding' (Knoll and Sherriff, 2017: 207) as they did not agree with the framing and objectives of the funds. While doubts remain on how to engage with an agenda aimed at strengthening return and reducing irregular migration through development cooperation, NGOs have found a modus operandi, balancing existing 'red lines' while still accepting funding from the EU and EU member states, which allows them to continue their work in a funding environment that is increasingly under pressure.

Some NGOs have gone further and declined any formal funding from the EU and its member states because of EU responses to the refugee crisis and its approach to migration in the Mediterranean. Médecins Sans Frontierès, for instance, decided to stop accepting any money from the EU or its member states, emphasising its objections to the EU–Turkey Deal of 2016 (Kingsley, 2016), which required Turkey to take back migrants that were irregularly entering the EU in exchange for financial aid to assist refugees and their resettlement. In addition to rejecting further funding, others declined to continue working as service providers for EU member states, in reaction to growing restrictions on their work. For instance, many NGOs operating in migrant and refugee camps and hosting structures in Greece have decided not to register with the Ministry of the Interior's new 'Register of Greek and Foreign Non-Governmental Organisations', thereby foregoing the right to continue their work.[22] Only 18 out of 40 NGOs did so and were granted the right to continue their work, while others criticised the new regulations for NGO operations as being 'stringent, disproportionate and arbitrary requirements for registration and certification, which create risks of violations of rights of civil society' (RSA, 2020: 2).

Such dynamics are likely to continue, as the EU agenda outlined in the new Pact on Asylum and Migration fails to break with the past, in many respects intensifying those migration governance approaches that NGOs have criticised in recent years. Specifically, 10 per cent of funding of the EU's development cooperation instrument in the next Multiannual Financial Framework – the EU's long-term budget – is likely to be reserved for migration-related activities (Knoll and Veron, 2019). This priority may continue to bring civil society actors into uncomfortable positions having to defend their ground and make choices about the extent to which cooperation with EU member states can be justified and seen as compatible with their own values.

Conclusion and the way forward

Civil society actors will continue to form an important pillar of the GCM implementation in Europe and beyond. This chapter has outlined their roles and engagement with European governments and identified several challenges they face in a changing global context. The first review process of the GCM at the end of 2020 reiterated the need for inclusive processes and the importance of a 'whole-of-society' approach as key guiding principles of the GCM.

NGO coalitions have already pointed out that the implementation of the GCM should be taken further at the level of the EU and by individual member states. The above examples on the challenges and deviations in practice from the GCM's vision and principles show that there is still a long way to a successful GCM implementation (Brot für die Welt et al., 2020). New challenges have also impeded the effective implementation of the GCM. For instance, some of the responses to the COVID-19 pandemic have been harmful to migrants' rights and have exacerbated their vulnerabilities, and there is a risk that the global community is currently rolling back on global migration commitments (UN, 2020).

Four policy interventions should be considered by the EU, European governments, and civil society actors for the future implementation of the GCM to help mitigate some of the discrepancies that exist between the GCM aspirations and their implementation:

First, safeguard the space for civil society actors in the field of migration. CSOs are important actors for upholding democratic principles and rights. Democratic backsliding and the emergence of new actors has put pressure on the civil society sector. The EU should do more to safeguard the space for civil society actors to operate and take stances so that the current trend of shrinking spaces does not intensify across EU member states.

Second, establish more formal processes for the GCM implementation, specifically at the level of EU member states. Some EU member states do not follow dedicated processes in support of the implementation of the GCM goals and engagement with civil society on its objectives. While some states have reached out to civil society, in most EU member states coordinated processes to discuss and implement the GCM, following multi-stakeholder mechanisms, reportedly do not take place (ACT Alliance, 2020). For instance, regular working groups could be organised for specific clusters of GCM objectives to bring the technical understanding and practical experience of civil society actors together with the policy-making experience of governments. Furthermore, and especially during crisis situations such as the COVID-19 pandemic, consistent consultations with civil society on migration governance issues would support more effective responses for migrants.

Third, keep the GCM on the agenda. Civil society actors need to continue to hold governments to account and push even more strongly to keep the GCM on the European agenda. Amid rapid measures and policy changes due to the COVID-19 pandemic, as well as non-alignment of EU frameworks with the GCM, Europe could easily renege on its commitment to the GCM. This persistent engagement should go beyond periodic inputs to review processes. Lobbying activities need to be constant to increase the opportunities for a sustained discussion on the implementation of GCM objectives. This could include being more explicit on the GCM objectives when reacting to EU frameworks that are not framed in relation to the GCM.

Fourth, increase outreach and build collaborations with multiple stakeholders. Civil society actors have been active at building coalitions among themselves. Yet, to achieve true multi-stakeholder approaches to migration governance, civil society actors could take a more proactive role in seeking collaboration with UN agencies, the private sector, academia and local authorities.[23] The migration implications of the COVID pandemic bring renewed opportunities to reinvigorate the principles of the GCM for effective migration management, and to safeguard the rights of migrants. An example of a multi-stakeholder process involving local authorities, NGOs, foundations and research organisations, aimed at strengthening African migrants' rights in the context of EU-Africa relations, is the 'Mayors Dialogue on Growth and Solidarity'. It is a city-led initiative aimed at implementing practical solutions for human mobility in cities in Africa and Europe.[24] European and African civil society is bound to continue to play a crucial role in this context and to be instrumental in implementing the GCM. Yet, this will work only if all stakeholders play their part in seeking enhanced cooperation and inclusive partnership approaches to migration governance.

Notes

1   For more information, see MADE (n.d.).

2   For more information, see the entry for 'civil society organisation' in the Glossary of summaries of the EUR-LEX. Online at: https://eur-lex.europa. eu/summary/glossary/civil_society_organisation.html#:~:text=Civil%20 society%20refers%20to%20all,nor%20managed%20by%2C%20the%20 State.&text=Article%2015%20of%20the%20Treaty,in%20the%20EU's%20 good%20governance (accessed 6 November 2020).

3   For more information, see the entry for 'civil society' at the United Nations website. Online at: https://www.un.org/en/sections/resources-different-

audiences/civil-society/index.html (accessed 6 November 2020).

4   Umbrella organisations are so-termed 'networks of networks', which aim to represent the interests of migrants at the national, regional or global policy level. See Rother (2020).

5   MADE is a global civil society movement, which organises activities in various regions, including in Europe. See http://madenetwork.org/node/59.

6   Article 13 of the EU Treaty notes that the European Parliament, the Council and the Commission shall be assisted by an Economic and Social Committee acting in an advisory capacity. See European Union (2016).

7   Interview with a researcher contracted by the EU Commission to carry out research on the EU Trust Fund for Africa, June 2020. This follows about 40 per cent of activities implemented by international organisations and about 30 per cent by EU member state agencies. It has to be noted, however, that international organisations as well as EU agencies may subcontract international and local NGO partners to implement interventions.

8   The European External Action Service (EEAS) and the European Commission, for example, fit most of their initiatives under the GCM in their input to the GCM regional review (see EEAS and European Commission, 2020). Brot für die Welt has noted that Germany is 'repackaging' existing approaches and initiatives rather than utilising the GCM as a guiding framework for policy-making. See Braun (2020).

9   All contributions are online at: https://migrationnetwork.un.org/country-regional-network/europe-north-america (accessed 6 November 2020).

10 There also had not been a systematic exchange with civil society groups on the GCM's implementation until September 2020 in light of the upcoming review.

11 The EU Commission regularly launches consultations. Most recently a 'Public consultation on attracting skills and talents' has invited stakeholders, including civil society, to provide input. See Council of the European Union (2020).

12 For instance, Spencer (2017: 30) found that in some countries, civil society engages more directly with policy-makers on future migration policy (Germany and United Kingdom) and in others this seems less the case (France and Greece).

13 See EESC (2016) for examples of CSOs active in the EU since the 2015 refugee crisis.

14 For the full text of the Global Compact for Safe, Orderly and Regular Mi-

gration, see https://www.un.org/en/ga/search/view_doc.asp?symbol=A/RES/73/195.

15 See also Cuttita (2018).

16 The COVID-19 is an infectious disease caused by the coronavirus. It spread rapidly throughout the world in 2020 causing a global pandemic. Most common symptoms include fever, a dry cough and fatigue.

17 The NGO Médecins Sans Frontières highlighted that 'European governments are using the COVID-19 pandemic as an excuse to shirk responsibilities' (MSF, 2020).

18 For more information, see the Vienna Declaration (2020).

19 Serbia is not an EU member state but is part of the EU's accession process.

20 These have also been termed 'right-wing populist' civil society or 'uncivil' society. See Ruzza (2020).

21 Several other examples exist, such as the NGO 'Einprozent' active in Germany as a 'protest' NGO with anti-immigrant views. See https://www.einprozent.de/ueber-uns.

22 See RSA (2020) for more information.

23 Also see the recommendation of the CSA Committee (2020).

24 For more information see https://www.odi.org/projects/16889-mayors-dialogue-on-growth-and-solidarity-reimagining-human-mobility-in-africa-and-europe.

References

ACT Alliance. 2020. 'Submission to the 2020 United Nations Economic Commission for Europe (UNECE) regional review of the Global Compact for Safe, Orderly and Regular Migration (GCM), Online at: https://migrationnetwork.un.org/sites/default/files/docs/act_alliance_unece_2020_gcm_regional_review_submission.pdf (accessed 6 November 2020).

Amnesty International. 2020a. 'Greece: Regulation of NGOs working on migration and asylum threatens civic space'. Amnesty International Public Statement, 31 July 2020. Online at: https://www.amnesty.org/download/Documents/EUR2528212020ENGLISH.pdf (accessed 6 November 2020).

Amnesty International. 2020b. 'Punishing compassion: Solidarity on trial in Fortress Europe'. London: Amnesty International. Online at: https://www.amnesty.org/download/Documents/EUR0118282020ENGLISH.PDF (accessed 6 November 2020).

Banulescu-Bogdan, N. 2011. 'The role of civil society in EU migration policy:

Perspectives on the European Union's engagement in its neighbourhood'. Washington, DC: Migration Policy Institute. Online at: https://www. migrationpolicy.org/pubs/EUcivilsociety.pdf (accessed 6 November 2020).

Braun, K. 2020. 'Die Menschenrechte aller Migrant*innen schützen'. Brot für die Welt Blog Entry, 24.01.2020. Online at: https://www.brot-fuer-die-welt.de/blog/2020-die-menschenrechte-aller-migrantinnen-schuetzen/ (accessed 6 November 2020).

Brot für die Welt; Misereor, Dakonie, Katholisches Forum, Koordinierungskries gegen Menschenhandel e.V, 2020: 'German NGO Submission L Regional Review Global Compact, Paritätischer Gesamtverband, Caritas. Online at: https://migrationnetwork.un.org/sites/default/files/docs/german_ngo_submission_gcm_regional_review_2020_0.pdf (accessed 6 November 2020).

Civicus. 2019. 'Civic freedoms under threat in Europe and Central Asia: Two countries downgraded and no major improvements across others. Europe Central Asia Press Release, 4 December 2019. Online at: https://monitor.civicus.org/EuropeAndCentralAsia.PeoplePowerUnderAttack2019/ (accessed 6 November 2020).

Civil Society Action (CSA) Committee. 2020. 'Civil Society 2019 engagement in Global Compact for Migration implementation – with a post-COVID-19 outlook'. Online at: https://csactioncommittee.org/wp-content/uploads/2020/07/Mapping-report-FINAL.pdf (accessed 6 November 2020).

Council of the European Union. 2020. 'The future of legal migration in the EU: State of play and possible way forward – Presidency discussion paper'. 12026/20 Limite, Brussels, 16 October 2020. Online at: https://www.statewatch.org/media/1430/eu-council-presidency-paper-future-legal-migration-12026-20.pdf (accessed 6 November 2020).

Cusumano, E. 2019. 'Straightjacketing migrant rescuers? The code of conduct on maritime NGOs', *Mediterranean Politics*, 24(1): 106–14.

Cuttita, P. 2018. 'Pushing migrants back to Libya, persecuting rescue NGOs: The end of the Humanitarian Turn (Part II)'. Oxford University Faculty of Law Blog entry. 19 April 2018. Online at: https://www.law.ox.ac.uk/research-subject-groups/centre-criminology/centreborder-criminologies/blog/2018/04/pushing-0 (accessed 6 November 2020).

Deutsche Welle (DW). 2019. 'Germany: Identitarian movement classified as right-wing extremist', *DW News*, 11 July 2019. Online at: https://www.dw.com/en/germany-identitarian-movement-classified-as-right-wing-extremist/a-49550414 (accessed 6 November 2020).

Ebner, J. 2019. 'Who are Europe's far-right identitarians?' Politico Opinion. Online at: https://www.politico.eu/article/who-are-europe-far-right-identitarians-austria-generation-identity-martin-sellner/ (accessed 6 November 2020).

ECRE and PICUM. 2019. 'Implementing the Global Compact on Refugees and the Global Compact on Safe, Regular and Orderly Migration: What role for the EU?' 2019 Summary Report. Online at: https://picum.org/wp-content/uploads/2019/02/GCR-and-GCM-joint-event-report-1.pdf (accessed 6 November 2020).

European External Action Service (EEAS) and European Commission. 2020. 'Contribution to the regional review of the Global Compact for Safe, Orderly and Regular Migration in the UNECE region (12–13 November 2020)'. Online at: https://migrationnetwork.un.org/sites/default/files/docs/contribution_by_the_eeas_european_commission_services_to_the_regional_review_of_the_global_compact_for_safe_orderly_and_regular_migration_in_the_unece_region.pdf (accessed 6 November 2020).

European Economic and Social Committee (EESC) (2016). 'How civil society organisations assist refugees and migrants: Successful experiences and promising practices from the 2016 EESC Civil Society Prize'. Brussels: EESC. Online at: https://www.eesc.europa.eu/sites/default/files/resources/docs/qe-02-17-304-en-n.pdf (accessed 6 November 2020).

European Commission. 2020a. Communication from the Commission to the European Parliament, the Council, the EESC and the Committee of the Regions on a New Pact on Migration and Asylum. COM (2020) 609 Final. Online at: https://eur-lex.europa.eu/resource.html?uri=cellar:85ff8b4f-ff13-11ea-b44f-01aa75ed71a1.0002.02/DOC_3&format=PDF (accessed 6 November 2020).

European Commission. 2020b. 'Commission staff working document accompanying the document Proposal for a regulation of the European Parliament and of the council on asylum and migration management and amending Council Directive (EC)2003/109 and the proposed Regulation Asylum and Migration Fund', COM (2020) 610 final. Online at: https://eur-lex.europa.eu/legal-content/EN/TXT/PDF/?uri=CELEX:52020SC0207&from=EN (accessed 6 November 2020).

European Union. 2016. 'Consolidated versions of the Treaty on European Union and the Treaty on the Functioning of the European Union', *Official Journal of the European Union*. Information and Notices, Volume 59, 7 June 2016. Online at: https://eur-lex.europa.eu/legal-content/EN/TXT/?uri=OJ:C:2016:202:TOC (accessed 6 November 2020).

European Union Agency for Fundamental Rights. 2020. '2020 update: NGO ships involved in search and rescue in the Mediterranean and legal proceedings against them'. Website entry 19 June 2020. Online at: https://fra.europa.eu/en/publication/2020/2020-update-ngos-sar-activities (accessed 6 November 2020).

Gianetto, L. 2020. 'Frontex, civil society organisations, and human rights at EU borders: A complex relationship', Oxford University Faculty of Law Blog Entry, 28 October 2020. Online at: https://www.law.ox.ac.uk/research-subject-groups/centre-criminology/centreborder-criminologies/blog/2020/10/frontex-civil (accessed 6 November 2020).

Gordon, E. and Larsen, H.K. 2020. '"Sea of Blood": The intended and unintended effects of the criminalisation of humanitarian volunteers rescuing migrants in distress at sea'. Online at: https://onlinelibrary.wiley.com/doi/pdf/10.1111/disa.12472?casa_token=lXyYZvMijTUAAAAA%3AH8kXP9knBSmN4-TI9Aiq2vjgk2zTjuM6GHfhsvxWrBCMQZ25FMzhsvb1pvTdzqFD6bxsx0elwfXAyrg (accessed 6 November 2020).

Kingsley, P. 2016. 'MSF rejects EU funding in protest at refugee deal', *The Guardian*, 17 June 2016. Online at: https://www.theguardian.com/world/2016/jun/17/refugee-crisis-medecins-sans-frontieres-rejects-eu-funding-protest (accessed 6 November 2020).

Knoll, A. and Veron, P. 2019. 'Migration and the next EU long-term budget: Key choices for external action'. ECDPM Discussion Paper No. 250. Online at: https://ecdpm.org/wp-content/uploads/DP250-migration-next-EU-long-term-budget-Key-choices-external-action-ECDPM-Knoll-Veron-March-2019.pdf (accessed 6 November 2020).

Knoll, A. and Sherriff, A. 2017. 'Making waves: Implications of the irregular migration and refugee situation on official Development Assistance spending and practices in Europe'. EBA Report 01/2017. Online at: https://eba.se/wp-content/uploads/2017/02/EBA_2017_01_Making-waves_.pdf (accessed 6 November 2020).

Körmeling, J. 2020. 'Was 20 Jahre gesät wurde, wird jetzt geerntet'. Interview with Michael Nattke. Online at: https://www.neues-deutschland.de/artikel/1140187.rechte-hegemonie-was-jahre-gesaet-wurde-wird-jetzt-geerntet.html (accessed 6 November 2020).

Médecins Sans Frontières (MSF). 2020. 'EU states use COVID-19 to shirk search and rescue obligations as MSF ends Ocean Viking partnership'. Press release, 17 April 2020. Online at: https://www.msf.org/eu-states-use-covid-19-shirk-search-and-rescue-obligations (accessed 6 November 2020).

Migration and Development Network (MADE) n.d. 'European regional civil society consultation'. Online at: https://www.madenetwork.org/european-rcsc (accessed 6 November 2020).

Negri, G. 2020. 'How European civil society is pushing back against democratic erosion', *Carnegie Europe*, 20 March 2020. Online at: https://carnegieeurope. eu/2020/03/12/how-european-civil-society-is-pushing-back-against-democratic-erosion-pub-81254 (accessed 6 November 2020).

Novakova, N. 2020. 'The conservative–liberal clash reshaping Poland's civil society'. German Marshall Fund Blog Entry, 10 March 2020. Online at: https://www.gmfus.org/blog/2020/03/10/conservative-liberal-clash-reshaping-polands-civil-society (accessed 6 November 2020).

Oxfam. 2020. 'The EU Trust Fund for Africa: Trapped between aid policy and migration'. Online at: https://www.oxfam.de/system/files/eu-trust-fund-africa-migration-politics-en.pdf (accessed 6 November 2020).

PICUM. 2020. 'Implementation of the GCM in the European Union: Written submission ahead of the Regional Review of the Global Compact for Safe, Orderly and Regular Migration (GCM) in the UNECE region'. Online at: https://migrationnetwork.un.org/sites/default/files/docs/written_ submission_ahead_of_the_regional_review_of_the_gcm_in_the_unece_ region.pdf (accessed 6 November 2020).

Pornschlegel, S. 2020. 'Countering shrinking spaces: Recommendations to support EU civil society'. European Policy Centre Discussion Paper, Connecting Europe Programme, 11 June 2020. Online at: https://www. stiftung-mercator.de/media/downloads/3_Publikationen/2020/2020_06/ Countering_shrinking_spaces.pdf (accessed 6 November 2020).

Refugee Support Aegean (RSA). 2020. 'New rules on civil society supporting refugees and migrants in Greece'. RSA Comments. Online at: https:// rsaegean.org/wp-content/uploads/2020/05/RSA_Comments_NGO_ Registry.pdf (accessed 6 November 2020).

Rother, S. 2020. 'A Global Compact for Migration from below? The role of migrant civil society', *Newsletter of the American Political Science Associations' Organized Section on Migration and Citizenship*, 7(2): 16–20. Online at: https:// www.researchgate.net/publication/342425703_A_Global_Compact_for_ Migration_from_below_The_role_of_migrant_civil_society (accessed 6 November 2020).

Ruzza, C. 2020. 'Civil society between populism and anti-populism', in: O. Norocel, A. Hellström and M. Jørgensen (eds). *Nostalgia and Hope: Intersections between politics of culture, welfare, and migration in Europe*. IMISCOE Research Series. Cham: Springer.

Spencer, S. and Delvino, N. 2018. 'Cooperation between government and civil society in the management of migration: Trends, opportunities and challenges in Europe and North America'. Paper for the Global Exchange on Migration and Diversity, Autumn Academy 2018. Online at: https://www.compas.ox.ac.uk/wp-content/uploads/AA18-Background-paper-FINAL.pdf (accessed 6 November 2020).

Spencer, S. 2017. 'Migration policy making in Europe: Challenges and opportunities for civil society'. A short review for the Social Change Initiative. Online at: https://www.compas.ox.ac.uk/wp-content/uploads/Migration-Policy-Making-in-Europe-Challenges-Opportunities-for-Civil-Society-short-review-2017.pdf (accessed 6 November 2020).

Statewatch. 2020a. 'EU: Tracking the Pact: Reinforced cooperation against migrant smuggling with Balkan and African "partners"', News Entry, 15 October 2020. Online at: https://www.statewatch.org/news/2020/october/eu-tracking-the-pact-reinforced-cooperation-against-migrant-smuggling-with-balkan-and-african-partners/ (accessed 6 November 2020).

Statewatch. 2020b. 'Joint statement: The Pact on Migration and Asylum: To provide a fresh start and avoid past mistakes, risky elements need to be addressed and positive aspects need to be expanded'. A Joint statement signed by 70+ NGOs and human rights organisations from across Europe and beyond, October 2020. Online at: https://www.statewatch.org/news/2020/october/joint-statement-the-pact-on-migration-and-asylum-to-provide-a-fresh-start-and-avoid-past-mistakes-risky-elements-need-to-be-addressed-and-positive-aspects-need-to-be-expanded/ (accessed 6 November 2020).

United Nations. 2020. 'COVID-19 and people on the move'. Policy Brief, June 2020. Online at: https://www.un.org/sites/un2.un.org/files/sg_policy_brief_on_people_on_the_move.pdf (accessed 6 November 2020).

United Nations (UN) General Assembly. 2019. Global Compact for Safe, Orderly and Regular Migration, Resolution adopted by the General Assembly on 19 December 2018. A/RES/73/195. Online at: https://www.un.org/en/ga/search/view_doc.asp?symbol=A/RES/73/195 (accessed 6 November 2020).

Vienna Declaration. 2020. 'Vienna Declaration on effectively combating irregular migration along the Eastern Mediterranean Route', Ministerial Conference, 22–23 July. Online at: https://www.statewatch.org/media/1402/vienna-declaration-combating-irregular-migration-eastern-med-7-20.pdf (accessed 6 November 2020).

Vohra, A. 2018. 'Was macht eine rechte deutsche NGO im Libanon?'. Quantara. de entry, 16 October 2018. Online at: https://de.qantara.de/inhalt/ identitaere-bewegung-was-macht-eine-rechte-deutsche-ngo-im-libanon (accessed 6 November 2020).

Vosyliūtė, L. 2020. 'What is the EU's role in implementation of the Global Compact for Migration?' ReSOMA Policy Option Brief. Brussels: Centre for European Policy Studies. Online at: https://migrationresearch.com/ storage/app/uploads/public/5ef/b3c/62a/5efb3c62a5553833120649.pdf (accessed 6 November 2020).

Wintour, P. 2017. 'NGO rescues off Libya encourage traffickers, says EU borders chief', *The Guardian*, 27 February 2017. Online at: https://www. theguardian.com/world/2017/feb/27/ngo-rescues-off-libya-encourage-traffickers-eu-borders-chief (accessed 6 November 2020).

Xiang, B. and Lindquist, J. 2014. 'Migration infrastructure', *International Migration Review*, 48: 122–48.

Youngs, R. (ed.). 2018. 'The mobilisation of conservative civil society'. Carnegie Endowment for International Peace. Online at: https:// carnegieendowment.org/files/Youngs_Conservative_Civil_Society_ FINAL.pdf (accessed 6 November 2020).

Part VII
UN Perspectives

Chapter 17

The role of the UN High Commissioner for Refugees in African–EU migration

Nompumelelo Ndawonde

Introduction

On 14 December 2020, the office of the United Nations High Commissioner for Refugees (UNHCR, 2019a) celebrated 70 years since its adoption. In 1951, in response to the large number of displaced people in the aftermath of World War II, a diplomatic conference in Geneva adopted the Convention Relating to the Status of Refugees (the Refugee Convention). The Refugee Convention spelled out who was a refugee, and their legal rights and social statues. It was originally mandated to provide protection and humanitarian assistance to displaced, largely European, populations crossing international borders after the war. This Convention was later amended by the 1967 Protocol to remove geographical limitations as the problem of displacement spread around the world. Currently, the Convention plays a pivotal role in providing refugee and subsidiary protection regimes to all people who have been forced to leave their homes against their will (UNHCR, 2019a).

The UNHCR estimates that 30 million internally displaced persons, refugees and asylum seekers live on the African continent (UNHCR, 2022a). Conflict and political instability, and to a lesser extent climate-related displacements, have been the main drivers of forced migration on the continent. Violence from intercommunal clashes, the threat of terrorist attacks, and the lack of a unified central government have destabilised countries such as Nigeria, Eritrea, South Sudan, and the Democratic Republic of Congo (DRC), leaving thousands fleeing for their lives into neighbouring countries or further afield. For instance, attacks by Boko Haram resulted in the death of 32,800 Nigerians in eight Northern States between 2011 and 2021, while another 10,000 Nigerians were killed and 300,000 others displaced during the same period as a result of conflicts between herders and farmers (Akinola, 2021). In 2020, the Dadaab refugee complex in Kenya, one of the UNHCR's largest refugee settlements in Africa, registered 218,873 refugees and asylum seekers, many of whom were from Somalia and South Sudan (UNHCR, 2019e). In the Sahel region, jihadist terrorism and an escalation of intercommunal violence have displaced over 2 million people since 2015, the majority of whom have remained within their countries of origin.

In addition to the challenges posed by these and other displacement situations in Africa, the UNHCR operations and mandate have been severely tested by the so-called 'migration crisis' in Europe. In 2015 more than 1 million migrants arrived in Europe, propelled primarily by the Syrian conflict, but also thousands of Afghans and Iraqi nationals fleeing their war-torn countries in search of asylum in the EU. To escape violence and persecution, many refugees and other migrants, including sub-Saharan African nationals, have risked and lost their lives while attempting perilous journeys across the Mediterranean Sea via Libya, or using the Eastern Mediterranean route from Turkey to Greece in inflatable and/or decrepit boats, unfit for sea travel and filled beyond capacity. The International Organization for Migration (IOM) reported 7,400 deaths on migration routes across Africa between 2014 and 2019;[1] 4,400 in North Africa; 1,171 in the Horn of Africa; and another 1,830 in sub-Saharan Africa (IOM, 2019).

The influx of refugees and other migrants created a crisis for European Union (EU) countries, who were unprepared and thus overwhelmed by the sheer numbers they were receiving, most notably via the Central Mediterranean route used by African migrants; for example, 116,000 migrants arrived on Italian shores in 2015 (OECD, 2015). While some EU countries welcomed the refugees, others restricted entry at their borders, and there was a rise in underlying prejudices such as Islamophobia and xenophobia. This contradicted the universal right to migrate, which was 'founded on the principles of freedom of movement, the equality of all human beings, or the right to go abroad in search of dignified life conditions whenever they are not guaranteed in one's home country' (Zanfrini, n.d;, Satgar, 2019; Nwabuzo and Schaeder, 2017).

In an attempt to curtail this ongoing threat to the safety and dignity of migrants seeking refuge in the EU and elsewhere, the UNHCR implemented the 2018 UN Global Compact on Refugees as a comprehensive response to the refugee and migrant crisis affecting millions all over the world. The 11th UN High Commissioner for Refugees, Filippo Grandi, maintained that Africa is the region with a true migrant crisis as 'poor countries take care of more than 80 per cent of forcibly displaced persons' and that what happened in Europe during 2015–16 was not a crisis at all but 'a steep surge in arrivals, initially as an effect of the worsening of the Syrian war'. He further argued that 'while Europe has had a very good asylum system for many decades, it was designed for small numbers. When that system collapsed, it generated a perception of crisis in Europe that was bigger than it was' (Mukoya, 2019). These sentiments by Grandi have informed the nature of the response of the UNHCR to African–EU migration, which is the focus of this chapter.

This chapter assesses the role of the UNHCR in African–EU migration and its implementation of the four key mandates to address the challenges of this migration. The discussion draws on Libya as a case study, and reflects on the influence of the Italian–Libyan agreement, as well as African regional organisations such as ECOWAS, the SADC and the African Union (AU) on the UNHCR GCR in addressing African/EU migration. It illuminates the impact of the UN Global Compact on Refugees (GCR) on African–EU migration, particularly on the lives of African refugees through support to their countries of origin, and more broadly in terms of the implications for their countries of transit and destination.

The statutory roles of the UNHCR

The office of the UNHCR is premised on article 14 in the UN Declaration of Human Rights of 1948 and the UN Convention and Protocol of 1951, amended in 1971. The UN Convention and Protocol of 1971 ensures the universal coverage and protection of all people with its three overarching principals, namely 'non-discrimination,[2] non-penalization[3] and non-refoulement'[4].

The Convention of 1971 offers a universal definition of a refugee as 'someone who is unable or unwilling to return to their country of origin owing to a well-founded fear of being persecuted for reasons of race, religion, nationality, membership of a particular social group, or political opinion' (UNHCR, 2019a). The overarching role of the UNHCR is to supervise, promote, and safeguard the international instruments that seek to protect and assist refugees.

The mandate of the UNHCR is formally stipulated in the Statute of the Office of the United Nation High Commissioner for Refugees of 1950 paras 8*(c)* and *(b)*, 9 and 10 (UNHCR, 2019b). Principally created as a legal framework for the protection of refugees, the UNHCR's mandate has been expanded to include stateless and internally displaced people, as well as returnees (UNHCR, 2013). Furthermore, it remains the responsibility of the UNHCR to oversee the compliance of states in adhering to the principles related to the treatment of some of the most vulnerable people in the world.

Despite the inclusion of stateless people and returnees, the principal focus of the UNHCR is refugees. Its role in relation to other categories of migrants was further restricted by the establishment of the International Organization for Migration (IOM) in 1951, as an agency of the United Nations. Since its inception, the IOM has worked alongside governments and non-governmental partners in the pursuit of the promotion of safe, humane and orderly migration through four key areas of its own: 'migration and development, facilitating migration, regulating migration and forced migration' (IOM, 2014).[5] Although the IOM and the UNHCR are formally different entities, with different responsibilities, some of their responsibilities overlap. Although the UNHCR's chief mandate is the plight of refugees, stateless people, returnees, and internally displaced people, its impact is visible in African–EU migration governance.

The Global Compact for Refugees

The New York Declaration for Refugees and Migrants was adopted on 16 September 2016 as a strong commitment of UN member states to collectively protect refugees and migrants. Member states who joined the declaration,

> (i) expressed profound solidarity with those who are forced to flee; (ii) reaffirmed their obligations to fully respect human rights of refugees and migrants; (iii) agreed that protecting refugees and supporting the

countries that shelter them are shared international responsibilities and must be borne more equitably and predictably; (iv) pledged robust support to those countries affected by large movements of refugees and migrants; (v) agreed upon the core elements of a Comprehensive Refugee Response Framework (CRRF); and (vi) agreed to work towards the adoption of a Global Compact on Refugees (GCR) and a Global Compact for Migration (GCM).

This Declaration for Refugees led to the later establishment of the Global Refugee Forum and the Comprehensive Refugee Response Framework (CRRF); both initiatives seek to amplify the response to the global refugee crisis. As an extension of the UNHCR's mandate, the Global Compact for Refugees (GCR), founded on 17 December 2018, is framed on the principles of international human rights law and the obligation to protect refugees.

To the UNHCR, the GCR is a framework representing the 'political will and ambition of the international community as a whole', to assist in the management of refugees as the mass displacement of people across the world continues to grow (UNHCR, 2019e). The GCR was established on the understanding that the current scale of displacements constitutes a global refugee crisis, which requires global intervention. The underlying reasoning suggests that such international commitments are in the shared interests of the displaced populations, their countries of origin, and the receiving states alike. For all states to enjoy peace and stability, they need to make a concerted effort, alongside actors in the private sector and civil society, to assist all those fleeing conflict, violence and persecution. The GCR's key objectives are to: '(i) ease pressures on host countries; (ii) enhance refugee self-reliance; (iii) expand access to third-country solutions; and (iv) support conditions in countries of origin for return in safety and dignity' (UNHCR, 2019a).

Against this backdrop, the following section addresses how the four objectives of the GCR and the UNHCR's mandate have impacted African–EU migration in practice.

The UNHCR and African–EU migration

In 2019, the UNHCR reported 26.4 million persons of concern in sub-Saharan Africa, accounting for 35 per cent of the global total of 74.8 million. Of this 26.4 million, 14.1 million are in East Africa and the Horn of Africa, 8 million in Central Africa and the Great Lakes, 3.8 million in West Africa, and 0.5 million in southern Africa (OCHA, 2018). Currently, 30 million internally displaced persons, refugees and asylum seekers live in Africa (UNHCR, 2021b). Considering that there are a reported 48 million internally displaced persons globally, it is highly alarming that Africa accounts for a majority of this (UNHCR, 2021b).

These people of concern are victims of abject poverty, internal conflicts, and persecution in countries such as the Central African Republic (CAR) and South Sudan. The instability in one country generally has a direct spill-over effect on the neighbouring countries. For example, the tumultuous 2020 elections in the CAR resulted in an influx of refugees in neighbouring DRC. For many in the host countries, who are already living below the poverty line, the influx of those seeking asylum further exacerbates their difficult circumstances. As an illustration, in 2019, the UNHCR reported 1,428,999 refugees (93,719 returned) and 6,302,108 internally displaced people (2,578,256 returned) in Central Africa and the Great Lakes region.

Table 17.1: The groups of people of concern in Africa in 2019

Internally displaced persons	17.7 million
Refugees	6.3 million
Returned IDPs	584,000
Stateless persons	712,000
Asylum seekers	484,000
Others of concern	319,000
Returned refugees	341,000

Source: OCHR (2018a)

In 2019, the sub-Saharan African countries with the largest people of concern are the Democratic Republic of Congo at 4.5 million; Somalia at 2.6 million; Ethiopia at 2.6 million; Nigeria at 2.2 million; South Sudan at 1.9 million, and Sudan at 1.9 million (OCHA, 2018). Many have had to flee their homes as a result of the political and electoral governance crisis in Burundi, ongoing clashes between armed forces and non-state armed groups in Cameroon, and the struggle for resources, as well as the outbreak of the Ebola virus and cholera in the DRC.

In the East and Horn of Africa, the drivers of regular and irregular migration are attributed to low human and economic development, violent conflicts, as well as political oppression, and persecution in Ethiopia, Somalia, South Sudan and Sudan (Marchand et al., 2017: 3). In these regions, the key countries of origin are Somalia and South Sudan; countries of destinations are Ethiopia and Uganda, while Kenya, Sudan, and Djibouti are transit countries for irregular migrants making their way to Yemen or the Gulf coast (Marchand et al., 2017: 3). As in many other parts of the world, these displacements expose irregular migrants to violence, extortion, and human trafficking, often intended for forced labour and sexual exploitation.

On the continent, West Africa is central to the debate on African–EU migration. According to the UN Department of Economic and Social Affairs (UN DESA), there were a reported 7.6 million international migrants residing in the subregion, 90 per cent of whom are from other countries in the region (IOM, 2020). The top five destination countries for migrants are Côte d'Ivoire (2,564,857 migrants), Nigeria (1,308,568), Burkina Faso (723,989), Mali (485,829), and Ghana (476,412) (IOM, 2020). The main reasons for the migration were reported to be economic hardship, poverty, and the desire to seek better business opportunities.

While the majority of African migrants remain within their immediate subregion, approximately 400,000 African nationals enter the EU by regular means every year, and around 40,000 pursue irregular migration to Europe.

It has become increasingly clear that the irregular routes and means of migration from the African continent towards Europe are being used by migrants with highly diverse profiles, ranging from economic migrants, and students on long- or short-term visas to people displaced by violence, disaster, or political persecution. This has lead the UNHCR and other agencies to embrace the notions of 'mixed movements' or 'mixed migration', which describe 'flows of people travelling together, generally in an irregular manner, over the same routes and using the same means of transport, but for different reasons' (UNHCR, 2021a) Irregular migrants that fail to make the crossing from the North African coast to southern Europe become displaced or stranded in the Maghreb. In 2020, 625,638 migrants were accounted for in Libya, with nationals from five countries making up 72 per cent of the registered migrants: Niger (21 per cent), Chad (16 per cent), Egypt (16 per cent), Sudan (12 per cent), and Nigeria (7 per cent) (IOM, 2020).

A smaller percentage of those that seek refuge in neighbouring African countries, risk their lives to make the perilous onwards journey to

Europe. The Maghreb countries bordering the Mediterranean Sea, namely Morocco, Algeria, Tunisia and Libya, thus become both destination and transit countries for sub-Saharan African migrants, including international refugees. The Mediterranean crossing from North Africa to Italy or Spain is not a new phenomenon but dates back to the 1990s (De Haas, 2006). During the 2015 crisis, the IOM reported 3,149 deaths of migrants who perished in the sea, while 170,100 African migrants, including refugees, arrived in the EU via the Mediterranean Sea. In 2020, 33,418 new arrivals were recorded in Europe, and another 983 deaths recorded (IPATC/NAI, 2021: 3). At the time of writing, in late 2021, migrants from West Africa are usually headed to Spain's Canary Islands. OCHA reported in 2020 that 16,760 migrants used the irregular Western African Maritime Route to reach the Canary Islands, which was a staggering 1,019 per cent increase on 2019 (IOM, 2020b). It should be noted, however, that the crossings using the central and eastern routes decreased significantly over the same time period.

As a result of the irregular movement of Africans to Europe, migration has been framed as a security threat to states and societies in the EU, despite the fact that 53.2 per cent of African migrants move within the continent, and only 12.9 per cent of sub-Saharan Africans contribute to the European migrant population (Abebe, 2020). The increased securitisation of borders has reduced African–EU migration, but it has created greater problems in the following five key areas: 'the disruption of livelihoods, increased regional destabilisation, continued smuggling, increased violation of migrants' human rights, and the erosion of citizen–government relations' (Abebe, 2020).

As a response to the reality of African migrants and the challenges they face in Europe, the UNHCR has responded in it is own way on how best to address the issue. At the beginning of the 2015–16 European refugee crisis, the UNHCR was at the forefront of presenting emergency policies to deal with the chaotic scenes unfolding around the Mediterranean. In their efforts to accommodate those arriving via the sea route, the UNHCR initiated the:

Immediate creation of facilities in Greece, the expansion of existing facilities in Italy with a robust capacity **to receive, assist, register and screen people who arrive by sea, the immediate start of the relocation process for 40,000 from Greece and Italy,** strengthening **the mechanisms for the humane return of people not in need of**

international protection (UNHCR, 2015a).

In relation to African–EU migration, the role of the UNHCR was to be a buffer between European states wanting to strengthen their borders and migrants vulnerable to harm and human smuggling (Meandzija, 2018: 4). In essence, the UNHCR has a particular role to play in supporting governments to reconcile their measures to address the smuggling of refugees with ensuring the protection needs of those on the move are met. For example, the UNHCR is involved in ensuring that national laws on smuggling do not criminalise smuggled persons or persons who support refugees to cross state borders for humanitarian reasons.

As migration is a cross-border phenomenon, facilitating the harmonisation of African and EU policies proved challenging. The Common European Asylum System (CEAS), founded on the ideals of the Geneva Convention, was established as a framework[6] to facilitate a common asylum procedure between EU countries (Baumgartner and Wagner, 2019: 3). However, the CEAS soon became overwhelmed by the sheer number of arriving migrants and with increased tensions among participating countries. Indeed, 'the Dublin system collapsed under its own weight. Only then the Union was forced into action. The failure of the ordinary government of the refugee challenge led to the emergency government of the refugee crisis. A major challenge had become a crisis' (Menendez, 2016: 397). As a response, the UNHCR launched the Central Mediterranean Sea Initiative (CMSI), which was a 12-step plan to minimise the deaths at sea (Orav, 2015), which will be discussed in more detail.

In order to illustrate the UNHCR's role in African–EU migration governance, the following section uses Libya as a case study to discuss the recent shift in the European governance agenda and its impact on humanitarian responses and the management of mixed migration flows.

From transit route to containment: A case study of Libya

Libya, in addition to being a destination for aspiring labour migrants from sub-Saharan Africa, especially prior to the fall of the Gaddafi regime, is also a transit country for many Africans, who use it as a point of entry and exit to reach their desired destination in Europe. Over the past five or so years, however, many who sought refuge within its borders have been unable to transit further, and have become stuck in Libyan detention centres, in makeshift camps on the outskirts of urban centres, or in other precarious situations. It is difficult to categorise or identify people in these situations as being either refugees or migrants, since displaced people and aspiring migrants find themselves in similar circumstances, and they sometimes change their strategies for onward travel and livelihood.

Trans-Saharan migration to Libya was facilitated by Muammar Gaddafi's Pan-African policies, developed in the 1990s as a response to the mounting crises in Somalia, Ethiopia and the DRC (Millar and Bob-Millar, 2013: 62). However, 'a policy volte-face in 2007 led to the imposition of visas on both Arabs and Africans ... turning thousands of immigrants into "irregulars", many more fleeing after the Libyan 2011 uprising known as the Arab Spring' (Grange and Flynn, 2015).

The fall of Gaddafi in October 2011 saw the rise of conflicts between tribal regimes and authority groups, most notably the struggle for power between groups such as the UN-supported Government of National Accord (GNA) and those in support of the Khalifa Hafta's Libyan National Army (Kuschminder, 2020). The main contention has been between the Toubou and the Tuareg groups, located in the southeast region of Libya. This region has become the main entry point into the country for African migrants, as well as the major region for human trafficking and the slave industry (Kuschminder, 2020). With the governance crisis and the lack of control over issues such as migration in the post-Gaddafi era, migration in Libya has become commercialised, involving the kidnapping and sale of migrants as commodities, for ransom and trafficking for sex and labour.

After the 2015–16 European migration crisis, African migrants – who once moved and worked freely in Libya, and potentially moved onwards to Europe via Italy – became victims of kidnapping, racism, extortion and detention. As reported by Kuschminder, one migrant recounted how he had been kidnapped and forced to work off a debt of 1,200 dinar (approximately US$850) per person, to liberate himself, his sister, and his brother. Earning only 300 dinar (US$214) per month, he faced working for his captor for a year, which eventually drove him to attempt an irregular crossing of the Mediterranean Sea:

The day we entered into the boat, I saw ... they were bringing people out of the water, dead people, so I was very scared ... 'God,' I said, 'please show us the way; show us Italy way…' I was just praying, that's all I was doing until the moment we saw the rescue ship (Kuschminder, 2020).

Although this man was lucky to reach the Italian shore, many do not survive the dangerous journey and for many more, the true difficulty begins once on the other side of the Mediterranean. The high number of migrants arriving on Italian shores led to the Libyan–Italian agreement, established in 2017 under the title, 'Memorandum of Understanding on cooperation in the fields of development, the fight against illegal immigration, human trafficking and fuel smuggling and on reinforcing the security of borders between the State of Libya and the Italian Republic' (European Commission, 2017).

This agreement was signed by Italian Prime Minister Paolo Gentiloni and the head of the UN-backed Libyan Government of National Accord, Fayez al-Serraj. One of the key objectives of this agreement was to address 'the clandestine immigration phenomenon and its impact, the fight against terrorism, human trafficking and fuel smuggling' (European Commission, 2017). As a result of the agreement, Libya has become increasingly hostile to migrants. It has become less of a transit country, and more of a country of containment, where migrants have found themselves stuck in a dangerous limbo, unable to move onwards yet reluctant to return to an unsafe country of origin.

According to UNHCR, before the outbreak of the Libyan conflict in 2009, approximately 4,000 people were placed in 'arbitrary, indefinite detention in facilities where they face a high risk of exploitation and violence, including rape' (Human Rights Watch, 2020). The mounting hostilities and safety concerns resulted in the UNHCR announcing on 30 January 2020 that it would be closing its Gathering and Departure Facility (GDF) in Tripoli, Libya, a facility intended to house those awaiting resettlement or evacuation. The UNHCR's departure left many vulnerable and predestined migrants in official detention centres, to which humanitarian organisations such as UNHCR have minimal access (UNHCR, 2020e).

Despite the Libyan–Italian agreement 'forcefully' reducing the number of migrants attempting to travel to Italy via the Mediterranean Sea, there remains a real crisis in Libya, with reports of deplorable conditions in detainment centres and the unlawful detention of migrants, while kidnapping and smuggling practices are still in operation. The US Secretary-General has urged countries to 'revisit policies that support the return of refugees and migrants' (Council of Europe, 2020). To mitigate the closing of its GDF, on 15 November 2022, the UNHCR facilitated the resettlement and evacuation of migrants to third countries. With the support of the IOM, the UNHCR resettled 71 refugees in Canada, 37 of whom were children (UNHCR, 2021a). Quick impact projects (QIPs) – small projects that are speedily implemented to target areas such as health, education, shelter, or water and sanitation – were further implemented by the UNHCR to alleviate the pressure. In conjunction with the QIPs, the UNHCR has 12 disembarkation points in western Libya, working in community development centres and advocating for alternatives to detention (UNHCR, 2020d). Despite the UNHCR's intervention, the migration crisis in Libya remains rampant. The UNHCR's key figures for people of concern in Libya, as of 19 November 2021, are shown in Table 17.2.

Table 17.2: Groups of people of concern in Libya in 2019

Key figures	
Internally displaced persons (IDPs)	199,949
IDP returnees	648,317
Registered refugees and asylum seekers	41,404
Monitoring visits to detention centres in 2021	297
Refugees and asylum seekers released from detention in 2021	465
Vulnerable refugees and asylum seekers departed since 2017 (627 to date in November 2021)	6,826

Source: UNHCR (2021b)

To achieve its goals, the UNHCR requires €70 million for the Libyan migration project in 2022. By 15 February 2022, 22 per cent of this total has been contributed by Germany, Austria, Netherlands, Italy, the EU and Malta (UNHCR, 2022b).

The following section examines the UNHCR's role in implementing the GCR in Libya to get a better understanding of what it is currently doing, not just for the migrants and their countries of origin, but also for the countries of transit like Libya, and the countries of destination like Italy. In addition, it assesses the role of the Economic Community of West Africa (ECOWAS) and the African Union (AU) in addressing the crisis of irregular migration in Africa, and beyond.

Migration governance in post-Gaddafi Libya: The impact of the GCR

Clearly, the post-Gaddafi Libyan migration policy is completely different from that implemented during his regime. The current conflict and the absence of a rule of law mean that the situation for migrants remains dire and desperate. The UNHCR has sought to aid and protect those who have been forced to flee their homes, which is one of the core mandates of the GCR. The GCR, under the office of the UNHCR, has outlined four key objectives for member states, which are used here as a framework to discuss how the GCR has been implemented as a response to the human-rights violations and the grave crimes against humanity inflicted on desperate migrants in Libya.

GCR Objective 1: To ease pressures on host countries

The primary objective, outlined in the GCR, is the desire to provide assistance to and ease pressure on host countries such as Italy, which has been responsible for rescuing, processing, settling and placing African migrants. To assist host countries such as Italy, the UNHCR developed the Central Mediterranean Sea Initiative (CMSI) in 2015, which outlined 12 steps on how the EU could be involved in the rescue of those stranded at sea (UNHCR, 2015b). Despite the CSMI's call for solidarity with the EU member states, there were reports from migrants on Libyan shores of officials' 'lethal disregard' for their obligations to search, rescue and protect migrants in the Mediterranean Sea, with ship masters, shipping companies and flag states failing and delaying to respond to those in dangerous situations at sea. The COVID-19 pandemic further exacerbated the issue, with reports of migrants being denied access to humanitarian vessels (UN, 2021).

Furthermore, the UNHCR has assisted in the harmonisation of EU migration policies. As a response to the mounting political pressure around the issue of irregular migration, many European countries have implemented stronger border controls. Coastal countries, such as Italy and Spain, have intensified their protectionist immigration policies by erecting fences, toughening immigration laws, and drawing on the Common European Asylum System (CEAS), as well as the Dublin Regulation, which is 'a strategy becoming known as the internationalisation or externalisation of EU migration policies' (Düvell, 2006). As members of the international community and signatories of the Geneva Convention, states still have the responsibility to ensure that EU law, international law and country-specific immigration policies do not interfere with one another.

In the case of African–EU migration, a central issue of contention arises when host countries refoul refugees who are protected under international law. The main point of dispute is differentiating between migrants and refugees, as the Commissioner of the UNHCR, Filippo Grandi, explained:

> Refugees are often lumped together with migrants – people who have left their homes in search of work and a better life. But they are different. Refugees do not travel in search of economic opportunity but to escape war, persecution, death, torture and rape, and because they do not have a home to go to. They are entitled to the protection and assistance of other states under international law, and under shared principles of human decency (Grandi, 2016).

Given the UNHCR's mandate not to interfere in politics, how does the organisation exert its influence on sovereign states to comply with international law? Similar to other international organisations, the UNHCR has no formal authority to coerce adherence to laws or its mandates, but relies on the goodwill of states. The UNHCR works alongside the EU institutions, such as the Council of the European Union, the European Commission, the European Parliament, and the European Court of Justice, to advise and uphold its mandate (Meandzija, 2018). Furthermore, the UNHCR consults within its European Union Agency for Fundamental Rights, the ultimate goal being to engage in 'regular and systematic exchanges of information and analysis on particular issues arising from Member States' (Einarsson, 2011).

Despite these attempts to relieve host countries of the mounting pressures of refugees and migrants, the ultimate authority remains with sovereign states. Thus, there is no surety that countries such as Italy will uphold international law to protect migrants.

GCR Objective 2: To enhance refugee self-reliance

As part of the objective to enhance refugees' capabilities to become self-reliant and self-sufficient, the UNHCR has implemented several projects. Between January and August 2021, the UNHCR provided the following assistance to migrants in Libya: 2,148 migrants received legal assistance; 12,300 received food aid; 11,818 received emergency life-saving items – 2,716 of these were individuals with disabilities; and 154 received special support (UNHCR, 2021c). Providing medical assistance, training and protection measures not only protects the human dignity of these migrants but also ensures their physical survival in conditions in which they would not otherwise have survived. Although these projects are helpful and lifesaving, other concerns remain unaddressed. For instance, the assistance is usually temporary and does not demonstrably enhance their long-term self-reliance. Furthermore, without accompanying efforts to resolve the dangerous situations facing refugees and migrants in Libya, either through larger scale voluntary return programmes or by assisting sustainable resettlement, the UNHRC's temporary relief assistance is unlikely to improve refugee self-reliance.

GCR Objective 3: To expand access to third country solutions

To support the countries of origin, safeguard the dignity of refugees and facilitate their safe return, the UNHCR has assisted with durable solutions aimed at 'resettlement to third countries, return to countries where they have previously been granted asylum or to voluntarily return home' (UNHCR, 2018b). In 2021, 12 flights were chartered to resettle 224 people from Libya (113 females and 111 males) (UNHCR 2020b). The resettled migrants were from Syria, Sudan, Eritrea and South Sudan, and the three main destination countries were Canada, Sweden and Norway. The resettlement criteria were children at risk, legal and physical protection needs, medical needs, survivors of violence and torture, and women at risk (UNHCR, 2020b).

There is still much debate around whether Libya is safe enough to be considered a third country for disembarkation, following rescue at sea. In 2018, a GDF was established by the UNHCR, in collaboration with the Libyan Ministry of Interior, as a safe space to host those pending evacuation (UNHCR, 2020a). Boat embarkations on 18 November 2021 revealed 302 survivors (including 50 women and 20 children); 348 people were reported missing and 112 bodies were recovered. The UNHCR and the International

Rescue Committee (IRC) provided aid and medical assistance. The Libyan Coast Guard continues to intercept boats and rescue people; by November 2021 they had picked up 29,427 asylum seekers, refugees and migrants, (UNHCR Libya Update, 2021).

The countries of origin of those rescued are Sudan (3,929); Eritrea (1,462); Syria (1,105); Ethiopia (489); Somalia (320); South Sudan (35); Yemen (20); Palestine (4), and Iraq (1) (UNHCR, 2020a). On 23 September 2020, the UNHCR and the IOM have called for the EU to adopt a more cooperative and principled approach to the African–EU migration crisis through the launch of the European Commission's new Pact on Migration and Asylum. This pact is aimed at curtailing the protectionist policies of EU countries and increasing their responsiveness to saving lives at sea, in light of the 'delays in disembarking migrants and refugees rescued at sea, increasing reports of pushbacks and the devastating fires at the Moria Registration and Identification Centre (RIC) on the Greek island of Lesvos' (UNHCR, 2020d).

Despite these efforts, the Libyan Coast Guard has been criticised for its search and rescue operations, with some accusing the guards of smuggling, and using firearms on migrants (UNHCR, 2020b). This calls into question the effective implementation of the GCR, which was designed to protect the interest of migrants. This backlash further calls into question the credibility of the claims that international organisations, such as the UN, are upholding human rights at the global level.

A key challenge to the effectiveness of the UNHCR in Libya could be traced to Libya's refusal to ratify the 1971 UN Convention and Protocol Relating to the Status of Refugees. However, Libya has officially ratified the 1969 Convention dealing with the specific aspects of refugee governance in Africa, and the African Charter on Human and Peoples' Rights, suggesting that the fundamental problem lies in implementation rather than informal ratification of international treaties. Thus, despite the presence of the UNHCR in Libya and the country's formal commitment to (some) of the international protocols, migrants remain at risk of unlawful and prolonged detention and persecution. The passivity of the UNHCR in the face of Libya's disregard for the plight of its refugee population is symptomatic of the limitations of the organisation's mandate and operations.

CGR Objective 4: To support conditions in countries of origin for return in safety and dignity

In November 2017, the UNHCR established two Emergency Transit Mechanisms (ETMs) in Niger and signed a Memorandum of Understanding (MOU) with Niger in December 2017, later extended in December 2019 for two years. The ETMs were established to provide for the safe evacuation of refugees and asylum seekers from detention centres in Libya to Niger. Since 17 December, about 1,723 flights from Libya to Niger have evacuated 3,208 refugees and asylum seekers (UNHCR, 2020c).

In alignment with the GCR Objective 4, to support countries of origin for the safe and dignified return of refugees, the UNHCR partnered with African regional organisations, namely the AU, ECOWAS, and the SADC. As a regional organisation, ECOWAS has developed a less protectionist approach to migration. In November 2001, a MOU was signed by the UN High Commissioner for Refugees, Ruud Lubbers, and ECOWAS, aimed at protecting refugees in West Africa, especially the most vulnerable, who are women and children (UNHCR, 2001). Later, in 2012, the Banjul Plan of Action was adopted between ECOWAS, the UNHCR, and Côte d'Ivoire. The Banjul Plan of Action was an ECOWAS initiative dedicated to eradicating statelessness in Africa (UNHCR, 2019d). More recently, the UNCHR and ECOWAS have collaborated to build their humanitarian response capacity to deal with emergency situations in West Africa. From 26–31 August 2018, Emergency Management Training (EMT) for ECOWAS commenced in Jaji, Kaduna State, Nigeria, to equip trainees with the skills to prepare, manage and respond to emergency situations (Relief Web, 2018).

The UNHCR also signed a MOU on the ETM with the government of Rwanda and the AU to evacuate more refugees from Libya to the Republic of Rwanda. Under this MOU, Rwanda will provide protection and assistance to refugees and asylum seekers currently held in detention centres in Libya. The 'UNHCR has evacuated more than 4,400 refugees and asylum seekers out of Libya to other countries since 2017, including 2,900 through the Emergency Transit Mechanism in Niger and 425 to European countries through the Emergency Transit Centre in Romania' (UNHCR, 2019c). The African Commission on Human and Peoples' Rights (ACPHR) has also collaborated with the UNHCR to achieve the overall objective of protecting the human rights of refugees, asylum seekers, returnees and other persons of concern (ACPHR, 2022).

Conclusion

This chapter has discussed the role of the UNHCR in addressing African–EU migration. As the champion of the Geneva Convention, the UNHCR has been active in upholding the standards of international law, which seek to protect migrants. Even though the end of the African–EU migration crisis is nowhere in sight, efforts to manage it are evident. The UNHCR's mandate to protect and serve is exemplary in principle, but in practice it has fallen short. Its efforts to provide migrants with health care, food, money, shelter and the opportunity to resettle in third countries are commendable, as they do help to enhance refugees self-reliance in terms of the GCR's second mandate. These efforts have undoubtedly provided temporary relief to some, but considerable challenges remain to ensure the long-term and sustainable protection of Libya's vulnerable migrant population.

Although the GCR is clear on its mandates, the guidelines on its implementation have not been clearly outlined, thus creating room for host countries to interpret the mandate under the guise of compliance. While the UNHCR's mandate is said to be 'non-political', politics remain evident in practice. The GCR's first objective seeks to ease pressures on host countries, but the UNHCR seems to be bargaining with European host countries, while the plight of refugees and other vulnerable migrants is at stake. Instead of strongly advocating for refugees, the UNHCR has established partnerships such as the Italian–Libyan Agreement, which is less focused on the protection of refugees than the protection of European borders. It is unfortunate that humans continue to be disregarded in this way. Perhaps due to its Western orientation, the UNHCR seems to have been yielding to the wishes of the EU, rather than defending the interests of migrants. Consequently, the organisation has been unable to influence the EU and its member states to implement the objectives of the GCR.

The implementation of the GCR's objective to expand access to third countries has been slow. Given the unprecedented number of migrants that entered Europe in 2014–16, which temporarily overwhelmed the European asylum system, surely more could have been achieved by this time? The UNHCR's 'non-political' stance on migration matters is alarming as migrants, many of whom are youths, women and children, continue to fall victim to sexual violence, human trafficking and labour exploitation.

Refugee camps are effective in providing some measure of safety. However, with the number of refugees continuously increasing in facilities like the Dadaab refugee camp in Kenya, because residents are left waiting for resettlement for years or even decades, this is not a sustainable, long-term solution. Furthermore, the UNHCR's collaboration on the Central Mediterranean Sea Initiative (CMSI) has been riddled with inconsistencies, with reports of Italian officials refusing to assist irregular migrants on the dangerous sea, and even forcefully overturning their boats. Such initiatives were meant to protect migrants from the pushback of European protectionist policies but, instead, have only served to solidify them.

Regional organisations such as the AU and ECOWAS, as well as African heads of states, have a responsibility to support, safeguard, defend and resettle their citizens. Countries such as South Africa, Kenya and Botswana have the capacity to open their borders further to accommodate migrants. Although such an initiative may not prevent irregular migrants from seeking better opportunities in Europe, it would expand their choices. Although African labour markets are currently unable to offer all African citizens the opportunity to put their skills and education to work, leaving some to see irregular migration to Europe as the only viable option, intra-African labour mobility may also be an alternative to refugee resettlement outside the continent.

Xenophobia rears its ugly head in conversations like these, as the reality of the intolerance and violence towards non-nationals in countries such as South Africa deters other Africans from seeking opportunities within African borders. It is a sobering and depressing truth that when Africans in danger have knocked on the doors of their safer African neighbours, they have often been rejected or faced persecution. The solution to these challenges lies within the African continent, especially at a time when the UNHCR and other international organisations who are entrusted with the protection of vulnerable populations continue to struggle to live up to their mandates.

Notes

1   The records are based on hundreds of eyewitness accounts collected from migrants through surveys by the Mixed Migration Monitoring Mechanism Initiative (4Mi). The interviews with migrants were conducted by 4Mi between December 2018 and April 2019 in West, North and East Africa and were analysed by the Missing Migrants Project team before being added

to its MMP database. See: 'Over 7,400 deaths on migration routes across Africa in last five years, IOM figures show', 10 December 2019, International Organization for Migration.

2   The 'non-discrimination' principle speaks to the fact that no refugee or asylum seeker be discriminated against on the basis of 'race, age, religion, disability or country of origin' (UNHCR, 2019a). See UNHCR, Convention and Protocol Relating to the Status of Refugees.

3   The 'non-penalization' principle speaks to the fact that refugees or asylum seekers should not be punished for the means in which they seek asylum, as some of them may have to breach immigration rules (UNHCR, 2019a). See UNHCR, Convention and Protocol Relating to the Status of Refugees.

4   The 'non-refoulement' principle speaks to the fact that 'no one shall expel or return (refouler) a refugee against his or her will, in any manner whatsoever, to a territory where he or she fears threats to life or freedom' (UNHCR, 2019a). See UNHCR, Convention and Protocol Relating to the Status of Refugees.

5   The IOM currently supports 122 countries through its development fund; it targeted 46.8 million beneficiaries through its crisis response efforts between 2020–21, and assisted 1.7 million migrants to return home voluntarily (IOM, 2021).

6   At its special meeting in Tampere on 15 and 16 October 1999, the then 15 EU member states agreed in the European Council to work towards establishing a Common European Asylum System, to be implemented in two phases (Tampere Programme, 1999–2004). The vision of establishing a Common European Asylum System was based on the full and inclusive application of the 1951 Geneva Refugee Convention, thus ensuring that nobody is sent back to persecution, that is, maintaining the principle of non-refoulement (Tampere Conclusions, para. 13). The instruments that were negotiated and adopted, consisted of (in chronological order) the EURODAC Regulation, the Temporary Protection Directive, the Reception Conditions Directive, the Dublin Regulation, the Qualification Directive, and the Asylum Procedures Directive. See the International Centre for Migration Policy Development, 'In search for a vision of the Common European Asylum System (CEAS)', 19 June 2019. Online at: https://www.icmpd.org/blog/2019/in-search-for-a-vision-of-the-common-european-asylum-system-ceas (accessed 22 May 2022).

References

Abebe T. 2020. 'Fewer migrants to Europe, bigger problems for Africa'. Pretoria: Institute for Security Studies. Online at: https://issafrica.org/iss-today/fewer-migrants-to-europe-bigger-problems-for-africa (accessed 17 October 2021).

African Commission on Human and People's Rights. 2022. Memorandum of Understanding between ACHPR and UNHCR. Online at: https://www.achpr.org/presspublic/publication?id=23 (accessed 17 February 2022).

Akinola, A. 2021. 'The Mali coup and instability in Africa', *Premium Times*, 9 June. Online at: https://www.premiumtimesng.com/opinion/466684-the-mali-coup-and-instability-in-africa-by-adeoye-o-akinola.html (accessed 17 February 2022).

Baumgartner, P. and Wagner, M. 2019. 'In search for a vision for the Common European Asylum System (CEAS)'. Commentary. Vienna: The International Centre for Migration Policy Development. Online at: https://www.icmpd.org/file/download/52101/file/In%2520search%2520for%2520a%2520visio n%2520of%2520the%2520Common%2520European%2520Asylum%2520S ystem%2520%2528CEAS%2529.pd (accessed on 11 October 2021).

Bob-Millar, G.M. and Bob-Millar, G.K. 2013. 'The politics of trans-Saharan transit migration in the Maghreb: Ghanaian migrants in Libya, c. 1980– 2012', *African Review of Economics and Finance*, 5(1). Online at: https://www.african-review.com/journal/v5(1)december2013/Bob%20Milliar%20 and%20Bob%20Milliar_The%20Politics%20of%20Trans-Saharan%20 Transit%20Migration%20in%20the%20Maghreb.pdf (accessed 17 February 2022).

Council of Europe. 2020. 'Commissioner calls on the Italian government to suspend the co-operation activities in place with the Libyan Coast Guard that impact on the return of persons intercepted at sea to Libya'. Online at: https://www.coe.int/en/web/commissioner/-/ommissioner-calls-on-the-italian-government-to-suspend-the-co-operation-activities-in-place-with-the-libyan-coast-guard-that-impact-on-the-return-of-p (accessed 17 February 2022).

De Haas, H. 2006. 'Trans-Saharan migration to North Africa and the EU: Historical roots and current trends'. Washington, DC: Migration Policy Institute. Online at: https://www.migrationpolicy.org/article/trans-saharan-migration-north-africa-and-eu-historical-roots-and-current-trends (accessed 13 October 2021).

Düvell, F. 2006. 'Crossing the fringes of Europe: Transit migration in the

EU's neighbourhood'. Compas Communications, WP-06-33. Centre on Migration, Policy and Society (COMPAS), School of Anthropology, University of Oxford. Online at: https://www.compas.ox.ac.uk/wp-content/uploads/WP-2006-033-D%C3%BCvell_Fringe_Migration.pdf (accessed 16 October 2021).

Einarsson, S. 2011. *The European Union and International Human Rights Law*. Office of the Commissioner, United Nations Human Rights. Online at: http://www.europe.ohchr.org/Documents/Publications/EU_and_International_Law.pdf (accessed 15 October 2021).

European Commission. n.d. Migration and Home Affairs. In *European Commission*. Online at: https://juridice.ro/wp-content/uploads/2017/03/factsheet_-_the_dublin_system_en.pdf (accessed 13 October 2021).

European Commission. 2017. Memorandum of understanding on cooperation in the fields of development, the fight against illegal immigration, human trafficking and fuel smuggling and on reinforcing the security of borders between the State of Libya and the Italian Republic. In *Odysseus Network*. Online at: https://eumigrationlawblog.eu/wp-content/uploads/2017/10/MEMORANDUM_translation_finalversion.doc.pdf (accessed 15 October 2021).

Goodwin-Gill, G.S. n.d. 'Protocol relating to the Status of Refugees'. United Nations Audiovisual Library of International Law. Online at: https://legal.un.org/avl/ha/prsr/prsr.html (accessed 11 October 2021)

Grandi, F. 2016. 'Refugees deserve action and investment, not indifference and cruelty'. Geneva: World Economic Forum. Online at: https://www.weforum.org/agenda/2016/05/refugees-deserve-action-and-investment-not-indifference-and-cruelty (accessed 15 October 2021).

Grange, M. and Flynn, M. 2015. Immigration Detention in Libya. Global Detention Project, February 2015. Geneva: Global Detention Project. Online at: https://www.refworld.org/pdfid/5567387e4.pdf (accessed 19 October 2021).

Human Rights Watch. 2020. 'Italy: Halt abusive migration cooperation with Libya: As abuse is known, material assistance makes Rome complicit', 12 February. Online at: https://www.hrw.org/news/2020/02/12/italy-halt-abusive-migration-cooperation-libya (accessed 17 February 2022).

Institute for Pan-African Thought and Conversation and The Nordic Africa Institute (IPATC/NAI). 2021. 'Centering the voices of African migrants in Africa/European Union (EU) migration debates', *Policy Brief 9*. Online at: https://ipatc.joburg/wp-content/uploads/2021/06/ipatc-policy-brief-

9-centering-the-voices-of-afri9can-migrants-in-africa-eu-migration.pdf (accessed 12 October 2021).

International Organisation for Migration (IOM). 2020a. 'Migration data in Western Africa'. Migration Data Portal. Online at: https://www. migrationdataportal.org/regional-data-overview/western-africa (accessed 11 October 2021).

International Organisation for Migration (IOM). 2020b. 'Western African Route: Migration to the Canary Islands – Irregular migration towards Europe, January–November 2020', (18 November 2020). United Nations Office for the Coordination of Humanitarian Affairs. Online at: https:// reliefweb.int/report/world/western-african-route-migration-canary-islands-irregular-migration-towards-europe (accessed 12 October 2021).

International Organization for Migration (IOM). 2020c. 'Libya's migrant report: Round 30, March–April 2020', *Displacement Tracking Matrix*. Online at: https://displacement.iom.int/system/tdf/reports/DTM_R30_Migrant_Report.pdf?file=1andtype=nodeandid=9067 (accessed 14 October 2021).

International Organization for Migration (IOM). 2019. 'Over 7,400 deaths on migration routes across Africa in last five years, IOM figures show'. Geneva: IOM. Online at: https://www.iom.int/news/over-7400-deaths-migration-routes-across-africa-last-five-years-iom-figures-show (accessed 10 October 2021).

International Organization for Migration (IOM) and Libya Ministry of Displaced Peoples Affairs. 2021. 'Internal displacement in Libya: Displacement from Tripoli during hostilities 2019–2020'. Geneva: IOM. Online at: https:// displacement.iom.int/system/tdf/reports/DTM_MinistryOfDisplaceme nt_2019-2020_Report_ENGLISH.PDF?file=1andtype=nodeandid=10894 (accessed 13 October 2021).

Jaji, R. 2012. 'Social technology and refugee encampment in Kenya', *Journal of Refugee Studies,* 25(2): 221–38.

Jordan, B. and Franck Düvell. 2003. *Irregular Migration: The dilemmas of transnational mobility.* Cheltenham: Edward Elgar.

Kuschminder, K. 2020. 'Once a destination for migrants, post-Gaddafi Libya has gone from transit route to containment'. Washington, DC: Migration Policy Institute. Online at: https://www.migrationpolicy.org/article/once-destination-migrants-post-gaddafi-libya-has-gone-transit-route-containment (accessed 14 October 2021).

Marchand, K., Reinold, J. and Dias, R. 2017. 'Study on migration routes in the East and Horn of Africa'. Maastricht Graduate school of Governance.

Online at: https://i.unu.edu/media/migration.unu.edu/publication/4717/ Migration-Routes-East-and-Horn-of-Africa.pdf (accessed 15 October 2021).

McConnachie, K. 2016. 'Camps of containment: A genealogy of the refugee camp', *Humanity*, 7(3): 397–412.

Meandzija, B. 2018. 'The UNHCR's role in the harmonization of EU migration policies during the refugee and migrant crisis' Seminar paper. *Research Gate.* Online at: https://www.researchgate.net/publication/338611883_The_ UNHCR%27s_Role_in_the_Harmonization_of_EU_Migration_Policies_ during_the_Refugee_and_Migrant_Crisis (accessed 11 October 2021)

Menendez, A.J. 2016. 'The refugee crisis: Between human tragedy and symptom of the structural crisis of European integration'. Editorial, *European Law Journal*, 22(4): 388–416. Online at: 311892117_The_Refugee_Crisis_ Between_Human_Tragedy_and_Symptom_of_the_Structural_Crisis_of_ European_Integration_Editorial (accessed 13 October 2021).

Mercator Dialogue on Asylum and Migration. 2018. 'Flexible solidarity: A comprehensive strategy for asylum and immigration in the EU'. Online at: https://www.ceps.eu/wp-content/uploads/2018/06/MEDAM-assessment-report_2018.pdf (retrieved 10 September 2021).

Mukoya, T. 2019. '"There is a crisis, but not in Europe", UN High Commissioner Filippo Grandi answers questions about migration and refugees', *Deutschland de.* Online at: https://www.deutschland.de/en/topic/politics/refugees-in-europe-filippo-grandi-interview (accessed 10 October 2021).

Newhouse, L.S. 2015. 'More than mere survival: violence, humanitarian governance, and practical material politics in a Kenyan refugee camp', *Environment and Planning*, 47(11): 2292–307.

Nwabuzo, O. and Schaeder L. 2017. 'Racism and discrimination in the context of migration in Europe'. European Commission. Online at: https://ec.europa. eu/migrant-integration/library-document/racism-and-discrimination-context-migration-europe_en (accessed 10 October 2021).

Orav, A. 2015. 'EU migration policy: Calls for holistic approach and closer international cooperation'. European Parliamentary Research Service. Online at: https://epthinktank.eu/2015/05/13/eu-migration-policy-calls-for-holistic-approach-and-closer-international-cooperation/ (accessed 12 October 2021).

Organisation for Economic Co-operation and Development (OECD). 2015. 'The unfolding humanitarian crisis: How does it compare with previous ones?' Migration Policy Debates. Online at: https://www.oecd.org/migration/Is-this-refugee-crisis-different.pdf (accessed 13 September 2021)

Relief Web. 2018. 'ECOWAS and UNHCR collaborate to build humanitarian response capacity in West Africa'. Online at: https://reliefweb.int/report/world/ecowas-and-unhcr-collaborate-build-humanitarian-response-capacity-west-africa (accessed 17 February 2022)

Satgar, V. 2019. *Racism After Apartheid: Challenges for Marxism and anti-racism.* Johannesburg: Wits University Press. Online at: https://www.jstor.org/stable/10.18772/22019033061.9?seq=1#metadata_info_tab_contents (accessed 7 February 2021).

United Nations. 2021. *'Lethal disregard': Search and rescue and the protection of migrants in the central Mediterranean Sea.* Online at: https://www.ohchr.org/Documents/Issues/Migration/OHCHR-thematic-report-SAR-protection-at-sea.pdf (accessed 21 October 2021).

United Nations. 2020. 'Thousands suffer extreme rights abuses journeying to Africa's Mediterranean coast, say humanitarians', *UN News.* Online at: https://news.un.org/en/story/2020/07/1069231 (accessed 13 September 2021).

UN High Commissioner for Refugees (UNHCR). 2022a. Africa. Online at: https://www.unhcr.org/africa.html (accessed 7 February 2022).

UN High Commissioner for Refugees (UNHCR). 2022b. Libya Funding. Online at: https://reporting.unhcr.org/libya-funding-2022 (accessed 17 February 2022).

UN High Commissioner for Refugees (UNHCR). 2021a. Asylum and Migration. Online at: https://www.unhcr.org/asylum-and-migration.html#:~:text=Mixed%20movements%20(or%20mixed%20migration,transport%2C%20but%20for%20different%20reasons(accessed 17 February 2022).

UN High Commissioner for Refugees (UNHCR). 2021b. Figures at a glance. Online at: https://www.unhcr.org/afr/figures-at-a-glance.html (accessed 17 February 2022).

UN High Commissioner for Refugees (UNHCR). 2021c. UNHCR Libya Monthly Response Factsheet (January-August 2021). UN Refugee Agency. Online at: https://reporting.unhcr.org/sites/default/files/Libya%20Response%20Dashboard-20%20August%202021.pdf (accessed 21 October 2021).

UN High Commissioner for Refugees (UNHCR). 2020a. 'Durable Solutions Fact Sheet: Libya'. UNHCR Operational Data Portal. Online at: https://data2.unhcr.org/en/dataviz/110?sv=0andgeo=666 (accessed 18 October 2021).

UN High Commissioner for Refugees (UNHCR). 2020b. 'Libya Evacuation Factsheet'. UNHCR. Online at: https://data2.unhcr.org/en/dataviz/111?sv=0andgeo=666 (accessed 13 October 2021)

UN High Commissioner for Refugees (UNHCR). 2020c. *UNHCR Position on the Designations of Libya as a Safe Third Country and as a Place of Safety for the Purpose of Disembarkation Following Rescue at Sea.* UN Refugee Agency. Online at: https://www.refworld.org/docid/5f1edee24.html (accessed 17 October 2021)

UN High Commissioner for Refugees (UNHCR). 2020d. 'Emergency Transit Mechanism', Fact Sheet. Online at: https://reliefweb.int/sites/reliefweb.int/files/resources/UNHCR%20Niger%2C%20Niamey%20CO%20%20Factsheet%20Update%20ETM%20May%202020.pdf (accessed 17 February 2022).

UN High Commissioner for Refugees (UNHCR). 2020e. 'UNHCR to suspend operations at GDF in Tripoli amid safety concerns'. Online at: https://www.unhcr.org/news/press/2020/1/5e32c2c04/unhcr-suspend-operations-gdf-tripoli-amid-safety-concerns.html (accessed 17 February 2022).

UN High Commissioner for Refugees (UNHCR). 2020f. 'UNHCR and IOM call for a truly common and principled approach to European migration and asylum policies'. The UN Refugee Agency. Online at: https://www.unhcr.org/news/press/2020/9/5f69deff4/unhcr-iom-call-truly-common-principled-approach-european-migration-asylum.html (retrieved 14 October 2021).

UN High Commissioner for Refugees (UNHCR). 2019a. *Convention and Protocol Relating to the Status of Refugees.* UNHCR. Online at: https://www.unhcr.org/protection/basic/3b66c2aa10/convention-protocol-relating-status-refugees.html (accessed 10 September 2021).

UN High Commissioner for Refugees (UNHCR). 2019b. 'Joint Statement: Government of Rwanda, UNHCR and African Union agree to evacuate refugees out of Libya'. UNHCR. Online at: https://www.unhcr.org/news/press/2019/9/5d5d1c9a4/joint-statement-government-rwanda-unhcr-african-union-agree-evacuate-refugees.html (accessed 21 October 2021).

UN High Commissioner for Refugees (UNHCR). 2019c. 'Country – Libya'. UNHCR. Online at: https://data2.unhcr.org/en/country/lby (accessed 20 October 2021).

UN High Commissioner for Refugees (UNHCR). 2019d. 'UNHCR West Africa Eradicating statelessness in West Africa: ECOWAS, UNHCR and Côte d'Ivoire celebrate the 2nd anniversary of the Banjul Plan of Action'. https://

data2.unhcr.org/en/documents/details/69738 (accessed 17 February 2022).

UN High Commissioner for Refugees (UNHCR). 2019e. 'Dadaab Refugee Complex'. UNHCR Kenya. UN Refugee Agency. Online at: https://www.unhcr.org/ke/dadaab-refugee-complex (accessed 12 September 2021).

UN High Commissioner for Refugees. 2018b. 'Resettlement'. UNHCR. Online at: https://www.unhcr.org/resettlement.html (accessed 14 October 2021)

UN High Commissioner for Refugees (UNHCR). 2017. 'Quick Impact Projects'. Online at: https://www.unhcr.org/libya.html#:~:text=Our%20overall%20objective%20in%20Libya,asylum%2Dseekers%20and%20host%20communities.andtext=Libya%20also%20hosts%2043%2C113%20refugees,through%20dangerous%20routes%20towards%20Europe (accessed 17 February 2022).

UN High Commissioner for Refugees (UNHCR). 2015a. 'UNHCR Central Mediterranean Sea Initiative (CMSI), EU solidarity for rescue-at-sea and protection of asylum seekers and migrants'. Online at: https://www.unhcr.org/protection/operations/531990199/unhcr-central-mediterranean-sea-initiative-cmsi-eu-solidarity-rescue-at.html (accessed 20 October 2021).

UN High Commissioner for Refugees (UNHCR). 2015b. 'UNHCR outlines proposals to manage refugee and migration crisis in Europe ahead of EU Summit. UNHCR'. Online at: https://www.unhcr.org/news/latest/2015/9/56015ba86/unhcr-outlines-proposals-manage-refugee-migration-crisis-europe-ahead-eu.html (accessed on 12 October 2021).

UN High Commissioner for Refugees (UNHCR). 2013. 'Note on the United Nations High Commissioner for Refugees and his Office'. UN High Commissioner for Refugees. Online at: https://www.refworld.org/docid/5268c9474.html (accessed 13 September 2021).

UN High Commissioner for Refugees (UNHCR). 2009. 'Central Africa and the Great Lakes', UNHCR Global Appeal, 2009, Update. UN Refugee Agency. Online at: https://www.unhcr.org/4922d40d0.pdf (accessed 15 September 2021).

UN High Commissioner for Refugees (UNHCR). 2001. ECOWAS–UNHCR Memorandum of Understanding. Online at: https://www.unhcr.org/news/briefing/2001/11/3bfa4a962/ecowas-unhcr-memorandum-understanding.html (accessed 17 February 2022).

United Nations Office for the Coordination of Humanitarian Affairs (OCHA). 2018a. 'Africa: Sub-Saharan: Total population of concern to UNHCR, end 2018'. Online at: https://reliefweb.int/map/world/africa-sub-saharan-total-population-concern-unhcr-end-2018 (accessed 17 February 2022).

United Nations Development Programme (UNDP). 2019. *Scaling Fences: Voices of irregular African migrants to Europe*. Online at: https://www.undp.org/ publications/scaling-fences#modal-publication-download (accessed 20 October 2021).

United Nations Development Programme (UNDP). 2018. 'The future of human mobility: UNDP in Europe and Central Asia'. Online at: http:// www.eurasia.undp.org/content/rbec/en/home/blog/2018/the-future-of- human-mobility-4-things-to-keep-in-mind-when-debat.html (accessed 19 October 2021).

Zanfrini, L. n.d. 'Europe and the refugee crisis: A challenge to our civilization'. Academic Impact. United Nations. Online at: https://www.un.org/en/ academic-impact/europe-and-refugee-crisis-challenge-our-civilization (accessed 19 October 2021).

Chapter 18

Towards lasting solutions to the Africa–European Union migration challenge

Ahunna Eziakonwa

Introduction

Migration is as old as human history. Contrary to the current predominant narrative, the flow of people, goods and services across Europe and Africa dates to ancient civilisation and has been part of the broader ecosystem of trade. The debate on migration must be framed in a more balanced manner that does not depict a one-sided story of desperate Africans risking high seas in shoddy boats to get to the promised land – Europe. In fact, the trend of migration between these two continents is one of duality. Europeans have migrated to Africa from precolonial times – and continue to live and thrive on the continent. The scramble for Africa and search for raw materials for European industries and, in more recent decades, for jobs in multinational companies (MNCs), remains the central *pull factor* that makes Africa a home of choice for many Europeans. Though contextually and operationally different (Europeans go with jobs whereas Africans go with dreams to find jobs), the incentives or pull factors are essentially the same for both European and African economic migrants: a search for enhanced or new and better economic opportunities for their families.

Finding lasting solutions and political consensus to Europe/Africa migration starts from the point of recognising the relationship's true dynamics. This recognition must bring all partners to the table to dialogue about how to protect migrant workers, both formal and informal, and create win–win solutions for both regions, so that migration can work for sustainable development. COVID-19 has exacerbated the urgency to seek solutions, as the other side of the equation – the push factors – have increased considerably with the pandemic's impact of *reversed development* globally, and in Africa (UNDP, 2020a: 3).

This chapter assesses the duality of migration, teases out the similarity in pull factors in both Africa and Europe (the green pastures phenomenon), highlights the impact of COVID-19 on migration, and offers comprehensive, sustainable and equitable policy frameworks for solutions, while shedding light on a development approach including engagement from the United Nations Development Programme (UNDP).

The duality of migration

The one-sided story of migration between Africa and Europe is problematic because of its non-recognition of the hospitality Africa has accorded European migrants for generations, and its implicit message that the pursuit of better lives in other territorial jurisdictions is acceptable only in a unidirectional sense. It also ignores the contributions Africans have made to the European economy over centuries. The story often depicted is one of desperate Africans drowning in the Mediterranean Sea off Lampedusa (*Guardian*, 2013) and other European shores – in an exodus to the promised land (Asserate, 2019). However, the history of European migration into Africa tells of a commonality in some of the reasons that initially pushed Europeans to search for greener pastures in Africa – such as the attempts to flee poverty and overpopulation (Oualdi, 2018). This commonality confirms that migration is a natural phenomenon for which we need development solutions.

Data on African migration trends to Europe remains misrepresented. Contrary to the dominant narrative, more than 80 per cent of African migration occurs within the continent (UNDESA, 2019a). According to the United Nations Department for Social and Economic Affairs (UNDESA), migration dynamics are changing. In 2019, the regional distribution of international migrants grew faster in northern Africa and sub-Saharan

Africa than in other regions. Unfortunately, there is paucity of data on the pattern of European migration to Africa, particularly official data on European economic migrants in Africa.

Similarity in pull factors

Migration is an inevitable consequence of growing economies and open societies. Ill-informed responses often have dire consequences, and lead to more irregular migration through unprotected routes complicating migration governance and heightening the risk of abuse and violations (European Council on Foreign Relations, 2018). The calls to 'stop' migration are inherently contradictory to humanity's curiosity – both from Europe and Africa – judged from accounts of Africa's discovery of Europe (Northrup, 2014).

Migration between Africa and Europe results from pull factors on both sides. A common denominator is the economic incentive that drives migration. On the one hand, development institutions, MNCs and other external actors have been pulled by the attractive compensation, resource extraction and other socio-economic benefits in Africa. On the other hand, Africans move to Europe because of a gap in the European market that requires companies to use African labour (formally or informally) in different contexts, such as (historically) fighting wars, and building railways, bridges and other infrastructure, or more recently, in health, agriculture, education, production and service delivery.

The type of migrant this chapter addresses moves by choice. In the case of Africa, the story of some respondents during a recent UNDP study – *Scaling Fences: Voices of irregular African migrants to Europe* – was not one of desperation, but a search for a better future (UNDP, 2019). These individuals were already an educated group, on a development trajectory of ascendance, representing the positive story of development gains in Africa. Their plans were to make money and return to Africa (UN News, 2019).

A pull factor for this is the labour market gaps that have been filled by Africans in various European countries. Despite the official policy positions, companies offer Africans jobs in those parts of the economy that locals would prefer not to engage in. The phenomenon of undocumented African workers in communities in Europe has been around for decades. Stopping migration as a policy goal is ineffective if there is a continued strong demand in the labour markets. Many countries have specific schemes and visa categories for such workers (Institute for Public Policy and Research, 2015). Overall, however, Africans face unnecessarily harsh conditions in Europe, designed to create sufficient hardship, in terms of living conditions and overall protection, to make them give up and return home (UNDP, 2019).

COVID-19: An unwanted push factor

COVID-19 has created renewed pressure for (re)migration, as millions of Africans are being pushed back into poverty (UN, 2020), increasing their resolve to attain their dreams elsewhere (IOM, 2020). Since much more migration takes place within Africa, many African countries are likely to see more movements into their countries. In 2017, out of 100 immigrants in Africa, 79 were categorised under intra-African migration (UNCTAD, 2018).

According to the International Organization for Migration (IOM), which has been tracking the impact on movement daily during the COVID-19 pandemic, there is a special concern for youth living in conflict regions (IOM, 2020). The fear is that greater levels of poverty will trigger civil unrest or expose these young people to radicalisation, terrorism, and violent extremism. The reality of closed borders also means that youths are likely to move through non-formal routes. Thus, offering alternative pathways for lives and livelihoods is urgently needed. Meanwhile, Europe's economy is also struggling (UNDESA, 2020), and many Europeans will be looking for opportunities far and wide, and historically Africa has been an attraction, and a welcoming host.

Towards long-term solutions

The promotion of safe, orderly, and regular migration is a key goal of the UN through the Global Compact for Migration (GCM) (UN, 2018). The UN frames its work on migration in ensuring that the opportunities presented by migration are harnessed for development and in addressing adverse drivers and structural factors that hinder people from building and maintaining sustainable livelihoods in their countries of origin. This framework strives to create conducive conditions for migrants to enrich societies – both origin and destination countries – through their human, economic and social capacities. The following are some of the ways in which longer-term solutions can be shaped to leverage the migration–development nexus for win–win solutions for both the European Union (EU) and Africa.

The role of multilateral cooperation in creating decent jobs for migrants

Tourism – the exportation of a service through hosting foreign consumers – is one of the few sectors in which Africa is a net exporter. Resuscitating Africa's tourism sector by increasing opportunities in the airline industry and other areas of hospitality is an important driver of employment. Other ways of increasing employment include constructing more hotels and lodges, conserving the continent's historic sites, and incentivising tour companies/operators, including those in the transport logistics sector of the tourism industry.

Currently, centralised travel-related computer reservation systems offer full packages to European travellers – covering their flights, accommodation and transportation – leaving Africans to benefit only from visa fees (for governments) and perhaps handcrafts (for those engaged in the informal economy and small and medium-sized enterprises (SMEs)), because many of the large hotels that are part of these package tours are likely to be foreign-owned. European governments can help by conditioning the licensing of local travel companies to partnerships with African SMEs – to increase the financial value and content of what is left on the ground in Africa.

In the education sector, African countries have a unique advantage in being able to offer courses on history and culture, or around health services such as the treatment of complex infectious diseases. Access could be carved out in the European market for the provision of such professional services, which might be tied to temporary contracts in Europe. There is a sufficient body of multilateral legal instruments that would allow for this. For instance, the World Trade Organization's (WTO) General Agreement on Trade in Services (WTO–GATS, 1995), as well as most new generation regional trade agreements cater for the presence of foreign nationals supplying services on a temporary basis.

Europe should transform its skills gaps realities into an offer for lower skilled workers from Africa based on fixed-term contracts. Such an offer could allow African migrants to work without hiding under the radar, thereby contributing to filling existing market needs. These migrant workers would be duly recognised, remunerated and protected. In return, they would pay their taxes and would, after a given time, return home – with the possibility of applying to return after a requisite break.

Shifting portfolios – from extractive to inclusive investments

Sustainable development-oriented management of investment regimes offer plenty of opportunities to strengthening Africa–Europe partnerships on migration. At the core of this reframing is the transformation of the extractive character of investments into more inclusive partnerships, particularly ones that add value to Africa's raw materials within the continent. This would create quality jobs in Africa through increased foreign direct investment (FDI) ventures. It is important to foster new partnerships anchored on value addition *within* Africa that creates employment for African youth, capitalising on the continent's lower labour costs; partnerships that encourage technological innovation and invention, as well as digitalisation and industrial progress, including agro-allied industries. Value addition should also include the creation of 'greener' industries that promote biodiversity and renewable energy usage and the sustainable governance of natural resources such as water, to address desertification.

The advent of the African Continental Free Trade Area (AfCFTA) Agreement creates important opportunities for investment in Africa for those countries that are willing to deepen their productivity by partnering with local companies. Africa is home to many of the resources that advanced nations need for their industries, such as inputs into hi-tech Fourth Industrial Revolution products. A post-COVID-19 recovery requires emphasis on the type of relationship that fills the gaps in the development deficit in Africa caused, inter alia, by footloose investment regimes.

This approach is in line with Africa's aspirations for structural transformation anchored in both the Sustainable Development Goals (SDGs) and the African Union (AU)'s Agenda 2063. In this model, which emphasises value addition and not extraction of raw materials, Africa can realistically assume that economic-induced migration to Europe will reduce, as greater opportunities for Africans to fulfil their aspirations are created on the continent. Europeans could also seek work permits for highly skilled parts of these investments, based on local market needs (UNCTAD, 2019).

Figure 18.1: Top investor economies in Africa, 2013 and 2017
(Billions of dollars)

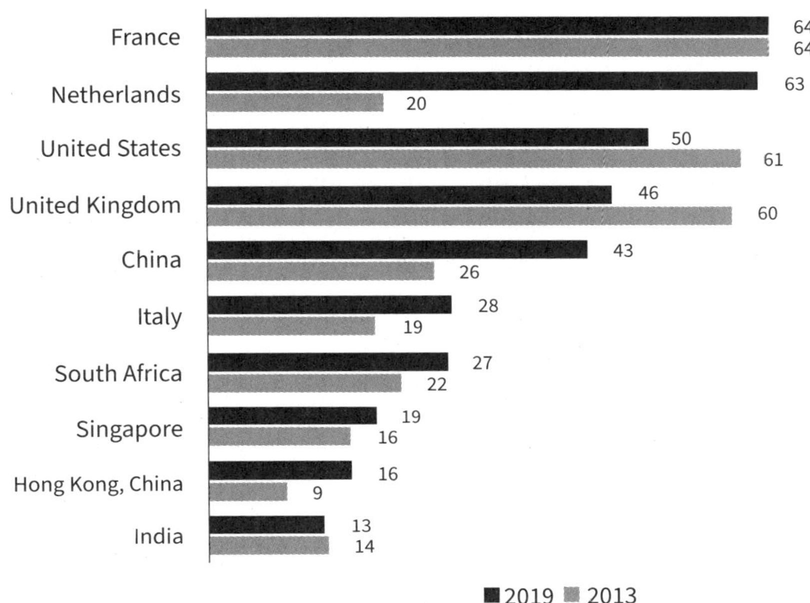

Source: UNCTAD (2019)

Promoting governance of Africa's natural resources to stem push factors

Strengthening capacities for the sustainable management of Africa's natural resources will create the financial base for the public goods needed to improve human development in Africa and reduce inequality in access to basic services. Strengthening effectiveness in this area will create an enabling environment for Africa's population to harness the opportunities within the continent, which could reduce the likelihood of irregular migration from Africa to Europe. The urgency for this shift is strengthened by the negative impact of COVID-19 on Africa and its devastating effect in Europe. More than ever before, Africa needs to step up the use of its own money and resources to fund its development – a major part of which stems from how FDI is managed.

Ensuring that MNCs pay their taxes where their substantive business operations are located is important to increase the pot of Africa's resources to fund its development. This is also a win–win situation from a business perspective. For example, taxes are important to ensure that the MNCs can receive the necessary services and infrastructure, such as electricity, roads and Internet connectivity, and operate in a sound business environment. More fundamentally, tax payment is the general standard applied to African companies that operate outside of Africa and should be expected from foreign companies working in Africa. Investment agreements that contain tax holidays should be revised to ensure that MNCs contribute to national development. Other important measures that should be applied to foreign MNCs in Africa include employment of local talent and restrictions on international hires to the dictate of economic needs, and mandatory joint ventures with local companies, including technology transfers and learning-by-doing, value addition, and local content, as well as lifting the veil to stem capital flight and illicit financial flows.

African governments must be decisive and committed to improving the governance of foreign companies and to transforming its contracting systems, fighting corruption, and consolidating the transparent use of fiscal revenues. Furthermore, the strengthening of oversight and efficient governance of African natural resources and the MNCs is also required to ensure that these companies comply with the conditions for operating in Africa.

Adoption of new generation policies: Putting people first

COVID-19 has demonstrated that economic models that do not invest in people must be abandoned. The weaknesses in health systems the world over, including in Africa, which were exposed by the COVID-19 pandemic are a case in point. The UN has prioritised a focus on a crisis-oriented socio-economic recovery. This involves bolstering Africa's health systems; providing social protection; and investing in SMEs and the informal sector, in macro-economic policies and multilateral cooperation, and in social cohesion.

Delivering on this mandate in a COVID-19 response and recovery context can be a powerful way to twist the tide of push factors into *incentives to remain*, offering opportunities for Africa's people, especially the youth and women, to enjoy productive lives in Africa. This should be done for its own merits, and for its appropriateness as a continent-wide response and investment in its people, and not only from the prism of keeping Africans out of Europe. This frame is important to give Africans the opportunity to participate in rebuilding their continent.

Over 90 per cent of African businesses are SMEs (IFC, 2020) and there are even more in the informal sector. Many of those who migrate could be failed entrepreneurs, or those with degrees and diplomas from institutions of learning that have failed to find employment in the local market. These people do not see themselves as contributing to the construction and prospects of their own economies. These are often professionals – teachers, doctors, nurses and lawyers – who have tried to make a living in their countries. While some may have recorded successes, they have not quite achieved their dreams or they cannot see the possibility of socio-economic shifts and opportunities within their nations. It is logical, therefore, that much of the intervention that needs to go into supporting Africa's youth is about creating that new reality of possibility through effective policies.

One of the few silver linings emerging from the COVID-19 pandemic has been the quality of the stewardship that African leaders have demonstrated in tumultuous times. Many African leaders have been swift and purposeful: imposing lockdowns (restriction of movements and capital) to contain the spread; offering social protection where they are able – less than 20 per cent of Africans have access to social protection (ILO, 2020) – and putting in place fiscal measures to support SMEs.

Decisive leadership is also relevant for migration governance because strong leadership will offer motivation and opportunities for *would-be migrants* who have demonstrated great ingenuity in producing goods for domestic markets faced with border closures and export bans. The kind of leadership that shows support for SMEs and innovators will contribute to boosting confidence and hope for prospects at home. Africa's youth have demonstrated that they are up to the task: from Eritrea's masks to Burkina Faso's respirators; from Nigeria's mobile testing facilities to Senegal's test kits; and from Mauritania's contact tracing to Rwanda's robot doctors, African responses and innovations have shown that, as a continent, Africa can stand up for itself when pushed against the wall.

This potential was bottled up owing to the saturation of imports coupled with punitive policy and regulatory frameworks in Africa. The same African leaders that stood up to COVID-19 should secure markets for the craftsmanship and products of Africa's youth, nurturing their ideas so that the green shoots of their innovations become pillars of national and continental recovery. Creating space for these ideas to transform into innovative industries with a societal character in terms of jobs creation, should be the immediate focus of leadership.

Government procurement could be a powerful recovery tool to ensure that the goods produced by Africa's youth have a market. Similarly, trade policy could play a role in ensuring that flexibilities are provided in multilateral treaties to assist countries that can support only low levels of development.

Consulting youth in the coordination of COVID-19 responses is important to send the message that they matter; that they can cocreate a new development future for their countries; and to ensure that they see themselves as being at the centre of this plan, and feel that their governments are rooting for their success. In turn, and as the youth begin to change their perspectives, they will be encouraged to invest their time and energy in building their nations. They will see themselves progressing if they stay.

This development of trust and social capital is critical to create new social contracts that can stem the outflow of African youth. This is particularly important given that many of these migrants would have been the beneficiaries of a national investment in education. Their emigration supports the development objectives of the countries to which they migrate, at the expense and detriment of the country that invested in their education. Post COVID-19 recovery is an opportunity to reset the development button to focus on Africa's people, particularly its youth.

COVID-19 has also brought changes to Africa's education systems, providing new incentives to tap the opportunities afforded by digital learning. Considering these changes, Africa must strengthen its digitalisation capacities to export services through digital means. UNDP studies have revealed that most of the migrants from Africa are target workers (UNDP, 2019). They come with an objective to improve the conditions of those they left behind, many of whom have invested heavily in their travel to Europe. If Africans were given the certainty and the opportunity to provide services in Europe and then return home without stringent restrictions on re-entry, they would be more disposed to leaving Europe at the expiration of their entry permits or visas. Many of those interviewed in the UNDP study emphasised that they were willing to return home once they had earned sufficient money that would allow them to establish businesses at home (UNDP, 2019). In this increasingly digitalised world, migrants often see improvements in their home countries and many would like to be influencing the progress. They would also go back to reunite with their families, if they knew that there was the possibility to return in the future.

African governments need to prioritise the protection of their people working in foreign countries as a duty of care issue. Unfortunately, stories about human trafficking, sexual exploitation, organised crime, and drug trafficking are increasingly common (UNODC, 2020). Safe and orderly migration, anchored in protection, offers a compelling solution that will put these gangs out of business.

Leveraging opportunities in intra-African migration

While much attention has been directed towards African migration to Europe, it is critical to view migration from the perspective of influencing opportunities in intra-African trade. The African market offers wider opportunities for Africans to engage both through the AfCFTA Protocol on Trade in Services, which is the framework of liberalisation of intra-African trade in services, and the AU Protocol on the Free Movement of Persons, which seeks to facilitate broader movement for the continent's citizens (AU, 2018). Removal of restrictions on trade and people, as mandated by these instruments, will open access for Africans to supply their services across the continent or within Regional Economic Communities (RECs). Most of the RECs also have provisions for promoting free movement, which should be used.

In addition, centres of excellence are critical in key areas like tourism, hospitality, the treatment of infectious diseases, the production of personal protective equipment (PPE), innovative agriculture, and the Fourth Industrial Revolution. This investment will be important to create the beacons of light that can empower a cadre of African practitioners with upgraded skills, which can be used for the African market, in either creating or finding gainful employment. Mutual recognition of African qualifications and certificates of competence issued by other African institutions – be they vocational or tertiary – is important in facilitating opportunities for Africans to find work across the continent. This is also likely to reduce African migration to Europe.

Towards a developmental approach to migration: UNDP's response

The UNDP is concerned about the development response required for a paradigm shift on migration; in particular, the need for global, regional, and national policies to support governments in attaining their development objectives through migration. To maximise the development gains of migration, and to promote actions that create sustainable development frameworks, as envisaged under the GCM, the UNDP invests in knowledge creation with products that tell these stories in ways previously unexplored. The UNDP's 2019 report on the voices of irregular migrants opened the eyes of policymakers to the reality of the human suffering within their backyards (UNDP, 2019). It opened the conversation in a way that was not possible before. But more needs to be done to emphasise the duality of migration dynamics between Europe and Africa to create a more balanced debate, and to bring all parties to the table to find solutions.

In addition to knowledge creation and policy support, the UNDP supports specific areas such as strengthening governance, a people-centred response and recovery from COVID-19, enhancing the skills and potential of African youth and women, and the productive capacities of African SMEs, and addressing the push factors through climate change mitigation, strengthening social protection, providing economic opportunities and access to services, and sustainable management of natural resources.

Migration is as emotive as it is contentious and often lends itself to silo-designed and politically charged conversations. The UNDP offers platforms that encourage dialogue to promote exchange and reconsider impactful policy responses. Stakeholder engagement should be encouraged from a basis that portrays a balanced appreciation of the issues at hand so that this discussion is taken out of a charity lens and put into an effective policy one that works for both sides. This conversation should tackle issues in the entire ecosystem – from push and pull factors, to the conditions of stay, to return and renewed opportunities for re-entry. A cross fertilisation of ideas is important and can be encouraged by listening to migrants on both sides – Europeans in Africa and Africans in Europe. Putting the faces and voices of those experiencing migration into the discourse is important to understand what policies could yield a lasting development impact.

The UNDP's Renewed Strategic Offer in Africa prioritises initiatives that seek to unlock, once and for all, the bottlenecks that have held back Africa's quest for sustainable development. The offer places the UNDP's human capital and programming resources across 46 African countries, to work with African governments on six priority area: (1) natural resource governance; (2) structural transformation; (3) youth and women employment and empowerment; (4) climate change mitigation and adaptation; (5) affordable and sustainable energy; and (6) peace and security (UNDP, 2020b). These interventions will help to scale back push factors and enhance the creation of opportunities for self-actualisation in Africa.

The UNDP's focus on empowering women and youth to create and sustain entrepreneurial activities seeks to endow 100,000 youth with skills to start and scale businesses (UNDP, 2020b). Through the partnership with the Tony Elumelu Foundation Initiative on Youth Empowerment, work is ongoing to expand and reach more young people – a matter that is even more urgent in the context of COVID-19. The basket of fruits showcased in the COVID-19 PPE local production by youth offers a menu of options to engage going forward (UNDP, 2020c).

Lifting the lid off the potential of the informal sector as an important segment in the African economy, is another priority of the UNDP's work. This requires breaking mindsets to ensure that government incentives protect and nurture, and not penalise and cast out the informal economy. Investing in the informal sector is the stock that will guarantee development dividends across Africa for reasons of scale and reach to households.

Financing both the informal sector, and SMEs and micro, small and medium enterprises (MSMEs) is an area the UNDP is supporting through specific packages to resuscitate businesses affected by COVID-19. Creating the knowledge base that drives governments to develop financing instruments, such as tax breaks for local entrepreneurs that can give them room to stay afloat and grow, is an important feature of the socio-economic analyses that the UNDP offers to African governments.

Ramping up development and investment financing and remittances is required to invest aggressively in opportunities for Africans in Africa. This can be done by plugging holes in illicit financial flows and other haemorrhaging of capital out of the continent. It is vital to ensure that remittances, which are a key source of development financing, continue to support and be redirected to assist investment in SMEs and local development projects in Africa. Europe can contribute to this drive by reducing the costs of remittance transactions. One way to achieve this is by making it a performance requirement for granting licenses to companies operating in Europe so that more financial resources can reach the African homes to fight some of those challenges that push people to emigrate. Mobilising the African diaspora through the Transfer of Knowledge Through Expatriate Nationals (TOKTEN) programme can also allow for highly skilled people to contribute to the development of their countries.

Conclusion

There are positives for both Europe and Africa in facilitating migration in both directions. Finding solutions requires a renewed partnership between Africa and Europe that ensures that opportunities for self-actualisation are increased in Africa, so that if people must migrate, it is not out of desperation, and does not take away from locals the opportunity to work and to grow.

The evidence for the positive net benefits of migration, irrespective of geography, is irrefutable. However, pragmatic solutions remain elusive. Notwithstanding the lack of political consensus, migration trends have persisted with irregular migrants risking their lives as Europe adopts containment and securitised measures to curb inflows. At the same time, Africa's policymakers have not maximised the economic incentives, which have historically attracted Europeans to Africa, to strengthen their own sustainable development. Recognising the mutually reinforcing benefits of Africa–Europe migration, and of Africa hosting migrants from outside, is required for a changed narrative, reality and renewed approach to an Africa–Europe partnership on migration.

In addition, it is important for Africa to harness its resources and wealth effectively, to create conditions on the continent that offer Africans viable pathways to actualise their dreams in Africa. Investment in vehicles that create jobs and opportunities for livelihoods will tap into that growing positive narrative of intra-African migration, which can play a critical role for the socio-economic progress of the continent, as well as for its economic transformation through the contribution made to local economies, and to home countries through remittances, new skills brought back, better access to social services for family members left behind as a result of remittances, and the dynamic potential of diaspora trade and investment.

The COVID-19 pandemic will create stronger push factors – yet is also likely to strengthen restrictive measures given that economies the world over are struggling. The solution lies in dialogue, based on mutual interest and the promotion of safe and orderly migration. African migration to Europe can be mutually beneficial, if the conditions of entry, residence and employment are made more conducive and better regulated.

References

African Union (AU). 2018. 'Protocol to the Treaty Establishing the African Economic Community Relating to Free Movement of Persons, Right of Residence and Right of Establishment'. Online at: https://au.int/sites/default/files/treaties/36403-treaty-protocol_on_free_movement_of_persons_in_africa_e.pdf (accessed 18 February 2021).

Asserate, A.-W. 2019. *African Exodus: Migration and the future of Europe.* (Trans. P. Lewis). London: Haus Publishing.

European Council on Foreign Relations. 2018. 'The Mediterranean and migration: Postcards from a "crisis"'. Online at: https://www.ecfr.eu/specials/mapping_migration (accessed 3 March 2021).

Guardian. 2013. 'Death toll of African migrants rises after boat disaster near Lampedusa'. Online at: https://www.theguardian.com/world/2013/oct/12/african-migrants-boat-lampedusa-capsizes-mediterranean (accessed 18 February 2021).

Oualdi, M. 2018. 'Migrants: When Europeans once flocked to North African shores', *The Conversation,* 25 March. Online at: https://theconversation.com/migrants-when-europeans-once-flocked-to-north-african-shores-93696 (accessed 16 February 2021).

International Financial Corporation. 2020. 'Sub-Saharan Africa: SME initiatives'. Online at: https://www.ifc.org/wps/wcm/connect/REGION__EXT_Content/Regions/Sub-Saharan+Africa/Advisory+Services/SustainableBusiness/SME_Initiatives/ (accessed 18 January 2021).

International Labour Office. 2020. 'Social Protection in Africa'. Online at: https://www.ilo.org (accessed 15 November 2020).

International Organization for Migration. 2020. 'COVID-19 in the Sahel and Lake Chad Basin: Background Brief – April 2020'. Online at: https://rodakar.iom.int/sites/default/files/document/publications/Sahel%20and%20Lake%20Chad%20Background%20Brief%20-%20COVID-19.pdf (accessed 16 January 2021).

Institute for Public Policy and Research. 2015. 'Migrant employment outcomes in European labour markets'. Online at: https://www.ippr.org/files/publications/pdf/migrant-employment-outcomes-in-europe-labour-markets_April2015.pdf (accessed 16 January 2021).

Northrup, D. 2014. *Africa's Discovery of Europe: 1450–1850*. Oxford: Oxford University Press.

United Nations (UN). 2018. Global Compact for Safe, Orderly and Regular Migration. Online at: https://refugeesmigrants.un.org/sites/default/files/180713_agreed_outcome_global_compact_for_migration.pdf (accessed 10 February 2021).

United Nations (UN). 2020. 'Policy Brief: Impact of COVID-19 in Africa'. Online at: https://www.un.org/sites/un2.un.org/files/sg_policy_brief_on_covid-19_impact_on_africa_may_2020.pdf (accessed 16 February 2021).

United Nations Conference on Trade and Development (UNCTAD). 2018. *Economic Development in Africa Report: Migration for structural transformation.* Geneva: United Nations.

United Nations Conference on Trade and Development (UNCTAD). 'Foreign direct investment to Africa defies global slump, rises 11%'. Online at: https://unctad.org/news/foreign-direct-investment-africa-defies-global-slump-rises-11 (accessed 16 February 2021).

United Nations Department of Economic and Social Affairs (UNDESA). 2019a. 'African migration to Europe: How can adequate data help improve evidence-based policymaking and reduce possible misconceptions?'. Online at: https://publications.iom.int/system/files/pdf/gmdac_data_briefing_series_issue_11.pdf (accessed 16 February 2021).

United Nations Department of Economic and Social Affairs (UNDESA) 2019b. 'International migrant stock'. Online at: https://www.un.org/en/development/desa/population/migration/publications/migrationreport/docs/MigrationStock2019_TenKeyFindings.pdf (accessed 16 February 2021).

United Nations Department of Economic and Social Affairs (UNDESA). 2020. 'The COVID-19 pandemic: A speedy and balanced recovery of Europe will remain critical for the world to return to the trajectory of sustainable development'. Policy Brief No. 63. Online at: https://www.un.org/development/desa/dpad/publication/un-desa-policy-brief-63-the-covid-19-pandemic-a-speedy-and-balanced-recovery-of-europe-will-remain-critical-for-the-world-to-return-to-the-trajectory-of-sustainable-development/ (accessed 16 February 2021).

United Nations Development Programme (UNDP). 2019. *Scaling Fences: Voices of irregular African migrants to Europe.* Online at: https://www.undp.org/content/undp/en/home/librarypage/democratic governance/ScalingFences.html (accessed 16 February 2021).

United Nations Development Programme (UNDP). 2020a. 'Beyond Recovery: Towards 2030'. Online at: https://www.undp.org/content/undp/en/home/librarypage/hiv-aids/beyond-recovery--towards-2030.html (accessed 10 February 2021).

United Nations Development Programme (UNDP). 2020b. 'Renewed Strategic Offer in Africa'. Online at: https://www.africa.undp.org/content/rba/en/home/library/outreach-material/undp-strategic-offer-africa.html#:~:text=The%20Strategic%20Offer%20aims%20to,found%20within%20the%20continent%20itself (accessed 14 February 2021).

United Nations Development Programme (UNDP). 2020c. 'Socio-economic impact of COVID 19 in Africa'. Online at: https://www.africa.undp.org/content/rba/en/home/library/covid-19-briefs.html (accessed 16 February 2021).

UN News. 2019. 'More than 90 per cent of Africa migrants would make perilous Europe journey again, despite the risks'. Online at: https://news.un.org/en/story/2019/10/1049641.

United Nations Office on Drugs and Crime (UNODC). 2021. 'Human trafficking and smuggling of migrants'. Online at: https://www.unodc.org/westandcentralafrica/en/newrosenwebsite/TIPSOM/Human-trafficking-and-smuggling-of-migrants.html (accessed 14 February 2021).

World Trade Organization. 1995. General Agreement on Trade in Services. Online at: https://www.wto.org/english/tratop_e/serv_e/mouvement_persons_e/mouvement_persons_e.htm (accessed 14 February 2021).

Chapter 19

The role of the International Organization for Migration in African–European Union migration

Leonie Felicitas Jegen

Introduction

This chapter explores the role of the International Organization for Migration (IOM) in the African context through a double approach, which is necessary if one is to understand the rationales behind the organisation's work. It provides a meta perspective on firstly, *which* donor governments fund the biggest chunk of the IOM's earmarked projects in Africa. It then examines *what* activities are being sponsored by the most important donors. These meta-level findings are complemented by two case studies that zoom in and examine the IOM's role in two specific policy fields, namely, return and state capacity-building. This more micro-level perspective provides further insight into the organisation's entanglement with receiving governments and the power dynamics of donor governments.

Literature on the IOM is largely fragmented and heterogenous (Bradley, 2020). An extensive body of work has considered different aspects of the organisation, including its history (Perruchoud, 1989; Lebon-McGregor, 2020), its role in co-creating an international mobility regime (Geiger and Pécoud, 2010; Ashutosh and Mountz, 2011; Pécoud, 2015), its role in knowledge production (Pécoud, 2015; Bartels, 2018; Korneev, 2018) and migration governance in an age of global capitalism (Georgi, 2010; Georgi and Schatral, 2012). Other works have considered the IOM's position in the external dimension of EU migration governance (Lavenex, 2016), it's role in returns (Collyer, 2012; Koch, 2014), or its information campaigns (Heller, 1996; Nieuwenhuys and Pécoud, 2007; De Jong and Dannecker, 2017; Musarò, 2019). A more comprehensive analysis of the IOM's work in the African context is so far missing.

Most studies on the IOM in the African context have focused on the organisation's role as an implementer of EU migration control policies (Poutignat and Streiff-Fénart, 2010; Heller, 2014; Brachet, 2016; Bartels, 2017). Trauner et al. (2019) found that since the EU's increased attention on West Africa, after the so-called '2015 refugee crisis', the IOM's position has become more connected to the political ambitions of the EU. Indeed, a policy-maker in Senegal has referred to the IOM as a 'workforce of the EU' (Trauner et al., 2019). Other research on the IOM in Africa has considered the role of the organisation with regard to specific policies or country-specific contexts, such as border management (Dini, 2018; Frowd, 2018a, 2018b; Scherf, 2020), return and reintegration (Koch, 2014; Mensah, 2016; Trauner et al., 2019), information campaigns (Heller, 2014; Musarò, 2019), or the IOM's emergence as a humanitarian actor (Bradley, 2017, 2020). Bradley (2020) has criticised this body of work for its overt focus on the IOM as an EU implementing actor, resulting in a one-sided picture of the IOM's activities (Bradley, 2020). This focus might stem from the fact that research has focused mostly on particular projects in specific countries.

Thus, this chapter aims to reflect on who funds the IOM's interventionist roles in Africa, and examines the IOM's politics with regard to return and capacity-building. It therefore aims to tackle this research gap and review the claim that the organisation acts as an implementing actor of European interests on the African continent. It addresses two key questions: (1) Who pays the IOM in Africa? and (2) What are IOM's largest donors paying the organisation to do in Africa? This chapter shows that the largest proportion of the IOM's earmarked funding for projects in Africa in 2019 originated from European governments and the EU. Furthermore, the majority of the projects funded by European donors have a migration governance or control dimension. These findings are complemented by an exploration of three fields of IOM involvement in Africa, namely, so-called voluntary return, reintegration and (border) capacity-building.

This chapter examines the IOM's earmarked funding in its 2019 financial report to analyse its activities and priorities. Donors have been clustered into six different categories: European donor governments (including the European Commission); African donor governments; donor governments from non-African and non-European countries; United Nations (UN) organisations and funds; private actors, and other organisations. The distinction between the three types of government donors enables a more nuanced understanding of *whose* projects the IOM is implementing in Africa and, secondly, it allows for an engagement with the assumption that research on the IOM in Africa has focused disproportionately on European-funded projects.

The analysis is delimited to include projects executed within Africa, including projects that might not have an immediate effect, such as funding for research projects. Funding for IOM staff in Africa, such as junior professional officers, and projects without a specific reference to African countries, regions or cities have been excluded. The latter includes projects with titles such as 'Emergency water, sanitation and hygiene along migration and transhumance routes'. This might exclude projects that are carried out on the African continent, but have imprecise titles, from the calculation. Another factor that could impair the accuracy of the estimation of the total amount of earmarked funding stems from the inclusion of projects with a multi-country focus, including both African and non-African countries. Here the full project sum was added to the calculation, as exact distribution per country is not identified in the funding overview. This might inflate the calculation of earmarked spending in African countries. Hence, the numbers in Figure 19. 1 should not be seen as the absolute value of earmarked funding per donor country, but rather as an indication of earmarked funding per donor government.

Following the analysis of funding trends, funding from the largest set of donor countries, namely, the EU and European countries, is scrutinised. To capture the broader funding patterns, categories of IOM activities, such as 'return', 'resettlement', 'humanitarian projects', 'root causes' or 'information campaigns', have been deduced from the different project headlines and projects clustered accordingly. In cases where project headlines were vague, secondary project information was obtained, where possible. However, in some cases, the exact project components were not transparent and in others, the activity allocation was based on imperfect information. Further, in projects that had more than one activity component, the sum was calculated twice, as information on the exact allocation per project component was not available. This contributes to an artificial inflation of spending. Hence, the calculations in the second section (Figures 19.2 and 19.3 and Table 19.1) serve more as an indication of the IOM's activities in Africa. Furthermore, while funding allocated per cluster might serve as an indication of the political importance allocated to it, some activities require less funding than others; for example, carrying out information campaigns is less cost-intensive than state capacity-building. Further, some activities, such as resettlement, traditionally fall under the mandate of the UN High Commissioner for Refugees (UNHCR), so projected funding allocation serves only as an indicator but not fully mirror the political importance granted to each activity cluster.

This chapter proceeds with a general introduction to the IOM to show why earmarked funding is a suitable way to gain a better understanding of its activities in Africa. Then it investigates *who* funds the IOM and *what* earmarked projects on the African continent are being funded by its most important donors. Finally, it draws on existing research and complements the empirical analysis by considering two key IOM activities in Africa, namely, so-called voluntary returns and reintegration, and second, state capacity-building. Zooming into these activities provides an understanding of how IOM projects become intertwined with European rationales for migration control while remaining dependent on the national political context.

The IOM and its funding structure

The IOM was founded in 1989, emerging from its predecessor, the Provisional Intergovernmental Committee for the Movement of Migrants from Europe (PICCME), which was renamed the Intergovernmental Committee for European Migration (ICEM) a few months later, and the Intergovernmental Committee for Migration (ICM), which was founded in 1980 (IOM, 2011). At inception, the organisation's role was defined by the post-World War II context – the 'overpopulation' of Europe as a result of the high number of displaced populations, which were seen to be impairing economic rehabilitation and facilitating the spread of communism (Pécoud,

2018). In this context, the role of the IOM's predecessor was to facilitate European migration to non-European countries, mainly Latin America. From its outset, what became the IOM was 'closely associated with US leadership and with a homogenous group of developed, "white" and capitalist Western states' (Pécoud, 2018: 1624).

Since its inception, the IOM has grown on an international level, especially over the past 20 years: in 1998, the organisation had 67 member states, while by 2019, the numbers had risen to 173. With 12,600 staff members and 400 field locations in 2019, the IOM has become one of the world's largest intergovernmental organisations (Bradley, 2020). Until 2016, the IOM operated outside the UN framework. While the IOM presents itself as the UN Migration Agency, it does not hold full UN membership status. This hybrid status accounts for its exclusion from the binding provisions of the UN framework (Pécoud, 2018). According to the UN, the IOM is considered an 'essential contributor in the field of human mobility, [including] in the protection of migrants' (UN General Assembly, 2016, Article 2 (2)). Its overall objective is to 'manage migration' and its work focuses on a wide range of activities: humanitarian assistance to displaced people; providing migration policy advice; facilitating high-level migration dialogues; capacity-building projects; as well as knowledge production on migration (Pécoud, 2018). Despite its focus on migration, much of its work is, de facto, *against* migration, for example, through its involvement in the return activities of some host states and projects that aim to halt certain types of mobility in some countries of origin (Pécoud, 2018; see also Bradley 2020).

To understand the IOM's work, it is crucial to take a closer look at the organisation's funding structure (McGregor, 2019). The overall budget has increased steadily over the past 20 years, reaching US$242.2 million in 1998, and US$1.8 billion in 2019 (Bradley, 2020). At the same time, the organisation has adopted a projectisation[1] budgetary model and a decentralised structure, which were captured in the IOM Council Resolution No. 1309 of 24 November 2015, as one of the essential elements of the organisation to be preserved after its affiliation with the UN (IOM, 2016a).

Indeed, in 2013, about 97 per cent of the financial contributions to the IOM were earmarked for specific projects (Bradley, 2020). The project funding structure has, on the one hand, resulted in a general entrepreneurial spirit within the organisation, which is marked by a drive for cost-efficiency and the will to provide competitive services to states (Bradley, 2017). On the other hand, it has allowed donor states to assert more influence over the operational activities of the organisation (Pécoud, 2018; Bradley, 2020). According to a government official quoted in Bradley (2020), the project finance model has resulted in the IOM becoming a 'consulting firm for the international community'. The European Commission is among the organisation's most influential donors, ranking as the third largest donor of earmarked contributions between 2000 and 2016; from 2007 to 2011 The European Commission was behind the United States, Peru and Columbia; and from 2012 to 2016, it was behind the Unites States and Peru (Bradley, 2017).[2]

The projectised budget structure has resulted in the IOM being involved in a wide range of issues (McGregor, 2019). These include projects and research activities that are not explicitly linked to migration, such as disarmament, the management of land claims, and projects in response to the 2013–2016 Ebola outbreak in West Africa, most importantly in Guinea, Liberia and Sierra Leone (IOM, 2016b; Scherf, 2020). An illustration of projects without an explicit focus on migration is the organisation's involvement in infrastructure projects in countries such as Peru. Between 2007 and 2016, the Latin American country was among the top donors to the organisation in terms of its absolute contribution to earmarked funding. During this time, the IOM constructed a convention centre in the capital, Lima, and supported the construction of the Central Bank headquarters (McGregor, 2019; Bradley, 2020). The projectised budget structure has also resulted in unlikely donors, such as the British Petroleum (BP) Exploration (Caspian Sea) Ltd. In 2019, BP financed a project to establish more effective migration management in Azerbaijan (IOM, 2020).

Beyond the widened scope of IOM's project and donor range, the projectised funding model has resulted in donor governments outsourcing their politically contested or sensitive projects to the IOM (Van Criekinge, 2009). This has led to the observation that the IOM operates as an implementing actor, a 'subcontractor' and 'transmitter' (Lavenex, 2016) to get donor countries' 'dirty' work done (Andrijasevic and Walters, 2010; Georgi, 2010; Ashutosh and Mountz, 2011). Overall, the IOM's financial and political dependence, resulting from the projectisation mode, has decreased its scope for engagement in projects that go against donor interests (Pécoud, 2018).

Who funds the IOM in Africa?

The importance of African states in the IOM's operational activity becomes evident when one examines its presence on the continent. Besides its headquarters in Geneva, the organisation has nine regional offices, four of which are in Africa, two in Latin America, one in Asia and two in Europe. It also has two special liaison offices in New York and Addis Ababa, as well as numerous field offices. In the overall geographic distribution of IOM offices, in 2019, Africa came second – 121 offices in total – just after Asia and Oceania, where 123 offices are located. There are 67 offices in Europe and Central Asia and 24 in the Middle East. Overall, in 2019, the second biggest allocation of funds was spent in Africa (US\$653,904,911), just after field spending allocations to Asia (US\$687,332,252) (IOM, 2020).

When considering the earmarked funding for projects on the African continent, it is evident that the IOM's biggest donors are the European countries[3] and the European Commission. This main bloc of donors is followed by non-European and non-African governments, most importantly, the United States, followed by Japan, Canada, South Korea and China, and UN organisations. The three most important ones in 2019 were the Central Emergency Response Fund, the UN Peacebuilding Fund, and the UN Office for project services. African governments also contribute, such as the Democratic Republic of Congo (DRC), Chad, the Central African Republic and Somalia, as well as other organisations such as NGOs and universities and the private sector (see Figure 19.1).

In 2019, European contributions made up 59.72 per cent of the total earmarked projects implemented in Africa. Non-European and non-African donor governments were the second largest, contributing 23.65 per cent of the total earmarked contributions. This group comprised five states, namely, Canada, China, Japan, South Korea and the United States. The largest contributor was the United States, followed by Japan, with China contributing the least, financing only one project aimed at providing humanitarian aid to conflict affected populations in Nigeria. The third biggest group comprised UN organisations and funds, who contributed 11.64 per cent of the total earmarked funding in 2019. African donor states, namely the Democratic Republic of Congo (DRC), Chad, the Central African Republic and Somalia made up only 3.35 per cent of the total contributions to IOM projects. While both Chad and the DRC funded humanitarian projects, the Central African Republic funded a project for the reintegration of disarmed and demobilised persons, falling within the field of post-conflict stabilisation rather than migration. In Somalia, the funding was for an urban water supply and sanitation project, again moving the organisation's activity beyond migration. Other organisations – such as NGOs and universities – funded 1.6 per cent and the private sector 0.04 per cent of earmarked projects in Africa in 2019.

Figure 19.1: Earmarked non-UN/non-private funding of the IOM in Africa, 2019

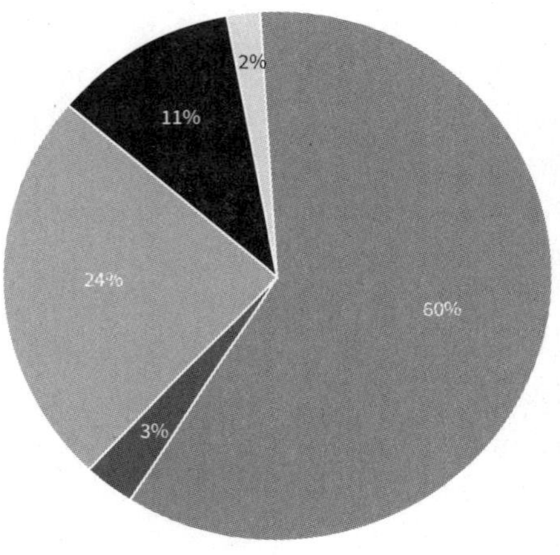

Source: IOM Financial Report 2019 (author's calculations)

Having established that the bulk of IOM projects are financed by European donors, the chapter tackles the question of what kind of activities are funded by these donors.

Financed to do what? European-funded IOM projects in Africa

Looking at the different projects funded by European earmarked contributions, activities were clustered under the following categories: return and reintegration; assisting migrants en route;[4] humanitarian assistance (mostly to internally displaced persons (IDPs); state capacity-building; post-conflict-related activities; data gathering; non-migration-related activities (other); root causes of migration; information campaigns; diaspora support; and resettlement-related activities (see Figure 19.2).

Figure 19.2: Earmarked European funding to the IOM by policy field in 2019 (in US$)

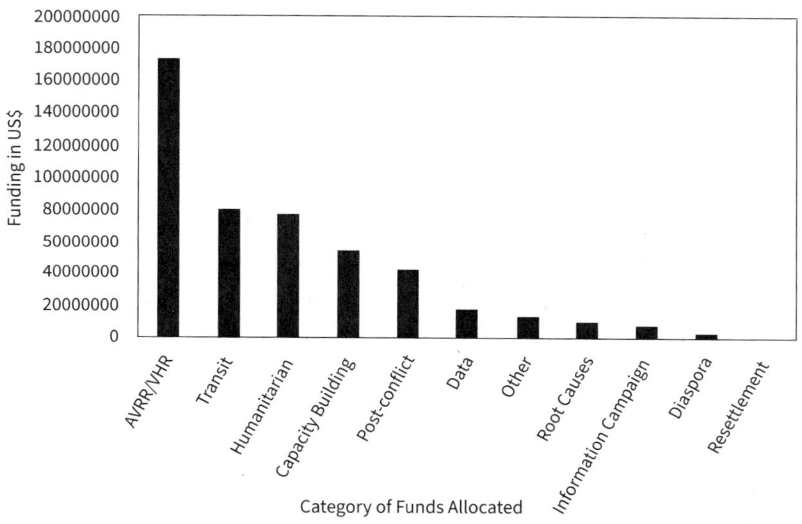

Source: IOM Financial Report 2019 (author's calculations)

In 2019, the largest amount of funding (35.65 per cent) was spent on projects with a return and/or reintegration component. These projects encompassed both assisted so-called voluntary returns and voluntary humanitarian return (AVRR/VHR). These projects included, for example, the return and reintegration programmes under the EU–IOM Joint Initiative.

The second largest amount, which constituted 16.49 per cent of the total funding, went to projects aimed at assisting migrants who were understood to be in transit to Europe. In view of UN reports stating that IOM assistance at the so-called transit centres in Niger was conditional on migrants agreeing to return 'voluntarily' to their country of origin (Morales, 2018), these types of projects were clustered independently from humanitarian support. These projects included support to vulnerable migrants in Tunisia, assistance to migrants in Libya, or to unaccompanied minors in Morocco.

Humanitarian support for populations that were not considered to be on the move to Europe received the third largest proportion of funding. In 2019, 16.01 per cent of the entire European funding was for humanitarian projects. These included projects that tackled the living conditions of populations affected by drought in Somalia; projects supporting the response to the Ebola outbreak in the DRC; life-saving assistance in Nigeria; and shelter assistance in Mozambique.

Capacity-building projects, constituting 11.3 per cent of the total funding, were generally aimed at building the capacities of state and non-state actors to deal with specific migration management components. These included projects that aimed to strengthen state border management capacities in Kenya, Niger and Somalia; strengthening the response capacity of the Mauritanian government to address the issue of unaccompanied minors; and strengthening local initiatives to manage migration in Côte d'Ivoire.

Furthermore, 9 per cent of funding was granted to projects with a post-conflict component, mostly dealing with the stabilisation of post-conflict situations or facilitating the return of conflict displaced populations or former combatants. Such projects include human security and stabilisation of coastal areas in Kenya or facilitating the sustainable return of Somali migrants.

The remaining 11.58 per cent of funding was allocated to projects that aimed to enhance data gathering (3.78 per cent); projects that address the so-called root causes of migration (2.23 per cent); information campaigns (1.8 per cent); diaspora engagement (0.67 per cent); and resettlement (0.15 per cent). Projects aimed at strengthening data gathering included initiatives to enhance data on regional displacement situations or migratory routes from Africa to Europe. Projects that did not deal directly with migration and conflict-related issues included election observation, and community stabilisation in northern Niger. The community stabilisation projects in northern Niger were not directly a post-conflict exercise, but were aimed at addressing the shifting political economy that resulted from the implementation of the 2015 anti-smuggling law in the country, which was funded mostly by the EU (Jegen, 2020a).

The projects in Table 19.1 were clustered according to their overarching aim based on four different subcategories: (1) restricting/governing mobility; (2) humanitarian assistance; (3) post-conflict support; and (4) benefitting from/enabling mobility. The category called humanitarian assistance comprises projects that fund humanitarian work, as well as data gathering projects to facilitate such activity.

Table 19.1: Overarching aim of EU-funded projects (in US$)

S/N	Categories	Funding
1.	**Restricting/governing mobility**	**329,341,657**
	AVRR/VHR	173,132,927
	Capacity-building	54,888,230
	Root causes	10,843,363
	Information campaigns	8,750,502
	Data migratory routes	1,626,698
	Transit	80,099,937
2.	**Other**	**14,179,923**
3.	**Humanitarian assistance**	**94,498,211**
	Humanitarian	77,752,299
	Displacement data	16,745,912
4.	**Benefitting from/enabling mobility**	**3,962,137**
	Diaspora	3,240,340
	Resettlement	721,797
5.	**Post conflict**	**43,720,048**
TOTAL		485,701,976

Source: IOM Financial Report 2019 (author's calculations)

Based on this clustering exercise, it can be established that 69.85 per cent of European earmarked funding in Africa is spent on projects that aim to restrict or govern mobility; 20.23 per cent on humanitarian projects, 9.27 per cent on post-conflict-related activities and 0.84 per cent on projects resonating directly with African key interests of diaspora engagement and resettlement (see Figure 19.3).

Figure 19.3: European earmarked funding to the IOM per project cluster in 2019

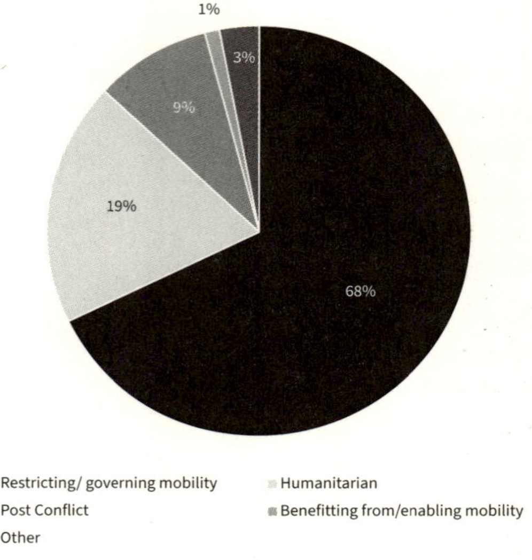

Source: IOM Financial Report 2019 (author's calculations)

With most of the funding going to what seems to be projects that restrict or at least aim to render mobility 'governable', the question arises: should the IOM be viewed as an actor that mainly implements European migration control objectives. This will be investigated drawing on research conducted on the IOM in general, and on its activities in the African context. To complement these findings, two case studies will be discussed. These show how the IOM's projects are intertwined with European rationales for migration control, beyond the mere funding aspect, while at the same time becoming entangled with the different project implementation contexts.

The IOM in Africa: An implementing actor of European migration control?

Two types of IOM activities, which fall under the 'restricting/governing mobility' cluster, are considered: the organisation's work in the field of return and reintegration in Africa, and its work in (border) capacity-building. These case studies illustrate how the IOM's work contributes to changed migration/mobility governance and the conceptions thereof – notwithstanding the fact that it sees itself as being neutral.

Case 1

The IOM's involvement in return and reintegration in Africa: An implementer of EU return governance?

The IOM is, to varying degrees, involved in two types of return activities that are relevant to the African context: first, the so-called 'voluntary' returns from transit countries (including both assisted voluntary returns and humanitarian returns); and second, the reintegration efforts. Questions pertaining to forced return have been a sensitive issue at the heart of EU–Africa migration cooperation (Mouthaan, 2019; Zanker et al., 2019; Adam et al., 2020; Lücke et al., 2020). Forced return carries high political, social, and economic consequences for (West) African actors. As many households live off remittances, migration to Europe is often a family investment, and beyond that, individuals who are forced to return often face exclusion and poor economic prospects (Zanker et al., 2019). At the same time, fostering deportations has been a key interest of European countries, becoming ever more prominent since the so-called migration crisis in 2015 (Zanker et al., 2019; Adam et al., 2020). It is within this context that return-related activities have gained considerable support, especially from European donor countries (Koch, 2014).

The so-called voluntary returns has traditionally encompassed returns from destination countries. In the context of the strongly divergent interests of European and African states, and the prospects of forced return, so-called voluntary return has become the alternative to deportation and, thus, a field for cooperation, and the IOM has become a key implementing partner. While politically less salient ((Zanker et al., 2019), in most cases voluntary return schemes have not actually been voluntary (Collyer, 2012; Koch, 2014; Mensah, 2016; Pécoud, 2018) but often constitute a less violent alternative, sometimes offered with coercive and incentivising elements, to people facing an order to leave.

Voluntary return schemes have also been used increasingly to return migrants en route to Europe. Return from African transit countries to African origin countries can be tied directly to the European desire to stop unwanted movement from Africa, following the so-called 2015 migration crisis (see also Pécoud, 2020). Just like other types of so-called voluntary return, transit returns are often not *de facto* voluntary. In 2018, the UN Special Rapporteur on the Human Rights of Migrants, Felipe González Morales, raised concerns over the practice of making access to shelter and other humanitarian aid in the IOM-run transit centres in Niger conditional on an agreement to 'voluntarily' return (Morales, 2018). This is funded under the IOM–EU Joint Initiative, which represents a key investment in return and reintegration from and to African countries (transit returns) (EEAS, 2017). This initiative, which is funded by EU development aid, was launched in 2016 to carry out voluntary returns of African migrants from transit countries, most notably Libya and Niger, but also Mali, Morocco and Algeria (Zanker et al., 2019).

While being tied to European 'containment' objectives (Duffield, 2006), and similar to voluntary returns from host countries, returns en route have been more acceptable to many African governments, as they go in hand with a narrative of protection concerns. Following a 2017 CNN documentary on the situation of transit migrants in Libya, many African governments have raised concerns about the safety of their citizens while they are en route to Europe (Arhin-Sam, 2019; Mouthaan, 2019; Zanker et al., 2019; Adam et al., 2020; Jegen, 2020b).

Linked to questions of forced and so-called voluntary returns are projects providing reintegration assistance, for both deported and so-called voluntarily returned migrants. This reintegration support has been an important demand by some African governments such as Senegal (Jegen, 2020b), Nigeria (Arhin-Sam, 2019), Ghana (Adam et al., 2020), and The Gambia (Altrogge and Zanker, 2019). However, the actual implementation of reintegration assistance has often been accompanied by tensions between African governments and the IOM, on one hand, and between the IOM and returnees, on the other. In regard to the questions over whether state and non-state actors should receive reintegration, funding has been an issue, for in Senegal (Jengen 2020b). With regard to the latter, incidents of contestations have occurred when reintegration support has failed to live up to the expectations of returnees. In Senegal and Ghana (Trauner et al., 2019), for instance, many returnees have stressed that reintegration support from the IOM was insufficient (Jegen, 2020b). Studies have also highlighted the general failure of reintegration support under the EU–IOM Joint Initiative to address the complex challenges faced by returnees (Alpes, 2020).

Case 2

Capacity-building: Building state capacity to restrict mobility?

Research has considered state capacity building as a deviation from the narrow

European return and control-oriented agenda, and at the same time, an intrinsic part of it. On the one hand, an increased focus on capacity-building from 2007 has been understood as a response by European actors to the demand by West African states to extend cooperation beyond the security-oriented focus on return (Van Criekinge, 2009). On the other hand, it has been seen as an important part of the externalisation of migration control to African countries (Paoletti, 2010; Anderson, 2014; Vives, 2017). Externalisation has been described most generally as 'policing at a distance' (Bigo and Guild, 2005), and 'outward shifting' (Lavenex, 2006) of immigration control. In the context of EU–African migration cooperation, capacity-building is mostly focused on the drafting of policies and strengthening border-control capacities.

With regard to the former, the IOM functions as a hub for discussions and policy debates on migration (Pécoud, 2018). The IOM's role in providing migration policy advice and assisting states in the drafting of policies has resulted in destination countries using the IOM increasingly to influence the policies of transit and origin countries. Meanwhile, capacity-building has also been launched at the request of African countries (Bradley, 2020), for example, under the EU–ACP initiative, which provides demand-driven facilities for capacity-building. IOM capacity-building projects have included financial and technical support for the national migration policy formulation process in Senegal (Jegen, 2020b), Ghana (Adam et al., 2020), The Gambia (Altrogge and Zanker, 2019), Nigeria (Arhin-Sam, 2019), and Morocco (Bartels, 2018). While considered a 'neutral' actor that proposes value-free migration policy advice to all parties (Lavenex, 2016; Bartels, 2018), the IOM's bias towards European interests becomes evident in some cases. For example, in Ghana, where the national migration policy gives more weight to European migration interests than to those of Ghanaian stakeholders – for instance, one of their crucial interests is responding to rural–urban mobility (Segaldo, 2021). Additionally, the adoption process of the National Migration Policy (NMP) in Senegal received additional coercive elements. Here, the successful adoption of a national migration policy was made a condition for receiving budget support through EU development funding (Jegen, 2020b).

In regard to the latter, an important focus of the IOM's capacity-building programmes has been the ability of African states to control their borders. The organisation has been involved in building border posts, drafting border control strategies, providing support for legislation and calling for the implementation of biometric entry–exit governance through border management databases, such as the Migration Information and Data Analysis System (MIDAS) (Frowd, 2018b). Through the IOM's African Capacity Building Centre on Migration Management (ACBC), founded in 2009, the organisation has circulated training manuals and trained border and immigration officials across Africa. These initiatives have been rolled out in a range of countries, including Djibouti, Mauritania, Senegal and Niger.

In Djibouti, the IOM carried out border capacity-building projects that were financed jointly by the EU and Japan, and focused on reforming the country's entry–exit governance and building border posts (Dini, 2018). Under the EU-funded Integrated Border Management Initiative, the IOM built new border crossings at the Senegalese borders with Mauretania and Mali, and renovated existing posts, in addition to training and equipping 250 border guards (Frowd, 2018a). In Niger, since 2015, the IOM has been implementing numerous border capacity-building projects, financed by multiple donors, including the EU and European governments, Canada, Japan and the United States. Border capacity-building activities in Niger entailed building and modernising border posts, renovating the headquarter of the Nigerien border police, launching mobile border units, and supporting the drafting of a national border strategy (Jegen, 2020).

These forms of border capacity-building tend to take place in spaces in which conceptions of belonging and mobility differ from Eurocentric conceptions (Asiwaju, 1985; Flynn, 1997; Chalfin, 2010; Nyamnjoh, 2017; Dini, 2018). Nyamnjoh (2017) finds that postcolonial African states' borders are marked by intercommunal cross-border mobility, which questions the compartmentalisation of Africans into contained and 'nationalised' units of belonging. Prior to the IOM intervention in Djibouti, individuals without identification documents – but with physical attributes of belonging to a clan geographically situated across the border – could cross without the registration of their fingerprints or showing documentation (Dini, 2018). Similar, research has found that cross-border mobility has characterised the lives of nomadic populations in Northern Niger (Molenaar et al., 2017). In this regard, research has found that the governance of mobility in many African contexts surpasses the state, and is, indeed, localised and in the hands of mobile populations. Hüsken (2017) captures this through the concept of 'shared sovereignty', which he develops to capture the Awlad Ali Bedouin's agency in governing mobility in the Egyptian–Libyan border lands.

Contrary to these conceptions and cross-border practices, the IOM's border management projects in Africa tend to promote sedentarism and institutionalised citizenship (Dini, 2018), and hence an international mobility regime that connects sovereignty and statism (Schiller and Salazar, 2013). Furthermore, in Djibouti, IOM capacity-building workshops have strongly advocated for the idea that Africans (and Djiboutians) should stay on African soil – an interest strongly aligned with European policy objectives (Dini, 2018). Boarder capacity building must also be understood in relation to European donor objectives of migration control. Similarly, in the Senegalese context, the IOM was a key implementing partner for externally funded migration control measures, which became a donor priority in the context of the so-called Canary Island crisis (Casas-Cortés et al., 2013; Vives, 2017; Jegen, 2020b). As the example of Djibouti shows, not only did the IOM rhetoric of patriotism and African pride conceal wider questions of who has access to mobility on a global scale, it was also clearly in line with the political agenda of the Global North, which aims to halt unwanted migration (Dini, 2018). In this sense, the IOM, as a border capacity-builder, can be considered as an 'idea generating organisation' (Frowd, 2018a), with an important role in the rebordering of global society (Andrijasevic and Walters, 2010).

Yet, it is important to note that the IOM's capacity-building projects are not executed in a political vacuum. Beyond the interests of donor states, the projects must also be contextualised in terms of their national political dynamics (Dini, 2018). In the context of both Senegal and Ghanaian border control measures, governments were interested in border control measures to strengthen national security apparatuses in view of a volatile regional security situation (Frowd, 2018a; Adam et al., 2020;). Additionally, in both Djibouti and Mauritania, border measures were embedded in ethnic politics and a wider process of redefining citizenship (Dini, 2018; Frowd, 2018b). More generally, capacity-building measures are also a way to reap 'migratory rent' or to gain funding for the underfunded public sector (Adam et al., 2020). At the individual level, participating in IOM training has been considered a way to 'gain relations, resources and recognition in the transnational field of migration management' (Bartels, 2018: 51), and to attain per diems for attending training (Jegen, 2020). Further, Djiboutian security professionals drew a sense of pride from their new role as guardians and performers of both sovereign powers and a sense of nationhood (Dini, 2018).

The two case studies have shown that while both return programmes and capacity-building initiatives have material outcomes, they also have an important impact on shaping knowledge on mobility and migration. On a more general level, the IOM has aimed to produce knowledge on migration that creates categories of *what* migration is, as well as what *bad* and *good* cross-border mobility entails (Pécoud, 2010; Bartels, 2018). Through various projects, often funded by financially stronger states, knowledge produced by the IOM has resulted in unquestioned assumptions and recommendations on how to govern mobility (Korneev, 2014). Through the creation of these categories, the knowledge produced by the IOM appears neutral and rational (Kalm, 2012; Pécoud, 2015). This contributes to the depoliticisation of the organisation's work (Ashutosh and Mountz, 2011; Pécoud, 2015) and the consolidation of its standing as a cooperation partner preferred by some African governments over European actors (Van Criekinge, 2009). Through the spread of these ideas on migration, the IOM is promoting an 'international conduct of conduct' both to states (Andrijasevic and Walters, 2010) and to individuals (Pécoud, 2010).

Conclusion

This chapter has provided empirical evidence to the claim that the IOM acts as an implementing actor for European migration control objectives on the African continent. It has shown that in 2019, the most important donors of IOM's earmarked activities in the African contexts were European governments and the European Commission. They made up 60 per cent of the total funding attributed to earmarked projects in the African context. A closer look at what projects have been funded by European governments and the European Commission reveals that by far the largest proportion of European funding was spent on projects aimed at restricting or governing mobility (68 per cent of all European funding). The IOM's funding structure establishes a foundation for the organisation's bias towards donor government's interests. The IOM has a 'projectised' budgetary model, which means that the organisation's staff and office costs are linked to the implementation of a specific project and covered by the project's cost. In this funding structure, donor agents fund specific projects through earmarked funds, making the organisation financially dependent on donor states' funding and interests. It is, therefore, not surprising that the IOM largely acts as an implementing actor of the European migration-control agenda in the African context, *de facto* turning it into more of an anti-migration organisation than a migration organisation. In this way, the IOM can be understood as constituting a device for its donor states 'to make governable a world marked by tensions and conflicts, without having to govern it directly' (Brachet 2016: 287, quoting Shore et al., 2011).

This is also highlighted in the case studies, which showed that the (self)perception of the IOM as a value-neutral projector of international expertise covers up its implication in the expansion of European logics of and interests in migration governance, and the reproduction of power relations in policy elaboration processes (Bartels, 2018). In this sense, projects that aim to render migration 'governable' in the African context may challenge the sovereignty of non-Western states, without imposing on the sovereignty of its donor governments (Georgi, 2010). Andrijasevic and Walters (2010) describe the IOM as a 'post-imperial' actor that does not work towards policy changes in countries by imposition but by persuasion. Yet, it is important to note that the case studies have shown that projects are not carried out in a political vacuum. African states and their representatives have used the IOM projects to foster their own strategic interests, on the political, financial, as well as professional levels (Bartels, 2018; Frowd, 2018a). Hence a consideration of its funding structure grants a valuable insight into the *raison d'être* of many of the projects implemented by the organisation in the African context, whether and how these migration control objectives are reached or used strategically to obtain other political interests, are only revealed when zooming in and considering the political dynamics of a given project.

To expand an understanding of how European migration control interests have played out in the role of the IOM in Africa, the analysis of funding streams to the IOM budget should be expanded over a longer timeframe. Further, the rather obvious, yet necessary, analysis of European migration-related interests in African migration governance, could be complemented by additional research into the roles of non-European donors, such as Canada, the United States, Japan and South Korea, as well as African states such as Chad, the Central African Republic, the DRC and Somalia. This research agenda would be an important contribution to understanding the role of the IOM in Africa. Furthermore, the emerging role of the IOM in interventions that are not explicitly linked to migration or mobility, most significantly in post-conflict stabilisation, but also in relation to election observation, remains largely unexplored and constitute an important aspect of understanding the expanding role of the IOM in Africa.

Notes

1   Projectisation denotes an organisational funding structure whereby staff and office costs linked to the implementation of a specific project are covered by the project costs. In this structure, donor agents fund mostly specific projects through earmarked funding, rather than the overall operational activity of the IOM.

2   When considering the average annual voluntary earmarked contribution to the IOM in US$ between 2000 and 2016, the EU ranked third behind the US and Peru (McGregor, 2019)

3   European donors are the governments of Austria, Belgium, Denmark, Finland, France, Germany, Italy, The Netherlands, Norway, Spain, Sweden, Switzerland, and the United Kingdom, as well as the European Commission.

4   Drawing on Casas-Cortés et al. (2015) "Fortress Europe" continues to fail as an effective means of controlling irregular migration. As a consequence, European states are restructuring their border regimes by externalizing migration management to non-EU countries beyond the border and creating new programs and policies to do so. With European political prominence granted to movement towards Europe, in many cases the actual direction remains constructed, as many people on the move may be targeting other destinations in Africa.

References

Adam, I., Trauner, F., Jegen, L. and Roos, C. 2020. 'West African interests in (EU) migration policy: Balancing domestic priorities with external incentives', *Journal of Ethnic and Migration Studies*, 46(15): 3101–18.

Alpes, J. 2020. *Emergency Returns by IOM from Libya and Niger: A protection or a source of protection concerns?* Analysis No. 96. Berlin/Frankfurt am Main:

Brot für die Welt/Medico International e.V.

Altrogge, J. and Zanker, F. 2019. *The Political Economy of Migration Governance in the Gambia*, MEDAM Dialogue. Freiberg: Arnold Bergstraesser Institute and Mercator Foundation.

Anderson, R. 2014. *Illegality Inc.: Clandestine migration and the business of bordering Europe*. Berkley, CA: University of California Press.

Andrijasevic, R. and Walters, W. 2010. 'The International Organization for Migration and the international government of borders', *Environment and Planning D: Society and Space*, 28(6): 977–99.

Arhin-Sam, K. 2019. *The Political Economy of Migration Governance in Nigeria*, MEDAM Dialogue. Freiberg: Arnold Bergstraesser Institute and Mercator Foundation.

Ashutosh, I. and Mountz, A. 2011. 'Migration management for the benefit of whom? Interrogating the work of the International Organization for Migration', *Citizenship Studies*, 15: 21–38.

Asiwaju, A. 1985. *Partitioned Africans: Ethnic relations across Africa's international boundaries, 1884–1984*. London: Palgrave Macmillan.

Bartels, I. 2018. 'Practices and power of knowledge dissemination. International organisations in the externalization of migration management in Morocco and Tunisia movements', *Journal for Critical Migration and Border Regime Studies*, 4(1): 44–66.

Bartels, I. 2017. 'We must do it gently: The contested implementation of IOM's migration management', *Migration Studies*, 5(3): 315–36.

Bigo, D. and Guild, E. 2005. *Controlling Frontiers: Free movement into and within Europe*. Aldershot: Ashgate.

Brachet, J. 2016. 'Policing the desert: The IOM in Libya beyond war and "peace"', *Antipode*, 48(2): 272–92.

Bradley, M. 2017. 'The International Organization for Migration (IOM): Gaining power in the forced migration regime', *Refuge: Canada's Journal on Refugees*, 33(1): 97–106.

Bradley, M. 2020. *The International Organization for Migration: Challenges, commitments, complexities, global institutions*. New York: Routledge.

Casas-Cortés, M., Cobarrubias, S. and Pickles, J. 2015. 'Riding routes and itinerant borders: Autonomy of migration and border externalization', *Antipode*, 47(4): 894–914. doi.org/10.1111/anti.12148.

Casas-Cortés, M., Cobarrubias, S. and Pickles, J. 2013. 'Rebordering the neighbourhood: Europe's emerging geographies of non-accession integration', *European Urban and Regional Studies*, 20(1): 37–58.

Chalfin, B. 2010. *Neoliberal Frontiers: An ethnography of sovereignty in West Africa*. Chicago, IL: Chicago University Press.

Collyer, M. 2012. 'Deportation and the micropolitics of exclusion: The rise of removals from the UK to Sri Lanka', *Geopolitics*, 17(2): 276–92.

De Jong, S. and Dannecker, P. 2017. 'Managing migration with stories? The IOM "I am a migrant" Campaign', *Journal für Entwicklungspolitik*, XXXIII(1): 75–101.

Dini, S. 2018. 'Migration management, capacity-building and the sovereignty of an African state: International Organization for Migration in Djibouti', *Journal of Ethnic and Migration Studies*, 44(10): 1691–705.

Duffield, M. 2006. 'Racism, migration and development: the foundations of planetary order', *Progress in Development Studies*, 6(1): 68–79.

European External Action Service (EEAS). 2017. 'One year of EU partnership with IOM: Migrants protection and reintegration in Africa'. EEAS – European Commission. Online at: https://eeas.europa.eu/headquarters/ headquarters-homepage/37353/one-year-eu-partnership-iom-migrants-protection-and-reintegration-africa_en (accessed 1 August 2019).

European Commission. 2016. 'Commission announces New Migration Partnership Framework: Reinforced cooperation with third countries to better manage migration'. Online at: http://europa.eu/rapid/press-release_IP-16-2072_en.htm (accessed 18 June 2019).

Flynn, D. 1997. '"We are the border": Identity, exchange, and the state along the Bénin–Nigeria border', *American Ethnologist*, 24(2): 311–30.

Frowd, P.M. 2018a. 'Developmental borderwork and the International Organization for Migration', *Journal of Ethnic and Migration Studies*, 44(10): 1656–72.

Frowd, P.M. 2018b. *Security at the Borders: Transnational practices and technologies in West Africa*, 1st ed. Cambridge: Cambridge University Press.

Geiger, M. and Pécoud, A. (eds). 2010. *The Politics of International Migration Management*, Migration, Minorities and Citizenship Series. London: Palgrave Macmillan. doi.org/10.1057/9780230294882.

Georgi, F. 2010. 'For the benefit of some: The International Organization for Migration and its global migration management', in: M. Geiger and A. Pécoud (eds). *The Politics of International Migration Management*, Migration, Minorities and Citizenship Series. London: Palgrave Macmillan, pp. 45–72. doi.org/10.1057/9780230294882_3.

Georgi, F. and Schatral, S. 2012. 'Towards a critical theory of migration control: The case of the International Organization for Migration (IOM)', in: M.

Geiger and A. Pécoud (eds). *The New Politics of International: Migration Management and its Discontents*, pp. 193–222.

Heller, C. 2014. 'Perception management: Deterring potential migrants through information campaigns', *Global Media and Communication*, 10: 303–18. doi. org/10.1177/1742766514552355

Heller, K.J. 1996. 'Subjectification and resistance in Foucault', *Substance*, 25(1): 78–110.

Hüsken, T. 2017. 'The practice and culture of smuggling in the borderland of Egypt and Libya', *International Affairs*, 93(4): 897–915.

International Organization for Migration (IOM). 2020. 'Financial Report for the Year Ended 31 December 2019'. Financial Report No. C/111/3. Geneva: IOM.

International Organization for Migration (IOM). 2016a. Council: First Special Session. Improved legal arrangements between IOM and the United Nations. Geneva: IOM.

International Organization for Migration (IOM). 2016b. *Health, Border and Mobility Management*. Geneva: IOM.

International Organization for Migration (IOM). 2011. Director General's Report to the 100th Session of the Council. Geneva: IOM.

Jegen, L. 2020a. *The Political Economy of Migration Governance in Niger*. Freiburg: Arnold Bergstraesser Institute (ABI) and Mercator Foundation.

Jegen, L. 2020b. *The Political Economy of Migration Governance in Senegal*, MEDAM Dialogue. Freiburg: Arnold Bergstraesser Institute (ABI) and Mercator Foundation.

Kalm, S. 2012. 'Global migration management, order and access to mobility'. IMIS-Beiträge, Issue 40. Lund University. Online at: https://www. lunduniversity.lu.se/lup/publication/7083155d-e67b-43b8-89fe-2657da3a0b87 (accessed 25 December 2021).

Koch, A. 2014. 'The politics and discourse of migrant return: The role of UNHCR and IOM in the governance of return', *Journal of Ethnic and Migration Studies*, 40(6): 905–23.

Korneev, O. 2018. 'Self-legitimation through knowledge production partnerships: International Organization of Migration in Central Asia, *Journal of Ethnic and Migration Studies*, 44: 1673–90. doi.10.1080/136918 3X.2017.1354057.

Korneev, O. 2014. 'Exchanging knowledge, enhancing capacities, developing mechanisms: IOM's role in the implementation of the EU–Russia Readmission Agreement', *Journal of Ethnic and Migration Studies*, 40: 888–

904. doi.org/10.1080/1369183X.2013.855072.

Lavenex, S. 2016. 'Multi-levelling EU external governance: The role of international organizations in the diffusion of EU migration policies', *Journal of Ethnic and Migration Studies*, 42, 554– 70. doi.org/10.1080/13691 83X.2015.1102047.

Lavenex, S. 2006. 'Shifting up and out: The foreign policy of European immigration control', *West European Politics*, 29: 329–50. doi. org/10.1080/01402380500512684.

Lebon-McGregor, E. 2020. *A History of Global Migration Governance: Challenging linearity*. IMI Working Paper Series No. 167, pp. 1–35.

Lücke, M., Sundberg Diez, O., Jegen, L. and Zanker, F. 2020. *European and African Perspectives on Asylum and Migration Policy: Seeking common ground*. MEDAM Assessment Report. Kiel: Kiel Institute for the World Economy.

McGregor, E. 2019. *Money Matters: The role of funding in migration governance*. IMI Working Paper Series No. 149, pp. 1–37.

Mensah, E.A. 2016. 'Involuntary return migration and reintegration. The case of Ghanaian migrant workers from Libya', *Journal of International Migration and Integration*, 17(1): 303–23.

Molenaar, F., Ursu, A.-E., Tinni, B.A., Hoffmann, A. and Meester, J. 2017. *A Line in the Sand: Roadmap for sustainable migration management in Agadez*. Clingendael, Netherlands Institute of International Relations, CRU Report No. 45.

Morales, F.G. 2018. OHCHR/End of mission statement of the UN Special Rapporteur on the human rights of migrants, Felipe González Morales, on his visit to Niger (1–8 October 2018) (End of Mission Statement). OHCHR.

Mouthaan, M. 2019. 'Unpacking domestic preferences in the "policy-receiving" state: The EU's migration cooperation with Senegal and Ghana', *Comparative Migration Studies*, 7(37): 35.

Musarò, P. 2019. 'Aware migrants: The role of information campaigns in the management of migration', *European Journal of Communication*, 34: 629–40.

Nieuwenhuys, C. and Pécoud, A. 2007. 'Human trafficking, information campaigns, and strategies of migration control', *American Behavioral Scientist*, 50: 1674–95.

Nyamnjoh, F. 2017. 'Incompleteness: Frontier Africa and the currency of conviviality', *Journal of Asian and African Studies*, 52(3): 253–70.

Paoletti, E. 2010. *The Migration of Power and North-South Inequalities: The case of Italy and Libya*. London: Palgrave Macmillan.

Pécoud, A. 2020. 'The IOM and "voluntary return" programmes in Africa'

AMMODI. Online at: https://ammodi.com/ammodi-blog/ (accessed 26 November 2020).

Pécoud, A. 2018. 'What do we know about the International Organization for Migration?' *Journal of Ethnic and Migration Studies*, 44(10): 1621–38. doi.org/10.1080/1369183X.2017.1354028.

Pécoud, A. 2015. 'Depoliticising migration'. In: A. Pécoud (ed.). *Depoliticising Migration: Global governance and international migration narratives, mobility and politics.* Basingstoke, UKLondon: Palgrave Macmillan, pp. 95–123. doi.org/10.1057/9781137445933_8

Pécoud, A. 2010. 'Informing migrants to manage migration? An analysis of IOM's information campaigns', in: M. Geiger and A. Pécoud (eds). *The Politics of International Migration Management*, Migration, Minorities and Citizenship series. London: Palgrave Macmillan, pp. 184–201. https://doi.org/10.1057/9780230294882_9.

Perruchoud, R. 1989. 'From the Intergovernmental Committee for European Migration to the International Organization for Migration', *International Journal of Refugee Law*, 1: 501–17. doi.org/10.1093/ijrl/1.4.501.

Poutignat, P. and Streiff-Fénart, J. 2010. 'Migration policy development in Mauritania: Process, issues and actors', in: M. Geiger and A. Pécoud (eds). *The Politics of International Migration Management*, Migration, Minorities and Citizenship Series. London: Palgrave Macmillan.

Scherf, T. 2020. 'The IOM's humanitarian border management in the West African Ebola crisis (2014–2016)', in: M. Geiger and A. Pécoud (eds). *The International Organization for Migration: The new 'UN Migration Agency' in critical perspective*, International Political Economy Series. Cham: Springer International Publishing, pp. 217–44. doi.org/10.1007/978-3-030-32976-1_10.

Schiller, N.G. and Salazar, N.B. 2013. 'Regimes of mobility across the globe', *Journal of Ethnic and Migration Studies*, 39: 183–200. doi.org/10.1080/1369183X.2013.723253.

Segaldo, N. 2021. 'Navigating through an external agenda and internal preferences: Ghana's national migration policy'. Discussion Paper No. 8. Bonn: German Development Institute.

Trauner, F., Jegen, L., Adam, I. and Roos, C. 2019. 'The International Organization for Migration in West Africa: Why its role is getting more contested'. Policy Brief No. PB-2019/3. UNU-Cris Working Paper. Brugge: UNU-Cris.

UN General Assembly 2016. 'Agreement Concerning the Relationship Between the United Nations and the International Organization for Migration: Resolution adopted by the General Assembly'. UN General Assembly, Session 70. United Nations Digital Library. Online at: https://digitallibrary. un.org/record/837208?ln=en (accessed 10 February 2022).

Van Criekinge, T. 2009. 'Power asymmetry between the European Union and Africa? A case study of the EU's relations with Ghana and Senegal'. PhD dissertation, London School of Economics and Political Science.

Vives, L. 2017. 'The European Union–West African sea border: Anti-immigration strategies and territoriality', *European Urban and Regional Studies*, 24: 209–24.

Zanker, F., Altrogge, J., Arhin-Sam, K. and Jegen, L. 2019. *Challenges in EU–African Migration Cooperation: West African Perspectives on Forced Return.* Policy Brief No. 2019/5, MEDAM Dialogue. Kiel: MEDAM and ABI.

Part VIII
Future of Africa–EU Migration Governance

Chapter 20

Renegotiating Africa–EU migration governance

Adeoye O. Akinola

Introduction

This volume has offered a nuanced exploration of the ways in which migration governance has occupied the top agendas in policy-making and public debates in Africa and the European Union (EU), particularly in the wake of the so-called 2015 migration crisis in Europe. The depth of the crisis has increased the importance of migration to European and African actors because of the convergence of migration, conflict and development. This book was inspired by a shared concern over African and European decision-makers' tendency to stand worlds apart in their understanding of, and approaches to, migration governance.

This collection presents carefully selected themes and case studies for unravelling the securitisation of African–EU migration. It proffers sustainable policy frameworks for effective and mutually beneficial migration relations between Africa and the EU. The imperativeness of improved migration relations between Africa and Europe was central to the establishment of the Africa–EU Partnership (AEP), which presented a platform for both continents to have meaningful conversations on African–EU migration, during the first Africa–EU Summit in Cairo in 2000.[1]

Disturbingly, Africa and the EU have approached migration from different standpoints – as reflected in the volume – due to what Jan Bade calls 'differences in levels of prosperity and demography'.[2] African actors see migration as natural, developmental, and beneficial to both continents, but their EU counterparts perceive it through the lenses of security and migration control. Indeed, migration from Africa was not the main cause of border security in Europe – it was the Syrian refugee crisis in 2015 that moved migration policy to the forefront of European politics and policy-making, leading to its categorisation as an existential threat and a security concern to the EU and its member states. The protracted conflict in different African countries has also resulted in massive human displacements, contributing to the rise in the number of African migrants in the EU. While there are other push factors of migration, conflict is one of the direct root causes of forced displacement, while the displacement – both as a consequence and a potential cause of further conflict – leads to outbound migration (AU, 2006: 6). Many regions in Africa, including the Sahel, have become epicentres of human displacements caused by conflict. Despite the global agenda for a friendly approach to irregular migration, the EU has continued to devise ways to counter irregular migration from Africa, which is seen as a priority area of European policy on migration.

Since 2012, migrants have entered Europe using tourist visas or fake documents, or smuggled in ferries and vehicles (Arnold 2012; Idemudia and Boehnke 2020: 21). In 2018, it was reported that Nigerians (390,000), South Africans (310,000), Somalis (300,000), Senegalese (270,000), and Ghanaians (250,000) constituted the highest number of migrants from African countries to the EU, Norway and Switzerland (Pew Research Centre, 2018: 7). The report also maintained that 72 per cent of migrants from sub-Saharan countries are living in four European countries, namely Portugal (360,000), Italy (370,000), France (980,000), and the United Kingdom (1.27 million) (Pew Research Centre, 2018: 8). Under the EU's influence, some African countries, such as Libya, have become part of the process of 'migration containment and control' (Chandler, 2018: 84–5). In the 2000s, President Muammar Gaddafi of Libya became an important partner of the EU in fighting irregular migration. After his departure from power in 2011 and the protracted violent conflict in the country, many African migrants saw an opportunity to use Libya as a gateway to Europe and subsequently moved in tremendous numbers to Libya.

Europe has pursued migration policy on two fronts (d'Humières, 2018). The first are preventive measures to act on the root causes of migration by supporting development programmes and facilitating trade or foreign direct investment (FDI), as well as expanding employment opportunities in both countries of transit and origin. The EU remains Africa's most important foreign investor, the main source of financial transfers, and the greatest supplier of humanitarian and development assistance (d'Humières, 2018). However, in reality, the EU's so-called humanitarian aid is no longer humanitarian. Since the rise of migration to the EU in 2015, the EU's response to African–EU migration has not necessarily been out of concern for the vulnerable and those fleeing conflict zones. The EU has ceased prioritising human capacity and developmental initiatives but has focused on preventing irregular migrants from reaching the EU. The second policy is the securitisation of migration. This is aimed at preventing the irregular movement of migrants across the borders of partner countries by implementing several policies to keep Africans out of Europe. This focuses on border controls and the efforts to counter illegal entries and the trafficking of migrants. The EU has consistently used development and financial assistance to manage external migration, including influencing the transit countries such as Libya to strengthen their border security.

Rethinking migration governance

This section focuses on the reality of African–EU migration and how actors from both continents could partner for improved migration relations. It presents several thematic migration issues that are reflected in this volume, and tries to proffer sustainable policy options to strengthen the quest for a more human and reflective African–EU migration governance.

Addressing the root causes of migration

Generally, most people migrate across borders for reasons related to work, family and study, while others move due to several compelling and sometimes tragic reasons, such as climate change, conflict, human rights abuse and catastrophe. While those in need of humanitarian assistance, such as irregular migrants, refugees and internally displaced persons (IDPs), represent a relatively small percentage of all migrants, they also attract the most attention in international policy-making or national discourse on migration (IOM, 2019). Since the root-causes analytical framework originated in Europe as a response to the 2015 migration issue, the EU's longer goal should be directed at addressing the root causes of irregular migration.[3] Threats to human security such as economic crisis, climatic change, structural violence and infrastructural depletion, as well as political instability and violent conflict, are top of the list of the push factors for African–EU migration. Contrary to expectations, conflict continues to proliferate in Africa, leading to an increase in international migration. Indeed, several studies and several chapters in this volume have established the nexus between conflict and African–EU migration.

According to ACCORD's COVID-19 Conflict and Resilience Monitor, the pandemic and the quest for its containment continue to worsen the fragility of weak states and their formal and informal social institutions (ACCORD and AU, 2020). This has imposed additional pressures on African states' social capital, resilience and social cohesion, and jeopardised their capacities to generate additional resources to cope with the COVID-related stress. This is more likely to engender negative coping strategies, social unrest, and even violent conflict, as the latter has intensified in some African countries, particularly in the Sahel zone. Africa, particularly the Sahel, has been declared the epicentre of armed conflict in the world, and these conflicts have led to human displacements. For instance, South Sudan produced the highest number of refugees in Africa in 2018 (2.3 million), and ranked third in the world, with most hosted in neighbouring countries such as Uganda (IOM, 2019). Somalia occupied the second position in the region and ranked fifth in the world, with the majority of its refugees hosted in Kenya and Ethiopia. For the past few years, Uganda has been the highest receiver of refugees in Africa, hosting about 1.2 million people, mostly from Sudan, the Congo and the DRC (IOM, 2019: 59).

The number of IDPs in Ethiopia, due to conflict, had risen to 1.2 million by the end of 2018, up from 700,000 in 2017. By March 2022, the Ethiopian government's crackdown on Tigray had reportedly led to the death of more than half a million people, internally displaced over 2 million others, subjected more than 100,000 women and girls to sexual violence, and accounted for the starvation of about 4.5 million people (Wildermichel, 2022). Furthermore, South Sudan recorded over 2.2 million refugees and about 1.9 million IDPs, while about 1 million refugees left Somalia due to protracted conflict and over 250,000 IDPs due to disasters such as drought

(IOM, 2019: 61). Xenophobic violence in countries such as Ghana and South Africa, and border security in Europe have added to the rate of irregular migration to Europe.[4] Some migrants who would have chosen South Africa as their destination, have found their way into Europe instead because of the xenophobia and insecurity experienced by foreign nationals in the country.

In 2020, the number of forcefully displaced persons in Africa was estimated at 32 million, up from 29 million recorded in 2019 (Africa Center for Strategic Studies, 2021: 1). Of these, 75 per cent (24 million) were displaced within Africa. The DRC tops this list with 6 million IDPs, followed by Sudan (4 million), and Nigeria (3.3 million). Terrorist attacks by Boko Haram and Islamic State militants in West Africa have accounted for the displacement of 2.5 million Nigerians, while the spill-over effects of the violent attacks in Mali have resulted in 1.2 million human displacements in Burkina Faso, representing a 900 per cent increase in Burkinabe IDPs in 2019 (Africa Center for Strategic Studies, 2021: 3). Many of these populations have found their ways into transit countries like Libya.

Apart from Libya, many other Maghreb countries are a gateway to Europe. With the colonial-inclined destruction of the agricultural economy of the Maghreb countries and subsequent rural–urban migration, which has aggravated the unemployment crisis in cities, migration to the EU has become the obvious escape route for thousands of citizens of the region. States in the region have encouraged migration into Europe to ease tensions in the economy and provide remittances to strengthen the quest for development of the region. Stakeholders in both Africa and the EU should address the root cause of migration in the region by expanding employment opportunities, particularly for the highly skilled population, instead of committing enormous resources for border control. Rather than relying on the EU to create a friendlier migration environment, the Maghreb countries should also initiate and implement policies on how the region would benefit from African–EU migration.

The Horn of Africa seems to have been more proactive than the Maghreb member countries in benefitting from African–EU migration. The regional body, the Intergovernmental Authority on Development (IGAD), has coordinated efforts to limit the negative impact of migration and harness the gains of migration for the development of the region and the benefit of the citizens. The Horn presents a complex pattern of migration, as people on the move comprised different categories of people – from displaced people to those seeking better economic opportunities in the EU. The Horn is a high-risk society with different forms of protracted armed conflicts, which account for the high rate of emigration. The Great Lakes Region is in a similar situation, as conflict and human displacement have led to migration and blurred the distinction between irregular and regular migrants.

Despite the high number of migrants from the Great Lakes countries to the EU, European policy-makers have shown less interest in addressing the plight of the migrants. This situation is similar to that in southern African, where political and economic instability, and conflict in countries like Zimbabwe and Mozambique, have distorted the historical pattern of migration in the region (intra-region), leading to a high number of both regular and irregular migrants to Europe.

It is thus crucial to address the push factors for migration. In addition to influencing the EU and its member states to invest in the demilitarisation of Africa and combat conflict by strengthening national and regional efforts to create peace and security, poverty and unemployment are other drivers of migration that require attention. The present template for African–EU relations is too state-centric and counterproductive, since some state leaders have constituted a stumbling block to peace in Africa. It is high time that the EU took its engagement with civil society groups more seriously. The responsibility to manage migration falls more on donor organisations and civil society groups, than the EU. The main push factors in the region are conflict, drought and hunger – three closely related root causes of migration. Instead of directing most of the efforts at the quest for peace and security in the Horn of Africa, the priorities should include implementing policies that would improve the livelihood of families, and investing in infrastructure that would limit the effect of drought on the predominantly farming communities. In short, the EU has focused on and invested heavily in controlling migration to the detriment of implementing poverty alleviation programmes in Africa. African actors should put the development of Africa at top of the priority list for African–EU dialogue.

One way to combat household poverty could be a focus on investment in the labour-intensive agricultural sector, which would generate employment opportunities for both skilled and unskilled Africans. Migration knows no status – both the rich and poor, skilled and unskilled, are prone to migration, although under different circumstances. Based on the Organisation for Economic Co-operation and Development's (OECD's) categorisation, over 50 per cent of Nigerian migrants have high levels of education, 26 per cent have completed at least up to upper-secondary education, while the remaining 18 per cent have completed lower-secondary education or below (Adhikari, Chaudhary and Ekeator, 2021: 64). While data have shown that both the rich and the poor migrate, there is compelling evidence that most of the irregular African migrants are either victims of conflict or harsh economic conditions in their home countries.

Mitigating against the European concerns on migration

Over 87 million international migrants lived in Europe in 2019, which was an increase of about 10 per cent from 2015, when over 75 million international migrants were hosted by the region. This represented the largest number of international migrants in any region of the world (IOM, 2019: 85). Between 2008 and 2017, there were about 7.4 million irregular migrants from developing countries in the EU (Idemudia and Boehnke, 2020: 22). Stricter border laws implemented by the EU have since reduced these figures.

Irregular migration to Europe reached its peak in 2015, with about 1.8 million migrants crossing the Mediterranean Sea. It was discovered that 50 per cent of the migrants who went missing or were found dead in the Mediterranean were of African origin (Idemudia and Boehnke, 2020: 21). Socio-economic and political circumstances in Africa keep driving people from their countries, and the EU is relatively close to African borders. Table 20.1 shows the percentage of citizens of selected African countries that choose to migrate to other countries.

Table 20.1: Percentage of those who would leave for another country if given the chance to migrate

	Country	Percentage
1.	Ghana	75
2.	Nigeria	74
3.	Kenya	54
4.	South Africa	51
5.	Senegal	46
6.	Tanzania	43

Source: Pew Research Centre (2018)

Providing basic infrastructures, creating employment opportunities, increasing the economic performance of African states, and guaranteeing peace and security would reduce the number of people who are ready to move.

Despite the balanced perspectives by some European actors and the rhetoric on migration governance, migration continues to be highly contested in the EU and remains a priority for policy-making by member states. Since 2017, far-right-wing political parties and groups have continued to mobilise Europeans against immigration, through well-coordinated, online campaigns, petitions and videos (IOM, 2019: 94). While migration continues to attract divergent perspectives in the EU, a 2018 European Commission survey found that 40 per cent of Europeans conceive of immigration as more of a problem than an opportunity (IOM, 2019: 94). Apart from the impact migrants have on meagre European resources, many anti-immigration Europeans have pointed to the illicit activities (drugs and human trafficking, and prostitution) perpetuated by irregular migrants and feared the distortion of the EU's social value system. A cross-section of EU actors believed that many of the irregular migrants are people with shady characters.

As has been seen in Libya, a high number of spontaneous and irregular migrations can influence national and international stability and security, and have the propensity to hinder countries' capacity to effectively exercise control over their borders (AU, 2006). This could easily create hostilities between home, transit and destination countries, as well as within the host societies. Migration, if not managed with sincerity and commitment by both sending and receiving countries, has the tendency to deepen illicit business transactions, small arms proliferation, terrorism and other social vices in the destination countries.

Policy-makers from both continents should focus on different partnership models to bridge the gap on African–EU migration, and adopt a common understanding of migration issues such as the root causes of migration (push and pull factors), the plight of irregular migrants, the importance of migration, and migration as a human right. While we can broadly sketch European perspectives on migration, we must also be mindful of different voices – even within Europe – with regard to conceptualising migration. For instance, Eastern and Western European countries have different attitudes to accepting immigrants.[5] In many of these countries, more permissive deportation pacts still dominated the

African–EU migration narratives, but a more constructive engagement by African actors and CSOs from both continents, based on genuine migration data, could bring about attitudinal changes and a more positive response to migration. For instance, migrant smuggling and trafficking, and other abuses of migrants on the move could be halted by creating more opportunities for legal migration pathways, and raising public awareness on the risks of using illicit routes such as the Sahara Desert and the Mediterranean Sea (African Union Commission, 2018: 6). The media and CSOs have a great responsibility to provide balanced reports of migration issues to the public.

Desecuritisation of migration and expansion of legal pathways

Since 2015, migration has become a top security issue in Europe, with the sole aim of keeping migrants away from European borders. To achieve this, the EU has partnered with transit countries like Libya and Niger to shut down both old and new migratory routes (Dockery, 2017). Zanker (2019: 1) correctly reported that EU perspectives on migration have shifted from the 'management-orientated discourse' to the 'restriction-orientated practice'. Her study exposes the EU's rhetorical pronouncements and policy implementation. While the securitisation conversation became popular during the so-called 2015 'migration crisis' in Europe, it actually dated back to the 1980s (Zanker, 2019: 2). Since the Schengen Agreement in 1995, the EU has strengthened its external borders and elevated migration to a security concern (d'Humières, 2018). As the EU and its member states perfect their strategies to strengthen border control, thousands of desperate African migrants continue to risk their lives by attempting to reach Europe via the Mediterranean Sea and the Sahara Desert from Libya and Niger.

Migrants are being abandoned in the desert by human traffickers, thus being exposed to exceedingly hot conditions without food and water. As an IOM personnel revealed, 'cars break down, drivers get lost, and migrants get abandoned … the conditions are dire … [the] desert is a bigger cemetery than the Mediterranean Sea' (Dockery, 2017). Sadly, those who survive the desert in Niger, still have to confront the risk of being killed in Libya by the smugglers, jihadists, tribal factions and other criminal networks. Migrants who manage to manoeuvre through the desert and confront the other risks, must now contend with the sea route. The tragic story of Samia Omar, an

Olympian who died while trying to reach Europe, represents the reality of many migrants whose stories sank with them in the Mediterranean Sea.[6] Through migration *mis*governance, the EU has endangered the lives of many irregular African migrants, who are so desperate that they would explore several life-threatening routes to escape the 'unbearable' conditions in their home countries.

While the number of migrants entering the EU legally has exceeded the number of irregular entries, there is still a need for Europe to abolish several restrictive policies and expand access to the EU through legal pathways. This is the most decisive point that African actors should keep emphasising to their European counterparts. West African actors have tried to implement policies to expand legal pathways between West Africa and Europe,[7] but the EU has not created an enabling environment for easy access to Europe-bound migrants from West Africa. The opening of the labour market has remained the prerogative of the EU and its member states (d'Humières, 2018). There is a need for more commitment and sincerity by both African and European actors to address the question of expanding legal pathways, which would reduce the rate of irregular migration and reduce the casualties recorded on the illegal and dangerous routes to the EU, such as the Sahara Desert and the Mediterranean Sea.

The EU also pursued a regional approach to migration issues. In 2014, representatives from both continents met in Rome to launch the EU–Horn of Africa Migration Route Initiative, tagged the Khartoum Process, to address migration issues between the Horn of Africa and Europe (Chandler, 2018). Indeed, the Khartoum Process sent a clear signal to the Sudanese government that controlling migration was top of the EU's agenda on African–EU migration. European governments have asked their African counterparts for their cooperation on migration in exchange for aid to the tune of €1.8 billion via the EU Emergency Trust Fund for Africa (Chandler, 2018: 82). In addition, EU member states have established several bilateral agreements. For instance, in 2008, Italy signed a pact with Libya to increase security over its coastlines in a deal involving US$500 million worth of electronic monitoring devices (Chandler, 2018: 82).

Centring the link between migration and human rights

Since 2014, over 600,000 African migrants have arrived in Italy through the perilous Central Mediterranean route, and nearly 120,000 arrived in

2017 alone (Kirwin and Anderson, 2018). The high casualties reported on the Mediterranean Sea routes have not deterred desperate Africans from crossing into Europe.[8] Indeed, these deaths are underreported for many reasons, including the clandestine nature of human trafficking (Kirwin and Anderson, 2018). Many migrants have also died in the Sahara Desert, while others have lost their lives in the inhuman detention centres and other miserable conditions in transit countries such as Libya.

African migrants have had to endure human rights abuses and discrimination and racism, before and during the COVID-19 pandemic. They have been subjected to 'exploitation, mass expulsion, persecution, and other abuses in both transit and destination countries' (AU, 2006). Migration should be seen as a human rights issue, and the lives and wellbeing of migrants, particularly irregular ones, should be protected by international laws on human rights. The practice of harassment, discrimination, and other abuses by European states' security should be declared a human rights issue. European actors should protect the economic and socio-cultural rights of migrants, because this is a fundamental component of balanced migration management systems. For instance, the right to development should be non-negotiable.

Engagement with non-state actors

Africa–EU summits have been state-centric, and fewer platforms have remained open to civil society and international organisations. Global organisations such as the UNCHR, the UNDP, the IOM and civil society groups involved in the management of migration, should be accorded more space to intervene in African–EU migration.[9] These organisations have the capacity to influence actors in Africa and Europe, and invest more in the governance of African–EU migration. States are at the centre of refugee management, which makes it appropriate to explore the role of states and non-state actors in migration governance. Migration cannot be separated from human displacement, and this speaks to the blurring of the categories of people on the move.

While there are several institutional templates for addressing migration issues by states and regional organisations such as the AU, several challenges have impeded effective migration governance both in Africa and Europe. As reflected in this book, the interests of the EU have continued to dominate

African governments' policies on migration and refugees.[10] Interestingly, countries like Nigeria and Rwanda have been made to facilitate the return of several African migrants stranded in Libya. This serves the interests of the EU. Thus, the voices of African-based non-state actors are urgently needed, given the questionable compromises introduced by multinational organisations – for example, the IOM's handling of so-called Voluntary Repatriation Programmes from Libya, or the UNHCR's passivity in relation to the outsourcing of asylum processing from the United Kingdom and Denmark to Rwanda. When the credibility of the biggest players in the field is compromised, sustained dialogue with less powerful actors may provide much-needed reality checks.

The need for accurate data on migration

The dearth of accurate data is not peculiar to Africa; European policy-makers also lack reliable data. Therefore, it is in the interest of both continents to invest in building a reliable database to inform migration policies and to implement them effectively. All actions must be based on evidence. It is instructive to bear in mind that about 80 per cent of international migration occurs within Africa. This narrative seems to be lost in many European media reports and by leftist parties who present the narrative as if entire African populations were headed for Europe. There is also a misconception in Europe that Africans are the top sending countries, whereas no African country was on the list of the top 20 countries of emigration in 2019 (IOM, 2019: 27).

Bjarnesen (2020) argued that political debates were selective and misleading on African migration, and that the European public has received distorted facts about African–EU migration through the media. These narratives should be supported by valid data, but most of the rhetoric has no empirical basis and weaves in political misconceptions. For instance, the fact that regular migration exceeds irregular migration from Africa is not popular among many EU actors. Natalie and Isaacs (2020: 4) noted that 'the media is lazy and often report data as they are reported without undertaking specialized reporting'. Western media also tend to focus on stories of displacement, especially refugees and irregular migrants, giving the impression that large numbers of African are bound for Europe.

African civil society organisations lack access to data, and most of them do not have the capacity to generate data. They have to rely on data generated by their EU counterparts and the accuracy of such data is difficult to verify. African governments should invest in research and development to obtain accurate data to develop sustainable policies on migration. For instance, it is not widely recognised that Africa is also a major destination for migrants from all over the world. In 2000, about 15.1 million international migrants were hosted by Africa, and by 2019, this figure had increased to 26.6 million (Natalie and Isaacs, 2019: 16). This is the sharpest relative increase (76 per cent) of all the major continents in the world.

Migration as mutually beneficial

Africa and the EU have platforms on which to engage on issues of mutual benefits. For instance, Morocco 2005 opened the channels for establishing the link between migration and development, while the Rabat Process in 2006 provided a platform for the EU to discuss migration issues with North, West and Central Africa. The EU–Africa Migration, Mobility and Employment (MME) partnership was launched in Lisbon in 2007, where the First Action Plan (2008–2010) and a framework for dialogue and cooperation with the AU were adopted. One of the highlights was the adoption of a common asylum policy. It was at the Fourth EU–Africa Summit in Brussels in 2014 that deliberations took place on the future of African–EU migration, with the aim of fighting irregular migration through a comprehensive approach, addressing the root-cause narratives, and strengthening migration governance (d'Humières, 2018).

By 2015, the externalisation of European migration policy had become a central pillar, as reflected during the Valletta Summit on Migration held in November 2015, at the height of the 'migration crisis'. The summit reinforced the importance of Africa–EU cooperation in the management of migration. These summits always conclude with joint statements on migration governance, but decisions usually favour European interests over those of their African partners (Zanker, 2019). While it may be a difficult demand to recommend equality in this partnership, because of the power relations between the two continents, involving African actors in decisions and taking their issues seriously would certainly improve African–EU migration governance.

Migration is beneficial to both continents. Destination European countries are top gainers in the African–EU migration process due to the migrants' economic contributions. Furthermore, irregular, and even regular, migrants provide cheap labour and volunteers for dirty, dangerous and low-paid jobs, which the locals would usually reject (Rainer et al., 2006). European shadow economies have always relied on both documented and irregular migrants for cheap and exploitable labour. Europe has been 'confronted with an ageing population, stagnating or even declining native populations' (Rainer et al., 2006: 7). The use of undocumented migrants in the EU is motivated by the reality of aging populations, low fertility rates and the imperativeness of guaranteeing a sustainable labour force.

The mobility of young, skilled labour from Africa has created a brain drain on the continent, which has enhanced the development of the EU countries. African states tend not to oppose this movement as long as those who have gained employment status in the EU are 'permitted' to send back remittances to families and friends in their home countries. Migrants fill critical labour shortages and pay taxes when they have high-income employment, thereby contributing to the development of the receiving countries (Adhikari, Chaudhary and Ekeator, 2021). They have been critical in the agricultural and hospitality sectors in Europe, particularly during the COVID-19 pandemic. Thus, it is important to integrate migrants into the productive and labour sectors of destination countries to maximise the benefits of their skills and expertise. To this end, a more progressive labour-friendly mobility strategy should be implemented by the EU actors.

In 2020, there were 281 million international migrants (including refugees). Of the top 10 destinations in 2020, only three countries were in Europe: Germany (with 16 million was second), France (with 9 million was seventh), and Spain (7 million in the tenth place). Russia had 12 million and was fourth, while the United Kingdom, with 9 million was fifth (World Bank/KNOMAD, 2021: 4). Despite the outcry over African–EU migration, the United States remains the top destination for African migrants, although Europe remains Africa's greatest partner. In 2020, the EU foreign direct investment, estimated at €222 billion, was the largest investment in Africa, exceeding that of the United States (€42 billion), and China (€38 billion) (EU, 2020: 6). The EU has invested in transport, clean energy and agricultural sectors, including the region's thriving private sector. The aim is to enhance the developmental capacity of African states, which is beneficial to both countries (EU, 2020: 7). Aid serves the dual function of supporting Africa's quest for sustainable development and keeping Africans in Africa. The EU should focus more on empowering Africans through skills transfer in different sectors, and African actors should seek assistance beyond conventional financial aid.

Fostering partnership on remittances

Chapter contributors have laid the claim that poverty and harsh economic reality, including unemployment, are some of the push factors for migration. The COVID-19 pandemic increased the number of 'new poor' in 2020 to between 119 million and 124 million. The Sahel constitutes the poorest region in the world. Thus, remittances should be seen as a mechanism to address some of the financial challenges faced by African households. As has been discussed in the volume, remittance is one of the most tangible benefits of migration.[11] It has the potential to reduce the level, scope, depth and severity of poverty in many African countries. For instance, research in Ghana showed that the poorest households under study received 22.7 per cent of their total income from remittances.

Remittances have improved people's resilience to shocks and have become a means for human capacity development, as well as an instrument for combatting poverty, as remittances are invested in income-generating projects. African actors, including the AU, see remittances as a potent instrument for national and regional development, and they want to remove every impediment to the easy transfer of funds and other materials from the EU to Africa. However, European policy-makers have shown resistance to the transfer of funds from the EU to other countries, particularly in Africa. Indeed, Africa is currently the most expensive region for money transfers because of institutional constraints. It is important that European policy-makers see remittances as part of Europe's contribution to the development of Africa, and facilitate an easy and less costly mechanism to transfer legitimate funds, which the AU has consistently supported (AU, 2018: 5). Another way to enhance the flow of remittances to Africa is by increasing the legal pathway of migration and expanding job opportunities for migrants in both the formal and informal sectors of the European economies.

The Global Compact for Safe, Regular and Orderly Migration (GCM), which is not legally binding, provides guiding principles to enhance migration governance and regulate states' behaviour in respect of migration. It presents a holistic approach to achieving regular and safe migration through its 23 actionable targets.[12] Systematic implementation of these recommendations would ameliorate the burdens of both regular and irregular migration to both continents. International organisations such as the UNDP have championed effective migration governance and the protection of irregular migration. They have also emphasised the importance of remittances to poor countries and recommended that transfer costs to Africa should not exceed 5 per cent.[13]

Remittances continue to flow from Europe to Africa, contributing to the region's resilience during the COVID-19 pandemic. The Central Bank of Egypt declared a rise in the inflow of remittances into the country from US$29.6 billion in 2020 to US$31.5 billion dollars at the end of 2021 (Taiwo, 2022). This constitutes about 7 per cent of the country's GDP, at a very critical period, as the world continues to battle the devastating effects of COVID-19. The remittances have enhanced recovery from the pandemic, thereby stabilising Egypt's foreign reserves. Similar narratives have been reported in other African countries. Therefore, instead of using remittances primarily for household consumption, African actors should direct remittances to the creation of productive opportunities. African governments require concrete assistance from Europe to guarantee good governance, which is more important than financial aid and more effective in reducing African–EU migration. Effective governance enables human capacity development and a fulfilling life in the home countries.

Conclusion

This chapter has highlighted eight paths toward a more just and sustainable migration governance agenda, against the backdrop of the detailed reflections on the key policy priorities, drivers, regional dynamics, and actors influencing African–EU migration. As already stated, most of these paths are well trodden in scholarship and policy thinking, but this volume has reiterated the importance of a holistic and rights-based approach to migration governance, and a more concerted effort to challenge the Eurocentric and defunct agenda that has emerged over the past decade.

In this spirit, this chapter has traced the contributions of this volume back to the initial international engagement with the implementation of the GCM. The GCM, which draws on the 2030 Agenda for Sustainable Development, contains all the essential building blocks necessary for a fundamental shift in the way migration is approached and managed. The dwindling momentum of the framework can be attributed only to the lack of political will and leadership in the Global North. This claim is not just an indictment of the bureaucratic inefficiency in implementing a global framework for migration governance. In the case of African–EU migration, the European politicisation of migration governance has become an important root cause of insecurity in its own right, exposing migrants to unsafe and undignified migration, and to marginalisation and outright persecution as migrants of colour in the EU. This volume provides decision-makers and policy analysts on both continents with an elaborate framework to challenge the status quo and improve the conditions and prospects for African migrants, wherever they may wish to journey.

Notes

1   For more information, see Chapter 11.

2   For more information, see Chapter 12.

3   See chapters 1, 3 and 14

4   For more information, see Chapter 9.

5   For more information on this, see Chapter 12.

6   For more information, see Chapter 1.

7   For more information, see Chapter 8.

8   For information on the casualty through the sea route, see Chapter 2.

9   For more information on the roles of the UNHCR, UNDP and IOM in African–EU migration, see chapters 17, 18 and 19.

10 See Part II of this book.

11 See chapters 5 and 11.

12 See more on the UN Compact and the role of civil society organisations in driving migration governance in Chapter 15.

13 For more information on the role of UNDP in migration governance, see Chapter 18.

References

Adhikari, S., Chaudhary, S. and Ekeator, N.L. 2021. *Of Roads Less Traveled: Assessing the potential of economic migration to provide overseas jobs for Nigeria's youth.* Washington, DC: World Bank. Online at: https://openknowledge. worldbank.org/handle/10986/35995 License: CC BY 3.0 IGO.

Africa Center for Strategic Studies. 2021. '32 million Africans forcibly displaced by conflict and repression', 17 June. Washington, DC: Africa Center for Strategic Studies. Online at: https://africacenter.org/spotlight/32-

million-africans-forcibly-displaced-by-conflict-and-repression/ (accessed 6 October 2021).

African Union Commission. 2018. *Migration Policy Framework for Africa and Plan of Action (2018–2030)*. Addis Ababa: African Union.

African Union (AU). 2006. 'African Common Position on Migration and Development'. Addis Ababa, Ethiopia. Online at: https://www.unhcr.org/protection/migration/4d5257e09/african-common-position-migration-development.html (accessed 6 October 2021).

Arnold, G. 2012. *Migration: Changing the world*. London: Pluto Press.

ACCORD and AU. 2020. '2020 Review of the United Nations Peacebuilding Architecture African Regional Consultation Report'. 30 June. Online at: https://www.un.org/peacebuilding/sites/www.un.org.peacebuilding/files/2020_review_of_the_united_nations_peacebuilding_architecture_african_reg.pdf (accessed 6 October 2021).

Bjarnesen, J. 2020. 'Shifting the narrative on African Migration: The numbers, the root causes, the alternatives – get them right!' *The Nordic Africa Institute Policy Note* 2020:1.

Chandler, C.L. 2018. 'How far will the EU go to seal its borders?' *Dissent*, 65(3): 80–92.

d'Humières, V. 2018. 'European Union/African cooperation: The externalisation of Europe's migration policies,' *European Issues* No 472. Brussels: Fondation Robert Schuman. Online at: https://www.robert-schuman.eu/en/european-issues/0472-european-union-african-cooperation-the-externalisation-of-europe-s-migration-policies (accessed 6 October 2021).

Dockery, W. 2017. 'The Sahara route: A journey more deadly than the crossing from the coast', InfoMigrants, 28 August. Online at: https://www.infomigrants.net/en/post/4811/the-sahara-route-a-journey-more-deadly-than-the-crossing-from-the-coast?msclkid=65347df4aaaa11eca588df67ef5f16de (accessed 6 October 2021).

European Union (EU). 2020. 'Joint Communication to the European Parliament and the Council: Towards a Comprehensive Strategy with Africa'. Online at: https://ec.europa.eu/international-partnerships/system/files/communication-eu-africa-strategy-join-2020-4-final_en.pdf (accessed 6 October 2021).

Idemudia, E. and Boehnke, K. 2020. *Psychosocial Experiences of African Migrants in Six European Countries: A mixed method study*, Social Indicators Research Series No. 81. Springer Nature, pp. 15–31.

International Organization for Migration (IOM). 2019. *World Migration Report*

2020. Online at: https://publications.iom.int/system/files/pdf/wmr_2020.pdf (accessed 6 October 2021).

Kirwin, M. and Anderson, J. 2018. *Identifying the Factors Driving West African Migration*, West African Papers No. 17. Paris: OECD Publishing, pp. 1–22.

Münz, R., Thomas Straubhaar, T., Vadean, F. and Vadea, N. (2006). *The Costs and Benefits of European Immigration*, HWWI Policy Report No. 3. Hamburg: Hamburg Institute of International Economics. Online at: https://www.hwwi.org/uploads/tx_wilpubdb/HWWI_Policy_Report_Nr__3_01.pdf (accessed 6 October 2021).

Natalie, C. and Isaacs, L. 2020. 'Remittances to and from Africa', in: A. Adepoju, C. Fumagalli and N. Nyabola, *African Migration Report: Challenging the narrative*. Geneva: International Organization for Migration, pp. 117–31.

Pew Research Centre. 2018. 'At least a million sub-Saharan Africans moved to Europe since 2010'. Online at: https://www.pewglobal.org/2018/03/22/at-least-a-million-sub-saharan-africans-moved-to-europe-since-2010/ (accessed 6 October 2021).

Taiwo, J. 2022. 'Egypt: Foreign remittances increase to \$31.5b', News Central TV. Online at: https://newscentral.africa/2022/03/16/egypt-foreign-remittances-increase-to-31-5b/ (accessed 6 October 2021).

United Nations Department of Economic and Social Affairs, Population Division. 2020. 'International Migration 2020 Highlights' (ST/ESA/SER.A/452)', pp. 1–60. Online at: https://reliefweb.int/sites/reliefweb.int/files/resources/International%20Migration%202020%20Highlights.pdf (accessed 6 October 2021).

World Bank/KNOMAD. 2021. *Resilience: COVID-19 crisis through a migration lens*, Migration and Development Brief No. 34, pp. 1–40. Online at: https://reliefweb.int/sites/reliefweb.int/files/resources/Migration%20and%20Development%20Brief%2034.pdf (accessed 6 October 2021).

Wildermichel, T.G. 2022. 'Vårt Land's article titled "New Amnesty report reveals serious war crimes in Ethiopia" is troubling'. Online at: https://tghat.com/2022/03/18/vart-lands-article-titled-new-amnesty-report-reveals-serious-war-crimes-in-ethiopia-is-troubling/?noamp=mobile&msclkid=359215faa86011ecb603fd5e38ddcc9a (accessed 6 October 2021).

Zanker, F. 2019. 'Managing or restricting movement? Diverging approaches of African and European migration governance', *Comparative Migration Studies*, 7(17): 1–18.

Index

A

Abidjan Summit 276, 278

Abuja Treaty (1991) 179, 264, 265, 266

academic migration scholarship 333

ActionAid 374

Action Against Hunger 392

Action Plan on Maritime Security 251

Active population 142

Addis Ababa Action Agenda (4A) 126

Africa's 'brain drain' 62

Africa's tourism sector 445

Africa–EU migration 65, 117, 134, 220, 223, 225, 269, 273, 278

Africa–EU Partnership (AEP) 221, 266, 267, 485

Africa–EU Summit 50, 51, 61, 266, 485

Africa–Europe migration 454

Africa–Europe partnership 446, 454

African 'Boat People' 65

African 'exodus' 76

African Capacity for Immediate Response to Crises (ACIRC) 64

African Centre for the Study and Research on Migration (CARIM) 225

African Centre for the Study and Research on Migration in Mali

(ACSRM) 277, 325

African Charter on Human and Peoples' Rights 76, 86, 89, 179, 428

African citizens 29, 61, 62, 106, 223, 431

African Commission on Human and Peoples' Rights (ACPHR) 429

African Common Position on Migration and Development 179, 263, 321

African Continental Free Trade Area (AfCFTA) 39, 90, 97, 264, 280, 301, 379, 446

African CSOs 369, 370, 371, 374, 375, 377, 380, 381, 382, 383, 384, 385, 386

African diaspora 29, 263, 264, 271, 323, 454

African diaspora communities 61, 62, 64

African Economic Community 266

African economic migrants 441

African economies 63

African Governance Architecture (AGA) 277

African Great Lakes 167

African Great Lakes (AGL) region 239

African Institute for Remittances

(AIR) 63, 129

African labour market 292, 431

African migration landscape 316

African Migration Observatory 325

African natural resources 448

African Observatory on Migration in Morocco (AOM) 50, 277

African paradox 86

African pride 475

African Regional Economic Communities 244

African student mobility 330

African Union (AU) Revised Migration Policy Framework for Africa (MPFA) 370

African Union Convention on Preventing and Combatting Corruption 80

African Union Migration Policy Framework for Africa (AUMPFA) 76, 126

African Union's Migration Policy Framework for Africa (AU-MPFA) 180

African youth 51, 348, 446, 450, 452

African youth cohorts 372

African, Caribbean and Pacific (ACP) states 250

African, Caribbean and Pacific States (ACP)–EU Dialogue on Migration 306

African, Caribbean, and Pacific (ACP)–EU Partnership Agreement 267

African/EU migration 415

African–EU dialogue 490

African–EU migration governance 40, 416, 421, 487, 497

African–EU migration narratives 493

African–EU mobility 128

African–European relations 115

Afro-centric understanding 279

Afro–European relations 330

AGL countries 241, 245, 254, 256

agrarian reforms 139

aid disbursement 159

Alternative Help Association (AHA) 399

American 'war on terror' 346

anti-corruption initiative 80

anti-immigrant politicians 76

anti-immigrant sentiments 372

anti-immigration efforts 354

anti-immigration Europeans 492

anti-immigration sentiments 101

anti-immigration stances 399

anti-Islam stances 399

anti-smuggling law 103

apartheid 222, 224, 225, 226

apartheid regime 25

apartheid state 227

Arab Maghreb Union (AMU) 249

Arab Spring 87, 422

armed conflict 332

assisted voluntary return and voluntary humanitarian return (AVRR/VHR) 467

assisted voluntary returns 471

asylum applications 344, 346, 347, 353

AU Constitutive Act 279

AU Free Movement Protocol 107

AU Member States 276

AU/IGAD member states 188

AU–EU partnership 63

AU–EU relations 63

AU-EU-UN Task Force 279

authoritarian governance 85

authoritarianism 332

B

Balkan war 344

Banjul Plan of Action 429

Bantu people 225

Better Migration Management

(BMM) programme 184
bilateral agreement 194, 195
biometric entry–exit governance 474
black majority 224
Boko Haram 414
border capacity-building projects 474
border conflict 178
border control measures 475
border control strategies 473
border enforcement programme 116
border security measures 157
brain circulation 231, 263
brain drain 62, 77, 124, 125, 225, 231, 233, 264, 269, 301, 323, 498
brain drain debate 225
brain gain 231, 301, 307
Brexit 270
British Petroleum (BP) Exploration (Caspian Sea) Ltd 464
Bush administration 346

C
Cable Network News (CNN) 173
Canary Island crisis 475
capital flight 448
causal mechanisms of migration 355
Central African Republic (CAR) 418
central imperium philosophy (China) 302
Central Mediterranean route 494
Central Mediterranean Sea Initiative (CMSI) 421, 431
Centre for Migration Information and Management (Centre d'Information et de Gestion des Migrations [CIGEM]) 197
Central Bank headquarters 464
Chinese Belt and Road Initiative (BRI) 303
cholera 418
circular migration 59, 161, 199, 200, 220, 305, 306, 308

civil society landscape 399
civil society organisations (CSOs) 369, 392
climate change 331
climate change mitigation 452
closed borders 444
Cold War 318
colonial centre 150
colonial centres 343
colonial conquests 222
colonial geopolitical power dynamics 343
colonial masters 128
colonial powers 100
colonial subjects 223
Commission on the Root Causes of Displacement (2019) 394
Common African Position on Assets Recovery 80
Common African Position (CAP) on Migration and Development 279
Common European Asylum System (CEAS) 195, 299, 421
Common Perspectives Paper 200
Common Position 322, 323
Community Court of Justice 244
Community Legislative Assembly 244
community refugee issues 246
complex infectious diseases 445
Comprehensive Refugee Response Framework (CRRF) 75, 300, 305, 380
Confederation for Relief and Development (CONCORD) 391
conflict-related displacement 359
conflict-related forced migration 343
Congo–Rwanda border zones 42
conspiratorial territory 360
Constitutive Act of the African Union 86
Consultative Forum on fundamental rights 396

Continent-to-Continent Migration
    and Mobility Dialogue
    (C2CMMD) 278
Continental Operational Centre
    (COC) 278
coronavirus disease 88
Cotonou Agreement 249
Council of the European Union 426
countries of origin 159, 444
countries of transit 159
COVID-19 Conflict and Resilience
    Monitor 488
COVID-19 crisis 131, 278
COVID-19 curve 188
COVID-19 epidemic 99
COVID-19 outbreak 228
COVID-19 pandemic 48, 53, 58, 74,
    88, 90, 91, 107, 117, 119, 120, 127,
    130, 133, 134, 149, 188, 189, 194,
    231, 232, 278, 385, 396, 402, 403,
    425, 444, 448, 449, 455, 495, 498,
    499, 500
COVID-19 protocols 396
COVID-related stress 488
Crimea 302
crisis of irregular migration (Africa) 424
crisis-oriented socio-economic
    recovery 448
cultural remittances 117

D

Dadaab refugee camp (Kenya) 101, 430
decolonisation 317
Defend Europe 399
democratic idealism (United States) 302
democratic remittances 118
Democratic Republic of Congo
    (DRC) 414
dependency ratio 142
dependency theorists 360
dependency theory 343
destination countries 140

development architecture 128
development discourse 133
devolution of power 373
dialogues 212
diaspora activities 377
diaspora communities 128
diaspora community 200
diaspora investments 118
Die Identitären (Identitarian
    Movement) 399
digital economy 203
Digital Explorer project 203
digital financial services 134
disaster-induced migration 379
discrimination 495
Djibouti shows 475
domestic gaps 198
domestic labour markets 151
domestic labour shortages 197
domestic legitimacy 101
demographic disparities 346
donor categories 461
donor governments 459
donor leverage 102, 104
Drivers of migration in Africa (2017)
    326
Dublin Regulation 425
Dutch East India Company 222

E

EAC Common Market 244
East African Community (EAC) 244
Eastern Europe 344
Eastern Mediterranean route 414
Eastern migration corridor 171-172
Ebola 100, 418
Ebola epidemic 1132
Ebola outbreak (2013–2016) 464
ECGLC identity card 242
ECGLC special card 242
ECGLC states 244
Economic Community of West

African States (ECOWAS) 244,
379, 424
economic dominance 223
economic dynamics 140
economic emigration 140
economic factors 175
economic incentives 454
economic migrants 116, 317, 377
economic migration 359
economic models 448
educated elite 223
educational trajectories 331
Egyptian–Libyan border lands 475
election management bodies
(EMBs) 82
election-related violence 74
electoral violence 81
Emergency Transit Centre 429
Emergency Transit Mechanisms
(ETMs) 428, 429
Emergency Trust Fund for Africa 349
entry–exit governance 474
environmental crises 220
environmental migrants 332
Erasmus and Marie Curie fellowships
211
Ethiopian National Intelligence and
Security Services (NISS) 188
ethnic fault lines 74
EU Agency for Fundamental Rights
(FRA) 396
EU asylum system 359
EU Emergency Trust Fund (EUTF) 75
EU Fund for Asylum, Migration and
Integration 399
EU migration and asylum policy 303
EU migration policy adviser 187
EU Pact for Migration and Asylum
(PICUM) 393, 396
EU Partnership Framework on
Migration 75
EU policy-makers 115

EU Trust Fund for Africa (EUTF)
252, 253, 392
EU-Africa relations 403
EU–Africa Summit (Abidjan) 102
EU–AU cooperation 299
EU-funded anti-trafficking measures
357
EU–Horn of Africa Migration Route
Initiative 494
EU–IOM Joint Initiative 467
Euro-African Dialogue on Migration
and Development 224
Euro–African migration governance
348
Euro-African Summit on Migration 253
European Agenda on Migration 200,
299
European asylum applicants 346
European Asylum Support Office
(EASO) 397
European asylum system 361
European border governance 390
European Commission 195, 206, 464
European conquest 222
European 'containment' objectives 472
European Council on Refugees and
Exiles (ECRE) 391
European Court of Human Rights 249
European dream 147
European earmarked funding 469
European Economic and Social
Committee (EESC) 391
European economic migrants 441
European El Dorado 62
European External Action Service 393
European governance agenda 421
European governments 401
European immigration regimes 331
European logics 477
European migration control
objectives 476
European migration crisis 422

European Migration Forum 391
European migration governance 347
European Neighbourhood Policy 75
European Pact on Migration and
    Asylum (2020) 195
European perspectives 492
European policy-makers 318, 347
European populist politics 372
European refugee crisis 299, 359
European shadow economies 358
European Union Agency for
    Fundamental Rights 426
European Union Emergency Trust
    Fund (EUTF) 105, 159, 195
European Union (EU)–Africa
    relations 315
European Visa Centre 247
European–southern African
    migration 222
Europe's international borders 339
exclusionary political rhetoric 102
exploitative labour practices 230

F
failed entrepreneurs 449
fall of Gaddafi 422
family reunion 175
far-right-wing political parties 492
fertility regulation 141
Fifth AU–EU Summit 279
financial lifelines 116
First World War 150
Flow Monitoring Report (2018) 175
forced displacement 73, 75
foreign aid 116
foreign direct investment (FDI) 115
foreign inflows 119
foreign relations 194
formal government structures 385
formal governmental response
    strategy 174
former colonies 343

Fourth EU–Africa Summit, Brussels
    (2014) 497
Fourth Industrial Revolution (4IR)
    232, 451
Fourth Industrial Revolution
    products 446
Free Movement of Civil Servants 242
Free Movement of Persons, Right
    of Residence and Right of
    Establishment Protocol (PFMP)
    77, 280
free movement schemes 198
free trade zones 346
Frontex 396
Frontline States (FLS) 226

G
Gaddafi regime 421
Gallup Migrant Acceptance Index
    289, 295
Gallup World Poll 295
Gathering and Departure Facility
    (GDF) 423
gender effect 147
gender-based violence 229
Geneva Convention 421
geographic information systems 385
geographical variations 239
geostrategic needs 105
German Red Cross chairs 394
German–British–Belgian colonial
    past 247
Global Commission on International
    Migration (GCIM) 320
Global Compact for Safe, Orderly and
    Regular Migration (GCM) 75,
    202, 300, 356
Global Compact on Refugees (GCR)
    75, 300
Global financial crisis (2008–9) 117
Global Forum for Migration and
    Development (GFMD) 199, 390

Global gross domestic product (GDP) 86
global hierarchy of nation-states 342
global income inequality 360
global intervention 417
global migration commitments 402
global mobility dynamics 346
Global North 29, 36, 231, 234, 318, 339, 340, 350, 370, 371, 372, 375, 377, 475, 501
global North–South relations 372
global perceptions, of refugees 181
global political economy 345, 348, 360
global social protection systems 119
Global South 21, 29, 39, 95, 96, 121, 317, 320, 331, 350, 359, 360, 370, 371, 372, 380
global sustainable development agenda 340
global visa regime 342
good border management 382
good governance 372
governance push factors 73
Government of National Accord (GNA) 422
governmental ministries 385
Grandi, Filippo 415
grassroots projects 399
Great Lakes highlands 240
Great Lakes Region 490
green pastures phenomenon 442
greener industries 446
Gulf Cooperation Council (GCC) 169
Gulf States 181

H
health infrastructure 144
health status, of the population 143, 144
High-Level Panel on Migration for Africa (HLPM) 301
historic world order 302
historical economic hegemony 223
HoA/EU migration 168

Horn of Africa (HoA) 167
host country 154
Housing and Population Census 178
human and economic development 418
human capacity development 499
human capital 124
human dimension 378
human mobility 304, 341, 403, 463
human rights abuses 173
human rights organisations 398
human rights sensitivity training 100
human rights violations 74, 85
Human Rights Watch 173
human security 488
human traffickers 118
human trafficking 169
humanitarian aid 472
humanitarian assistance 469
humanitarian credentials 102
humanitarian emergency 348
humanitarian help organisation 399
humanitarian intervention 102
humanitarian returns 471
humanitarian search and rescue (S&R) activities 395
humanitarian work 381, 469

I
identity cards 242, 298
ICT specialist firms 203
IGAD member states 84
IGAD Security Sector Program 172
illegal border crossings 232
illegal immigration 101
illicit activities 492
Illicit financial flows (IFFs) 78, 448, 453
IMF Working Paper 298
immigration restrictions 101
immigration rules 341
improved migration relations 487
incentives to remain 448
inclusive governance 373

independent civil society 396

industrial economies 139

industrialised economic centres 220

inequality 86, 87, 99, 288, 326, 329, 332, 356, 358, 360, 362, 378, 447

inequality gap 130

information and communication technology (ICT) 231

Infrastructures for Peace (I4Ps) 83

inhuman detention centres 495

inhumane detention centres 372

Institute for Security Studies (ISS) 228

institutionalised citizenship 475

intercommunal clashes 414

intercommunal violence 414

Intergovernmental Authority on Development (IGAD) 167, 251, 489

Intergovernmental Committee for European Migration (ICEM) 462

intergovernmental fora 369

internal displacement 74, 175

internal regional inequalities 140

internally displaced persons (IDPs) 487

international agenda 331

International Centre for Migration Policy Development (ICMPD) 203

international conduct of conduct 475

international migrants 115

international migration 75, 76, 140

international migration governance 389

International Organization for Migration (IOM) 88, 169, 414

international out-migration 74

International Peace Institute 82

international protection 240

International Refugee Rights Initiative 172

International Rescue Committee (IRC) 392, 427

intra-Africa migration 76, 324, 444

intra-African labour mobility 431

intra-European migration 302

involuntary immobility 333

irregular migration 118

Iron Curtain 318

Islamic terrorism 346

Islamophobia 414

Italian–Libyan agreement 415

J

Jihadist terrorism 414

job consolidation 132

Joint Africa–EU Declaration on Migration and Development 269

Joint Experts Groups (JEGs) 268

Joint Research Centre (JRC) 290

Joint Strategy and Action Plan (2008–2010) 268

Joint Valletta Action Plan (JVAP) 75, 183, 271, 273-274

JRC scenario study 291

K

Kakuma Refugee Camp 182

Kalobeyei Integrated Socio-Economic Development Plan (KISEDP) 182

Khartoum Process 251

Kigali Summit 278

L

labour data collection systems 228

labour market imbalances 140

labour migration arrangements 193

Labour Migration Policy Framework

labour migration programmes 198, 211

labour-intensive agricultural sector 490

labour-intensive economic growth 304

legal migration pathways 201

legal mobility arrangements 210

legal pathways principle 201

legal principles of asylum 360

legal residence status 154

liberation struggle 178
Liberian refugees 100
Libyan coast guard 360
Libyan conflict (2009) 423
Libyan detention camps 103
Libyan detention centres 360, 421
Libyan–Italian agreement 423
Libyan migration crisis 103
Libyan Ministry of Interior 427
Libyan National Army 422
lockdowns 449
long-term development
    interventions 359

M

macro-economic growth 358
macro-economic policies 448
MADE-Afrique 370
Maghreb countries 139
Maghreb economies 139
Maghreb–Europe migration 151
mainstream economists 343
management-orientated discourse 493
Marrakesh Declaration and Action
    Plan (2018–2020) 271
market-oriented liberalisation 197
market-reform-orientated structural
    adjustment plans 104
mass deportations 117
mass displacement 31, 332, 417
mass emigration 262
mass irregular immigration 307
mass migration 325, 350
mass mobilisation 100
mass movement 85
mass repatriations 89
massive human displacements 486
Mayors Dialogue on Growth and
    Solidarity 403
Mbeki High Level Panel on Illicit
    Financial Flows 80
Mbeki report 80

Médecins Sans Frontières 395
Mediterranean Basin 139
memoranda of understanding
    (MOUs) 227, 428
meta-level findings 459
Mfecane Wars 219, 225
migrant insecurity 357
migrant-centred agenda 340
migrant-centred approach 340
migrant-centred understanding 324
migrant-receiving destinations 327
migrant-sending states 327
Migration and Development Civil
    Society Network (MADE) 370, 391
migration cooperation 193, 196, 198,
    199, 201, 206, 207, 208, 211, 240,
    241, 242, 245, 246, 247, 249, 250,
    255, 256, 269, 308, 471, 472, 473
migration corridors 78, 118, 167, 168,
    175, 176
migration crisis 32, 108, 128, 201,
    208, 228, 273, 348, 350, 414, 422,
    424, 428, 430, 471, 485, 493, 497
Migration Dialogue for Southern
    Africa (MIDSA) 224
migration governance reform 230,
    233, 351, 361
Migration Information and Data
    Analysis System (MIDAS) 474
Migration of African Talents through
    Capacity building and Hiring
    (MATCH) project 204
Migration Policy Framework for
    Africa (MPFA) 279
*Migration Policy Framework for Africa
    and Plan of Action (2018–2030)* 321
migration policy instruments 198
migration policy thinking 326, 341,
    343, 345
migration scholars 25, 37, 322, 355,
    359, 360
migration scholarship 317, 326, 333, 342

migration strategic outline 346

migration transition theories 297

migration worker programmes 198

migration/mobility governance 470

migration–asylum nexus 318

migration–development nexus 98, 265, 318, 319, 325, 340, 341, 353, 356, 445

migration–development question 320

migration-related activities 188, 401

migration-related agenda 354

migration-related CSOs 375

migration-related frameworks and guidelines 168

migration-related interests 477

migration-related interventions 25

migration-related issues 25, 375, 385

migration-related problems 383

migration-related projects 105, 276

migration-related subgoals 38

migration-stimulating role of education 330

mineral revolutions 219, 222

ministry of education 385

Missing Migrants 374

mixed migration 168, 175, 181, 318, 419

Mixed Migration Centre (MMC) 175

mixed migration flows 189, 421

mixed migration patterns 167

mobile transfers 134

Mobility and Employment (MME) partnership 497

mobility partnership 195, 197, 308

modern services sector 304

modern slavery 173

modernisation 343

monetary flows 129

monetary remittances 118

monetary transfers 379

Moria Registration and Identification Centre (RIC) 428

Multiannual Financial Framework 401

multinational companies (MNCs) 441

multinational organisations 496

N

National Focal Points 270

National Human Rights Institutions (NHRIs) 86

National Peace Committees (NPCs) 83

national political agendas 36

national political context 462

national political dynamics 475

national recovery plan 178

national security 82, 201, 227, 380, 475

national service programme 178

nationalist NGO 399

nationalist parties 194

nationalist politicians 76

naturalisation certificates 102

naturalisation laws 101, 102

neoliberal consensus 106

neoliberal global agenda 104

neo-liberal globalization 354

neoliberal ideas 197

net migration 152, 289, 290, 307

Netherlands, Senegal and the Africa Business Council (NABC) 204

neutral humanitarianism 319

new global order 303

new humanitarianism 319

new nationalism 100

New York Declaration for Refugees and Migrants 59, 75, 416

nomadic pastoralists 293

nomadic populations 474

non-cash assistance 117

non-European countries 461, 463

non-European donor governments 465

non-European donors 477

non-European governments 465

non-European refugees 35

non-European states 207, 209

non-governmental organisations

(NGOs) 180, 204, 373, 391, 398
non-governmental partners 416
non-OECD countries 346
non-refoulement 279, 376, 415
non-state actors 125, 133, 373, 375, 385, 386, 389, 468, 495, 496
North–South inequalities 357, 358
North–South migration 25, 26, 221
North–South relations 372
North–South trajectory 222
northbound mobility 360
northern migration corridor 172-173

O
off-continent migration 324, 329
official development assistance (ODA) 78, 116, 119, 159, 263, 275, 305
oil crisis 151, 157
Operational Platform for the Eastern Mediterranean Route 397
Organisation for Economic Co-operation and Development (OECD) 115, 316, 490
Organisation of African Unity (OAU) 76, 86
origin countries 124, 158, 161, 206, 263, 273, 317, 319, 323, 327, 334, 345, 355, 471, 473
out-bound migration 74, 75, 78, 81
out-migration 73, 74, 77, 78, 85, 87, 89, 90, 321

P
Pact on Migration and Asylum 195, 224, 393, 428
Pan-African Forum on Migration (PAFoM) 277
pan-African migration and mobility frameworks 277
Pan-African Network in Defense of Migrants' Rights (PANiDMR) 370
pan-African policies 422
pan-African solidarity 97

Pan-African Thought and Conversation (IPATC) 37, 500
parliamentary scrutiny 397
partnership models 492
partnerships of equals 303
patriotism 475
People's Global Action on Migration, Development and Human Rights (PGA) 375
policy coherence for development (PCD) 304
political citizenship 102
political crises 224
political deadlock 356
political destabilisation 332
political economy approach 73
political instability 124, 334
political leverage 102
political opportunism 228
political oppression 332
political polarisation 361
political reframing of development assistance 400
political vacuum 475, 477
politically charged atmosphere 357
politically charged conversations 452
politically motivated demands 36
politically motivated investment 357
politically motivated objectives 400
politically polarising confusion 358
politically unstable countries 140
politically vulnerable position 354
poor governance 48, 49, 62, 74, 77, 87, 89, 118, 321, 322
Population pyramid of Africa (2019) 292
Population pyramid of Europe (2019) 291
positive political orientation 140
post-2015 era 358
post-2015 European migration governance agenda 353
post-2015 root causes approaches 358

post-colonial conflict situations 317
post-colonial period 221
post-colonial political boundaries 261
post-colonialism 303
post-conflict exercise 468
post-conflict reconstruction 319
post-conflict situations 83, 468, 478
post-conflict stabilisation 466
post-conflict support 468
post-conflict-related activities 467, 469
post-COVID rescue packages 107
post-COVID-19 recovery 446
post-Gaddafi era 422
post-Gaddafi Libya 425
post-Gaddafi Libyan migration policy
    425
post-independence era 332
post-war period 343
post-war reliance 343
post-war violence 83
post-World War II context 462
post-World War II guest worker
    programmes 199
power blocs 302
precolonial era 115
precolonial times 441
pre-departure training and education
    200
pre-GCM negotiations 374, 376
primary transit countries 177
principles of national sovereignty
    and regional collaboration 360
progressive civil society 397
progressive civil society activities 397
progressive labour-friendly mobility
    strategy 498
progressive NGOs 399
progressive pre-existing refugee laws
    104
project finance model 464
projectisation budgetary model 463
projectisation mode 464

Protocol to the Treaty Establishing
    the African Economic Community
    Relating to Free Movement of
    Persons, Right of Residence and
    Right of Establishment 76, 97,
    264, 277, 379
Provisional Intergovernmental
    Committee for the Movement of
    Migrants from Europe (PICCME)
    462
public services 100, 143, 244
pull approaches 296
pull factors 175, 296, 297, 322, 441,
    442, 443, 452
push approaches 296
push factors 62, 73, 79, 87, 89, 141,
    296, 297, 323, 442, 448, 452, 453,
    455, 486, 488, 490, 499

Q
quota refugee programme 347

R
Rabat Process (2006) 224, 251, 269,
    270, 271, 276, 497
racially white 341
racism 89, 222, 230, 341, 422, 495
readmission 51, 106, 157, 195, 201,
    202, 208, 250, 256, 271, 273, 276,
    278, 279, 299, 306, 307, 376, 377
readmission agreements 106, 157,
    158, 208, 306
readmission negotiations 206
readmission programmes 184, 188
rebordering of global society 475
red lines 397, 400
Refugee Amendment Act 174
refugee camps 98, 99, 104, 107, 171,
    172, 401, 430
refugee laws 104
refugee status 97, 249, 289, 299
regional economic communities 256
Regional Economic Communities

(RECs) 80, 167, 179, 226, 262, 263, 301, 370, 380, 451
Regional migration 224, 251
Regional Migration Action Plan (R-MAP) 180
Regional migration governance 16
regional migration management policies 264
regional migration plans 386
Regional Migration Policy Framework (RMPF) 180
Register of Greek and Foreign Non-Governmental Organisations 401
reintegration activities 382
reintegration assistance 472
reintegration component 467
reintegration efforts 471
reintegration support 472
rejected asylum seekers 157, 299
religious supremacism (political Islam) 302
remote technologies 232
resettled refugees 300
residence permits 32, 33, 210, 211, 248, 342
restricting/governing mobility cluster 470
restriction-orientated practice 493
restrictive migration policies 122, 140, 157, 198
restrictive migration regimes 36
return, readmission and reintegration 278
Returns Directive 392
reversed development 442
right-wing leadership 399
right-wing NGOs 399
right-wing political parties 59, 492
right-wing radical civil society actors 399
right-wing voices 128
rights-based principles 392

Rome Declaration and Programme (2014–2017) 271, 273
root causes approach 339
root causes conversation 334
root causes logic and narrative 354
root-causes analytical framework 488
rural exodus 140, 143
rural underdevelopment 321, 334
rural-to-urban mobility 330
rural–urban migration 140, 262, 329, 489
rural–urban mobility 473
rural–urban transformation 329

S
SADC Labour Migration Policy Framework 227
SADC Protocol on Employment and Labour 226, 227, 228
SADC Regional Labour Migration Action Plan (2013–2015) 228
Sahan Foundation 172, 173, 174
Sahel countries 331
Sahel region 32, 118, 275, 357, 414
Sahel window 196
Sahel zone 488
Sana'a Declaration 181
Scaling Fences: Voices of irregular African migrants to Europe 128, 443
Schengen Agreement 493
Schengen agreements 34
Schengen Area 287, 289
Schengen statistics 247
Schengen visa applications 247
School of Oriental and African Studies (SOAS) 172
Search and Rescue 390
search and rescue missions 65
search and rescue operations 64, 428
seasonal jobs 198
securitisation 226, 227, 228, 229, 232, 233, 234, 274, 395, 420, 485,

487, 493

sedentarism 475

selective migration 158

sending–receiving dichotomy 219

settler colonialism 223

shared sovereignty 474

short-term humanitarian responses 359

short-stay entry visas 209, 210, 247

skilled job market 155

Skills and Talent Packages 394

skills gap changes 194

skills gaps realities 445

smuggling activities 170, 396

smuggling industry 229

smuggling practices 423

social cohesion 230, 231, 448

social media platforms 100, 171

socio-economic analyses 453

socio-economic benefits 160, 443

socio-economic challenges 57, 161

socio-economic conditions 321

socio-economic context 156

socio-economic crises 147

socio-economic development 26, 49, 80, 141, 339

socio-economic discrepancies 34

socio-economic disparities 35

socio-economic effects 131

socio-economic exclusion 84

socio-economic fabric 240

socio-economic factors 118

socio-economic impacts 130

socio-economic inequalities 48

socio-economic malaise 90

socio-economic production 124

socio-economic profile 209, 329

socio-economic progress 145, 454

socio-economic realities 261

socio-economic recovery 448

socio-economic rights 85, 86

socio-economic shifts 449

socio-economic stability 158

socio-economic welfare 201

socio-economic wellbeing 61, 372

socio-political conflicts 256

socio-political crises 247

socio-political exclusion 100

socio-political stabilisation 317

soft power relations 194

SOS Méditerranée 395

South African exceptionalism 101

South African politicians 230

South–North migration 29, 221, 342, 358, 359, 362

South–South migration 232

Southern African Development Community (SADC) 48, 175, 226, 380

Southern African Development Coordination Conference (SADCC) 226

southern corridor 168, 173

Southern migration corridor 173-175

Soviet bloc 344

Soviet Union 318

state–civil society relations 394

state–society relations 73

Statistics South Africa (Stats SA) 223

Statute of the Office of the United Nation High Commissioner for Refugees (1950) 416

Strategic Initiative for Women in the Horn of Africa (SIHA) Network 172

Strategy for the Gulf of Guinea 251

student mobility 200, 330

subregional bodies 62

subregional economic communities 241

subregional migration repercussions 242

sub-Saharan African migrants 34, 76, 103, 140, 420

sub-Saharan African nationals 348, 414

survival mechanism 231

survival strategies 374

sustainable development 38, 87, 126, 133, 158, 161, 233, 266, 267, 378, 382, 442, 453, 454, 498

Sustainable Development Goals (SDGs) 126, 202, 266, 356, 369, 375, 384, 446

sustainable development process 145

Swiss Development Corporation 270

Syrian conflict 414

Syrian crisis 103

Syrian refugees 28, 31, 103, 297

system of readmission 157

T

technical mobility agreements 382

technology transfers 263, 448

third country nationals 193, 210

third country resettlement 252

third-country solutions 300, 417, 427

Tony Elumelu Foundation Initiative on Youth Empowerment 18, 453

total fertility rate (TFR) 142

Toubou and Tuareg groups 422

tourist visas 300, 486

Transfer of Knowledge Through Expatriate Nationals (TOKTEN) programme 454

transit centres 467, 472

transit countries 174, 177, 328, 419, 420, 471, 472, 487, 489, 493, 495

transit migrants 187, 472

transit stations 171

transition approach 297

transnational response 390

transnational security field 106

Transparency International 77, 79

Trans-Saharan migration 422

Treaty Establishing the African Economic Community 76, 90, 97, 180, 264, 277, 379

Tripoli Ministerial Conference on Migration and Development 183, 268

U

UN Conference on Trade and Development (UNCTAD) 262

UN Convention (51) 376

UN Convention and Protocol (1971) 415

UN Convention and Protocol Relating to the Status of Refugees 415, 428

UN Declaration of Human Rights (1948) 415

UN Department of Economic and Social Affairs (UNDESA) 226, 371, 419

UN Global Commission on International Migration (GCIM) 320

UN Global Compact 58, 61, 134, 333

UN Global Compact for Safe, Orderly and Regular Migration (GCM) 48, 202, 300, 320, 325

UN Global Compact of Refugees 63

UN Global Compact on Migration 64

UN Global Compact on Refugees (GCR) 415

UN High Commissioner for Refugees (UNHCR) 63, 249, 415, 429, 462

UN Office on Drugs and Crime 173, 184

UN Special Rapporteur on the Human Rights of Migrants 471

United Nations Development Programme (UNDP) 18, 19, 21, 49, 84, 442

United Nations Economic Commission for Africa (UNECA) 78

United Nations General Assembly 377

United Nations Humanitarian Commission for Refugees (UNHCR) 27, 176, 181

Universal Declaration of Human Rights 89

unskilled Africans 490

unskilled labour 150, 151
unskilled migrants 228, 230
unskilled migration 141
unskilled workers 299
unskilled workforce 147
unwanted migration 475
urbanisation 143, 145, 304, 307, 326, 329
US–Mexico border 305

V

Valletta Summit on Migration 195, 200, 201, 202, 210, 212, 271, 273, 320, 348, 349, 350, 497
Vienna Declaration 397
violence/oppression 332, 333
violent extremism 444
virtual education 232
virtual healthcare 232
visa-free entry 221, 227
visa-free trend 221
visa regulations 155
visa regimes 62, 277, 342
visa restrictions 101, 107, 157
voluntary labour migration 178

W

war/conflict 176
war-torn countries 414
Water, Sanitation and Hygiene (WASH) standards 188
welcome home programme 156
welfare policies 198
Western African Maritime Route 420
Western Balkan governments 397
Western model of democracy 372
Western orientation 430
Westphalian Peace (Europe) 302
white minority 225
White Paper on International Immigration for South Africa (2017) 230

whole-of-society approach 385, 401
whole-of-society commitments 397
whole-of-society engagement 389
winner-take-all system 82
women's migration 151
work permits 104, 298, 377, 446
working-age group 149
working-age population 142, 262, 290
World Bank 79, 104, 119, 120, 125, 126, 128, 129, 131, 132, 182, 231, 371
World Bank/NOMAD 128
World Health Organisation (WHO) 88
World Order: Reflections on the character of nations and the course of history 302
world systems theory 343
World Trade Centre 346
World Trade Organization's (WTO) General Agreement on Trade in Services 445
World War II 30, 199, 413, 462

X

xenophobia 21, 35, 36, 85, 89, 202, 228, 230, 415, 431, 489
xenophobic acts 62
xenophobic attacks 85, 229, 230
xenophobic attitudes 85
xenophobic discourse 99, 100
xenophobic rhetoric 101
xenophobic robes 59
xenophobic sentiments 35
xenophobic undertones 35
xenophobic violence 229, 489

Y

youth empowerment 90
youth unemployment 61, 62, 148, 338

Z

Zulu nation 225